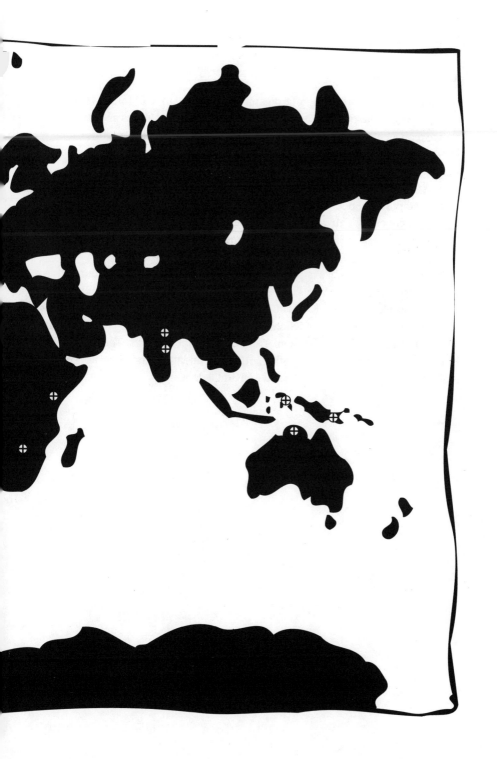

About Island Press

Island Press is the only nonprofit organization in the United States whose principal purpose is the publication of books on environmental issues and natural resource management. We provide solutions-oriented information to professionals, public officials, business and community leaders, and concerned citizens who are shaping responses to environmental problems.

In 1994, Island Press celebrates its tenth anniversary as the leading provider of timely and practical books that take a multidisciplinary approach to critical environmental concerns. Our growing list of titles reflects our commitment to bringing the best of an expanding body of literature to the environmental community throughout North America and the world.

Support for Island Press is provided by The Geraldine R. Dodge Foundation, The Energy Foundation, The Ford Foundation, The George Gund Foundation, William and Flora Hewlett Foundation, The John D. and Catherine T. MacArthur Foundation, The Andrew W. Mellon Foundation, The Joyce Mertz-Gilmore Foundation, The New-Land Foundation, The Pew Charitable Trusts, The Rockefeller Brothers Fund, The Tides Foundation, Turner Foundation, Inc., The Rockefeller Philanthropic Collaborative, Inc., and individual donors.

NATURAL
CONNECTIONS

Natural Connections

Perspectives in Community-based Conservation

Edited by
David Western and R. Michael Wright

Shirley C. Strum, Associate Editor

Washington, D.C. • Covelo, California

Library of Congress Cataloging-in-Publication Data

Natural connections : perspectives in community-based conservation / edited by David Western and R. Michael Wright : Shirley C. Strum, associate editor.
    p.   cm.
    Proceedings of a workshop held in Airlie, Va., Oct. 18–22, 1993.
    Includes bibliographical references (p.) and index.
    ISBN 1-55963-345-X (cloth). — ISBN 1-55963-346-8 (paper)
    1. Nature conservation—Citizen participation—Congresses.
2. Ecosystem management—Citizen participation—Congresses.
I. Western, David.   II. Wright, R. Michael.   III. Strum, Shirley C. (Shirley Carol), 1947– .
QH75.A1N337   1994   94-38977
333.7'2—dc20   CIP

Contents

Part I Case Studies

Part II Case Study Profiles

Part III Themes

Part IV The Workshop

Preface

Natural Connections: Perspectives in Community-based Conservation is the proceedings of a workshop on community-based conservation held in Airlie, Virginia, from October 18–22, 1993. Both the origins and the outcome of the workshop need some explanation if the collaborative effort that went into the creation of this book is to be fully appreciated.

The workshop began to take shape in the unlikely setting of 650 Fifth Avenue, New York City, during a board meeting of the Liz Claiborne Art Ortenberg Foundation (LCAOF). The foundation's meetings are always about conservation directions and philosophy as much as they are about projects and budgets. The meeting on April 24, 1991, was typical except in one respect: The directors—Art Ortenberg, Liz Claiborne, David Quammen, and David Western—and the program manager, Jim Murtaugh, all felt more than usually excited about the community-based direction conservation was taking and troubled by the failure of projects to live up to their promise.

Proposal after proposal alluded to the need to reconcile human needs and conservation at the local level. The words were there—*local participation, empowerment, tangible benefits, sustainable development*—but, somewhere along the line, most programs either failed to come to grips with the human dimension or failed to tackle conservation issues.

Why did some projects fail despite a surfeit of funds and personnel, while a few succeeded on next to nothing? As the foundation pumped conservation organizations for details, a few salient lessons surfaced. Most organizations appeared to pay lip service to the goal of involving local communities in conservation but, in reality, went about their business as usual. Projects tended to be short term in nature and overreliant on expatriate expertise; those involved seemed disinclined to work through or build up local institutions in the developing world. Most personnel had not resolved the problem of building local sustainability into their projects. Most also had no clear criteria through which to determine whether local people did benefit from conservation or whether conservation did better for having involved local people.

LCAOF decided the time was ripe to draw together a wide range of conservation-minded people to review success and failure in community-based projects and ask for their advice on the way ahead. The first workshop planning session, convened by the LCAOF board, took place in Washington, D.C., on November 14, 1991, with representatives of the World Bank, USAID, Wildlife Conservation International, World Resources Institute, World Wildlife Fund, and Conservation International in attendance. The Nature Conservancy joined in the meetings that followed during the next year. Once the size and scope of the endeavor became apparent, LCAOF contracted Michael Wright, senior vice president of World Wildlife Fund, to coordinate workshop planning activities.

In keeping with the spirit of community-based conservation, the planning group envisaged a participatory approach to the workshop from the outset. The first step involved choosing fifteen case studies from a long list recommended by members of the planning group. The final selection was intended to provide workshop participants with a sample of community-based conservation activities from around the world, as well as a common set of materials for evaluation and discussion.

The second step entailed identification of common themes that cut across the case studies, for which analyses would be commissioned. Case study authors contributed suggestions of their own. The planning group and outside reviewers contacted by Michael Wright suggested theme authors once the topics had been selected. Each theme author was to review the case studies and other relevant materials and to draw out broad conclusions for the workshop participants.

A few months prior to the workshop, once the need for a synthesis of the issues became obvious, a final background document was commissioned. David Western and Michael Wright, with input from the LCAOF board and program manager, sifted through the case studies and theme papers to draw out the key points and lay out a logical structure for the workshop discussions.

Once the background materials were under way, the planning group drew up a list of prospective workshop participants. Suggestions included a cross section of landowners, resource managers, government agencies, conservation organizations, international donors, development agencies, and a variety of specialists involved in community-based conservation. The final selection of sixty participants, based on geographical coverage and a balance of interests, was heavily biased toward those with firsthand experience.

The case studies were circulated to all participants three months prior to the workshop, followed by the theme papers six weeks later and then by the issues paper. Each participant was asked to review the case studies and theme papers and recommend topics for discussion. Their suggestions were reviewed and incorporated into the workshop agenda.

The workshop was staged at Airlie House, set in the superb fall colors of Virginia. The participants from Latin America, Africa, Asia, Oceania, Europe, and North America included indigenous peoples, politicians, anthropologists, game wardens, forest managers, scholars, and conservationists. The group could not have been more mixed or more steeped in the issues.

This book follows the structure of the workshop. The case studies, theme papers, and issues paper gave each participant a common set of documents to stimulate their thinking prior to arrival at Airlie. At the workshop, paticipants reviewed the linkages between conservation and local community interests. The group then split into parallel groups to examine the lessons contained in each major theme, identify areas of uncertainty, and draw up recommendations. The groups later reconvened to compare notes and draw out common threads. They then split once more into working groups for Asia and the Pacific region, Africa, Latin America, and the Developed World. Each regional group reviewed the findings from the earlier sessions and defined its own priorities and agenda. Two additional groups met to outline the role of donor agencies and suggest the most appropriate methods for skills and technology transfer.

The final plenary session reviewed the workshop proceedings, drew responses from the participants, and mapped out a series of regional follow-up activities. On the final morning, Bruce Babbitt, United States Secretary of the Interior, met with the entire group over breakfast and gave a thoughtful talk on the politics of community-based conservation.

The Airlie House workshop captured the excitement of community-based conservation in its formative stages. The atmosphere was charged with expectation, indignation, anger, fire, compassion, and humor. With so many different faces, cultures, voices, and experiences—so many individuals all eager to fill the void between people and nature—drawn together in one place, the workshop took on a life of its own, to everyone's surprise and delight. No one came knowing what to expect; no one left disappointed.

Something unique happened at Airlie—something beyond words, recommendations, resolutions. Perhaps it is best described as a vision of a new conservation. That vision and its accompanying spirit have been elegantly captured in the foundation's summary of the workshop, "The View from Airlie: Community-based Conservation in Perspective" (1994).

The workshop proceedings presented here draw on the background materials and the discussions at Airlie House. Four case studies have been dropped, and an additional theme paper on economics has been added. The issues paper has been rewritten and divided between chapters 1 and 22 to better fit the information to the book's format. The outcome of the Airlie meeting, presented in Part IV, summarizes the workshop discussions. We have added some material for the sake of completeness and fleshed out the text to make the proceedings as readable as possible. Above all, we have tried to transmit, as truly as possible, the voices, the excitement, and the hopes of Airlie.

Acknowledgments

The Airlie House Community Based Conservation Workshop—the proceedings of which comprise this volume—would not have been possible without the personal, passionate conviction and leadership of Art Ortenberg and Liz Claiborne and the foundation that bears their names. In addition, the editors owe a particular debt of gratitude to the sixty participants from throughout the world whose insight and candor during the October 1993 workshop broadened our understanding and deepened our conviction regarding the role of communities in managing our biosphere. The workshop was their product, and so too are these proceedings.

James Murtaugh and Ellen Trama, respectively the program officer and program assistant of the Liz Claiborne Art Ortenberg Foundation, ably coordinated and handled the complex logistics of the workshop. Each case study was reviewed by at least two reviewers whose efforts are most appreciated but who, by prior agreement, must remain anonymous. We most appreciate the support of Island Press in preparing this volume and the editing of Lisa Lawley, without which this would be a less literate effort. We are grateful also to Silicon Graphics for help with the design. Finally, we wish to thank U.S. Secretary of the Interior Bruce Babbitt, whose remarks on the closing day of the workshop linked the concerns of communities throughout the world with those of rural areas in the United States.

In addition, David Western would like to thank the Wildlife Conservation Society for supporting his efforts in preparation for the workshop and Zippy Wanakuta for her support in its aftermath. Michael Wright wishes to thank the World Wildlife Fund and The Nature Conservancy for their support and Hilary Barbour for her assistance from the inception of this project.

Note to the Reader

The ideas in this book, particularly those related to the themes discussed in Part III, have been extensively cross-referenced in order to make them as accessible as possible. For ease of reading, each chapter therefore has been assigned a shortened name, derived, whenever possible, from the full chapter title. For instance, Chapter 6, "Kakadu National Park: An Australian Experience in Comanagement," has been shortened to KAKADU, and Chapter 14, "Cultural Traditions and Community-based Conservation," is referred to as CULTURE for cross-referencing purposes. To make locating cross-referenced materials as effortless as possible, these shortened titles also appear as the running heads at the top of each right-hand page within their respective chapters.

For quick reference, a complete listing of these shortened chapter titles follows:

Chapter 1	BACKGROUND	Chapter 14	CULTURE
Chapter 2	AMBOSELI	Chapter 15	PARTICIPATION
Chapter 3	INDIA	Chapter 16	TENURE
Chapter 4	MALUKU ISLANDS	Chapter 17	POLICY
Chapter 5	AMAZON	Chapter 18	INSTITUTIONS
Chapter 6	KAKADU	Chapter 19	ECONOMICS
Chapter 7	CAMPFIRE	Chapter 20	ECOLOGY
Chapter 8	CRATER MOUNTAIN	Chapter 21	INITIATION
Chapter 9	BOSCOSA	Chapter 22	LINKAGE
Chapter 10	NIGER	Chapter 23	LESSONS LEARNED
Chapter 11	ANNAPURNA	Chapter 24	RECOMMENDATIONS
Chapter 12	NORTH YORK MOORS	Chapter 25	CHALLENGES
Chapter 13	NEOTROPICAL FORESTS	Chapter 26	THE FUTURE

Grateful acknowledgment is expressed to the John Muafangejo Trust for permission to reproduce the linocuts found on the opening pages of Chapters 1 and 14–26. Following are their titles in order of appearance: *Thinking Man* (1986); *He Is Killing an Ox to Collect the Corn* (1987); *A Good Family in Ovambo* (1985); *An Interview of Cape Town University in 1971* (1971); *A Jealousy Man* (1976); *Muafangejo's Kraal* (1979); *Men Are Working in Town* (1981); *An Ark Noah* (1979); *A Beautiful Ovamboland* (1984); *A Man Is Hunting an Eland* (1974); *Shiyane Home* (1969); *Kuyanjama Kings. Manduma Has Assagal* (1983); *Lions Are Wanting the Two Boys up the Tree* (1985); and *Hope and Optimism. In Spite of the Present Difficulties* (1984).

These illustrations (©1992 by John Muafangejo Trust) were reproduced from *The African Dream* by Orde Levinson (London: Thames and Hudson, 1992).

CHAPTER 1

The Background to Community-based Conservation

David Western and R. Michael Wright

The focus of conservation concern and debate has changed throughout history in response to new problems, concerns, and knowledge. One approach, newly emergent, is community-based conservation, or CBC. Community-based conservation arises from within the community—or at least at the community level—rather than internationally or nationally. The irony, of course, is that community-based conservation is hardly new. Communities down the millennia have developed elaborate rituals and practices to limit offtake levels, restrict access to critical resources, and distribute harvests (Croll and Parkin 1992).

Conservation in History

Traditional conservation practices revolved around sustaining food supplies such as fruiting trees or wildlife or protecting cultural symbols, whether totemic animals or religious sites. Conservation, in other words, originated in prehistory as practices that satisfied human needs, not as an altruistic concern for animals and plants. Despite the conservation practices of ancient times, as early as the Paleolithic period of the Stone Age the survival of the wild had more to do with low human population density, limited technology, and undeveloped or restricted markets than with self-imposed human restraint. When resources ran out, new lands for human habitation were always available.

Moving on in pursuit of fresh resources remained an option during the early Neolithic, even as pastoralism and shifting agriculture emerged. Movement, whether nomadic, transhumant, or wholesale relocation, enabled humans to optimize resource use and sidestep the consequences of overexploitation.

Movement didn't entirely obviate the need for conservation or inhibit compassion for other forms of life. Evidence from contemporary traditional societies suggests that a holistic sense of the world was common to most cultures. Many cultures and religions (including the faiths of Hindus, Buddhists, and native

Americans) still retain a strong sense of the indivisibility of humanity and nature (Kemf 1993).

Where space was lacking and prey species had evolved in isolation from humans, conservation practices often were ineffective. Evidence from oceanic islands, for example, shows a sharp rise in extinction rates with the arrival of seafaring peoples (Olson 1989). Large-mammal exterminations in the New World during the Pleistocene bear evidence of overkill by early hunters (Martin and Klein 1984). Indeed, traditional conservation practices probably evolved more to maximize and allocate harvests than to conserve supplies (see MALUKU ISLANDS). Moreover, many traditional societies, given modern weapons, overhunt their prey, as discussed in NEOTROPICAL FORESTS. Traditional conservation beliefs, in other words, are not ready-made prescriptions for today's world.

The Rise of Modern Conservation

Populations expanded and grew more sedentary during the Neolithic. Historical evidence points to localized resource depletion and abandonment of agrarian and urban centers as early as 3000 B.C. (Southwick 1976). In classical Greece, Aristotle and Plato wrote almost as persuasively as the twentieth century's Aldo Leopold about landscapes withering under the onslaught of livestock. "What now remains compared with what then existed," Plato noted, "is like the skeleton of a sick man, all the fat and soft earth having been wasted away, and only the bare framework of the land being left" (Rodes and Odell 1992).

By pharaonic times, wildlife was scarce in Lower Egypt. The ruling elite there established the first recorded wildlife reserves in order to assure themselves of quarry on hunting expeditions. A similar devastation of wildlife was repeated across the Middle East, Asia, and Europe as populations grew, settled, and transformed the natural landscape for arable farming, husbandry, and forestry. The same issues arose time and again with each cycle of settlement and resource depletion: Who owns wildlife? Who owns the forest? Who owns the land?

The aristocracy almost invariably won such disputes and denied the peasants who lived on their land or around royal hunting preserves access to wildlife (Thomas 1983). Disputes over forest land and products were particularly contentious, culminating in the rise of forestry practices in eighteenth-century Europe (Nash 1967) and the first forest conservancies, established by the British Raj in India during the mid-nineteenth century (Vedant 1986).

By the 1850s, a new conservation sensibility emerged alongside the romantic movement in Europe and the United States (Nash 1967; Thomas 1983). Humanitarian concerns for the poor, the enslaved, and the disenfranchised soon spilled over into demands for ethical treatment of animals. By 1869, expanding sensibilities led John Stuart Mill to advocate the preservation of species for their own sake, independent of their utility for humans (Thomas 1983).

The rise of a modern conservation consciousness and conscience gathered mo-

mentum in the late nineteenth century, as the wilds disappeared and rural communities became urban. Forest reserves, national parks, and hunting laws familiar
to twentieth-century conservationists came into being, although nineteenth-cen-
tury motives were decidedly more political and utilitarian than preservationist.
The question of who owned wildlife and who had the right to shoot it, for example,
intensified and became closely tied to egalitarianism in the United States and, to
a lesser extent, in Europe (Tober 1981). Early national parks mostly were intended
to save natural monuments and open space for recreation rather than to preserve
vignettes of nature (Runte 1979).

Sustainable use nevertheless was the best way to preserve nature, according to
U.S. President Theodore Roosevelt's chief forester, Gifford Pinchot. Pinchot, the
self-proclaimed founder of American conservation, advocated efficiency and pru-
dence in the profitable and sustainable use of natural resources. Conservation, in
this new doctrine, was "the application of common sense to the common problems
for the common good" (Shabecoff 1993). Stripped of its rhetoric, Pinchot's sustainable-use policy signaled President Roosevelt's intention to restrain big businesses' abuse of public lands.

The sustainable-use doctrine also lent legitimacy to efforts to conserve land for
the public good. The movement gained an aura of scientific respectability in later
years, when mathematical population models were used to calculate maximum
sustained yields for natural-resource harvests (Holt and Talbot 1978). But the very
pragmatism of Pinchot's wise-use conservation proved abhorrent to the spiritual-
ists and romantics led by preservationist John Muir. The first salvo signaling a
deep rift in the conservation movement was about to be fired.

The Diversification of Conservation

The standoff first arose over plans to dam and flood Hetch Hetchy Valley within
Yosemite National Park to provide water for San Francisco. Roosevelt and Pinchot
came down on the side of exploitation and Muir on the side of preservation. The
gap between pragmatists and preservationists widened after World War II, when
the archdruid of modern preservationism, David Brower, assumed the directorship
of Muir's Sierra Club and opposed dams in Dinosaur National Monument and the
Grand Canyon (Shabecoff 1993). In later years, the split widened further when the
animal rights and deep ecology movements surfaced and began to champion the
interests of species and nature on ethical and moral grounds (Nash 1989).

The preservationists had reason to be skeptical. Impressive as early conservation successes had been in the United States, powerful commercial counterforces
waged war on the preservationists. These forces were behind the introduction of
laws and policies that encouraged, mandated, and often subsidized the private exploitation of public water, land, timber, minerals, and fisheries (Wilkinson 1992).
The underlying goals, which foreshadowed similar resource policies elsewhere,
were to boost the United States' national economy, encourage settlement, and

strengthen international trade. Once the forces of utilization were unleashed, however, they ran on, blind to ecological limits and environmental destruction. In many other cases, society's ability to sustainably manage living resources ranging from wild species in the Peruvian rain forest (see AMAZON) to trochus shells in Indonesia (see MALUKU ISLANDS) also has proved illusory (Talbot 1993).

Preservationists scored victories in 1908, with the introduction of the wildlife refuge system in the United States, and with the establishment of a series of game reserves and parks in Africa at much the same time. In the developing world, conservation by and large became the state's responsibility, both during and after the colonial era.

State policies and legislation both regulating the use of natural resources and protecting nature continued apace, however, throughout the early part of the twentieth century as population and commerce burgeoned. The rationale echoed those common to Britain's Indian conservancies and Roosevelt's national forests: commercialism and local interests were said to cause environmental destruction inimical to the state. Using this well-honed argument, governments intervened time and again to secure land and resources in the larger interest of society. State land ownership and conservation became unquestioned norms, whether or not they were called for or worked.

Renewable-resource use and preservation have served the environment well, but neither approach has proved sufficient. Both often have fared badly in the face of population growth, poverty, and commercialism. At one extreme, international forces such as trade and economic incentives undermine conservation efforts. At the other, government indifference and incompetence—often intensified by commercial greed, nepotism, corruption, and local hostility—have swelled the tide of destruction. Finally, both utilization and preservation policies falter wherever land tenure and access rights are ill defined. The problem is most acute in areas where national policies deprive local communities of the right to use the resources on their own land. The resulting us-versus-them rush to harvest is the root of resource depletion.

The weaknesses in Pinchot's and Muir's philosophies raise the question of whether prevailing policies, which isolate the interests of local communities from those of the state, are the only or even the best ways to go about conservation. A countertrend, based on the belief that local participation in decisions and benefits could reduce hostility toward conservation efforts, began to emerge in the late 1960s and 1970s (see AMBOSELI). The resulting first small steps in the direction of community participation in conservation were hastened by several developments.

Prelude to Community-based Conservation

The first development involved mounting threats to the environment in the face of careless technology, consumerism, and the population explosion. Rachel Carson's

Silent Spring (1962) and the Ehrlichs' *Population Bomb* (1968) alerted the public to these threats. Earth Day 1970 made *environment* a household word in much of the world, and the surrounding issues later gained political recognition through the United Nations Conference on the Global Environment held in Stockholm in 1972. Recognition paid off: International conservation conventions mushroomed in the years that followed.

Despite some progress, conservation efforts still revolved around saving high-profile species and habitats. This was to change in the next decade, once the oil crises instilled conservation in Western consciousness and conservationists broadened their horizons to encompass biodiversity and biological processes (IUCN, UNEP, and WWF 1980). Conservation's expanded horizons stretched far beyond parks onto rural lands, where the ultimate threat to biodiversity lay. Just how conservation was to be tackled in rural areas was an issue that remained disturbingly vague, invoking the aspirations of future generations while ignoring the problems of the rural poor (Western 1984).

The second precipitating factor involved grass-roots development. The centrally planned, capital-intensive aid projects begun in the 1950s and based on both altruism and self-interest had done little to alleviate poverty and income disparity in the developing world, despite the grandiose dams, irrigation projects, power stations, roads, and industrial developments that resulted. Integrated rural development (IRD) projects became fashionable but, again, failed with disconcerting regularity. The causes included continued centralization of planning and overly ambitious projects. The grass-roots approach, in contrast, focused on participation and local aspirations (Chambers 1983). To a significant degree, small-scale projects based on resource use did emerge during this period, thus laying a foundation of experience for community-based conservation.

The grass-roots approach recognized rural communities' dependence on sustainable use of natural resources such as soil, water, grazing land, forest products, and wildlife. This recognition conceded the case long made by the Pinchot school. What had been missing in Pinchot's approach, according to rural sociologists, was a local say and stake in resource use. Free to define their own priorities, local communities, in theory, would develop at their own pace and in their own way. They would learn their own lessons and build up their own skills in everything from health care and education to water management and communal forestry (Uphoff 1985).

Grass-roots development was not an unqualified success. The 1970s oil crisis, in particular, put severe economic strain on developing countries. Recently, however, the grass-roots approach has matured and come to play an ever larger role in development programs around the world (Durning 1989; Hirschmann 1993).

The third precipitating factor involved the human rights and indigenous peoples movements. Both drew attention to disenfranchised rural communities such as the Yanomami in Brazil and the Aboriginals of Australia (Berger 1979; Miller

1993). Internationally, developing countries' claims of North-South inequality led to demands for a new world economic order based on redistribution of wealth. Radical grass-roots organizations promoted populist movements as an alternative to government assistance (Hellinger, Hellinger, and O'Regan 1988). As a result, groups that linked social justice for ethnic minorities with environmental health became increasingly vocal.

Environmentalism and Democracy

The upshot of these convergent developments was a heightened sensibility about the environment and the interests of local people. A shift away from the elitism that had dogged the largely urban and Western preservation movement finally was under way. As much as anything, the shift acknowledged the fact that the fate of most of the earth's biological diversity lay in the hands of poor people in the Third World. Conservation and development no longer were John Muir's irreconcilable forces on either side of the divide. In a startling turnaround from the protectionism of earlier conventions, the theme of the Third World Parks Congress of 1982 was CONSERVATION FOR SUSTAINABLE DEVELOPMENT. The published proceedings drew on a handful of case studies to show how protected areas could contribute to human welfare and increase security in the process (McNeely and Miller 1984). The emphasis was still decidedly on buffering parks, but the move from preservation to multiple use of protected areas was clearly under way.

By the mid-1980s, conservation took on new urgency as environmental degradation accelerated and ecologists' warnings of impending mass extinctions captured public attention. Chernobyl, confirmation of greenhouse warming, and the development of a hole in the ozone over the Antarctic left no doubt about the connection between consumer habits and the state of the environment. The heightened awareness created fertile ground for economic development in a greener shade. The World Commission on Environment and Development's (1987) *Our Common Future*—or the Brundtland Report, as it became known—brought political respectability to the marriage of ecology and economics. The link was not simply academic; neither was it lost on politicians confronted with public demands for clean air and water, curbs on insecticides and pesticides, and a halt to whaling and tropical-forest destruction.

Several other events presaged a sharp turn toward local participation and rural-based conservation during the last decade. The end of the Cold War provided perhaps the biggest fillip to environmental issues and conservation. The environment and sustainable development quickly assumed high priority on the international agenda, culminating in the United Nations-sponsored Earth Summit. The summit, held in Rio de Janeiro, Brazil, in 1992, drew together 120 heads of state to discuss the state of the environment.

Calls for democratization and liberalization, spurred by the collapse of communism, also triggered demands for equitable resource allocation and a local voice in conservation. Centralized control over conservation and natural resources, tightened over decades, began to loosen. Regional and local autonomy took hold—although not without their own weaknesses.

Yet another significant shift was the new emphasis on biodiversity and bioethics. Demonstrations of the strategic value of biodiversity, for example, added weight to the argument for sustainable development advocated in the Brundtland Report. The animal rights movement, with a voice grown powerful in calls for whaling and ivory trade bans, developed its own strong following. Both approaches, unfortunately, also deepened tensions and disagreements over conservation, particularly between rich and poor nations.

At the root of these tensions are two opposing rights: the right of communities to assume control over their land and resources, and the right of outsiders to deny them the use of species and resources. One force of liberalization is pushing for community rights; the other, as in the case of the animal rights movement, calls for even more stringent controls.

New terms such as *ecotourism, green economics, intergenerational equity, debt-for-nature swaps, green consumerism,* and *people-based conservation* sprang up, tracking the shifting environmental sensibilities. Out of this ferment of concern and flurry of activity has arisen the ill-defined concept called community-based conservation. In community-based conservation, the emphasis has moved from the top to the bottom, from the center to the periphery, from the elite to the poor, and from the urban to the rural. The shift has opened the door on the biggest conservation challenge of all: how to deal with the vast majority of the earth's surface, where there are no parks and where the interests of local communities prevail.

A Shift in Focus: Community-based Conservation

Community-based conservation includes, at one extreme, buffer-zone protection of parks and reserves and, at the other, natural resources use and biodiversity conservation in rural areas. The term covers both new and traditional conservation methods, as well as conservation efforts that originate within or outside a community, so long as the outcome benefits the community.

Community-based conservation reverses top-down, center-driven conservation by focusing on the people who bear the costs of conservation. In the broadest sense, then, community-based conservation includes natural resources or biodiversity protection by, for, and with the local community (see INSTITUTIONS).

The deeper agenda, for most conservationists, is to make nature and natural products meaningful to rural communities. As far as local communities are concerned, the agenda is to regain control over natural resources and, through conservation practices, improve their economic well-being.

Defining community-based conservation any more precisely would be futile and even counterproductive. As the case studies demonstrate, community-based conservation intentionally includes a range of activities practiced in various corners of the world that directly or indirectly lead to conservation. The coexistence of people and nature, as distinct from protectionism and the segregation of people and nature, is its central precept.

If community-based conservation can not be defined simply, detailed case studies from around the world at least can convey a sense of what it entails. But gauging the strengths and weaknesses of this new and growing emphasis in conservation requires a further step: an appreciation of the very diversity encapsulated within the many approaches to community-based conservation. The disagreements on definition, too, are significant in themselves. Both diversity and disagreements draw attention to the many actors involved and to the reasons why they see things differently.

The broad meanings of *community* and *conservation* also make community-based conservation hard to pin down. Should *community* be defined by ethnicity or traditions, by the length of a group's residency, or by a sense of common purpose? Or, given the great flux and transition in most societies—the global village in the making—is *community* best defined by geographical and conservation context? *Community*, in this case, would have to include immigrants, cultures in transition, and those with no ancestral ties to the land or to each other. As development professionals have discovered (see PARTICIPATION), even traditional communities are rife with internal conflicts and divergent interests and often split along economic, gender, and social lines.

And what of *conservation*? Does this term exclusively connote the preservation of pristine natural ecosystems and species, as many preservationists argue? If so, few areas today qualify for conservation; fewer still have escaped humankind's imprint at some point in the intervening ages since the Pleistocene. Is conservation about the right of any and all species to find a living space on this overcrowded planet? Is it, more broadly yet, about maintaining the diversity of life, albeit modified by humanity? Or, more vitally, is it about the global ecological processes that sustain natural resources and the environment and, ultimately, our physical and emotional well-being?

The meaning of *community* varies with context, just as perceptions of nature vary around the world (see CULTURE). Cultural views, attitudes, and values are no less varied than biodiversity and defy a unified ethic of the natural world (see CHALLENGES). Simply sticking a label on locally based efforts does not create a new field of conservation.

Community-based conservation is growing of its own accord, despite the obstacles. What is most needed is recognition of a neglected set of participants and acknowledgment of the rural landscape's significance in conservation. Above all, the opportunities and challenges of community-based conservation need to be explored and encouraged.

The Potential of Community-based Conservation

Fortunately, a loose definition of community-based conservation does not preclude exploration of its potential or the challenges it poses. Clearly, community-based conservation is essentially about the locus of action. The locus may define the place but not necessarily the opportunities or what is at stake. Community efforts open up the bulk of the earth's landscape, often written off as ecologically sterile and hopeless for conservation. Ecologists and conservationists have only just begun to turn their attention to rural areas and seriously examine (or, more correctly, rediscover) the options for coexistence. If these efforts succeed, biological losses will be minimized, and protected areas will become less important (Western 1989).

At stake is nothing less than the fate of the natural world and its resources. In rural areas, humankind has the chance to value land, live within it sustainably, and learn how to coexist with nature. The alternative is a biologically and physically degraded world. Overexploitation will lower the productivity of ecosystems and the self-replenishing capacity of soil, water, and atmosphere. The stability of planetary processes will be at risk. Nature will be reduced and confined to hypermanaged ecological islands and megazoos. The eight thousand or so protected areas that currently cover 4 percent of the earth's surface form a vital biological storehouse, but even if their area were doubled, the storehouse would be unable to prevent mass extinctions. Habitat fragmentation, ecological isolation, edge effects, poaching, and other forces will greatly impoverish these isolated biological islands.

If nothing else, community-based conservation can help buffer protected areas from ecological impoverishment. A bigger opportunity by far lies in conserving and using the bulk of rural land productively and sustainably for its inhabitants, stemming the loss of biological wealth that necessitates protected areas (Western 1989).

The Uncertainties

We must avoid simple prescriptions and romantic illusions of returning to a less-complicated bucolic past in tackling community-based conservation. We must also avoid the pitfalls of integrated planning (IRD), in which overly ambitious goals and timetables and heavy dependence on outside expertise for specialist skills undercut indigenous administrative institutions (Lewis and Carter 1993).

Enormous obstacles block the potential for conservation in the rural landscape. The breakdown of traditional societies, population and commercial pressures, nepotism, corruption, and lack of awareness, knowledge, skills, and enforcement are only a few examples. Perhaps the greatest obstacle lies in the parochialism of communities and the difficulties they face in conceding the rights and interests of other communities.

Furthermore, no community today stands alone. In some cases, communities share resources such as the Pacific salmon or the Serengeti wildebeest. Others find that common interests arise indirectly, for example, over the impact of deforestation on river flows. Every community now depends on outside markets and is therefore subject to the vagaries of pricing policies and marketing structures outside its control.

Community-based conservation, under these circumstances, is not simply a question of recognizing the rights of local communities and landowners to use resources. In the absence of a sense of responsibility to society and the appropriate management capacity, devolving to local communities the right to use resources carries the risk of even worse destruction.

Given the risks and uncertainties, can governments realistically abrogate their responsibilities to society in the interest of devolving proprietary rights to local communities and individuals? This raises the difficult question of which right is more fundamental: that of the community or that of society? Does this mean, then, that responsibilities and capabilities should be linked to rights to use and manage natural resources?

All three factors—rights, responsibilities, and capabilities—were once more or less internalized within traditional communities and imposed by resource limitations. The integrity and interrelatedness of these factors broke down once local communities entered a larger constellation of communities within nation states and, more recently, a global community of nations.

While community-based conservation and talk of the new conservation paradigm have engendered a rush of optimism, the troubling question of whether communities actually can resolve resource conflicts and slow environmental degradation better than a centralized authority remains (Wells and Brandon 1992). The scale and complexity of environmental problems is far greater today than anything traditional communities ever had to deal with. Even where cultural institutions are still intact, poverty, commerce, and politics play havoc with them.

The chapters that follow take a hard look at community-based conservation in order to shed light on its strengths and weaknesses. Parts I and II present case studies from around the world. Part III is concerned with the urgent themes that arise from the case studies. The chapters in Part IV present the conclusions of the Airlie House workshop and convey a sense of the common ground and differences that emerged from discussion among the diverse participants. The final chapter, "Visions of the Future: The New Focus of Conservation," speculates on the future of conservation in the rural landscape.

SOURCES

Berger, J., ed. 1979. *Indigenous Peoples: A Global Quest for Justice.* Report for the Independent Commission on International Humanitarian Issues. London: Zed Books.

Carson, R. 1963. *Silent Spring.* Boston, Massachusetts: Houghton-Mifflin.

Chambers, R. 1983. *Rural Development: Putting the Last First.* London: Longman.

Croll, E., and D. Parkin, eds. 1992. *Bush Base: Forest Farm, Culture, Environment and Development*. London:Routledge.

Durning, A. 1989. *Action at the Grassroots: Fighting Poverty and Environmental Decline*. Worldwatch Paper 88. Washington, D.C.: Worldwatch Institute.

Ehrlich, P. R., and A. H. Ehrlich. 1968. *The Population Bomb*. Maltituck, New York: Amereon.

Hellinger, S., D. Hellinger, and F. O'Regan. 1988. *Aid for Just Development: Report on the Future of Foreign Assistance*. Boulder, Colorado: Lynne Rienner.

Hirschmann, A. 1993. *Getting Ahead Collectively: Grassroots Experences in Latin America*. New York: Pergamon Press.

Holt, S. J., and L. M. Talbot. 1978. "New Principles for the Conservation of Wild Living Resources." Wildlife Monograph No. 59. Supplement to *Journal of Wildlife Management* 43(2):1–33.

International Union for the Conservation of Nature and Natural Resources, the United Nations Environment Program, and World Wildlife Fund (IUCN, UNEP, and WWF). 1980. *World Conservation Strategy*. Washington, D.C.: IUCN, UNEP, and WWF.

Kemf, E., ed. 1993. *The Law of the Mother*. San Francisco: Sierra Club Books.

Lewis, D., and N. Carter, eds. 1993. *Voices from Africa: Local Perspectives on Conservation*. Washington, D.C.: World Wildlife Fund.

Martin, P. S., and R. G. Klein, eds. 1984. *Quarternary Extinctions: A Prehistoric Revolution*. Tucson, Arizona: University of Arizona Press.

McNeely, J. A., and K. R. Miller, eds. 1984. *National Parks, Conservation, and Development. The Role of Protected Areas in Sustaining Society*. Washington, D.C.: Smithsonian Institution Press.

Miller, M. S., ed. 1993. *State of the Peoples: A Global Human Rights Report on Societies in Danger*. Boston: Beacon Press.

Nash, R. F. 1967. *Wilderness and the American Mind*. New Haven, Connecticut: Yale University Press.

———. 1989. *The Rights of Nature. A History of the Environmental Ethics*. Madison, Wisconsin: University of Wisconsin Press.

Olson, S. 1989. "Extinction on Islands: Man as a Catastrophe." In *Conservation for the Twenty-first Century*, eds. D. Western and M. Pearl, 50–53. New York: Oxford University Press.

Rodes, B., and R. Odell, compilers. 1992. *A Dictionary of Environmental Quotations*. New York: Simon and Schuster.

Runte, A. 1979. *National Parks: The American Experience*. Lincoln, Nebraska: University of Nebraska Press.

Shabecoff, P. 1993. *A Fierce Green Fire: The American Environmental Movement*. New York: Hill and Wang.

Southwick, C. H. 1976. *Ecology and the Quality of Our Environment*. Boston: Prindle, Weber and Schmidt.

Talbot, L. M. 1993. *Principles for Living Resource Conservation: Preliminary Report on Consultations*. Washington, D. C.: The Marine Mammal Commission.

Thomas, K. 1983. *Man and the Natural World: A History of the Modern Sensibility*. New York: Pantheon.

Tober, J. A. 1981. *Who Owns the Wildlife? A Political Economy of Conservation in Nineteenth Century America.* Westport, Connecticut: Greenwood Press.

Uphoff, N. 1985. "Fitting Projects to People." In *Putting People First,* ed. Michael Cernea, 359–395. New York: Oxford University Press.

Vedant, O. S. 1986. "Afforestation in India." *Ambio* 15(4):254–255.

Wells, M., and K. Brandon. 1992. *People and Parks: Linking Protected Areas with Local Communities.* Washington, D.C.: World Bank.

Western, D. 1984. "Conservation-based Rural Development." In *Sustaining Tomorrow: A Strategy for World Conservation and Development,* eds. F. R. Thibodeau and H. H. Field, 94–110. Hanover, New Hampshire: University Press of New England.

―――. 1989. "Conservation Without Parks: Wildlife in the Rural Landscape." In *Conservation for the Twenty-first Century,* eds. D. Western and M. Pearl, 158–165. New York: Oxford University Press.

Wilkinson, C. F. 1992. *Crossing the Next Meridian: Land, Water, and the Future of the West.* Washington, D.C.: Island Press.

World Commission on Environment and Development (WCED). 1987. *Our Common Future.* New York: Oxford University Press.

PART I

Case Studies

CHAPTER 2

Ecosystem Conservation and Rural Development: The Case of Amboseli

David Western

The conservation efforts in Amboseli National Park, Kenya, described in this case study began as an exploratory project looking into new ways to secure a future for wildlife in Africa. In the course of time, those efforts broadened to involve many different people. They also became inextricably bound up with policy reform, legislation, and institution building. In the description that follows, I have tried to convey the flavor of the actors, ideas, and circumstances that influenced the direction of conservation programs in Amboseli and, eventually, a shift in national policy toward local participation.

Conservation Background

The Amboseli area (see Map 2.1) has long been recognized for its abundant wildlife. Located in southern Maasailand on the northern slope of Mount Kilimanjaro, Amboseli lay on a slave and trading route connecting the coast with the Great Lakes of the interior. Amboseli's large herds soon came to the notice of colonial administrators, and the area was incorporated into the Southern Reserve— what remained of Maasailand after expropriations for British settlers. The reserve, set up under the Special Districts Ordinance of 1902, was expanded in 1911 under a treaty between the colonial administration and Lenana, the Maasai's spiritual leader. The treaty was intended to prohibit further annexation of Maasailand and leave the Maasai people free to develop along their own lines (Kantai 1971). In the process, the Amboseli ecosystem was protected inadvertently from hunting and settlement.

The treaty, guaranteed "for as long as the Maasai shall exist as a race" (Kantai 1971), was soon challenged by the National Parks Ordinance of 1945. The ordinance signaled a shift in conservation policy from protection through hunting legislation to preservation through land protection (Simon 1962). The new position arose largely in response to burgeoning human and livestock numbers. Several areas including Nairobi, Tsavo East and West, Aberdares, and Mount Kenya were gazetted as national parks. Most of the parks lay within former Maasai territory.

Map 2.1

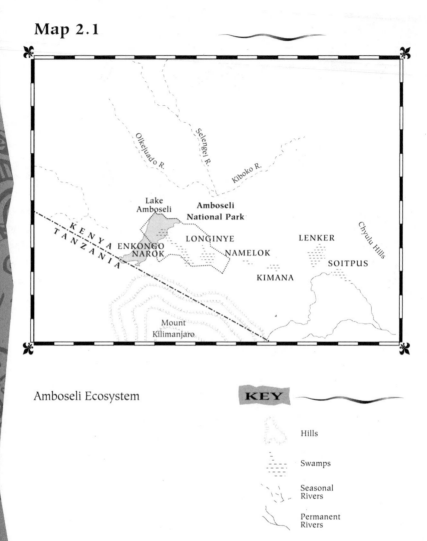

Amboseli Ecosystem

KEY

Hills

Swamps

Seasonal Rivers

Permanent Rivers

0   10 km

Amboseli and Mara were problematic, since they fell within the Southern Reserve covered by the Maasai Treaty. This did not stop the colonial government from trying to usurp Amboseli, but their efforts met stiff resistance. As a temporary solution, a 3,260-km² area was established as the Amboseli National Reserve. Although the Maasai were not excluded, the reserve, administered by the Kenya National Parks (KNP) board, was viewed by the Maasai as an impending land grab.

The Maasai's continued resistance prevented the loss of Amboseli and Mara to the parks, even in the pre-Independence rush to set aside new land for wildlife conservation. Instead, game reserves were established under the administration of district, or "county," councils. This alternative was partly the result of efforts by Lynn Temple-Boreham, then Narok District warden, who wanted to see the Maasai benefit from the area around the Mara (Talbot and Olindo 1990). Amboseli National Reserve became the Amboseli Game Reserve, administered by the Maasai Kajiado County Council under a similar arrangement.

Despite Temple-Boreham's motive, the traditional occupants were banned not just from Mara, but from virtually every other reserve, without compensation. The councils' primary reason was to protect tourist revenues—the main source of income for many councils—from possible depletion due to encroachment by pastoralists. Consequently, local hostility toward the new county council reserves was at least as great as it had been toward the national reserves. Amboseli differed from Mara in that the Maasai were not prohibited from using the reserve, except for a 7,800-ha stock-free area at Ol Tukai.

By 1967, county councils were well established as the form of district administration in Kenya. The weakness of this system soon became obvious. Where Kenya National Parks was concerned solely with conservation (and, toward that end, reinvested all its income in the parks), the councils used the reserves' income to finance development in the more populous areas of their districts. Very little money was spent within the reserves. In 1969, for example, of earnings of some Ksh2 million (US$285,000), the Kajiado County Council spent less than Ksh50,000 (US$7,100) to run the reserve (Mitchell 1969). In short, the councils ignored the concerns of local people even more than Parks had, and they also did far less to protect wildlife.

Amboseli came to national and international attention in the late 1960s because of four factors. First, Amboseli became a pivotal tourist destination in East Africa, rivaling the Serengeti and Ngorongoro in Tanzania. Amboseli owed its popularity to its remarkable diversity of wildlife; to long-horned rhinos Gertie and Gladys; and to Odinga, one of the biggest tuskers in Africa. Amboseli—with its superb setting of yellow-barked acacias (*Acacia xanthophloea*), marshes, and plains beneath the striking backdrop of Kilimanjaro—was the most widely advertised wildlife spectacle in East Africa. Tourism grew at 22 percent per year between 1965 and 1969 (Mitchell 1969) and contributed more than 70 percent of the Kajiado County Council's income for the entire 20,000-km² district (Western 1969b).

Second, the growth in wildlife tourism, particularly in Amboseli, soon caught the interest of and raised concern within the Kenyan government. The government's interest, as with the county council's, lay in Amboseli's income.

The third factor, a strong conservation movement, was driven by international forces and an expatriate lobby within Kenya. The lobbyists insisted that the only assurance for wildlife's future lay in parks, and they successfully played on the government's interest in the fast-growing tourist economy.

The threats to wildlife were rooted in the fourth factor, a 4 percent annual increase in the human population. This increase was beginning to lead to land shortages and strident demands for more land. Rural communities became openly hostile to wildlife and parks when their pleas went unheeded (Yeager and Miller 1986).

Amboseli, the last renowned wildlife area in Kenya occupied by people, was the target of a well-publicized conservation campaign. Conservationists blamed livestock for turning the area into a dust bowl (Western 1969b) and Maasai herders for spearing dozens of rhinos, including Gertie. Numerous fingers pointed to the Kajiado County Council, which was accused of milking Amboseli and doing nothing to conserve it.

The threats to Amboseli sparked my own interests. My perspective—to find a solution that would both satisfy the Maasai and preserve wildlife—was at variance with the strong protectionist ethos of the time. It needs some explanation, since it would have a major influence on the conservation approach adopted in Amboseli.

I had grown up in Tanzania in the late 1940s and 1950s, when protectionist policies first were being implemented. My father, a part-time hunter, became an honorary warden in the Tanganyika Game Department and alternately protected wildlife from poachers and farmers from wildlife, with little sense of the inherent contradiction. He later lobbied for the creation of Mikumi National Park to protect the threatened herds from encroachment and poaching and to promote tourism.

Two impressions of that period stand out. First, there was no such thing as wilderness in East Africa. Human activity was a natural and historical factor everywhere. Second, it was difficult to ignore local enmity toward colonial hunting laws and game reserves. Reserves were tellingly called *shamba la bibi*—literally, "the woman's garden" in Swahili, referring to the British queen. The suffering of farmers and traditional hunters was acute. Wild animals regularly destroyed their crops and livestock. Many farmers lost their lives to wild animals each year. Most rural Africans expressed resentment over being denied the right to hunt or use traditional land within the protected areas. In short, protectionist policies seemed to be doing more harm than good. It was difficult not to develop a strong sympathy for the people most affected by these policies.

My misgivings about the adequacy of parks were reinforced by my training in biology, a deep interest in ecosystems, and a survey of protected areas I made in 1967, prior to settling on Amboseli as a subject of study. No park covered an entire ecosystem, and most were far too small to survive in ecological isolation. Moreover, the unnecessary hardship that wildlife caused people was virtually ignored in the postcolonial years (Yeager and Miller 1986).

For the most part, after Independence, conservation remained the preserve of expatriates (mainly ex-colonial officers). Not surprisingly, then, the protection-against-people view of parks persisted. Researchers drawn to East Africa to look at pristine ecosystems (as they saw it) reinforced the view that parks were laboratories of nature. The largely mechanistic views of nature in vogue reinforced protectionist policies and hands-off management (Botkin 1990). The absence of human activity, itself an artifact of the establishment of parks, seldom was mentioned or considered.

Amboseli Game Reserve was the logical place to investigate the conflicts between wildlife and people. I began work there in 1967, looking at the entire ecosystem and trying to resolve conflicts between Maasai and wildlife interests. The first phase of the study focused on the numbers and seasonal movements of wildlife and livestock, the ecology of the Maasai, and their attitudes toward wildlife. A description of Amboseli's ecological, socioeconomic, and political background sets the stage for what followed.

Ecology

The Amboseli ecosystem (see Map 2.1) is, for the most part, typical of the bushed grassland covering most of East Africa. Classified as Ecological Zone V (Pratt, Greenway, and Gwynne 1966), Amboseli sits on basement soils. Wildlife biomass and diversity is low and limited by seasonal water pans that dry soon after the rains.

Local geological forces make this otherwise unremarkable ecosystem distinctive, productive, and diverse. Volcanic upheaval lifted the Kilimanjaro massif to nearly 6,000 m—4,800 m higher than the surrounding plain. Subsequent geological and climatic influences created an alkaline lake—the Amboseli Basin—at the northern slope of the mountain (Williams 1967). North of the basin, where the seasonal discharge backs up before entering the Kiboko-Sabaki River (Western 1975), the Ol Kajiado River forms a floodplain, favored by migratory ungulates.

Kilimanjaro today creates opposing climatic and hydrological influences. Climatically, Amboseli is cradled in the rain shadow of the mountain. Rainfall (on average, 300 mm a year) comes in two seasons. The mountain discharges much of its forests' 1,500-mm annual rainfall to the plains below through underground aquifers (Lahi 1967). Many springs fed by the aquifers dot the arid plains in a wide arc around the northern foot of the mountain (Map 2.1). The Amboseli basin has two main swamps, Longinye and Enkongo Narok, each used by migratory ungulates during the dry season.

Kilimanjaro's influence in Amboseli also extends to vegetation. The dry bushed grassland in the mountain's northern rain shadow responds quickly to rain and attracts migrants from the Amboseli basin for as long as the rain pools last. The Amboseli basin is quite different. Plant production—low over most of the northern basin, where the water table is deep—is dominated by a few grasses tolerant of alkaline conditions (Western and Sindiyo 1972). This otherwise simple habitat is complicated by the hydrologic influence of the mountain. The many swamps and shallow water table create a rich tapestry of habitats (Western 1973). The shifting swamps, fluctuating water table, and impact of elephants and Maasai on these habitats create continually changing relationships between them (Western and van Praet 1973).

Amboseli's diverse habitats support a richer variety of large mammals than the adjacent Tsavo East and West national parks, which are fifty times as large. All conservation efforts in Amboseli's history, even the most current (KWS 1991), have focused on this high biodiversity.

The Amboseli ecosystem is circumscribed by seasonal wildlife migrations (see Figure 2.1). Large aggregations of zebra, wildebeest, gazelle, and elephant migrate from the basin to the surrounding bush lands and Ol Kajiado River floodplain during the rains. The migrants spread erratically over an area of roughly 8,000 km² (Figure 2.1), depending on rainfall patterns.

The dry season forces migrants to concentrate close to permanent water in the basin (Western 1975) and limits the size of populations. All ungulates show some degree of habitat selectivity in the basin (Western 1973), and they move along a gradient of increasing abundance and declining quality of forage as the season progresses (Western and Lindsay 1984). Maasai livestock—cattle, sheep, and goats—traditionally follow a similar migratory pattern (Western and Dunne 1979).

The plans to resolve the conflict in Amboseli drew heavily from this research, highlighting the importance of the area's high ecological diversity, the annual migrations, and the interactions of the Maasai and wildlife.

Maasai Life-style and Politics

Pastoralism has been a factor in the East African savannas for three thousand years, and probably longer (Marshall 1989), although the Maasai themselves only moved down from the north as little as five hundred years ago (Kituyi 1990). Traditional Maasai pastoralists depended on cattle for milk and on cattle, sheep, and goats for meat. They bartered for agricultural products from neighboring tribes when milk supplies dried up (Galaty 1982). Large herds, mobility, and sophisticated herding practices helped the Maasai survive drought (Western and Finch 1986). Human herders shadowed the wildlife migrants through the seasons but made greater use of the forest-edge pastures on Kilimanjaro. The area used and defended most vigorously was Amboseli, the Maasai name for the basin.

Maasai attitudes toward wildlife since colonial times have ranged from indifference to antagonism. Many Maasai elders claim that wildlife traditionally was used as "second cattle" to see them through droughts when their own herds were

Figure 2.1

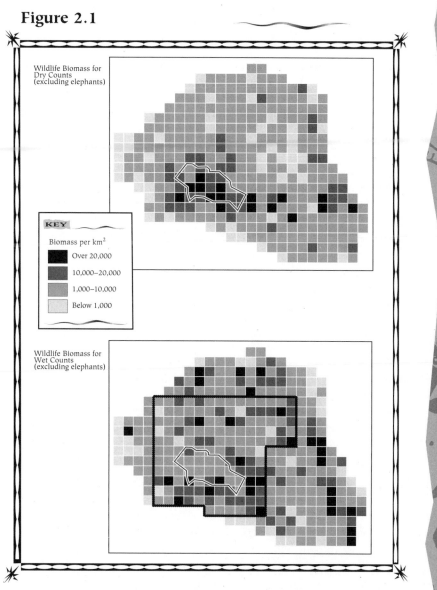

Wildlife Biomass for
Dry Counts
(excluding elephants)

KEY

Biomass per km²

■ Over 20,000

■ 10,000–20,000

■ 1,000–10,000

□ Below 1,000

Wildlife Biomass for
Wet Counts
(excluding elephants)

Wet and dry distribution of Ilkisongo wildlife biomass averaged over the years 1973 to 1991. The wet season map shows the Amboseli ecosystem defined by the range of migratory herbivores. Each cell is 5 km². Data from the Amboseli Ecological Monitoring Program.

depleted (Western 1982a). Reliance on second cattle helps to explain the traditional Maasai tolerance toward wildlife. This relationship was to become the basis
of the *Development Plans for Amboseli* formulated in the mid-1970s.

Maasai land and resource ownership was typical of East Africa's pastoral societies until two decades ago (Galaty 1982). Land was communally owned, and
forage was freely available to all members of a section. Each section was politically autonomous and made up of a number of clans (Sankan 1971). Battles
within Maasailand usually were over sectional access to forage during drought.
One section, the Ilkisongo, covers the whole basin and most of the ecosystem.
Two adjacent sections, the Matapatu to the west and the Kaputei to the north,
border the ecosystem. Grazing disputes between the Ilkisongo and Kaputei sections in the last few decades have arisen over sectional boundaries, often during
drought.

By contrast, the Ilkisongo section associated with the Amboseli area did not
deny grazing to any of the clans within the ecosystem. Water, often contested
within other pastoral societies (Galaty 1982), is not disputed, since the main
sources are large, open bodies.

The Maasai had no centralized government because they were mobile and had
low population densities. Individual families owned their own herds and made
their own foraging decisions (Kituyi 1990). Consequently, they had little need to
reach communal decisions, except when it came to ceremonies, raids, defense,
and, sometimes, access to pasture and water. Political authority in the age-graded
Maasai society was vested in the ruling elders (Jacobs 1975), whose gatherings
were egalitarian. The elders' decisions grew out of consensus. A spokesman (the
Olaigwenani) was selected for each age group by the "fire-stick elders," or patrons,
of the age group (Kituyi 1990). In the Amboseli region, traditional political institutions, including those for resolving grazing disputes, weakened in the face of official governmental structures but were not entirely undermined (Spencer 1988).

Maasai life-style and politics are directly relevant to conservation and development programs that rely on community participation. Neither the Maasai traditional social structure nor the mobile life-style readily lends itself to community-
based programs. Although the Maasai are egalitarian to an unusual degree,
authority nevertheless rests with the ruling elders. Women traditionally had no
formal role in decision making and even today have little say.

Government chiefs and elected members of Parliament (MPs) complicate the
picture further. In many cases, chiefs are traditional leaders. But over the last few
decades, chiefs and MPs have consolidated their power in parallel with the centralization of power by government (Kituyi 1990). One important consequence
has been the weakening of the district councils' authority, including that of the Kajiado County Council (KCC), which administered the Amboseli Game Reserve.
The council was, until the mid-1970s, a powerful political and development force
within the area. All the communal lands—effectively the entire district—were
vested in the council. That influence declined sharply when the communal lands

were subdivided into group and individual lands in the 1970s, and diminished further with the centralization of political power in Kenya throughout the 1980s.

History also has played an important role in the Maasai psyche. Smallpox, drought, and rinderpest had a crippling effect on their society and economy in the early colonial period. Thus the colonial perception was that Maasailand was underutilized, resulting in a series of land grabs for white settlement (Kituyi 1990).

The Maasai subsequently withdrew to the Southern Reserve and into themselves. Independence found them ill prepared for the rapid modernization and free-market economy ushered in by the government of Jomo Kenyatta. The Maasai had one of the lowest literacy levels in Kenya at that time, with less than 10 percent of their children entering primary school in the 1960s (Ochilo 1991). Another factor in the political and economic marginalization of the Maasai after Independence was the antipathy the central government showed toward pastoralists in general (Galaty and Salzman 1980).

The Maasai's seeming reticence in the face of modernization was viewed as fierce traditionalism at best and plain backwardness at worst. The traditionalism reflected the Maasai's strong cultural values. But until the 1970s, circumstance played as much a part as attitude. The Maasai had become wealthier without changing their traditional system, as stock recovered from the disasters of the late 1800s and then increased sharply with veterinary services and water development in the 1940s and 1950s (see Figure 2.2). Per capita stock holdings rose, and market incentives to sell—when markets were accessible—remained weak (Kituyi 1990). The Maasai's revitalized subsistence economy remained robust until human population increase and drought whittled down family holdings in the mid-1970s (Figure 2.2).

In addition, around Independence, Kikuyu and Kamba people started settling Kilimanjaro and some of the swamps east of Amboseli. This added to the land shortage and pressure on Amboseli. By the late 1960s, pressure increased for legal land ownership, and Maasai tolerance of wildlife quickly evaporated. The Maasai's antagonism toward any takeover of Amboseli or concession to wildlife must be seen in this historical context.

Working Toward a Locally Based Conservation Plan

I began work in Amboseli shortly after Daniel Sindiyo's appointment as warden. Sindiyo's background and influence did much to foster the locally based conservation plan. As a Maasai brought up in Narok District, he was keenly aware of the coexistence of wildlife and pastoralists. He had a strong interest in conservation and, as a young indigenous Kenyan, an equally strong commitment to development. Sindiyo received a diploma in wildlife management from Colorado State University. Afterward, he spent three years as an education officer in the Kenyan

Figure 2.2

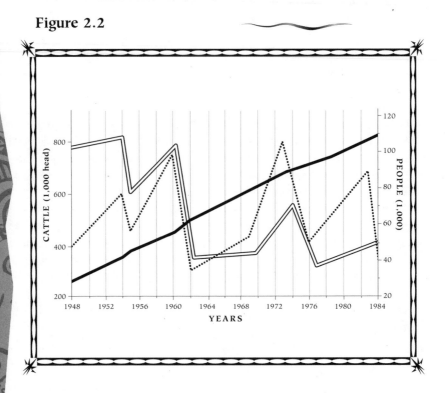

Livestock and human population trends in Kajiado District. The per capita stock holdings show the progressive decline in Maasai livestock subsistence. The strong downturns are associated with drought. Data from Grandon 1991.

KEY

——————— Per Capita Livestock (= People/10)

•••••••••• Number of Cattle

━━━━━━━ Number of People

Game Department. There he used money from the sale of wildlife trophies to build dams and health clinics for Samburu herders (Sindiyo 1968). Sindiyo's background and education distinguished him from other wardens of the time, and our views on Amboseli were similar from the outset.

The first phase of my research helped to provide ecological data upon which subsequent conservation plans were based. The finding of most immediate significance was that the game reserve, which was being promoted as a national park within government and conservation circles, held little of the wet-season migrations. Furthermore, Maasai and wildlife migrations were more or less identical. The combination meant that wildlife migrants would not be fully protected, even if the Maasai were totally excluded from the reserve. The total exclusion of the Maasai was in itself an obstacle, given their political antagonism. Both the ecological and socioeconomic realities began to suggest a radically different conservation alternative to segregating the Maasai and wildlife.

Sindiyo and I both began working with the local community in different ways. Sindiyo, as warden, set up a wildlife committee of influential elders to resolve conflicts within the game reserve. I befriended a number of elders and warriors to learn more about their life-style, ecology, and attitudes toward wildlife. Many of the insights on which subsequent plans were based were a direct result of these close associations.

Some of my friendships with Maasai elders and warriors, among them Parashino Ole Purdul and Kerenkol Ole Musa, were formalized through an exchange of livestock. As stock associates (Jacobs 1975), we openly discussed the future of the Maasai, wildlife, and Amboseli. The Maasai were fully aware of my commitment to conservation; they made their own priorities and welfare equally clear. Our exchange of ideas was easier because I was a student of wildlife and not a wildlife officer. I was seen as someone willing to listen and talk openly on a topic about which they felt strongly.

Ole Purdul's ideas and insights helped clarify options and shape plans in the years 1968 to 1974. Even by Maasai standards, Ole Purdul had a deep understanding of wildlife ecology and livestock husbandry. He contributed much to the 1973 *Development Plans for Amboseli*. Kerenkol Ole Musa, the *Olaigwenani* spokesman of the warrior age group, was another important influence during this early stage.

The pace of Sindiyo's and my own efforts was forced into high gear by a plan under discussion at the Ministry of Tourism and Wildlife (MTW). The plan, which originated with a wealthy industrialist, Royal Little, proposed setting aside a 500-km^2 national park in exchange for providing the Maasai with alternative sources of water. The plan, backed by the New York Zoological Society (NYZS), won ministry approval and was put to the Kajiado County Council. The council tentatively agreed but quickly backed away after the plan was rejected at an elders' meeting in 1968. Both Sindiyo and the area MP, Stanley Oloitiptip, were present. Oloitiptip, then assistant minister of health, insisted on a local solution

rather than one imposed from outside. Although he was caught between government and local interests, Oloitiptip sided squarely with the Maasai. The elders
deeply resented the proposal and wrote a strong letter articulating their views
(Lwezaula 1970). Much as they favored positive returns from Amboseli, they had
received no remuneration, despite their accommodation of wildlife.

The elders' rejection of the plan led to renewed pressure on the government to
take over Amboseli. Conservationists argued forcefully for decisive action to avoid
the destruction of Amboseli through overgrazing. The result was a race between
the government's little-disguised takeover efforts and Oloitiptip's search for a local
solution.

Oloitiptip was unrealistic in thinking that the Maasai would come up with their
own conservation plan, given their deep antipathy to wildlife at that time. The alternatives were either to let the Maasai's decision stand and risk losing Amboseli
to the government, or to press for action in the Maasai's long-term interests.
Sindiyo believed it was necessary to pursue the latter course.

I had my own reasons for following a similar course. First, the livestock and
human population trends showed an impending collapse of the Maasai's traditional cattle economy (see Figure 2.2). There seemed to be no alternative to even-
tual diversification. The Maasai had, in fact, already voluntarily entered the
market economy. Despite a centralized government marketing system that discouraged Maasai sales, herders regularly sold livestock to make cash purchases of
blankets, tea, sugar, flashlights, livestock drugs, and other consumer items
(Western 1973). Younger warriors found the task of building up their herds increasingly difficult and were entering the wage economy in increasing numbers.

Few Maasai elders, however, were willing to admit the inevitability of change,
although they were aware of their faltering economy. Only elders such as Simon
Salash, who had some education and experience outside Maasailand, saw hard
times ahead for their people. In contrast to the traditional elders, these men felt
that, in competition with more educated and politically savvy Kenyans, the
Maasai would be consigned to second-class status.

My second reason was that wildlife offered the only economic alternative to
stock keeping in the arid Amboseli area. This was no longer a vague prospect,
given the demonstrable growth of tourist income within the reserve (see Figure
2.3).

Tentative steps toward the first locally based conservation plan for Amboseli
came out of discussions with Maasai elders and my own observations. The main
elements that I felt would balance Maasai and wildlife interests and conserve the
ecosystem as a whole were

- A nominal area (about 6 percent of the ecosystem) should be set aside to secure
  viewing facilities and protect the abundance and diversity of the large-mammal
  community from future land annexation and development. The area, defined
  by ecological surveys, would be set aside as a "Maasai park." The move would

Figure 2.3

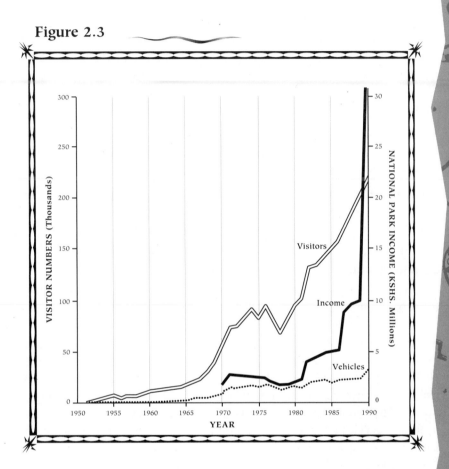

Annual gate earnings and visitor statistics for Amboseli National Park.

safeguard the area against government annexation, channel tourist benefits to the Maasai as the elders requested (Lwezaula 1970), and assuage the government and conservationists in the process.

- Some 94 percent of the ecosystem, including some of the dry-season and all of the wet-season grazing area, would be secured for the Maasai. This proposal rested on the premise that the ecologies of the Maasai and wildlife were intertwined and historically compatible. The proposal would, in other words, degazette all but some 10 percent of the Amboseli Game Reserve and hand it over to the local Maasai for livestock use.

- Wildlife from the park would have free access to these Maasai livestock lands. In exchange, the Maasai would receive specified benefits from the park and the right to utilize wildlife over the rest of the ecosystem.

I continued my own investigations and discussions with Maasai associates through early 1969, although my role was informal. Sindiyo, meanwhile, discussed the options more formally with the wildlife committee.

Reactions and Response

I put a preliminary proposal to the East Africa Natural History Society in Nairobi in 1969, with the intention of sparking wider discussion and greater appreciation of problems and options within the conservation community. The presentation was couched in terms of optimal land use, but from a local and national rather than a conservation perspective. The controversial elements in the proposal included making Amboseli into a Maasai park, giving benefits to the local residents, and degazetting most of the reserve for livestock use. The premise was that *wildlife would have to pay its way*. The plan was not well received by conservationists, nor by the Maasai elders at first. The only positive backing came from the Institute for Development Studies (IDS) at the University of Nairobi.

IDS support contributed a strong multidisciplinary component to the plan. In collaboration with IDS, I expanded my study to include a number of economic analyses of wildlife tourism and livestock development as well as anthropological, political, and administrative issues. Our interdisciplinary effort looked at conservation options within the framework of both the potential national and local benefits accruing from the ecosystem (Western 1969a; Mitchell 1969). The studies involved dialogue between IDS members and Maasai in Amboseli, but the pastoralists continued to distrust any wildlife plan. Suspicions were eased only by talk of tourist income, livestock development, and health facilities for the Maasai.

The expanded planning phase, like the preliminary round, drew from local discussions and looked explicitly at locally based solutions. While the initiative did not come from the community as Oloitiptip had hoped, it was nonetheless rooted in long-term local interests. There were protracted on-the-ground discussions with the Maasai, as well as with their wildlife committee.

One immediate and portentous outcome of the land-use study was an economic analysis that revealed enormous economic returns, both actual and potential, from wildlife tourism (Mitchell 1969). These large wildlife revenues drew considerable press interest, resulting in a double-page spread in the Kenyan daily *Standard*. This article featured in all later discussions, locally and nationally. Frank Mitchell, the social economist behind the analysis, would become an influential figure in promoting local involvement of the Maasai within government circles and at the World Bank.

Sindiyo, after further local discussions, put the plan before the Kajiado County Council and the Amboseli elders in August 1969. The plan was purposefully simple and rudimentary (Western 1969a, 1970), leaving detailed discussion to the Maasai. It was debated over a two-day period by the elders, Oloitiptip, the Kajiado County Council, and Sindiyo. The reception was mixed. The elders remained distrustful and dubious. Their attitude was, "If the government hasn't given us anything in the past, why should it now?" They had the same feelings about the Kajiado County Council.

Oloitiptip, together with the other educated Maasai (including councilors and Sindiyo), finally persuaded the elders to adopt the essence of the plan and continue to work out the details. Oloitiptip stressed the potential benefits of a Maasai park as outlined in the *Standard* article, the inevitability of change, the need for a long-term view, and the threat of a government takeover. Those at the meeting finally agreed and opted to accept the NYZS's monetary offer. The significance of this meeting should not be overlooked: The plan was commissioned and adopted locally within a traditional framework and prevailing political and administrative structures.

Six weeks later, however, the plan foundered, and opposition candidates in the impending parliamentary elections played on Maasai fears of land annexation. The answer, as far as the Maasai were concerned, lay in private and group ownership of land. The government saw "group ranches" as a way to improve livestock control and development by partitioning communal lands into smaller holdings based on traditional seasonal movements. The Maasai saw the issue differently: By effectively privatizing the communal lands under joint title, the group ranches legitimized their claim to all Maasailand, making wildlife concessions unnecessary. Oloitiptip read the political mood and began to oppose the Amboseli plan on the basis of losing "not one more inch" of Maasailand.

Amboseli's wildlife undoubtedly would have dwindled within a decade had Amboseli been incorporated as a group ranch. Namelok Swamp, adjacent to Amboseli, illustrates the trend: Once Namelok was adjudicated and title granted to group ranches, the swamps were drained for farming and wildlife was driven out. By 1980, the herds had all but disappeared from Namelok.

The die was cast for government intervention. Sindiyo resigned shortly afterward, when the Kajiado County Council's financial support for the reserve waned. The council, in a move that can only be described as suicidal, cut back expenditures further, installed a corrupt and inept warden, and effectively abandoned the reserve. Failure of the local plans and the council's pullout fed directly into the hands of the conservationists who wanted a national park. The Ministry of Tourism and Wildlife appealed to President Kenyatta to act on Amboseli in the "national interest."

Cycles of Planning and Lobbying: Opening the Dialogue

The threat of government takeover was realized in 1971. President Kenyatta decreed that an unspecified 200 mi.^{2} of Amboseli would be set aside as government land and the Maasai compensated with alternative water sources. The Maasai were irate. Large numbers of lions, leopard cubs, hyenas, rhinos, and elephants were killed in the next few weeks. The point could not have been made more clearly: The government could annex Amboseli, but its fate lay squarely with the Maasai. Oloitiptip promptly led a Maasai delegation to see the President and won back 50 mi.^{2}.

At this stage, I became an unofficial arbitrator between the Maasai and the government. My immediate aim was to salvage as much of the locally based plan as I could within the constraints imposed by the presidential decree. In Amboseli I met regularly with an informal network of Maasai, including Ole Purdul and Ole Musa, in an attempt to defuse the crisis and promote local involvement. Both men had begun to appreciate the opportunities that the Amboseli plan held for the Maasai, but they had little hope of securing them.

In Nairobi, I articulated the need for local involvement and the danger of ignoring the Maasai by citing the protest spearings. Both Daniel Sindiyo and Frank Mitchell played important advocacy roles. Sindiyo, who had risen to the position of deputy chief game warden, urged the Ministry of Tourism and Wildlife to consider local benefits. Mitchell, recently appointed an advisor to the Ministry of Finance and Planning, cogently articulated the economic case for integrating wildlife and livestock development in the Amboseli ecosystem. This ministry would have an influential voice.

One outcome of this joint effort to salvage something of the original plan was the reallocation to the Kajiado County Council of a 156-ha land parcel around the two existing lodges. The Ol Tukai parcel was explicitly handed back to the Maasai to give them an economic stake in Amboseli and to calm the fears of other district councils vis-à-vis the future of the game reserves. Getting the ministry to accept the wisdom of truly local benefits proved more difficult. But there was an even greater obstacle: Now that Amboseli was national land, no local involvement was possible until government policy and legislation was changed. Since the ministry remained implacably opposed to revising its protectionist policies, change had to come through the backdoor.

The opportunity arose in 1971 during negotiations between the Ministry of Livestock Development and the World Bank on a US$40 million extension to a livestock development program for the Kenyan rangelands. Working with the World Bank appraisal mission for the Livestock 2 program, Mitchell and I alerted its team to the enormous potential wildlife held for landowners. These potential benefits— and the tourist industry—were threatened by plans to develop the rangeland areas for livestock production without regard to alternative economic options. Interestingly, the link between conservation and landowner income, which had eluded the Ministry of Tourism and Wildlife, was immediately obvious to livestock planners. The Ministry of Agriculture and the World Bank agreed to fund water projects around Amboseli, Kitengela, and Mara if the Maasai received benefits from wildlife. They also agreed to finance a Kenya Rangeland Ecological Monitoring Unit to monitor ecological changes on the rangelands.

The Ministry of Lands also was pressured into accepting a single large group ranch around Amboseli rather than a series of smaller holdings. The basic premise was that the revenue distribution from Amboseli to the surrounding landowners, as called for under the Livestock 2 loan agreement, would be greatly simplified by a single holding. Data on Maasai migratory patterns, derived from the ecological monitoring programs, were also instrumental, since they stressed the need for Maasai herding flexibility in this drought-prone area. The resulting 120,000-ha Ololorashi Ogulului Group Ranch ultimately would greatly simplify revenue-sharing programs established by Amboseli National Park in 1977 and 1991.

The Livestock 2 proposal and the terms relating to Amboseli (the only program ultimately implemented) led to an overall review of national wildlife policy. The terms relating to Amboseli would not have been adopted without the backing of the New York Zoological Society. NYZS backing (and funding) gave the World Bank the assurance it needed that this new and untested conservation approach had the support of at least one influential conservation body. NYZS also recognized the centrality but official weakness of my own position and later insisted on funding me in an oversight capacity as a precondition of the grant to the ministry. The involvement of the NYZS and the formal backing it gave the project would prove crucial to subsequent planning, monitoring, and institution building.

The Amboseli plan opened up a second and more important opportunity. Mitchell convinced the World Bank of the need for a scaled-up economic package for parks and reserves based on the principle of landowner participation. The loan package of approximately US$40 million drew the ministry directly into the planning process and face to face with the need for policy reform. Mitchell and I were asked to prepare an Amboseli plan as a working model, spelling out the principles, details, and financial implications. The plan was intended to provide the economic justification and overall rationale for a scaled-up national tourism and wildlife project involving training, institution building, planning, enforcement, and wildlife utilization.

Mitchell soon moved from the Kenyan Ministry of Finance and Planning to the World Bank headquarters in Washington, D.C. Economist Philip Thresher of the Kenya Wildlife Management Project took over the task of helping to prepare what was called the *Development Plans for Amboseli* (Western and Thresher 1973). In this instance, the Amboseli plans helped legitimize the national program and not the reverse, although implementation of the Amboseli plan itself depended on national policy reforms. These would not have been necessary had Amboseli become a Maasai park rather than a national preserve.

The *Development Plans for Amboseli*, which rationalized the integration of livestock and wildlife economies (see Table 2.1), included utilization schemes on the group ranches, payment of the opportunity costs incurred by the ranches in accommodating Amboseli's migratory herds, Maasai involvement in the tourist industry, and various other benefits including a community center on the park periphery. Although focused primarily on tourism, the plan was explicitly an ecosystem conservation plan and stressed the need for wildlife utilization on Maasai group ranches outside the protected area. This integration required an amalgamation of the traditionally divided roles of the Game Department and the national parks.

The broad support for the new policies proved decisive. At a meeting on June 26, 1974, the Ministry of Tourism and Wildlife reluctantly adopted the position that wildlife must pay its way on private and communal lands, in reference to Amboseli, and tacitly accepted the need for a national overhaul of wildlife policy.

The protracted maneuvers over policy did not involve the Maasai, much as they rested on principles they had voiced (Lwezaula 1970). But the terms of the NYZS/World Bank water project changed that situation, since it required an agreement, at least in principle, between the Maasai and the ministry. An increasing number of government and World Bank visits to Amboseli had talking with the Maasai as their focus. Although at first this involved government experts handing ideas to the Maasai—usually through Oloitiptip—rather than discussing them, at least an exchange was under way. The dialogue improved quickly in 1973 and 1974, especially when the Kenya Wildlife Management Project (KWMP) became formally involved.

The Food and Agriculture Organization funded the Kenya Wildlife Management Project, set up in 1971 to develop wildlife utilization plans in Kajiado District. Initially, the expatriate advisers were interested only in hunting-management programs, not in tourism or local benefits. But the ailing KWMP hunting program was redirected toward wildlife tourism and utilization projects and landowner benefits after Thresher helped to prepare the *Development Plans for Amboseli*. Sindiyo again was a strong catalyst.

Several events led to more open dialogue on development plans for the ecosystem. First, the Ministry of Tourism and Wildlife announced in 1974 that Amboseli would be taken over as a national park. The move did not come as a complete surprise. Kenya National Parks recently had posted a warden, Joe Kioko, to Amboseli to avert the crisis created by Kajiado County Council's abandonment of the reserve after the presidential decree. The takeover nevertheless outraged the Maasai, who saw Parks as their implacable enemy. The Maasai had good reason

Table 2.1

Gross revenues from existing and potential uses of Amboseli as calculated in 1973

	Park	Ecosystem
Total wildlife 1972	US$1,200,000.	US$1,202,710.[+]
Total livestock 1972 (cash returns only)	3,000.	4,200.
Subsistence value livestock 1972	199,188.	597,562.
Wildlife potential (no livestock)	6,560,000.	8,030,000.[+]
Commercial livestock potential (no wildlife)	69,300.	445,930.
Combined wildlife and commercial livestock potential	6,560,000.	8,285,580.

to believe they would once again be evicted from a park without receiving any benefit.

Kioko, encouraged by Parks Director Perez Olindo to engage in constructive dialogue as Sindiyo had done, averted the crisis. Kioko acted in the spirit of principles yet to be legislated rather than that of existing Parks policy. He reconvened the Maasai's wildlife committee, calling on representatives of the four group ranches that had been identified as encompassing the wildlife dispersal area for Amboseli. The group ranches eventually would change Maasai attitudes toward property rights and wildlife. But at the time, given the prevailing Maasai conservatism and government paternalism, common ground was hard to find and mutual agreement difficult to come by.

Ironically, the 1973–1977 drought, which took a heavy toll on Maasai livestock, helped change attitudes. Per capita stock holdings plunged by half (see Figure 2.2), stock prices fell, and grain prices rose (Kituyi 1990). The poorer Maasai survived largely on famine relief. The more progressive, like Ole Purdul and Ole Musa, began to diversify economically through livestock sales, small-scale farming, and wage employment. Their interest in wildlife benefits also grew. Ole Purdul, in the course of our many discussions on the subject, again pointed out that the Maasai had traditionally hunted wildlife during droughts and regarded them as second cattle—a relationship that had been destroyed by the colonial government. Monetary and other benefits from wildlife, in other words, could be seen as a Maasai tradition in modern guise. Ole Purdul's revelations helped garner support for Maasai participation among agencies in Nairobi. With Ole Musa, he campaigned assiduously and effectively among the Amboseli Maasai.

From my own continuing ecological studies and discussions with Ole Purdul, Ole Musa, and other influential elders, I was convinced that the Maasai could not survive the drought without swamp grazing, all of which lay within the designated park boundaries. The elders suggested two access points. I put the proposed changes to the Ministry of Tourism and Wildlife and pushed for discussions. As a result, the ministry met with the Maasai for the first time on January 24, 1974. The Maasai were represented by more than one hundred elders, warriors, and leaders and the ministry by the permanent secretary and other officials. Subsequently, the park boundaries were surveyed and redrawn. More important, the meeting broke the ice between the two parties. The wildlife utilization fee, new water points, and the prospect of income from lodges on the group ranches were debated. The parties reached an agreement, at least in principle, at this meeting. In the final analysis, the local public participation that the January meeting initiated would prove its most enduring impact.

Other public meetings followed, including the establishment of a Maasai hunting association. The association, engineered by the Kenya Wildlife Management Project and put to the Maasai by Oloitiptip at Sindiyo's urging, was launched at a large public *baraza* held in Kimana on March 19, 1975. Under this plan, the Maasai group ranches leased out hunting concessions as envisaged in the *Development Plans for Amboseli*. These concessions, involving a great deal of local participation, brought in more than Ksh1.9 million (US$271,000) for southern Kajiado group ranches between 1975 and 1977. Poaching levels dropped sharply.

Direct dialogue had become common practice by the time the new wildlife policy (Sessional Paper No. 2) was introduced in 1975 and the Wildlife Act was passed in 1977. The policies, based on the principle of wildlife paying its way outside parks, called for direct negotiations on the future of wildlife in dispersal areas between the Ministry of Tourism and Wildlife and landowners. The Wildlife Act also called for the creation of an implementing agency, the Wildlife Conservation and Management Department (WCMD), to put the new policies into effect. The agency would prove disastrous not just for Amboseli, but for the locally based approach and Kenya's wildlife generally. The first mistake lay in making the institution a government department within the ministry rather than a parastatal organization similar to the former Kenya National Parks; the second lay in appointing as director the former head of the game department, a man heavily implicated in poaching rackets.

By 1976, top-down policy decisions made in Nairobi rapidly gave way to on-the-ground planning through the wildlife committees and public *barazas*. Issues were debated and resolved through the newly constituted group ranch committees. The most important were discussed at widely attended annual general meetings. The Kenya Wildlife Management Project held two successful workshops on the locally based approach, one for government agencies (PBFL 1977a) and another for the Maasai, specifically addressing people's participation in conservation (PBFL 1977b). This is not to say that dialogue was fully communal; but inasmuch as the elders and group ranch committees were the traditional and legal authorities, local participation had become the means of pursuing implementation of the *Development Plans for Amboseli*. But with the new policies passed, alternative water sources in place, and the US$37.5 million tourism and wildlife loan agreed, the project was ready for implementation. Nearly US$6 million was earmarked for Amboseli.

The exclusion of the Maasai from the park was delayed for a year because of the drought. Another public *baraza* brought the Maasai and the Ministry of Tourism and Wildlife together to agree on the final terms of Maasai relinquishment. The Maasai extracted their own preconditions, including the Kajiado County Council's retention of the 156-ha Ol Tukai inholding, an annual grazing fee to cover the opportunity cost of the Amboseli migrants' use of the adjacent Maasai ranches, the Wildlife Conservation and Management Department's assumption of responsibility for the four southern boreholes, and a new swamp for Maasai livestock outside the park that would be fed by Enkongo Narok spring. WCMD also was to pay the Kajiado County Council a further Ksh460,000 (US$65,000) for the right to manage the council's land at Ol Tukai. The ministry did not, however, extract management rights from the council, despite regular payments. That failure would prove troublesome in future years, when the council, as anticipated, tried to overdevelop Ol Tukai.

The agreement was reached at a public *baraza* in accordance with Maasai wishes. The elders eschewed any written agreement, given their past experience of failed contracts. They insisted that a public *baraza*, in the time-honored way, was open to all and based on consensus. This too would prove a costly mistake. The government abrogated every term of the agreement within four years, creating a legacy of distrust that the successor to WCMD, the Kenya Wildlife Service, inherited more than ten years later.

At the *baraza*, the first wildlife payments—Ksh1.9 million (US$271,000) from the hunting concessions—were given out to the members of the group ranches in the Amboseli region. As the first affirmation of the new policies, this did much to convince the Maasai to vacate the park. The elders at the *baraza* responded to what they hailed as a new era of cooperation and mutual benefit by saying, "Wildlife have become our second cattle once more. We will be able to milk them when our own cows run dry in droughts. The national park has gained two thousand extra pairs of eyes to help watch out for poachers."

Implementation and Outcomes

The implementation of the *Development Plans for Amboseli* and subsequent events occurred in three phases: the formal project phase, the period when the Wildlife Conservation and Management Department collapsed, and the period following establishment of the Kenya Wildlife Service.

Phase 1, 1977–1981: Implementation of the Plan

The period from 1977 to 1981 saw most of the *Development Plans for Amboseli* under way. During this phase, the park viewing tracks were completed, the headquarters and Maasai community center were built, and a detailed management plan was drawn up by the newly instituted Wildlife Planning Unit (WPU) of WCMD. Improved roads and heightened visitor management contributed to a drop in off-road driving, from around 150,000 km per year to less than 25,000 km.

Most programs involving the Maasai and the larger ecosystem also were implemented. The wildlife utilization fee was paid twice yearly during the dry seasons, with allocations based on the opportunity costs to the four group ranches within the dispersal area: Ogulului, Kimana, Mbirikani, and Selengei. The ranches earned additional revenues from quarries that provided road ballast and from firewood collection. WCMD and the lodges hired many local Maasai. Revenues from wildlife now exceeded costs and began to contribute to the Maasai's development needs.

The Maasai wildlife committee, representing the four group ranches, met monthly with the Amboseli warden and functioned fairly well. The group ranch committees received grazing compensation directly and decided how it should be spent. My inputs declined sharply and became largely advisory in nature. The institutions created to implement the plan appeared to work, at least initially.

Ogulului built a primary school at Maarba with the wildlife utilization fee. Oloitiptip opened the school, the first in the area. At a large public rally, he pointed out that wildlife should now be seen as Maasai cattle and stressed that wildlife income had made Ogulului the wealthiest group ranch in Maasailand. Several other *barazas* reinforced the link between wildlife and development. Spearing and poaching became rare. Rhino and elephant populations began to recover (Western 1982a). Overall, wildlife biomass in the ecosystem rose quickly after the drought and in the absence of poaching (see Figures 2.4 and 2.5). Total biomass—most particularly that of zebra and wildebeest—eventually would far exceed pre-drought levels in the park (Figure 2.4). The wildlife committee regularly informed the warden of legal infractions and helped track down the few Maasai who speared animals.

A final indicator of success was the impact the Amboseli approach had on national policy in Kenya and elsewhere in Africa, including Zimbabwe, Namibia, and Zambia. Amboseli, as originally intended, became a test case for an integrated approach to wildlife conservation and development.

Ironically, the Amboseli plan began to falter after 1981, just as it began to be widely touted as a model for local participation. The reason, as will become evident further on, lay with government.

There were also some notable failures in the implementation of the Amboseli plan. One was the government's decision to ban hunting. The decision was taken during the tourism and wildlife loan negotiations. The ban was an assurance to the World Bank that Kenya intended to clean up poaching, in which the Wildlife Conservation and Management Department was heavily implicated. However, the ban reduced the potential wildlife income in nontourist areas, where hunting was regarded as a complementary land-use activity.

Another failure was the community center designed for the Maasai. This would remain little used until the late 1980s, due to poor siting and low demand from the Maasai.

The elders also rejected a public campsite on their land (a project I had promoted assiduously since 1972), despite the revenues it would bring. The elders saw the move for a campsite as a trick to secure more ground for the park. Later, when suspicions began to subside, the elders bolstered their position by insisting that the loss of *Acacia tortilis* trees associated with the campsite would deprive their goats of nutritious seeds needed as food.

Finally, the Wildlife Conservation and Management Department did not maintain the water pipeline satisfactorily or take over the southern boreholes as promised. Low government allocations to the department at this stage reflected

Figure 2.4

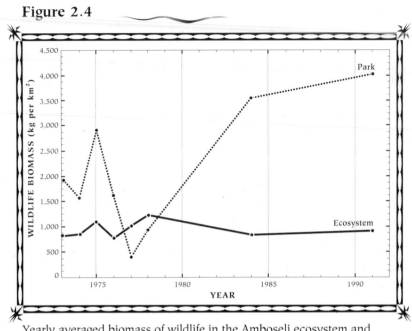

Yearly averaged biomass of wildlife in the Amboseli ecosystem and national park. The drop in the 1970s coincides with drought. Increase in the park is to levels higher than before the drought.

Figure 2.5

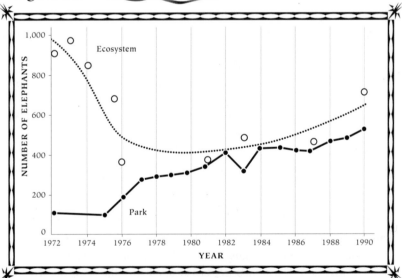

Number of elephants in the Amboseli ecosystem and national park. The trend in the early 1970s shows a rapid loss in numbers consistent with trends throughout East Africa. The initial increase in the park was due to immigration from the ecosystem. The increase in total population after 1977 runs against the continuing collapse of elephant populations elsewhere, a measure of the protection given by the Maasai around Amboseli.

public antipathy to wildlife and a flagging tourist market (see Figure 2.3), precipitated by the 1970s oil crises. An additional contributing factor was the high
turnover of senior ministry officials. Officers not present at the 1977 *baraza* refused to acknowledge the verbal contract. Consequently, the link between wildlife
and human welfare, which had taken so long to establish in Amboseli, evaporated.

At the conclusion of the implementation phase, the Amboseli Plan was a considerable success, if measured by the original goals: to create new ways to resolve
the human and wildlife conflicts in the ecosystem, to keep the ecosystem intact,
and to improve the prospects for wildlife and the Maasai alike. The project also established formal dialogue between WCMD and the Maasai group ranches through
the wildlife committee.

Still largely lacking was community willingness to take the initiative in diversi-
fying wildlife income, as in the case of the campsite. This in part reflected the developing political oligarchy in Kenya, with Oloitiptip becoming powerful after
helping Vice President Daniel T. arap Moi to succeed Kenyatta. Oloitiptip became
the mouthpiece for the Maasai in all matters, not only wildlife, thus short-cir-
cuiting community involvement. But the lack of initiative also stemmed from
Maasai conservatism and an individualism that precluded community action.

The Maasai, however, were in the process of rapid transition from subsistence
pastoralism to a mixed economy that included small-scale farming, wage employment (reflected in the emigration of young men), and—with the emergence of a lib-
eral livestock market and rapidly rising beef prices—commercial ranching. These
trends, and the rise of a young, educated cadre of Maasai with a more worldly
view, sowed the seeds of change that would alter Maasai aspirations and attitudes
in the 1980s (Kituyi 1990). Economic and social changes soon would become the
dominant forces shaping local initiatives.

Phase 2, 1982–1987: Alternatives to the Plan

The early successes of the *Development Plans for Amboseli* quickly faded after
1981. Heavy equipment and vehicles lay derelict, roads deteriorated, enforcement
activity declined, and visitor management was suspended. The ecosystem plans
also faltered. The annual wildlife utilization fee stopped, the water pipeline broke
down for lack of funds, livestock moved back into the park, the wildlife committee
rarely met, and the relationship between the Wildlife Conservation and Management Department and the Maasai became distinctly antagonistic. Spearing increased, and the wildlife committee did little to help apprehend the culprits. Rhino
numbers began dwindling again. Lindsay (1987) suggests, based on this period,
that the Amboseli plan was a failure. His conclusion that the reasons were lack of
local participation and lack of Maasai interest in economic benefits is, however,
erroneous. The Maasai themselves called for an economic stake in Amboseli in
the 1960s (Lwezaula 1970), and dialogue between the Maasai and the Ministry of

Tourism and Wildlife had been common practice prior to 1980–81. Why, then, did success falter after the first phase?

The failure can be directly attributed to the Wildlife and Conservation Management Department. The department was progressively starved of funds as other national priorities took precedence over wildlife. Total park expenditures slumped and by the mid-1980s were less than Ksh150,000 (US$8,000) a year—about 1 percent of the park's gross income. Allocations for the pipeline dropped from Ksh300,000 (US$16,000) per year to Ksh30,000 (US$1,600). Finally, WCMD refused to operate the southern boreholes, and the Ministry of Tourism and Wildlife no longer honored the wildlife utilization fee.

Even more than financial privation, developments within the Wildlife Conservation and Management Department were to blame for the problems at Amboseli. The department quickly lost its best officers due to paltry salaries, deepening corruption, poaching, and nepotism. Blame fell on the newly appointed director, Daniel Sindiyo, and there is no doubt that he failed to fulfill his early promise. But he was powerless without funds and snared in a web of corruption. Many of the nepotistic appointees in the department were behind elephant poaching. Sindiyo became more withdrawn and isolated and failed to halt the free-fall in WCMD. Bad as it was, WCMD was not exceptional as a government department during this period of deepening economic crisis and countrywide political malaise.

In addition, the Ministry of Tourism and Wildlife had never fully subscribed to the 1975 policies and the specific commitments it made to Amboseli. The reasons were perceptual as much as political. The ministry had been *coerced* to change its policy more than *convinced* to do so. As a result, strong antipathy to local involvement remained within the ministry. A great deal more effort on public relations might have made a difference. Too much emphasis had been placed on proving the case for the plan on the ground and not enough effort expended on raising political awareness and commitment at governmental level in Nairobi. Amboseli, as a result, was left isolated and with no institutional backing.

Ironically, the Wildlife Conservation and Management Department's failure and the social and economic trends among the Maasai sparked the first genuine local initiatives. Oloitiptip's political demise in the early 1980s and subsequent death were contributory factors. With no single voice to speak on behalf of the Maasai, they began to speak and act for themselves.

A preoccupation with their individual lives and lack of experience in community projects had restrained the Amboseli Maasai from embarking on their own wildlife projects. After several years in which my role had become little more than advisory, I became reinvolved. This time I concentrated on stimulating self-help programs by working with the officially elected group ranch committees. David Maitumo, my Maasai field assistant since 1977 and a member of the local community, was to play a significant role.

The committee responded quickly to the renewed suggestion of taking over the public campsite, but the elders continued to resist. The new generation of elders, however, included Ole Musa and two younger, educated Maasai, John Marinka and Jonathan Leboo, who worked at Serena Lodge in Amboseli. They were persuasive, pointing out the closing livestock options, made all the more obvious by the 1970s drought, and the wildlife alternatives. Marinka and Leboo, with their tourism training, left their jobs to run the public campsite and improve the facilities. By 1987 the campsite was earning in excess of Ksh300,000 (US$18,000) per year.

A second initiative involved an electrified fence at Namelok, an area that the Maasai had settled and farmed during the 1970s drought. Maasai farmers began growing subsistence crops at first, and then cash crops for market. While the gardens diversified Maasai income and relieved pressure on the grazing lands, more than half of their crop was being destroyed by elephants, buffalo, and other herbivores. I urged the Maasai to put up a solar electric fence to protect their crops. The farmers were to erect the fence under David Maitumo's supervision and subsequently maintain it themselves. Half the funds would be raised by the community and the other half through conservation donors.

The Wildlife Extension Project of WCMD initially tried to organize the fence program through a full community-participation approach involving workshops and seminars (Berger 1989). While the project did involve a large cross-section of the community in discussion, it failed to get the fence constructed. The failure resulted from a misunderstanding of both traditional leadership (Hannah 1992) and the role a handful of progressive Maasai played in catalyzing development.

Subsequent work with the committee of one group ranch, Ogulului, and a group of progressive elders resulted in a smaller demonstration fence set up around their own farms. This example quickly got the fencing program off the ground. The Ogulului group contracted farm laborers to build and maintain the fence under Maitumo's direction. Its rapid completion and demonstrable success in keeping wildlife out of crops influenced the rest of the community to follow suit.

A third project involved developing a tourist concession on Ogulului. Although I initiated the project and brought in the three prospective tour operators, the group ranch committee negotiated the Ksh500,000 (US$20,000) annual contract and has run the concession on its own since 1988. During this period, Kimana and Mbirikani group ranches reached similar agreements with other tourist concessionaires, as did Selengei Group Ranch with a bird-hunting consortium. By 1992, the four group ranches had initiated seven wildlife concessions with little or no government involvement.

Thus the mid-1980s saw a basic shift in the level and nature of Maasai participation in the Amboseli plan. The first-phase response to plans drawn up with the Maasai's input and for their benefit was soon superseded by self-initiated projects. While the full community may not have participated, the initiative undeniably came from the Maasai, both leaders and progressive individuals, with the backing of the community at large. The self-help conservation programs in the second phase purposely mimicked the successful agricultural programs that had diversified the

Maasai economy in the 1970s (see PARTICIPATION), often even involving the same individuals.

These initiatives, self-generated wildlife income, and the expectation of renewed benefits from the park accounted for the Amboseli Maasai's tolerance of wildlife. At a time of heavy poaching elsewhere in Kenya, wildlife increased in Amboseli throughout the 1980s. The increase was especially evident in the case of elephants (see Figure 2.5). Mara, the other exception to wildlife's general decline, had similar projects in place. In other words, despite the failure of the government program, WCMD's contribution to the collapse of park infrastructure, and a much-publicized poaching scandal (Douglas-Hamilton and Douglas-Hamilton 1992), the Maasai's own wildlife programs sustained and improved their development activities as well as wildlife numbers.

Phase 3, 1987–1992: New Institutions and New Initiatives

The failure of the Wildlife Conservation and Management Department and the collapse of elephant populations in Kenya became a national scandal by the late 1980s. WCMD's performance in Amboseli helped to persuade President Moi to make sweeping personnel and institutional reforms in 1987. Sindiyo was replaced by Perez Olindo, and the principles of local participation became a central plank in the terms of reference drawn up in 1988 for the Kenya Wildlife Service, which replaced WCMD in 1990. The word *Service* was purposefully included in the parastatal KWS's name to convey a sense of the contributions the new institution would be expected to make to the welfare of rural communities.

KWS, borrowing from some of the successful features of the former Kenya National Parks, has an independent board of trustees and direct control over its own revenues and expenditures. The main reasons for the failure of WCMD—lack of control over the funds it earned, lack of accountability, corruption, and nepotism—are, to a great extent, redressed within the new KWS institutional structure.

When Richard Leakey became director of WCMD in 1989 to oversee the launching of KWS, he initially announced his intention to fence all parks in the interest of protecting people from wildlife depredations and wildlife from poachers. This policy would have been disastrous biologically, due to insularization effects (MacArthur and Wilson 1967). Equally as important, fencing would have reversed the entire policy of local participation and severely reduced Kenya's wildlife tourism capacity. Fortunately, the fledgling KWS soon came out in favor of keeping park boundaries open where possible. By announcing a national revenue-sharing plan, it reinforced the policy of local participation.

A meeting convened in Amboseli in January 1990 by the warden and Wildlife Conservation International (the conservation division of the New York Zoological Society) quickly established dialogue between the group ranches, represented by forty members, and KWS. The workshop also involved other government agencies including the Ministry of Livestock Development. Broad agreements reached at the end of the two-day meeting included the need to resume revenue dispersal, reestablish a wildlife committee, allow for elephant migration from Kilimanjaro, and set up a system of local Maasai scouts to protect wildlife.

It is still too early to gauge the impact of the new community programs, but there is reason to believe that they will succeed, despite some initial setbacks. For example, although KWS promised to share 25 percent of the gate receipts from Amboseli with the ranch members, in reality, little more than half that amount, or roughly half the opportunity cost to the ranches, has been disbursed to date. The first payments were delayed by squabbles between the group ranches over how the payments should be apportioned. Further setbacks occurred when KWS refused to acknowledge the boundary realignments of 1973 (which would have allowed Maasai livestock access to swamps in the drought of 1992) or to assume responsibility for the southern boreholes. The wildlife committee has yet to be reestablished, and KWS is still inclined to make decisions unilaterally. Revenue-sharing programs are in a formative, ad hoc stage, and the important link between landowners' opportunity costs and benefits with respect to wildlife has not been made. There is, in short, little connection between the revenue-sharing programs and the conservation costs incurred in conserving the larger Amboseli ecosystem.

Despite the setbacks, successes are beginning to outweigh failures. Perhaps the most important factor in the successes is the changing balance of authority as the local Maasai realize their rights and begin to exercise them politically. One example is the assertiveness Ogulului Group Ranch showed in canvassing politically in Nairobi. A strongly worded letter to the director of KWS threatened to fence off the park unless they were given their legal share of the gate income. Such assertiveness paid off: The Amboseli group ranches were the first to benefit under KWS's revenue-sharing program.

Another measure of success is the Maasai's determination to resist subdivision of Ogulului Ranch in the interest of keeping the wildlife migratory routes intact and deriving wildlife revenues. The annual general meeting of the group ranch passed a resolution that only a small portion of the ranch on the arable slopes of Kilimanjaro would be subdivided for settlement, leaving the rest open to livestock and wildlife.

There are other measures as well. The four group ranches have set up a system of twenty game scouts, paid for with money from the revenue-sharing program, to protect wildlife on ranch land. Kimana and Mbirikani ranches have launched plans for their own electric fences to protect irrigated cropland east of Amboseli. New tourist concessions for Ogulului and a wildlife cropping scheme for Mbirikani are under discussion. The four schools on Ogulului have been built wholly or in part with wildlife revenues.

The new relationship between the Maasai and the official wildlife custodian, Kenya Wildlife Service, has been gaining strength. KWS is beginning to show commitment and the capacity to implement the community-based conservation programs needed in Amboseli and countrywide. KWS initially focused on antipoaching and security measures to reassure a tourist industry wary of rampant poaching and tourist assaults. KWS has been successful in these tasks. More recently, KWS has turned its attention to community-based conservation, establishing and securing funds for its own Community Wildlife Service and training programs. It also has begun to initiate several wildlife-utilization schemes on private land and group ranches. In 1993, however, the Maasai, dissatisfied with KWS's performance and its reluctance to push ahead with policy reforms, set up their own wildlife association. The new association includes Kuku and Rombo group ranches, which separate Amboseli from Tsavo West National Park. The association will pursue its own conservation programs, emphasizing the strong historical association between Maasai culture and wildlife. The association expects to draw up land-use plans to balance conservation and development. Legal contracts with KWS will form the basis of all agreements between the two parties.

In this present phase, strong empirical evidence shows that the original aim of maintaining the integrity of the Amboseli ecosystem and improving the welfare of the Maasai landowners is being achieved. Poaching levels remain low, attitudes toward wildlife are fairly positive, and wildlife income is steadily becoming a more significant component of Maasai income (see Figure 2.6).

Evaluation

The Amboseli program is enormously complex and beset with conflicts and problems. This has been partly because of the choice of Amboseli itself as a place to test new locally based approaches to conservation. Amboseli in the 1960s and '70s was the most controversial wildlife area in Kenya and presented a difficult challenge in resolving the clash of human and wildlife interests in the savannas.

The very intensity of the clash over Amboseli and the intertwined ecologies of the Maasai and wildlife ruled out a hard-edged national park, which simply never would have worked. Had a small area been set aside, the ecosystem would not have survived, nor would there have been the increase in wildlife seen during the last fifteen years. The Amboseli program should be judged by comparison with other ecosystems in Kenya, most of which have experienced both a decline in wildlife numbers and increasingly negative local attitudes toward wild animals.

The success of the program, measured against its original goals, is that new conservation approaches and policies bearing on reconciling human and wildlife interests did emerge. These principles also helped to maintain the integrity of the Amboseli ecosystem and improve prospects for both wildlife and the Maasai. There can be little doubt that the Amboseli program played an important role in changing national policies and had an international impact in bringing about recognition and acceptance of the need to direct conservation benefits to local communities (Hannah 1992).

However, the eight years consumed in promoting and implementing the new

Figure 2.6

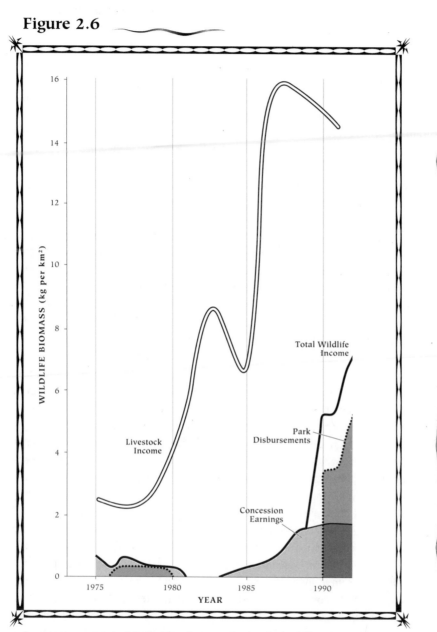

Income accruing to Maasai landowners in the Amboseli ecosystem. Livestock income is based on subsistence and commercial value. Wildlife income includes money accruing from the park, tourist concessions, hunting concessions, and miscellaneous other sources.

policies added a level of complexity to the Amboseli program that later integrated projects have been spared. The success of Amboseli hinged on new and untried policies, a new wildlife institution, and innovative management practices. In short, the Amboseli program depended on changing attitudes at the top as much as on the ground.

How well, then, did the program meet its original objectives? Ecologically, the success of the program can be judged by data derived from the monitoring program set up to evaluate trends. The data show that the ecosystem has remained open, migrations are viable, and populations are healthy (see Figures 2.1, 2.4, and 2.5). The main reason for the increase of elephants numbers in Amboseli, in the face of a continental plunge (Douglas-Hamilton and Douglas-Hamilton 1992), is the protection the Maasai have given the animals (Moss 1988).

The Maasai also have benefited in demonstrable ways (see Figure 2.6), although less than they should have on the basis of equitable distribution of costs and benefits. During the early implementation phase, wildlife income and other benefits contributed to Maasai welfare at a time of difficult cultural and economic transition (Figure 2.3). These benefits are now being reestablished under KWS's revenue-sharing program (Figure 2.6). Other measures of success can be seen in changes in attitudes and concrete achievements generated by the program—for example, Ogulului's decision not to subdivide the nonarable portion of the ranch in the interest of securing greater wildlife income; the ranches' provision, deployment, and payment of twenty Maasai scouts to protect wildlife outside the park; construction of schools and other facilities with wildlife income; and creation of tourist concessions negotiated and run by the Maasai.

It is worth restating that the original locally based plan failed. The Maasai (understandably, given their history) could not sufficiently overcome their phobia of land loss and suspicion of wildlife preservationism to come to grips with the socioeconomic realities and alternatives the initial plan offered. The follow-on stage was complex, involving a combination of top-end and open-dialogue approaches once the broad principles were in place.

Analysis of Amboseli emphasizes the point that many factors, some strongly interlinked, account for the successes and failures. Individuals played an all-important part in the Amboseli program at the outset. Ideas, initiative, and continuity all came from individuals who were motivated by the vision of a new locally based approach to conservation and development. These individuals, including Sindiyo, Ole Purdul, Ole Musa, Marinka, Leboo, Mitchell, Kioko, myself, and several others, were key players who worked together closely, often against national and local resistance. They became the focal point for the distillation and integration of ideas and helped the program survive and move ahead when the institutional framework failed in the post-1981 period. These same individuals, working cooperatively, provided the program's give-and-take dynamic. The iterative learning process became one of the program's survival tactics and a way of ensuring practical flexibility.

The use of ecological information, Maasai knowledge, economic analyses, and land-use assessments also proved important in looking at the options and trying to resolve conflicting interests. The support of an international organization—the New York Zoological Society—was decisive at many points, particularly in giving the new policies credibility and the entire program financial and institutional support over an unusually long period. Here, too, the participation of key individuals, including Royal Little, Bill Conway, Charlie Nichols, and Barclay Morrison, extended far beyond the confines of their institutions.

Unquestionably, the biggest single failing was at governmental and institutional levels. The strong persistence of colonial preservationist policies, coupled with a continuing paternalistic attitude toward nomadic pastoralists among senior administrators, put the brakes on open dialogue. And once the new policies were in place, the Wildlife Conservation and Management Department as an institution proved disastrous for wildlife. Some reviews (Lindsay 1987; Talbot and Olindo 1990) sidestep this politically sensitive topic and look to other explanations. The reality is that WCMD became such a national and international scandal that it took presidential intervention to scrap the department and start again with a new institution, the Kenya Wildlife Service.

If institutional shortcomings led the government to abrogate its part of the Amboseli agreements, local initiatives ultimately sustained the economic link between Maasai and wildlife welfare. The Maasai's local initiatives, and the direct income that resulted, were the deciding factors in sustaining the program, albeit at a much lower level than planned. That the Maasai gained some benefits during this time probably mattered more than whether the sum they received exceeded their losses. These benefits, and the expectation of more in the future as their livestock options narrowed, were an important element in sustaining Maasai commitment to wildlife conservation. The initiative and participation in turn depended not on the involvement of the entire community, but on traditional leadership and new institutional structures. A few individuals constituted the driving force among the Maasai no less than in government. And yet, to an important degree, the cohesiveness of traditional Maasai society made and continues to make consensus possible and binding. The collective memory and obligation of the Maasai was far greater than that of government officers, whether permanent secretaries or wardens. As these officers came and went, the Maasai collective commitment endured.

Two final points, linkage and enforcement, need mention. Stronger linkage and enforcement would have strengthened the program considerably. The fact that weak linkage and enforcement did not undermine the program needs some explanation. The link between Maasai benefits and wildlife conservation was fairly explicit in the *Development Plans for Amboseli*, to the extent that the wildlife utilization fee was tied to opportunity costs and the Maasai's impact on wildlife. An ecological monitoring project was set up to track the outcome and adjust the fees. The link was also explicit in terms of the agreement under which the Maasai vacated the park. That linkage broke down when the government abrogated the agreement unilaterally. Linkage of benefits and wildlife conservation has yet to be reestablished under the terms of the new revenue-sharing program. Failure to secure control over the council land at Ol Tukai in return for a management fee is another example of weak linkage. The council recently approved plans for a third lodge on the already crowded 156 ha, despite opposition from the local Maasai and KWS. For the most part, the link between Maasai benefits and wildlife survival has been implicit, rather than explicit. This did not matter much under traditional and relatively benign Maasai herding practices. It will matter a great deal more as the Maasai settle, fence, build upon, and physically develop their land.

Enforcement without doubt has been the weakest element in the entire program. Little has been done in the way of antipoaching since the original Amboseli Game Reserve was established in 1947. That laxity saw rhino numbers fall from 75 in 1967 to 8 in 1977 (Western 1982b) and elephants from more than 1,000 to about 480 over the same period. That elephants (and, for a brief period, rhinos) subsequently recovered, despite the lack of patrols, is a measure of Maasai tolerance. The attitudinal change did more to conserve elephants in Amboseli than law enforcement achieved elsewhere in Kenya. Amboseli and Mara make the point that community programs can minimize the need for law enforcement and reduce management costs substantially. But, as with the question of linkage, enforcement will be increasingly necessary as the traditional interaction of the Maasai and wildlife changes with development and new aspirations. Enforcement will be needed to keep wildlife out of Maasai farms, livestock out of the park, and poaching levels to a minimum—a reality the Maasai recognized when they commissioned twenty of their own scouts to protect wildlife on their ranches.

Pointers for the Future

The effects of political and economic liberalization on Maasai values and aspirations, as well as other inevitable changes, will present a challenge for community-based conservation in Amboseli. Future successes may well depend on local people's ability to adapt to change.

Effects of Political and Economic Liberalization

The maintenance of a viable ecosystem in Amboseli has succeeded to a great extent due to the traditionally benign relationship between the Maasai and wildlife. The community, although heterogeneous at the individual level, was unified to a far greater degree than most due to the demands of subsistence pastoralism, the strong cultural ideals of the Maasai, and traditional means of arbitrating disputes (Spencer 1988). The ecological benignity and relative cultural homogeneity was implicit in the early plans for Amboseli. Neither ecological nor cultural factors favoring coexistence will persist in the face of development, however. Individual economic and political interests will diverge progressively with the adoption of new life-styles, formal education, and changing aspirations (Kituyi 1990). Political and economic liberalization will further encourage demands for land and property rights that include wildlife utilization. The trend toward individual land ownership will continue over much and possibly all of the ecosystem as the subsistence livestock economy diminishes in importance.

The trends inevitably will accelerate the diversification of Maasai interests and voices. The relative homogeneity of interests will give way to a far more heterogeneous community—farmers, ranch members, wildlife entrepreneurs, traders, transporters, teachers, etc.—and one less easily represented by a few voices. The present system of representation is already proving inadequate; some spokesmen, for example, are siphoning off much of the wildlife income destined for the community at large. The monetary benefits clearly will have to reach all members of the community and, in the process, risk dilution.

The cultural, economic, and political transition under way in Maasailand is the single biggest challenge to future integrated planning for the Amboseli ecosystem. KWS and the Maasai increasingly will have to meet on equal terms, not on the paternalistic basis that dominated WCMD's attitude and KWS's formative approaches. Wildlife inevitably will become one of several Maasai interests rather than the only alternative to livestock. Land-use planning to balance the expanding range of interests will become imperative. The challenge to KWS is to adapt to the new reality of landowner rights and interests and see to it that wildlife opportunities are realized. Its interest, however, should continue to focus on the viability of the ecosystem. This will entail more and more involvement with other agencies and landowners, in the interest of less and less direct wildlife management. The alternative, a retreat to the confines of the park, will mean intensive wildlife management and the loss of ecological integrity and naturalness, the point most visitors value above all else (Gakahu 1992). The park, after all, was designed not as a self-sufficient unit but as part of a multiple land-use system (Western 1969a, 1973).

To believe that wildlife will be conserved for its own sake as long as Maasai traditions survive is unrealistic. The biggest challenge lies in continuing to find ways to accommodate both interests and in maintaining a large arena of physical overlap based on economic and noneconomic values that are meaningful to landowners. This will mean exploring development opportunities and reducing conflicts of interest when they arise. Formal plans and written contracts, already proposed by the Maasai, should become the focus of mutual endeavors. And, inasmuch as the type and nature of conflict will continually change as the Maasai themselves change, the plans and contracts will have to be continually revised.

Adaptability and Change

The conservation of Amboseli will require adaptability and change. Inevitably, the nature of benefits will have to change from communal to individual. Only so many schools and social services can be built around Amboseli, for example, and not everyone benefits from these. The ranches already are thinking of direct benefits to individuals in the form of cash handouts. Under such a system, each landowner would become a shareholder in commonly held stock (wildlife), which would yield annual dividends.

Finally, KWS will have to manage wildlife in the interest of maintaining biodiversity and ecological integrity as the dynamic ecological processes that maintain diversity weaken. Much as management is anathema to many conservationists, it becomes a necessity when human activity threatens these essential processes (Western and Gichohi 1993). An overpopulation of elephants in the park, partly due to the demise of their seasonal migration (Western 1989), has severely reduced Amboseli's biological diversity and caused great hardship to Maasai farmers close by. There is no longer sufficient open space to absorb the elephant population, and management, in one form or another, will be essential if biodiversity is to be maintained.

Much the same can be said of the greatly expanded migratory herds of wildebeest and zebra. Utilization in one form or another not only will ease the conflict between wildlife and herder but will help contribute greater financial benefit to Maasai living away from the park, where there is no prospect of tourist income. KWS has been loath to implement utilization policies but is gradually considering doing so at the urging of landowners.

SOURCES

Berger, J. 1989. "Wildlife Extension: A Participatory Approach to Conservation." Ph.D. dissertation, University of California, Berkeley.

Botkin, D. 1990. *Discordant Harmonies: A New Ecology for the Twenty-first Century.* New York: Oxford University Press.

Douglas-Hamilton, I., and O. Douglas-Hamilton. 1992. *Battle for the Elephants.* New York: Doubleday.

Galaty, J. 1982. "Being 'Maasai,' Being 'People of Cattle': Ethnic Shifters in East Africa." *American Ethnologist* 9: 1–20.

———, and P. C. Salzman, eds. 1980. *Changes and Development in Nomadic Pastoral Societies.* Leiden, Holland: Brille.

Gakahu, C. G., ed. 1992. *Tourist Attitudes and Use Impacts in Maasai Mara National Reserve.* Nairobi: English Press.

Government of Kenya (GoK). 1977. *The Wildlife Act.* Nairobi: Government Printer.

Grandon, B. E. 1991. "The Maasai: Socio-historical Context and Group Ranches." In *An Analysis of the Livestock Production System of Maasai Pastoralists in Eastern Kajiado District, Kenya.* Addis Ababa: International Livestock Centre for Africa.

Hannah, L. 1992. *African People, African Parks.* Washington, D.C.: Conservation International.

Jacobs, A. 1975. "The Traditional Political Organization of the Pastoral Maasai." Ph.D. dissertation, Oxford University.

Kantai, B. 1971. "Foreword." In *The Maasai*, by S. Sankan, vii–xxxi. Nairobi: Kenya Literature Bureau.

Kenya Wildlife Service (KWS). 1991. *Amboseli National Park Management Plan (1991–1996)*. Nairobi: Kenya Wildlife Service.

Kituyi, M. 1990. *Becoming Kenyans: Socio-economic Transformation of the Pastoral Maasai*. Nairobi: ACTS Press.

Lahi, A. V. 1967. *Hydrology of Sinya Meerschaum Mine*. Dar es Salaam: Institute for Study and Development.

Lindsay, W. K. 1987. "Integrating Parks and Pastoralists: Some Lessons from Amboseli." In *Conservation in Africa: People, Policies and Practice*, ed. D. Anderson and R. Grove, 149–167. Cambridge, England: Cambridge University Press.

Lwezaula, F. M. R. 1970. *Analysis of Problems in Maasai Amboseli Game Reserve*. Mweka, Tanzania: College of African Wildlife Management.

MacArthur, R. H., and E. O. Wilson. 1967. *The Theory of Island Biogeography*. Princeton, New Jersey: Princeton University Press.

Marshall, F. 1989. "Rethinking the Role of *Bos indicus* in Sub-Saharan Africa." *Current Anthropology* 30(2): 235–246.

Mitchell, F. 1969. *Forecasts of Returns to Kajiado County Council from the Maasai Amboseli Game Reserve*. Institute for Development Studies Discussion Paper No. 87. Nairobi: Institute for Development Studies, University of Nairobi.

Moss, C. 1988. *Elephant Memories*. London: Elm Tree.

Ochilo, J. A. 1991. "Implications of Landuse Changes: Amboseli Biosphere Reserve Buffer Zone (Kenya)." Master's thesis, Institute of Aerospace Survey and Earth Sciences, Enschede, Holland.

Pratt, D. J., P. J. Greenway, and M. O. Gwynne. 1966. "A Classification of East African Rangelands." *Journal of Applied Ecology* 3:369–382.

Program for Better Family Living (PBFL). 1977a. *Kajiado District Workshop Report on Wildlife Conservation and Management Held at Amboseli National Park, Nairobi*. Paper No. 34. Nairobi: Program for Better Family Living.

———. 1977b. *Loitokitok Workshop on Wildlife and Local Communities, Nairobi*. Nairobi: Program for Better Family Living.

Sankan, S. 1971. *The Maasai*. Nairobi: Kenya Literature Bureau.

Sessional Paper Number 2. Wildlife Policy 1975. Government Printer, Nairobi.

Simon, N. M. 1962. *Between the Sunlight and the Thunder*. London: Collins.

Sindiyo, D. M. 1968. "Game Department Field Experience in Public Education." *East African Agriculture and Forestry Journal* 33: 237–240.

Spencer, P. 1988. *The Maasai of Matapatu*. Manchester, England: Manchester University Press.

Talbot, L., and P. Olindo. 1990. "Amboseli and Maasai Mara, Kenya." In *Living with Wildlife: Wildlife Resource Management with Local Participation in Africa*, ed. A. Kiss, 67–74. World Bank Technical Paper No. 30. Washington, D.C.: World Bank.

Western, D. 1969a. *Landuse in Maasai Amboseli Game Reserve: A Case Study for Interdisciplinary Cooperation*. Institute for Development Studies Research Bulletin No. 40. Nairobi: Institute for Development Studies, University of Nairobi.

———. 1969b. "Amboseli." *Africana* 3(12):17–20.

————. 1970. *Proposal for an Amboseli Game Park*. Institute for Development Studies Research Bulletin No. 53. Nairobi: Institute for Development Studies, University of Nairobi.

————. 1973. "The Structure, Dynamics and Changes of the Amboseli Ecosystem." Ph.D. dissertation, University of Nairobi.

————. 1975. "Water Availability and Its influence on the Structure and Dynamics of a Savannah Large-mammal Community." *East African Wildlife Journal* 13: 265–287.

————. 1982a. "Amboseli National Park: Enlisting Land Owners to Conserve Migratory Wildlife." *Ambio* 11(5): 302–308.

————. 1982b. "Patterns of Depletion in a Kenya Rhino Population and the Conservation Implications." *Biological Conservation* 24: 147–156.

————. 1989. "The Ecological Value of Elephants: A Keystone Role in African Ecosystems." In *The Ivory Trade and the Future of the African Elephant*, section 5.2. Oxford, England: Ivory Trade Review Group.

————, and T. Dunne. 1979. "Environmental Aspects of Settlement Site Decisions among Pastoral Maasai." *Human Ecology* 7(1):75–98.

————, and V. Finch. 1986. "Cattle and Pastoralism: Survival and Production in Arid Lands." *Human Ecology* 14(1):77–94.

————, and H. Gichohi. 1993. "Segregation Effects and the Impoverishment of Savanna Ecosystems: The Case for Ecosystem Viability Analysis." *African Journal of Ecology* 31:268–271.

————, and W. K. Lindsay. 1984. "Seasonal Herd Dynamics of a Savanna Elephant Population." *African Journal of Ecology* 22:229–244.

————, and D. M. Sindiyo. 1972. "The Status of the Amboseli Rhino Population." *East African Wildlife Journal* 12(1):43–57.

————, and P. Thresher. 1973. *Development Plans for Amboseli*. World Bank Report. Nairobi: World Bank.

————, and C. van Praet. 1973. "Cyclical Changes in the Habitat and Climate of an East African Ecosystem." *Nature* 241:104–106.

Williams, L. A. J. 1967. "The Kilimanjaro Volcanic Rocks of the Amboseli Area." Ph.D. dissertation, University of Nairobi.

Yeager, R., and N. N. Miller. 1986. *Wildlife, Wild Death, Land Use and Survival in East Africa*. Albany, New York: State University of New York Press.

CHAPTER 3

The Resurgence of Community Forest Management in Eastern India

Mark Poffenberger

Since the middle of the nineteenth century, large areas of forest throughout the Indian subcontinent have been declared designated public land. These lands were placed under the management of state forest departments for production and protection purposes. Millions of rural inhabitants throughout India who had utilized these lands to meet basic needs for food, fuel, building materials, fibers, and medicines effectively lost their access rights. By 1980, nearly 23 percent of India's land area had been placed under state management, displacing an estimated 300 million rural resource users.

As the rights of rural communities eroded, conflicts between state agencies and Indian villagers became increasingly evident. Disagreements over management priorities led to unsustainable patterns of forest exploitation and gradual degradation of India's vast forests. By 1990, less than 10 percent of the country possessed good forest cover.

During the last few years, planners and forest administrators have begun developing new policies to reduce the conflict between the state agencies and rural groups responsible for this resource crisis. These policies are designed to facilitate the emergence of collaborative forest-management systems that respond to national needs and local resource requirements. In eastern India, between six thousand and eight thousand villages have begun patrolling and protecting hundreds of thousands of hectares of degraded forest as part of the new comanagement (usually referred to as joint management in India) policies, often with dramatic results in terms of forest regeneration.

The community or cooperative forest-management systems emerging in West Bengal, Bihar, and Orissa (see Map 3.1) promise an alternative to the custodial policing systems of the past. They require a shift from commercial timber exploitation to the sustainable use of many nontimber products. They necessitate a move from centralized planning and bureaucratic management to decentralized community-based management. Currently, little is known regarding the structure and function of these community-based management groups, or about the processes through which they form forest protection committees.

Map 3.1

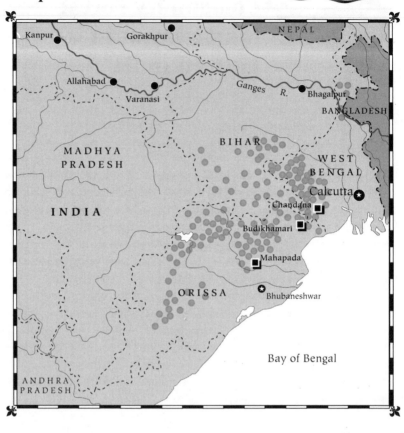

Eastern India

KEY

⊛ State Capitals

▣ Case Study Areas

● Areas with Extensive
Community Forest
Management Activity

The dearth of information prompted the commissioning of the two rapid diagnostic case studies presented here. The case studies were conducted by members of the Indian National Support Group for Joint Forest Management (NSG) during field visits from 1990 to 1993. (The NSG's objective is to disseminate learning from grass-roots movements and forest department programs that promote community-based resource conservation and management.) The NSG field researchers held discussions with community members and leaders, nongovernmental organization staff, and field foresters about forest comanagement activities in West Bengal and Orissa. A summary of their findings follows.

Community Forest Management in Southwest Bengal

Chandana and Harinakuri villages are located approximately 20 km south of Kharagpur, in the state of West Bengal. A 2-km dirt track off the main road crosses rain-fed rice fields and passes through regenerating forest lands on the way to Chandana village. Another kilometer down the road bordering the southern extension of the forest is Harinakuri village. The forest lands in the Chandana area total 160 ha; Chandana and Harinakuri villages border the forest on the south, and Nidata and Babunmara villages in the north (see Map 3.2).

Most of the villages in the area are inhabited by members of low-income scheduled castes (social groups that are outside the dominant majority of the caste system), tribals, and farming-caste families. Chandana village has thirty-eight households. Of these, half are Bhumi tribals and the rest members of scheduled castes, including oil makers. In Harinakuri, the thirty-one families are primarily of the Naik scheduled caste (untouchables also known as harijans). The Naik claim to have worked as mercenaries for a local raja until approximately one hundred years ago, when they moved into this forest area. At that time a large landowner, or zamindar, was opening the area for agriculture. Most of the villagers worked as agricultural laborers and tenant farmers until the state land-reform program of the early to mid-1970s granted them title in local rain-fed rice lands. Historically, these communities have depended on the neighboring forest lands in significant ways for fuel, fodder, supplemental food, medicines, and fibers.

Chandana Forest Management History

According to Lokhun Sahu, a sixty-five-year-old Chandana villager, the surrounding forest was once comprised primarily of first-growth *sal* (*Shorea robusta*) trees. During the years of British colonial rule, a zamindar named Bhuwan Chandra Pal, who lived 20 km away in Hundla, near Narayangar, controlled the forest tracts of Chandana. In part to pay his taxes to the British raj, the zamindar periodically leased tracts of jungle to contractors for logging. During the felling,

Map 3.2

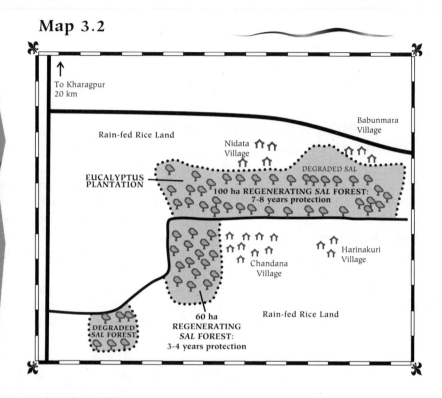

Chandana Village
and Protected Forests

local villagers were allowed to purchase lops and tops for fuelwood at the rate of Rs1 or 2 (US$.03 to $.06) per cartload. The zamindar didn't allow villagers to cut poles or logs and posted guards to protect the forest against local users. Periodically, the zamindar sent his men into the village to see if they had hidden poles or timber. The guards beat anyone found to have stolen wood, sometimes fatally. After a contractor finished logging his concession, the *sal* trees sent up coppice growth, and the forest reestablished itself. Older trees, including *sal, mahua*, and cashew were left to act as seed and fruit sources.

Little changed in forest-management practice during the early years following Independence in 1947. The zamindar continued to control the forest of Chandana until the early 1950s, when the Zamindar Abolition Law was passed. The new law gave the West Bengal Forest Department an opportunity to establish direct control over the forest lands of the southwestern part of the state. But first, seeing that he was about to lose control of the forest, the zamindar sold off the entire Chandana forest tract to contractors who felled the area, leaving only a few fruit trees. For the next six months, local communities faced a severe shortage of fuelwood. As coppice growth emerged, the forest resource supply also began to recover.

From the mid-1950s through the 1960s, the West Bengal Forest Department exerted control over the forests of Chandana. Throughout this period, the department continued the practices of the zamindars by leasing cutting rights to contractors. Consequently, *sal* trees were cut every ten to fifteen years and regenerated after a few years through coppice growth. The local field officer complained that the contractors often also cut the older *sal* and fruit trees. This practice is officially banned, as these mature trees, or standards, are important yielders of seeds for natural regeneration. When the forest guards or villagers attempted to stop the contractors, they were threatened by armed guards. The contractors reportedly enjoyed political support, so the field staff and villagers could do little to stop them.

According to Lokhun Sahu, political organizers began visiting the community in the early 1970s. They told the villagers that the forest was community property. In retrospect, Lokhun feels that "the political leaders misled the people to gain their political support." The villagers began cutting and selling trees indiscriminately. According to Lokhun, no control system existed, and everyone cut where they pleased. Lacking support from the community and threatened with physical violence by the contractors, the forestry field staff was helpless. By the early 1980s, the *sal* forests were badly degraded. In some areas, even the trees' root systems had been extracted for fuelwood. Lokhun reports that, with this degradation, the temperature seemed to become hotter, while rainfall diminished, and the earth became drier. The cooling breezes ceased to blow. The villagers had difficulty finding wood for their spade handles, plows, and other agricultural implements. The village ponds and well dried up faster, and the villagers had to rely on water from the river 2 km away. The forest had been so thoroughly cut that there were no standing trees outside the village environs. It was possible to see all the way to the river and beyond.

In 1983, Jyoti Naik, a man from the neighboring village of Harinakuri, began visiting Chandana village to discuss forest-management problems. Jyoti is a forty-five-year-old small farmer with only two years of formal education. He was convinced that some action had to be taken to reverse the process of forest destruction. Jyoti had been a landless laborer until the CPIM (Communist Party of India Marxist), which controlled the West Bengal state government, implemented a land-reform program in the 1970s. At that time, Jyoti and other families in his village gained small tracts of farmland. He felt that since the community now controlled its agricultural land, it should also manage its forest resources as well.

In the beginning, Jyoti visited each house separately in the evenings to talk about the problem. He told the villagers of Chandana that if they didn't begin protecting the forest, it would degrade to a point where even fuelwood and leaves no longer would be available. He told them they would be forest people with no forest, and their children would have no forest resources to utilize in their adulthood. Gradually, he began organizing village-level meetings. By 1984, a sufficient number of Chandana villagers were ready to call a meeting with the three neighboring villages to discuss a collaborative management program. At the meeting, each community decided to take responsibility for the forest area nearest its village. The subdivision of the 160-ha forest tract tended to follow footpaths and bullock cart tracks.

Chandana and Harinakuri villages began actively protecting the forest tracts near their communities. The villages to the north of the forest, Nidata and Babunmara, were less effective in controlling access, and commercial fuelwood cutting continued. Jyoti Naik and other village leaders since have met with local political representatives from the area and urged them to put pressure on the northside communities to begin protection activities. Jyoti says that the politicians are afraid they will lose votes if they do so. At present, however, a four-village forest protection committee coordinating board does exist. Jyoti Naik currently acts as chairman.

Experiences with Protection Activities

Outside pressures on the forest protected by the Chandana community continue. Women from other villages come in groups of five or six every two or three days to cut fuelwood. These women frequently come from Bhetia village across the river to the north, or from Pora and Simildanga villages in the south. When Chandana villagers catch the woodcutters, they ask them to go elsewhere; when necessary, they chase the women away with sticks. A more serious threat is from gangs of ten to twelve men who come in the night during the months from August through October and February through May, slack times in the agricultural season. These groups come to cut *sal* poles for commercial sale.

When outside cutting groups are active, the Chandana Forest Protection Committee tends to keep one man patrolling the area on two- to three-hour shifts. Other villagers are also watchful and notify the committee if cutting groups are seen approaching the area. Occasionally, the forest protection committee catches groups in the process of cutting. They then confiscate the men's axes and fine them.

Protection experiences in the neighboring village of Harinakuri are similar. Since the Harinakuri Forest Protection Committee was formed in 1979, Harinakuri has worked with neighboring Chandana and Telebanga villages to protect against cutting groups from villages to the north and east. According to Jyoti, pressure from outside villages is particularly high because many members of these communities depend on fuelwood sales as their primary source of cash income. Often tribal and scheduled caste members of these villages are contracted by high-caste families in towns and villages and at the Soluwa Army Base to cut fuelwood and timber for them. The cutting groups often band together to overcome local resistance.

In response, the Harinakuri Forest Protection Committee has to patrol in groups of eight to ten men armed with bows and arrows and spears. Boys with grazing animals also watch and listen for the sound of ax upon tree when cutting groups are active, so that they can warn the forest protection committee. When this occurs, the men attempt to encircle the cutting group so that they can catch them. In these cases, they turn offenders over to the forest department guard, which later fines the woodcutters.

Economic Costs of Protection

Jyoti believes the decision to protect the degraded forest land has had a significant impact on the economy of Harinakuri. Previously, Jyoti and the other villagers also had been engaged in cutting fuelwood for sale. If a number of family members were engaged in cutting, a household might collect two or three 40- to 50-kg bundles of wood each day. In 1979, these quantities generated Rs35 to 50 (US$1.16 to 1.66) per day; at 1991 prices (Rs1, or US$.03, per kilogram), they yielded three times as much. Fuelwood cutting and carrying could be done in three or four hours in the morning, leaving time for other work. In contrast to agricultural wage labor, which is available only during certain times of the year, fuelwood cutting was likely to generate two or three times more wages per unit of time spent.

For the Chandana and Harinakuri communities to discontinue this lucrative economic activity was a considerable sacrifice. Based on discussions with villagers in Harinakuri, their decision appears to have been made partly on the basis of their concern over the deteriorating environment. They also recognized that their former level of forest exploitation was not sustainable, and that they would have had to shift occupations, in any case, once the forest resources were exhausted.

The shift away from fuelwood cutting, and the loss of income it entailed, was softened by the land-reform program of the West Bengal Communist Party government. The program transferred title in rain-fed rice land from the landlords to

Jyoti and his neighbors, who had acted as tenant farmers in the past. Because they no longer had to share their harvests with the landlord, the villagers' incomes rose.

At the same time, Jyoti and his neighbors decided to begin producing puffed rice (*chira*) for the local market. The work involves buying small stocks of unhusked grain (*dhan*), usually 20 kg at a time. The rice is husked, winnowed, and roasted under a brushwood and leaf fire. The operation requires three men, who work from 4 A.M. until 5 P.M. During one shift, usually they process 20 kg of raw rice, worth Rs60 (US$2), into 10 kg of *chira* worth Rs240 (US$8). This means hourly income per man from *chira* making is approximately Rs4.60 (US$.15) per hour, or Rs60 (US$2) per thirteen-hour day. This is approximately three times the official minimum daily wage (Rs24.85, or US$.83) for agricultural laborers. It also closely approximates the income that might be generated by fuelwood headloaders if they had sufficient forest resources to exploit.

While Jyoti and his neighbors have been successful in finding an alternative source of income at least as lucrative as fuelwood cutting, many of their neighbors have not been so fortunate. They must suffer the lost income or continue to exploit the forest in defiance of their neighbors.

The amount of time the Chandana and Harinakuri forest protection committees spend patrolling the forest and the value of that time in terms of opportunity costs are difficult to calculate. Many of these activities take place during periods of high threat. These fall during the months of August through October, after rice transplanting has been completed, and from February to May, after the rice harvest, when little agricultural work or paid labor opportunities are available.

No regimented, full-time patrolling system has been utilized. Instead, villagers, especially women and children engaged in grazing, fuelwood collection, and other forest-related activities, act as an early-warning system. When given news of illegal activities, men then move into the forest for protection activities. While the time involved may not be great, many community members appeared to be available and alert to possible threats, which they perceived as significant.

Sal poles probably represent the single most valuable product in the regenerating forest. The villagers also use the small leaves of date palms to weave mats for sale. Many women in the community were involved in *sal* leaf plate making; their product is sold for packaging foods.

Other forest products include tubers, considered to be one of the most important products collected by community members. Although their value in local markets is low, they are an important source of starch and nutrients during food shortages. (Tuber preparation, however, is time- and fuel-consuming.) Mushrooms also provide a seasonal source of food and cash income. Of particular importance are *kurkuri, mudal,* and *parab* mushrooms. They bring Rs8 to 16 (US$.26 to $.53) per kg. When the mushrooms appear, during the rainy season from July to mid-October, households may collect up to 30 kg per day. Finally, grass and leaf fodder from the forest are important, especially from July to October, with forest leaf fodder (*sal* and others) of importance during the April-May dry season. By determining the number of kilograms of forest fodder consumed per household and placing an equivalent fodder value on it, it would be possible to estimate the cash saved through the use of forest fodder.

Ecological Impact of Community Forest Protection

The degraded *sal* forests of Southwest Bengal are known for their impressive regenerative vigor. In Chandana, for instance, after seven to eight years of protection, the trees had reached 6 to 8 m in height, and the forest canopy was nearly closed, creating a shaded, moist microenvironment. Accumulating leaf litter on the forest floor and expanding root systems appear to slow runoff during monsoon rains. Sun-loving species such as *kendu* (*Diospyros melanoxylon*) are being replaced by shade-tolerant herbs and fungi. With regeneration, villagers have reported the reappearance of a number of bird and plant species.

In villages near Chandana, after five years of protection, more than 214 species of flora and fauna were present in the forest. Of these, 189 were utilized by local people. Edible food plant species numbered 39, including 6 types of tubers and 11 species of mushrooms. Some 47 plants are used as medicinals. In addition, 79 species of birds, animals, and insects are consumed. Generally, the larger regenerating forest patches exhibit greater diversity. Tribal communities tend to possess greater ethnobotanical knowledge and practice more extensive species utilization than caste groups. Basal areas, reflecting the volume of standing timber, also increased from zero in unprotected *sal* forests to 71 m^3 after five years of protection and reached 164 m^3 after ten years.

Forest Protection Committee Expectations

Comanagement systems of the type emerging in Southwest Bengal are essentially partnership agreements between state forest departments and participating communities. To the extent that partnerships succeed, each party needs to share similar expectations regarding their roles and rights. The experience of Harinakuri village is typical of the kind of give and take necessary for successful comanagement.

In Harinakuri, the forest protection committee leaders indicated a desire to fell *sal* for pole harvest as soon as possible. The villagers indicated that they had protected their *sal* for ten to twelve years, and that it should have reached the end of the rotation. On walking through the area, the forest department staff saw that the *sal* was only of seven to eight years' growth and had not reached the 3-inch diameter at breast height (DBH) required to yield a good price as construction poles. The villagers' eagerness to harvest the poles appeared to be driven by concern over the continuing pressures exerted by the outside cutting groups. The villagers were worried that as the poles gained value, the threat of a mass looting by a group of outside villagers would grow.

The Harinakuri Forest Protection Committee leaders felt that a gradual harvest of the sal forest would be preferable, allowing for a 10 percent cut of the standing stock on an annual basis. The forest department had been considering such a system to provide a steady flow of yearly income to participating forest protection committees. Although the villagers thought that this would be a better system than a single felling every ten years, they feared that commercial felling would stimulate outside villagers to exploit their forest. They thought that this one time, as a demonstration to other communities of the financial benefits of protection, it might be better to cut the entire stand. Through this approach, other villagers finally might be induced to begin protection. All the surrounding communities would then start at the same point, with new coppice growth. At present, however, no decision has been made to go ahead with the pole harvest. Due to rapidly declining market prices for poles, the villagers may decide to preserve the forest and only selectively fell trees for local use in housing and as tools.

The committee leaders had little information about forest department policies on *sal* pole harvesting and revenue-sharing procedures. Members of both the Chandana and Harinakuri forest protection committees noted that they hoped to obtain 40 percent of the gross proceeds rather than the 25 percent authorized under forest department policies. They were also unaware that their share would be calculated from the net proceeds rather than the gross.

In Arabari, one of the only forest protection committee areas where harvesting and revenue distribution had taken place, the forest department overhead costs ran to 53 percent of the gross. This meant that, under the 25 percent policy, the Arabari Forest Protection Committee was entitled to only a little less than 12 percent of the gross. At the same rate, the 75 ha of forest land protected by the Harinakuri Forest Protection Committee would yield only Rs4,550 (US$151) per household during the ten-year rotation, or Rs455 (US$15) per year per family— far less than the Rs5,000 to 10,000 (US$167 to $333) a family might earn from a year of fuelwood headloading. Senior officers of the forest department later noted that the costs from Arabari were quite high, and they planned to reduce the overhead charges substantially when calculating the share going to forest protection committees like those of Harinakuri and Chandana.

The Harinakuri Forest Protection Committee did not have access to information regarding the income it might receive from management activities. At the same time, they were committed to working with the forest department on the basis of good faith. They were anxious to participate in the felling themselves. The forest department staff indicated that local forest protection committee members would be hired at the official state minimum wage of Rs24.85 (US$.83) per day. The villagers thought the wage rate was fair and agreed to undertake the work on that basis. Consequently, forest protection committee members derived additional benefits from labor opportunities generated through the felling operation. The forest department staff told the villagers that officers from the forest protection committees would be involved in supervising the counting of poles taken from the forest. The forest protection committee members felt such an arrangement also would be useful, since they lacked experience in commercial felling.

The forest protection committee wanted to maintain the revenues as a community fund rather than distribute them equally among the participating families. They had clearly spent some time considering how to utilize the funds and requested that the forest department assist them in establishing a community account with the local branch of the Punjab National Bank. The account was to be overseen by the eight-member Harinakuri Forest Protection Committee's managing committee and its secretary.

The committee planned to use the funds to construct a community rice-storage barn, which could also be used by families involved in *chira* making to allow them to buy grain at harvest time at lower cost. They also wanted to establish a cooperative store to sell groceries, stationery, and school supplies, since they currently had to travel some distance to the local markets to buy these goods. Finally, the forest protection committee wanted to form a savings and loan program to allow community members access to low-interest loans for medical needs, marriages, and agricultural inputs. Establishing a bank account and gaining tax exemptions on revenues generated from timber sales may require the formal registration of the forest protection committee under the Indian Societies Act. This also may require assistance from the forest department.

For future rotations, the forest protection committee would like to shift to an annual felling system. They note that the regeneration of the forest has had substantial environmental and economic benefits that will be lost temporarily if the entire area is clear-felled. The most important advantages emerging from forest regeneration have been improved groundwater infiltration and slowed runoff and the increased availability of such nontimber forest products as tubers, mushrooms, and fiber materials. The reestablishment of standing forest near Harinakuri village also has enabled a large population of birds to nest in the area. The birds are important in controlling insect pests that attack the rice crop. The forest protection committee also feels the forest has had a beneficial effect in cleansing the air of disease. When the forest was degraded, its members note, the incidence of disease had increased. They associate a healthy environment with a good standing forest.

Community Forest Management in Orissa

In the state of Orissa a grass-roots community forest protection movement has been growing for several decades. Two case studies from Orissa indicate the types of community-based management systems that are emerging.

The case of Mahapada village reflects the process through which a forest-dependent, low-status tribal group demonstrated the ways communities can organize to protect degraded forests. The management systems the villagers developed later were adopted by the higher-caste groups in the village. The second case, Budikhamari, tracks a single village's forest-protection group's expansion into a coalition of seventy-nine neighboring communities. This larger group formed an apex organization to coordinate forest-protection activities, conduct environmental education programs, and provide mutual assistance in dealing with the forest department.

In recent years, the Orissa Forest Department has taken a greater interest in village forest-protection groups. Resolutions passed in 1988 (GOO 1988) and 1990 recognized the villagers' right to a share of forest products and clarified their management responsibilities. (A resolution is a unique Indian legal form, a technical term that describes a process through which the intent or emphasis of broad legislative authority can be refined or clarified. Resolutions are often in the form of a government order promulgated by a technical agency such as the forest department.) Some foresters have been very effective in encouraging communities to organize. They have enhanced the groups' authority by formally registering them and providing local patrol groups with identity cards. Yet recent meetings with village forest protection group leaders indicate that few see any advantage in interacting with forest department staff or local government officials.

The Case of Mahapada Village

Sarangi Range is located in Dhenkanal Division, approximately 40 km to the northeast of Dhenkanal town. The range has extensive tracts of degraded forest land as well as large forest areas, including the 12,960-ha Kapilas Reserve Forest, which provides a habitat for up to sixty wild elephants. In 1987, a shortage of trees of harvestable girth led to a moratorium on further felling. Still, the range officer and his staff have serious problems with organized, illegal felling, especially in the eastern side of the territory. Fortunately, the emergence of community forest protection groups throughout the range has established effective access controls over an estimated 30 percent of the forest lands in the range.

In an attempt to strengthen these informal groups, I. Z. Khan, the range officer, has registered sixty-one local village forest protection committees. He notes that thirty of these community groups were active before the forest department began its program to encourage group formation in 1988, and more villages are forming groups as they observe the successful forest regeneration efforts of their neighbors. PIPAR, a local training and research NGO involved in assisting forest management groups, indicates that a number of groups may be operating without having been contacted by the forest department. PIPAR estimates that one corner of the range has sixty-five active forest protection committees and that an additional eighty-five villages are interested in forming management organizations. In summary, Sarangi Range may comprise up to one hundred active community-management groups, with the potential for up to two hundred or more forest protection committees to operate (see Map 3.3).

Map 3.3

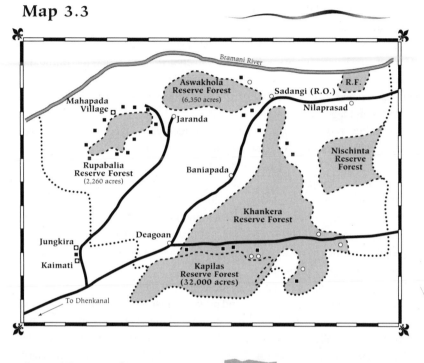

Sarangi Range and Forest
Protection Committees

KEY

.... Range Boundary

.-'-'-' Forest Boundary

———— Roads

■ Forest Protection
Committee

○ Village/Town

Forest Protection Committee Experiences

Mahapada Village is located at the northern side of Rupabalia Reserve Forest, a tract of more than 900 ha. The community was settled by Saura tribals approximately three generations ago. The Saura cleared the forest and developed rain-fed rice fields at the base of the hill. Brahman families who moved into the area gradually acquired all the farmland in the village and brought scheduled- and cultivator-caste families with them. The forest was well managed by the community to meet subsistence needs until about sixteen years ago, when the Brahmans sold clear-felling rights to outsiders, probably from Dhenkanal. With the once-rich forest quickly being reduced to scrub, the Saura tribals went to the Brahmans and demanded to manage their share.

The Saura began protecting a 25-ha tract fourteen years ago, and rapid mixed-forest regeneration resulted, encouraging three other groups to form committees two years later. These forests are now more than 10 m in height and support a diverse range of tree, shrub, climber, and herb species, generating significant flows of valuable nontimber forest products. Wildlife, too, has begun to reappear, witnessed by the recent sighting of a bear emerging from the forest. Two years ago, the Brahmans also began protecting their 40-ha section of the forest. The five forest protection committees now operating in Mahapada are shown in Figure 3.1, and their territories are delineated in Map 3.4.

The Saura tribal community bases its survival for at least six months of the year on forest tubers (*tumbualu*, *kanta alu*, and *panial*), mushrooms, edible leaves, and other forest foods. For an additional two months of the year, their subsistence is dependent on the collection of *kendu* (*Diospyros melanoxylon*) leaves, used for making *bidi* (cheroots), in the forest. They receive Rs10 (US$.33) for two thousand leaves of high quality. The Mahapada forest protection committees meet monthly to make forest-management decisions.

The committees determine when community members can collect fuelwood (generally five to six times per month), how often each household head is responsible for forest patrolling duties (usually twice a month), and fines for community members who break management rules. Special meetings are held to discuss major timber or pole requirements for roof or house construction. Women generally do not get invited to *sahi* meetings, which are held in a men-only community center. The forest protection committees are basically a component of the clan or tribal council (*sahi samiti*), which also handles village disputes, festival organizing, road repairs, and school activities.

Some time ago, the forest protection committees of Mahapada village asked the Orissa Forest Department beat officer to supervise the digging of trenches to demarcate the boundaries between each committee's managed forest patch. Their request indicates that, at least in this area, communities perceive a need for forest department recognition of their boundaries and rights and wanted the beat officer to be knowledgeable regarding their territorial responsibilities. Similar needs for demarcation and recognition likely will be found elsewhere. Special training for

Figure 3.1

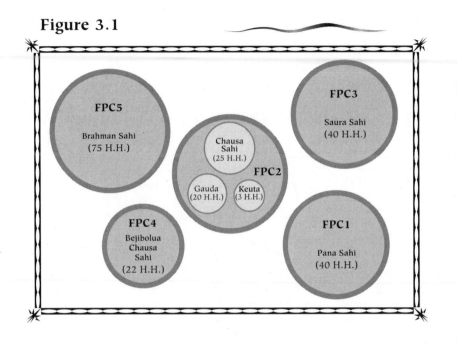

Venn diagram of forest protection groups
in Mahapada Village by social composition.

Map 3.4

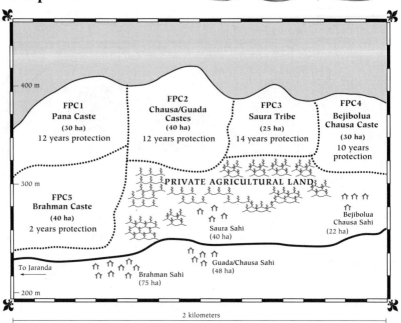

Mahapada Forest
Protection Committee
(FPC) Territories

forest department field staff in these procedures might be useful, after operational guidelines have been developed.

Budhikhamari Joint Protection Party

Budhikhamari is at the center of a forest protection movement that has evolved in northern Orissa during the last ten years. Until the 1960s, villagers report, good standing forests existed. These produced a wide range of products used for home consumption and commercial activities. A prolonged drought in the late 1960s led to more rapid exploitation of forest resources, as destitute villagers turned to fuelwood headloading and worked for town-based timber smugglers. By the late 1970s, most of the surrounding forest had been reduced to scrub. The disappearance of the forest meant that local households had great difficulty obtaining the many forest products they needed to meet a wide range of recurring needs, including materials for housing, tools, medicines, food supplements, fodder, and fuelwood. By 1993, seventy-nine villages had established a network of forest-protection groups guarding 3,247 ha of once degraded moist deciduous forest.

The actual process through which communities began to organize is not clear. As early as 1983, some community members, in response to forest product scarcities, began discussing strategies to control access and regenerate small patches of forest neighboring Budhikhamari village. The community adopted the *thengapali* (bamboo-stick rotation) system, in which each household must allocate a young male member for patrol duties when its turn arises. Patrols are usually done in groups of four to five people. In Budhikhamari, if someone fails to patrol, he is fined Rs5 (US$.17). When patrols encounter outsiders carrying out illegal headloading or timber harvesting, they are fined.

Both local people involved in illicit timber and fuelwood extraction and some forest officers initially questioned the villagers' efforts. By 1986, however, S. C. Mohanty, the divisional forest officer, and K. C. Mishra, the local range officer, became aware of the concern and initiatives of the community. They began a series of support activities. The Orissa Forest Department staff worked with Gorachand Mohanta, a local community leader, to initiate a series of meetings with other villages in the area. The local forest department staff began assisting villagers in demarcating forest tracts to be placed under the protection of each participating community.

By January 1987, sixty people from eight neighboring villages had reached an agreement to conserve plots of forest with the approval of the forest department. Within two months, seven other local communities also began guarding degraded forests surrounding their villages; by 1988, twenty-five villages in the area had formed forest protection committees.

Representatives from participating villages formed an apex body known as the Budhikhamari Joint Protection Party to facilitate communication among participating communities. The party is an important example of nongovernmental, intervillage forums for forest-management coordination. Since its formation, the party has conducted numerous public meetings, environmental marches, and nature camps for schoolchildren and local community members. The party also has provided a unified front through which the seventy-nine participating villages can deal with the forest department, as well as with more powerful timber smugglers and fuelwood middlemen.

Representatives from the Budikhamari Joint Protection Party are reluctant to establish any formal ties with the local *panchayat* (formal village government system), and they reject the idea that *panchayat* headmen (*sarpanch*) should become chairmen of forest protection committees, as required by the Orissa state government. While the party remains skeptical of government officials, community leaders feel that the local forest department staff has been supportive of their attempts to stabilize forest use.

The Budhikhamari Joint Protection Party has gained greater legitimacy among its membership and with outsiders through its dealings with foresters. Since the Orissa Forest Department passed resolutions to formalize community protection groups in 1988 (GOO 1988) and 1990, it has begun issuing identification cards to villagers involved in forest patrolling. The forest department staff from neighboring Simlipal National Park hopes that the party movement might extend its activities to that area in the future.

As the forests surrounding Simlipal have experienced greater protection from local communities, extractive pressures inside the park from fuelwood headloaders as well as organized logging gangs have increased. Whether communities and the forest department can develop a comprehensive management plan for production forests and the national park remains to be seen.

Policy and Institutional Challenges in Comanagement

The emergence of tribal and scheduled-caste leaders who are able to organize forest protection is a testimony to the broad sociopolitical changes that have occurred in Orissa and West Bengal during the last twenty years. Community members clearly are concerned about environmental degradation in their areas and are willing and able to take action to respond to the challenge. In some cases, they are increasingly encouraged by supportive forest department programs and helpful field staff.

Community Initiatives

The cases of Chandana, Mahapada, and Budikhamari indicate that communities often are mobilized by local leaders who draw attention to the villages' deteriorating forest resources and related environmental problems. These case studies provide useful glimpses into the context and process of emerging forest protection committees. They highlight communities' ability to organize and take control of their natural resources. The villages' experiences also indicate the vast potential of *sal* forest ecosystems to renew themselves, provided human disturbance patterns are halted. At the same time, the case studies indicate that many institutional, economic, and ecological problems continue to threaten the sustainability of these new community-based resource management systems.

In Chandana, despite success in protecting at least 100 of the 160 ha of disturbed natural *sal* forest neighboring their village, the community continues to be confronted by threats from other villages in the area whose residents depend on fuelwood cutting for a substantial portion of their income. The tribal and scheduled-caste people who illegally exploit these forests are driven by economic necessity and encouraged by local and urban higher-income and -caste groups. Until all communities neighboring the forest can be effectively brought into the comanagement program and their economic needs met, these emerging local-management systems will remain threatened and their sustainability questionable.

The Role of National Policy

In West Bengal, many management issues still need attention as communities and the forest department attempt to develop sustainable partnerships. As the *sal* pole harvest approaches, the forest protection committees and the forest department will face a new set of issues. The forest department needs to clarify procedures for harvesting and communicate them to participating forest protection committees well in advance. Profit-sharing terms also need further consideration.

Ideally, the forest protection committee share should be based on an economic assessment of the opportunity costs each community incurs through protection activities and the income lost when the community ceases other forest-exploitation activities. A floating rate based on the ratio of protected forest area to households also may be necessary. In Harinakuri, where the ratio is more than 2 ha per household, the returns from protection will be relatively attractive. By contrast, in forest protection committees with only 0.5 ha or less per household, forest conservation income may be insufficient to provide an adequate incentive to stimulate effective management actions. The forest department also needs to reassess the management costs that are deducted from gross profits. It may be possible to set a clear percentage figure as a maximum, therefore ensuring the forest protection committee share would not be subject to major reductions due to management costs.

More generally, forest departments need to relax felling requirements and revise working plans in areas where communities primarily are managing for conservation.

Forest departments should respect situations in which villagers prefer not to carry out any commercial timber cutting but rather leave the forest for nontimber forest products and its hydrological and microclimatic functions.

Newly drafted national and state resolutions support the establishment of forest comanagement systems in India and provide an attractive opportunity for experimentation with community–forest department collaboration (GOI 1988; MEF 1990). These guidelines will need revision based on experience with forest comanagement activities. Changes are likely to be in the direction of providing communities with adequate managerial authority, tenurial security, and appropriate economic incentives.

Research on the process of community forest management group formation indicates the existence of a great deal of grassroots organizing for environmental management in various parts of India (see Dhar, Gupta, and Sarin 1990; Gadgil 1991; Malhotra 1991a; Pandey 1991; Poffenberger 1990, 1992; Poffenberger, McGean, and Bhatia 1990; Poffenberger and Singh 1992; Roy 1991; Shashi, Singh, and Singh 1991). In response to deteriorating forest conditions, thousands of communities from south Bihar, eastern Gujarat, Orissa, eastern Maharashtra, southwest Bengal, and other parts of the country have attempted to restrict exploitation and halt the process of environmental degradation. A number of state forest departments have supported these local activities for some years. Where state forest departments are supportive, village forest management groups often are able to sustain protection effectively, even under pressure from other communities and the private sector. With the support of state forest comanagement resolutions, these groups can receive formal legitimacy, further strengthening their authority. One policy question concerns the form this recognition should take and the legal nature of these local management organizations.

Forest Protection Committee Relationships with Local and National Governments

There is some concern that the emerging forest management organizations may not fit well within the system of local government (*panchayati raj*) or may be in conflict with the customary rights of the larger local-user population. Experience concerning the possible relationships between community forest-management organizations and local government is limited. Most resolutions give local *panchayat* institutions an oversight role in monitoring the activities of village groups, as is the case in West Bengal. If a forest tract and managing communities are spread over a large area covering several *panchayats* (*gram sabha*), coordination may be more difficult.

One option for dealing with the extralegal nature of community forest-management groups and their relations with local government bodies, as the Orissa joint-management resolution has suggested, is to extend membership in forest-management groups to all members of the *panchayat*. In some areas, however, this would create other problems. Since many joint forest management groups are comprised of members from a single small hamlet, incorporating all communities within the *panchayat* would expand membership significantly. The community that originally formed a joint forest management group would have to join other villages in creating a new management system. In the process, the original community's authority over forest management decisions would be eroded. Finally, where existing community management groups are functioning, they would be obligated to share forest produce with other communities that have been incorporated into the management committee. The West Bengal Forest Department has attempted to form multivillage forest protection committees, in some cases joining together smaller community forest protection committees. Here, the component communities generally agree to keep their independent identities within the larger group, maintain clear boundaries for their areas, and retain exclusive control over harvests in their territories. At the same time, the larger group does seem to play a helpful role in facilitating joint protection activities and resolving disputes. According to the West Bengal resolution (GOWB 1989, 1990), these larger groups can be linked to the village *panchayat*.

Another concern is that if forest comanagement groups were absorbed by the village *panchayat*, vested interests influential in many communities might exert control over decision making. More democratically elected village *panchayats* are developing in Karnataka and West Bengal, where the new *panchayati raj* system has been adopted. These also exist in many communities in other parts of India. In many states, though, traditional elites still effectively manipulate village *panchayat* decision making. Since many small, community-based forest protection groups are comprised of less powerful groups and communities within the larger *panchayat*, they might lose authority to elites if the management groups became a direct adjunct of the *panchayat*.

In addition, twenty years' experience of Indian social forestry programs suggests that *panchayats* may not even be able to effectively manage community woodlots. In some cases, this incapacity was due to the *panchayats'* inherent political nature and the often diverse constituencies that make reaching consensus about the management of community forest resources difficult. Recent experiences in both India and Nepal demonstrate that smaller community groups (often comprised of ten to fifty households) can more effectively mobilize to establish management systems, including protection activities, harvesting and sharing systems, and dispute arbitration. This results from the smaller groups' economic and social homogeneity and their physical proximity to the forest. While there is a need to clarify the relationships between local forest management groups and local government institutions, simply subsuming these groups in the local government body could threaten their effectiveness.

Exploration of the role local governments could play in collaborating with forest departments to assist with planning and monitoring the forest management activities of local groups within their jurisdiction may be a more useful approach. A formal institution, such as the local government body, could play a role in dispute arbitration among communities and, when the need arose, between communities and the forest department. All state resolutions should deal more clearly with arbitration among communities and should discuss the handling of disputes between the communities and the forest department.

While the resolutions that have been promulgated are generally vague when addressing relationships between community management groups and the local government organization, the West Bengal resolution may have been overly specific in terms of the role of the forest department and local government in determining committee members. The original 1989 resolution stated, "The beneficiaries shall be identified from amongst the economically backward people living in the vicinity of forests concerned," and that the local *panchayat* land management committee "shall select beneficiaries for construction of the forest protection committee." This statement indicated that local government representatives from outside the community would determine who could and could not participate. In 1990, the West Bengal resolution was revised to allow every family in the village to be a member of the management group. However, the new resolution maintained the clause that the *panchayat* land-management committee and the forest department should determine families eligible to benefit from the program.

If membership is selective and determined by outside agencies and local government bodies, there is a possibility that some families already participating in forest comanagement activities might be denied membership and would be excluded from the program. Having final authority over their own membership seems fundamental for community-based organizations. Studies in West Bengal (Malhotra 1991b; Roy 1991) indicate that many villages organize their own forest protection committees and determine their own membership. Forest protection committees comprised of all or most households in the community had more effective forest-management organizations than those with partial membership.

In areas where local groups function effectively, the forest department and local government may only need to formally empower them and provide technical assistance. This, generally, is what is occurring in West Bengal. Since the West Bengal resolution and those from a number of other states imply that the forest department and local government direct the formation of community forest management organizations, the policy does not entirely fit the realities of the rural context in which the program is being implemented. Forest departments and policy makers need better information about how and why communities organize to manage forest resources, and about how they might best relate to local government bodies.

Recent resolutions also could stimulate the proliferation of numerous new community-level organizations that are completely dependent on the forest department, rather than local initiative, for their existence. This could undermine the possibility of greater self-governance at the lower level or the development of more democratically elected or selected institutions or processes. Community forest management groups, as the little brothers in the partnership with the forest department, then would have little say over policy and management decisions. Most state resolutions possess clauses that allow the forest department to dissolve forest management organizations if they fail to perform according to the expectations of the department. While forest departments will require some statement in the resolution to enable dissolution of the management agreement if their community partners fail to uphold their responsibilities under the joint forest management program, it is also important that the identity of village resource management organizations be respected. In Rajasthan and Haryana, where the resolutions (GOH 1990; GOJK 1992; GOM 1992; GOMP 1992; GOR 1991) require communities with active forest-management groups to become registered societies, protection committees have a separate legal identity and, consequently, greater independence. Some committees in Haryana and West Bengal have requested assistance from members of the legislative assembly and other politically elected leaders to strengthen their bargaining power. In the Pinjore area north of Chandigarh, fourteen community management groups met together to request that the Haryana Forest Department modify the terms of the grass-lease pricing and payment system. These experiences suggest that community forest management groups will want to maintain a separate identity and utilize local governance bodies, elected leaders, and group apex organizations as mechanisms to express their needs and negotiate more effectively with forest department partners. The need for autonomy and democratic process at the community level is currently lacking in state resolutions, but these should be part of any revisions.

Satisfactory agreements between forest departments and community management groups also might be facilitated by representatives from both groups developing a joint plan for the area. Although some resolutions mandate community input into microplans, current forest department working plans do not incorporate this community input. The result, especially if there are different viewpoints, is an unresolved tension between the community and the forest department plan. Mechanisms need to be developed to ensure that forest department and management-group plans for areas under comanagement are compatible with and satisfactory to both parties.

Policy and Women's Participation

Most resolutions do not adequately address the role of women in forest comanagement systems. While the Gujarat resolution (GOG 1991) specifically requires at least two women members on community management committees, and revised guidelines for the joint forest management program in Haryana require both male and female household heads to be members of the community forest management society, most resolutions do not refer to women's participation. Since women are frequently the primary users of forest resources, this is a serious omission.

For women to play a central role in management decision making and be formally recognized as voting members of local management groups is both logical and important. In some rural contexts, men migrate from the village for extended periods or are too busy with agricultural work to allocate time to management activities. In these cases, the establishment of community management groups solely comprised of women may be appropriate. This has taken place already in a number of states. Resolutions need flexibility to successfully support emerging community initiatives. They should not assume a single model of community management.

Conflicting Ownership and Use Rights

Perhaps more problematic is the question of preexisting user rights. In many forest areas in India, communities and *panchayats* already possess a range of customary legal rights over forest resources (*nistar, dafavati,* etc.) granted under the earlier forest acts of 1878 and 1927. Emerging forest department comanagement programs are entering into new agreements with communities and extending a new set of rights targeted to local groups. This process can create problems if earlier rights-holders are excluded from the new agreements. Existing rights need to be reviewed before new management agreements and rights, previously granted as appropriate under the earlier forest act, are formalized.

Some forest protection committees operating in Southwest Bengal negotiated with neighboring communities to clarify rights and territorial responsibilities when they began to initiate protection activities. In many cases, communities have the strongest incentive to avoid conflicts with their neighbors over forest rights. These villages have demonstrated that they can conduct much of the negotiation on their own or with the assistance of the local government. The forest department, however, holds ultimate responsibility for seeing that its agreements with management groups do not create conflicts over real or perceived preexisting use rights. Once an intervillage consensus about forest management rights has been reached, agreements need some type of formal legal approval.

Some government agencies also are empowered with certain rights and interests. *Panchayats* and parastatal organizations, as well as local cooperatives, often have harvesting and marketing rights to timber and nontimber products. These rights must be recognized or settled when the forest department is developing agreements with community management groups.

With the exception of clauses in the national (GOI 1988; MEF 1990) and West Bengal (GOWB 1989, 1991) resolutions, most state program guidelines do not address the long-term rights of participating communities who protect and hope to benefit from forest lands under comanagement. Clear tenure security enhances community-management groups' authority to carry out protection activities, especially when they are under pressure from neighboring villages and private interest groups. Participating communities that invest labor in protection activities and defer exploitation of forest resources to benefit from future production may need greater assurance of the government's commitment to their participation in the program.

Since state forest departments are creating management partnerships with village groups, the timeframe for such agreements, as well as the basis for extensions, necessarily must be clear. It may be appropriate for the time period of the agreement to correspond to the production cycle (rotation) of the primary products. In West Bengal, this is the ten- to twelve-year rotation of the *sal* poles. Without a clear temporal mandate, community management groups may fear that their labor investments will not yield benefits, since the forest department could revoke the agreement prior to the harvest.

Aside from providing tenure security through specific clauses in state forest co-management resolutions, management groups should be aware of their tenurial rights and formalize them through countersigned agreements, certificates of usufruct rights, and symbols of authority. When outsiders question the authority of community-management groups, or when a group must challenge offenders, such documents are important in demonstrating the group's legitimacy.

Ecological Limitations of Policy

The level of biological productivity is another important consideration in setting policies regarding produce sharing. For example, in semiarid western India, tree growth and biomass production will be slower than in high-rainfall areas. Some disturbed forest land in Southwest Bengal still possesses healthy *sal* stumps and other root systems that regenerate secondary forest growth through coppicing very rapidly. Within a few years of harvesting, a community may possess a substantial secondary forest that generates multiple products. In other forest areas, where stumps have been removed for fuelwood and soil erosion has been extensive, flows of forest products will be considerably lessened and slower to materialize. If community management costs are to be met in such contexts, the forest department will need to invest in more capital-intensive enrichment planting and possibly provide additional employment opportunities. Currently, forest comanagement policy documents do not address the need for flexibility in ensuring an equitable flow of benefits to participating community-management groups operating in different ecological contexts.

Conclusion

Resolutions alone may have little or no effect on reality. They need to be effectively communicated to the forest department staff and village families and translated into local languages. Meetings will need to be organized with forestry staff and participating communities to explain the content and discuss the implications of resolutions. New ideas will emerge through diagnostic research, program monitoring, and open discussion with participating groups; these should result in improvements to the programs. To the extent that policies and program activities can respond in a supportive manner to the problem-solving strategies being developed by communities and foresters, forest comanagement offers a promising opportunity to respond to India's forest management problems in a socially and ecologically sound manner.

ACKNOWLEDGMENTS

The author would like to thank the communities and all NSG colleagues who contributed to the collection and analysis of these field reports. Particular thanks are due to the West Bengal and Orissa forest departments, S. B. Roy, Mitalee Chatterjee, Kailash Malhotra, Arvind Khare, Madhav Gadgil, N. H. Ravindranath, Jeff Campbell, S. Palit, Neera and Kundan Singh, Samar Singh, Syed Rizvi, Shekhar Singh, K. R. Raghutnathan, and Betsy McGean.

SOURCES

Dhar, S.K., J. R. Gupta, and M. Sarin. 1990. *Participatory Forest Management in the Shivalik Hills: Experiences of the Haryana Forest Department*. Working Paper No. 4, Sustainable Forest Management Series. New Delhi: Ford Foundation.

Gadgil, M. 1991. *Natural Regeneration through Community Participation in Degraded Forest Lands in the Western Ghats*. Bangalore, India: Centre for Ecological Sciences, Indian Institute of Science.

Government of Bihar (GOB). 1990. Resolution No. 5244. August 11.

Government of Gujarat (GOG). 1991. Resolution No. FCA-1090-125V (3). March 13.

Government of Haryana (GOH). 1990. Resolution No. 1370 FL-1-90/15610. June 13.

Government of India (GOI). 1988. National Forest Policy. December.

Government of Jammu and Kashmir (GOJK). 1992. Resolution No. SRO-61. March 19.

Government of Madha Pradesh (GOMP). 1991. Order No. 16/4/10/2/91. October 12.

Government of Maharashtra (GOM). 1992. Resolution No. SLF-1091/P/K/119-191/F/11. March 16.

Government of Orissa (GOO). 1988. Resolution No. 10 F (Pron) 47/88/17240/FFAH. August 1.

Government of Rajasthan (GOR). 1991. Circular No. F-7 (39)/FOREST/90. March 16.

Government of West Bengal (GOWB). 1989. Resolution No. 4461-For/D/15-16/88. July 12.

———. 1990. Modification Resolution No. 5062-For D/15-16/88. July 27.

Malhotra, K. C. 1991a. "People, Biodiversity and Regenerating Tropical Sal Forest in West Bengal, India." Paper presented to the International Symposium on Food and Nutrition in the Tropical Forests, September, Paris, France.

———. 1991b. *Joint Forest Management in West Bengal: A Study in Non-Timber Forest Produce and FPC Structure in Jamboni Range, Midnapore District*. Calcutta: Indian Institute of Biosocial Research and Development.

Ministry of Environment and Forest (MEF), Government of India. 1990. Resolution Regarding Involvement of Village Communities and Voluntary Agencies for Regeneration of Degraded Forest Lands. No. 6-21/89 F. P. June 1.

Pandey, D. 1991. "Joint Forest Management in Rajasthan." *Yojana* (Oct. 15).

Poffenberger, M. 1990. *Joint Management for Forest Lands: Experiences from South Asia*. Working Paper No. 2, Sustainable Forest Management Series. New Delhi: Ford Foundation.

———. 1992. "The Resurgence of Community Forest Management in the Jungel Mahals of West Bengal." Paper presented at the Conference on South Asia's Changing Environment, March 16–20, Bellagio, Italy.

———, B. McGean, and K. Bhatia, eds. 1990. *Forest Management Partnership: Regenerating India's Forests*. Executive Summary of the Workshop on Sustainable Forestry, September 10–12, New Delhi. Working Paper No. 3, Sustainable Forest Management Series. New Delhi: Ford Foundation.

———, and S. Singh. 1992. "Forest Management Partnership: Regenerating India's Forests." *Unasylva* (Food and Agriculture Organization, Rome) 43 (170).

Roy, S. B. 1991. *Forest Protection Committees in West Bengal, India: Emerging Policy Issues*. Honolulu, Hawaii: East West Center.

Shashi, K., N. Singh, and K. Singh. 1991. *Community Forest Management in Orissa: Case Studies*. Bhopal and New Delhi: Indian Institute of Forest Management/ Swedforest.

Transforming Customary Law and Coastal Management Practices in the Maluku Islands, Indonesia, 1870–1992

Charles Zerner

Leave the *pinang* alone!
Leave the coconuts alone!
Leave the bananas alone!
Leave the trochus there!
From the mountains to the coast,
Leave it all alone!

Ritual chant, Saparua Island

In 1989, I sat in the office of the head of Nolloth village on Saparua Island, one of the Lease Islands of the Central Maluku of eastern Indonesia. There Mr. Metekohy, one of two chief *kewang*s of the village, chanted a portion of the announcement he recites each year to communicate that the period of prohibitions on entry, harvest, or hunting in community-controlled areas, known throughout the islands as *sasi*, is in effect.

In his role as *kewang*, Metekohy combines the responsibilities of a resource monitor with the power to enforce community resource-management rules. While walking the paths on the periphery of the community-management territory, or *petuanan*, he announces the temporary closing of the area. "As I circumambulate the outermost limits of each community-management area," Metekohy explained, "I stop wherever paths intersect to repeat my ritual chanting." His chants are accompanied by the lowing, plaintive sounds of an assistant blowing on a conch shell trumpet.

Among many agricultural and fishing communities throughout the Maluku Islands, *sasi* is an historic family of institutions and practices that has been used to regulate access to particular resources and territories under a variety of property regimes. Although a systematic study of *sasi* over a broad geographic range has never been undertaken, it is clear that these practices have been and, in many areas throughout the 1,029 or more Maluku Islands (see Map 4.1), continue to be followed.

Time and space are among the most important media through which many Moluccan communities regulate access to resources and territories that are important from subsistence and commercial perspectives. When an area is *ditutup* (closed), entry prohibitions are in effect, and the area under *sasi* is marked by signs placed at strategic locations. Temporary signing of individual trees, groves, or entire territories is accomplished with striking ritual constructions of paired coconut palm fronds jutting outward from a central sugarcane trunk crowned by a young coconut; sound-producing "instruments" at the apex of the assemblage make percussive sounds when struck by the wind. This is one of the fundamental ways in which the boundaries of resource areas under *sasi* are marked. In the case of Nolloth, only the chief *kewang* and his assistants, a group of ten *anak-anak kewang* charged with enforcing the closure of the area and implementing the prohibitions within the community-management territory, are permitted to enter freely during the closed period; a host of other prohibitions on gear, behavior, and identity of entrants also is put into play. When *sasi* is opened, entry prohibitions and other associated restrictions are lifted; the *kewang* circumambulates the territory formerly under *sasi*, unties the *sasi* signs or bindings, and announces that the prohibitions governing the territory have been lifted.

Although the practice of demarcating "cultural regions" is problematic because it suggests historically fixed and homogenous regions, it may be useful to consider the Maluku Islands as the westernmost edge of a cultural and institutional Wallace's line. Beginning with the Maluku, and extending east through New Guinea and the islands of the Southwest Pacific, marine tenure institutions, rules, and practices have played an important role in regulating access to reefs and inshore marine waters. To the west of the Maluku, beginning with Indonesia's orchid-shaped island, Sulawesi (formerly Celebes), open-access, freedom-of-the-seas ideologies and practices are mixed with a variety of marine tenure practices that only now are beginning to be understood and documented (see Bailey and Zerner 1992; Zerner 1992, 1994a, 1994b).

The Development of *Sasi* Institutions and Practices

Historically, and in many contemporary Moluccan communities as well, *sasi* practices are not just a body of changing rules but also a diverse set of institutional roles that have varying degrees of relationship to central governmental and religious authority. *Sasi* role holders, including *kewang*s and *mauweng*s as well as other practitioners, combine religious, civil, martial, and commercial functions. Attempts to characterize *sasi* ahistorically, as though these practices, rules, and institutional roles had a fixed essence, would be inadequate and inaccurate.

Zerner (1994b) and von Benda-Beckmann, von Benda-Beckmann, and Brouwer

Map 4.1

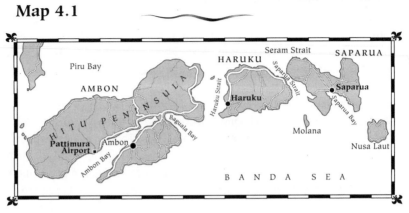

Major Maluku Islands

Map 4.2

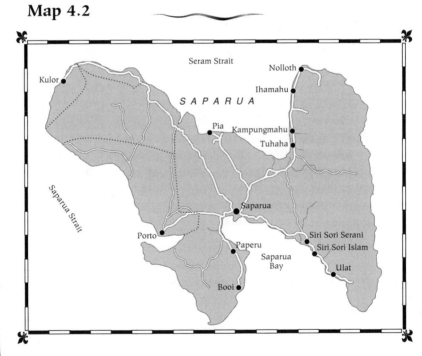

Saparua Island

(1992) speculate that *sasi* practices initially may have been directed toward ancestral spirits believed to inhabit Moluccan marine and terrestrial landscapes. Such spirits were said to control the luck of the hunt, the fertility of crops, and individual fate. Those who violated areas marked by *sasi* signs risked sickness or even death at the hands of these spirits, in addition to a variety of civil punishments and fines implemented by the *kewang*.

During the late nineteenth century and the first three decades of the twentieth, Zerner and von Benda-Beckmann, von Benda-Beckmann, and Brouwer suggest, *sasi* practices were recrafted and deployed by local elites, assisted by Dutch colonial administrators who sought access to sources of income realized by the control of the sale of valuable agricultural and, to lesser extent, marine commodities.

Sixty-nine years before Mr. Metekohy chanted a few *sasi* verses for me, a villager recalled the anxious atmosphere surrounding ritual closure of the coconut groves around Siri Sori Serani village in 1920:

> In the village very ripe coconuts were in the trees, ready to be plucked. After consultation with the chief kewang, the village council decided to impose the sasi. . . . Following this, a sasi proclamation was made. One evening in the dark of the moon, the chief kewang, attended by his assistants, walked around the village. . . . [T]he kewang called out loudly . . . [and] the assistant kewang blared his great shells to produce a long and somber sound. The chief kewang chanted a long-lasting "silo . . . o . . . o!" [a word that means *sasi*]. Whereupon his assistant answered "mese . . . o . . . o! [is laid down]". As they went around the village, I heard the sounds. I was but a child sitting in my house, and I began to tremble in my seat. *(Volker 1925:298–299)*

As a young boy, fears of spirits, as well as fears of being apprehended by the *kewang*s on their nightly patrols, prevented the narrator from entering the grove of coconuts on which the *sasi* prohibition had been laid:

> From this evening the sasi was laid down and the work of the kewang began: they saw to the implementation of sasi. For no one can escape entrapment and punishment, if he plucked something out of a garden. Personally, it is enough to come up against a kewang on a dark evening, far away from the vicinity of your own house. In order to quell suspicion, men will reverse and criss-cross their paths to avoid the bush police; for if a man cannot give a clear and polished explanation for being out so late beyond his house, then he must bear the punishment anyway. *(Volker 1925:299)*

The teller of this tale cringed at the prospect of violating the coconut grove *sasi* because he was terrified of the potential response of watchful spirits. These impalpable witnesses might inflict a catastrophe upon him or the community:

I still remember this very well, that we boys in the time of sasi played in the groves, and an old dry coconut fell down [we would not pick it up]. [Normally] we wouldn't think twice about grabbing it and whisking it away. This was because we felt a sort of holy awe, and we knew we would cause a great flood if we took the coconut. We had a secret terror of the ghosts. *(Volker 1925:299)*

Sasi and the Regulation of Access to Agricultural Commodities

The effectiveness of *sasi* practices has waxed and waned throughout its recorded history, depending, in part, on the source(s) of authority and the political and economic interests these authorities and rules represented. Whether, and in what circumstances, local villagers were interested in or willing to submit to *sasi* regimes is not clear. Religious sanctions and practitioners, Dutch colonial authority, and local Moluccan elites dependent upon the colonial enterprise for legitimization of their power and income were among the varying sources of authority behind imposition of *sasi* in different times and places. Recently, as we shall see, Indonesian village-level government officials as well as environmental nongovernmental organizations have begun to restructure *sasi* rules, practices, and ideologies in attempts to reconstruct *sasi* in ways that further their own (very different) interests.

In certain areas of the Maluku Islands, *sasi* developed as an instrument for facilitating commercial regulation of access to valuable agricultural crops, especially coconuts, betel and *kemiri* nuts, and possibly cloves. Indeed, the pivotal historical role of the Central and North Maluku Islands (including Ambon, Saparua, Seram, Banda, Buru, Haruku, Ai, Hatta, and Ran, as well as Halmahera, Ternate and Tidore) as supply centers for the world spice trade suggests the strong possibility that, in certain areas, these practices may have been stimulated by markets for agricultural commodities.

Prior to the arrival of Europeans in the sixteenth century, traders from Makassar, East Java, the Philippines, and Banten were sailing to Moluccan ports to seek agricultural commodities (Andaya 1993). Like their European successors, these traders needed to establish and secure access to prized crops grown in remote village groves. During the sixteenth century, Portuguese, British, and Dutch traders also arrived, eager to establish monopolies on the Moluccan spice trade for European markets. The development of institutional control mechanisms, whether superimposed on already existing indigenous practices or invented by local native elites, traders, and, later, Dutch government officials, may have been driven by commercial opportunities. If this speculation is correct, then the codification of *sasi* customary law in Dutch and Malay-Ambonese texts becomes more easily understandable. These texts may have constituted attempts to control, codify, and commercially rationalize *sasi* customary law, practices, and institutions.

At least one account from the island of Ambon in 1920 reveals a *sasi* institutional structure in which the proceeds of harvest auctions were used to pay for surveillance of agricultural territories under *sasi* and to provide salaries for resource monitors. This particular kind of *sasi* elaborated the arrangements for timing and manner of harvest and the rules for gathering, marking, and auctioning individual and clan-controlled crops that had been gathered into central warehouses. Prices for the yearly crops were negotiated and allocations made to distribute profits to individual and clan landowners. As in many villages practicing *sasi* today, the Siri Sori Serani rules of 1920 stipulated that the market price for the commodities sold from one *sasi* were negotiated at a meeting of local government officials, *sasi* and clan leaders, and elders. Apparently, portions of each year's profits also were distributed to village government and religious institutions. Money obtained from the sale of certain *sasi* harvests occasionally was donated to the mosque or used to buy oil for the *mesjid* (Volker 1925).

The elite leaders of Siri Sori Serani village elaborated one such arrangement during the early twentieth century:

> During the imposition of sasi, the rightful landlord is permitted to enter his own garden in order to clean up the grounds and to gather already ripened and fallen coconuts. He must take these to the village meeting place, where they are branded and stamped with the sign of his clan group and stockpiled. So I saw at the conclusion of the sasi-period almost the entire space under the village meeting place filled with piles of coconuts. *(Volker 1925:299–300)*

The imposition of *sasi* in this particular village seems to have been initiated by a rural elite working in collaboration with a Dutch colonial official. A letter signed by leaders of this village to a local regent implores him to issue a "strong promise" reinforcing and further codifying *sasi* rules because local villagers apparently *did not want to obey them*. According to the letter,

> Because it is clear that we villagers pay little attention to sasi regulations which are usually implemented by us according to custom . . . apparently villagers do not yet understand that sasi regulations implemented under each rule will improve the lives of the inhabitants themselves, we request that this matter will hopefully be taken care of by Sir [the *controleur*] through issuing new orders using a strong promise to confirm that this sasi is for the good of the inhabitants. *(Volker 1925:301)*

In response to this collective request from local leaders and *sasi* enforcers for assistance, the regent issued a letter intended to strengthen villager compliance by regularizing and codifying *sasi* procedures, purposes, and penalties. His "strong promise" and new rules constituted an attempt to enforce *sasi*, to "fix this *sasi* for the lifetime of the inhabitants" (Volker 1925:307). In the past, as in the present, *sasi* presented problems of institutional design, compliance, and articulation with markets. In his letter, the regent stipulates that "in the event someone wants to buy or to contract the coconut *sasi* one year in advance" (Volker 1925:309), all the district officials, "old ones of the land" (Volker 1925:309), and young inhabitants are ordered to gather and meet on that issue.

At one such meeting, the regent asked,

> Whoever wants to enter all his fertile coconut trees into the prohibition, his fruits will be channeled within the sasi, his fruits will never be stolen because the kewang officers have purchased them, [and] the prohibition will be guarded every day until the contract is finished. *(Volker 1925:310)*

The lands of farmers who declared their coconut groves within that year's *sasi* were monitored, patrolled, and protected by the *kewang*, aptly described by at least one Dutch official as the "bush police." If the *kewang* discovered any villager other than the rightful owners within the protected groves, they were arrested, tried, shamed publicly, and fined. Fines levied on outsiders, whether nonlocal traders or villagers, were higher than those levied on local villagers.

It is not at all clear that the common farmers and fisherfolk of local villages supported these *sasi* regulations. In Siri Sori Serani village, for example, not all coconut growers wished to participate in this scheme of community-enforced production and market access. The colonial official's response to the letter sent by local leaders suggests that participation in market-oriented *sasi* in that one village may have been coerced:

> Whoever does not want to follow these "sasie" [sic] rules and does not want to sign his name to this letter, then that person will be viewed as a person who does not want to be governed and order[ed] and wants to use his own desires in a free manner only. *(Volker 1925:307–308)*

The proceeds from agricultural lands entered within a particular yearly *sasi* were distributed according to various schemes. According to one scheme, the total amount of coconuts from an individual farmer's or clan's land was tallied and the coconuts marked. The proportional amount of profit due to individual farmers or clans, obtained from the proceeds of a collective auction of all crops sold to a particular trader in that year, was returned to them. In alternative arrangements, a certain percentage of profits from a particular *sasi* was allocated for the public good (for example, the purchase of lamp oil and a donation of cash for the Siri Sori Serani mosque). Administrative costs for imposition and implementation of the *sasi* were provided by allocating a share of each farmer's coconut crop to the *kewang*, who thus had a direct incentive to guard the ripening coconuts under *sasi*, prevent theft, and convey the harvest to the village hall without loss or damage. In Siri Sori Serani village of 1920, for example, the chief *kewang* "receives one-tenth of all gathered fruits" (Volker 1925:310).

Whether designed, invented, or fused with previous religious practices, agricultural *sasi*, as practiced in the late nineteenth and early twentieth centuries in the Central Maluku Islands, apparently provided an institutional and legal framework in which the security of agricultural crops could be guaranteed for individual groves or collectively held areas. Ripening groves of coconuts, betel, and candle-wood or *kemiri* nuts were protected from theft through the watchful eyes and mobile patrols of *kewangs*. Moreover, *sasi* institutions provided political and economic arrangements whereby individuals could coordinate their decisions—for example, to enter or not to enter into a particular *sasi*—through collective institutions. Although the equitable consequences of these relationships are not known, village-based *sasi* linked individual production to a larger market manifested by the yearly arrival of traders. *Sasi* arrangements allowed a forum for collective decisions on allocation of benefits to *sasi* officials, to individual cultivators, and for the collective good.

T. Volker, a Dutch colonial legal observer, commented on the institutional benefits of *sasi* in 1921. His remarks anticipate the arguments and even the rhetorical strategies of contemporary common-property theorists and community-management enthusiasts who extol the virtues of direct economic incentives to local communities. Explaining the purported benefits of *sasi* as a collective institution, Volker waxes enthusiastic:

> The young fruits remain on the trees and are not plucked before their prime, for whatever purposes. Because the kewangs have a stake in the outcome, the production is increased. They see to it that the grove renters keep their groves clean, and guard against harmful wild animals such as boars, badjings, and crawfish. It is more advantageous that a significant amount of fruit should be harvested in one fell swoop and taken en masse to be processed as copra. This [collective harvest and processing] insures that it will be traded in good quantities, and so that the proprietor can conduct a lively business with honest neighbors. This is better than selling the coconuts in increments of four and five fruits, or drying them and selling them to a Chinese for a few cents that are quickly spent. Thus, as a result of sasi, an entirely different situation comes to pass. The right of sasi is still an undervalued source of education, for the little peoples are, in general, still self-willed and pig-headed. Sasi brings with it a discipline that has an important educative element. *(Volker 1925:300–301)*

The picture of *sasi* that emerges from Volker's own account, as well as from the letter from an indigenous elite linked to and dependent upon the colonial enterprise, suggests that *sasi*, as practiced in the Central Maluku during the early twentieth century, was a set of institutional arrangements and rules based on state-sponsored policing of productive areas. These arrangements implied control over harvesting, market negotiations for sale of the product, and allocational decisions. The implication that local elites, with the benign or possibly smug connivance of the Dutch regent, were imposing "discipline" on "self-willed, pig-headed little peoples" and manipulating local practices in the service of particular economic interests is also apparent. By the early twentieth century, and probably for decades before written records were produced, *sasi* was a changing, hybrid institution that arose in a border zone of intercultural contact, crosscutting interests, and competing claims on resources.

Sasi on the Seas: A Marine Common-Property Institution in Flux

Sasi institutions and rules also regulated access to nearby marine environments in local coves, bays, and estuaries. Historical materials suggest that until the 1960s marine *sasi* regulations were far less differentiated and well developed than their agricultural counterparts. In the Central Maluku, markets for marine commodities apparently did not gain significance before the late 1950s or later.

Moluccan coastal communities historically possessed well-defined marine territories under the control of particular villages. In the Central Maluku, these areas are known as *petuanan laut*, from the Malay *tuan*, or "owner," and *laut*, which means "sea." Lateral boundaries frequently are associated with natural features in the landscape, such as promontories or points. In Teluk Kau on Halmahera, according to Shalan, a young student who grew up in the area, an imaginary line between two promontories located on opposite sides of a cove 15 km deep and 40 wide constituted the boundary of a single village's *petuanan* (Shalan 1991).

While promontories often are regarded as the lateral boundaries of *petuanan*, the outermost edge of community-controlled waters is usually located at the juncture of coral reef and drop-off. The inshore waters under community control, from the low-tide line to the farthest edge of the reef (sometimes called "white water"), are known as *meti* in the Central Maluku. This area is scrupulously monitored during the imposition of *sasi* by the *kewang*, his assistants, and local villagers. Several island communities also claim and control rights over submerged atolls and underwater reefs, known locally as *negeri tengelam* (literally "submerged communities"), which may be several miles from the island on which the community is located.

During the performance of *sasi* closure rituals, the boundaries of a marine *petuanan* are made visible and communicated. At the inception of the closing ceremonies, ritual practitioners carry incense and offerings of food to sacred places. These places may include the tips of promontories and points along the shoreline, as well as special places in the mountains believed to be inhabited by ancestral spirits. During the imposition of *sasi* on Ai Island in the Central Maluku, semipermanent ritual "trees" (lengths of wood crowned with a fringe of banana leaves and topped with a young coconut) are anchored offshore. With their fringe of banana leaves and coconut crown visible on the surface of the sea, these constructions function as a ritual sign of the *sasi* prohibition and a boundary marker signifying the outermost edge of the marine *petuanan*.

Marine *sasi* has differed from land-based *sasi* in several ways. Unlike the variety of property regimes and rights-holding bodies that seem to have characterized agricultural *sasi*, local communities, rather than individuals, most commonly possessed ownership or control rights. In some coves, however, individuals were able to acquire rights to operate lift-net platforms or other gear in particular places. Also unlike agricultural *sasi*, which was deployed in the Central Maluku to regulate access to productive land and forest areas for subsistence and for commercial purposes, marine *sasi*, until very recently, only regulated access to the *petuanan* for subsistence purposes.

With certain exceptions, marine *petuanan*s were closed only during the arrival of schools of pelagic fish such as tuna and the thousands of *lomba* fish (*Thrisina baelama*) that yearly returned to the mouths of certain rivers for days at a time:

> The sea sasi and on the reef drop-off is implemented during that time of year when many fish migrate to the bays or into river mouths. If a fisherman discovers that the influx is beginning, he warns the village council as quickly as possible. . . . The kewang . . . sets a branch as a sasi symbol on the edge of the reef drop-off just in front of the place where the fish swim in. . . . After a couple of days, if there are enough fish in sufficient quantities in the signed places, the entire population ventures out in boats with nets, ropes, and driftnets. They hang out large sheets to drive the fish into the nets. The men break up into communal fishing parties. *(Volker 1925:302)*

Prior to the 1950s or 1960s, marine *sasi* regulations focused on increasing hunting success and coordinating collective drives of fish that were temporary, possibly migratory residents of local bays and river mouths. When a school of fish entered a marine *petuanan*, the ocean *kewang* dived into the water and observed the movements of the school. Until the school settled down, he declared *sasi* closed, and no one, whether a local or an outside villager, was permitted to fish or enter the area. In Porto village, for example, only after this happened was *sasi* opened and a collective fish drive begun. In this regulated free-for-all, villagers' access rights were equal, and each fisher's share depended only on personal skill, luck, and position in the hunt.

The few written rules concerning early marine *sasi* practices all relate to timing, equipment, and coordination of fish drives. They focus on maximizing the catch and minimizing the possibility of startling the fish and scattering them through disruptive behaviors (such as standing up in a boat) or the use of improper gear. As long ago as 1870, rules concerning marine *sasi* in Porto village stated that

> [w]hen schooling fish have just entered our harbor, no one may toss his net while standing in the water, and from time to time [it is forbidden] to use a redi, because these actions will panic the fish, they will not stay close to land and be accessible to people [trying to] net them. Whoever violates this rule, the person that stands up in his boat, he will be fined three rupiah and the [user of] the redi will be fined ten rupiah that will be placed in the village treasury. *(Aponno 1977:20)*

Gear restrictions continue to play an important role in the Central Maluku today. In the spring of 1991, Shalan, a high school student, recalled that only certain kinds of scoop nets were permitted during fish drives within a bay along the jagged coast of Kau Bay on Halmahera Island:

> Everyone within the village is entitled to fish for any kind of fish within our bay. It is only when school fish enter the bay that strict prohibitions on timing of the drive, gear and behavior go into effect. If schooling fish are sighted by a local, they are reported to the saniri negeri [a *kewang*-like resource monitor] who goes out to observe them. If the saniri opens up sasi, then our fish drive begins. About forty boats from our village, each with a crew of four, paddle toward the school and surround them. They may not use motors and they may not use any other gear than scoop nets. As they surround the school, the fish are driven wild and into a panic. They try to escape from our circle of boats and in the process, they jump right into our scoop nets. *(Shalan 1991)*

In the 1990s, on Saparua Island (see Map 4.2, page 82) as schooling fish swim to sea from an estuary they had entered, the *kewangs* of Porto village signal the relaxation of gear restrictions and the opening of *sasi*.

In 1870, the marine *kewang* of Porto village (known as the *laukewanno*) also enforced regulations concerning the use of large nets that could close off an estuary or an entire cove. Fees levied on users of large gear provided the *kewang* with a salary and an incentive to perform his duties assiduously. In return, the *kewang* guarded the nets, prevented theft, and reduced conflict:

> Whoever uses a closed net (*djarin tutop*), when he wants to close [off] the cove in our land, must pay fifty cents each time to the community treasury so that the kewang can guard against other people entering the net and taking fish, at their whim, which causes conflict and curses with dirty words with the result that people make the Rajapatti dizzy and there is no tranquillity within the community. *(Aponno 1977:20–22)*

People who were foolish or avaricious enough to enter the area near these big nets during the temporarily closed-off time were fined: "Whoever dares to enter within [the area of the] closed net mentioned in article 86 without permission from the owner will be fined twenty five cents [that is deposited in] the community treasury" (Aponno 1977:20–21). Other rules from 1870 Porto prohibit the use of fish poison and prescribe sanctions for violators.

A Shift in Punishment Standards: From Shame to Money

In the 1920s, if a man stole fruit from his own grove before *sasi* was opened, he might have been fined a block of white cloth, a bottle of palm wine, a gong, or a quantity of gold. If he stole from another person's garden, however, he was not only fined but shamed:

If a sasi transgressor in the community was found to have stolen something from another's grove, then a completely different punishment is
levied. Aside from the fine, he is punished as follows. If someone is
caught red-handed who is clearly the thief, he is nabbed, stripped, and
his body is wound round with young coconut leaves. . . . [He] is followed
around by the drum beater, gong bangers, [gangs] of howling children
and dragged through the community. He must then call out in the local
language or [in] Malay: "Don't steal like me, don't steal like me." In general people believed that the man wouldn't live much longer. What was
certain, even if he lived, was that life for him in his community or in
neighboring communities was no longer possible or desirable. All honor
was stripped from him. He was shamed in every sense of the word.
(Volker 1925:301–302)

While fishermen in 1991 recalled stories of violators being bound and shamed
with the *sasi* sign who were forced to walk about the community shouting, "I have
violated *sasi!*", most punishments implemented today involve money. "People
would no longer submit to being bound today," explained a head of Nolloth village on Saparua Island. "They would find such a punishment intolerable"
(Matatula 1991).

Changes in Marine *Sasi*, 1953–1991: A Market in Mollusks

Prior to the 1960s, although reefs were within the boundaries of marine *petuanan*s, few rules regulated access to reef fish or mollusks. *Trochus niloticus*, a reef-
resident mollusk, was gleaned freely from the shallow waters and reefs. The
animal inhabiting the shell was extracted and eaten and the shells thrown away.

During the 1960s, a commercial market developed for trochus shell, which is
used to make paint pigments and a variety of ornamental items, including buttons,
for East Asian markets in Taiwan and Japan as well as for European consumers
(Reid 1992). From this beginning, and continuing through the 1970s and 1980s,
trochus extracted from Central Moluccan reefs became the object of an international system of commerce linking local fishermen and fisherwomen, *sasi* institutions and laws, local-level government officials, marine commodities traders, and
international exporters. The market for trochus has driven changes in the focus,
structure, and operation of marine *sasi* institutions and practices for the last three
decades.

Historically, coastal fishing communities have been among Indonesia's poorest
peoples. Fishing, even when combined with agriculture in small gardens and
swidden plots, is a notoriously risky way of making a living. In the Central
Maluku, the rise of a commercial market in trochus created a window of economic
opportunity for local traders on the islands of Ambon and Banda, village-level government officers searching for funds to supplement their cash-starved routine budgets, and local fishermen. During the early 1950s, merchants based on Banda

Neira Island began buying trochus and other shell products from fishing communities on nearby Hatta, Ai, and Ran islands. At roughly the same time, merchants based on Ambon Island journeyed to Saparua, Haruku, and Ceram islands and began offering cash for trochus.

Government officials soon realized that the *sasi* system offered an institutional and legal means to control the trochus harvest and its profits. In 1968, for example, Mr. Matatula, the village-level government head of Nolloth village (Saparua Island), issued a proclamation declaring the existence of a trochus *sasi* within community waters and asserted control of the *sasi* on behalf of local government (Matatula 1990; Matatula et al. 1990). The formerly "free" access of individual local families to the community-managed marine *petuanan*, he declared, was forevermore prohibited. Matatula's unusually candid "History of the Trochus *Sasi* in Nolloth Village" states,

> Until 1968 . . . the trochus gathered even more attention, because the market became better and better by day. It was [in 1968] that the community was never again permitted to take trochus in a free manner. . . .
> [B]ased on the decision of the Government Body, all the income from the trochus must be allocated to all community needs and the Village Government generally and [this income] will not be permitted [to be used] for private [needs]. *(1990:1)*

Indeed, by 1988 trochus exports were big business throughout Maluku Province. In a single year, the province's total volume of shell exports tripled, from less than 80,000 kg in 1987 to more than 256,000 kg in 1988. From the shallow shelf and reef of Kei Besar, an island in southeastern Maluku Province, a total of 7.5 tons of trochus shell with an approximate value of US$65,000 was harvested in 1989 (Abrahamsz 1991). By 1991, trochus shell was selling for Rp16,750 (more than US$8) per kg.

Governmental responses to trochus depletion throughout the Maluku, however, were far from uniform. At the same time that village-level governments began revising *sasi* in their own interest and asserting their control over community territories and revenues, higher-level government actors in Jakarta moved in different directions. In 1972, Decisional Letter of the Minister of Agriculture No. 327 already had declared *Trochus niloticus* a creature that "cannot be found" or is "rare" throughout Maluku Province (Soelaiman 1978:4). In 1987, as trochus extraction soared, the minister of forestry declared *T. niloticus* a protected species (MOF 1987). His decision meant that trochus harvests had become illegal. Ideas about conservation were emerging from the political center, in government ministries far from Moluccan shores.

As prices and the pace of trochus extraction increased, the geographical extent of government-driven revisions of *sasi*, including reallocation of benefit streams and rights, spread throughout the Central Maluku. On Hatta Island, for example, rights to harvest reef-resident creatures, including trochus, remained open to all local residents before and after the late 1960s. In 1965, however, a village-level governmental regulation (MOF 1987) established that the village government was entitled to 6 percent of the total trochus harvest. The motives of the impoverished village head, who explained "that village government income in Hatta is derived solely from the trochus profits" (Saidjan 1991) were clear. By 1991, on Ai Island, several kilometers northwest of Hatta, the local government share of the trochus *sasi* was one shell out of every three harvested, or 33 percent of the entire reported harvest. In that same year, on Saparua Island, village governments in Porto and Paperu asserted or considered asserting government entitlement to 100 percent of the total trochus harvest; Nolloth's government had staked its 100 percent claim as early as 1969.

While the government share of the profits from trochus *sasi* varied widely from island to island, a relatively rapid, market-driven restructuring of the legal, economic, and institutional aspects of *sasi* clearly had occurred between 1970 and 1990. This restructuring was in the direction of centralization and control of access to reef areas and commodities in government hands. Developments in several communities on Saparua Island exemplify these changes.

In 1990, for instance, a Nolloth village head issued another version of *sasi* regulations (Matatula et al. 1990). This entailed progressive seizure and tightening of governmental control over the marine *sasi* area through narrowly drawn regulations controlling the space and time regulations, as well as others specifying the behavior, identity, and gear of those permitted to enter the *sasi* area. These regulations, signed by four customary officials (the *pakter*, the *kewang besar*, the *ukulima*, and the *ukulua*) as well as by the government head (a former police officer), demonstrate how formal government has effected rapprochement and operational collaboration with customary authorities. Through government proclamation, *sasi* rules, roles, and institutions have been seized and squeezed in a progressively more centralized governmental embrace. Moreover, the language of the Nolloth regulations—legalistic, scientific, precise and bureaucratic, peppered with spatial coordinates and fixed on maps, numbers and alphabetized remarks—presents a striking contrast to the ritual speech, incense, and silent offerings of *sasi* ritual.

Consequences of a Revised *Sasi*: The Distributive Justice Question

The social and economic consequences of governmental codifications and creative manipulations of the *sasi* system such as those implemented on Saparua Island in Nolloth, Porto, and Paperu villages are not yet clear. How do local villagers, *sasi* office holders, and government officers evaluate these dramatic changes? The question of distributive justice inevitably arises in assessing the consequences of increasing governmental control of *sasi*.

In 1990, the Nolloth village head painted a positive image of these changes:

Beginning in 1969 and continuing to the present day, management of trochus has developed progressively, in accordance with the growth of the world and our country, with the result that we, as Village Leaders, are always working and making strenuous efforts to provide guidance and explanations concerning village-level economic development generally, and trochus particularly, as well as various kinds of shells, coral, rocks, sand, gravel, decorative fish, and sea cucumber. *(Matatula 1990:1–2)*

Nolloth's village head points with pride to the material improvements in village life he has implemented with the proceeds from trochus sales. Since 1986, these have included the construction of a drainage ditch for expelling excess rainwater, a seawall, streetlamps, two wells, a village coconut grove, and two police posts. A village museum is now being built with *sasi* proceeds.

In contrast, a fisherman from Paperu village, commenting on the rumored imposition of a 100 percent government monopolization of the trochus *sasi* in Porto village in 1991, strongly rejected the idea of government control of profits and key decisions on labor, timing, and gear:

> The sasi on schooling fish is an heirloom [*pusaka*] handed down from the grandfathers, while the sasi on sea cucumber and trochus is completely new and only began in 1989. I do not agree with what is being proposed in Porto village. The idea of a corporate village right [*hak negeri*], separate from the rights of individual families to fish and harvest in community waters, was never asserted before. In the old days, people made contributions, on a voluntary basis, to the village government or they gave privately, as families, to the Raja. *(Kewang Paperu 1991)*

The same man, a respected marine *kewang*, focused on the potential for corruption and diversion of profits if village government succeeded in centralizing *sasi* administration and control of the economic flow it generates:

> If the Porto government controls all trochus rights, who knows how many trochus or sea cucumber will be gathered? Who knows who will make profits from those operations? People could get all kinds of hidden profits from this procedure, and steal our property for their private gain. We have an expression, "Small fish are eaten by the big ones." It means that small people, the common people, who are like small fish, are eaten by the big ones, like the silvery Bobara' fish. The common people may die making the big people rich. *(Kewang Paperu 1991)*

Government assertion of control over *sasi* often means control of the identity of laborers (villagers or workers hired from outside), the bidding process through which marine commodity traders are selected as purchasers, the minimum price accepted per kg of shell, and the technologies and manner in which trochus is extracted. All of these decisions have allocational as well as environmental consequences that as yet are not clear.

Private exporters as well as local governments also vie for control of inshore fisheries resources. In the southeastern Maluku islands Aru and Kei, Indonesian entrepreneurs based as far away as Bali have succeeded in acquiring rights to community-owned fishing grounds by advancing loans—for which the *petuanan*, or the right to harvest it, is given as security—to individual families during the monsoon season. Once indebted, many families transfer their rights to these entrepreneurs. In some communities, outsiders have acquired sole rights to harvest local marine resources, resulting in loss of local control of the community's resource base. Recent studies from Aru and Kei document significant loss of income by local residents as a result of these transfers (Abrahamsz 1991; Khouw and Simatauw 1991).

A Crisis in Environmental Management?

The rise of a market for trochus, in conjunction with widespread rural poverty in coastal communities and increased motorization of small craft, also may have generated a crisis in reef-resource management throughout the Maluku Islands (Reid 1992). In the inshore waters of many islands, trochus, mother-of-pearl, and other reef-resident species are being overexploited and depleted (Abrahamsz 1991; Reid 1992; Zerner 1991a, 1991b). Beginning in the 1960s, *sasi* prohibitions against harvest of trochus lasted from three to five years, a period sufficient to allow populations to mature and reproduce at least once (Kastoro 1991:22–23). As trochus prices have risen and local needs have increased, including those of fishing families and government offices, the interval between harvests has declined progressively on many islands. On some islands, divers are permitted to use scuba tanks to conduct the trochus harvest. Rapid motorization of small-scale Sulawesian craft has made it possible for local reefs to be depleted by roving crews of opportunistic fishermen from other islands (Reid 1992). The result of this constellation of developments is that Moluccan trochus stocks have been seriously depleted.

On Saparua Island, for example, annual trochus harvests are yielding only 800 kg, whereas previous harvests on a three-year cycle were 3,000 to 4,000 kg (see Figure 4.1). During the Japanese occupation of Hatta Island in the 1940s and the immediate postwar confusion, trochus was not harvested for eight years; when harvesting resumed, in 1950, the yield was 30 tons. From 1950 through 1984, *sasi* was opened at two-year intervals on Hatta, with yearly yields of approximately 2 tons. Since 1984, *sasi* has been opened every year on Hatta, and yields are down to about 1 ton.

Marine Environmental Problems and the Cultural Construction of the Idea of Nature

The causes of overexploitation are multiple and converging. In addition to local governmental needs for routine budget funds, the national government also has

Figure 4.1

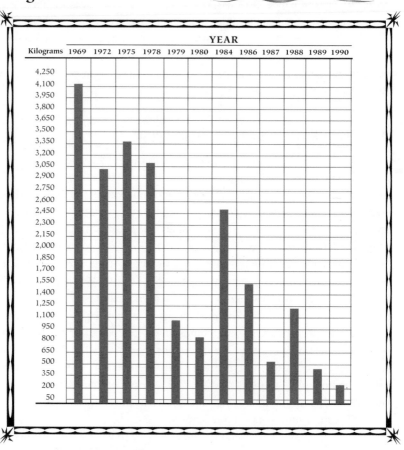

Trochus shell yield management,
Nolloth Village, 1969–1990.

stimulated village-level competitions that exhaust local coffers and place additional pressure on extractive industries. But local governments are not the only nor invariably the primary source of pressure for trochus extraction.

Rapidly rising consumer desires, stimulated by television images of a growing Indonesian middle class and its consumption patterns, are pushing local government and customary officials to shorten the interval between *sasi* harvests. Increased population densities on isolated Moluccan islands, in addition, are leading to increasing needs for alternative sources of income. Despite evidence that shortened intervals result in drastically decreased stocks, local officials claim that villagers' need for income—to perform religious rituals, to pay school fees, and to acquire consumer goods—are forcing them to extend the harvest period. In response to a question about the decreasing interval between harvests, the village chief of Hatta replied,

> We open sasi so frequently now because there are more people on this island and making a living is very difficult. It is hard to make a living on this island. In order to meet the operational needs of the village and its inhabitants we must use village-wide auctions of the trochus harvest as well as sea cucumber. *(Saidjan 1991)*

Although conventional community-based development narratives often demonize private-sector agents and government officials in analyzing the depletion of local environments, in the Maluku, and probably elsewhere, the story is more complex. Both government and private-sector actors may be exerting positive restraining influences on pressures toward overexploitation driven by local community desires. Private-sector trading companies that establish strict minimal size limits for acceptable trochus may discourage extraction of immature trochus indirectly.

In some areas, local officials claim they have attempted to resist local villagers' desires to shorten the interval between harvests:

> Local people do not understand ideas of sustaining the environment. They just want new things, good things, beautiful things. They are looking for their own happiness. From their perspective, the best way of getting a satisfactory life cheaply and easily is from a yearly auction of the trochus. I am convinced that we must lengthen the interval between trochus harvests to at least three or four years, but my community does not grasp why we need to limit harvests. *(Matatula 1991)*

Local communities, moreover, may not grasp the need to limit harvests because their conceptions of the nature of the marine environment differ radically from contemporary scientific understanding of marine population dynamics and the effects of extraction pressures on stocks.

The complexity of Moluccan cultural conceptions of the marine environment and societal relationships is apparent in the following interchange with Mr. Matatula, the government head of Nolloth village:

Charles Zerner (CZ): Why have trochus yields decreased? Why didn't you keep *sasi* closed for a few more years?

Government head (GH): There is a difference of opinion between my own views and what many people feel about this question. Many people think that the amount of trochus found by divers depends on the proper performance of *sasi* rituals.

CZ: What is the relationship between ritual performance and the amount of trochus found on the reef?

GH: I'll give you an example. Before I permitted trochus *sasi* to be opened in 1991, we sent out some men to dive and investigate the condition of the trochus. On a single dive each of them found four large shells within minutes. We took this as an indication that there were plenty of mature trochus, so we opened the *sasi*. On the first and second days of the season, trochus were plentiful. But by the third day it became more difficult. In the following weeks it was almost impossible to find a single trochus.

CZ: Perhaps there weren't many trochus to find?

GH: People here suspect that the trochus were made to vanish. Disappeared. They reason that the ritual opening of *sasi* must have been incomplete. The ritual must have not been performed in accordance with customary rules [*peraturan adat*]. (Matatula 1991)

This interchange, which occurred early in my exploration of *sasi*, suggests that Moluccan societal relationships and conceptions of causation in the natural world are culturally distinct and laden with implications for natural resources management.

Further conversations with Moluccan fishermen revealed that many imagine the marine world to be populated by a highly responsive community of invisible spirits. These spirits are believed to inhabit particular places within the Moluccan terrestrial and marine landscape, including promontories, graves, knolls, and mountaintops, as well as submerged places within the marine *petuanan*. Watchful spirits listen, see, and respond to the everyday practices as well as the ceremonial performances of the community. A fisherman's fate, as well as his luck in fishing—whether fish cluster about his net or disappear from sight—depends upon his relationship to these fractious spirits of the place.

From this Moluccan perspective, the effects of shortened harvest intervals on trochus stock replenishment or the consequences of increased extraction pressure through the use of scuba gear may not be relevant questions. For many Moluccan fishermen, the key question concerns the status of their personal relationships to a local community of ancestral and environmental spirits. Spirit polities can draw a school of fish to the scoop nets and can just as easily "disappear" them and the fishermen's nets in an instant. Fishermen also can be disappeared.

Late at night, on the island of Halmahera in North Maluku, my research assistant, Hasmi Bandjar, and I learned more about how Moluccan fishermen construct images of the marine environment and about the ways they conceptualize relationships between marine rituals and the presence of fish. Shalan, who grew up in an isolated cove in Kau Bay, told us many stories of growing up on a bay protected by unique practices and a family of local guardian spirits. In response to my repeated question, "Why are only scoop nets permitted and other gear prohibited during fish drives?", he quietly revealed a landscape in which fish, spirits of the cove, gear restrictions, and ritual performances are linked in a dynamic, morally sensitive relationship:

Shalan: If you actually use a net, the net will disappear and the fish will not be catchable. They can disappear.

CZ: Why?

Shalan: Because there are guardians there. They will only permit us to capture fish in scoop nets. For example, if a school of fish came to a place and they disappeared, it means that people will be compelled to say prayers and scatter offerings in the spot. The offerings are given symbolically, to suggest that there is food. Yellow rice, eggs, and a chicken are offered in a little scoop net. Offerings are not only performed when a school of fish disappears. Each year a group of village elders sails to both promontories flanking the bay and makes offerings of incense and yellow rice in a ritual known as *cakalele*. In the center of the bay, they sacrifice a white female chicken, place it in a small, floating fish scoop, and set it adrift. The bay is believed to be the site of a former village whose inhabitants fled when the waters rose. The places where offerings are now made are believed to be inhabited by a spirit family descended from the inhabitants of the inundated former village. Before a fish drive is commenced, village elders sail to the center of the bay and inform the female spirit believed to inhabit that spot that they wish to begin the drive. (Shalan 1991)

Shalan's and other stories provide a window onto local ideas of the marine world and fishermen's moral relationship to it. At the same time, the cleavage—indeed, the chasm—between these conceptions of the natural world and the societal relationships they entail and contemporary scientific notions of the interactions between natural dynamics and social practices is striking. While the scientific value of local fishermen's environmental knowledge increasingly has been recognized, the cultural, aesthetic, and ethical values of indigenous fishers' models and metaphors of nature and society often have been ignored. From the perspective of conservation or environmental management, however, the slippage between these indigenous conceptions of nature and societal relationships to it, and Western scientific models of environmental dynamics, also must be addressed.

Inventing a Green *Sasi*, 1968–1991

The historical trajectory of a community-management structure, like that of any political and legal institution, is in part the product of the way interested parties and institutions have imagined its purposes, narrated its history, and attempted to shape it to suit their own purposes (Bowen 1989; Hobsbawm 1985). The history of *sasi* in remote coastal hamlets of the Maluku Islands is largely the product of the ways various powerful and differently positioned interests have interpreted, and continue to interpret, this institution's administrative structure, rules, and most importantly, purposes.

In Indonesia during the early 1980s and continuing into the 1990s, new kinds of talk about the environment, economic development, and, later, social equity, began to inform central government policy, institutions, and the discourse of political leaders and policy makers. Indonesia's Basic Law of the Environment was passed in 1982 (GOI 1982), and the influential Department of Population and Environment was formed in 1978. WALHI, the Indonesian Environmental Forum, an umbrella agency for more than one hundred nongovernmental environmental- and social-activist groups scattered across the archipelago, was formed in 1980.

Between the remote villages of Maluku Province and the political center in Jakarta, people, ideas, and new ways of talking about the environment and communities moved across the seas. Since the 1980s, environmental and governmental representatives have begun to interact. Discourse among Java-based governmental and nongovernmental institutions; academic and scientific institutions in Ambon, the Moluccan capital; and formal and customary village leaders in remote Moluccan hamlets has resulted in changes in the interpretation and, possibly, in the implementation of *sasi*.

The story of Haruku village on the Central Maluku island of the same name is representative of these changes and the emerging new institutional actors. In Haruku, Mr. Ririmasse, a charismatic government head influenced by contemporary ideas about conservation and sustainable development disseminated by a national-level institution, decided to revive *sasi* and, in the process, make it environmentally acceptable. In 1992, Mr. Ririmasse recalled, "The situation of *sasi* was weak in the 1980s. No one on the island knew about or obeyed the rules. The local elite had no idea of resource conservation or sustainable management. The local youth were not interested in *sasi*. They were leaving the village and moving to the city" (Tjitradjaja 1992).

The Haruku head, however, was a close friend of an official representative of the Indonesian Department of Population and Environment, Pak Daisy, whose influential ideas led to the reshaping of *sasi*. According to the head, he "got ideas from Pak Daisy and . . . reformulated *sasi* as an instrument of conservation. I saw the youth rejecting the *sasi*, so I typed them up and added a few rules" (Tjitradjaja 1992).

More than "a few rules" were added when Haruku's *sasi* law was codified in 1985 (Ririmasse, Kissya, and Ririmasse 1985). In the process of reviving *sasi*, the institution was actually being reinvented. As represented in the new rules, *sasi's* purposes were articulated as "sustainable management and protection of living stocks as well as the equitable distribution of economic benefits." Community practices laden with a surplus of meanings and functions were being recast as community-based resource-management institutions focused on equity and protection of stocks.

Government-generated shifts in the functions of *sasi*, moreover, were paralleled in the political and aesthetic spheres. The "voice" and the appearance of *sasi* were changing. Rather than make pronouncements with a conch shell trumpet and the chanting of a ritual poem, *sasi's* new bureaucratic voice announced, in tightly constructed sentences, that

> sasi is a prohibition against the taking of various kinds of specific natural resources within a specified time period in order to conserve while guarding [its] quality and population [level] as well as conserving the social rules of local society and the equitable distribution of economic returns for the whole society. *(Ririmasse 1984:4)*

Sasi not only was being "greened," it was being married to the government. In one village in the Central Maluku, a government head proudly announced that *kewangs'* assistants had been made to wear uniforms, suggesting the development of an increasingly rationalized and bureaucratized structure. In a section entitled "The Legal Basis Supporting *Sasi*," this newly written constitution acknowledges the dual sources of *sasi* authority: "*Sasi* contains rules that are ordered through village legal decisions and the *Kewang* Institution that is a customary institution which is delegated [the responsibility] to monitor implementation of the aforementioned *sasi* rules" (Ririmasse, Kissya, and Ririmasse 1985:4).

Rather than use the imprecise but familiar, even familial, toponyms (named topographical features of coastal promontories, rocks, and marine drop-offs that are the landscape power spots and naturally visible cleavages in the marine landscape), the Haruku *sasi* constitution specifies boundaries of the marine management area in meters and topographically fixed coordinates located on a map. As local perceptions and memories about particular marine landscapes were being transformed, mapping reefs and *sasi* boundaries and positioning them within a grid of mathematical coordinates constituted a means through which governmental definition of and dominion over community-held sea space is advanced (Vandergeest and Peluso 1993).

New Rules and New Purposes

The codification of Haruku's *sasi* rules in 1984 was not a rote recapitulation of rules already transcribed and manipulated by the Dutch. Mr. Ririmasse, the Haruku government head, inserted several new rules directed toward conservation and sustainable management of resources. Rule B.8 is directed toward prevention of erosion and stabilization of riverbanks: "People are prohibited from cutting down trees near the river bank throughout the area under coastal sasi with the exception of sago trees" (Ririmasse, Kissya, and Ririmasse 1985:1). Under a division titled "For Men," Rule 6 mandates: "People are prohibited from entering [the estuary and river] with a motorized boat or any kind of a speed boat while the motor is on" (Ririmasse, Kissya, and Ririmasse 1985:1).

Prior to his term in office, Mr. Ririmasse explained, "there were only two basic kinds of *sasi*, a *sasi* on clove production and on the ocean." By the time he came into office, motorboats had begun to travel into the estuary and up the river, disturbing the migration of marine fishes and cutting them up with their blades. "Local people opposed the entry of the motor boats," he explained, "and I added a rule prohibiting entry" (Tjitradjaja 1992).

Environmental problems are not static but change over the course of time. The role of contingency in shaping legal institutions, moreover, can not be underestimated. After Mr. Ririmasse's retirement, a new problem emerged: the entry of *bagan,* or fine-mesh lift-net platforms, into the estuary area. The new government head claimed that he was "unable to act to prohibit the entry of bagan because 'There was no *sasi* rule prohibiting the entry of bagan'" (Tjitradjaja 1992).

In the early 1990s, frustrated local fishermen took matters into their own hands, working with a courageous *kewang* and a vibrant nongovernmental organization known as HUALOPU. In a burst of creative advocacy, the *kewang*, nominally the traditional *sasi* authority, relied on national fisheries laws prohibiting the use of fine-mesh nets (which indiscriminately capture fish of all kinds and at all life-cycle stages) and pressed his case for expulsion of the *bagan* with local police. HUALOPU members successfully supported the *kewang* in his attempt to goad the police into action by taking photographs documenting the illegal entry of the *bagan* into the community-controlled rivermouth.

The alliance of a *kewang* with a nongovernmental organization and the novel use of national fisheries statutes and documentary evidence to expel the *bagan* would have been unimaginable two decades ago. Indeed, the alliance parallels the productive diffusion of leading-edge conservation and economic-development strategies from the political center to the political periphery that led to the revision and rescripting of the purposes and positive regulations of *sasi.*

In the 1990s, the development of *sasi* purposes, institutions, and rules continues to be fueled by a volatile mixture of environmental and social values, innovative conservation planning, and economic-development schemes brought into productive conjunction with local institutions and traditional resource-management practices. *Sasi,* initially conceived as a traditional management institution, is now being strategically edited, revised, and integrated into current environmental ideas and plans.

Far from having germinated in an indigenous institutional or political vacuum, these ideas are being nurtured and disseminated by a variety of sophisticated institutional bodies with overlapping and often intersecting interests. Among these organizations are the Department of Population and Environment and the Indonesian Environmental Forum (Jakarta); the Environmental Studies Center, Faculty of Law, and Fisheries Faculty of the University of Pattimurra, Ambon; and the innovative, energetic HUALOPU, which focuses on improving the lives and livelihoods of coastal peoples throughout the Maluku while seeking to integrate conservation with sustainable development.

The role of the Department of Population and Environment has been particularly important. As the governmental bully pulpit, this department and its eloquent, charismatic former minister, Dr. Emil Salim, constituted a national voice for environmental affairs. Under Salim's direction, the department addressed a wide variety of constituencies within and beyond Indonesia's national boundaries. The department's annual award of the *Kalpataru*, a kind of national seal of approval initiated in 1981 for good local environmental housekeeping that is awarded to communities throughout Indonesia, authorizes and honors these constituencies.

Awarding the *Kalpataru* engenders further developments. Indeed, an assistant minister avidly explained that "the *Kalpataru*'s purpose is to drive conservation, preservation, and restoration of the environment, and sustainable development. Our office, although a State department, can not implement policies. It can only promote policies, disseminate articles, issue guidelines, and advise the president." The award—one that generates considerable prospective pressure—"is an incentive," he continues. "But the *Kalpataru* is not just given to those who do things well. During the *Kalpataru* presentation session, the minister also points to places or problem areas in the district which still need attention. Public discussion of these areas forces local district heads to act" (Tadjoedin 1992).

During the 1980s, the *Kalpataru* was awarded to several Central Moluccan communities practicing *sasi*. In 1982, for example, based on the positive recommendation of the Environmental Studies Center of the University of Pattimurra, Ihamahu village on Saparua Island was awarded the *Kalpataru*. Recognition of the village also generated the impetus for further development. In acknowledging receipt of the award, the Ihamahu village leader looked backward in history and, at the same moment, forward, retrospectively reconstructing the historic intentions of former *sasi* practitioners:

> When the regulations that were implemented along with the sasi system
> that was performed since the old days are viewed historically, it may be
> stated that Moluccan society, particularly Ihamahu society, through the
> kewang, were already conscious of the importance of their environment
> in terms of its importance to them as individuals. All of this was put into

effect through custom *[adat]*, without knowing that the modern world needs acts of conservation toward living resources. Whatever was done by the Ihamahu kewangs since the times of the old rulers—perhaps they understood conservation issues, even though [this understanding] was only based on realities and signs from their own observations which were still rather old-fashioned. *(KKI n.d.:9)*

Although from a narrow, positivist perspective the retroactive assessment of *sasi* as an intentionally conservationist institution from its "beginnings" is probably inaccurate, these interpretive fictions play a positive role as enabling myths (Bowen 1989; Cole 1986; Hobsbawm and Ranger 1983). They are used to ground and guide future action at the governmental center and in remote provinces, and to advocate for historically marginalized and disenfranchised communities. Historic *sasi* practices in Ihamahu village, for example, have been reconfigured retroactively as directed by current institutional goals. In these reconfigurations, historic *sasi* is imagined as a "good conservation system" executed by environmentally conscious practitioners.

The certification of *sasi* practices and institutions through awards from the Indonesian political center also compels future institutional changes. An Ihamahu official emphasized that "after receiving the Kalpataru, it [became] clear that the responsibilities of the Ihamahu Kewang became heavier in the sense that the Kalpataru goblet was a reminder to the Kewang to always protect the living environment. . . . Because this group [the *kewang*] is conscious, [they] provide an Environmental Support Group with the consequence that several activities have been added in addition to the routine performed since the beginning [of *sasi*]" (KKNI 1987:9–10).

Since award of the *Kalpaturu*, the "Ihamahu Kewang [now] perform in a regular manner" (KKI n.d.:9) a variety of new activities, including planting vegetation near the sites of key water sources; building fences; and planting mangroves for coastal stability, water purification, and protection of the marine and coastal fisheries. Other rules prohibit commercial extraction of sea cucumber, coral, trochus, and *garu* wood (used for incense) from the reefs and forests under community control. Moreover, the Ihamahu *kewang* make periodic reports on their activities to the Environmental Studies Center and the Department of Population and Environment, communicating personally with Dr. Salim.

Projecting a conservationist past onto current *sasi* practices, these interpretations authorize supportive actions by important central governmental and NGO actors and, at the same time, guide or goad local communities toward conservation-promoting behavior. By directing the attention of those at the political center, especially the respected Dr. Salim, toward the political periphery, these enabling fictions link the energies, knowledge elites, and, potentially, the financial flows of powerful Indonesian and transnational cosmopolitan centers to singularly remote locations throughout the archipelago. Indeed, Salim has informally remarked that the "purpose of these awards is to recognize the achievements of these communities and to stimulate them to go even further" (Salim 1992).

By the early 1990s, *sasi* in the Maluku was marked by intense interaction between diverse kinds of organizations. The Department of Population and Environment, HUALOPU, and the University of Pattimurra's Environmental Studies Center continue to be key institutional players interested in the social and environmental potential of *sasi*. Both of the latter two groups are interested in practical attempts to shape and develop *sasi*. Both are intensely committed to exploring the possibilities they envision: *sasi* as the institution with the greatest potential for supporting sustainable environmental management and biological diversity in reefs, rivers, and inshore waters and, most importantly, as an instrument for promoting distributive equity and democratization. By 1992, a representative of the World Bank had visited the HUALOPU office in Ambon and traveled to a neighboring island in search of new "institutional alternatives and opportunities for marine resource development in Indonesia" (Leibenthal 1992).

Conclusion

In the past *sasi* was constituted as rules, practices, and sanctions that must be implemented to avoid the punishments of spirits and *sasi* enforcers. *Sasi* also has been imagined and manipulated as a secular social-organizational armature facilitating commerce between traders from distant Asian and European lands, local rulers, and small Moluccan communities. In an era when concern for equity in development, the political and cultural rights of indigenous communities, biodiversity, and sustainable growth have become global as well as national issues, *sasi* is now being imagined and discursively constructed as a changing embodiment of these values and aspirations. What is not at all clear is whether these discursive changes will result in significant or lasting changes in the purposes or practices now known as *sasi* and what the environmental and socioeconomic consequences of these changes will be (Zerner 1994a, 1994b).

Imagine *sasi* as a palimpsest—a parchment or writing tablet on which, at previous moments in its history, several kinds of inscriptions have been superimposed. Like a palimpsest, *sasi* contains traces and fragments of its previous incarnations. In its totality, *sasi* contains regions of translucence as well as areas of opacity, archaic residues as well as recent overlays that may never be understood. Obsession with the original intentions or motives for *sasi*, like similar preoccupations in constitutional law, are beside the point. For everyone except interpretative fundamentalists attempting to prove a singular and simple original motive for *sasi* (conservation, for example), understanding why and how this institution has changed, and how to generate positive changes in the future, is far more important.

Above all, the *sasi* emerging in the 1990s is a hybrid creature, shaped in a cultural border zone where traders, fishers, and markets interact with global conservationists and social nongovernmental organizations. *Sasi* is, and was, as much a product of local religious fears and practical purposes as it is the product of continuous cosmopolitan influences such as the desires of Javanese and Portuguese traders sailing to Moluccan shores on monsoon winds and, more recently, the intentions of contemporary trochus merchants cruising from cove to cove in speedboats and calibrating world market prices electronically. Given the changing cross-currents and competing interests in this complex interaction, how can coexistence of Moluccan reef and human communities be improved?

The most recent interpretations of *sasi*, particularly those created by inspired ministers and aspiring NGOs, constitute a social mandate and environmental constitution for change. Like all constitutions, the broad-ranging collection of *sasi* pronouncements needs to be interpreted and operationalized through specific and concrete actions. *Sasi* can and should be reread as legal mandate and institutional armature deployed in the service of reef and inshore marine fisheries conservation, sustainable development, and community equity.

Many foundational elements for such a contemporary reading, including access imitations to fisheries in terms of territory, season, gear, and people, already are present. A second and key element is that of the "*kewangate*," the implementatory, judicial, and enforcement institution that plays a central role in putting *sasi* into effect. Third, but not last, *sasi* is an ongoing practice or habit with which local people are familiar. These three pillars of *sasi*—its institutional, legal, and cultural core—can and should be used in the attempt to create new ways to conserve reefs and assist local-community development.

To effect such a transformation, a host of other actions is necessary. Among these steps should be a series of major research initiatives, community-based environmental education and alternative economic development programs, and, possibly, political and legal reform. Baseline investigations into sustainability of current practices and their relationship to *sasi* are needed. For example, how does *sasi* affect resource bases in communities under varying conditions of sociopolitical control, population pressure, gear use, reef conditions, and harvesting practices. More quantitative information is needed on site-specific catch levels, *sasi* restrictions, and resource availability, not only for trochus but for a variety of reef species. Such studies, conducted in a variety of sites, could reveal the dynamic links between social and legal organization, markets, and population pressure, and their effects on habitat as well as on species conservation and management.

Much more information needs to be gathered about the socioeconomic effects of marine *sasi* regimes under different conditions of property rights and market penetration. For example, we need to know how recent changes in *sasi* codification affect the differential access of poor families, women, and nonindigenous communities to marine resources for subsistence as well as economic needs. Poor families or individuals may be made even poorer by these changes, decreasing any economic incentives to sustainably manage reefs.

The extent to which *sasi* is practiced throughout the Maluku, or where and how, is not clear. Several sources suggest that *sasi* practices are "on the wane" or "wilting" (Lokollo 1988; von Benda-Beckmann, von Benda-Beckmann, and Brouwer 1992). If we do not yet know how extensive these practices are or why they are described as "wilting," then expending considerable financial resources on revitalizing or restructuring these practices for socioeconomic and conservation purposes may be unwarranted.

Several long-term ethnographic accounts of *sasi*, conducted in sites that vary in degree of market interaction, governmental control, and NGO influence, would be extremely useful in tracking the institution in action. A comparative, Malukuwide survey of *sasi* that assesses the relative strengths of the factors driving change in *sasi* and regional variation in the processes of social, political, and economic control should complement long-term ethnographic research. Team research pairing marine biologists with ethnographic researchers would yield the most useful kinds of results.

If *sasi* is to become an institution that embodies the emerging global values of biodiversity and habitat conservation, social equity, and economic development, a variety of research probes are not the only kinds of action needed. To assist in the creation of a sustainable *sasi*, a program in environmental education at the village level, effectively implemented by local NGOs and village youth, is much needed. At the technical and economic level, exploration of the potential of other forms of marine cultivation or management, including cultivation of giant clams, trochus, and pearl oysters, would be very useful. The Philippines, Japan, and other places in the South Pacific whose communities have experimented along these lines have lessons to offer.

The further development of *sasi* also may require administrative and legal reforms that recognize community-based jurisdictions for management. Indeed, representatives of HUALOPU, the Environmental Studies Center, and the legal bureau of the Moluccan governor's office are collaborating to draft regulations along these lines, although it is too early to tell whether these reforms will succeed or what their effects will be.

Attempts to recognize marine tenurial areas vested in local communities, however, must avoid the pitfalls of romanticism or naive optimism. Proponents of legal recognition for community-based marine-management areas must deal with evidence of long-term, historical community conflict over the issue of boundaries. As the government head of Porto village on Saparua Island explained, "there hasn't been a time when Porto has not been at war with neighboring communities over the size of its own area. The history of our boundaries is the history of conflicts and burnings, right through the last few decades" (Aponno 1991). In the marine sector, Abrahamsz (1991) notes repeated instances of intercommunity theft from mother-of-pearl beds. Marine *sasi*, like their agricultural counterparts, are apparently discrete and not overlapping. Rather than move for unilateral decentralization of management authority to particular villages or clusters of villages, imposition of areas of comanagement (such as those proposed for forests and marine bays in the Philippines, in which the various strands of rights in the bundle of authority are apportioned among local villages, provinces, and the provincial government) may be more realistic.

Ultimately, a series of pilot projects could implement a "green" form of *sasi* around several Moluccan reefs. Among the most notable examples of innovative reef management and conservation projects are several in the Philippines and other areas of the South Pacific that seek to integrate the idea of a marine reserve, or totally restricted area, with a marine conservation area that allows for fishing under sustainable local controls. Perhaps a Moluccan form of reef reserve and fishing area that borrows from Philippine examples as well as transnational conservation theory and builds upon already existing forms of Moluccan *sasi* may one day be implemented.

Whether—and how—particular Moluccan fishing communities are able or eager to rejuvenate and redirect the multitude of practices and institutions clustered under the *sasi* umbrella is one of the key questions to be answered in the next chapter in the history of this remarkable and changing set of social ideas, laws, and institutions. Whether the *sasi* that develops actually will promote social equity, environmental sustainability, or biological diversity is uncertain.

From this brief history, however, it is clear that a new constellation of government policy makers, nongovernmental social and environmental activists, and scholars is seeking to invent new forms and new purposes for *sasi*. Local notions of institutional structure and law, nationalist ideology and pride, and global, transnational conservation ideas are being mixed, not melted, into these institutional forms and narratives in ways that are unpredictable, yet characteristic of the processes of global change everywhere (Appadurai 1990; Bremen 1988; Rouse 1991). Although the site of *sasi* is specifiable as a series of coordinates and contours on a map of the Maluku, the actions and values injected into and through this "structure" are inevitably and quintessentially transnational, relying on information and ideologies that flow between Washington, D.C., Jakarta, and remote Moluccan coves. Transforming *sasi* these days is an act of global imagination and improvisation.

ACKNOWLEDGMENTS

Due to limited opportunity for field work, this chapter should be regarded as a speculative and preliminary attempt to deal with *sasi*'s complex history. It is based on two months' field research in the Maluku Islands during 1991, sponsored by the Fisheries Research and Development Project (FRDP) based at the Central Fisheries Research Institute, Agency for Agricultural Research and Development, Department of Agriculture, Indonesia; a brief visit in 1992; and the analysis of archival materials. The project was funded by the U.S. Agency for International Development. Support for preparation of this paper was provided by the Woodrow

Wilson International Center for Scholars (Asia Program) and the Liz Claiborne Art Ortenberg Foundation. Archival research and translations were completed during my tenure as a Woodrow Wilson Fellow. Revisions were completed with the support of the Rockefeller Brothers Foundation and the Rainforest Alliance, Natural Resources and Rights Program.

Many people and organizations have contributed to my understanding of *sasi*. I wish to acknowledge the assistance of Carla Sapsford, whose translations of a Dutch text made accessible an important historical window on *sasi*; Hasmi Bandjar, my research assistant and colleague during field research; Frances Gouda, whose passion for history and the Dutch colonial project in Indonesia has been an inspiration; and Toby Alice Volkman, who has contributed her insights and clarity of perception to this paper. Productive discussions with Iwan Tjitradjaja (University of Indonesia); Sandra Moniaga and Suraya Afif (Indonesian Environmental Forum); Cliff Marlessy (HUALOPU); Meentze Simatauw, Kalvein Khuouw, and many other HUALOPU staff members; as well as the staff of the Environmental Studies Center (PSL, University of Pattimurra) have contributed to my understanding of recent developments in *sasi* and coastal community management. The fishermen, local government leaders, and *kewang*s of Saparua, Halmahera, Hatta, Ai, and Ran Islands made this intellectual journey possible.

An earlier version of this chapter was presented at the Second Annual Meeting of the International Association for the Study of Common Property (Winnipeg, Canada, 1991). Michael Wright, David Western, and John Cordell provided insightful comments on a draft, encouraging the chapter's further development. The chapter was substantially completed in September 1992. During final revisions in 1994, the author had the opportunity to read von Benda-Beckmann et al.'s manuscript, which provides a parallel view of *sasi*. Unfortunately, this manuscript came to my attention only as this chapter was going to press, so I have not been able to include ideas presented in it. I have cited it, however, for the benefit of the reader. All the usual disclaimers apply.

Sources

Abrahamsz, J. 1991. "Nasib Lola dan Lembaga Sasi di Kepulauan Kei, Maluku Tenggara" (Fate of Trochus and *Sasi* Institutions in the Kei Archipelago, Southeast Maluku). *Kabar Dari Kampung* (*News From the Village*) 48(IX):52–61.

Andaya, L. 1993. *The World of Maluku*. Honolulu: University of Hawaii Press.

Appadurai, A. 1990. "Disjuncture and Difference in the Global Cultural Economy." *Public Culture* 2(2):1–24.

Aponno, J. 1977. "Peraturan Kewan Negeri Porto Tahun 1870" (Kewan Regulations from Porto Village in 1870). Typescript.

———. 1991. Interview with the author and H. Bandjar, Porto Village, Saparua Island, Indonesia, March 29.

Bailey, C., and C. Zerner. 1992. "Community-based Management of Fisheries Resources in Indonesia." *Maritime Anthropological Studies* 5(1):1–17.

Bowen, J. R. 1989. "Narrative Form and Political Incorporation: The Uses of History in Aceh, Indonesia." *Comparative Studies in Society and History* 31(3): 627–693.

Bremen, J. 1988. *The Shattered Image: Construction and Deconstruction of the Village in Colonial Asia.* Dordrecht, Holland: Center for Asian Studies/Foris Publications.

Cole, David. 1986. "Agon at Agora: Creative Misreadings in the First Amendment Tradition." *Yale Law Journal* 95 (5):857–905.

Government of Indonesia (GOI). 1982. Undang Undang Nomor 4 1982 (Law Number 4 Concerning Basic Provisions for the Management of the Environment).

Hobsbawm, E. 1985. "Introduction: Inventing Traditions." In *The Invention of Tradition*, ed. E. Hobsbawm and T. Ranger, 1–14. Cambridge, England: Cambridge University Press.

———, and T. Ranger, eds. 1983. *The Invention of Tradition.* Cambridge, England: Cambridge University Press.

Kastoro, W. W. 1991. "Two Commercial Mollusks: Giant Clams and *Trochus Niloticus.*" *Voice of Nature* 23:22–23.

Kewang Paperu. 1991. Interview with the author and H. Bandjar, Paperu Village, Saparua Island, Indonesia, March 28.

Khouw, K., and M. Simatauw. 1991. "Hasil Survei Sosial Ekonomi Masyarakat Pulau-Pulau Aru, Maluku Tenggara" (Results of Socioeconomic Survey of the People of the Aru Islands). Ambon: Yayasan HUALOPU (HUALOPU Foundation). Typescript.

Korps Kewang Ihamahu (KKI). n.d. Korps Kewang Ihamahu Dan Peraturan-Peraturan Sasi (*Kewang* Corps and *Sasi* Regulations of Ihamahu). Yayasan HUALOPU (HUALOPU Foundation), Pusat Dokumentasi Dan Informasi HUALOPU (HUALOPU Documentation and Information Center), Ambon, Indonesia. Mimeograph.

Korps Kewang Negeri Ihamahu (KKNI). 1987. "Korps Kewang Negeri Ihamahu Dan Lingkungan Hidup" (*Kewang* Corps of Ihamahu Community and the Living Environment). Paper presented at the Nature Conservation Seminar (Marine), July 2–9, TOISAPU, Ambon, Indonesia. Ambon: Yayasan HUALOPU, Center for Information and Documentaton. Mimeograph.

Leibenthal, A. 1992. Interview with the author at the World Bank, Washington, D.C., September 4.

Lokollo, J. E. 1988. "Hukum Sasi di Maluku: Satu Portret Bina Mulia Lingkungan Pedesaan Yang Dicari Oleh Pemerintah" (*Sasi* Law in the Maluku: A Noble Portrait of the Village Environment Sought By the Government). Paper presented on the twenty-fifth anniversary of the University of Pattimura, May 11, Ambon, Indonesia.

Matatula, A. 1990. "Sejarah Bia Lola (*Trochus niloticus*) di Desa Nolloth (Kecamatan Saparua)" (History of the *Lola* [*Trochus Niloticus*] in Nolloth Village [Saparua District]). Nolloth Village Office, Saparua Island, Indonesia. Mimeograph.

———. 1991. Interview with the author and H. Bandjar, Nolloth Village, Saparua Island, Indonesia, March 28.

———, U. Manuputty, J. Huliselan, and P. Metekohy. 1990. "Peraturan Sasi Desa Nolloth" (Sasi Rules of Nolloth Village). Nolloth Village Office, Saparua Island, Indonesia. Mimeograph.

Ministry of Agriculture (MOA). 1972. Keputusan Menteri Pertanian No. 327 (Decisional Letter of the Minister of Agriculture No. 327). Government of Indonesia, Jakarta.

Ministry of Forestry (MOF). 1987. Keputusan Menteri Kehutanan Nomor 12/Kpts-II/1987 tentang Penetapan Tambahan Jenis-Jensi Binatang Liar Yang Dilindungi Di Samping Jenis Jenis Liar Yang Telah Dilindungi (Ministry of Forestry Decision No. 12 Concerning Determination of Additional Kinds of Wild Animals Which Are Protected Along with Wild Animals That Already Are Protected). Government of Indonesia, Jakarta.

Reid, A. 1992. "Indonesian Fishermen Detained in Broome: A Report on the Social and Economic Background." In *Illegal Entry!*, 1–11. Occasional Paper Series, No. 1/1992. Casuarina, Australia: Center for Southeast Asian Studies, Northern Territory University.

Ririmasse, B. 1984. "Peraturan Sasi Desa Haruku" (Sasi Rules of Haruku Village). Yayasan HUALOPU (HUALOPU Foundation), Pusat Dokumentasi Dan Informasi (Center for Documentation and Information), Ambon, Indonesia. Photocopy.

———, E. Kissya, and E. Ririmasse. 1985. Peraturan Sasi Desa Haruku 1984 (Sasi Rules of Haruku Village, 10 July 1985). Yayasan HUALOPU (HUALOPU Foundation), Pusat Dokumentasi Dan Informasi (Center for Documentation and Information), Ambon, Indonesia. Photocopy.

Rouse, R. 1991. "Mexican Migration and the Social Space of Postmodernism." *Diaspora* 1(1):8–23.

Saidjan, A. F. 1991. Interview with the author, Hatta village, Hatta Island, Indonesia. April 1.

Salim, E. 1992. Interview with the author, Jakarta, Indonesia, October 8.

Shalan. 1991. Interview with the author and H. Bandjar, To Belo, Halmahera Island, North Maluku Province, Indonesia, April 6.

Soelaiman. 1978. "Daftar Jenis Margasatwa Yang Dilindungi Dan Yang Terdapat Di Maluku" (List of Protected Creatures Which Inhabit the Maluku [through 1978]). Department of Fisheries, Nature Conservation and Protection Section, Ambon, Indonesia. Circular.

Tadjoedin. 1992. Interview with the author, Jakarta, Indonesia, October 5.

Tjitradjaja, I. 1992. Interview with the author, Ambon Island, Indonesia, May 17.

Vandergeest, P., and N. L. Peluso. 1993. "Fixing Property in National Space: Territoriality of the State in Siam/Thailand." Paper presented at Yale University Agrarian Societies Seminar, February 23, New Haven, Connecticut.

Volker, T. 1925. "Het recht van *sasi* in de Molukken (1921)" (The *Sasi* Right in Maluku [1925]). *Adatrechtbundels* 24:296–313.

von Benda-Beckmann, F., K. von Benda-Beckmann, and A. Brouwer. 1992. "Changing 'Indigenous Environmental Law' in the Central Moluccas: Com-

munal Regulation and Privatization of *Sasi.*" Revised version of paper presented to the Congress of the Commission on Folk Law and Legal Pluralism on
Resouces, Rules and Identity in State and Unofficial Laws, August 27–30, Victoria University, Wellington, New Zealand.

Zerner, C. 1991a. *Community Management of Marine Resources in the Maluku Islands, Indonesia.* Report prepared for the Center for Fisheries Research and Development, Jakarta, Indonesia.

———. 1991b. *Key Issues in Indonesian Fisheries Law and Institutional Development: Implementation, Environmental Management, and the Rights of Small-
Scale Fishers.* Report prepared for the Center for Fisheries Research and Development, Jakarta, Indonesia.

———. 1992. "Sea Change: Toward Community Management of Coastal Resources in Insular Southeast Asia." World Resources Institute, Washington,
D.C. Typescript.

———. 1994a. "Tracking *Sasi*: Transformation of Moluccan Reef Management
Practices." In *Community-based Coral Reef Management: Lessons from Experi-
ence,* eds. A. White, L. Hale, and L. Cortese, 19–32. West Hartford, Connecticut:
Kumarian Press.

———. 1994b. "Through a Green Lens: Constructing Customary Environmental
Law and Community in Indonesia's Maluku Islands." Paper presented at the
Annual Meeting of the Association of Asian Studies, March 25, Boston.

CHAPTER 5

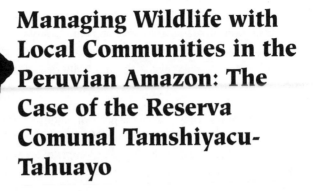

Managing Wildlife with Local Communities in the Peruvian Amazon: The Case of the Reserva Comunal Tamshiyacu-Tahuayo

Richard E. Bodmer

Conservation of tropical rain forests is one of mankind's greatest challenges because of the delicate balance that needs to be developed between a complex and fragile ecosystem and an impoverished rural population. Amazonian forests comprise a fragile ecosystem of very high diversity and endemism inhabited by rural folk in need of an ecologically sustainable and economically sound future.

Forests are important to local inhabitants for the market and consumption benefits obtained from hunting and fishing (Redford and Robinson 1987) and from extraction of nontimber plant products (Vasquez and Gentry 1989). But rural households overexploit some species, and deforestation often occurs when inhabitants no longer gain sufficient economic benefits from game and nontimber plant products to meet their needs (Browder 1992). Therefore, a system of sustainable use of animals and plants should help retain the value of intact Amazonian ecosystems.

The recently established Reserva Comunal Tamshiyacu-Tahuayo (RCTT) (see Map 5.1) links rural community programs with protected-area management in a region of upland Amazonian forest. The management of natural resources within the reserve includes conservation and community programs for game meat, fish, and nontimber plant products (Bodmer et al. 1990b). An understanding of the relationship between population biology, economics, and rural communities' use of wildlife within the RCTT is essential to community management plans for sustainable use of the reserve's natural resources. Toward this end, an examination of biological, social, economic, historical, and legal aspects of wildlife use in the Peruvian Amazon follows.

Sustainable Utilization in the Peruvian Amazon

The term *sustainable development* has become an important phrase for conservation policy since the UNCED Earth Summit held in Rio de Janeiro in 1992. The official definition of sustainable development, formulated in 1987 by the World Commission on Environment and Development, combines two important issues: economic development and ecological sustainability. Environmental groups often question whether development can result in successful conservation, since these two issues traditionally have been oppositional.

Can Amazonian wildlife fulfill the goals of sustainable development by bringing sustained economic growth combined with the conservation of species? History suggests that this may be difficult. One example of an attempt to use free-ranging wildlife in the Peruvian lowlands to secure sustained economic growth is the professional pelt-hunting period that began after the Amazonian rubber crash in the early part of this century and continued until the prohibition on professional pelt hunting in 1973.

When the rubber boom in the Amazon ended around 1920, rural inhabitants looked for other forest products with which to earn income. One such product was the pelts of wild species that had growing markets in Europe and North America. For the next fifty years, rural inhabitants of the Peruvian Amazon tried to build a system of sustained economic growth from the sale of animal pelts. The most commonly exported pelts during the professional pelt-hunting period were those of jaguars, ocelots, peccaries, deer, Amazon and giant river otters, and caimans.

Up until 1945, during the early period of the professional trade, pelt exports were not counted, so no detailed study of the impact of pelt hunting on animal populations during these years is possible. In 1946, the Peruvian Ministry of Agriculture began to report pelt exports from Iquitos. These data can be used to approximate the impact of professional pelt hunting on animal populations. An FAO study conducted during 1970 supplements this pelt export data (Hvidberg-Hansen 1970a–e).

Europe and North America imported the greatest quantities of skins during the professional pelt period. Pelt imports differed between countries, depending on the animal species. Germany, for example, was the major importer of peccary pelts, England was the major importer of otter skins, and the United States was the major importer of jaguar pelts.

The combined income for all hunters in the professional pelt-hunting period averaged US$461,000 per year, with a total gross income of around US$12,106,200 between 1946 and 1973. This income was not evenly divided between species; ocelots brought the greatest profits, followed by collared peccaries. Giant and Amazon river otters brought the least profits. The economic value of individual species' skins did not influence the gross income for that species. For example, jaguars and giant otters had the most valuable skins, but they were not the most profitable animals due to the lower number of skins extracted.

Map 5.1

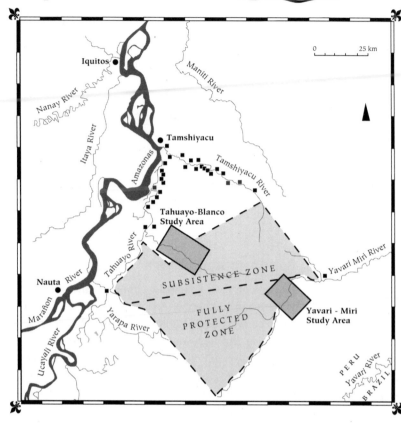

Reserva Comunal Tamshiyacu-Tahuayo

KEY

- Towns
- Villages of the Permanent
  Settlement Zone

PERU

**Area Shown
in Detail**

Economic returns from pelt hunting in the Peruvian Amazon steadily increased between 1946 and 1969 (Figure 5.1). Then, in 1970, economic returns crashed to a fifteen-year low. This economic crash was paralleled by a decrease in pelt exports (Figure 5.2). A need for increased income had influenced harvests and led to overhunting, which apparently caused the decrease in pelt exports.

The case of professional pelt hunting in the Peruvian Amazon calls into question whether *sustained economic growth* is a realistic option for the utilization of most wild species in Amazonia. On the other hand, the *sustainable utilization* of wild species, as opposed to sustained economic growth, is possible in Amazonia and is a realistic way for rural inhabitants to obtain subsistence products and income. Sustainable utilization implies extraction of species at a level that does not affect the recruitment of populations and therefore maintains stability in the number of individuals. Sustainable utilization of wild species in Amazonia usually will not present opportunities for rural inhabitants to realize sustained economic growth, but might yield stable long-term economic and subsistence benefits.

Peruvian Wildlife Management Laws

The first management law that attempted to regulate offtake in the lowland Amazon was legislated by the Peruvian Ministry of Agriculture. This legislation was enacted in 1951 and sought to curb excessive hunting of animals that became trapped on floodplain islands during the high-water season (Pacheco Gomez 1993). In addition, seasonal restrictions on hunting were intended to limit hunting in isolated forest blocks that could be reached during high water, because of improved navigation capabilities. This attempt to manage wildlife had little success due to the difficulties of enforcement in rural areas.

In response to excessive hunting during the professional pelt-hunting period, the Ministry of Agriculture enacted a national management law in 1973 that prohibited this activity in the Peruvian Amazon. This legislation, however, did permit the use of certain game for subsistence by rural Amazonians (Table 5.1). Skins of these species, if obtained by "subsistence" hunters, could be commercialized. Thus trade in deer and peccary pelts remained legal after 1973 if the skins originated from subsistence hunters. The management law of 1973 significantly decreased the commercialization of peccary and deer hides from an average of 211,099 pelts per year before the 1973 law to around 88,186 pelts per year. These numbers reflect a real decrease in hunting pressure and suggest a successful implementation of the 1973 law. The law apparently was more successful than restrictions on hunting seasons because enforcement was at the level of legal business operations in large urban centers, not in isolated rural areas. These registered businesses dealt with a variety of import and export products and abided by the pelt law to maintain their legal status.

In 1976, a new threat emerged as the Ministry of Agriculture noted increasing

Figure 5.1

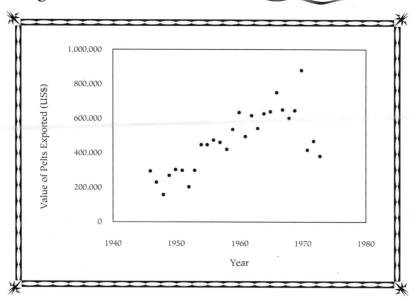

Economic returns from pelt sales in the Peruvian Amazon.

Figure 5.2

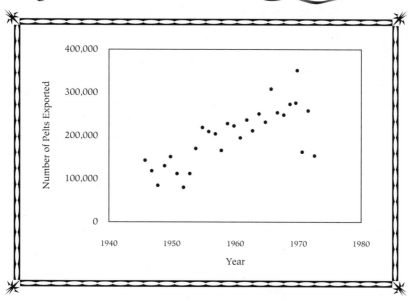

Number of pelts exported from the Peruvian Amazon.

Table 5.1

Game species that rural inhabitants are permitted to hunt for subsistence under Peruvian law

Latin Names	Common Names
Mammals	
Tayassu pecari	White-lipped peccary
T. tajacu	Collared peccary
Mazama americana	Red brocket deer
M. gouazoubira	Grey brocket deer
Tapirus terrestris	Lowland tapir
Hydrochaeris hydrochaeris	Capybara
Agouti paca	Paca
Dinomys branickii	Pacarana
Dasyprocta fuliginosa	Black agouti
Myoprocta pratti	Green acouchy
Dasypus novemcinctus	Nine-banded armadillo
Birds	
Mitu spp.	Curassow
Nothocrax spp.	Curassow
Penelope spp.	Guan
Ortalis spp.	Chachalaca
Crypturellus spp.	Tinamou
Columba spp.	Pigeon
Collumbigallina spp.	Pigeon
Reptiles	
Geochelona spp.	Tortoise

Source: Government of Peru 1973.

sales of game meat in the city markets of Iquitos. To curb professional meat hunting, the ministry enacted a third management law in 1979 to restrict the sale of game meat to cities with fewer than 3,000 inhabitants. Again, only animals listed as sources of subsistence game meat could be commercialized for their meat. The professional meat law apparently curbed hunting, but implementation was fraught with difficulty. Management authorities could not control small, unlicensed meat vendors in city markets effectively. Urban populations' demand for wild game meat added to the problem of controlling meat sales.

The Peruvian experience suggests that legislation governing wildlife functions best when directed toward middle- or upper-income urban population groups. Government wildlife-management policies are not as successful when directed toward rural people or lower-income groups of urban populations due to the difficulties of enforcement. Informal legislation developed by rural communities apparently is more successful than government legislation in achieving wildlife management in natural habitats of the Peruvian Amazon. But community regulations must concur with government legislation and therefore require government approval or sanctions that are difficult for rural inhabitants to obtain.

The Reserva Comunal Tamshiyacu-Tahuayo

Management of natural resources in the Reserva Comunal Tamshiyacu-Tahuayo is an example of community-based regulations that have achieved government approval. Community-based management of the RCTT began long before the establishment of the reserve, when local communities realized the extent of natural-resources degradation occurring in the forests and began to take the initiative in protecting their natural resources. These community environmental actions in the upper Tahuayo were a major influence in the creation of the RCTT.

Study Area

The Reserva Comunal Tamshiyacu-Tahuayo is in northeastern Peru, within the state of Loreto, and extends over an area of 322,500 ha of Amazonian forest. The reserve comprises the upland *terra firme* forest habitats that divide the valley of the Amazon from the valley of the Yavari. The geography of this area apparently has contributed to its extraordinary biodiversity, which includes fourteen primate species, giant Amazonian river otters, and manatees, along with many other prominent species and unusual ecological features (Puertas and Bodmer 1993).

The human inhabitants of the RCTT are detribalized communities of diverse origins, including colonists from the Andean foothills region, the Peruvian and Brazilian Amazon, and non-Amazonian countries. These people, known as *ribereños*, practice hunting, fishing, shifting agriculture, and gathering of non-timber plant products. *Ribereños* are well aware of the damage inflicted by their activities and are themselves trying to develop nondestructive uses of the forest. In this context, the communities of the Tamshiyacu and Tahuayo rivers eventually acted with the Ministry of Agriculture in Iquitos to form the Reserva Comunal Tamshiyacu-Tahuayo, legislated in June 1991 (GOP 1991).

The RCTT is divided into three distinct land-use zones: a buffer zone of subsistence use, a fully protected core area, and an area of permanent settlement. The fully protected and subsistence areas fall within the official limits of the reserve and contain no human settlements. The zone of permanent settlement along the Tamshiyacu, Tahuayo, Yarapa, and Yavari Miri rivers is adjacent to the reserve and comprises thirty-three villages with about five thousand people. To avoid conflict over land-use practices, this area was not officially incorporated into the reserve, but it is an important part of the RCTT management plans (Bodmer et al. 1990b).

The three zones form a continuum of land uses, with intensive activities such as agriculture confined to the permanent settlement zone, natural-resource extraction carried out in the subsistence zone under community-management rules, and no activities permitted in the fully protected area. Game hunting is the major extractive activity within the subsistence zone of the reserve, followed by the extraction of nontimber plant products. In the flooded lakes of the permanent settlement zone, fishing is the most important extractive activity.

Community Wildlife Management

The open-access system that began with the abolition of estates after the enactment of the agrarian law of 1969 stimulated the uncontrolled extraction of natural resources. After 1973, in the area that now encompasses the RCTT, timber, game animals, palm fruit, and fisheries were exploited extensively by both local residents and small businesses operating from the city of Iquitos. At first, the communities benefited from the increased access to resources. Eventually, as resources became depleted, small business operations cut their employment costs by hiring a select group of city-based employees, often bypassing the local labor force, thus providing less benefit locally. Natural resources were scarce by the mid-1980s.

Natural resources had fulfilled both economic and subsistence needs of local inhabitants, who were threatened by resource depletion and loss of employment. As a result, the *ribereño* communities organized a system of controls that began to prohibit the extraction of resources by nonresidents. This led to greater consensus among local people regarding management of resources and a desire to obtain greater control over resource use. Communities were particularly unhappy about harvests of fish by freezer vessels, extraction of timber by city-based operators, and hunting of meat by lumbermen and merchants from Iquitos.

The communities initially began management programs on the fisheries of lakes in the permanent settlement zone. These lakes are close to *ribereño* communities, and overharvesting of fisheries affected the subsistence and commercial activities of rural inhabitants. In 1984, the villages of the upper Tahuayo set up a community-based fisheries management program that included prohibition of nonresident commercial fishing vessels and restrictions on harvest methods.

Restrictions on the types of individuals allowed to hunt were the first community-initiated hunting regulations. In Tahuayo, lumbermen were the most significant hunting class before 1988, contributing more than 50 percent of the hunting pressure on mammals (Bodmer, Fang, and Moya 1988). Small-scale lumber operations supplied workers with shotguns and cartridges instead of basic foods, thus decreasing their operational costs by utilizing game meat and overhunting many species. The communities expressed their concern to government officials, who proposed the area as a "reserve in study," a classification that ended timber concessions in 1988 and so decreased the overexploitation of game. This management program apparently helped mammal populations to rebuild. Subsequently, in 1991, the communities realized that many commercial meat hunters were beginning to enter the area. With the help of extension workers, local people of the upper Tahuayo set up a vigilance system that prohibited city-based hunters from entering the reserve.

Community representatives approached both the Ministry of Agriculture and scientists working in the area to gain support for their community-based conservation initiatives. The ministry and the scientists acted in concert with these communities to initiate the legal actions required to legislate a reserve. Fortunately, the Peruvian government recently had created a new protected-area category: the community reserve. This type of reserve coincided with the community's requirements and the conservation ambitions of the Regional Ministry of Agriculture.

Currently, communities of the upper Tahuayo and Yavari Miri have established a series of community-management rules for the extraction of natural resources in and around the RCTT. Rules for land use and extraction of resources are determined by consensus within each community. These rules not only govern titled land officially owned by communities, but also forest and fisheries resources in neighboring areas. Agreements between communities regarding access rules and vigilance posts also have been signed.

A Study of Wildlife Sustainability

Implementation of sustainable management of wildlife by communities requires integrating information on the biology of game species and the economics of sustainable use with the desires of local communities. Communities and extension workers often are unclear about the best management techniques with which to ensure ecological sustainability. For this reason, strong links must be developed between scientists, extension workers, and community representatives if a true system of sustainable use is to be realized.

Following legislation of the reserve and cancellation of lumber concessions, studies were conducted on the population biology of mammals in the RCTT to determine whether hunting was sustainable by examining the biology and harvest of mammals in two sites. One site was the Tahuayo region of the reserve, which experiences persistent hunting pressure; the other, the Yavari Miri region, experiences light hunting pressure. Three methods were used to evaluate whether mammals were overhunted, causing or threatening population declines—an indicator of the complexity of making such a determination.

First, animal biomasses were compared in the lightly hunted Yavari Miri and in the persistently hunted Tahuayo sites, which are only 40 km apart and located within the same continuous forest. Biomasses were determined by multiplying the average bodyweight of a species by the density of individuals. Bodyweights of mammals came from hunted samples and densities of mammals from estimates of Fourier-series expansion of line-transect sightings.

Second, the age structure of peccary, deer, and tapir populations was compared in the Tahuayo site and in a site at Taperinha, 40 km east of Santarém in the eastern Brazilian Amazon, which had been under persistent hunting pressure since the 1850s (see Roosevelt et al. 1991). Age-structure curves of game species respond to hunting pressures and provide an index of survivorship that can be used to evaluate the condition of a population. Tooth wear from animal skulls was used to estimate the ages of hunted ungulates.

Third, examining the condition of harvested females yielded information on the reproductive productivity of ungulates. Lactating females and those with developing fetuses were considered reproductively active. Litter sizes also were recorded during the examination. This method estimated sustainability of hunting by comparing the reproductive productivity of a given species to actual harvests. Overhunting occurs when harvests are greater than production. If harvests only constitute a small percentage of production, then hunting is likely to be sustainable.

Excluding small rodents, 1,278 mammals were harvested during one year in a 500-km² area of the Tahuayo site (Table 5.2). This hunting pressure resulted in the extraction of 22,136 kg of animal biomass. Ungulates represented 78 percent of this biomass and were harvested in greater numbers than primates, marsupials, edentates, large rodents, and carnivores (Bodmer et al. 1994). The biomass data for deer, peccaries, and large rodent species from the persistently hunted Tahuayo site were similar to those from the lightly hunted Yavari Miri site (Table 5.3). This suggests that these groups were not greatly affected by hunting. In contrast, biomass of primates in Tahuayo was considerably less than in Yavari Miri, which suggests that primates had been overhunted in Tahuayo. Lowland tapir biomass also was lower in Tahuayo than in Yavari Miri.

The age-structure curve of lowland tapir in Tahuayo concurs with the results of the biomass comparison. The curve declines more rapidly than expected in such a long-lived species and suggests overhunting. Also, lowland tapir were prevalent

Table 5.2

Number of mammals hunted and biomass extracted in Tahuayo from October 1990 to October 1991

Latin Names	Common Names	Number Hunted	Biomass Extracted (kg/yr.)
Artiodactyls			
Tayassu pecari	White-lipped peccary	166	5,312.0
T. tajacu	Collared peccary	165	4,125.0
Mazama americana	Red brocket deer	60	1,980.0
M. gouazoubira	Grey brocket deer	28	560.0
Perissodactyls			
Tapirus terrestris	Lowland tapir	38	5,320.0
Primates			
Saguinus spp.	Tamarins	11	5.5
Cebuella pygmaea	Pygmy marmoset	1	0.1
Saimiri spp.	Common squirrel monkey	9	7.2
Cebus albifrons	White-fronted capuchin	20	60.0
C. apella	Brown capuchin	46	161.0
Callicebus cupreus	Titi monkey	76	91.2
Aotus nancymae	Night monkey	4	3.2
Pithecia monachus	Monk saki monkey	57	114.0
Cacajao calvus	Uakari monkey	23	92.0
Alouatta seniculus	Red howler monkey	22	187.0
Ateles paniscus	Black spider monkey	8	62.4
Lagothrix lagothricha	Common woolly monkey	58	632.2
Rodents			
Coendou bicolor	Bicolor-spined porcupine	8	40.0
Hydrochaeris hydrochaeris	Capybara	10	300.0
Agouti paca	Paca	174	1,531.0
Dasyprocta fuliginosa	Black agouti	97	446.0
Myoprocta pratti	Green acouchy	13	9.8
Sciurus spp.	Squirrels	15	12.0
Marsupials and Edentates			
Didelphidae	Opossums	25	17.5
Myrmecophaga tridactyla	Giant anteater	5	157.5
Tamandua tetradactyla	Collared anteater	17	78.2
Bradypus variegatus	Three-toed sloth	4	16.0
Priodontes maximus	Giant armadillo	1	30.0
Dasypus novemcinctus	Nine-banded armadillo	19	110.0
Carnivores			
Canidae	Free-ranging dogs	2	20.0
Nasua nasua	South American coati	49	151.9
Potos flavus	Kinkajou	4	12.0
Eira barbara	Tayra	14	67.2
Lutra longicaudis	Southern river otter	1	10.0
Felis spp.	Ocelot/margay	25	180.0
Puma concolor	Puma	3	225.0

Source: Bodmer et al. 1994:31.

Table 5.3

Biomass of peccaries, deer, tapir, primates, and large rodents in Yavari Miri and Tahuayo

Latin Names	Common Names	Biomass (kg/km²)	
		Yavari Miri	Tahuayo
Artiodactyls			
Tayassu pecari	White-lipped peccary	64	45
T. tajacu	Collared peccary	82	82
Mazama americana	Red brocket deer	63	59
M. gouazoubira	Grey brocket deer	14	16
Perissodactyls			
Tapirus terrestris	Lowland tapir	96	64
Primates			
Saguinus spp.	Tamarins	20	21
Saimiri spp.	Common squirrel monkey	46	14
Cebus albifrons	White-fronted capuchin	23	17
C. apella	Brown capuchin	40	27
Callicebus cupreus	Titi monkey	3	2
Pithecia monachus	Monk saki monkey	10	7
Ateles paniscus	Black spider monkey	19	4
Lagothrix lagothricha	Common woolly monkey	280	79
Rodents			
Agouti paca	Paca	42	31
Dasyprocta fuliginosa	Black agouti	13	14
Myoprocta pratti	Green acouchy	8	4

Sources: Bodmer et al. 1994:33; Puertas and Bodmer 1993:590.

in Taperinha during the 1850s (Smith 1879) but were virtually absent from this site between 1912 and 1942, presumably because of overhunting. The age-structure curves also show evidence of overhunting in the case of Taperinha's deer and peccary populations.

The data on reproductive productivities were consistent with the biomass comparisons and age-structure data. Production of peccaries and deer was compensating for hunted offtake and ranged between 15 and 38 percent of recruitment (Table 5.4 and Table 5.5). This suggests that hunting of these animals in Tahuayo was at a sustained level, because the harvest offtake leaves ample room for the effects of natural mortality. In contrast, the production of tapir in Tahuayo did not appear to compensate for the hunted offtake, which was 160 percent of recruitment. This offtake overexploits the tapir population and is not sustainable.

Biomass and production data suggest that deer, peccaries, and large rodents are sustainably hunted in the RCTT, but age-structure data show that increasing current hunting levels might have a negative effect on the populations of these species. The population data also show that lowland tapir and large-bodied primates are not being sustainably hunted in the RCTT; their populations appear to be declining.

Economic Costs of Sustainable Hunting

The economic value of game mammals is probably the major factor leading to overhunting. Game meat is the most valuable product extracted from the subsistence zone of the RCTT. Fortunately, the major income of local people living next to the RCTT is from agricultural products and fisheries located in the permanent settlement zones, not from game meat (Coomes 1992). There are, however, economic costs incurred by limiting hunting to more sustainable levels.

Hunters in Amazonia obtain economic benefits from both market sales and consumption of game mammals (Bodmer et al. 1990a). In Tahuayo, for example, hunters receive cash for the meat of peccaries, deer, tapir, and two of the large rodents (*Hydrochaeris hydrochaeris* and *Agouti paca*) in city markets of Iquitos. Hunters take these mammals because of their market value and only occasionally consume parts of these species. Peccary hides also have a market value for hunters. Mammals with no market potential have consumption value and substitute for purchases of animal protein. Hunters of the RCTT seek out primates and other small-bodied mammals to use as subsistence food, so as to avoid consuming the marketable meat of ungulates and large rodents. Thus hunting of primates and other small-bodied mammals is intricately linked to the economic factors of game hunting.

Commercial sale of meat during a one-year period in Tahuayo earned US$17,270 for all hunters combined and constituted 82 percent of the total economic benefits obtained from mammalian game (Table 5.6). Peccary meat constituted 57 percent of this income; in addition, hunters received US$662 from the

Table 5.4

Reproductive rates of Amazonian ungulates in the Tahuayo study area

Species	Litter Size	Percentage of Females Reproductively Active	Number of Gestations per Year	Productivity of Females: (average no. of young/female/year)	Total Productivity (average no. of young/individual/year)
Tayassu tajacu (collared peccary)	1.7	43.6 (N=62)	1.5	1.11	0.55
T. pecari (white-lipped peccary)	1.6	51.4 (N=37)	1.5	1.23	0.61
Mazama americana (red brocket deer)	1.0	45 (N=40)	1.5	0.67	0.33
M. gouazoubira (grey brocket deer)	1.0	50 (N=16)	1.5	0.75	0.37
Tapirus terrestris (lowland tapir)	1.0	50 (N=8)	0.5	0.25	0.12

Note: N=number of samples examined.
Source: Bodmer et al., in press.

Table 5.5

Sustainability of current hunting of Amazonian ungulates in the Tahuayo study area

Species	Total Productivity (average no. of young/individual/year)	Density (individuals/km^2)	Production (individual/km^2)	Hunting Pressure (individual/km^2)	Sustainability (% of production taken by hunters)
Tayassu tajacu (collared peccary)	0.55	3.3	1.83	0.27	15
T. pecari (white-lipped peccary)	0.61	1.3	0.80	0.30	38
Mazama americana (red brocket deer)	0.33	1.8	0.60	0.13	22
M. gouazoubira (grey brocket deer)	0.37	0.8	0.30	0.06	20
Tapirus terrestris (lowland tapir)	0.12	0.4	0.05	0.08	160

Source: Bodmer et al., in press.

Table 5.6

Economic benefits of the current harvest in Tahuayo
and costs of converting to a more sustainable
harvest over a one-year period

Species	Price/Animal	Number Taken	Total Value
Tayassu pecari	US$30	166	US$4,980
T. tajacu	30	165	4,950
Mazama americana	30	60	1,800
M. gouazoubira	20	28	560
Tapirus terrestris	80	38	3,040
Hydrochaeris hydrochaeris	20	10	200
Agouti paca	10	174	1,740
Total commercial meat value	—	—	US$17,270
Commercial pelt value	US$2	331	US$662
Total commercial value for hunters	—	—	US$17,932
Direct consumption value	US$1/kg	3,008 kg	US$3,008
Total direct benefits of mammalian harvests for hunters	—	—	US$20,940

Economic costs of prohibiting hunting on overharvested species

Tapirus terrestris	US$3,040
Primates (1,419 kg)	1,419
Edentates and carnivores (1,075 kg)	1,075
Total costs	US$5,534 or US$11/km^2

Source: Bodmer et al. 1994.

331 peccary pelts extracted. A total of 3,008 kg of game meat was not suitable for commercial use and had a consumption value of US$1 per kg. In Tahuayo, economic benefits obtained from mammals with market value were much greater than benefits obtained from mammals used for consumption. Also, harvests of mammals with commercial value were greater than harvests of mammals with consumption value (Bodmer et al. 1994).

Population analyses of game species in Tahuayo suggest that peccaries, deer, and large rodents currently are not overhunted. Populations of primates and tapir probably are overhunted, and it is assumed that populations of marsupials, edentates, and carnivores can not sustain current hunting levels because of their apparently low densities. Thus a more sustainable hunt would require cessation of hunting of primates, tapirs, marsupials, edentates, and carnivores and setting of artiodactyl and large-rodent harvests at or below current levels. Hunters would incur a 26 percent reduction of economic benefits if they ceased to harvest primates, tapir, marsupials, edentates, and carnivores, and extraction of mammalian biomass would be reduced by 35 percent.

Local inhabitants undoubtedly will incur short-term economic costs by enforcing a more limited—and hence more sustainable—harvest of wildlife. These costs might be alleviated either by subsidizing social services or by developing alternative economic activities in the permanent settlement zone. Focusing increased economic benefits in the permanent settlement zone while limiting exploitation in the subsistence zone would be consistent with the goal of approximating sustainable development in the RCTT through distinct land-use zones.

Managing for Sustainable Utilization

Wildlife management programs of the RCTT are intended to help local communities of the permanent settlement zone manage the natural resources of the subsistence zone sustainably and protect the core area. While the inhabitants of the permanent settlement zone take a true interest in managing natural resources, they have requested assistance in determining the best ways to secure economic gain from extraction using techniques that will not compromise future availability. Plans for natural-resource use will be determined from information on the ecological sustainability of extraction and the subsequent costs and benefits incurred by inhabitants of the permanent settlement zone.

How could the community manage a sustainable hunt by combining biological and economic considerations to conserve Amazonian wildlife in the subsistence zone of the RCTT? One possible management program would be to cull a greater proportion of male animals among species that are not currently overharvested and cease hunting of overexploited mammals. Implementing a male-directed hunting program should maintain a harvest that does not degrade game resources. Male-directed hunting is commonly used in ungulate management in North

America and Scandinavia to minimize the impact of harvests on reproduction (Gill 1990). This is because, in many mammals, lifetime reproductive success of males is determined by access to females, but female reproductive success is limited more by resources than by the number of males (Clutton-Brock 1988). Recruitment in such mammalian populations is therefore relatively unaffected by a reduction in the proportion of adult males if the population is not near its carrying capacity, which is apparently the case for Amazonian ungulates and large rodents (Terborgh 1989).

Age-structure curves of deer and peccaries in Tahuayo suggest that current harvests of artiodactyls should not be increased, and it is assumed that harvests of large rodents also should not be increased. An increase in the proportion of males taken is likely to increase recruitment only if it involves an actual reduction in females harvested.

Recognizing the substantial difference in the benefits of commercial and consumption (or subsistence) exploitation, one way to manage a male-directed hunt without increasing current harvests of peccaries, deer, and large rodents would be to establish a system that requires that market benefits be derived only from males and consumption benefits only from females of these species. This male-directed harvest of species that are not currently overhunted would concur well with predictions based on production models (Robinson and Redford 1991). The management program does not propose a male-only harvest because this might have repercussions for recruitment by altering too drastically the ability of females to find mates.

Interestingly, the economic considerations of this management program complement its biological justification. First, hunters will become more selective in harvesting male animals to maximize commercial benefits. Second, meat from females used for consumption will substitute for meat lost from prohibited species. Hunters will have less incentive to harvest primates, marsupials, edentates, or carnivores for consumption when meat from female artiodactyls and large rodents is available. Finally, benefits of the peccary hide trade will not be affected by this management scheme.

A management program that permits only male artiodactyls and large rodents to be sold at market would decrease total commercial meat benefits by 54 percent of the present hunt, using the sex ratio of the current harvest. Meat available for consumption would increase by 2.4 times the current level, and harvests of mammals with commercial value would be similar to those with consumption value. By implementing a male-directed management program, the harvested sex ratio should become male biased and increase the proportion of commercial benefits.

As a practical matter, how would such a program be implemented? A male-directed program for hunting of deer, peccaries, and large-bodied rodents could be managed through local communities. Hunters would be required to present the meat of male animals to community-appointed inspectors, who would then issue permits for transportation of the meat to markets upon confirmation of the animal's sex. The penis could be used for this purpose; because hunters butcher animals before transporting meat, a maximum weight would be permitted for each penis presented. For example, a transportation permit would be given for each 30 kg of fresh (or 15 kg dried) collared peccary meat presented with a penis. The community-appointed inspectors would collect the penises to prevent improper use.

A wildlife extension officer would be vital to the success of this type of management program. The extension officer would educate people on wildlife use and link social services and economic alternatives of the permanent settlement zone to the male-directed management program. Maximum hunting quotas (based on current hunting levels) would be communicated to hunters by community representatives, and transportation permits would not be issued once monthly quotas are filled. (The communities understand quota systems and recently set up a maximum monthly quota of three large mammals and five small mammals per hunter.) Resolving conflicts over the sale of female animals and maximum quotas would be a community responsibility. The wildlife extension officer would be available to assist in resolving conflicts and solicit support from the Regional Ministry of Agriculture, if necessary.

The proposed management program has been set up on a trial basis for a two-year period and is being supervised by the Regional Ministry of Agriculture. The densities, age structure, and harvested sex ratio of deer, peccaries, and large rodents and the densities of primates and tapir are being monitored over the trial period to evaluate management impact.

Palm Fruit and Wildlife Survival

Both game species and people eat many species of wild fruits in Amazonia. Some of these fruit species experience great harvesting pressure because of commercial demand. The extraction of fruits from natural habitats probably affects the nutritional condition of animals, which in turn may affect their population growth.

Ungulates of the RCTT, the most important game species, make up 78 percent of mammalian biomass extracted. These large-bodied mammals are primarily frugivores. For example, red brocket deer consume a diet composed of 81 percent fruit; grey brocket deer, 87 percent; collared peccaries, 59 percent; white-lipped peccaries, 66 percent; and lowland tapir, 34 percent (Bodmer 1989). The most important fruits for these ungulates are those of palm species. For red and grey brocket deer, the fruits of *Euterpe* spp. and *Iriartea* spp. palms are the two most important foods. Collared peccaries consume large amounts of *Astrocaryum* spp. and *Jessenia* spp., and white-lipped peccaries like *Mauritia flexuosa*, *Jessenia* spp., and *Astrocaryum* spp. Lowland tapir specialize in *M. flexuosa* and consume large quantities of this species.

People of the RCTT also harvest large amounts of palm fruit. Palm fruit is the most important nontimber plant resource in the Peruvian Amazon and contributes 61 percent of the market value for fruit production (derived from Peters, Gentry, and Mendelsohn 1989). The two most valuable palm resources are the fruits of *aguaje* (*Mauritia flexuosa*) and *ungurahui* (*Jessenia* spp.). Both species occur throughout lowland Amazonia, and stands of *M. flexuosa* account for 2.35 percent of the Peruvian rain forest (COREPASA 1986).

In the Peruvian Amazon, *M. flexuosa* and *Jessenia* spp. are being cut down at alarming rates to make fruit harvests easier (Vasquez and Gentry 1989). *Ribereños* cut palms because the physical structure and height of the trees render climbing almost impossible and very dangerous. For example, *M. flexuosa* trees often reach 40 m in height and have stegmata wood bark (containing silica bodies) that is extremely hard and slippery (Uhl and Dransfield 1987).

Harvesting of fruit is leading to localized extinction of *M. flexuosa* in many areas of the Peruvian Amazon. *M. flexuosa* occurs in almost monotypic stands within backswamp habitats that range in size from 1 to 10 ha or more (Uhl and Dransfield 1987). The patchy distribution of *aguaje* helps *ribereños* locate and collect fruit, and overexploitation quickly renders swamps useless. Because *M. flexuosa* has a dioecious reproductive system, only male trees remain in exploited swamps, rendering them reproductively dead. Harvesting of *M. flexuosa* has already destroyed many palm swamps close to villages. In the Tahuayo River area, most swamps within 10 km of villages were heavily damaged, and intact swamps of *aguaje* usually could be found only at distances more than 25 km away. Thus there is a negative relationship between the degree of damage to *M. flexuosa* swamps and proximity to villages.

Managing Palm Fruit for Wildlife

In addition to management of direct hunting pressure, wildlife management in the subsistence-use zone of the RCTT requires programs for the extraction of forest fruits to maintain and possibly increase the nutritional intake of game species.

Ribereños do not destroy fruit-bearing palm trees when they occur in small private plots but do collect the fruit, both for household consumption and market sale. Palm trees that occur outside village gardens are cut for commercial sale (Bodmer et al. 1990b). Also, palms outside village boundaries are used most by game animals.

Communities living next to the RCTT realize the damage inflicted by cutting palm trees and have begun an agroforestry system that incorporates these species. Interestingly, many palms only grow 2 to 5 m tall when planted in an open system without competition and therefore do not require cutting or special climbing equipment. Agroforestry plots that contain large numbers of *M. flexuosa* and *Jessenia* palms in the permanent settlement area of the RCTT are being promoted.

Harvesting the fruit of planted palms will have several advantages over cutting of wild trees. For one, inhabitants will have a renewable supply of palm fruit for market sale and subsistence consumption, and this alternative will be truly sustainable. In addition, palm fruit in natural habitats of the subsistence zone mostly will be left for animal food, which in turn should strengthen game populations.

Maximum Sustained Yield

Population studies of game in the RCTT suggest that deer, peccaries, and large rodents are not as susceptible to hunting pressure as primates, tapir, edentates, and carnivores. Sustained yields of deer and peccaries have been estimated at current population levels in the RCTT, but sustained yields can be obtained at any population level. If hunting of deer, peccaries, and large rodents is to continue, the level of hunting pressure that can provide maximum sustained yield and maximize recruitment at the greatest possible density must be calculated.

Offtake by natural predators must be considered when approximating maximum sustained yields of hunters. Predators probably hunt deer, peccary, and large rodent populations to well below their carrying capacities. The effects of natural predators in many areas may be reducing prey populations to near their maximum sustainable yields, which could leave only small proportions of the game production for hunters without pulling animal populations below the maximum sustainable levels.

The next step in wildlife management in the RCTT is to approximate the maximum sustained yields of these hunted species by studying intraspecific variance of recruitment against different population densities. Information on maximum sustained yields will enable communities to set quotas at levels that will maximize offtake of game without degrading animal populations, thus optimizing benefits of wildlife for local people over long periods.

ACKNOWLEDGMENTS

I thank T. Fang, P. Puertas, J. Penn, L. Moya, I. Vilchez, and J. Moro for their kind assistance. Logistical and financial support was provided by the Chicago Zoological Society, Proyecto Peruano de Primatología "Manuel Moro Sommo," Direccion Regional de Recurses Naturales y de Medio Ambiente-Loreto, and the Amazon Conservation Fund.

SOURCES

Bodmer, R. E. 1989. "Frugivory in Amazon Ungulates." Ph.D. dissertation, Cambridge University.

———, N. Y. Bendayin, I. Moya, and T. G. Fang. 1990a. "Manejo de Ungulados en la Amazonía Peruana—Analisis de la Caza de Subsistencia y la Comercializacion Local, Nacional e Internacional." Boletin de Lima 70:49–56.

———, T. G. Fang, and I. Moya. 1988. "Ungulate Management and Conservation in the Peruvian Amazon." Biological Conservation 45:303–310.

———, T. G. Fang, and I. Moya. 1990. "Fruits of the Forest." Nature 343:109.

————, T. G. Fang, I. Moya I. and R. Gill. 1994. "Managing Wildlife to Conserve Amazonian Forests: Population Biology and Economic Considerations of Game Hunting." *Biological Conservation* 67:29–35.

————, J. Penn, T. G. Fang, and I. Moya. 1990b. "Management Programmes and Protected Areas: The Case of the Reserva Comunal Tamshiyacu-Tahuayo, Peru." *Parks* 1:21–25.

————, P. E. Puertas, L. A. Moya, and T. G. Fang. In press. "Estado de las Poblaciones del Tapir en la Amazonia Peruana: En el Camina de la Extincion." *Boletin de Lima.*

Browder, J. O. 1992. "The Limits of Extractivism: Tropical Forest Strategies Beyond Extractive Reserves." *BioScience* 42:174–182.

Clutton-Brock, T. H. 1988. *Reproductive Success: Studies of Individual Variation in Contrasting Breeding Systems.* Chicago: University of Chicago Press.

Coomes, O. T. 1992. "Making a Living in the Amazon Rain Forest: Peasants, Land, and Economy in the Tahuayo River Basin of Northeastern Peru." Ph.D. dissertation, University of Wisconsin-Madison.

COREPASA. 1986. *Plan Maestro de la Reserva Nacional Pacaya-Samiria.* Loreto, Peru: Editoriale Imprensa DESA.

Gill, R. 1990. *Monitoring the Status of European and North American Cervids.* Nairobi: United Nations Environment Program.

Government of Peru (GOP). 1991 Decreto Supreme NO 934-73-AG, Lima, October 8.

————. 1973. Resolucion Ejecutiva Regional N" 080-91-CR-GRA-P.

Hvidberg-Hansen, H. 1970a. "Utilization of the Amazon otter (*Lutra incannun* Thomas) in Peru." FAO Forestry and Training Project UNDP/SF No. 116. Lima: Food and Agriculture Organization. Typescript.

————. 1970b. "Utilization of the Capybara (*Hydrochoerus hydrochaeris* Linne) in Peru." FAO Forestry and Training Project UNDP/SF No. 116. Lima: Food and Agriculture Organization. Typescript.

————. 1970c. "Utilization of the Collared Peccary (*Tayassu tajacu* Linne) in Peru." FAO Forestry and Training Project UNDP/SF No. 116. Lima: Food and Agriculture Organization. Typescript.

————. 1970d. "Utilization of the Giant Otter (*Pteronura brasiliensis* Gmelin) in Peru." FAO Forestry and Training Project UNDP/SF No. 116. Lima: Food and Agriculture Organization. Typescript.

————. 1970e. "Utilization of the Jaguar (Linne 1758) in Peru." FAO Forestry and Training Project UNDP/SF No. 116. Lima: Food and Agriculture Organization. Typescript.

Pacheco Gomez, T. 1993. "Efectos Positivos y Negativos de la veda de caza de 1973 en la Amazonia Peruana." Report to the Universidade Nacional Agraria la Molina, Peru. Typescript.

Peters, C. M., A. H. Gentry, and R. O. Mendelsohn. 1989. "Valuation of an Amazonian Rainforest." *Nature* 339:655–656.

Puertas, P., and R. E. Bodmer. 1993. "Conservation of a High Diversity Primate Assemblage." *Biodiversity and Conservation* 2:586–593.

Redford, K. H., and J. G. Robinson. 1987. "The Game of Choice: Patterns of Indian and Colonist Hunting in the Neotropics." *American Anthropologist* 89:650–667.

Robinson, J. G., and K. H. Redford. 1991. "Sustainable Harvest of Neotropical Forest Mammals." In *Neotropical Wildlife Use and Conservation*, eds. J. G. Robinson and K. H. Redford, 415–429. Chicago: University of Chicago Press.

Roosevelt, A. C., R. A. Housley, M. Imazio da Silveira, S. Maranca, and R. Johnson. 1991. "Eighth Millennium Pottery from a Prehistoric Shell Midden in the Brazilian Amazon." *Science* 254:1621–1624.

Smith, H. H. 1879. *Brazil: The Amazons and the Coast*. New York: Charles Scribners Sons.

Terborgh, J. 1989. Letter to the author, December 13.

Uhl, N. W., and J. Dransfield. 1987. *Genera Palmarum: A Classification of Palms Based on the Work of Harold E. Moore, Jr.* Lawrence, Kansas: Allen Press.

Vasquez, R., and A. H. Gentry. 1989. "Use and Misuse of Forest-harvested Fruits in the Iquitos Area." *Conservation Biology* 3:350–361.

CHAPTER 6

Kakadu National Park: An Australian Experience in Comanagement

M. A. Hill and A. J. Press

Aboriginal people have been present in what is now Kakadu National Park for more than fifty thousand years (Roberts, Jones, and Smith 1990). The Australian landscapes that variously welcomed, bewildered, or intimidated the first European settlers of the continent more than two hundred years ago were artifacts of millennia of Aboriginal activity and management. The early settlers (or, indeed, those who came later) had little or no appreciation that they had come to a managed environment. Rather, their efforts were directed toward "taming the wilderness" and anglicizing the landscape (Hallam 1975). An understanding of the role Aboriginal people played in shaping the Australian environment, and an appreciation of their knowledge of and ability to manage it, came very much later.

In the mid-1960s two events started a process that would culminate in the establishment of Kakadu National Park and its comanagement by a national government nature conservation agency and the traditional Aboriginal owners of the area. First, in 1965, the Northern Territory Reserves Board put forward an early proposal for the establishment of a major national park in the Alligator Rivers Region. Second, in 1967, the Australian Constitution was amended to make the commonwealth rather than the state governments responsible for Aboriginal affairs and the welfare of Aboriginal people.

During the ten years following 1965, interested individuals or agencies put forward a succession of modified proposals for a major national park in the region. These culminated, in 1975, with a formal proposal by the commonwealth government under the recently passed National Parks and Wildlife Conservation Act 1975 (COA 1975), which declared a major national park in the region. At that time the commonwealth directly administered the Northern Territory (which achieved self-government in 1978). The passage of the act was supposed to result in the creation of a number of major national parks in the territory.

Interestingly, and farsightedly, this legislation specifically authorized assistance to and cooperation with Aboriginal people in a variety of contexts. These included managing land vested in Aboriginal people or organizations, land held in trust for the benefit of Aboriginal people, and land occupied by Aboriginal people. The act originally permitted only the declaration of parks and reserves in areas of land owned or held under lease by the commonwealth. Still, this early recognition through legislation of the potential for cooperation with Aboriginal people in achieving nature-conservation objectives was to play an important part in the development of Kakadu National Park.

Natural History and Cultural Heritage

Kakadu National Park is situated in the wet-dry tropics of northern Australia and presents a broad array of landforms with diverse vegetation and fauna. The park extends 150 km from the coast in the north to a remnant Tertiary plateau to the south, and 120 km from the Arnhem Land sandstone plateau in the east through wooded savanna to the west. In contrast to the great antiquity of the underlying geological formations (around 2,000 million years ago), the riverine and coastal floodplains are modern phenomena (some around 1,000 B.P.). This conjunction of major landforms has produced an ecological diversity unique in northern Australia—one that has sustained a human population for at least 50,000 years.

The Arnhem Land plateau is an area of deeply dissected sandstone with rugged cliffs and spectacular escarpments. It contains relict rain forest vegetation, as well as essentially arid, spinifex-dominated grassland and wooded savanna. The area, of great floristic endemism (Russell-Smith et al. 1993), contains a number of unique vertebrates (ANPWS and DASETT 1991). Where the Arnhem Land plateau has eroded in the south of the park, the ancient rocks of the southern hills and basins have been revealed.

The lowland plains, stretching from the sandstone to the coastal plains, contain wooded savannas, forests, rivers, billabongs, and fringing vegetation. Although the soils are acidic, shallow, and infertile, the plant and animal communities are rich.

The four major river systems of Kakadu and the coast have produced extensive freshwater floodplains and backwater swamps, as well as estuarine communities, mangroves, and mudflats. During the last 100,000 years, the sea level fluctuated greatly, and the northern coast of Australia moved to within tens of kilometers of the Indonesian archipelago's coastline. Climate changes throughout the Pleistocene, changes in sea level, and the creation of freshwater ecosystems are all events that have had a profound impact on the region. Much of the magnificent rock art of the Arnhem Land escarpment and plateau records local changes at least through the Holocene (Chaloupka 1983), and the material cultural record reflects a long and diverse pattern of occupation and use (Sullivan 1990).

Kakadu's archeological record indicates one of the longest periods of human occupation in Australia (Roberts, Jones, and Smith 1990), with dates of up to

50,000 B.P. Some scientists speculate about much older dates. The first Australians most likely arrived to find a much drier landscape than that of the present, and the hunting-and-gathering technology and art from that time reflects a savanna-based economy. At the end of the Pleistocene, temperatures increased and the sea level rose.

Sea levels appeared to stabilize around 6,000 years ago, and establishment of the freshwater floodplains began. The rock art of Kakadu reflects changes in hunting weapons from this period, with the disappearance of boomerangs and the appearance of new spears and spear throwers. Archeological deposits show increasing use of freshwater foods and much greater use of wetlands as a resource (Brockwell 1989). The Aboriginal people made good use of these abundant resources, and the regional economies held great store in these readily accessible resources.

When the first Europeans attempted to settle in the area in the first half of the nineteenth century, the indigenous population of the Kakadu region was approximately 2,000. Decimation of the Aboriginal population through disease and social dislocation had occurred by the 1920s. Kakadu's Aboriginal community consisted of probably less than 100 individuals in 1979. Since that time, numbers have increased markedly, and some 300 Aboriginal people probably reside in the park today.

Many of these Aboriginal residents are traditional owners, and others have recognized social and traditional ties to the area. Permanent Aboriginal living areas are established at ten or more locations throughout the park. On occasion, small temporary living areas may be established.

The Aboriginal people, the legally recognized owners of much of Kakadu National Park, are the bearers of the longest continuous cultural traditions on earth. Management arrangements for Kakadu attempt to recognize this cultural heritage and successfully marry a traditional conservation ethic with the traditions and aspirations of the region's Aboriginal owners. The presence of a resident Aboriginal population in Kakadu National Park today is part of that continuing heritage and a reason for the park's nomination as a World Heritage Site in 1992.

Steps to Comanagement

Comanagement was a "discovered" principle for Kakadu, the result of a slow process in which the views and involvement of Aboriginal people living in the area came to be an integral part of policy and action. Kakadu National Park has almost never been out of the news or the political spotlight since it was established. It has generated intense emotion about issues such as mining (uranium mining, at that) and conservation; mining and Aboriginal interests; pastoral activities and conservation; tourism and conservation; conservation and Aboriginal interests; and

Aboriginal interests and tourism. Overlying all these issues has been the Northern Territory government's fundamental opposition to the commonwealth government's presence and involvement in the park, specifically through its nature-conservation agency, the Australian National Parks and Wildlife Service (ANPWS).

The 1965 proposal for a national park in the region included within its boundaries an Aboriginal reserve. Other controversial inclusions were two areas that were to come under pastoral lease in 1969 but at the time were licensed temporarily to commercial buffalo operations. The government made no formal response to the proposal. One minister, however, did suggest that although the government was sympathetic to the creation of more national parks, this particular proposal was complicated by an Aboriginal Reserve, a wildlife sanctuary, special-purpose leases, and pastoral and mining activities.

The modified proposals put forward in 1967 generally sought to exclude the Aboriginal reserve and the areas that were to become pastoral leases. One proposal included the suggestion that part of the area be managed as a game-hunting reserve. The government responded to these proposals by inviting an overseas expert to visit the area and respond to the proposal. The subsequent report recommended a national park substantially larger than had been suggested previously. The government responded by agreeing, in principle, to creation of a national park a little more than a quarter of the size proposed; it also established a planning committee to look into the park's extension.

Meanwhile, between 1967 and 1971, the government issued mining prospecting authorities (later called exploration licenses) covering most of the proposed park area. While this action further complicated the issues, work on determining appropriate boundaries for the park continued. When the boundaries finally were suggested, two significant areas were excluded from mining activity, and in 1972 most of the proposed park area was declared a wildlife sanctuary.

In the process of devising and modifying the various proposals for the national park, the views of the Aboriginal people living in the area were neither considered nor sought, despite an appreciation of the wealth of the Aboriginal rock art in the area as an important element worthy of preservation. The proposals were based on the conservative Eurocentric attitudes about national parks and nature prevalent at the time. The work did focus attention on the natural and, to a lesser extent, the cultural values of the area; subsequently, these values and the need to safeguard at least a portion of them never were questioned. Determining which parts of the area should be conserved was to prove too difficult in the face of competing land uses until 1977, when the concept of Kakadu emerged largely as it exists today.

In the early 1970s, the commonwealth established a commission of inquiry to analyze the issue of Aboriginal land rights in the Northern Territory and appointed a judge of the supreme court of the territory as its head. In his first report, the commissioner, Justice A. E. Woodward, addressed the issues of Aboriginal land rights, public reserves, and Crown land by suggesting that "it may be that a scheme of Aboriginal title, combined with National Park status and joint management, would prove acceptable to all interests" (Woodward 1973:42).

In his second report, Woodward further developed the concept of Aboriginal land, national parks, and joint (or co-) management in the context of reconciling Aboriginal interests with conservation. In the process, he identified a number of principles to be followed if Aboriginal interests were not to be subordinated unreasonably to those of conservation. He also identified a number of specific points to be addressed in planning the future of the Ayers Rock-Mount Olga National Park, now called Uluru-Katatjuta National Park.

By the early 1970s, three significant uranium deposits had been discovered in the area that is now Kakadu National Park—at Ranger, Jabiluka, and Koongarra. In 1975, the commonwealth government received a formal proposal to develop the Ranger deposit. The government initiated a commission of inquiry to study the proposal under the provisions of the Environment Protection (Impact of Proposals) Act 1974 (COA 1974).

After the Ranger Uranium Environmental Inquiry had commenced its work, the federal Parliament passed the Aboriginal Land Rights (Northern Territory) Act 1976 (COA 1976), largely as a result of the work of Justice Woodward. The act granted title to certain areas in the Northern Territory to the traditional Aboriginal owners. It also established the process whereby Aboriginal people could claim title to other areas of unalienated Crown land on the basis of being traditional owners, or of being entitled by tradition to its use or occupation. The act also specifically provided for the commission established to conduct the Ranger inquiry to determine the merits of a land claim in the Alligator Rivers Region.

In submitting their claim to the commission, the traditional Aboriginal owners had instructed their representative, the Northern Land Council (NLC), to propose that the director of national parks and wildlife should lease the land from them if their claim were successful. One of the claimants' concerns was that they might not be able to adequately manage and look after the land on their own in the face of growing and competing pressures. They believed that a national park would establish a management regime that could safeguard their interests and sympathize with their aspirations. This concept was supported by the commission.

No provision exists in the Aboriginal Land Rights Act for claims to alienated Crown land (i.e., Crown land in which a person other than the Crown has an estate or interest). However, provision was made, in the case of land actually granted to the traditional owners by incorporation in the schedule to the act, for title to be granted to areas in which other people had an interest; such title was to be held in escrow on behalf of the traditional owners. This provision was to play a part in the initiation of the first stage of Kakadu. At the time when Aboriginal title was granted, a limited number of small areas were held under lease, mostly by Aboriginal people or organizations. These areas were not included as part of the park, as title was held only in escrow; since they are mostly used for tourist-related activities or as Aboriginal living areas, these areas cause no problems for management of the surrounding park.

In May 1977, the commission commented in its final report, "Possibly no other part of Australia is faced with as many strong and concurrent competing claims for the use of land as this region" (Fox, Kelleher, and Kerr 1977:287). It saw the major land-use interests as the use and occupation of land by Aboriginal people, the establishment of a national park, uranium mining, tourism, and pastoral activities (Fox, Kelleher, and Kerr 1977).

The commission's principal recommendations included

- granting of title to the area claimed by the Aboriginal claimants,

- establishment of a large national park, to include the proposed Aboriginal land,

- resumption of two pastoral leases, to enable Aboriginal land claims to be made over the area and the area incorporated in the national park,

- inclusion in the park of a regional center (the town of Jabiru, established later) to service the uranium mining operations,

- prohibition of tourist development in the regional center, at least for the time being, and

- preparation of a plan of management for the park, in which Aboriginal views would be strongly represented.

The commission's recommendations relating to the national park, Aboriginal land, and management of the area accorded very well with the thrust and intent of the National Parks and Wildlife Conservation Act. But amendments were required to accommodate specific recommendations.

In making its submission to the commission, the Australian National Parks and Wildlife Service (ANPWS) proposed to use the section of the National Parks and Wildlife Conservation Act that provided for assistance to and cooperation with Aboriginal people in managing Aboriginal land. The commission, however, preferred to see Aboriginal land included in the proposed national park; to allow for this, the act needed to be amended. This was subsequently accomplished by including Aboriginal land leased to the director of national parks and wildlife as a type of area that could be declared a park or reserve under the act.

Although the act does provide for mining and mineral exploration in parks under very specific conditions, the commission recommended that if uranium mining were to proceed, the mining leases or project areas should be excluded from the park. However, the commission recommended that the regional center (Jabiru) that would be established to service the mines should be included in the park.

In August 1977, the commonwealth government announced its response to the recommendations of the Ranger Uranium Environmental Inquiry. It accepted virtually all of the commission's recommendations, including grant of Aboriginal title and establishment of a major national park. The park was to be established in stages, with the first stage including roughly the same areas proposed as Aboriginal land.

The concept of a national park on Aboriginal land was untried in Australia. In addition to amendment of the National Parks and Wildlife Conservation and Aboriginal Land Rights acts, realization of the concept would require negotiation of appropriate terms and conditions under which the Aboriginal land could be leased to the director of national parks and wildlife, allowing the land to be declared a national park. A lengthy negotiation period commenced, culminating in the signing of a lease agreement in October 1978. During the same period, the necessary amendments to the legislation, which also included provisions for incorporating a meaningful role for Aboriginal people into park management, were prepared. Since these objectives reflected proposals from both the Aboriginal people and the ANPWS, there was little or no concern about the amendments in these camps.

Negotiations over the lease agreement were more contentious. This was not because of any disagreement over the objectives of the agreement between the ANPWS and the NLC, but because the commonwealth government chose to include the lease agreement in a package of agreements it was negotiating with the NLC on uranium mining operations. Broadly speaking, Aboriginal people did not want uranium mining at Ranger, but they did want a national park. The negotiations on this matter were protracted and delayed finalization of the lease agreement for the park.

If Kakadu National Park was conceived in a period of conflict over land use in the mineral-rich Alligator Rivers Region, the park was born in a period of broader conflict. In 1978, the fledgling government of Northern Territory, which had just achieved self-rule, strenuously opposed the official proclamation of the first stage of Kakadu National Park on April 5, 1979, and the comanagement arrangements that went with it.

The commonwealth government had intended, in creating Kakadu National Park in stages, that further exploration for minerals should take place in the Stage 2 area during a five-year program that would determine which areas should be added to the park or retained for mining. For the moment, no exploration (or mining) was to take place in Stage 1 of the park.

A change of government occurred in 1983, before the exploration program began. The Stage 2 area was declared part of the park in the following year, even though it holds great potential for mineral extraction and many mining companies had claimed mining and/or exploration rights or had applications pending. The death of the exploration program amid such intense interest was linked to competing interests within the bureaucracy.

In many respects, the issues were similar to those that had so effectively precluded establishment of a park in the area during the previous decade. The fundamental conflict was between mining and conservation interests, with Aboriginal interests spanning both. Of the three major uranium deposits located on enclaves excluded from but located within the boundaries of Kakadu National Park, Ranger Uranium Mine is the only one operating. The other two have been constrained by current government policy, which limits the number of uranium mines in Australia. In spite of this, representatives of the traditional Aboriginal owners of the land on which these deposits are located have signed agreements with mining companies with the intention of proceeding with operations.

National and local conservation groups have opposed mining in the Kakadu region strenuously and vociferously. The fact that uranium is the principal product from the existing and proposed mines adds weight to their concerns. In opposing mining, they have partially succeeded in forming a coalition with the Aboriginal people. Although conservation groups implacably oppose all mining in the region, the Aboriginal people do not. While the Aboriginal people are pleased to see mining and exploration generally prohibited within the park, they are conscious of the very substantial financial benefits that may accrue to them if mining proceeds in the enclaves located on Aboriginal land.

Much to the dismay of the mining companies and the Northern Territory government (which invariably sided with them), in 1987 the commonwealth government finally legislated prohibition of any activities associated with mining and exploration within Kakadu National Park. The existence of the enclaves, though, means that the issue is still alive, and the Northern Territory government continues to argue strongly that mining should be allowed.

In considering Kakadu National Park as an example of community-based conservation, it is important to remember the environment of extreme and sustained political sensitivity in which it has operated. Throughout the history of the park, the Northern Territory government has sought to gain control of Kakadu and remove the ANPWS. Its intention has been to support major commercial development (including mining) in the park without any apparent consideration of the point of view of the traditional Aboriginal owners. The government's words and actions have greatly angered the Aboriginal people, and, paradoxically, the Northern Territory government's efforts well may have helped to strengthen the relationship between the ANPWS and the traditional owners and their representatives.

Comanagement Arrangements

The involvement and participation of the Aboriginal community in comanagement of Kakadu National Park is assured through a hierarchy of measures: statutory instruments, conditions of lease, and management arrangements. The responsibilities and role of the ANPWS in comanagement arrangements are determined by similar measures.

Statutory Instruments

The two pieces of legislation that fundamentally underpin the project, the Land Rights Act and the National Parks and Wildlife Conservation Act, required substantial complementary amendment in 1978 to implement the commonwealth government's decision on Kakadu National Park. Amendments to the National Parks and Wildlife Conservation Act in 1979, 1985, and 1987 provided the legal basis for further development and refinement of the arrangements.

The Land Rights Act provides the mechanism through which unalienated land in the Northern Territory may be claimed by traditional Aboriginal owners. It establishes procedures for claims to be argued before an Aboriginal Land Commissioner and, if upheld, for title to be granted to and held by the relevant Aboriginal land trust. It establishes Aboriginal land councils, which function in their respective areas to ascertain and express Aboriginal views on management of the land, protect the interests of traditional owners of land, consult traditional owners about proposals for use of their land, and negotiate on behalf of the traditional owners and assist Aboriginals in pursuit of their land claims.

The Northern Land Council (NLC) has jurisdiction over the Aboriginal lands within Kakadu National Park and elsewhere within the northern half of the territory. The NLC consists of an elected council of Aboriginal community representatives and a bureaucracy to administer its affairs. The council meets four times yearly to set policy and direction for the organization. Over the years, the NLC has played a major role in the establishment and development of comanagement arrangements for the park.

Aboriginal people also have formed associations to represent their local political and financial interests. In the Kakadu region three such organizations—the Gagudju, Djabulukgu, and Jawoyn associations—provide, inter alia, services to their members (e.g., health services) and run businesses and enterprises such as shops, tourist ventures, and contracting services. The local associations and the Northern Land Council exist side by side, with the council carrying out statutory functions under the Land Rights Act and the associations looking after the financial and other interests of their members.

Land trusts established under the Land Rights Act are the legal title holders of Aboriginal freehold land granted under the same act. In Kakadu, land has been granted to the Kakadu Aboriginal Land Trust and the Jabiluka Aboriginal Land Trust. The Land Rights Act also provides the necessary mechanisms for Aboriginal land to be leased to the director of national parks and wildlife, declared a national park, and managed accordingly.

The National Parks and Wildlife Conservation Act establishes the statutory

office of director of national parks and wildlife and directs the Australian National
Parks and Wildlife Service to assist the director in carrying out his functions. It
provides for Aboriginal land in the Alligator Rivers Region of the Northern Territory, which is leased to the director, to be declared a national park.

The act also requires that a plan of management be prepared for a park as soon
after its declaration as is feasible. More specifically, the act provides for the establishment of boards of management for parks on Aboriginal land (on which the
majority of representatives are to be Aboriginal). The functions of the board are to
prepare, in conjunction with the director, plans of management; make decisions
on management consistent with the plan of management; monitor management in
conjunction with the director; and advise, in conjunction with the director, the
minister responsible for the environment on future development. Additionally, the
act sets out in some detail the process the director and the board must follow in
preparing a plan of management and provides a means for resolving disagreements between them.

Once a plan of management has been prepared, it is submitted to the minister
for approval. If the minister accepts the plan, he or she must then table it in both
houses of the federal Parliament. Within a specified time, it can be disallowed by
either house; if this does not occur, the plan becomes a legal instrument, having
been accepted by both houses. Management of the park thenceforth must be in
accordance with the prescriptions of the approved management plan.

Conditions of Lease

The original lease agreement setting out the terms and conditions applying to the
lease of Aboriginal land for the park was between the NLC (representing the traditional owners) and the director. The primary concern of the agreement was to
ensure an appropriate level of involvement in the park's management among the
traditional owners. It required the director to consult with officers of the NLC, who
would ascertain and represent the views of the traditional owners on all matters
affecting Aboriginal people.

Under the terms of the agreement, the director accepted obligations to

- train local Aboriginal people in skills necessary to enable them to assist in
  management of the park,
- employ as many traditional Aboriginal owners as is practicable, under conditions that recognize their special needs and culture,
- promote among non-Aboriginals a knowledge and understanding of
  Aboriginal traditions, culture, and languages,
- engage Aboriginals in park interpretation programs,
- consult with the NLC in preparing a plan of management for the park, in
  order to ascertain the wishes and opinions of the traditional owners, and

- have due regard for the needs of traditional owners in their use of and movement through the park.

The agreement also required ANPWS supervising officers to live in the park. Annual rent was AU$7,502 (US$5,100) per annum. Because the traditional owners also received substantial royalties from the Ranger Uranium Mine, they were willing to accept this nominal rent for the park land.

The lease agreement was written in broad terms and made the NLC the principal contact for consultations with the traditional owners. At that time, the traditional owners had no formal local body to represent them, and the establishment of a board of management for the park was still some years away. Many felt the lease agreement did not give the Aboriginal people sufficient power over the decision-making process, but the system proved satisfactory for establishing the park and the needs of the early years thereafter.

In time, the original lease needed renegotiation to take into account evolving conditions in the park. Of particular significance were the incorporation of the Gagudju Association, whose members were the traditional owners; the huge expansion in the size of the park; the establishment of a board of management with an Aboriginal majority; the charging of park-use fees; and the increasing popularity of the park as a tourist destination. The original lease provided for a review of its provisions (except for the period of lease, which was set at one hundred years) every five years.

After the original Kakadu lease, the Aboriginal traditional owners of Gurig and Nitmiluk national parks negotiated leases with the Northern Territory government, and the traditional owners of Uluru-Katatjuta (Ayers Rock-Mount Olga) National Park negotiated a lease with the director of national parks and wildlife. In a sense, the terms and conditions of the new Kakadu lease have benefited from conservation agencies' experiences of these other lease arrangements.

The new Kakadu lease arrangements were negotiated over a number of years, from 1987 to 1990. The complex nature of the lease and proposed amendments were a major factor in the length of time required to finalize the amendments. The new lease arrangements also incorporated into the park areas granted to the Jabiluka Aboriginal Land Trust after the original lease had been signed. A further area of Kakadu (Stage 3, the last area to be added) is currently under an Aboriginal land claim. Negotiations have commenced between the director of national parks and wildlife and the Northern Land Council over proposed lease arrangements on behalf of the claimants if the claim is successful (see Map 6.1).

The new lease arrangements reflect a maturation of the relationship between the ANPWS (and, for that matter, the commonwealth government) and the Aboriginal traditional owners as represented by the Northern Land Council. The financial provisions now provide for an indexed annual rent based on AU$150,000 (US$102,000), plus 25 percent of income derived from Aboriginal land in the park (in effect, 25 percent of all park revenues). Income from this source is distributed to the Aboriginal traditional owners and their associations through the Northern

Map 6.1

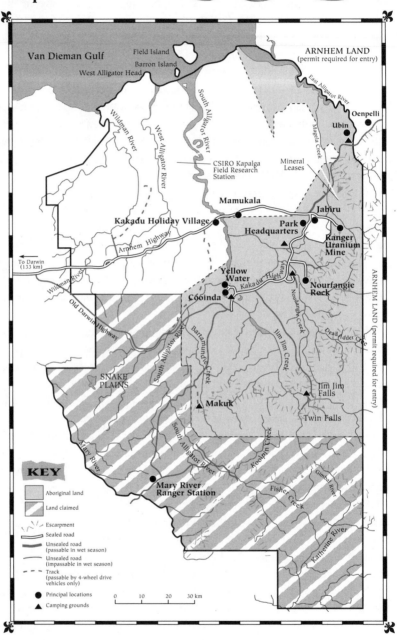

Kakadu National Park

Land Council. In the financial year ending in June 1992, payments to the Aboriginal traditional owners amounted to approximately AU$500,000 (US$340,000). The balance of the income derived from entry fees, licenses, and leases is available for the management of the park under a cost-sharing arrangement with the commonwealth government.

The new lease also requires the ANPWS to manage the park to the highest world standards. This reflects the commitment of the Aboriginal traditional owners to maintaining the park's natural and cultural heritage. The lease also provides for employment and training of Aboriginal people in all areas of park management.

A further provision of the new lease arrangements, which required much negotiation, involves termination of the lease if issues of detriment to the Aboriginal traditional owners can not be resolved. The lease provides detailed mechanisms for resolving conflict between the parties, and termination would occur only in extreme circumstances of complete breakdown of trust and cooperation.

Management Arrangements

The commonwealth government, in reaching its decision to establish Kakadu National Park, had stated that the park would be managed as though all of it were Aboriginal land, even if some areas had not been formally granted to Aboriginal people through the land-claim process. The lease provides the framework of ANPWS obligations to the Aboriginal traditional owners in Kakadu National Park, but the three major pillars of park management are the board of management, the plan of management, and day-to-day liaison with members of the Aboriginal community.

The Kakadu Board of Management, created in 1989, followed the lead of a board of management established under the National Parks and Wildlife Conservation Act in 1985 in Uluru-Katatjuta National Park. The Kakadu board comprises ten Aboriginal nominees (selected by the traditional owners), the director of national parks and wildlife, the regional ANPWS executive, an ecologist, and a person with expertise in tourism. The Aboriginal representation on the board reflects the geographic spread of Aboriginal people in the region, as well as the major language groupings.

The first task the Kakadu board took on was the writing of a new (third) plan of management for the park. As part of the process of developing this plan, the NLC established an Aboriginal consultative committee, just as it had for preparation of the second plan. The consultative committee consisted of representatives of all Aboriginal communities and groups in the park. Its task was to consult and advise on all aspects of the plan of management. Park staff and the board provided discussion papers and drafts of the plan to the consultative committee, and the board took cognizance of the committee's views in its actions. When it met to consider final amendments to the draft plan, the board had an extensive brief on public submissions, as well as the consultative committee's comments on the draft plan and proposed amendments.

The role of the board in the process of drawing up the plan was both as adviser to the drafters and final arbiter of the contents. The other major role of the board is to make decisions regarding the park that are consistent with the management plan. The board meets four times a year to fulfill this responsibility.

While the board provides the formal and ongoing expression of comanagement, the backbone of comanagement's success is embedded in the opportunities provided for direct involvement of Aboriginal people in day-to-day decision making and liaison. Specifically, Kakadu National Park's first ten years as a comanagement exercise can be measured by the successful negotiation of the new lease arrangements and the introduction of the Kakadu Board of Management. (The Third Plan of Management was completed at the end of 1991 and came into effect after approval by both houses of Parliament in April 1992.) The fact that mechanisms for involving Aboriginal traditional owners in the management of the park were put in place without the formal arrangements described above is testimony to the desire, in 1978, of all parties to make the Kakadu experiment work. Weaver's (1991) narrow, structuralist critique, in addition to being extremely outdated when published, also fails to appreciate fully the success of "informal" (i.e., nonstatutory) liaison arrangements in the early period of the park's history.

The maintenance of successful comanagement arrangements in the future also will depend on informal liaison arrangements, in addition to statutory and legal arrangements. These informal arrangements include, among other things, local meetings to discuss specific issues; the employment of (Aboriginal) cultural advisers to serve as a liaison between the ANPWS and the Aboriginal traditional owners; day-to-day working contact with the traditional owners; and the employment of increasing numbers of young Aboriginal people in all areas of park management. Success also will depend on the continuing commitment of the ANPWS, as well as the commonwealth government, to effective comanagement.

Evaluation of the Comanagement Process

The plan for Kakadu National Park easily could have failed because comanagement was a relatively new and untried concept, at least in Australian terms. There were no models to follow, and those involved in the project frequently had to improvise.

Interestingly, the controversy and conflicts that have surrounded Kakadu National Park since before its establishment may have contributed to the success of the initiative rather than worked against it. This is because the conflicts were not between the partners in the project—the ANPWS, the NLC, and the traditional owners—but rather lay in external factors that encouraged the partners to join together to deal with them, thus strengthening their relationship.

Although the Northern Territory government's constant attacks on the ANPWS and its role in Kakadu, on the NLC and its "manipulations" of traditional owners, and on the traditional owners themselves at times were somewhat debilitating, they also had the effect of hardening the resolve of the Kakadu partners. While all of the Aboriginal people living in the park did not hold the same views on many matters, the traditional owners and their representatives were consistent and strong in their support for the involvement of the ANPWS. The Northern Territory government, in choosing its line of action, appeared to ignore the traditional Aboriginal owners' publicly stated wish to work with the ANPWS and not a Northern Territory agency.

Despite (or possibly in part because of) this controversy, Kakadu National Park has survived and flourished. More important, it has been a beacon in guiding nervous and uncertain people and institutions toward a concept of comanagement of other protected areas in Australia. Had it failed in its early days, as some people hoped and others feared, the real involvement of Aboriginal people in the management of national parks and similar areas would have been set back by a decade or more.

The success of Kakadu National Park as a community-based conservation project is all the more remarkable because of the cross-cultural environment in which comanagement takes place. Aboriginal people have been willing to welcome and accept the involvement of non-Aboriginal people in the management of their "country," and the non-Aboriginal officers from ANPWS have been able to fit comfortably into this cross-cultural scenario.

Over the years, a number of incidents have strained the relationship between the Aboriginal people and the ANPWS. Some, involving the transfer of officers away from the park, have been serious. Others involved less tangible, longer-term issues such as the emphasis given to management of the natural and cultural resources of the park vis-à-vis management of tourism.

The feral water buffalo, introduced from Asia during the last century as a food and transport resource for early European settlers in northern Australia, provides an example of the types of stresses that can arise in comanagement. By the time Kakadu National Park was established, water buffalo had spread widely across northern Australia and multiplied enormously in the predator-free environment. They were the cause of serious environmental damage in the region and were also bearers of tuberculosis. Over the years, Aboriginal people living on the land had become dependent upon buffalo as a major source of protein.

Since 1979, when Stage 1 of the park was declared, the ANPWS has carried out an extensive program of buffalo eradication. The program has two objectives: to protect the park environment and meet the requirements of the government's Brucellosis and Tuberculosis Eradication Campaign. (The latter aims to eliminate brucellosis and tuberculosis from Australia in the interest of existing and future markets for the country's beef.) As buffalo numbers and density became substantially reduced, taking buffalo for consumption as either human or pet food became

uneconomical for commercial operators. Eradication shooting of buffalo from he-
licopters by park staff became the primary and almost only means of disposal.

As the density of buffalo diminished, the Aboriginal people's ability to obtain
buffalo meat from the park for their own consumption was adversely affected. This
created some tensions, ultimately resolved when the ANPWS and the traditional
owners agreed to establish a tested, disease-free herd of buffalo in a part of the
park that is not open to visitors. Strict environmental conditions were applied, and
the venture appears to be working well.

In another incident involving buffalo, during a routine helicopter shoot park
staff killed a number of pet buffalo, hand-raised by Aboriginal people, close to a
living area. The pet owners were incensed both by the killings and their proximity
to home, and relations between some traditional owners and some staff members
became seriously strained. The incident resulted in transfer of the personnel involved, both in their interest and because of concern for long-term relationships
in Kakadu.

Conservation and management of the park's cultural resources are additional
sources of tension. These cultural resources, considered to be of universal value,
generate much interest nationally and internationally among archeologists and
anthropologists who wish to carry out research in the area. The traditional owners
very strongly wish to keep control of their cultural resources and the intellectual
property associated with them. They are concerned about researchers who visit
the park briefly, collect materials, and remove them to laboratories elsewhere—
and do not return them. Generally, they are skeptical of research into Aboriginal
prehistory and believe that over the years researchers have benefited at the expense of Aboriginal people.

Two non-Aboriginal archeologists are employed in the park full-time to manage
the cultural-resource conservation program. Tensions arise in this area both because of the inherently sensitive nature of the program and because of personali-
ties, and issues have to be managed carefully. The current solution is for a group
of traditional Aboriginal owners to act as committee overseers (to whom the archeologists report regularly) of the program. Tensions have eased substantially
through this process, but the issues persist.

Another area of tension concerns allocation of resources to different aspects of
park management. The traditional owners, mindful of the needs of their country,
are concerned that too little of the park's human and financial resources is allocated to management of natural resources and too much is given over to management of tourism.

At an early stage, largely because of pressure from the traditional owners, the
ANPWS began putting very substantial resources into keeping the park clear of
the invasive weed *Mimosa pigra*, which has devastated large areas adjacent to the
park. The introduced water weed *Salvinia molesta* is a major threat to the park's
waterways, since it is well established in two catchments. Aboriginal people on oc-

casion have been critical of what they see as ANPWS's inadequate efforts to control *Salvinia.*

The current plan of management, reflecting the concerns of the Aboriginal people, places clear emphasis on management of Kakadu's natural resources. This emphasis is reflected in day-to-day operations and will begin to address Aboriginal concerns. Such actions, however, can not be expected to completely alleviate the tensions that competing demands on a finite budget always create.

The important thing about these incidents and issues is not that they occurred (which is inevitable), but that a process exists for discussing and resolving them while maintaining the relationship between the ANPWS and its Aboriginal partners. Relationships between the traditional Aboriginal owners and the non-Aboriginal staff of the ANPWS established in the early days and carefully fostered are, in many respects, the foundation upon which comanagement at Kakadu is based. Because of these relationships, which involve trust and mutual respect, significant issues can be worked through. In part, this is a result of ANPWS efforts over the years to recruit the "right" people to work in Kakadu. Even before the park was declared, recruitment of a small specialist team commenced the process. Each officer was selected specifically to work in Kakadu, and each had extensive direct experience in living and working with Aboriginal people.

Selection of these officers set a precedent for the future; to get a job in Kakadu now, applicants must demonstrate a capacity to work with and relate to Aboriginal people. The traditional owners are represented on all panels that select personnel for positions in Kakadu National Park. Nonetheless, despite the best intentions, this selection process has proven inadequate on several occasions, and remedial action has been necessary. The ANPWS (and the comanagement program) was fortunate to have as its first director a person who was fully committed and would not countenance any backsliding among his staff. This commitment was reflected in the attitudes of people specifically recruited to work in the program, who had a particular dedication to the ideal that the Aboriginal people should benefit from comanagement.

Benefits of Comanagement

The benefits of comanagement in Kakadu are concentrated in three areas: the Aboriginal community, nature conservation, and the economy. Besides receiving direct financial benefits through the lease arrangements, Aboriginal people also benefit from comanagement through a number of direct and indirect means. The mere existence of Kakadu as a national park is a major contribution to nature conservation, not only nationally but internationally. As a representative large regional conservation area, Kakadu has few rivals, even on the world stage. And the successful comanagement of Kakadu for tourism has had an important economic effect, felt throughout the region.

Community

The most obvious benefit Aboriginal people have derived from comanagement is access to traditional lands for cultural practices, including hunting and gathering. Related, although more intangible, are the social and spiritual benefits of owning, living on, and controlling traditional lands. The Aboriginal traditional owners see their deep and abiding commitment to "looking after country" as a continuous legacy for their children and grandchildren. The result of this commitment is not only an enhanced conservation estate but a parallel economic resource for the Aboriginal people.

The emphasis on Aboriginal interpretations of the park (e.g., the use of Aboriginal place names or Aboriginal interpretations of landscape, history, and culture) is an intangible element, but a benefit in which Aboriginal people place great emphasis and pride. This process also has a wider educational function, which leads to broader community understanding of Aboriginal culture and support for comanagement processes.

Employment of Aboriginal people in the ANPWS is a direct benefit. Of approximately sixty staff members, 35 percent are Aboriginal traditional owners or individuals who have close family ties to Kakadu. Aboriginal people are also employed in other agencies and businesses associated with Kakadu.

The resources available through the comanagement process for land-management initiatives in Kakadu are substantially greater than those available in other lands of the region. In addition, Aboriginal enterprises control, own, or partly own major tourism facilities in the park. And local Aboriginal organizations are currently developing additional tourism initiatives in the park.

The comanagement process addresses the issue of empowerment of Aboriginal people and organizations. Intertwined with all other issues, the social and political processes opened up by comanagement initiatives in Kakadu permeate the social fabric beyond the local community.

The park's non-Aboriginal community resides almost exclusively in the town of Jabiru, which is part of the park, or in ANPWS district ranger stations (see Map 6.1). Since Jabiru's founding in the early 1980s (to service Ranger Uranium Mine), it has established a limited role in regional tourism. With the downturn in the world's uranium market in the early 1990s, Ranger Uranium Mine shed many staff, and the population of Jabiru shrank by more than a third, to about nine hundred people. With the consequent downturn in the local economy, tension between the small business community of Jabiru and the ANPWS over the future direction of tourism has grown.

When local businesses have suggested that they or the town deserve preferential treatment in planning and initiatives, the ANPWS and the Kakadu Board of Management have tried to balance the long-term future of the park and the interests of the Aboriginal traditional owners against short-term economic advantage. As part of Kakadu National Park, Jabiru's development is subject to the park's plan of management. No major development can occur in Jabiru without the consent of the director of national parks and wildlife, and such developments must be provided for in the plan of management.

Nature Conservation

The ecological landscape that comprises Kakadu is substantially an artifact of extensive and prolonged Aboriginal use and occupation. The contribution of Aboriginal traditional knowledge to nature conservation is a most significant area of knowledge that has been pursued in comanagement of Kakadu National Park. Besides providing information on specific plants and animals, the Aboriginal traditional owners have been instrumental in providing understanding of ecological processes. The most obvious example is the study of fire management; another area currently under investigation is floodplain vegetation dynamics. Although marrying a "European" scientific paradigm with Aboriginal traditional knowledge is not a straightforward task, it is possible, and the benefits to conservation in maintaining the integrity and diversity of the ecosystem are potentially great (Reid et al. 1992).

The Aboriginal traditional owners' desire that their country be looked after properly is one other direct and tangible benefit of comanagement in nature conservation. The success of the Mimosa control program directly resulted from the Gagudju Association's efforts to convince the ANPWS that the program was both necessary and achievable. Kakadu National Park is now widely seen as a Mimosa-free island in a sea of the threatening weed.

Traditional owners also have been responsible for an emphasis on ecological restoration. For example, feral water buffalo had eroded and degraded some parts of the Kakadu floodplains, resulting in intrusion of tidal saltwater into freshwater habitats. The construction of small levees in these degraded areas has excluded saltwater, retained freshwater, rapidly ameliorated environmental damage, and returned floodplain vegetative associations (Skeat 1986).

Regional Economy

Kakadu National Park is the region's major drawing card for tourism and its biggest revenue earner after mining. Tourists visiting Kakadu spend an estimated AU$30 million (US$20.5 million) per annum in the region (Knapman, Stanley, and Lea 1991). Kakadu is also responsible indirectly for 6 percent of employment in Northern Territory (Knapman, Stanley, and Lea 1991). Clearly, Kakadu is an integral part of the Northern Territory economy, and investment of government funds in infrastructure and park-management programs is more than returned through direct and indirect revenues.

Issues in Comanagement

The greatest challenge for the future is to adequately address and reconcile the sometimes conflicting demands of tourists, Aboriginal culture, public-servants' work practices, and traditional conservation.

The Hidden Costs of Tourism

Tourism in the region is a double-edged sword, both for the Aboriginal traditional owners and the ANPWS. In 1982, tourists numbered around 40,000 per year; in 1992, some 220,000 people, who stayed an average of three or four days each, visited Kakadu.

With the increase in tourist numbers has come not only greater revenues from the trade but more pressure on natural and cultural sites in the park and intrusion into the life-style of the Aboriginal residents. Visitor pressure on particular natural sites in national parks is hardly a new issue. In this regard, Kakadu is little different from other popular national parks in Australia or around the world. Where it does differ is in the context of pressures on cultural sites and the impact visitors have on the traditional Aboriginal owners who are resident in the park.

In Kakadu, cultural sites are earlier manifestations of a culture that has flourished for more than fifty thousand years and is still alive and well today. The problem is that virtually the whole landscape of the park is a cultural site. While Aboriginal people generally welcome visitors to their land, visitors are not welcome in many culturally sensitive areas. No doubt Aboriginal residents believe that use of the park by visitors to a certain extent inhibits their own use of the land. Aboriginal people going about their own business generally avoid areas of the park where they are likely to meet visitors.

Very careful planning and consultation is needed to provide facilities for visitors that will enable them to better enjoy, appreciate, and understand the park. The selection of sites or areas to open up and development of particular facilities for visitors requires consideration not only of environmental but cultural sensitivities from the viewpoint of the Aboriginal people. During the board of management's deliberations in preparing the most recent plan of management, reconciliation of increased tourism with park-management objectives and the wishes and aspirations of the Aboriginal traditional owners was a major area of debate.

The current plan of management, in setting parameters for medium- and long-term park planning, addresses the issue of carrying capacity. Local strategies for popular areas of the park are being formulated. Within a few years, limits on the number of people allowed to visit sites at particular times are likely to be introduced. The next plan, due to take effect in 1997, most probably will cover a ten-year period. In this fourth plan, long-term tourism impacts and opportunities for tourism will be most important, particularly in the context of meeting Aboriginal concerns.

Other Costs of Comanagement

An aspect of comanagement that is hard to articulate or quantify is the "weight" of the bureaucratic process. Many Aboriginal people feel that the demands placed on them by the comanagement process, by cross-cultural issues, and the necessity of working "in European" are enormous. In seeking to ensure that it is managing the park in accord with the wishes of the traditional owners, the ANPWS has a mandate to consult almost constantly with Aboriginal people. Sometimes Aboriginal people are asked to attend meetings daily when particular issues need to be discussed, placing substantial strain on those involved. There is no simple solution to this predicament, since the consultations are necessary if the ANPWS is to meet its commitment to the traditional owners.

Another issue is how to reconcile Aboriginal employment with social and cultural requirements. The standard public-service conditions under which ANPWS officers are employed were not developed with Aboriginal cultural requirements in mind. Fortunately, the ANPWS has a limited amount of flexibility to modify these conditions to better meet the concerns, responsibilities, and requirements of its Aboriginal employees. The ANPWS has introduced systems that are sympathetic to the needs of its Aboriginal staff to be absent at short or no notice for Aboriginal "business." The ANPWS also seeks to maximize opportunities for Aboriginal people to work under contract—for instance, when the requirement is provision of a particular service. In this way, the ANPWS could contract the Gagudju Association, which could then employ Aboriginal people to carry out the work. Aboriginal people then choose how, when, and for how long they provide their labor. This system provides the needed flexibility, together with maximum employment opportunities for Aboriginal people in the park.

Conclusion

If a cross-cultural community-based conservation initiative such as comanagement of Kakadu National Park is to be effective and beneficial to both the community and nature conservation, a few fundamental elements are required.

First of all, comanagement needs to be clearly defined, since the term may mean different things to different people. The expectations of each party need not necessarily be identical, but each party must understand, appreciate, and, more important, respect the other's viewpoint.

Second, commitment to the success of the project is critical in any cross-cultural situation in which complex and sensitive problems not normally experienced in more common conservation programs often arise. This is particularly so in the case of the managing agency (e.g., the ANPWS in Kakadu), where commitment must come from the very top of the organization.

Third, the management agency must take particular care to select the right people for each job. Special qualities are required in nonindigenous or nonlocal staff employed to work in such a cross-cultural environment. No matter how good the legislative and administrative arrangements are, the right people are needed to implement them. As staff numbers increase, long-serving staff members move on to other areas, and on-the-ground management requirements become more and more onerous, maintaining the same level of commitment often becomes harder. However, exercising great care in staff selection can reduce the problem. Staff working in Kakadu, for instance, see themselves as privileged, and competition for such opportunities is very strong. This acts as an added incentive for the staff to maintain its level of commitment.

Finally, empowerment of indigenous or local people through legal ownership of some or all of the land involved and ensuring that they have the principal role in the decision-making process (for example, through a majority on the board of management) is vitally important. It is also important for the landowning group to be meaningfully involved through direct employment, extensive consultation, and solicitation of their advice on management issues. In employing local or indigenous landowners, it is important to recognize the social and cultural impacts of normal government-employment conditions and seek to alleviate them through innovative employment arrangements.

Clearly, a successful venture of this nature has many other requirements, including effective legislation and adequate resources. But no matter how abundant the resources or how effective the legislation, the project has no chance of fulfilling its potential without attending to these four essential elements.

Australia presents opportunities for other projects similar to Kakadu. The prognosis looks good as virtually all the states move toward greater involvement of Aboriginal people in nature conservation, specifically in variations on the theme of comanagement. A recent decision of the High Court of Australia (*Mabo v. Queensland* 1992), which overturned the long-held view of *terra nullius* and established a new concept of native title, will provide impetus for the expansion of comanagement projects throughout the country.

Arrangements adapted and refined to suit particular situations are perhaps the strongest need. Arrangements that worked at Kakadu, Uluru, Gurig, or Nitmiluk may not successfully transfer directly into other situations, but they make good models upon which to draw when developing the most appropriate arrangements for a particular area.

SOURCES

ANPWS, and DASETT. 1991. "Nomination of Kakadu National Park by the Government of Australia for Inscription in The World Heritage List." Report prepared by the Australian National Parks and Wildlife Service (ANPWS), Canberra, and the Department of the Arts, Sport, the Environment, Tourism and Territories (DASETT), Canberra. Photocopy.

Brockwell, C. J. 1989. "Archaeological Investigations of the Kakadu Wetlands, Northern Australia." Master's thesis, Australian National University, Canberra.

Chaloupka, G. 1983. "Kakadu Rock Art: Its Cultural, Historic and Prehistoric Significance." In *The Rock Art Sites of Kakadu National Park: Some Preliminary Findings for Their Conservation and Management*, ed. D. Gillespie, 1–33. Special Publication 10, Canberra: Australian National Parks and Wildlife Service.

Commonwealth of Australia (COA). 1974. Environment Protection (Impact of Proposals) Act 1974 (No. 164).

———. 1975. National Parks and Wildlife Conservation Act 1975 (No. 12).

————. 1976. Aboriginal Land Rights (Northern Territory) Act 1976 (No. 191).

Fox, R. W., G. G. Kelleher, and C. B. Kerr. 1977. *Ranger Uranium Environmental Inquiry Second Report.* Canberra: Australian Government Publishing Service.

Hallam, S. J. 1975. *Fire and Health: A Study of Aboriginal Usage and European Usurpation in South-western Australia.* Canberra: Australian Institute of Aboriginal Studies.

Knapman, B., O. Stanley, and J. Lea. 1991. *Tourism and Gold in Kakadu: The Impact of Current and Potential Natural Resources Use on the Northern Territory Economy.* Darwin: North Australia Research Unit.

Mabo v. Queensland. 1992. *Australian Law Journal Reports* 66: 408.

Reid, J., L. Baker, S. R. Morton, and Mutitjulu Community. 1992. "Traditional Knowledge + Ecological Survey = Better Land Management." *Search* 23: 249–251.

Roberts, R. G., R. Jones, and M. A. Smith. 1990. "Thermoluminescence Dating of a 50,000 Year Old Human Occupation Site in Northern Australia." *Nature* 345:153–156.

Russell-Smith, J., D. E. Lucas, J. Brock, and D. M. J. S. Bowman. 1993. *"Allosyncarpia* Dominated Rainforest in Monsoonal Northern Australia." *Journal of Vegetation Science* 4:67–82.

Skeat, A. J. 1986. "Wetland Management—Kakadu National Park." *Australian Journal of Environmental Education* 2:17–20.

Sullivan, H. 1990. "Kakadu Past and Present." In *A Sense of Place: Proceedings of a Workshop,* 7–14. Australian Heritage Commission Technical Publication Series, No. 1. Canberra: Australian Government Publishing Service.

Weaver, S. M. 1991. "The Role of Aboriginals in the Management of Australia's Cobourg (Gurig) and Kakadu National Parks." In *Resident Peoples and National Parks: Social Dilemmas and Strategies in International Conservation,* ed. P. C. Welt and S. R. Brechin, 331–333. Tucson: University of Arizona Press.

Woodward, A. E. 1973. *Aboriginal Land Rights Commission, First Report.* Parliamentary Paper No. 138 of 1973. Canberra: Government Printer of Australia.

PART II

Case Study Profiles

CHAPTER 7

The Zimbabwe Communal Areas Management Programme for Indigenous Resources (CAMPFIRE)

Simon Metcalfe

> To sum up, wildlife once fed us and shaped our culture. It still yields us
> pleasure for leisure hours, but we try to reap that pleasure by modern
> machinery and thus destroy part of its value. Reaping it by modern
> mentality would yield not only pleasure, but wisdom as well.
> —Aldo Leopold, *A Sand County Almanac* (1949:222)

Land resources in Zimbabwe today are governed by three overarching tenure systems: state, communal, and private. Before the beginning of the colonial era in 1890, all land was held communally, but today, both the communal and private sectors are subordinate to government regulations. Decision-making arrangements for the management of wildlife on private land have, for the last twenty years, involved an effective comanagement balance between private and public property interests, governed by statutory rules and regulations. With communal landholders, the case is somewhat different, since the state legally owns the land and manages it through line agencies, each responsible for its own sector (for example, the agriculture and environment ministries, forestry commission, and departments of national parks, wildlife, and natural resources, etc.), in coordination with the ministry responsible for local government. Although applicable to both private and communal lands, comanagement was adopted soonest on private commercial lands. The need for an appropriate synthesis of old, present, and emerging forms of social organization required to manage community resources effectively is a driving force in the country's ongoing search for land-use solutions.

In the late 1960s, Zimbabwe's Department of National Parks and Wild Life Management (National Parks) reviewed the country's wildlife policy. The result was a radical shift in direction. The old protectionist approach had been instituted at the turn of the century and reflected the country's colonial legacy. A strategy of linking protected areas with sustained utilization of wildlife on communal and commercial land ultimately replaced this protectionism.

Map 7.1

Zimbabwe/Zambezi Valley Area
Administrative District and
Provincial Boundaries

KEY

–·–·– International Boundary

– – – Provincial Boundary

- - - - - District Boundary

··········· Boundary of Zambezi
Valley Area

Major Land Use Areas

Communal Land

Forest Land

National Park

Safari Area

Other Lands

The impetus for this transformation of wildlife policy came from Fulbright scholars Thane Riney, Raymond Dasmann, and Archie Mossman in the early 1960s (Cumming 1990b; Dasmann and Mossman 1961; Mossman 1963). As long as wildlife remained the property of the state, the three posited, no one would invest in it as a resource. As a result, on commercial and communal rangeland, management efforts went into domestic livestock rather than wildlife; protected wildlife areas were in danger of becoming isolated and vulnerable ecosystems. The scholars' thinking on these matters provided the rationale for the 1975 Parks and Wildlife Act (GOZ 1975). The impact of this innovative legislation is apparent today in Zimbabwe's thriving wildlife industry on private land and, increasingly, on communal lands as well.

The Communal Areas Management Programme for Indigenous Resources (CAMPFIRE) was established to facilitate implementation of comanagement policies on communal lands. Conceptually, CAMPFIRE includes all natural resources, but its current focus is communal wildlife management in about a quarter of the country's fifty-five districts. CAMPFIRE is most active where substantial wildlife populations exist.

The Evolution of CAMPFIRE

The colonial powers virtually everywhere in Africa neglected the potential of indigenous resources. Colonists who concentrated their efforts on crops and livestock from Europe saw little need to learn from the indigenous people. After an initial exploitation phase, Africa's wildlife came to be regarded as recreational goods (Crosby 1986). European colonists also favored state and private-property systems rather than indigenous systems of communal resource management. In consequence, indigenous resources were formally made state property and managed by wildlife and forestry departments.

Encouraging people to see wildlife productively had both an ecological and an economic purpose. The 1975 act primarily aimed to give private commercial ranchers an economic rationale for conservation by promoting wildlife utilization on their land. Half of the Zambezi Valley, for example, had protected status, while the rest remained communal. Until recently, the incidence of bovine trypanosomiasis, carried by the tsetse fly (*Glossina* spp.), limited cattle grazing in the Zambezi Valley. Wildlife obviously thrived everywhere in the entire area, but on communal land, its existence was threatened because wild animals lacked utility for local farmers. Through tsetse-control programs, wildlife habitat in half the valley came under direct threat of land uses planned by government departments other than National Parks. (Thus CAMPFIRE, which grew out of the Parks and Wildlife Act, is also an attempt to create a social link with its economic and ecological objectives.)

Unlike most African countries in the 1960s and 1970s, Zimbabwe's national parks had a substantial base of applied research and a management arm capable of implementing plans. Underpinning the comanagement ideal was the research arm of National Parks, the Branch of Terrestrial Ecology, with its strong core of motivated and innovative ecologists (Graham Child, David Cumming, Rowan Martin, Russell Taylor, et al.). National Parks also had considerable management capability in its wardens and rangers. They were able to capture, translocate, and cull large herbivores as necessary.

CAMPFIRE was preceded by several abortive attempts to apply the new wildlife policy on communal lands. One of National Parks' first experiments, begun in the late 1970s, was the Sebungwe Regional Plan for the mid-Zambezi. National Parks teamed up with the Department of Physical Planning (Ministry of Local Government) and the Ministry of Finance to introduce the plan. Its basis was a progressive resource-management approach rooted in community participation and set within a broad-reaching strategic land-use plan. After Independence, the University of Zimbabwe's Department of Land Management and Centre for Applied Social Sciences (CASS) also became involved in the Sebungwe Plan. Unfortunately, the plan foundered because of inadequate interministerial coordination and lack of commitment from the Treasury.

A second pre-CAMPFIRE effort, known as Operation Windfall, sought to link elephant culling to local communities in northern Gokwe. Windfall collapsed as a result of its failure to establish sufficiently direct linkage between resources and incentives for community-based conservation practice.

A third attempt followed during the mid-1980s, when Clive Stockil, a naturalist, rancher, and professional hunter, contacted the Shangaan people living in the Mahenya community on the eastern boundary of Gona re Zhou National Park. Stockil attempted to facilitate an ad hoc comanagement agreement between National Parks and the Mahenya community of Chipinge District. He discovered that the mechanism by which wildlife revenues were supposed to be returned from the Treasury was too cumbersome and delayed, and therefore was an ineffective conservation incentive for the community. Instead, trophy-hunting revenues went to Treasury and remained there. Implementation of the resulting proto-CAMPFIRE Mahenya Project was delayed by the need to obtain "appropriate authority" for the Chipinge District Council. (While a private landowner can claim ownership over wildlife as a result of his land title, a community living on communal land, in contrast, only has statutory rights to use wildlife, land, or other natural resources when it has been constituted as part of a local authority—i.e., granted appropriate authority by the government.)

During the mid-1980s, drafts of the CAMPFIRE concept document, revised by Rowan Martin (National Parks), Marshall Murphree (CASS), and Norman Reynolds (Ministry of Finance), began to circulate (Martin 1986). The concept gained advocates, and in 1987, *The National Conservation Strategy: Zimbabwe's Road to Survival*, the proceedings of the first conference on Zimbabwe's National

Conservation Strategy, recommended adopting "a model along the lines developed in the CAMPFIRE programme, grazing schemes, and similar community based projects" (MNRT 1987:23).

CAMPFIRE did not initially begin working with community-based natural resources cooperatives. The Parks and Wildlife Act of 1975 only allowed for statutory authority over resources to devolve from the state to local authorities (in the form of a representative district council), not directly to communities—a very significant distinction. Further, without Treasury support, National Parks lacked the resources to launch a national program. For some time, CAMPFIRE remained an unimplemented concept.

Between 1981 and 1987, I worked in the mid-Zambezi Valley districts of Binga and Kariba (Nyaminyami) on rural development projects. As the field director of the British Save the Children Fund, a primary-health-care NGO, I sat in on a Sebungwe Plan workshop at Binga. From my perspective, the development challenge in the region was to ameliorate the chronically poor nutritional status of children. That the area had considerable protein and revenue resources in the form of terrestrial and aquatic wildlife but routinely imported food aid to make up for a local grain deficit was most ironic. I became driven by a vision in which the Tonga people's dependence on food aid, and their alienation from their environment, would be transformed into a culturally and biologically rich and sustainable future.

In 1985, I advocated a CAMPFIRE-style approach to the problem with the Nyaminyami District Council. I contrasted the small development investment coordinated by the council with the massive regional program aimed at eradicating the tsetse fly. The council meeting held in October 1985, supported by Russell Taylor of National Parks, resulted in the formation of an "institution, to be called the Nyaminyami Wildlife Management Trust, which would serve as the governing body to establish and implement a district-wide programme for the rational exploitation of the wildlife resources of Nyaminyami and the reinvestment of proceeds in the district" (NDC 1985:1; 1987:8). In June 1986, the Nyaminyami District Council organized a development conference to evaluate the district's progress since the country's independence in 1980. That conference brought together individuals involved with the CAMPFIRE concept (Norman and Pamela Reynolds, Marshall Murphree, Russell Taylor, Colleen Cousins, Julian Sturgeon), district workers, and local communities. The CAMPFIRE message captured the imaginations of participants in the Nyaminyami Development Conference and played a substantial role in preparing the district for a development future based on natural resources management.

When the steering committee finished its work, the newly created Nyaminyami Wildlife Management Trust's board of management asked if I would act as interim general manager to get the program under way. I agreed, still holding a romantic vision of both liberating poverty-stricken people and conserving wild habitat. I joined the NGO Zimbabwe Trust (ZimTrust) in 1988 to work with districts and communities; Rob Monro, general secretary of ZimTrust, obtained support from donors and coordinated interaction with government agencies.

I spent most of 1988 working in Nyaminyami District and liaising with National Parks. At the time, the central issue was when and how, under the 1975 act, the Nyaminyami District Council or its wildlife trust could be granted appropriate authority to manage its wildlife and receive benefits from an already existing safari operation. Despite National Parks' commitment to CAMPFIRE, the department seemed reluctant to actually grant the authority. National Parks thought it had greater control of the process and was still hoping for Treasury support. Also, National Parks had not yet reached an understanding with the Ministry of Local Government, which ruled the communal lands through the embryonic district councils established at Independence.

ZimTrust finally forced the issue by arranging for the question to be raised in Parliament. National Parks feared that devolution of authority to the local councils might result in power simply being recentralized under the control of the Ministry of Local Government. (In colonial times, the Ministry of Local Government was known colloquially as "the government within a government" because of its hegemony over all the tribal trust lands, now called communal areas.) Lacking the financial capacity to implement CAMPFIRE and fearing loss of control to a rival ministry, National Parks increasingly lent support for implementation to ZimTrust.

This began a mutual relationship that brought ZimTrust alongside National Parks and CASS as CAMPFIRE institutional players. A little later, the World Wide Fund for Nature (WWF—now the World Wildlife Fund) Multispecies Animal Production Systems Project, guided by two former members of the National Parks' Branch of Terrestrial Ecology, David Cumming and Russell Taylor, became involved in what was to become known as the CAMPFIRE Collaborative Group (CASS/WWF/ZimTrust 1989). Thus CAMPFIRE, in its formative stages, had input from ecologists, economists, and sociologists. While its implementation depended on rural development practitioners, institutionally it was launched by a mix of government agencies, NGOs, and the university.

Despite the CAMPFIRE document's carefully laid out plan, the devolution of authority is what actually set CAMPFIRE in motion as a new policy. Programmatically, CAMPFIRE began in 1989 with a de facto granting of authority over wildlife to the local authorities in Nyaminyami and Guruve districts. De jure gazetting of appropriate authority did not take place until 1990, when National Parks finally negotiated an understanding on CAMPFIRE with the Ministry of Local Government.

The backgrounds of Nyaminyami and Guruve's projects and preparation of subsequent CAMPFIRE projects were quite different. This variety meant that CAMPFIRE was perceived from the beginning as an adaptive management experiment within a specific conceptual and policy framework. The adaptive approach required establishing limited and achievable objectives and approaches. Monitoring the implementation process cleared the way for modifications to be made when necessary. CAMPFIRE's concern with resource tenure issues was linked to broad issues of representation, economic participation, and communal area governance. CAMPFIRE's programmatic environment is as concerned with complex questions regarding the nature of rural communities and collective decision making as it is with the technical challenges of sustainable use of wildlife.

Appropriate authority was granted when a district council's intentions and capacity to use the authority to wisely manage natural resources were deemed adequate by National Parks. Over time, the "intent" criteria translated into the councils' acceptance of the CAMPFIRE principles and National Parks' guidelines for quota setting and distribution of benefits. The "capacity" criteria have remained moot, as few districts have had much experience. With hindsight, the devolution of authority has been an essential part of a capacity-building learning process. National Parks requires an annual report from each authority and takes seriously any quota violations or deviations from the guidelines on revenue distribution. While it can, in principle, remove a district's authority, National Parks is naturally very reluctant to do this. Oversight, therefore, mainly proceeds openly and cooperatively.

The devolution of rights of access to wildlife resources placed CAMPFIRE in the middle of the ongoing land-use-and-rural-development debate in Zimbabwe. From their previous peripheral roles, wildlife and National Parks have now moved to the center of the tenure and planning-policy arena in strategic land-use areas. Although communally based wildlife often was situated in districts adjacent to protected areas, CAMPFIRE was never promoted as a way of creating buffer zones but as a rural development program within which wildlife utilization could be a substantial or complementary land use.

At first, only a handful of people were involved directly in the CAMPFIRE concept. By 1989, National Parks' main actor was its assistant director for research, Rowan Martin, supported by the director, William Nduku, and deputy director, George Pangeti. Professor Murphree, at that stage, had a fairly singular vigil over a small group of graduate students in CASS. David Cumming and Russell Taylor had moved from National Parks to set up the WWF Multispecies Project, while Rob Monro and myself, both from ZimTrust, took the program to the districts.

During 1989, I arranged three provincial workshops to promote CAMPFIRE in other districts. The combination of the policy, the district leadership, and the individuals involved proved very successful. By 1990, another ten districts had been granted appropriate authority, making CAMPFIRE active in twelve of fifty-five districts in the country. The districts responded positively because CAMPFIRE promised both local control over resources and a new source of rural revenue.

In mid-1989, participants in CAMPFIRE heard about the proposed international ban on trade in ivory products, which threatened the very core of the program (Zimbabwe Trust 1989). To rally a communal response to the ivory ban, the

CAMPFIRE Association of Wildlife Producing Communal Areas was created. During 1990, I handed over management duties in Nyaminyami to Elliot Nobula and took up the role of interim manager of the association. In 1991, I passed that role to the present incumbent, Tapfuma Maveneke, and in late 1992 joined CASS, with the support of ZimTrust, to analyze how CAMPFIRE has evolved.

The Cultural Context

The main story of CAMPFIRE is about the communities themselves rather than about those who assisted, although the two are related. An underemphasized aspect of CAMPFIRE concerns the diversity of cultures and customs of the people involved. The indigenous people of Zimbabwe are predominantly Shona. The Ndebele constitute another substantial group. Overlaid on these traditional cultures is an anglophone and pioneer "settler" cultural influence.

The Shona have a strong regional clan structure, with the Zezuru clan in the middle of the highveld around Harare, the Manyika in the east, the Karanga in the south, and the Korekore in the northeast. Of these groups, CAMPFIRE mainly involves the Korekore clan in the eastern Zambezi Valley. The Korekore are pejoratively characterized by other Shona as more rustic, less formally educated, and therefore less prominent in government elites than the other clans. Perhaps in part because of their remoteness, the Korekore are still very traditional in customs. The roles of chiefs and spirit mediums remain very important in land matters.

The Ndebele people have great cultural and political influence in western Zimbabwe, known as North and South Matabeleland and centered on Bulawayo. Development in this region in the last decade has been beset by conflict between Ndebele people and state authorities. Regionalism appears as an underlying and recurrent theme, with threatening undertones of potential conflict.

Under the hegemonic influence of the Shona and the Ndebele are several other small ethnic groups. Despite their lack of political power, these groups figure substantially in CAMPFIRE because of their strategic location on land that is poor for agriculture but good for wildlife. One of the most substantial cultural minorities are the Tonga, who live in the mid-Zambezi Valley districts of Binga, Kariba, and northern Gokwe. The eighty thousand Tonga of Binga District would prefer far more contact with the majority of their group, who now live in Zambia north of the Zambezi with a manmade lake and an international boundary as barriers. The Tonga in Zimbabwe are caught culturally and politically between regionally based Ndebele and Shona interests (ZAPU and ZANU). The few Tonga of Kariba District (Nyaminyami Council), separated from Binga, where 75 percent of Zimbabwe Tonga reside, fall more clearly under a Shona cultural and political mindset.

In Beitbridge District, in the south on the Limpopo River, the dominant customary influence is Venda. Beitbridge is also wedged between Shona and Ndebele political and customary influences. The Shangaan live east of Beitbridge and around the Gona re Zhou National Park. The Shangaan have cultural continuity with people in Mozambique and South Africa, while the majority of Venda people live in South Africa.

This brief social and cultural portrait indicates the complexity of planning and managing biological and cultural resources within the framework of national sovereignty and cultural diversity. Realities of political and economic power continually impact upon institutions that try to provide discrete and legitimate authority over natural resources or impart any sense of indigenous rural community.

CAMPFIRE's Conservation Setting

The role of communal lands and the development options that resulted in the evolution of the CAMPFIRE program were strongly affected by ecological conditions. Zimbabwe is a landlocked country of some 390,000 km². Most of this land is part of the Southern African biotic zone known as Southern Savanna Woodland. Although well within the tropics, the climate is generally subtropical because of high altitude. One-fifth of the country lies above 1,200 m and three-fifths between 600 and 1,200 m.

Zimbabwe has been classified into five agroecological regions based on rainfall reliability and soil characteristics (see Map 7.2 and Table 7.1). Regions I and II have good potential for production of crops and livestock. Region III is suitable for semi-intensive agriculture; it experiences annual rainfall of 650 to 800 mm but is subject to periodic seasonal droughts. The rainfall in Region IV is too low and unreliable for agriculture, except in a few localities where drought-resistant crops produce at subsistence level. Appropriate systems in Region IV are therefore based on livestock ranching and the wildlife utilization that is the focus of the CAMPFIRE program. Region V includes the hot, dry areas below 900 m in altitude and covers the lower reaches of the Save-Limpopo system in the south of the country and the Zambezi Valley below the escarpment in the north.

Rainfall in the Save-Limpopo system is the lowest and least reliable (450 mm) in the country. The area is typically used as communal or commercial ranchland. The Zambezi system has slightly better rainfall (600 mm), but tsetse fly infestation has precluded cattle ranching in the past. Apart from pockets of alluvial soils, agriculture is extremely risky, and farming should be based entirely on utilization of the natural veld. Extensive cattle or game ranching is the only sound farming system for this region. The Save River is extensively silted, a symptom of massive soil erosion in the catchment area. This is a consequence of overgrazing and inadequate conservation practices among the communal people whose areas are densely populated.

The communal areas represent 42 percent of the total land area of 390,760 km² and have a total population of 5 million people. More than 90 percent of communal lands are located within the less productive regions III, IV, and V, and 76

Map 7.2

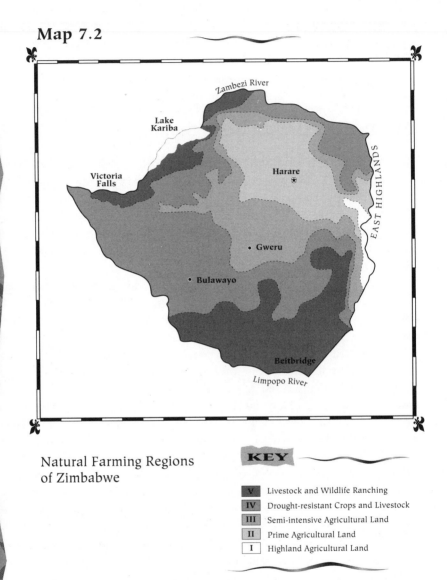

Natural Farming Regions
of Zimbabwe

KEY

V	Livestock and Wildlife Ranching
IV	Drought-resistant Crops and Livestock
III	Semi-intensive Agricultural Land
II	Prime Agricultural Land
I	Highland Agricultural Land

percent of the rural population lives within them (see Table 7.1). The majority of the population was dispersed in these marginal areas through the divisive land legislation introduced by the colonial administration (Thomas 1982).

There is an obvious relationship between natural regions and their human carrying capacity, with poorer soils and rainfall areas being more arid and capable of supporting only extensive rangeland use, since they are not reliable cropping areas. In addition, there is a stark contrast between the southern and western semiarid areas of Zimbabwe and the Zambezi Valley in the north. The Zambezi Valley provides extensive wildlife habitat with a low human population density. Control of the tsetse fly threatens to change that scenario and make the national parks islands in a sea of development. This threat, as much as anything else, was a major impetus for the policy that allows wildlife to be an agricultural land-use option.

The surface area of Zimbabwe is apportioned as shown in Map 7.3 and Table 7.2. The parks and wildlife estate includes 12 percent of Zimbabwe, half of which is comprised of safari areas (fifteen) where recreational hunting occurs for a fee set by market prices. Approximately 10 percent of communal land has sufficient large wild animals to support huntable populations. Game is run on 20 percent of commercial farmland in Zimbabwe. As the western state forest land is also under wildlife land use, more than 30 percent of Zimbabwe provides multispecies wildlife habitat. Both communal and protected land occur predominantly in regions where rainfall is too low and unreliable for agriculture. With 83 percent of the country's land area and 91 percent of communal land classified as semi-intensive to extensive grazing zones, Zimbabwe has a finite and fragile resource base (Cumming 1990a).

Zimbabwe's population will exceed its total production capacity by the year 2030, when the present population of 10 million will have grown to nearly 30 million. Of the 3.2 million ha presently under cultivation in Zimbabwe, a considerable proportion is in areas either regarded as unsuitable for the crops being grown or unsuitable for any cultivation.

In the communal half of the Zambezi Valley where the initial CAMPFIRE experiments began, the forced exclusion of cattle combined with low human population densities has meant low human impact on the environment. This contributes, along with the protected areas, to a favorable environment for wildlife, if not for humans. Migration of people and cattle into these northern districts, with resulting fragmentation and compression of wildlife habitats, is now the most pressing management problem. In the southwest of the country, the grassland in communal lands is extensively grazed, and the resilience of perennial grasses is threatened. Still, real possibilities for multispecies livestock production systems including both wildlife and cattle do exist on sparsely settled communal land near state-protected areas and private game-ranch areas.

Map 7.3

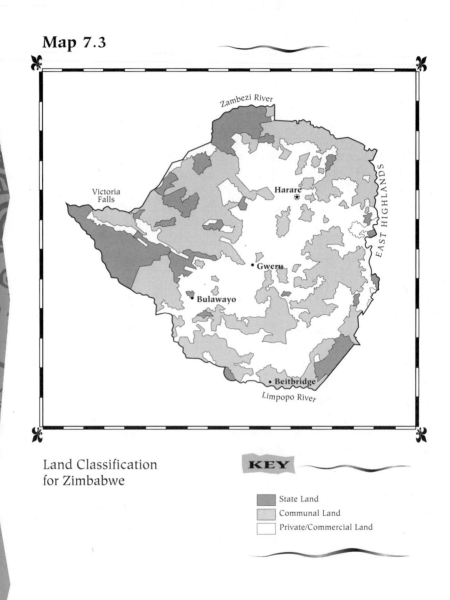

Zambezi River

Victoria
Falls

Harare ✪

EAST HIGHLANDS

• Gweru

• Bulawayo

• Beitbridge

Limpopo River

Land Classification
for Zimbabwe

KEY

▨ State Land
▨ Communal Land
☐ Private/Commercial Land

Table 7.1

Communal land distribution and population density by natural region

Natural Region	I	II	III	IV	V	Total
% Total Land Area	1.8	15.0	18.7	37.8	26.7	100.0
% Total Communal Land	0.3	3.7	7.2	19.9	10.8	41.9
Population Density (people/km^2)	99.5	60.0	46.5	18.11	2.5	25.5
Area as % of Total Communal Land Area	0.6	8.8	16.5	47.7	26.4	100.0

Table 7.2

National land allocation

Land-use Category	Proprietary System	Area (km^2)	% of Total Area
Communal Land	Communal	163,500	41.8
Resettlement Land	State/Common	26,400	6.7
Commercial Farming Land	Private	142,400	36.4
National Parks Estate	State	47,000	12.1
State Forest Land	State	9,200	2.4
Urban and State Land	Private/State	2,200	0.6

Implementation of CAMPFIRE

Short sketches of Nyaminyami and Guruve, and brief insights from Beitbridge and Hurungwe, provide a comparative context for CAMPFIRE. Each district in CAMP-FIRE, and the several communities, wards, and villages within each district, has had its own subjective experiences. Table 7.3 gives a comparative account of CAMPFIRE districts' financial performance in 1991, with a brief analytical comment on the distribution of benefits and the problems encountered.

Nyaminyami District

From the time of the creation of Nyaminyami's Wildlife Management Trust there was disparity between the council's and the National Parks' intent concerning the roles of local government and members of the community. The Ministry of Local Government argued for a locally based trust. The district council would dominate its policy board but be linked in turn to the ward and village development committees, known as Wadcos and Vidcos (NDC 1985). Thus the council desired a local quasi-government agency while, in contrast, National Parks desired a producer-based, group shareholder approach.

The issue of membership or participation in the Nyaminyami Trust divided the steering committee. The local government representatives (councillors) were a united majority, while National Parks, CASS, and the CAMPFIRE-supporting NGOs were in opposition. Finally, two constitutions were proposed: one with representation of the people through their councillors and another based on open membership with direct community representation. National Parks and the NGOs, who feared that the closed membership of councillors would ally the trust too closely to a paternalistic council, were overruled. At this point, Nyaminyami had only four years' experience with a democratic local authority, and the Ministry of Local Government felt that all activities within the district should reinforce the council rather than dilute its powers with the introduction of new institutions. In the end, Nyaminyami launched its own model of CAMPFIRE, one in which the district leadership defined what the district needed rather than allowing for a more market-oriented, community-level, production-based approach:

> The idea was that the Trust would act on behalf of the people . . . and that the flow of information and ideas from district level to the village level and vice versa would occur through the existing political and developmental structures of Wadco and Vidco. It was felt that contrary to widespread belief, the Vidco and Wadco structure was created not only for political but also for economic and developmental issues and that it would serve the purpose of mobilizing and engaging the mass of the people in economic and development projects. (NWMT 1990:11)

Table 7.3

Allocation of CAMPFIRE benefits: comparative district performance (1991)

District (CAMPFIRE Wards) (Wildlife Area, km²)	Population	Gross Revenue (US$)	Comments
1. Nyaminyami	30,000	190,000	Wards treated equally. Most decisons made at district level. Little identification between ward benefits and wildlife resource. Little expertise to implement ward projects. Poaching and immigration a threat.
2. Guruve	16,000	212,000	Only three wards that have active wildlife committees have good resources. Little expertise to implement ward projects. Poaching and immigration a threat.
3. Binga	37,000	79,000	Wards now receiving differential benefits. Wildlife committees formed. Little expertise to implement ward projects. Poaching and immigration a threat.
4. Gokwe	35,000	120,000	Wards receive differential benefits. WWCs formed. Household dividends offered. Immigration and poaching a threat.
5. Hwange	28,500	0	Lack of revenue a problem. Local regional land-use planning with state lands needed and tourist opportunities need development.
6. Tsholotsho	30,000	113,000	Ward dividends offered but management capacity of revenue needs development. Dependent on elephant revenue and suffers from lack of wildlife diversity. Range management needed to integrate with CAMPFIRE
7. Bulilima Mangwe	30,000	42,000	Equal benefits to ward. High amount of institutional development input to wards reflected in community-based resource management planning. Rangeland management for livestock necessary.
8. Beitbridge	18,000	34,000	Benefits distributed to wards, villages, and households with wildlife. Good linkage between costs and benefits. Positive council and executive staff support of village-based integrated resource management.
9. Gaza Khomenani	41,000	97,000	District-level control. Wards treated equally and benefits invested in district development plan and implemented at district level. Lack of community participation in resource management.
10. Gazaland	2,400	23,000	Ward-level project. Close collaboration between safari operator and community. Ward has choice over use of benefits and community-based management is developing.
11. Muzarabani	24,000	6,000	Revenue based on nonconsumptive protected area within communal land. Buffer communities need greater identification with project. Little connection between costs and benefits or appreciation of conservation goal.
12. Hurungwe	30,000	72,000 118,000	Revenue from first year spent on council lorry. Second-year dividends to villages and households.

Nyaminyami has a major wildlife resource including a population of 2,500 elephants, 7,000 Cape buffalo, and 30,000 impala, among other species. Utilization has been based on two substantial hunting concessions (see Tables 7.4 and 7.5), a cropping quota for 1,500 impala annually, and a set of quality tourist camps. Given the wealth of the district's wildlife resources and its top-down approach, Nyaminyami has established a substantial wildlife-management capacity based on the classic park rather than on a community-based model. Personnel are trained, uniformed, armed, and linked by radio communications. No other district in CAMPFIRE has followed this example. Nyaminyami District Council and its executive staff always have chosen to proudly stand somewhat alone in the CAMP-FIRE program. The community leadership so far has collaborated closely with the council's executive management.

Since the trust began, Russell Taylor of the WWF Multispecies Project has ensured that Nyaminyami has had the most sophisticated resource-monitoring procedures of all CAMPFIRE districts (Taylor 1990). For example, all trophy elephants shot have been aged and their tusks and body lengths and weights measured. Problem-animal reports have been logged and mapped and the information used to develop a protective fencing strategy. Crop damage has been monitored, estimated, and mapped and an experimental compensation scheme introduced. Monitoring revealed that compensation claims against the trust lacked any built-in mechanism for balancing individual costs against group benefits. As a result, Nyaminyami canceled compensation for wildlife damage as a right and now leaves such questions to the wards to settle. A cost-benefit relationship has been established, and now, for each dollar paid in compensation, the ward dividend is similarly reduced. Nyaminyami has further developed a lakeshore tourist plan and, with advice from accountants, has learned how to structure a tourist joint venture independently.

On many levels, Nyaminyami's achievements are laudable, but the district still faces problems. The communities themselves are not actively participating in the planning and management process and appear alienated from both the trust and the wildlife on which they depend for their existence. Reports of communal snaring of antelope and illegal settlement persist. There is little community organization below the district-based trust's board of management. Despite the ZimTrust Institutional Development Unit's encouragement, the council, having received the needed grant of authority, is less than keen to pass it on down to the wards and villages. So far, Nyaminyami has always given each ward an equal dividend, despite the fact that wildlife is not evenly distributed. Furthermore, those who receive the dividend are not allowed a choice in its use or the option to receive cash. Once a ward has selected a project such as a grinding mill or a roof for its school, it has been the role of the elected councillor or employed Wildlife Trust officer to facilitate the project's implementation. This oversight arrangement deprives the community of the opportunity to learn to manage funds and projects. Nyaminyami Trust sometimes seems to behave like a donor agency among its own

Table 7.4

Big game hunting quotas on communal lands (1993)

District	Total Trophy Fee Value Z$	Elephant[1]	Buffalo[2]	Lion	Leopard
Beitbridge	241,200	3	4	2	2
Binga	1,160,875	12	110	4	12
Gaza Komenani	816,628	10	17	18	11
Gazaland	239,015	4	4	3	1
Gokwe	484,038	5	34	2	6
Guruve	1,421,538	12	99	13	24
Hurungwe	663,895	7	39	8	15
Hwange	332,613	4	5	6	4
Nkayi	65,273	0	0	0	3
Mzarabani	210,688	2	20	1	2
Nyaminyami	1,858,725	14	129	7	25
Rushinga/Mudzi	128,030	2	1	1	2
Tsholotsho	384,138	13	18	12	7
Plumtree	258,753	4	10	4	3
Total	**Z$ 8,265,409**	**92**	**490**	**81**	**117**
	US$ 1,377,568				

Estimated daily revenue from elephant hunts is 92 × 21-day hunt × US$750 per day = US$1,449,000, added to trophy fees (92 × US$7,500) of US$690,000 dollars. Elephants are a major drawing card for US$2,829,000. Gross hunting revenue is approximately US$4 million.

1 Some districts have elephant problem animal control (PAC) quotas. If communities exceed these, they risk lowering the trophy quota in the following year: Binga PAC (4); Gaza Komanani PAC (5); Gazaland PAC (1); Gokwe PAC (3); Guruve PAC (4); Hurungwe (2); Hwange (4); Nyaminyami (8).
2 Some districts have a buffalo cropping quota: Binga (20); Guruve (30); Hurungwe (5); Nyaminyami may crop 50 and translocate 200 to another part of the district; Tsholotsho (4).

Table 7.5

Plains game hunting quotas on communal lands (1993)[1]

Species	Beitbridge	Binga	Gaza Komenani	Gazaland	Gokwe	Guruve	Hurungwe	Nyaminyami	Tsholotsho
Hippopotamus	2	3	0	1	0	8	1	9	0
Crocodile	3	3	4	1	0	11	1	9	0
Eland	3	5	4	0	1	4	4	5	4
Zebra	4	3	7	0	11	3	5	21	4
Waterbuck (M)	1	5	5	1	1	7	2	27	1
Kudu	5	16	22	1	6	21	3	31	12
Sable	0	3	2	0	0	10	10	9	4
Wildebeest	4	0	1	0	0	0	0	0	6
Tsessebe	0	1	0	0	0	0	0	0	0
Nyala	1	0	9	1	0	0	0	0	0
Impala[2]	40	85	127	2	19	142	3	230	16
Bushbuck	2	10	6	0	5	26	14	31	1
Duiker	4	25	14	4	10	23	11	33	13
Steenbok	4	0	8	0	0	0	0	0	13
Spotted Hyena	5	5	8	1	2	16	1	7	29
Jackal	5	4	6	0	3	5	3	9	10

1 A general feature of wildlife in communal lands is good big game populations due to proximity to protected areas and low human population densities, and poor plains game populations due to disturbed habitat and subsistence hunting activities.

2 Some districts with abundant impala have cropping quotas: Beitbridge (20); Binga (500); Gaza Komenani (500); Gokwe (30); Guruve (25); Nyaminyami (1,500).

people. Further, Nyaminyami has spent too high a percentage of its revenue on management, resulting in a smaller community benefit.

Critics of the Nyaminyami approach argue that if the trust spent less on salaried management, it might be able to stimulate far more community-based management. Because the Nyaminyami Wildlife Trust is only in its fifth year of operation, it is possible that the struggle for greater participation eventually will create a more participatory and sustainable institution. But Nyaminyami is threatened by immigration pressures and haphazard settlement. Unless it can pull plans and community commitment together, it runs the risk of closing off potential options for wildlife utilization.

All CAMPFIRE's advocates have urged the Nyaminyami Council and Trust to involve its communities more directly by giving them oversight of and direct access to wildlife revenues. One frustration of the program is that a potential CAMPFIRE "success" remains bureaucratized and controlled by a district-based elite.

At the end of 1993, the Nyaminyami Wildlife Management Trust decided to approve differential benefits that recognize the difference in quality of each ward's wildlife habitats. This change of heart recognizes that human immigration is a threat to the wildlife program and differential returns constitute an incentive for wards to recognize the relationship between settlement and wildlife habitat. The wards that can manage settlement patterns stand to gain the biggest wildlife benefits.

Guruve District

In contrast to Nyaminyami, the CAMPFIRE story in Guruve does not focus mainly on activities at the district level. Instead, the sense of a dialectical process between community and district institutions is much stronger. Wildlife is mainly found in the northern part of Guruve on the Zambezi Valley floor, on Dande communal land. The western part of Dande joins the Chewore Safari Area and has good wildlife populations; the eastern part has become more settled, and wildlife is now sparse.

Prior to the granting of appropriate authority, Professor Murphree of CASS visited the Kanyurira community and helped to develop the people's awareness of wildlife's potential, their rights to its benefits, and the general CAMPFIRE concept. To the north, in Chapota and Chisunga wards, the same input was not made. Murphree's selection of Kanyurira, a fairly homogenous community, was opportune; in Chapota ward, for example, apart from the usual ward-versus-district hierarchy problems, differences persist regarding traditional (chiefs') and democratic (councillors') authority. Of the two ethnic groups in the ward, the ChiKunda (agriculturalists) dominate the Dema (previously hunter-gatherers) (Hasler 1990).

In its first year of operation under the grant of authority over wildlife, the Guruve

District Council allowed revenues to be distributed according to the natural—hence unequal—distribution of wildlife. It also gave Kanyurira (but not the other wards) free choice in benefit distribution. Kanyurira Ward is geographically large (400 km²), with a small population of only 60 households (482 people) in 1988. The area is rich in wildlife and for many years has been exploited by professional safari hunters. Before CAMPFIRE, revenues went to the Treasury, and local benefits accrued only through nonsanctioned hunting and snaring. Attitudes toward wildlife were negative, and community aspirations centered on gaining more community services from the government (Murphree 1993), in part by encouraging new settlers. With CAMPFIRE and the distribution of direct benefits to the Kanyurira community, wildlife came to be seen as economically beneficial, a resource to be nurtured rather than eliminated. "We see now," says one elder, "that these buffalo are our cattle" (Spirit Medium 1990). The process has rekindled a proprietary attitude toward the ward's wildlife.

At the request of the Kanyurira community, CASS and WWF provided assistance in developing a village-based land-use plan that involved identification of arable and settlement land that was to be protected from surrounding wildlife by a game fence. (This simple participatory exercise contrasts with the elaborate top-down approach of the agricultural department, which elsewhere has mapped every field, homestead, and grazing area and initiated externally motivated village reform.) CASS also has undertaken a household survey to provide a baseline against which changes in Kanyurira can be measured over time. This will be useful in monitoring demographic changes and Kanyurira's success in excluding immigrants.

The impact of household dividends was profound. Internally, the community had to ask searching questions about what constitutes a household, the basic unit of participation. The community began to ask whether it wanted new settlers and, if so, what sort. The importance of rules of inclusion and exclusion became clear. The Kanyurira community has defended its proprietorship aggressively in the face of the council's centralizing tendencies. When it developed its land-use plan, the community charged its councillor and wildlife committee chairman with the task of taking the plan to the council for approval with these words: "Tell them that these are our animals and these are our plans. We will not accept any changes imposed by others." The importance of accountability—of council to community and community leaders to membership—is central to the success of Kanyurira to date (Murphree 1993).

A cautionary note on Guruve also must be sounded. In contrast to Kanyurira's experience, many other wards in the Dande have experienced rapid immigration and reduced wildlife-management opportunities. It is unlikely that a community could resist such top-down developmental and migratory pressures without full cooperation between community, council, and government departments. Without a community-based sense of proprietorship, such resistance probably is not possible at all. The experiences of Guruve and Nyaminyami districts are representative. Other wards in Guruve have experienced frustrations similar to those of wards in Nyaminyami. The Kanyurira experience provides a contrast to Nyaminyami and has reassured CAMPFIRE's advocates that community-based—in contrast to district-level—management is possible. The majority of CAMPFIRE programs fall somewhere between the extremes of the Nyaminyami and Kanyurira examples.

Other District CAMPFIRE Initiatives

Beitbridge District in the southeastern lowveld is a semiarid area suitable for extensive rangeland utilization. It was the second district, after Guruve, to distribute wildlife revenues in the form of cash to households. Beitbridge went further than Guruve, however, by instituting differential benefits and giving the village unit free choice of expenditure as a matter of principle. At the start of 1991, Beitbridge allocated each Chikwarakwara village household Z$400 (US$200). Households then voted some funds back to pay for a grinding mill and kept half as cash. This motivated Chikwarakwara village to become involved in its own land-use planning, and the people built wildlife into their rangeland management plan. All of this has made the project a role model within CAMPFIRE for benefits distribution (Child and Peterson 1991).

Agency inputs provided to Beitbridge have been in response to requests for assistance and not driven by any "blueprint" project approach. A demand-driven approach to the program, the Collaborative Group has learned, can work when a district supports devolution of decision making all the way to the village. When this happens, small groups of households are able to decide on critical issues related to trade-offs between private livestock, communal wildlife, and sustained use of the communal forage resources.

In many ways Beitbridge currently epitomizes the CAMPFIRE philosophy. The smallest accountable unit within the district has been empowered and feels secure enough to begin modifying long-standing rangeland practices incorporating a multispecies approach. Perhaps household dividends, and granting free choice over expenditure, could be central to the success of such a program. Certainly, the money-on-the-table approach helps wildlife overcome its disadvantage in comparison to privately owned livestock.

In January 1993, Hurungwe District also implemented differential benefits with free choice over expenditure down to the village level. Four out of six villages in Ward 1, which is immediately south of Mana Pools National Park and Chewore Safari Area, chose to distribute some US$36,000 among 849 registered households. Households that were not officially registered did not receive wildlife benefits. In this way, CAMPFIRE is tackling the critical membership or inclusion/exclusion issue. It is clear to local villagers that if human numbers rise, wildlife benefits will erode on two fronts: through less available wildlife habitat and more shareholders.

Institutional Design

CAMPFIRE's objectives are

> to initiate a program for the long-term development, management, and sustainable utilization of natural resources in the communal areas,
>
> to achieve management of resources by placing custody and responsibility with the resident communities,
>
> to allow communities to benefit directly from the exploitation of natural resources within communal areas, and
>
> to establish the administrative and institutional structures necessary to make the program work. *(Martin 1986:12)*

A set of CAMPFIRE principles has been developed to address the issue of balancing costs and benefits and to establish incentives, rules, and sanctions:

- "Effective management of wildlife is best achieved by giving it focused value for those who live with it" (Murphree 1993:6). People will seek to manage the environment when the benefits of management are perceived to exceed its costs.

- "Differential inputs must result in differential outputs" (Murphree 1993:6). An early CAMPFIRE proposition was that "those who pay the social costs should reap the economic benefits" (Martin 1986). Wildlife is an unevenly distributed and mobile resource. Wildlife costs (crop and livestock damage, threat to life) and the opportunity costs of other land uses are not equally shared. Consequently, the principle of equity is not applicable between wildlife management units. Benefit should thus be directly related to input, whether that input is in labor, in land, or in related costs.

- "There must be a positive correlation between quality of management and the magnitude of benefit" (Murphree 1993:6). Improved conservation, management, and marketing of wildlife should be directly rewarded.

- "The unit of proprietorship should be the unit of production, management, and benefit" (Murphree 1993:6). Proprietorship concerns who participates and makes decisions.

- "The unit of proprietorship should be as small as practicable within ecological and sociopolitical constraints" (Murphree 1993:6). Scale is an important factor in social dynamics. A communal resource-management regime is enhanced if it is small enough (in membership size) for all members to meet face to face, to enforce conformity with rules through peer pressure, and to create a long-standing identity.

Naturally, these principles will generate a diversity of CAMPFIRE plans *on the ground*, as expected of an adaptable approach to comanagement.

Resource Tenure

The relationship between modern and traditional authority in relation to access to land and natural resources is very important in understanding the development of CAMPFIRE. The two quotations that follow characterize some of the complex issues at stake:

> One of the central tragedies in the history of Southern African land and natural resource management is that the debate on tenure has largely been restricted to a discussion of the relative merit of state or private property regimes. Policy has assumed two options, privatize or nationalize, ignoring the further option of a communal property regime. *(Murphree 1993:4)*

> The government doesn't know where the land is. *(Sitauze 1992)*

The settler administration (1890–1980) attempted to control development in the tribal trust lands largely through statutes backed by coercive powers applied by district commissioners. In this process, the administration sometimes did and sometimes did not defer to traditional authorities, but ultimately preferred them to African nationalists. Since Independence, district "commissioners" have become district "administrators," with national and local authorities founded on universal franchise. Consequently, a collection of villages now forms a ward whose residents elect a councillor to the district level. This system largely parallels the traditional structure but also contradicts it and attempts to replace it.

If both the "modern" and "traditional" authorities agree on resource boundaries and rights of access to land, a positive sum solution is far more likely than if there is discord between them. Community-based land and resource management can be thwarted if democratic governance does not, whenever appropriate, recognize traditional values. This is most clearly seen in regard to migration of people between communal areas. This general guideline should not obscure the specificity of particular circumstances. Both formal and informal systems directly affect rights to participate in communally defined resource management. Fuzzy management boundaries in regard to rights of access to communal resources and their benefits make CAMPFIRE a complex program to implement. Rights and responsibilities need to be understood within different tiers of residence, as well by formal and informal authorities (Matose and Makamuri 1992).

The communal context—if it is to assure stable, efficient, equitable, and sustainable utilization—requires that locally established and legitimized rights and conditions of access to resource use be resolved. CAMPFIRE regards local proprietorship of wildlife resources as an essential first step toward community-based management. As Nyaminyami, Guruve, Beitbridge, and Hurungwe illustrate, local organization is an ongoing process of trial and error. Administrators and technical experts actually can inhibit local groups in the process of becoming responsible and capable managers if they highlight weaknesses more than strengths. External constraints and the internal difficulties associated with the complex social organization required, as well as failure to link costs and benefits, affect local communities' resource-management competence.

The experience of CAMPFIRE "successes" to date has been premised on recognition that the management of wildlife can not be separated from the control of its benefits and costs. Membership in a CAMPFIRE producer community rests on residency. Experience has demonstrated that it is important not to allow benefits to be shared between ward and district administrative units if environmental costs are incurred by households within village structures. Boundaries of both the resource and the parties who have access to it are very important but difficult to establish. An elephant, for example, may cross village, ward, district, and national park boundaries in a single day. A community has to have its own rules of behavior and get its neighbors to respect them. Apart from being units for resource decision making, producer communities have to cooperate with other villages and coordinate with wards and districts in a nested hierarchy of accountability.

The problems associated with uncontrolled use of natural resources (land, forest, grazing, wildlife) will persist until rules can be monitored and enforced effectively. One challenge is the need to control potentially detrimental intercommunal migration. With population growth, pioneering farmers are moving into more remote and marginal lands—the same lands where wildlife exists and CAMPFIRE is making headway. While the district councils in the Zambezi Valley assert that people can not settle without their permission, they are proving unable to control movement. Traditional authorities, represented by kraal heads, headmen, and chiefs, can influence this process. Unless modern and traditional authorities pull together locally, membership of CAMPFIRE producer communities will be threatened by a lack of exclusivity, spontaneous unplanned settlement, and fragmentation of wildlife habitat. The ability to exclude settlers, if necessary, may be a prerequisite for ultimate success.

The political dimension of land tenure and settlement remains contentious. New settlers create greater community heterogeneity. More participants sharing the natural wealth will lead to smaller household dividends from wildlife and less individual incentive for conservation. A downward development and environmental spiral provides a driving force for free access to resources. Uncontrolled resource access risks rapid loss of wildlife diversity through overexploitation. Unfortunately, access to arable and grazing resources is perceived as more important than access to wildlife. New farmers sometimes are not seen as sufficient threats to livelihood for a locally based consensus to stop the migratory process. Formal and informal authority over resources may be disunited and unable or unwilling to prevent encroachment into and disturbance of wildlife habitat.

Community and Government Comanagement

Zimbabwe's environment is—and will continue to be—the object of increased human impact through the uphill struggle for developmental progress. The outcome depends on how all social groups and communities sustain the resource base while working for economic growth. Rural people, living well beyond the effective grasp of administrative intervention, control much of the land. Pressure to refine and resolve land and resource tenure has been and remains a key issue.

Authority at the local level in Zimbabwe manifests itself mainly through two structures. The traditional roots of communal life are still strong, providing a web of affection and social and material security. African nations may have inherited the geopolitical units established by the colonial regimes, but to a great extent the modern state apparatus is a structure superimposed on communal Africa. The relationship between communal and national society has not always produced a positive synergy. Rather, all local institutions (democratic and traditional) largely are subordinated to the central authority of political party and state (Hyden 1983).

But for rural populations, the communal context remains the predominant social milieu, and will be for the foreseeable future. All the externally driven government communal conservation programs of this century prior to CAMPFIRE have foundered, while communal people have had neither the authority, the motivation, nor the technical training to establish new institutions for themselves. Quite simply, communal people have not had the requisite rights to establish their own forms of organization—until CAMPFIRE, which assumes that communities can become effective institutions for sustainable resource management if they are granted genuine proprietorship. In addition to being a wildlife management system, the CAMPFIRE approach has effectively set up a comanagement debate between protected areas and the surrounding communal land. It incorporates a parks-and-people approach by establishing a partnership between the significant local land authorities, National Parks, and district councils. While the government retains full control over the protected areas, CAMPFIRE strengthens National Parks' role in regional land-use planning. This situation is seen most clearly in the Zimbabwean portion of the Zambezi Valley, which is divided more or less equally into communal and protected areas. By establishing appropriate authorities for communal land, the possibility for joint planning between these authorities and National Parks is enhanced, along with the success of maintaining an integrated wildlife habitat big enough for the substantial elephant herds that exist in the region.

CAMPFIRE asks why people should be motivated to conserve the environment. Who benefits from conservation? Who pays the costs? Who manages the resources? Who has authority over them? It argues strongly that authority, management, production, and benefit all must be primarily situated with the producer community. Wildlife's high financial values generally have been realized by joint ventures between district councils and the private sector, with the latter paying high rents for exclusive resource marketing. This has left most communal people passive in the marketing process. Much of the debate and dispute in CAMPFIRE is about participation in managing the benefits from wildlife utilization, and about assessing and responding to wildlife costs related to crop damage, problem-animal control, and compensation issues.

At present, CAMPFIRE directly involves the participating councils and, increasingly, the producer communities. The active involvement of households within the villages is still a goal that has been realized only in distribution of household dividends, as in the cases of Beitbridge, Chipinge (Mahenya), and Hurungwe.

In regard to decision making, some communities are presently at the stage of developing the social organization necessary to evolve proprietary regimes capable of interacting with other communities, other districts, and the resource base. Others are still relatively powerless in the face of administrative, technical, and marketing domination. Several communities nevertheless are beginning to develop community-based resource management plans for which they themselves are accountable (e.g., Kanyurira, Mahenya, Beitbridge). In most communities, however, implementation is overseen by districts, the Collaborative Group, and private safari operators, who market hunts and assist with problem-animal control (e.g., Nyaminyami, Tsholotsho).

The logic underlying comanagement is that externally enforced rules break down if not maintained, but that internally defined and enforced rules require full devolution of tenurial rights over the resources in question to the lowest accountable unit. Prior to granting authority to the district councils, the government, through National Parks, was responsible for enforcing the regulations related to access to wildlife. Since devolution, this has become a comanagement responsibility. So far, enforcement of conservation rules has not received adequate attention. Antipoaching rules have been externally enforced and could now increasingly become internalized by the communities. In Hurungwe District, for example, village communities are debating methods of sanctioning transgressors of locally established bylaws related to the right of access to wildlife in an attempt to regulate local subsistence poaching. Nyaminyami has a reward system for information leading to capture of commercial poachers. In Kanyurira, subsistence poaching has reduced dramatically as the community has garnered legitimate wildlife benefits for themselves. However, the general opinion of those associated with CAMPFIRE is that councils and communities should avoid casting themselves in the role of law-enforcement agencies by establishing their own uniformed game guards. The costs of such activities are high and communities' perceptions of such law-enforcement units negative. Communities could control subsistence hunting but need external help from government to contain commercial poaching.

Institutional Policy

The 1975 Parks and Wildlife Act enabled commercial farmers on private land to use wildlife as a form of land husbandry. This has led to a thriving wildlife industry, with increased habitat being made available for wildlife to be managed with or replace cattle (Child 1991). Proving wildlife to be a competitive form of land use on private land is different and far easier than making it competitive on communal land. On communal lands, the management risk and effort and distribution of benefits can become diffused, providing ineffective incentives. The central thrust in CAMPFIRE is thus a belief that community-based proprietorship is necessary to motivate local institutions and to take into account the need to internalize conservation costs within the agricultural process.

By challenging the "open-access" nature of wildlife resources, CAMPFIRE has set in motion a growing communal debate. Since 1988, this has involved a widening circle of rural people and development and conservation agencies in active discussions related to the costs, benefits, and consequences of managing wildlife. What the 1975 Parks and Wildlife Act accomplished for commercial farmers, the new CAMPFIRE policy sought to make possible in communal areas. The sustained use of wildlife by communal people and the relationship between protected and communal areas is central to National Parks' new policy. The policy aims, inter alia,

> to maintain the Parks and Wildlife Estate for the conservation of the nation's wild resources and biological diversity; to encourage the conservation of wild animals and their habitats outside the Estate recognizing that this is only likely to be successful if wildlife can be used profitably and the primary benefits accrue to people with wildlife on their land; to use the Estate to promote a rurally based wildlife industry; to harmonize the management of the Estate with the efforts of neighboring communities who are developing wildlife as a sustainable form of land use; to transform land use in the remote communal lands of Zimbabwe through its CAMPFIRE programme under which rural peoples have the authority to manage their wildlife and other natural resources and benefit directly from so doing. (MET 1992:2)

Despite its foundation in policy, CAMPFIRE relies on its practical appeal to local people. Although CAMPFIRE is supported by legislation, it can still be either accepted or rejected by rural communities. And despite CAMPFIRE's goals, it has not yet been possible to establish a unified national policy. Several crosscutting pieces of legislation affect conservation in the communal areas. In addition, the activities of sector agencies manifest built-in conflicts and contradictions at the program level. Although an imperative to coordinate exists at the local district level in the district development committees, each governmental and nongovernmental agency is often more concerned with accountability to its particular sector's hierarchy (agriculture, health, environment, etc.). Compounding this is the fact that most governmental agency budgets are centralized through the Treasury. Councils may attempt to balance and coordinate the interests of government, NGOs, the private sector, community, and individual needs, but it is a daunting task.

The government seeks to establish comanagement relations between itself and local authorities in the new Rural District Councils Act. This legislation administratively amalgamates the private farming sector (rural councils) with the communal sector (district councils). Under CAMPFIRE, the district council in turn should comanage wildlife populations with local communities. But there is stark contrast between the legal status and decision-making capacities of the private and communal sectors. CAMPFIRE argues that communal rights and institutions need strengthening, as it views the communal nature of land ownership as a rich, valid, and supportive system for the stewardship of wildlife.

CAMPFIRE was designed to address both the potential and the weaknesses of communal ownership of natural resources. It drew on a vision that combines customary practice within a modern democratic framework. Its basic premise is that the natural resources base was declining, partly because of the failure of adequate systems for resource allocation (rights) and their protection (exclusion). Although CAMPFIRE is intended to conserve and manage wildlife, grazing, and forestry, at this stage it is only concerned with wildlife, due to National Parks' active support for the policy and the contrasting lack of consensus among the other governmental agencies responsible for overall communal resource management.

Some key unresolved aspects of policy will have an impact upon CAMPFIRE's future programs. These concern legislation, communications, and information. The amalgamation of communal and private land administration promises stronger local authorities. On the one hand, this is a promise of decentralization from central government, but on the other, it poses the threat of more powerful local-government control over rural communities. Natural resources legislation, as it affects communal areas, is weak, outdated, and in need of reform. Decentralization in the private commercial sector, based on farmer participation, appears to be more satisfactory than the bureaucratic committees found in the communal areas.

Coordination between local authorities is poor, especially between districts in different provinces. Regional considerations around national parks, Lake Kariba, and in the Zambezi Valley need a regional planning structure. Coordination between ministries at the policy and implementation levels needs to be enhanced, particularly by local authorities setting priorities for sectoral inputs. All technical agencies need to improve their communications and participatory techniques. Environmental education literature is needed in vernacular languages.

Sustainability

In order to determine whether the program is ecologically sustainable, fundamental environmental indicators are monitored—for example, whether wildlife populations are increasing, decreasing, or static. The driving and restraining forces affecting these movements are analyzed. Socioeconomic and demographic trends, such as population density and distribution at micro and macro level, are closely tracked and the relevance of ratios of resources to beneficiaries ascertained. Changes over time in local perceptions of the wildlife resource are important in order to detect whether these are becoming more or less positive toward wildlife. CASS case studies and surveys trace these trends, as do all other agencies. Structural arrangements for collective decision making, and the conditions for the provision of individual and group incentives, also are being monitored and researched.

Expansion of CAMPFIRE

CAMPFIRE should be expanded to include all resources, not just wildlife, for holistic communal management. The CAMPFIRE principles also should be extended to include resettlement and small-scale commercial farming sectors. Any attempt to expand CAMPFIRE beyond its present focus on wildlife will first face some severe institutional constraints:

- Government control over communal land and natural resources tenure at the moment is too bureaucratic, pervasive, and vertically managed. Wildlife utilization as a land-use option is not fully supported by all ministries, especially agriculture, which is responsible for land-use planning and grazing schemes. Control over access to natural resources on communal lands is too dependent on poorly enforced externally based rules. Responsibility for land and resource degradation is not clearly defined. Uncontrolled and spontaneous settlement in communal lands is a threat to CAMPFIRE, and to ecosystem stability.

- There is inadequate legislation to empower subdistrict administrative units (the ward and village committees) to manage land tenure and resource use.

- Should councils or communities be the business enterprise in CAMPFIRE? How far should equity within district or even ward boundaries be applied? A clearer definition of the producer community as a unit of management needs to emerge. All are complex, even when the focus is limited to wildlife.

Conclusions

Conservation is a state of harmony between men and land. . . . In our attempt to make it easy, we have made it trivial.
—Aldo Leopold, "The Land Ethic," A Sand County Almanac (1949:243, 246)

CAMPFIRE has involved more than a quarter of a million people in a dialogue about managing the environment. Through their village and district wildlife committees, communities now can make land-use plans that incorporate the conservation and sustained use of wild species. Equally, conservation and development planners and agencies now have a forum and an evolving management structure through which to operate. Conducive proprietary structures and positive economic incentives will assist communities in the process of becoming resource-management institutions. Project management alone will not establish sustainable management without local commitment. The driving force for improved conservation must be based on the recognition of conservation's role in enhancing individual as well as group security.

At times, communally situated wildlife management has been threatened by the state and its bureaucracy. Unrealistic or manipulative demands for control, technical competence, and financial accountability often have undermined communal management. Wildlife could be part of the rural means of production and therefore an integral part of the social organization of rural communities. Material and aesthetic aspects have been, and could be again, much more clearly linked.

CAMPFIRE's assumption that communal people are competent to make management decisions rests on the prior establishment of institutional and financial incentives. But there can be no guarantee, in the real world, that the playing field will ever be level enough for communal people to overcome their disadvantages when faced with political and economic elites. These latter groups, however, can not ensure sustainable management of the local environment without the full cooperation of communal people. Ultimately, CAMPFIRE depends on the support of local people for its success and merely attempts to provide an enabling environment in which that support can occur. This rests on the assumed right of communities' group proprietorship over "their" resources. It also depends on both parties contributing to making access rights exclusive. Successful conservation and development activities are unlikely unless government provides appropriate legislation and policy, as well as efficient and effective technical assistance and enforcement. The private sector also has a critical role in developing ethical, stable, and accountable joint marketing ventures with communities.

CAMPFIRE attempts to provide a means of harmonizing the needs of rural people with those of ecosystems. Whether it succeeds in sufficiently empowering communal producers remains a critical question. Clearly, biodiversity can not be perceived as an object of attention alone but has to become part of the subject matter related to community and individual identity in a world typified by the democratic and industrial revolutions. Zimbabwe's twentieth-century communal peoples have been alienated from both "their" society and "their" land. CAMPFIRE has some of the necessary ingredients to re-create a community identity that is in harmony with the environment.

SOURCES

Centre for Applied Social Sciences, World Wildlife Fund, and Zimbabwe Trust (CASS/WWF/ZimTrust). 1989. *Wildlife Utilization in Zimbabwe's Communal Lands: Collaborative Programme Activities.* Harare: University of Zimbabwe.

Child, B. 1991. *Wildlife Use on Zimbabwe's Rangelands in Developing World Agriculture, Animal Production and Health.* Hong Kong: Grosvenor Press.

———, and J. H. Peterson, Jr. 1991. *CAMPFIRE in Rural Development: The Beitbridge Experience.* Joint DNPWLM/CASS Working Paper Series, Paper 1/91. Harare: Branch of Terrestrial Ecology, Department of National Parks and Wild Life Management.

Crosby, A. W. 1986. *Ecological Imperialism: The Biological Expansion of Europe, 900–1900.* Cambridge, England: Cambridge University Press.

Cumming, D. H. M. 1990a. *Wildlife Conservation in African Parks: Progress, Problems and Prescriptions.* WWF Multispecies Production Systems Project Paper No. 15. Harare: World Wildlife Fund.

———. 1990b. "Wildlife Products and the Market Place: A View from Southern Africa." World Wide Fund for Nature Multispecies Animal Production Systems Project Paper No. 12, presented at the 2nd International Game Ranching Symposium, June 4–8, Edmonton, Canada.

Dasmann, R., and A. S. Mossman. 1961. "Commercial Utilization of Game Animals on a Rhodesian Ranch." *Wild Life* 3:7–17.

Government of Zimbabwe (GOZ). 1975. Parks and Wildlife Act, 1975.

Hasler, R. 1990. *The Political and Socio-economic Dynamics of Natural Resource Management: The CAMPFIRE Programme in Chapoto Ward 1989–1990.* Harare: Centre for Applied Social Sciences, University of Zimbabwe.

Hyden, G. 1983. *No Shortcuts to Progress: African Development Management in Perspective.* Berkeley: University of California Press.

Leopold, Aldo. 1970 [1949]. *A Sand County Almanac.* Reprint. New York: Ballantine.

Martin, R. B. 1986. *Communal Areas Management Programme for Indigenous Resources.* Revised version. CAMPFIRE Working Document No. 1/86. Harare: Branch of Terrestrial Ecology, Department of National Parks and Wild Life Management.

Matose, F. M., and B. B. Makamuri. 1992. "Rural Peoples' Knowledge and Extension Practice: Trees, People and Communities in Zimbabwe's Communal Lands." Paper prepared for the International Institute for Environment and Development (IIED) and Institute for Development Studies (IDS) Beyond Farmer First Workshop, October 27–29, Sussex University, Institute for Development Studies.

Ministry of Environment and Tourism (MET). 1992. *Policy for Wild Life—Zimbabwe.* Harare: Department of National Parks and Wild Life Management, Ministry of Environment and Tourism.

Ministry of Natural Resources and Tourism (MNRT). 1987. *The National Conservation Strategy: Zimbabwe's Road to Survival.* Harare: Department of Information.

Mossman, A. S. 1963. "Wildlife Ranching in Southern Rhodesia." In *Conservation of Nature and Natural Resources in Modern African States,* 247–249. IUCN Publications new series, No. 1. Salisbury (Harare), Rhodesia (Zimbabwe): International Union for the Conservation of Nature.

Murphree, M. W. 1993. *Communities as Resource Management Institutions.* International Institute for Environment and Development (IIED) Gatekeeper

Series, No. 36. London: Institute for Environment and Development. Previously published 1991 as *Communities as Institutions for Resource Management*. CASS Occasional Paper Series. Harare: Centre for Applied Social Sciences, University of Zimbabwe.

Nyaminyami District Council (NDC). 1985. Minutes and resolution arising from a special meeting of the Nyaminyami District Council, Bumi Hills Safari Lodge, October 24. Nyaminyami District Council, Siakobvu, Kariba District, Zimbabwe. Photocopy.

———.1987. "The Wildlife of Nyaminyami: A Proposal for the Improved Management, Control and Use of the Wildlife of Nyaminyami." Nyaminyami District Council, Siakobvu, Kariba District, Zimbabwe. Photocopy.

Nyaminyami Wildlife Management Trust (NWMT). 1990. "Report to the Nyaminyami Wildlife Management Trust First Annual General Meeting, 16 February, Bumi Hills Safari Lodge." Nyaminyami District Council, Siakobvu, Kariba District, Zimbabwe. Photocopy.

Sitauze, Chief. 1992. Interview with the author, Beitbridge District, November 11.

Spirit Medium. 1990. Statement to Headman Kanyurira's village, Masoka Ward First Annual General Meeting of CAMPFIRE Project, February 23, translated by the author.

Taylor, R. D. 1990. *Ecologists' Report for 1989 Nyaminyami Wildlife Management Trust Annual General Meeting*. WWF Multispecies Project Paper No. 9. Harare: World Wildlife Fund.

Thomas, S. J. 1982. *An Estimate of Communal Land Density in the Natural Regions of Zimbabwe*. Harare: Zimbabwe Trust.

Zimbabwe Trust. 1989. *Elephants and People: Partners in Conservation and Development*. Harare: Zimbabwe Trust.

CHAPTER 8

Local Initiatives and the Rewards for Biodiversity Conservation: Crater Mountain Wildlife Management Area, Papua New Guinea

Mary C. Pearl

The Crater Mountain Wildlife Management Area project combines tourism, research, and conservation with the development of alternative methods of improving economic returns from subsistence farming. The project designs programs to introduce environmentally friendly and more efficient farming methods, as well as develop small-scale businesses compatible with wildlife conservation. Employment with research projects and in ecotourism and scientific tourism generates other income. The project's goal is to help ensure that local people's strong preexisting conservation values are integrated into the area's economic development rather than lost through the process of change. Research is an integral part of the project, which provides information on the culture and traditions of local people and guidelines on hiring and employment practices to agencies working in the area. Research, of course, is also central to the project's main aim: gaining understanding of forest ecological dynamics so that important species can be identified and protected for both cultural and economic benefit.

The Research and Conservation Foundation (RCF) of Papua New Guinea, formed in 1986 to protect rain-forest flora and fauna throughout the country, has taken on the development of the Crater Mountain Wildlife Management Area as its first and most significant program. By managing and coordinating activities at Crater, the RCF is gaining the experience and expertise needed to develop community-based conservation programs in other parts of Papua New Guinea.

The Wildlife Management Committee, a policy-making and enforcement body whose members are drawn from the local population, is responsible for setting development and conservation priorities in Crater Mountain Wildlife Management Area.

General Country Background

Papua New Guinea consists of the eastern half of New Guinea, the world's second largest island (after Greenland), plus the Bismarck, Trobriand, Entrecasteaux, and Louisiade archipelagos and the island of Bougainville. At 475,020 km², Papua New Guinea is about the size of the states of Oregon and Idaho combined. Its population, at just 3.9 million, is low, and forest cover is still extensive (about 70 percent). However, more than half of the forest contains exploitable timber. The deforestation rate between 1986 and 1990 is estimated to have been 220 km² per year and is likely to escalate as a result of population growth. (The population growth rate is now 2.6 percent annually, and more than 50 percent of the population is less than 15 years old.) As international timber companies come to the end of the rapid exploitation of resources in Sabah, Sarawak, the Philippines, and parts of Indonesia, they will find Papua New Guinea's extensive exploitable forests appealing.

Since independence from Australia in 1975, Papua New Guinea has been a parliamentary democracy. The parliamentary system is ideally suited to symbolically replace the country's long cultural tradition of constant warfare between neighboring clans, although election campaigns sometimes escalate into violence. With universal adult suffrage vigorously exercised, the Papua New Guinea government is one of the most authentically representative in Asia and the Pacific.

Most Papua New Guineans live in rural villages, although drift to urban areas is high, causing cities to grow in population at an average rate of 6 percent per year. Of the work force of approximately 625,000 people, 85 percent is engaged in subsistence, 10 percent in commerce, and 4 percent in government. The population is fragmented geographically and also culturally, since more than 700 languages are spoken. Pidgin, Motu, and English are lingua francas, and the new popularity and availability of videos is increasing their use. While six years of education is compulsory, only 65 percent of school-age children attend school. Less than one-third of Papua New Guinea citizens are literate, life expectancy is less than 50 years, and the infant mortality rate, at 72 per 1,000 births, is high.

Most people have strong cultural and legal ties to their land. Despite a lack of formal education, village people are highly sophisticated negotiators of land-use issues, having negotiated among themselves for millennia such issues as in situ topsoil rental and trade based on forest fruit futures. The class system is not strong, in line with the traditional emphasis on acquired rather than inherited status. People who have had access to higher education tend to remain tied to family and clan obligations, and Papua New Guineans at all levels of education evidence a strong attachment to their land. Fully 97 percent of all land (and even coastal areas, including coral reefs) is communally owned by one of some 700 clans rather than by individuals or the government. Because land-use decisions must be made by group consensus in Papua New Guinea, resource-extraction companies find working quickly or in secrecy much more difficult than they have in Southeast Asia.

Papua New Guinea's gross domestic product, with an annual growth rate of 2 percent, was US$2.4 billion in 1988. The national debt was US$843 million in December 1989. Agriculture—principally coffee, palm oil, cocoa, copra, tea, and rubber—supplies 35 percent of the nation's budget; industry—copper and gold mining and, to a much lesser degree, manufacturing, food processing, and saw milling—provides 60 percent. The country's rich mineral resources, soon to be augmented by petroleum, keep the economy robust, with inflation below 7 percent, and provides the government with a fairly substantial income through royalties. The central government budget was nearly US$1 billion in 1986, US$4.34 million of which was supplied by multilateral and bilateral aid agencies. In 1984, imports totaled US$986 million; exports, led by gold, copper, and coffee, amounted to US$823 million. Japan, Germany, and Australia are major trading partners.

National Biodiversity Conservation Efforts

The Department of Environment and Conservation (DEC) is the government agency appointed to protect forests and wildlife. Like similar departments in other developing nations, Papua New Guinea's DEC is understaffed and weak in relation to the country's Department of Forestry. DEC runs its programs on an inadequate budget but remains committed to conservation, welcoming opportunities to work with nongovernmental organizations (NGOs) that offer assistance to achieve its goals.

Wildlife management area is a term the government of Papua New Guinea has devised to describe multiuse areas that include wildlife conservation. The wildlife management area, or WMA, is a useful legal entity in that it acknowledges ownership (which continues to rest with local people) in a variety of biogeographical areas. As a result, the country has sixteen wildlife management areas but only four national parks. The total area currently under strict protection, excluding Crater Mountain, is only 2 percent of Papua New Guinea's land area.

Crater Mountain Wildlife Management Area

The Crater Mountain Wildlife Management Area, while protected, is not set aside from human use. Any decision about conservation of land or wildlife is necessarily built on a consensus decision by local landowners. Conservation plans must reflect their aspirations and economic needs. While most of the 72 percent of the local population that exists purely within the subsistence economy is illiterate, these people are not unsophisticated in matters concerning land use. In addition, the strong traditional conservation ethic includes the idea of preserving resources for a generation of grandchildren.

As originally designed, the Crater Mountain Wildlife Management Area, located in the eastern Central Mountains south of Mount Michael, extended from Ubaigubi, a village in Eastern Highlands Province 50 km south of Goroka, to the Pio River in the south. The Tsoma River defined the area's southeastern boundary, and an unnamed river that flows north to south past the airstrip at Haia village defined the southwestern boundary. (As it was finally gazetted in 1993, the reserve is almost three times this original size. As a result, Haia is now close to the center of the reserve, and the Purari River defines the southern boundary; see Map 8.1).

Crater Mountain consists mostly of lower montane wet forest, although altitude ranges from under 600 m in the south to 3,056 m elsewhere. Crater Mountain is not a single peak but a series of detached pinnacles rising to just under 3,400 m. During the late Pleistocene, Crater Mountain was a huge active volcano. It is now a relict caldera, a series of giant Gothic spires almost always covered in cloud. The Crater area is the largest and least-known tract of hill and montane forest in the highlands fringe region (the broad wet-forest belt south of the main high peaks of East Highlands and Chimbu provinces). Of the land included in the WMA, 95 percent is still covered by primary forest or alpine scrub. The high country is dotted with water-filled fumaroles and hot springs. The area is biologically critical for its large, healthy populations of Pesquet's parrot, New Guinea harpy eagle, and two species of tree kangaroos.

The people of the Crater Mountain Wildlife Management Area belong to two language groups: the Gimi and the Pawaian. The Gimi-speaking people are perhaps more abundant, numbering about two thousand; for Pawaians, whose mostly nomadic existence in dense forest makes them hard to count, estimates of current numbers range between five hundred and three thousand. The Gimis hold customary tenure in a little less than half the land in the WMA; the rest belongs to the Pawaians. Together, these groups are the legal landowners. Because of this divided ownership, decisions regarding management of the WMA must reflect the common consensus of both groups.

The Gimis are subsistence farmers who practice shifting cultivation. The Gimi villages of Crater are traditional highland "big man" societies. Each clan has one or more big men, or chiefs, who maintain position through their skill as politicians or fighting leaders rather than through inheritance. The criteria for maintaining status as a big man in today's Crater society are changing rapidly. In addition to warrior skills, success in business, with government bureaucracies, or in Parliament leads to high status.

The Pawaian people, by contrast, are seminomadic. Their land extends beyond the Pio River and is situated at a lower altitude than the Gimis' holdings. The Pawaians practice hunting and gathering and limited short-term cropping,

Map 8.1

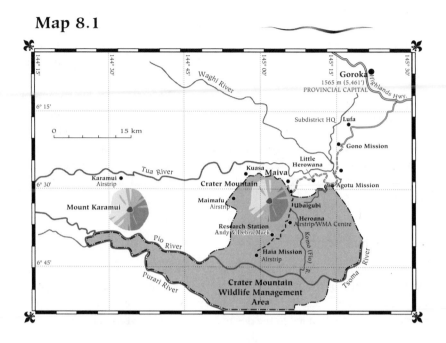

Crater Mountain
Wildlife Management Area

KEY

- Crater WMA
- Highway
- Secondary Road
- Jeep Track
- Walking Trail
- Major Rivers
- Secondary Rivers
- Extinct Volcano

growing or collecting sago palm as a staple. Although Pawaians do garden, this activity is not as central to their lives as to the Gimis'. Their society is built around the immediate family rather than a single big man, and they travel their forests in small bands usually numbering fewer than twenty.

Relations between the Gimis and the Pawaians are amicable, and there is some intermarriage between the two groups. According to the Gimis of Heroana, this arrangement is one way, in that Pawaian men buy Gimi wives but resist reciprocal marriages. Introduction of a market economy inevitably will modify life-styles and patterns of interpretation among local people. The Pawaians of Haia recently extended their wife buying to the Chimbu-speaking clans far to the north across the Tua River outside the Crater area. Many Chimbus are in need of land and may use marriage with Pawaians as a means to migrate into the wildlife management area. The situation is potentially critical and disrupts traditional control of migration into the area.

Origins of the Project

The Crater Mountain project did not begin as a major, organized program to develop a community-based management system for a protected area. Rather, years of discussions among local people and, later, with expatriates involved with and concerned about the area led to the desire for a community-based program.

Crater Mountain peoples' exposure to the outside world in 1958 was a critical triggering event. Australia took over the administration of the former German colony of New Guinea under a mandate from the League of Nations after World War I. Apart from some early German missionary activity in Western Highlands, and two patrols into Eastern Highlands during the 1930s, exploration and pacification did not begin until after World War II. The Australian patrols that reached the Crater area in 1957–58 were part of a broad-based Highlands pacification program that began around 1948.

The Australian patrol officials charged with persuading the Gimis and Pawaians to stop fighting and practicing cannibalism also discouraged them from hunting birds of paradise; a local taboo against killing one species, the Raggiana bird of paradise, already existed. Local people immediately explained the latter restriction in terms of religion: Since they believe the souls of their dead reside in some bird of paradise species, they assumed that the Australians, whom they perceived as returning ghosts, wanted to ensure the safety of their route to the land of the dead. From this first contact, Crater Mountain people have associated outsiders and "development" with conservation of wildlife.

External awareness of the area's wildlife began with the work of an Australian couple, anthropologists David and Gillian Gillison. Gillian's work, begun in 1973, centered upon the ritual life of Gimi-speaking people and the role of their forests in myth. David's companion study of the sources of imagery in Gimi art led him into the sacred male domain of the rain forest to observe firsthand the birds Gimi men said were their inspiration. For instance, the emergence of the fledgling hornbill (*Aceros plicatus*) from its nesting hole was said to be the men's model for initiation rites. The Gillisons also noted that the Gimis take many products from the forest to use in a variety of ways, with remarkable results in the treatment of migraine, diarrhea, malaria, and hepatitis.

Gimi rituals, and the birds whose behaviors inspired them, were beginning to disappear by the early 1970s. Less than a decade earlier, the Australian administration had opened this area of the highlands, allowing young Gimi men to travel far beyond the boundaries of their clan land. At the same time, increasing numbers of plumage and coffee traders and other outsiders began to enter Gimi villages and traditional lands. By 1979, big men were expressing to the Gillisons their alarm about both the disappearance of rituals and the emptying of clan forests by young men who killed birds and marsupials for valuable plumage to sell or meat to use as food.

The Crater Mountain project began as an effort to preserve birds of paradise. In 1982, David Gillison invited Donald Bruning, the curator of birds at the New York Zoological Society, to visit his field site in Ubaigubi. Bruning visited Crater during Gillison's absence and was flown to the site by Malcolm Smith, the owner of a Goroka-based aviation company and a keen amateur birder. As Bruning explored the extensive forests around the village with local guides, he took notice of the abundance of rare birds. These included the blue (*Paradisaea rudolphi*) and black (*Epimachus fastuosus*) birds of paradise and Lawe's (*Parotia lawesii*) and Queen Carola's parotia (*Parotia carolae*) birds of paradise. Other threatened or endangered bird species that Bruning observed included the *kokomo*, or hornbill (*Aceros plicatus*), Pesquet's parrot (*Psittrichas fulgidus*), and the *tarangau*, or New Guinea harpy eagle (*Harpyopsis novaeguineae*).

After his field trip, Bruning discussed conservation measures with the Gillisons, local and national bird enthusiasts, and government officials in the Department of Environment and Conservation (DEC). Karol Kisokau and Navu Kwapena of DEC, Bruning found out, wanted to create six wildlife management areas (WMAs) in various parts of the country. The two men made several visits to Crater, were impressed with local enthusiasm for creation of a WMA, and recommended moving ahead.

Bruning and Archie Carr III of Wildlife Conservation International (WCI) asked Gillison to approach interested and suitable individuals to help form an ad hoc conservation group in Papua New Guinea. Bruning and Carr reasoned that such a group could become a national conservation organization. At this point, Kisokau and Kwapena joined the group on behalf of DEC; they were joined by local bureaucrat and nature photographer Bill Peckover and expatriate conservationist Carlene Lohberger.

This informal group of local, national, government, and international people eventually was to create a national NGO, the Research and Conservation Foundation (RCF) of Papua New Guinea. But the group's immediate goal in Crater was to create a line of communication between landowners and national and provincial authorities. The fledgling RCF quickly became the neutral intermediary, trusted as an honest broker outside any local systems of sorcery or clan bias on the one hand and free of bureaucratic entanglements and the distractions of government on the other. From DEC's perspective, the RCF was just the sort of organization that could help its understaffed department achieve part of its mandate to create more protected areas.

In 1984, RCF members, following the lead of Kisokau, Kwapena, and others in government, suggested creation of a wildlife management area as a suitable official mechanism for formalizing the conservation program at Crater. Gillison immediately initiated negotiations with the Gimi-speaking people who live in Ubaigubi and six other villages in the Crater Mountain area to obtain their approval. In Crater, there is no such thing as "common" or "public" land. Instead, individuals hold or claim land that will be passed on to a member of the landowner's clan. For instance, in two villages of Crater, Heroana and Ubaigubi, there are a total of seven clans: Furakele, Kayumo, Labiabe, Lakaba-Faya, Danapisa, Fayu, and Hawkowe. Any land planning for the area must address the concerns of all of these clans.

At Crater, traditional negotiations take place at a gathering of the major participants, who sit facing each other in a large circle inside a fenced compound in the center of the village. Supporters of each faction stand with their leaders behind a barrier, usually a low pig fence. Having all parties to the discussion in clear sight of each other in a restricted space lessens the danger of sudden attacks, subterfuge, or private plotting. Customarily, participants speak at top volume so that everyone can hear. The villagers thus exchange views until they reach consensus—after an hour, a month, or even years.

During the two years of negotiations, Gillison attended numerous interclan meetings. He also held dozens of informal clan-level meetings in men's houses (known as *haus man* in Pidgin) and in private houses throughout northern and central Crater. Discussions first began within families, at which level women have major input into decisions. In later discussions about the relationship of conservation and development held at clan level, male views held supremacy. (Only in 1992 were clan members comfortable about extending the dialogue beyond the clans.) The people finally achieved consensus in 1986. Their decision was ratified by the Wildlife Management Committee, a representative body that David Gillison had helped form by balancing interests and needs and the ideas of big men from all clans within the proposed Crater Mountain Wildlife Management Area.

The committee, which included clan representatives from all the area villages, established seven operating rules. The clans that are party to the agreement (some have elected not to participate, and one family from the otherwise participating Danapisa clan does not take part)—not the national government—ratified and continue to enforce these rules:

- The committee will consist of members elected by the representative villages in the wildlife management area (one member per clan). Elections will be held once every three years. The committee requests that a representative from the Research and Conservation Foundation (RCF) be present during elections.

- The committee's annual general meeting will be held at the Research and Development Center, Heroana Village. Minutes will be kept, signed by all present, and mailed to the executive secretary of the RCF for filing. The committee requests that an RCF-designated person be present at the meetings.

- The committee will appoint a business management group comprised of one member from each village.

- For the committee to conduct business, a quorum of 40 percent of the active membership must be present. In order to change or add to the existing rules, all committee members must receive a ballot through the mail. For a motion to be carried, a four-fifths majority of the Crater WMC is required.

- The business management group will open and maintain a bank account in Goroka. To protect against fraud, any withdrawal from the account must be countersigned by three designated committee members from three villages and approved by a representative of RCF or the Crater Mountain Work Group, made up of Goroka business people, researchers, and government officials familiar with the goals and objectives of Crater Mountain Wildlife Management Area.

- The committee declares a total ban on the hunting of birds of paradise and bower birds in the WMA. The committee will make selective bans on the hunting of other animals such as parrots, eagles, tree kangaroos, echidnas, megapodes, and pythons. The committee will, at a later date, designate certain areas as hunting- and cutting-free zones. The committee will designate fines and other punishments for people who contravene WMA rules.

- The Crater Mountain Wildlife Management Committee recognizes the Research and Conservation Foundation as its sole representative in dealing with government agencies, nongovernmental organizations, and companies that do business in Crater WMA. The committee and RCF will work jointly to manage the WMA resources.

Ecotourism for Conservation at Crater Mountain

In the course of negotiating consent for the wildlife management area, the Gillisons had discussed with village leaders ways to conserve the local peoples' cultures as well as the birds in the face of increasing development pressure. They decided that ecotourism might be a means of both conserving and initiating appropriate local development. Following a presentation outlining their plans for ecotourism in Ubaigubi, WCI responded with support for Malcolm Smith's proposal to build a tourist lodge in the forest. Craig McConaghy, executive assistant to the premier of Eastern Highlands Province, witnessed a formal joint-venture agreement between the landowners and Smith, with the new Research and Conservation Foundation acting as intermediary.

Smith supervised and paid for construction of the tourist lodge, with the understanding that ownership eventually would rest jointly with the clans living at Ubaigubi. (Smith himself stood to gain from increased helicopter traffic to the site, should it become a tourist attraction.) Local people were hired to build the lodge from local materials. Bruning and Carr used their international networks to rally support for the ecotourism program.

In 1984, the Research and Conservation Foundation held its first annual general meeting at the newly completed but unused tourist lodge at Augumahatai, just above the village of Ubaigubi. Later that year, Bill and Kate Bray flew to Ubaigubi and became the lodge's first managers. Subsequent managers were Mal Smith's brother, Ken, and his wife, and George and Kathy Dodge of Los Angeles. The New York Zoological Society's (NYZS) travel department handled the tourist schedule. Under this plan, tourists flew by helicopter to Crater and the simple bush accommodation of the Ubaigubi lodge.

In addition to hiring men for construction work, the organizers of the ecotourism project trained other villagers to maintain and staff the lodge and serve as forest guides for tourists. Villagers agreed not to hunt ten species of birds of paradise and a bower bird that were targeted for conservation, and a cooperative was set up for activities to profit from wildlife protection. A short walk from the lodge, local landowners had built a series of hides where visitors could watch birds of paradise displaying and courting. Naturally, some hides close to the lodge were visited more frequently than others; therefore, a scheme was worked out where all members of the cooperative received a fee whenever tourists visited any one of the hides. At the suggestion of international tour operators and the lodge manager, Ubaigubi men made artifacts for sale and performed ritual theater for the tourists.

Upon the lodge's opening, a number of problems appeared almost immediately:

- The only access to the lodge was by helicopter or an arduous four-hour drive in a Land-Rover. The high cost (US$350/hour minimum) of shuttling tourists in by helicopter made visits only marginally profitable. The already high fares became unreasonable once international tour operators such as Abercrombie and Kent added a 33 percent markup.

- Nationally based tour operators were not enthusiastic about including the lodge in their "adventure safari" packages. When they did, their connecting flights to Goroka did not fit daily weather patterns, which preclude afternoon helicopter rides. This forced an additional expensive overnight stay in Goroka, which further discouraged international tour bookings.

- Apart from the first lodge managers, who left at the end of the opening season for personal reasons, the succeeding managers were notably unprofessional, unfamiliar with the tourist or hotel industry, and, in one case, egregiously ignorant of local customs. The enterprise could not afford the kind of management it needed to compete successfully with other high-priced adventure tours.

- The locals did not maintain the lodge to the standard wealthy American tourists expected.

- Because appreciation (and tips) from tourists rose for the sexier or more violent parts of ritual theater, the dancers increasingly tended to overplay or extend such sections. These distortions of tradition were deeply upsetting to some villagers, who saw the changes as a desecration of sacred rites, setting off new village conflicts. Ironically, anthropologist Gillian Gillison had predicted this problem and argued vigorously that displaying selected "bites" of ritual to outsiders who at best might be sympathetic but were ethnographically ignorant is destructive.

- Because birds of paradise and bower birds only display seasonally, tourists were not interested in visiting the area in the off season. This left the village with no tourism revenues for half the year.

- Just about the time the lodge was finished, growing unrest in urban centers began to be publicized internationally, devastating the Papua New Guinea tourist industry.

Despite these problems, the lodge managed to operate at the break-even point for the first three seasons. The villagers grew increasingly enthusiastic, and the Ubaigubi branch of the Crater Mountain Wildlife Management Committee wanted to buy out Smith. In contrast to his own initial US$100,000 investment, he accepted the figure of 30,000 kina (US$30,000). The IndoSuez Bank offered a loan, and Smith agreed to guarantee it.

During this time, Gillison and Smith met with Abercrombie and Kent and various national tour operators. The tour companies promised support, but there was no follow-up. After the United Nations issued a second international travel advisory because of fighting in Western Highlands Province, bookings dried to a trickle, the loan agreement failed to be approved, and the last full-time manager had to be laid off.

Smith's helicopter company continued operating the lodge as a weekend getaway for its executives for one more season. When faced with the need to rebuild the facility because of its aging bush-timber construction, however, the company withdrew support. For several years, the lodge sat slowly decaying while RCF continued to pay the salary of Omorido Kotapa, who acted as game warden and watchman at the site.

Despite these setbacks, scientists continued to visit the area, and local people maintained blinds for them. This led RCF to consider focusing on scientific tourism rather than adventure or ecotourism. Scientists expect fewer amenities, do not expect artificial "culture shows," and are less likely to heed travel advisories. However, they tend to spend a lot less money than other types of tourists. Clearly, other sources of income were needed in order to meet the growing aspirations of the Gimi clans.

In 1993, RCF/WCS decided that paying a salary to Kotapa, who continued to keep watch over the unused lodge, no longer made sense; the Padu clan subsequently pulled the lodge down.

Crater Mountain Conservation after Ecotourism

In 1989, representatives of WCI and RCF met with David Vosseler and David Wyler from the Foundation for the Peoples of the South Pacific, a rural-development organization that receives the bulk of its donations from U.S. agencies. They helped to secure a Peace Corps couple to help improve the local economy. In September 1990, the two volunteers, Steve and Kristi Booth, moved into a house just outside Ubaigubi that had been constructed for researchers some years earlier. With the sponsorship of the Foundation for the Peoples of the South Pacific, they encouraged small-scale businesses such as market gardening, bee keeping, butterfly farming, fish farming, and improved coffee production. Their gardening suggestions were slow to be adopted, but they did note one instance in which a farmer successfully marketed his tomatoes, one of the new cash crops the two had introduced. The farmer netted about US$10—enough to get the attention of everyone in the community. Even though quite modest by city standards, this economic return was regarded as satisfactory progress locally.

Unfortunately, the Booths' promising work later suffered under a legacy from the last expatriate lodge managers. Three years before, the managers somehow had acquired the skull of the father of a senior member of the Fayu, the most powerful clan in Ubaigubi. Whether the couple purchased the skull, thought it was a gift, or agreed to take it on consignment for sale in America is unclear. Regardless of the terms, the two clearly were ignorant of the Gimi people's relationship to their ancestors.

The skull's owner eventually demanded its return. The RCF located the skull in California, and it passed through several sets of hands before the Booths ultimately were charged with returning it to the Gimi owner. Upon receiving the box holding the skull, empty but for the human remains, the owner, apparently disappointed because he had not received a large rental fee or payment for the skull, accused the Booths of stealing roughly 10,000 *kina* (a little more than US$10,000) from the box.

Fayu clan members, perhaps as dubious as other villagers about the accuracy of this claim, had no choice but to back up their kinsman. They refused to have anything to do with the Peace Corps couple after the incident, an episode that illustrates how closely local people relate all outsider-generated activities, however unconnected they may seem from an external perspective. Poor performance or damaging behavior on the part of one actor can poison the effectiveness of others.

Nonetheless, the arrival of the Peace Corps volunteers in Crater brought the project to a new level of activity and interest. Other area villages aspired to have volunteers move into their communities. An enterprising community leader at Heroana, Avit Wako, built an airstrip for fixed-wing planes, making much cheaper transportation to the area possible.

RCF responded in July 1992 by agreeing to erect a house to serve as a residence for new Peace Corps volunteers, a guest house for visitors, and a storehouse for items headed for market. In consultation with villagers and various researchers, David Gillison decided, on behalf of the board of RCF, that having a building that could withstand the annual 7.5 m of rainfall without constant maintenance was important. Smith, who had underwritten the guest lodge, agreed to provide the shell of a metal helicopter hangar at cost, and Heroana men were hired to construct the interior. Smith also agreed to fly items from Heroana to Goroka, the nearest city with sizable markets, once produce and products were organized for sale.

Wako, in turn, constructed a coffee-buying ground and storage facility adjacent to the new house. He also is supervising construction of another guest house, which will be available for rent.

In October 1992, Bob and Donna Merlina, the new Peace Corps couple sponsored by the RCF, moved into the new house. They have begun working with Wako and other Heroana villagers to reexamine their farming options in light of new opportunities for marketing their products and the opportunities for some modest tourism.

Development of the Research and Conservation Foundation

The Research and Conservation Foundation (RCF) grew out of the efforts of an informal group of nationals and expatriates who had come to know one another while putting together the wildlife-management-area concept. Although it had been functioning informally since 1984, RCF formally incorporated in Port Moresby in 1986 "to promote and preserve, for the benefit of all the people of PNG and the world, the country's rich and unique flora and fauna." RCF has excellent credentials, and its board includes a number of Papua New Guinean leaders and decision makers: Gideon Kakabin (chairman), managing director, Software Laboratories; Alkon Tololo, chairman, National Broadcasting Corporation; Iamo Ila, secretary, Department of Environment and Conservation; Simon Saulei, senior lecturer, Department of Biology, University of Papua New Guinea; William Lawrence, former representative to the ADB and private businessman; and the Honorable Margaret M. Taylor, Papua New Guinea ambassador to the United States. The board also includes some expatriates: D. Bruning, chairman of the Ornithology Department, New York Zoological Society; A. Risser, general curator,

San Diego Zoo; David Gillison, Lehman College; William Peckover, retired director of telecommunications, Papua New Guinea; and Roy MacKay, retired director of Baiyer River Sanctuary, Papua New Guinea. Despite these human resources and yearly meetings, in the first few years the board effected little in the way of achieving its goals because the organization lacked the funds and board members the time to set up an effective administrative structure.

Wildlife Conservation International (WCI), recognizing the board's energy, leadership, and good intentions, eventually offered assistance with production of a membership brochure and locating sources of support. In the fall of 1991, the Liz Claiborne Art Ortenberg Foundation agreed to cover the first-year costs of setting up an office in Port Moresby with a full-time director and program officer. Gideon Kakabin, chairman of the RCF board, together with trustee Bill Peckover, advertised the position of general manager in newspapers and interviewed a number of candidates. Kakabin and Peckover recommended that the board hire former Secretary of the Department of Environment and Conservation Karol M. Kisokau. WCI Research Fellow Eleanor Brown agreed to be seconded to RCF as program officer.

The board also set up a scheme to make money through the sale of stamps. The retiring head of the Papua New Guinea philatelic bureau, experienced in stamp manufacture and marketing, volunteered to oversee the scheme and prepared a business plan to prepare and market a series of four parrot stamps. Parrots were chosen over the more spectacular birds of paradise because of the preexisting market for parrot stamps. The RCF secured the right to sell the stamp packets as one of four kinds of souvenirs offered at the Papua New Guinea pavilion of the World Exposition in Seville, Spain, in 1992.

With Kisokau installed as director, RCF developed a three-year plan to build up the Port Moresby office with the addition of an education director and several education projects in cooperation with the DEC, as well as continue expanding activities in Crater. A proposal to do this was submitted to the MacArthur Foundation, which responded with a grant covering half the total budget.

As with the Crater project the foundation manages, RCF members have encountered some obstacles and some growing pains.

Slow Period after a Fast Start

When the tourist industry dried up, the RCF did not have contingency plans. By 1989, the lodge was decaying, WCI's research house where the Gillisons had stayed was crumbling, and a number of area leaders began to question the wisdom of the decision to set up the Crater Mountain Wildlife Management Area. Falau Idoru, the chief guide at Ubaigubi, Geoffrey Kuave (now a minister in the Eastern Highlands provincial government), and Mr. Bathanimi of Heroana, a big man (and a major figure in establishing the Heroana delegation of the Wildlife Management Committee) all wrote letters, ranging in tone from polite concern to outright indignation, about the RCF's failure to live up to agreements. Their central complaint was that after having placed an embargo on killing birds of paradise, and having given over land and time to establish a tourist lodge and numerous field sites for potential research, they had received nothing in return. The complaints were not entirely justified, since many people had earned significant sums during construction of the lodge and in the first years of tourism. But their points were well taken, since the central goal of the program, as discussed during the establishment of the WMA, was a continuous flow of activity and income from the lodge and researchers working in the area. While the program began successfully enough, a hiatus of two years occurred before the arrival of WCI researchers Andrew Mack and Debra Wright and Peace Corps volunteers Steve and Kristi Booth renewed activity in the area.

The Stamp Scheme

The RCF board decided that it had the expertise to use special-issue stamp sales as a major source of publicity and fundraising for the foundation's work in Crater and, later, elsewhere in the country. The goal was to become self-sustaining as a national organization. However, shortly after the artwork for the stamps was completed and RCF signed a contract with an Australian engraver, the Australian government embarked on a major postal issue that engaged the services of all its engravers. By the time the engraver RCF had contracted with was free, the contract had to be renegotiated. These delays caused the RCF to miss the deadline for stamp sales in Seville. Even if the stamps had been ready in time for the World Exposition, quite likely they would have been consumed by the fire that later destroyed the Papua New Guinea exhibit.

The RCF Conflicts

The arrival of a large amount of unrestricted money can be very threatening to the integrity of a new organization. While the board of directors had decided to use the MacArthur Foundation money primarily on Crater Mountain, the general manager had determined that his priority was to hire a secretary and set up a grade-school environmental program. Rather than settle the matter through open consultation, which might have resulted in a compromise budget, bad feelings resulted when board member David Gillison went ahead and spent nearly all the MacArthur money on the Heroana Peace Corps/research/trade house. This very public conflict started rumors in Port Moresby that the RCF was in administrative disarray and controlled by foreigners. Within RCF, however, the division highlighted several structural flaws in the organization, including too few formal meetings between board and staff and too much day-to-day decision-making power in the hands of the board. Positive changes resulted: The staff is now preparing a more forceful management plan, the board is considering creation of a local executive committee for faster consideration of staff proposals, and mutual discussion is underway, auguring well for smoother management in the second year of the three-year plan. Several board members have suggested that the expatriate founder members retire to an advisory board in order to clarify the RCF's status as a national organization.

The Role of Wildlife Conservation International

Wildlife Conservation International, the international field division of the New York Zoological Society, supports biological field research applied to conservation. It has been active in Papua New Guinea since the early 1970s, when it began a research program on crocodilians and birds of paradise.

Starting in 1982, WCI supported most of the conservation work described in this case study, including surveys; dialogue among locals, nationals, and expatriate researchers; and investigation of wildlife ecology. For the last two years, with some assistance from the Claiborne Ortenberg Foundation, WCI has supported Andrew Mack and Debra Wright's research on rain-forest dynamics and the ecological importance of the dwarf cassowary. Dwarf cassowaries are the largest vertebrates in the forest and the crucial link in the regeneration of several species of large-fruited trees. They are also culturally and economically important; at local weddings, for example, gifts of cassowaries are a must, and their feathers are used in rituals and art.

Mack and Wright's work has been remarkable in its scope and in its demands. The team set up a field camp and a 12-km network of marked trails. They have documented previously unknown ecological patterns of cassowaries; some of these are critical for ensuring uphill seed distribution and explain the persistence of trees high on the steep slopes that characterizes the area. The researchers also have examined the growth strategies of a number of previously unknown tree taxa.

Mack and Wright have had an important social impact too. Because they live at Haia rather than at the northern end of the WMA, they have been able to act as "consultants" to and advocates for participation in WMA planning by the nomadic Pawaians, whom they have employed in rotating teams as field assistants. In their role as consultants, Mack and Wright have responded to Pawaian requests to explain the possible long-term outcomes of current decisions regarding land use.

Future Prospects at Crater Mountain

The work on the Crater Mountain project illustrates that community-based conservation demands a continuing commitment if local people's needs and aspirations are to be made compatible with ecological realities. New pressures and needs require new responses. One goal is to ensure that national and local leaders provide an increasing share of the day-to-day management as well as the long-term planning for the area. Since the nomadic Pawaians participate at a different level than the settled Gimis at this point, RCF or expatriate participation in decision making on their behalf is essential if the project is not to be controlled by Gimi speakers. Some changes seen on the horizon include:

Leadership Training

A series of leadership training workshops led by David Gillison, in conjunction with the management committee, will aim to develop local leadership.

New Subsistence Activities

The Division of National Policy Development Planning and Implementation, an agency that reports to the Department of the Prime Minister, has announced that up to 20,000 *kina* (US$20,000) will be available for the Crater Mountain WMA. A representative of this office has suggested introducing goats and/or cattle, animals not raised in the WMA at present. The Peace Corps volunteers and RCF staff are more enthusiastic about the possibility of increasing chicken production, since the birds are already part of local diets and do not disturb the habitat on the same scale as hoofed animals.

Health

A full-time aid-post officer who will provide basic health care and some social services is due to arrive next year, accompanied by a technician who will test the drinking water. Judging from the prevalence of skin lesions, respiratory infections, and swollen abdomens among children, people in the area have a poor health and nutritional status.

International Aid

In the last several years, delegations of international development specialists, including USAID, the Peace Corps, the diplomatic community, the World Bank, the United Nations Development Program (UNDP), the European Community, and freelance consultants and writers all have helicoptered to Crater. Aside from the Peace Corps, none has delivered any "cargo," to use a local term. Ironically, these visits from the "Development Set" have engendered rumors that the Global Environment Facility (GEF) funds to be managed by UNDP will be spent on sites that receive less "attention." Unless some real projects develop, local cynicism will grow from violated expectations as international aid agencies continue to visit the site without follow-up.

Population Growth

In 1973, 450 adults lived in Ubaigubi. Nearly twenty years later, there are more than 1,000, due to increases in family size deriving from better nutrition. According to Dr. Carol Jenkins of the Medical Research Institute in Goroka, explosive growth followed the availability of canned fish and rice, which in turn came as a result of road construction in the area; the experience at Crater bears out this theory. Until recently, local people have rejected any notion of population control, citing the need for sons as warriors, as protection against sorcerers, or as gardeners. This attitude may change as the share of household income from outside markets grows and subsistence activities lessen in importance.

Discovery of Oil or Gold within the WMA

In nearby Karamui, an international company's mining camp imported Chimbu workers who poached wildlife, squatted on land, and cleared it for agriculture. The lesson was not lost on Crater villagers. Heroana villagers have said that they want to have a say in who comes to work on their land and how long they stay. While inhabitants own the surface of their land, the rights to minerals under the surface belong to the government. Just as the villagers expect the government to sell concessions to mine their land, they expect the government to respect local guidance on what happens to the villagers' forests, fields, and wildlife. The RCF presence in Port Moresby may become critical in helping villagers communicate their concerns and demands about resource-extraction companies' behavior.

An Increasing Array of Development Projects

Local people can expect a growing number of changes in their lives. The two sets of Peace Corps couples (one at Ubaigubi since 1990, another at Heroana since October 1992) will continue to bring the market economy of the nation to the local villages and intensify agriculture among local gardeners. Researchers will continue to come to the area. The Peace Corps volunteers will be replaced every two years and researchers almost as frequently. The national government is interested in setting up a youth corps similar to the California Conservation Corps in the United States, which hires poor urban youths from Los Angeles and other cities to clear trails and perform other park maintenance. The RCF at one point suggested that the Ubaigubi lodge would make an ideal training center for local rural youth. By training bored, unemployed young men in various trades, urban drift could be slowed and the pool of trainees would be an excellent source of workers and guides for the WMA. Bringing in outsiders such as urban youths would only serve to alienate local communities from the WMA. The United States-based organization Conservation International has expressed interest in spearheading the project on behalf of the United States and Papua New Guinea. Conservation International and the Foundation for the Peoples of the South Pacific/Papua New Guinea both have expressed interest in commercial exploitation of nontimber forest products. The Medical Research Institute of Goroka might well participate in health and family-planning activities, should they be invited.

With so much activity looming ahead, the RCF has recognized the importance of having a cultural go-between—someone who will act as an ombudsman to monitor local attitudes and concerns about changes, bringing the managers of various activities together and helping villagers make sense of these projects as an integrated program of improvement for their community. Local people will need help as they find various ways of dealing with the national and international personnel they will be meeting.

Representatives of various aid agencies also will need to consult a central source of information on the sociocultural and microeconomic landscape, local mores, and appropriate wage scales and employment practices.

WCI will second Seldon James to RCF to fill this role when Mack and Wright depart in June 1992. James will rove among all villages, continually updating and monitoring the activities of Gimi and Pawaian community members, development specialists, and researchers. He will be accompanied initially by Samantha Gillison, who grew up in a local village before moving to the United States with her parents. She will focus on women's concerns. Local male and female counterparts will work alongside James and Gillison prior to taking over in 1993.

Conclusion

Although it has sometimes been sporadic, much community-based conservation and development activity has taken place at Crater Mountain in the last six years, with some important successes:

- The agreement of all clans in ten villages to set aside a portion of their lands for wildlife conservation;

- The restoration of rare bird populations whose numbers had declined steeply during the previous decade;

- The perceived linkage between conservation and an improved standard of living on the part of Crater area leaders;

- The establishment of a national conservation NGO with the potential to manage a multidisciplinary and comprehensive conservation program;

- Increased understanding of how Crater's forests regenerate and the role of key wildlife in that regeneration;

- Increased publicity for the region as a potential "model" for integrated conservation and development. Visits to the area from national and international agencies have resulted in more national resources, such as the promise of an aid-post officer and development funds from the Prime Minister's office, and international resources, such as Peace Corps volunteers;

- Increased local cash income from sales of new crops and handicrafts, construction work, tourism, and research assistance;

- Local experience with running a lodge.

On the other hand, the Crater WMA development program has experienced some significant difficulties:

- The generally steep decline in PNG tourism, which contributed, in large part, to the failure of tourism as a reliable local source of income;

- The failure to constantly follow up on the promised returns on the conservation investment. Many villagers questioned the point of a continued conservation program after the tourism project failed and many months passed before other projects could be initiated;

- The slow and sometimes contentious role of the RCF as the linchpin of the WMA's development;

- The failure to address women's needs. Women in Crater society have very constricted roles and are excluded from decision-making committees and discussions at all but the family level. Responding to the needs of women and girls without doing violence to local traditions is imperative for the future;

- The failure to communicate as fully with the nomadic Pawaian people as with the settled Gimi speakers. Conservation workers, no matter their origin, find it easier to live in a settlement. There is no precedent to serve as a model for Peace Corps volunteers who might choose to live alongside nomads.

The Decision-making Process

Finding fault with the unintegrated range of activities that have been tried at Crater is easy. The lack of a qualified central agency capable of directing operations from the start certainly contributed to the disarray. The RCF, as a budding NGO, had to create itself as it endeavored to practice conservation, so the organization was not always effective in its coordinating role. But experimentation and a diversity of projects may be a requirement for achieving genuine local involvement in an exuberantly egalitarian and pluralistic society like Papua New Guinea. While no one today is satisfied with the status quo at Crater, all parties continue to be vitally engaged in the process of community-based conservation and development and feel it will give them a strong stake in a better future. Although achieving consensus among villagers on the value of having a conservation management area took years, that conviction, held by all participants, is sincere.

In Papua New Guinea, land use, by both custom and law, is a never-ending dialogue about the activities of local people. Contracts, for example, can be reopened by descendants of the original parties—in sharp contrast to the belief, prevalent in most other countries, that land can be set aside forever through legal decree. Often the result of such decrees is polarization of local communities and governments when a mandated land use becomes untenable for ecological, social, or demographic reasons. Such conflicts reduce the likelihood of reconciling the values of conservation and development in the future, since the community usually comes to perceive the government agency responsible for wildlife as the enemy of local development aspirations.

Looking Ahead

Community-based conservation at Crater is unruly, contentious, rumor-filled, open-ended, and slow—but also broadly consultative, inclusive, and, potentially, uniquely effective. In Papua New Guinea, both government and local people express both conservation and development values—a good foundation for building conservation policy. In practicing conservation in Papua New Guinea, as elsewhere, benefits must accrue to local people or they will choose another option for the use of their land.

An important point to keep in mind is that, in this context, a positive return on conservation decisions does not have to be dramatic or large by Northern standards. Therefore, embarking on large-scale schemes to secure income from non-timber forest products in the absence of information on their abundance and the reliability of the supply is both unwise and unnecessary. Far too little is known about the forest "warehouse" of Papua New Guinea. Current research suggests that most trees fruit and cycle on multiyear schedules influenced by phenomena such as the Southern Oscillation Event (El Niño). The ecology and behavior of primary pollinators and seed-dispersing animals unique to New Guinea also is too little known. Continued applied research clearly is needed.

The Crater Mountain Wildlife Management Area's objective of successfully integrating Gimi and Pawaian society into national and international market economies as an incentive and reward for the protection and management of biodiversity on their land raises some other human considerations. The role of social and medical anthropologists will be imperative in addressing the social transitions that come with bringing subsistence farmers into world markets. At Crater Mountain, WCI has sponsored anthropological investigations alongside conservation action and research. Those of us involved in helping to preserve the essence of what it is to be Gimi or Pawaian while aspiring to positive social change have learned how truly interdisciplinary successful community-based conservation must be.

An RCF workshop planned for mid-1993 will address many future concerns by examining the decision-making process and enforcement of conservation regulations by the Wildlife Management Committee. The agenda includes the following issues:

- Land zoning and use patterns.

- Land monitoring: Who will monitor wildlife health and compliance with local regulations and who will adjudicate?

- What do clans expect to gain from resource conservation?

- What role can/will people outside Crater play?

- How should the Wildlife Management Committee's access to the RCF staff and board be structured?

- What species will receive priority protection?

- How will the two language groups communicate? Can clans continue to honor their own and others' land boundaries while retaining the integrity of the wildlife management area?

- How will future proposals for development be discussed (e.g., a proposed Chevron Oil pipeline)?

- Any other issues the committee raises.

The workshop also will provide training in monitoring and conduct a survey of marketable products that are more reliable and less invasive than coffee. The Crater Business Group, formed in conjunction with the lodge project, will help with this process.

ACKNOWLEDGMENTS

This case study was prepared in consultation with a number of people involved in setting up the project. I particularly thank Karol Kisokau, O.B.E., former secretary of the Papua New Guinea Department of Environment and Conservation; the Honorable M. M. Taylor, PNG ambassador to the United States; Dr. Donald Bruning, chair of ornithology, New York Zoological Society; Dr. Bruce Beehler, WCI and CI's Country Program Director for PNG; WCI research fellows and staff at Crater Mountain, Andrew Mack and Debra Wright; and Seldon James, WCI conservation fellow. I also thank Peter Little and an anonymous reviewer for their comments.

I also used information from Steve and Kristi Booth, David Vosseler, and Fred Bartu. My greatest debt is to David Gillison, who spent a number of years living and studying in Crater and has been central to its conservation and development. Much of my description of Gimi life is taken from his research.

CHAPTER 9

BOSCOSA: Forest Conservation and Management through Local Institutions (Costa Rica)

Richard Donovan

In 1987, the Osa Peninsula Forest Conservation and Management (BOSCOSA) Project was developed, in collaboration with the Neotropica Foundation of Costa Rica, as the first field project of the Tropical Forestry Program of World Wildlife Fund (WWF). For the last six years, BOSCOSA has attempted to arrest the rate of deforestation on the Osa Peninsula in southwestern Costa Rica by providing sustainable economic land-use alternatives to the region's inhabitants.

The Osa Peninsula is a 280,000-ha humid lowland area in southwestern Costa Rica (Map 9.1). The area is troubled by insecure land tenure, a lack of natural resources protection, unclear or inconsistent governmental development policies, and pressure from gold mining, timber felling, and uncontrolled agricultural expansion. The Osa currently loses up to 5 percent of its forest land each year (Campos 1991).

The Osa is the site of constant, sometimes volatile confrontations between gold miners, loggers, farmers, conservationists, biologists, foresters, and government administrators. Over the last ten to fifteen years, the government has thrown gold miners into jail for mining or hunting illegally in Corcovado National Park. Independent miners have reaped unknown profits, been compensated with land and living stipends, shot and wounded park guards, and complained about the unknown profits reaped by international mining consortiums. Administrators at the Ministry of Planning and Development; the Ministry of Natural Resources, Energy and Mines; and the Institute for Agrarian Development have made policy decisions without consulting local people or their own staff, provoking local farmers to retaliate by threatening the government's staff in the region. Nongovernmental organizations have attempted to mediate between the government and local union organizers.

The conflict on the Osa amounts to a tug-of-war between a growing population

Map 9.1

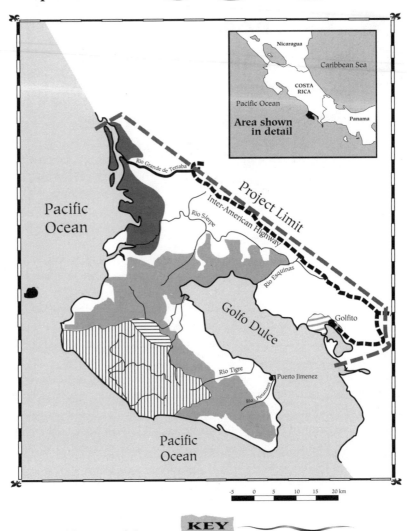

Protected Areas of the
Osa Peninsula

KEY

- Corcovado National Park
- Golfo Dulce Forest Reserve
- Isla del Cano Biological Reserve
- Golfito Wildlife Refuge
- Guaymi Indian Reserve
- Sierpe–Terraba Mangrove Reserve

and national and international interests aimed at conserving the unique biological resources of the area. The Osa is a region in transition made up mostly of subsistence farming families (average cash income: US$100 to $150 per month) who have migrated to the region since 1960 from other parts of Costa Rica. Typical family size is seven (two adults, five children). During the 1980s, up to 2,000 transient gold miners migrated into the region annually. Most worked independently, living in plastic-covered shacks on streamsides and relying on pick and shovel to extract gold. Over the years, some miners have continued their search for gold, while others have become established as small farmers, store owners, or laborers. In addition to gold miners and farmers, roughly 120 Guaymi, an indigenous people, live just outside the northeastern border of Corcovado National Park. Increasingly, foreigners (mostly North Americans and some Europeans) have come into the region to purchase land, either for farming, retirement, or operation of small-scale tourism businesses. Most residents of the Osa have tended to clear forest for agricultural purposes; the Guaymi are the only people in the region who maintain the forest while using it.

Conservation Setting

From a biological perspective, the Osa is the only large remaining block of lowland rain forest on the Pacific side of Central America. The Osa's unique traits stem from its geographic location as part of the land bridge between North and South America and the resulting uncommon mix of climate, soils, vegetation, and animals. The climate provides extreme wetness from August to November (averaging more than 500 mm rainfall/month) and relative dryness from December to April (around 100 mm/month). Climatic variation in terms of wind, cloud cover, and rainfall is significant, creating many highly localized microclimates that contain unique biological communities.

The Osa contains at least 27 different vegetation communities and roughly 2,000 species of plants. These include more than 500 tree species (possibly as many as 750), of which 40 to 45 are commercial hardwood species. For reasons not yet fully explained, the Osa contains a number of trees and other plants found in South America but nowhere else in Central America. At least 50 endangered or threatened plant species have been recorded on the Osa. Research has revealed that about 10 percent of new plant collections from the region contain either undescribed species or new records for Costa Rica. Roughly 50 percent of the endangered or threatened tree species in Costa Rica have genetically viable populations on the Osa, which hosts at least 370 species of birds, 120 species of reptiles and amphibians, 40 species of freshwater fish, and more than 8,000 species of insects.

Corcovado National Park (41,789 ha), the Osa's centerpiece, is often referred to as the crown jewel of the Costa Rican park system. Other protected areas in the Osa complex include the Golfo Dulce Forest Reserve (61,350 ha), Isla del Cano

Biological Reserve (300 ha), Guaymi Indian Reserve (2,700 ha), Sierpe-Terraba Mangrove Reserve (22,600 ha), and Golfito Wildlife Refuge (2,810 ha).

Project Born of Conflict

The intense level of conflict on the Osa Peninsula is due largely to human population pressures, the existence of valued natural resources, and ill-managed government conservation initiatives. The latter include the establishment of Corcovado National Park (1975), Golfo Dulce Forest Reserve (1978), and Guaymi Indian Reserve (1981) and the expansion of Corcovado from 1984 to 1985. From a local perspective, the establishment of Corcovado National Park and other protected areas has been forced upon the people of the Osa.

Until recently, local people have not wanted the park. They see it as representative of a highly centralized national government that is more interested in foreign tourists and the conservation of jaguars than the quality of life of people on the Osa. Although some people on the Osa are conservationists—and some even advocate sustainable development—there is deep-seated resentment of the government and the park. Land purchases by outsiders, whether the government or foreigners, evoke constant and recurring paranoia. Some farmers' land has been claimed consecutively as forest concession, forest reserve, and Indian reserve. Inconsistent policies in government agencies and the desires of interest groups dominated by people from outside the Osa often have dictated the conditions under which the Osa's campesinos live. Until recently, local people have had little say in plans or policies for the Osa's development or the management of its protected natural areas.

The fiercest resentment has been directed toward the government (especially the National Park Service) and Osa Forest Products, Inc. (or Osa Productos Forestales—OPF). Certainly the most caustic remarks almost always are aimed at OPF, an international company dominated by American interests. In the 1960s, OPF purchased from the Costa Rican government roughly 40,000 ha of forest land covering most of present-day Corcovado National Park.

With a lack of inclusiveness that would be typical of future government actions, those who agreed to the sale and subsequent OPF forestry concession ignored the existence of farm families living in the affected area. Once OPF received its concession, the company pressured the farmers to leave and attempted to control the land-clearing activities of those who stayed. Also typical of the times, the establishment of protected areas on the Osa also was undertaken with minimal involvement of the local population. Corcovado National Park was established in 1975 with seed funds from Rare Animal Relief Effort (RARE), WWF, and The Nature Conservancy, led by the crucial brokering of local conservationists Alvaro Ugalde and Joseph Tosi. At the time of the park's establishment, gold miners were not numerous, nor were they perceived as dangerous to the integrity of the park.

Although hunting and farming were banned, miners were allowed to continue panning for gold inside the park, a policy that would change.

Several years later, in 1978, the government of President Daniel Oduber established the Golfo Dulce Forest Reserve. The new forest reserve did not clarify the future of farmers who found themselves living inside the 66,000-ha area. Costa Rican law, then as now, mandated that land tenure conflicts in any newly created forest reserve be resolved through land-use assessments and the development of plans creating management units for forest protection and farmer resettlement. In the Osa, such a process did not begin for almost fourteen years. As of 1990, less than 10 percent of the families on the Osa Peninsula (and only 5 percent in the Golfo Dulce Forest Reserve) had title to their land (Meana Piñole 1989). Because the government has not planned or funded any resettlement scheme, the alternatives, for most small farmers in the region, have been either to move out or to become squatters.

The complications of OPF in the 1960s and the conservation actions of the 1970s were the foundation upon which the growing conflict of the 1980s would be built. In 1980, the government expanded Corcovado National Park by a third to its present total of more than 40,000 ha. The new areas provide the park with more defensible natural boundaries.

In the early 1980s, the Costa Rican economy began to suffer the effects of the global recession. Additional pressure on the Osa occurred with the shutdown of Standard Fruit Company banana plantations in nearby areas, which caused widespread unemployment; with the rise in the worldwide price of gold, which made gold mining more attractive as an economic alternative; and with construction of an all-weather road into the Osa, which provided better access for newly unemployed settlers, gold miners, and loggers seeking access to the commercially rich forest. Further complications arose through the establishment of the Guaymi Indian Reserve by CONAI in 1981. This reserve bordered the park on land that previously had been part of both the Osa Forest Products concession and areas specifically designated for settlement (*baldio nacional*).

As a result of these events, pressure on both the park and surrounding protected areas increased. In late 1984, the Ministry of Planning formed the Osa Inter-Institutional Technical Committee to coordinate government programs in the region and figure out a way to attack socioeconomic and environmental problems. The National Park Service assigned more than seventy members of its staff to the Osa. These park personnel worked not only in park protection, but in an aggressive environmental education campaign to elicit local support for the park, explain its benefits, and try to generate positive momentum in the region.

In mid-1985, an international team of scientists assessed the environmental impact of gold miners working in the park. The resulting report recommended that gold mining in the park should cease, that the National Park Service and other Costa Rican government institutions needed to embark on a program to use the park more innovatively, and that the use of the park as an economic and recreational resource should involve local people and generate income through services provided to park visitors. Some months later, in response, the government issued an emergency decree that placed priority on providing socioeconomic assistance to the people of the Osa. At that time, gold miners were forcibly removed from Corcovado, and the period of greatest conflict, commonly called the Gold Miners' Crisis, then occurred.

Ultimately, the government's emergency decree, designed to bring critical resources to the region, proved a somewhat empty promise. To the extent that the decree provided support for removing and resettling gold miners working in the park, and for establishing and enforcing more sensible boundaries, its impact was positive. But projects and programs that were supposed to provide economic alternatives for local people never were implemented. For people on the Osa, this inaction represented business as usual for the government. They continued to perceive Corcovado National Park as providing few benefits. In truth, most park visitors have been scientists, low-budget backpackers, or nature lovers traveling via expensive San José-based tour companies. A small percentage of visitors have been Costa Rican tourists who have provided relatively few benefits to the local economy—although this has begun to change.

By 1987, deforestation and natural resources degradation on the OSA were occurring at alarming levels. The volume of timber cut under official permit has risen each year, from 11,000 m^3 in 1988 to 17,000 m^3 in 1991. The BOSCOSA project staff estimates that wood harvests were causing deforestation on roughly 2,400 ha of the peninsula per year. With only about 27,000 ha of good, productive forest land left in the region outside the national park, all remaining forest needs to be conserved for watershed protection.

The impact of gold mining also has increased dramatically. As of 1990, thirty-nine active concessions had been registered, and a waiting list held one hundred additional concession requests. Gold miners who use old-time pick-and-shovel techniques process about 1 m^3 of material a day, producing about 1 kg of sediment per day. New larger-scale commercial operations process about 2,000 m^3 of material per day, producing roughly 2 tons of sediment. As a result of gold mining, ecologists estimate that 90 percent of the reef complexes in the Golfo Dulce have been destroyed by sediment.

Handling these threats has proved most difficult for the National Park Service and other Ministry of Natural Resources agencies, whose staff members regard the Osa as a Costa Rican Siberia—a place for new, inexperienced, or problematical staff members. Turnover in government positions in the Osa has been high. To a degree unheard of in almost any other park in Costa Rica, in Corcovado the staff has had to face potentially violent conflict. The situation was no better for employees in the seriously understaffed Golfo Dulce Forest Reserve. Increased access brought more settlers and loggers. A band-aid government policy seemed to dominate, aiding deforestation through benign neglect; creating dissension among government staff members; and increasing tension between public officials, loggers, settlers, and gold miners.

BOSCOSA Design

The growing number of threats and the limited impact of park protection and environmental education programs convinced WWF, Neotropica Foundation, and the Ministry of Natural Resources—an international and a national NGO and a government ministry—that a more comprehensive and consistent package of solutions had to be developed. They realized that new resources had to be brought to bear to support conservation of protected areas through the creation of viable economic alternatives to logging and gold mining for campesinos in the region.

Since its beginning, BOSCOSA has been viewed as a nongovernmental initiative supported by, but independent from, the Ministry of Natural Resources. The importance of this independent identity can not be overemphasized. In spite of attempts to bridge the gap between the ministry and local people, the Ministry of Natural Resources still was regarded as a protectionist organization with little or no concern for local people. In order to work effectively at the grass-roots level, BOSCOSA needed to gain the confidence of local people and be seen as working first and foremost in the interest of the historically disenfranchised local farmers.

The initial project emphasized a flexible framework that would allow staff and local communities and organizations to interact in the creation of future project designs. Past Osa projects had stalled after a long period of design. For this reason, BOSCOSA was designed and started in three to four months, with scaling up envisioned to take place during a process of years rather than months. The approach was to get project staff out in the field and develop the program more fully in collaboration with the local campesinos and local government staff. Through this process, the staff hoped, a strong sense of local ownership of the project would be created in the region.

Although designed outside the Osa by conservation-oriented NGOs, BOSCOSA was not designed or envisioned as a biological conservation project. In particular, due to historical antagonism toward land purchases for conservation, BOSCOSA did not include such a land-purchase program. BOSCOSA was to complement a separate, unrelated protection program by fomenting grass-roots-level sustainable economic alternatives for people in Corcovado's buffer zone. The assumption was that deforestation could be slowed by providing rural campesinos with economic alternatives.

The key principles of the BOSCOSA design were

- Development and/or consolidation of local grass-roots community organizations (i.e., the project would not work with unorganized farmers);

- Local people would be the decision makers, selecting the forestry, agriculture or other development alternatives that they wanted (i.e., ultimately, they would design and implement their own projects);

- BOSCOSA would provide only technical assistance, not financing, materials, or work payments;

- Local community organizations and BOSCOSA would form partnerships to attract financial and other resources for projects through a process called "resource leveraging." The resources so obtained were to be managed directly by the local community organizations;

- BOSCOSA would encourage a mix of local, regional, and national activities, complementing grass-roots development with local organization and project-staff participation in regional or national policy and planning.

Building Community-based Institutions

BOSCOSA's fundamental thrust has been the development and consolidation of community organizations to conserve and manage natural resources on the Osa. Many different participation methods have been used. Some activities have involved farmers and local community organizations in sustainable economic activities in agriculture, forestry, or ecotourism. Other activities include improving the quality of local participation in processes that affect public policy in the region. BOSCOSA's efforts aim to create synergy between activities at the grass-roots level and those at the national or regional planning and policy level. At the grass-roots level, BOSCOSA encouraged local people to get involved with data collection, selection of production alternatives, determining the distribution of costs and benefits, and sharing of project financing.

BOSCOSA did not start working with the best farmers but with those who were committed to working as a group toward ecologically sound and economically viable alternatives. The project began with groups of as few as ten farmer families.

Community Organizations: Designed or Discovered?

In April of 1988, BOSCOSA began activities in the community of Rancho Quemado and by year's end had helped the campesinos form a producer association, ASOPRAQ. By June 1992, BOSCOSA was working directly with twelve community organizations on the Osa, involving approximately seven hundred individuals.

Four criteria were used in the selection of project sites and/or collaborative organizations:

- location on the fringes or in a buffer area of a national park or biological reserve;

- existence of natural forest (usually primary) that, although threatened, was still large and diverse enough so that management and production might be explored as an economic development option;

- relatively stable land tenure and demonstrable interest in retaining land under forest cover;

- past record of success in development efforts.

Having practiced the application of these criteria, however, BOSCOSA has found that communities that are critically located from a conservation viewpoint may not have an appropriate organization, thus necessitating the formation of new organizations. On the other hand, local organizations that show promise of demonstrating alternatives to deforestation may not be found in the most crucial geographic locations.

BOSCOSA's experience with ASOPRAQ in Rancho Quemado and CoopeAgro-muebles in La Palma reflects the two situations described above. ASOPRAQ was organized, with BOSCOSA assistance, as a result of a focus on a specific community located on the border of Corcovado National Park—a critical position in terms of biological conservation. In contrast, CoopeAgromuebles is an organization that antedates BOSCOSA.

Rancho Quemado is a fairly isolated community of roughly four hundred subsistence farmers. Over a period of nine months, the residents slowly developed their focus and decided to form ASOPRAQ to pursue commercial and subsistence agricultural and forestry alternatives. The organization of ASOPRAQ was "induced" by BOSCOSA. Other community organizations already existed, but they either had major operational flaws (e.g., management problems at a community-managed bank) or were focused too specifically (e.g., school or health committees). Soon after BOSCOSA started working in the community, residents suggested that a new, production-oriented organization was needed. BOSCOSA suggested a producer's association because it seemed appropriate and was an institutional form that would gain support from the Institute for Agrarian Development (IDA).

In contrast, CoopeAgromuebles had existed independently for about a year before BOSCOSA became involved. CoopeAgromuebles was located in a town just outside the forest reserve La Palma, but the co-op's members came from all over the reserve. Because CoopeAgromuebles members already knew that they wanted to focus on forestry, BOSCOSA's work with them proceeded rapidly. In less than three months, a tree nursery had been designed, funded, and began operating. In Rancho Quemado, the same work took a year.

The difference in progress is typical of the advantages of working with an already existing local group whose members share a common vision. If the leadership, objectives, and philosophy of an existing local organization are appropriate, experience suggests that supporting an existing organization is the quickest way to successful grass-roots development.

Community Participation: Gold Miners and Farmer-Foresters

The IDA and Ministry of Natural Resources established Cañaza and Sándalo as settlements for gold miners and subsistence farmers who had been removed from Corcovado National Park during its establishment and expansion in 1975 and 1985 respectively. In both cases, the settlement process created dependency on the government, which initially gave the new settlers a living allowance, food for work, new houses, promises of secure title to the land, and technical assistance in agriculture. Both settlements faced a common problem: soils compacted by previous large-scale mechanized rice cultivation. Although the government had recognized the soil problem and promised to help make the land more productive, it was never able to do so; neither were the settlers, who were independent gold miners with limited agricultural experience. As a result, the miners became increasingly cynical of government-sponsored alternatives to gold mining.

At project start-up, BOSCOSA faced an immediate conflict with the Ministry of Natural Resources. The staff at Corcovado National Park believed that since gold miners were the principal immediate threat to the integrity of the park, BOSCOSA should target them for immediate and intensive technical assistance in sustainable forestry and agriculture. The BOSCOSA staff, however, was skeptical that any success could be achieved with gold miners, a group historically anarchistic and transient. BOSCOSA acknowledged that ultimately the project would have to take on the challenge of working with gold miners, but the project chose not to go to the most difficult groups first. BOSCOSA believed that if it began its community organization work with the gold miners, the technical assistance it had to offer might be seen as one more "gift" in response to the miners' past pressure tactics. Also, because of time and resource constraints, saying yes to the miners would have meant saying no to groups such as CoopeAgromuebles that already had shown initiative.

The immediate negative impact of BOSCOSA's approach was that gold miners and some Ministry of Natural Resources staff questioned why the project was not dealing with the greatest visible threat to Corcovado. They suggested that BOSCOSA was working with less difficult groups in a quest for quick success. By late 1988, the positive impacts of BOSCOSA's approach began to emerge. Two groups of ex-gold-miner/farmers of the Cañaza and Sándalo settlements, favorably impressed with activities in Rancho Quemado and at CoopeAgromuebles, solicited BOSCOSA technical assistance. Since then, activities at Cañaza and Sándalo have begun to show some promise. A small group of farmers in each community is organized and working toward commercial cultivation of *pejibaye* (*Bactriz gasipaes*) and *guanábana* (*Annona muricata*); they also are looking at other alternatives such as black pepper and reforestation. The positive trend of the work in Cañaza and Sándalo, plus the work with ASOPRAQ and CoopeAgromuebles, has sparked interest in a number of other gold-miner communities.

Reasons for successful involvement of the Cañaza and Sándalo miners are

- The farmers sought assistance from BOSCOSA on their own initiative;

- The work started with small, self-selected groups of farmers in each community; there was strong participation on the part of each farmer, reflecting an emphasis on the quality rather than the quantity of farmer participation;

- The farmers identified, researched, and selected their own commercial alternative;

- BOSCOSA deliberately downplayed farmers' expectations, explaining that they would confront many problems, that the path to success would be difficult, and that the path was not risk free and depended on farmer participation in everything from design to donor negotiation to reporting; and

- IDA supported the establishment of each association, endorsing credit or funding proposals and providing subsequent follow-up.

Relations with SIPRAICO (Independent Agricultural Producers' Union of the Canton de Osa) presented a strikingly different picture. The union has been both a supporter and an adversary of BOSCOSA. At one point, late in 1990, a conflict arose in which potentially violent confrontations between the two groups, as well as local groups such as ASOPRAQ and CoopeAgromuebles, were narrowly averted.

In 1987, SIPRAICO had roughly fifty to one hundred members concentrated in the northeastern (or Mogos) section of the Golfo Dulce Forest Reserve. SIPRAICO's main activity was obtaining annual wood-harvesting permits from the Department of Forestry for its members, campesino farmers. These permits enabled the farmers to cut down between five to twenty trees per family. Timber harvesting was beneficial to SIPRAICO members because it provided cash income, facilitated clearing of land for agriculture or grazing, and, through logging, provided farmers with better road access. Members were able to obtain harvesting permits because the government had offered no other economic alternatives. Loggers and sawmill owners from the cities also strongly supported the government granting the permits.

BOSCOSA's interaction with SIPRAICO started tentatively in 1987. SIPRAICO asked for assistance in developing tree nurseries for the reforestation required to compensate for trees cut down under permit. The BOSCOSA staff objected to SIPRAICO's idea of (and the Department of Forestry's implicit support of) clearing natural forest to reforest. By 1990, SIPRAICO's membership had climbed to more than three hundred families, covering almost all of the forest reserve. This growth was due largely to its success in getting wood-harvesting permits in 1987, 1988, and 1989 and led to the BOSCOSA and SIPRAICO conflict.

In a public letter to the Department of Forestry, BOSCOSA accused SIPRAICO of failing to meet its reforestation obligations, of constructing unplanned roads, and, through indiscriminate tree felling, of damaging a hectare of forest for every three trees felled. In addition, not only had SIPRAICO requested more wood-harvesting permits for 1990, but it had called for government support to pay for reforestation—which under the BOSCOSA plan was supposed to have been covered by profits generated by timber harvesting. SIPRAICO retaliated with public accusations that BOSCOSA and the Ministry of Natural Resources planned to buy out farms, expand Corcovado National Park, and eliminate timber harvesting, one of the few economic alternatives for farmers on the Osa.

As a result of this conflict, SIPRAICO and BOSCOSA began a process of negotiation and institutional soul searching. BOSCOSA became more active in publicizing its activities, communicating its goals, problems, and accomplishments on a broader basis to the Osa's population. At SIPRAICO, some members began to consider the long-term implications of unplanned timber harvesting. BOSCOSA offered to work with SIPRAICO in natural forest management and reforestation (but only in areas already cleared or degraded). Although many members of SIPRAICO at first rejected this initiative, some members were receptive.

SIPRAICO is still evolving, and the long-term impact of this conflict on the organization continues to unfold. However, the impact on BOSCOSA, Neotropica, and the Ministry of Natural Resources has been important. To all involved, this conflict graphically demonstrated the difficult issues in the Osa: the pull between reforestation vs. natural forest management and between short-term timber harvesting vs. long-term forest management. It also drew attention to the need to address the continuing socioeconomic plight of poor farmer-colonists. This was the first time that community organizations, the Ministry of Natural Resources, and BOSCOSA jointly confronted a major crisis. The crisis catalyzed more effective coordination between all the participating institutions.

Resource Management Options: Whose Priority?

During the project design phase, the suggestion arose that BOSCOSA should avoid involvement in agriculture because it would dilute the emphasis on natural forest management and conservation; others suggested that a strong agroforestry and agricultural intensification program would relieve pressure on protected or forested areas. In the end, BOSCOSA retained agriculture as a potential activity because the project was committed to the notion that farmers on the Osa should work in their own interest, on alternatives that they themselves identified.

Sustainable Agriculture

In practice, the project used agriculture as a first entrée into local communities. After selecting a particular community or organization to work with, BOSCOSA's first extension activity usually was to work in farmers' fields to establish mutual confidence, discuss forestry, and begin to determine which alternatives farmers were interested in. Initially, the project provided help to improve farmers' production of crops such as cacao, rice, beans, and corn; it also helped farmers research their other alternatives. Some groups were clear on the options they wished to pursue, and after brief analysis, BOSCOSA staff agreed, and activities moved ahead. Such was the case with CoopeAgromuebles; in other cases, either the groups' production choices were questionable or more information was needed before a decision could be made. In these cases, the project helped farmers get better information on options so that choices would be more sound.

Before pursuing a particular alternative, BOSCOSA staff and farmers examined each option from a number of perspectives. Diversification of crops to spread risk was a prime consideration, as were crop combinations with both subsistence and cash value. Perennial crops that required fewer long-term inputs and had better ecological adaptation also were emphasized. But whatever agricultural technology is chosen for a given project, BOSCOSA's experience indicates that without an explicit link or agreement at the grass-roots and governmental levels that ties assistance or improvements in agriculture or forestry to specific conservation actions, intensification of agriculture may have no impact whatsoever on forest conservation.

Reforestation

Reforestation and natural forest management can be complementary techniques for maintaining or reestablishing forest cover. As practiced on the Osa, there is often a conflict between them. Ironically, well-meaning policy directives or initiatives taken by government and private interests (even environmental organizations' plant-a-tree programs) sometimes have resulted in deforestation for reforestation purposes or reinforcement of the idea that tree plantations are more "productive" than natural forest. As a result, communities lose opportunities for productive management of primary, secondary, or degraded natural forest, and the relative role of reforestation in fighting deforestation becomes confused. The predilection toward reforestation as the solution to deforestation can be pernicious. Financial incentives for reforestation have caused deforestation on the Osa Peninsula.

Reforestation can help to redress deforestation, but its limitations for the conservation of biological diversity should be kept in perspective. Tree plantations usually do not provide the same benefits as natural forest in terms of biological diversity, watershed protection, or nontimber forest products. In order to consistently produce high-quality trees, foresters have sought to reduce variables and concentrate their efforts on monoculture plantations.

Like agriculture, reforestation—in response to local interest—became an unexpectedly large BOSCOSA activity. Soon after project start-up, the Osa campesinos' interest in reforestation became obvious. Among the reasons for this:

- Campesinos who saw the heavy logging in the region were impressed by the value of desirable species and concerned about future supply of those species for their own and commercial uses;

- Farmers on the Osa Peninsula easily relate to reforestation technology because of its similarity to traditional agriculture (e.g., row planting, clearing land);

- Government staffers generally regard reforestation projects as improvements (*mejoras*), a demonstration that campesinos are working their land, potentially helping them to gain title or, if they should be bought out or expropriated, increasing the land's compensation value;

- The Costa Rican government has placed tremendous emphasis on reforestation, providing strong financial and legal incentives for reforestation programs that farmers on the Osa had not been able to tap into.

The BOSCOSA staff never believed that reforestation would be the solution to deforestation on the Osa. It also was aware that, except for the small population of Guaymi Indians, no strong forestry tradition existed among the people of the Osa, whose first interest was agriculture. Thus when BOSCOSA staff supported reforestation, it did so with the strategy of simultaneously emphasizing conservation and management of natural forest.

BOSCOSA's approach of using reforestation, primarily with native species, as an initial forestry activity has been successful. Four groups are designing or beginning to implement natural forest management projects, in most cases after participating in reforestation. BOSCOSA technical assistance in reforestation was not explicitly "conditioned," either verbally or in written contract. Rather, the staff emphasized that reforestation was a means of developing forestry expertise to be utilized, ultimately, in managing and maintaining the remaining natural forest.

Natural Forest Management

Management of natural forest only recently has been of interest to many people in Costa Rica, even to foresters. In the media and among foresters, reforestation concerns overwhelm issues of natural forest management, and although there are promising natural forest management initiatives in the country, information about them remains largely in the hands of a few technicians or researchers.

When WWF initiated the BOSCOSA project, natural forest management was expected to be one of its principal foci. In practice, three to four years of grassroots development work were required before community organizations became actively involved in such activities.

BOSCOSA's work in natural forest management on the Osa Peninsula has had to accommodate a number of conditions. First, the people on the Osa are predominantly highly individualistic colonists who have moved to the region during the last ten to thirty years. Although many have valuable knowledge of the forest, they are not "forest peoples"; traditionally, they have viewed forests as obstacles to be cleared to make way for agriculture rather than as a resource to be managed. Second, most residents of the Osa Peninsula individually hold 5 to 100 ha of land. For viable management, these pieces of land have to be grouped together, requiring landowners to organize themselves.

Rather than force acceptance of natural forest management as a production alternative, BOSCOSA sought to help each group develop its own ideas. By working with them primarily on agricultural alternatives, it sought to gain their confidence. Often the first forestry activities involved reforestation, followed (because of constant promotion by the project) by increased involvement in management of the natural forest itself. An exception was the Guaymi Indian Reserve, where there was interest in managing the natural forest from the beginning.

The BOSCOSA approach to natural forest management has emphasized

- Developing a viable local organization that has a general interest in sustainable development and a specific interest in natural forest management. Often such development takes up to three years before commercial natural forest management projects can be started;

- Utilizing the structure of a local organization to group together smaller, individually owned forest blocks and put them under management—creating a "community rain forest," to be managed by local people through their own local organizations, whether cooperatives, producers' associations, or for-profit companies;

- Gradual incremental improvements and scaling up of forestry practices, wood processing, and commercial forestry development (i.e., taking a series of small steps to improve forest practices or wood processing rather than attempting quantum-leap changes); and

- Use of appropriate wood-harvesting and -processing technologies that can be operated and maintained by local people after minimal capital and training; these also must be available at low cost.

Secure land tenure, technical assistance, and training opportunities are incentives that BOSCOSA has provided community organizations. Since 1988, the Ministry of Natural Resources has provided concessionary credit to small farmers throughout Costa Rica for reforestation (as well as major incentives to industrial producers). Although BOSCOSA has suggested that the level of monetary reward provided for reforestation is too high, most of the project's efforts have focused on ensuring that management of natural forest receives equal support. Starting in 1990, BOSCOSA began to design a forest conservation and management incentive fund for organizations that conserve and manage natural forest. The incentive, called PROINFOR, is channeled through FIPROSA, a trust fund overseen by a committee of local people, NGOs, and government. PROINFOR provides a small initial cash incentive for land put under conservation easement, with the bulk of the incentive paid into an interest-generating account or bonds:

> Farmers receive the interest earned on the trust fund according to their contribution, half as an annual lump sum payment, half as an annual deposit in an escrow account established in the farmer's name. The escrow is intended to build equity to leverage future funding for productive activities once the incentives expire. After five years, the easement is evaluated by the farmer, the community organization, and BOSCOSA to decide whether it should be discontinued or extended for another three years. During the sixth through ninth years of the easement, three-quarters of the interest generated from the trust fund is paid to the farmer as income and the remaining quarter is invested in the farmer's escrow account. Once the easement expires, the PROINFOR program will be transferred to other communities and their residents who live on the margins of Corcovado National Park. Farmers who graduate from the PROINFOR program are expected to invest their newly acquired capital in productive activities that do not degrade the forest. *(Cabarle et al. 1992)*

National Policy and Tenure

BOSCOSA has struggled to address two complex policy issues: interagency coordination and land tenure. Despite three years of effort by BOSCOSA and more than fifteen years of continuous, although inconsistent, attempts by the National Park Service and other government agencies, policies and plans for the region remain inconsistent and vague, for many reasons. The "capital-city complex" in Costa Rica means that virtually all major decisions are made in San José with little or no input from people or government staff in the Osa or other regions. Symbolic participation by government officials takes place in public meetings, to temporarily reduce conflict, quiet detractors, and move ahead with personal or institutional agendas. Increasing politicization of conservation in Costa Rica also has begun, including turf fights and infighting among national and international professionals. These problems complicate government policy and planning in an already complex region.

BOSCOSA's first strategic emphasis has been to work on alternatives with grass-roots organizations. But this approach would have had limited impact unless the project also were able to change the standard operating procedures of government agencies in the region. To do this, the project combined grass-roots development activities with strategic interventions at the level of government policy and planning for the region.

BOSCOSA began its involvement in regional policy and planning with informal coordination between government agencies in the field. As an explicit philosophical statement, the project's first step was to work with local people, help them develop alternatives, and identify barriers. The project attempted to forge a coalition of local people and supportive government staff to tackle identified barriers. In theory, by working closely with small farmers, project staff members would come to better understand the "campesino reality," become their allies, and work with them to change government policy.

Within six months of start-up work with communities, BOSCOSA began to test the waters of regional and national government collaboration. In June 1988, BOSCOSA informally organized a meeting between local people, government staff members, and local project personnel. This meeting began a process of spontaneous and constructive interaction between people who previously had rarely communicated. Monthly meetings were initiated, with a new topic receiving priority at each occasion. Although nothing official took place at the meetings, the discussions began to affect the field operations of government programs, leading to government-NGO cooperation and collaboration between government agencies.

In August of 1988, this informal grouping named itself the Osa Inter-Institutional Committee (CIO). Although still informal, CIO meetings made clear that government field staff from different agencies were confronting similar institutional problems (e.g., lack of resources, little decision-making authority, etc.). Collaborative efforts through the CIO began to improve the situation, resulting in successful funding proposals, collaborative planning, and monitoring of conservation activity. Even though CIO fostered joint action at the field level, attempts to restructure resource management throughout the country were frustrated by a lack of commitment in San José.

Successful long-term forest conservation also requires resolution of the second major policy challenge: land tenure conflicts. As previously noted, less than 10 percent of the people on the Osa have secure title, and the average size of a forested parcel is less than 60 ha. Such fragmentation makes forest management or conservation extremely difficult. In addition, farmers can not borrow money because, in the absence of title, banks will not recognize their land as collateral for loans. Yet in spite of insecure tenure, land transactions are common. Untitled land is bought and sold because there is a tradition of spontaneous land settlement (e.g., homesteading), and also because Costa Rican law recognizes occupancy as a step in gaining title. Even if a farmer lives on a parcel of land for only a few years, when the land is expropriated by the government, the government must pay the farmer for clearings, buildings, and other investments. This situation is made even worse in the Osa, because cleared land still sells for more than prime virgin timberland. The link between such "improvements" and grants of title, along with confused government policy regarding land tenure, has been the major cause of deforestation on the Osa.

In response, BOSCOSA has not suggested that secure land tenure alone will stop deforestation. Rather, the project suggested that secure tenure be part of a package of incentives to stimulate forest management and disincentives that penalize forest clearing or overexploitation. The development of solutions to insecure tenure has taken more than three years and is still incomplete.

At the individual farmer level, BOSCOSA has proposed that the government grant title to individuals for most of the land, with conditions of title specifying that portions of the land must be maintained in agriculture, housing, or forest. At the local level, the proposal is that community organizations will manage blocks of forest land for production or protection under the Ministry of Natural Resources' supervision, with BOSCOSA technical assistance.

Conclusions

The ultimate goal of BOSCOSA has been to maintain forest cover on the Osa Peninsula through the development of alternatives for residents of the region. BOSCOSA's approach to halting deforestation has been to develop a coalition of community organizations and regional government staff members to fight deforestation.

Overall, success or failure for BOSCOSA should be judged, at least in part, by evaluating what has happened in terms of maintenance of forest cover on the Osa Peninsula outside Corcovado National Park and the ability of local residents to meet their cash and subsistence needs through activities that maintain or improve the quality of the natural resources base.

The hopeful tone of much of BOSCOSA's work can not obscure the reality that, in terms of both objectives, the Osa still faces a difficult struggle. The region continues to suffer deforestation at an annual rate of approximately 5 percent, and many local people and organizations still are searching for better economic alternatives. Corcovado National Park continues to suffer illegal hunting and gold-mining pressure, and forest degradation proceeds within the Golfo Dulce Forest Reserve.

On the other hand, BOSCOSA's accomplishments fall under the categories of institutional development, regional natural resources planning and management, and grass-roots development with community organizations. In terms of institutional development achievements, BOSCOSA has

- helped to establish eight community organizations and consolidated four;

- established a permanent Centro BOSCOSA as a center for farmer-oriented training, research, and extension in forest conservation and management, agriculture, environmental education, ecological research, and ecotourism;

- helped the Ministry of Natural Resources establish the National Conservation Areas System and the Osa Peninsula Conservation Area, a regional conservation plan;

- helped to redirect IDA's efforts on the Osa Peninsula toward sustainable development and forest conservation; and

- provided a base of field experience that has had a positive impact on the development of the Neotropica Foundation as a leader in buffer-zone management and integrated conservation and development in Costa Rica.

In terms of regional natural resources planning and management, the project has initiated cooperation between community organizations and government agencies, and a number of regional initiatives have been designed and implemented.

At the grass-roots community organization level, BOSCOSA has helped to implement improved land-use practices on 6,439 ha (Cabarle et al. 1992) of land owned by members of community organizations. These practices include reforestation, natural forest management, forest conservation, improved annual and perennial cropping, and agroforestry.

Overall, some things have changed on the Osa; others have not. Because of the efforts of the last five years, local resistance to forest conservation and management no longer appears to be the major factor limiting success. The question now is how the nucleus of interested and committed local people can function as a stepping stone to future successful conservation. A continued emphasis on farmer-level forest conservation and sustainable development remains necessary. Unfortunately, the government still speaks with an inconsistent voice about resolving land tenure, timber harvesting, and gold-mining threats. Community groups seeking to sustainably manage forest still confront almost as many bureaucratic barriers as before. Commercial logging and mining interests continue to move ahead, and insecure land tenure is yet to be resolved.

SOURCES

Cabarle, B., J. Bauer, P. Palmer, and M. Symington. 1992. "BOSCOSA: The Program for Forest Management and Conservation on the Osa Peninsula, Costa Rica." Project Evaluation Report (August). Photocopy.

Campos, J. 1991. "The BOSCOSA Project: Case Study of Sustainable Natural Resource Management and Community Development in the Osa Peninsula, Costa Rica." Paper presented at the Humid Tropical Lowlands Conference: Development Strategies and Natural Resources Management, DESFIL, Panama, June 17–21.

Meana Piñole, A. 1989. *Estudio sobre Tenencia de Tierra en la Península de Osa.* BOSCOSA Document # 8. San José, Costa Rica: Neotropica Foundation.

CHAPTER 10

Profile of National Policy: Natural Forest Management in Niger

Jonathan Otto and Kent Elbow

Niger and the other countries of the West African Sahel zone have suffered twenty-five years of subnormal rainfall. Drought conditions combined with demographic pressures, a legacy of centralized resource-management policies and practices, and other factors have had a profoundly negative effect on the country's natural-resources base. Once-vast tracts of natural forest land are dwindling at an alarming rate. Within the span of human memory, entire forests have disappeared—forests that provided wood, food, fodder, fiber, and other products essential for the survival of both rural and urban Nigerien populations.

Amid this environmental degradation, one of the few hopeful signs is a series of recent experiments intended to increase the involvement of local resource users in managing some of the remaining forest lands. By adapting principles of natural forest management (NFM) to the unique conditions of Niger, these projects are attempting to incorporate rational management and popular participation in the development of economically viable and environmentally sound strategies for exploitation of forest resources. On one level, these projects are ground-breaking policy experiments that challenge long-standing legislative codes and forest management practices. On another, they are technical and socioeconomic experiments that test an array of issues, from biological regeneration rates to the civil society's capacity to evolve new, decentralized resource-governance systems.

Community-based management of forest lands, particularly in the politically repressed environment of Niger, will require many years of evolution before meaningful patterns emerge and data can be extracted to predict long-term sustainability. When fieldwork for this report was carried out in 1991–92, at one site the new type of local institution called the forest cooperative was only months old. Likewise, experimental conservation and coppiced cutting, forestry activities that take years to show their impact, had been underway for just a few seasons at two other sites. Crucial changes in government policy, necessary to legitimate these new NFM regimes, have yet to be enacted; in fact, the very form of national government is under a protracted period of negotiation. Given these conditions, a decade may be a reasonable period after which to review Nigerien experiments in radical reform of resource-management regimes.

Attempting to draw conclusions about the long-term effectiveness of community-based NFM projects in Niger is premature. Whether those involved in nascent NFM efforts will make wise choices, forge compromises acceptable to multiple stakeholders, and enjoy the requisite legal structures is unknown at this juncture. In the absence of data collected over time, a description and analysis of what is known of these NFM projects' gestation and the context in which they must function probably is most useful. However, a major theme that runs through NFM projects in Niger is the dampening impact of the policies, practices, and attitudes inherited from the colonial period, many of which remain intact despite the passage of thirty years. These juridical, political, and social parameters work together to slow decentralization and inhibit innovation in resource management. These forces have severely circumscribed possibilities for effecting critically needed changes that favor user-based governance of natural resources. If progress is to occur in NFM, fundamental changes in policy and practices are required.

Despite this inability to draw definitive conclusions, the early phases of these pioneer efforts and the complex environments in which they function merit scrutiny for several reasons. Chief among these is that, given the dearth of viable alternatives, such NFM experiments undoubtedly will proliferate in Niger and elsewhere in the Sahel. Without careful consideration of the formidable constraints these projects face, unrealistically high expectations may obscure small but significant successes.

Sahel Geography and Climate

Niger is a landlocked country in West Africa (see Map 10.1), one of a series of countries that stretch across the continent just south of the Sahara from the Atlantic Ocean to the Red Sea. This zone—known as the Sahel, from the Arabic word for "edge" or "border"—is characterized by low levels of rainfall unevenly distributed in a brief rainy season. Beneath such surface uniformity is a variety of peoples (including mobile and sedentary pastoralists, farmers of rain-fed and irrigated crops, fisherfolk, hunter-gatherers, oasis dwellers, and many other nonexclusive categories of resource users) who exploit complex ecosystems and microenvironments. For all of these groups, the controlling factor in their cycles of activity (and, often, their survival) is water.

Wetter and drier periods have alternated throughout recorded Sahelian history, with lengthy droughts chronicled as early as the fifteenth century. Despite some wetter-than-average decades in the middle of this century, taken as a whole, the twentieth century may be the West African Sahel's most arid period in this millennium. Since the late 1960s, much of the West African Sahel (i.e., the region from Senegal to Chad) has been in the grips of a downward spiral of reduced

Map 10.1

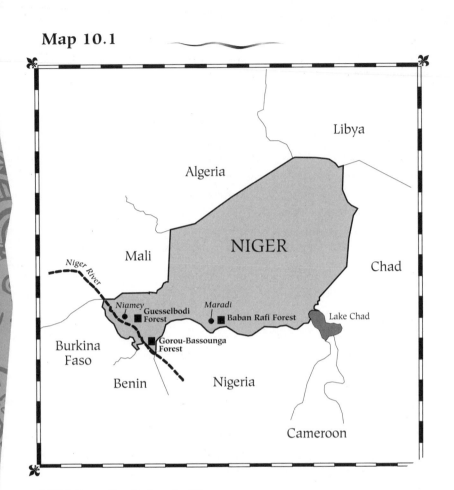

NFM Case Study Areas, Niger

rainfall and degradation of the fragile resource base. Severe and widespread drought has occurred twice in recent years: from 1968 to 1974 and again in the early 1980s. Natural forest lands, once a major feature of the Sahelian landscape, have suffered high mortality rates during this prolonged drought—losses that have been compounded by drought-intensified exploitation of surviving trees and other forest resources by herders and farmers alike.

Agricultural expansion into marginal lands during an interlude of atypically high rainfall throughout the 1950s and early 1960s has had tragic results during the stretches of subnormal precipitation that have followed. The alarming degradation of the natural-resources base that has captured international attention in the last twenty years had its origins in the colonial era, a period that, in the case of Niger, dates back less than a century.

During the colonial period, Niger's modern boundaries were cut with little regard for ethnoenvironmental systems, and the legislative and economic frameworks established then still strongly influence natural-resources management. Also in this era, the Sahel's elite class was imprinted with a mindset of central governmental control and entitlement that is largely intact thirty years after Independence.

Colonial Policies and Practices

In a study of natural forest management in the 1990s, only a brief examination of the enormous impact of the colonial era is possible. Yet to leave out the colonial period completely would be to ignore the very force that helped set in motion the resource-abuse problems that NFM is meant to resolve. Well-documented influences on Niger's environmental decline from the colonial period include cultivation of exportable cash crops, particularly peanuts; forced labor; obligatory centralized grain-storage schemes; controlled prices for grains; taxation and the need for monetized income; inappropriate new agricultural technology; and disruption of customary transhumant pastoralist patterns, among others.

The mindset that Nigerien officials inherited from the French, which has now passed to a new generation of government leaders, includes a number of ingredients particularly germane to the issue of present-day problems in NFM. The colonial power, France, suffered from an abiding misunderstanding of the complex Sahelian ecology that was coupled with the economic goal of transforming rural systems in order to maximize exportable production. The colonialists also manifested a combination of ignorance and disinterest concerning peasant farming systems, including the indigenous knowledge that produced and sustained them.

A central colonial concept of power views the state as entitled to appropriate virtually all authority to itself. French policies had a far-reaching impact on Niger and other Sahelian regions; yet France's administration of the vast interior of the Sahel was too extenuated to constitute detailed control. Elements of precolonial resource-management arrangements continued to hold sway. Nonetheless, colonial authority established the hegemonic right of central government over rule making, rule enforcement, and revenues from these resource-management functions.

Political Situation Since Independence

In 1974, a military coup replaced the authoritarian rule of President Hamani Diori that had evolved since the Independence elections of 1960. The new regime, led by strongman Seyni Kounche, held sway until 1987, when it was replaced by another military government under Ali Saibou. The same public pressure that swept through much of francophone Africa around the time of the collapse of the European communist regimes led to a protracted national conference in Niger beginning in 1991 and, finally, to a multiparty presidential election early in 1993.

Of all the trends and contradictions of these postcolonial regimes, those most relevant to community-based conservation concern policies and practices in popular institutions and an ongoing power struggle between local and central institutions. To some degree, Nigerien leaders attempted to continue French patronage relationships within customary leadership. But Diori and his successors also sought to circumvent local elites through new state-controlled structures designed to reach into individual rural communities. Initially, this was through government-controlled cooperatives meant to "mobilize" the peasantry into modernizing agriculture and increasing production of cash crops.

Local political and commercial interests eventually were to sabotage and co-opt these attempts at centralized organization of the rural population, and by the 1970s the cooperatives' function was reduced to monopolizing cash crops. The Kounche regime went even further in marginalizing the cooperatives' community-mobilization role by reviving the colonial-era Association of Traditional Chiefs and creating the national *Samariya* youth movement, ostensibly based on traditional Hausa groupings. A few years later, his government came up with a pyramidical plan for tightly regimented "participation" that was to dominate relationships between local communities and the government during the 1980s and into the 1990s. This corporatist system of central control was called *La Societe de Developpement,* or the Development Society.

The Nigerien state's strategy of integrating traditional authorities into state-directed networks responsible for tax collection and other functions of the state has created a powerful channel between centralized authority and scattered populations. More direct, although fragmented, channels between the state and rural societies persist through the activities of state agents including agricultural extension agents, cooperative advisers, foresters, and other officials in rural areas. A common characteristic of nearly all these channels is that communication is one way: from the state to rural populations.

To say that official state policies and politics in Niger sometimes appear remote and irrelevant to the daily lives of rural inhabitants is an understatement. The perception of irrelevancy stems from (1) the presence at village level of alternate nonstate authority systems and institutions, and (2) the general absence at village level of resident administrative or advisory installations of the state.

Throughout the entire postcolonial period, with the partial exception of the early cooperative movement of the 1960s, rural Nigeriens have not been allowed to form autonomous organizations. They have been coerced to "join" and work for a series of government-sponsored institutions in which they do not have a significant voice. As bystanders, they are aware, perhaps only dimly, of the competition among the central government, the bureaucratic class, and elite groups at various levels for control of this apparatus of mass organizations. Rural Nigeriens understand that "traditional" leaders, often selected by the state or serving in positions created by the state, also did not want to encourage local initiatives or see control of resources pass to the people. Consequently, rural resource users' experience of modern forms of organization is one of coercion, manipulation, and exploitation—an experience that NFM and other community-based conservation efforts will overcome only slowly, if at all. The legislative framework for management of forest resources is, unfortunately, no more user friendly than the institutional framework that has been imposed on rural Nigeriens.

Elaborate legislative texts such as forest codes and policies of the state and the movement to create the Development Society rarely arrive in the villages in unadulterated form. State machinery capable of delivering state policy to rural populations in implementable form is, in many cases, inadequate for the task if it exists at all. Yet in spite of the state's frequent inability to govern in the rural context in exact accordance with stated intentions of legislation or policy, the state nevertheless continues to plays a central role in the lives of rural populations. The state's claim of the ultimate authority in the land appears not to have been seriously questioned in the context of rural southern Niger. In northern Niger, on the other hand, some Tuaregs have been engaged in a low-level violent conflict with the government in recent years.

The situation is not uniformly bleak, however. At present, an apparently committed movement in Niger is attempting to redefine state-civil relations, although the situation remains in flux and defies any confident prediction. The military government's peaceful acquiescence in allowing a national conference on democracy to take place in October 1991 opened new possibilities for increased popular participation in setting policy priorities, with potential repercussions for community-based conservation. This process finally led to multiparty elections in 1993, another promising sign. The policy profile of forest resource management in Niger is significant not only for the legacy it has created among policy makers and rural populations, but particularly in the current context of evolving state-civil relations, which finally may make state policies directly and literally meaningful to rural populations. To what degree, or even in which direction, state-civil relations will evolve from historical patterns remains to be seen, as does the degree to which the policy trends toward increased popular participation chronicled below will come to typify state-civil relations in the rural context.

Natural Forest Management in Niger

As a term, *natural forest management*, or *NFM*, is relatively new in the Sahel, since until the 1980s the vast majority of forestry efforts aimed to transform forested lands rather than enhance and preserve indigenous forests. For reasons that seem to parallel the urban elite's discounting of peasant farming systems and indigenous knowledge, outsiders have long considered Niger's very landscape *la brousse inutile*—"useless bush." Enormous efforts have gone into clearing forests so that they could be replanted with exotic species. In Niger, as elsewhere in the Sahel, these schemes increasingly are discredited as technically unsuccessful and economically unjustifiable. The alternative to these failed invasive approaches, and to the adversarial practices of the Forestry Service, is to work in partnership with local resource users to manage and exploit the forests sustainably using natural forest management techniques.

Origins of NFM in Niger

The colonial forestry code and the manner of its enforcement survived without any basic change in orientation for more than half a century. An international call for reform emerged during and following the severe drought years of 1968 to 1973, when the threat of desertification in the Sahel became an international issue. The message from studies and seminars was that Sahelian states had been unsuccessful in efforts to police the use of natural resources and that the time had come for radical change in natural-resources policies.

As early as the 1960s, the Peace Corps, NGOs, and development workers attempted to assist Niger's Forestry Service in engaging local populations in forestry work. Typically, a nursery with tens of thousands of tree seedlings was established, and villagers were "mobilized" to plant and protect trees for fuelwood, windbreaks, shade, fruit, construction, and other uses. Hundreds of communities were urged to set up village woodlots using exotic and, in some cases, indigenous seedlings. Technical and organizational problems plagued these communal projects, from poor transplant survival rates and lack of fencing against untethered animals to difficulties organizing volunteer workers and unclear tenure rights for community woodlot trees. Even when exotic species survived, they often did not meet local needs. Eucalyptus wood, for example, gives off a pungent odor that makes it unacceptable for cooking fires.

During the 1980s, the major agencies involved in forestry came to seriously question or actually abandon the woodlot approach. The challenge to modify traditional state policies in forest-resource management was formulated in international as well as domestic forums. Natural regeneration techniques were getting more and more attention in field research and test projects, but legal and practical problems continued to stymie progress in agroforestry. Increasingly, observers began to question whether all efforts should focus on infield or agricultural and village areas when the vast forested lands were receiving little or no positive attention. The environmental degradation of these forested lands, coupled with the lessons of community-action forestry, compelled USAID and other donor agencies to attempt more direct intervention in the forests themselves. The evolution of a new policy stance in natural-resources management within Niger began in the early 1980s and displayed a progression in state willingness to allow local populations to assume responsibility and a share of the benefits from forest use and management.

Principles of NFM

In Niger, as an outgrowth of work by Peace Corps volunteers, a few NGOs, and some dedicated Nigerien forestry personnel, a new approach to managing natural forests has emerged in the last decade. In hindsight, the principles of NFM may seem little more than codified common sense, but each principle challenges the status quo of forestry policies and practices. Also, NFM principles remain ideals and are not yet fully realized in practice. Here is how they came to be viewed by the technical experts who guided early NFM efforts in Niger's Guesselbodi Forest, the country's first comprehensive NFM experiment:

Participation of Local Resource Users

The key to managing and controlling the exploitation of the forest territories in Africa lies in the direct, substantive involvement of local people in the development and implementation of sound forest management plans. Local participation has long been espoused by development planners and governments, but only recently have real partnerships—in which local user groups are officially accepted as the rightful users and stewards of a given forest tract—been established.

One of the most positive aspects of these initial NFM endeavors is the redefinition of the forester's role and relationships with local populations in the arena of natural-resources management. This redefinition of roles and relationships is a first step toward breaking away from the present situation, wherein farmers and pastoralists live in fear and disdain of Forestry Service agents who appear to do little more than impose fines.

Multiple Use

This concept is gaining more recognition from foresters throughout the world. In essence, the concept puts forward a view of forests and forestry that is much broader than the classical "timber" approach that has been the basis for most forest-management schemes in the past. A multiple-use approach is especially important in Africa, where forests have always provided food, medicine, forage, game, and other essential commodities, as well as timber. Indeed, local forest users, especially in the Sahel, often consider commercial wood products to be of secondary importance.

Financial and Economic Independence

Given the limited financial resources of Niger and other African countries, forest-management schemes should strive for economic self-sufficiency, ensuring that recurrent costs of management such as road maintenance, fire control, guards, and replanting are covered with revenues from forest use. Financial independence (i.e., local administration and control over revenues, expenditures, and budgeting through creation of a forest-management fund account) is important for long-term sustainability of each forest-management scheme.

The method by which revenues generated by forest exploitation are reinvested in the forest is conceptually simple but operationally complex, given the normal risks encountered and controls required in the handling of public funds. Although several models of self-financing forest management are being tested in NFM projects in Niger, they have not resulted in systematic changes in the legal code to permit or encourage the replication of comprehensive forest-by-forest management. In other words, the country has not legally institutionalized a forest-management fund system that provides for equitable sharing of benefits and reinvestment to ensure biologically sustainable systems.

Respect for the Existing Ecosystem

In the past, many failures in the field of forestry throughout the Sahel were due to attempts to "upgrade" the natural forests through the introduction of exotic species. Often this meant removing existing vegetation and planting in its place trees that were ill adapted to Sahelian soils and climate. Few attempts were made to work with local species to maintain the integrity of the existing ecosystem.

Because of the degraded state of most natural forests in Niger, most NFM projects have soil-conservation and site-restoration activities as integral components of their management plans. Intensive investment in this environmental work is essential in many locations and has produced some remarkable results in a few years' time. Once the initial phases of NFM schemes are completed and external funding assistance tapers off or ends, such investments in sustainability will have to compete against other, arguably more productive, uses for limited forest budgets.

Sustainable Use of Resources

While perhaps unattainable in its purest form, sustained yield remains a basic tenet of natural forest management. All efforts should be made to avoid cutting, grazing, gathering, or hunting in a fashion that compromises the permanence of an existing resource. From the perspective of productivity, many classified forests in the Sahel, including some in southern Niger, are overmature due to the influence of protective policies. Conservative cutting would help to remove older growth and promote regeneration through coppicing and natural seeding. Given the lack of inventories and growth data that are vital to establishing carrying capacity and offtake policies, harvesting schemes should remain conservative until better data become available. This does not mean, however, that in the interim harvesting should be delayed.

Adequate Legal Framework

Essential for the functioning of the new forestry management arrangement is the promulgation of legislative texts that clearly sanction all its legal aspects. Among the necessary elements are

- the right of association for user groups and other extragovernmental management units,

- tenurial rights for such groups to negotiate with the government for exclusive use of forest resources and for long-term contractual revenue sharing, and

- forestry regulations that permit scientific, sustainable exploitation of resources.

Niger does not have the legal framework required to meet most of these needs. A partial exception is the right of local communities to negotiate control over forest lands. Under pressure from external donors, Niger's land-use laws recently were changed to permit rural communities to negotiate for rights to forest lands and forest products in their customary territories. These laws make provision for communities to appropriate these usage rights by participating in the management of their forest lands according to established technical norms. Despite this breakthrough, rural communities will require considerable assistance to develop and implement comprehensive management plans acceptable to the government.

Niger, like other former French colonies in West Africa, inherited colonial-era structures and conceptions of ownership that centralized land rights in the hands of the state. These colonial-era tenurial concepts, superimposed on traditional systems, cast doubt and confusion on the customary tenurial systems that provided local governance structures for natural resources prior to the twentieth century and survive, piecemeal, today. Although detailed examination of customary tenure is beyond the scope of this discussion, in general these traditional systems regulated intra- and intergroup use of resources. Often resources were allocated sequentially between various user groups. Whether carefully negotiated allotment of agricultural lands, wood-cutting rights within the territorial boundaries of sedentary communities, or the controlled use of water points and seasonal grazing lands by pastoralist groups, time-tested rule systems controlled resource use.

Niger no longer has the option of returning to precolonial resource-management structures that were based on extensive production systems that are no longer adequate for modern population densities and the shrinking resource base. A new set of structures must now be created to balance the national government's overall responsibility for patrimonial resources with effective local-level management of local resources.

A Natural Forest Management Plan

NFM is based on developing and implementing a rational approach to forest use such as dividing the land into parcels and harvesting trees and other resources in sequence. The management plan also sets out the rights and responsibilities of various parties, including the Forestry Service, local administration, and local resource users. A management plan is a blueprint for exploitation, maintenance, and conservation of the forest.

The possibility of substantially redefining roles and responsibilities is best illustrated by presenting a simplified overview of the steps that Guesselbodi and other NFM efforts attempt to follow in developing and implementing a management plan based on participation of the local population. For readers familiar with community-based conservation planning in other countries, this model may sound quite top-down in nature. In Niger, it seems radical indeed.

In Niger, the management-planning process begins with a series of basic preliminary studies to acquire the information necessary to develop the management plan. These studies should be limited to essential information pertinent to the practical aspects of managing a particular forest. The local population is integrated into the preliminary-study phase. This allows outsiders to introduce the proposed activity to the community and initiators to benefit from the vast indigenous knowledge of the forest, particularly pertaining to how it has been used in the past and how it could be better managed. The preliminary-study-and-local-consultation phase also should include a training and animation component to organize and prepare local user groups and discuss the basic concepts of the envisaged management scheme.

The management plan is drafted based on the results of the preliminary studies. This overall plan is augmented by detailed annual work plans that spell out the scope and sequence of activities for each year. Continual consultation and negotiation with residents and with the organizations that they create to represent them is an integral part of establishing the management plan. In many cases, this means that, simultaneously with the elaboration of the technical aspects of the management plan, the initiators invest considerable effort in creating and strengthening local organizations.

New Role for the Forestry Service

In the past, implementation of management plans, to the extent that they exist, has been the responsibility of the Forestry Service. In fact, few functional management plans have been developed in Niger (or elsewhere in Africa) due to lack of personnel and equipment, and other resources.

Under the new community-oriented natural forest management arrangement, local user groups are granted exclusive rights to exploit a particular forest as long as they abide by the terms and conditions set forth in the management plan that they help to develop. In essence, the management plan serves as a contract between the local user groups and the government. The departure from the status quo is the active, legally sanctioned involvement of local communities in forest management stewardship, control, and benefits.

The role of the forester in this scenario, like that of the community, is based on the management plan. The forester is to ensure that the management plan is respected and provide technical assistance to local user groups. In return for the right to exploit the forest rationally and securely, local user groups will share responsibility for maintenance and conservation of the forest as negotiated in detail in the management plan.

Current State of NFM Efforts in Niger

The explosion of NFM projects under way in Niger traces its origin to the groundbreaking work of the Forest and Land Use Planning Project (FLUP) of USAID that began in 1981 and implemented its first experimental activities at the Guesselbodi National Forest in 1983. Subsequently, FLUP's Model Sites Program was extended to the Gorou-Bassounga National Forest, but intensive work there, sponsored by Lutheran World Relief, did not begin until 1988. FLUP also funded preliminary investigations of the Baban Rafi Forest near Maradi. FLUP's formal funding by USAID ended in 1988 after seven years, a regrettably short period of direct investment in this promising effort. Some USAID counterpart funding for NFM did continue in the forests of Boyanga, Guesselbodi, and Koure, all of which are quite near Niamey, the capital, and its markets for fuelwood, hay, and other forest products. News of the Guesselbodi experiment has spawned an increasing number of other donor-designed NFM efforts—clear evidence that the international community recognizes the great potential for community-based resource management.

Besides the government of Niger and its donors, a third major player in these early NRM efforts is foreign NGOs and volunteer agencies such as the Peace Corps and its European counterparts. Two of the three NFM projects described here are managed by NGOs, and all three are heavily dependent for local organizational development on an American NGO, the Cooperative League of the USA (CLUSA). Likewise, Peace Corps volunteers are (or were) assigned to two of these projects and play a supporting role in the third. No two institutional arrangements are identical, but the general pattern involves one NGO taking a management role (as does CARE in Baban Rafi), with technical support in popular participation from CLUSA and further assistance from volunteers, who may be foresters or community development workers.

Three Nigerien NFM Projects

Three case studies are presented in brief summary here and referred to later in various contexts.

Guesselbodi

Guesselbodi Forest, located 25 km east of Niamey on a major paved road, is the original NFM effort in Niger. The forest straddles two cantons in the Kollo Arrondissement and is surrounded by nine communities that now make up the forestry cooperative. Niamey's proximity provides an excellent urban market for Guesselbodi firewood, hay, straw, and other forest products, all with minimal transport costs. This location also has meant that USAID and Nigerien project personnel, aided by Peace Corps volunteers, have had ready access to national decision makers while working on the site.

After an initial period of negotiating, planning, and surveying that began in 1981, experimental cutting and conservation efforts were launched in 1983. Formal management activities in this 5,000-ha forest began in earnest in 1985, when Guesselbodi became the first site in FLUP's Model Sites Program. The severely degraded forest in this area of 500 mm annual rainfall was to be progressively treated with soil- and water-conservation techniques such as earthworks and some replanting of trees and perennial grasses. These improvements, which use hired casual labor, have been funded by the project.

The project, with assistance from CLUSA, also assisted a local forestry cooperative, the organization that facilitates participation of the local population in the management of this forest. (As explained on page 250, the cooperative structure is the only legal option for popular organization.) Forestry co-op members from the nine villages that surround the forest (total population: about three thousand) have now undertaken firewood harvesting in six of the ten forest parcels. Due to Niamey's demand for fodder for penned animals, hay, and straw, cutting of these products has grown into a major economic activity. Like firewood cutting, hay and straw harvesting is controlled through a permit system.

The firewood operation, from which the co-op receives 25 percent of permit revenues, is dominated by the relatively few individuals who have carts for transportation and who live in the communities nearest the roadside marketing center. The hay and straw cutting has much wider participation, and all the permit money from these activities goes to the cooperative. With a twentyfold increase in the number of hay permits in the last five years, the value of hay now may exceed that of firewood—and certainly will if firewood yields decline in the years ahead.

Although the forest has corridors for animal passage, more than 70 percent of Guesselbodi is closed to grazing. No grazing permit policy has been worked out at Guesselbodi, a major piece of the forest-management puzzle that must be addressed. But without clear governmental grazing policies, the situation is not likely to change in the foreseeable future.

Permit cutting of hay, rather than natural grazing, illustrates the complexity of NFM interventions. While banning animals from certain parcels for certain periods of the year is probably necessary to permit new growth to become established, the long-term impact on soil nutrients of the exclusion of animals is unknown.

Young as the Guesselbodi project is, it is the only NFM experiment in Niger with enough history to yield even preliminary findings on its impact and potential sustainability. On a technical level, much has been accomplished. The microcatchment earthworks have survived several years of substantial rainfall with impressive regeneration of the much-appreciated *Andropogon gayansus* grass. New growth is seen on previously denuded slopes, and some *Acacia* species have grown well. Spreading leafy material on barren areas after wood cutting has encouraged termite activity and improved water infiltration and some natural seeding. Regeneration rates from coppiced trees in parcels are variable, although generally encouraging. On the other hand, naturally seeded regeneration of some trees such as *Combretum* spp. has been discouraging, even in the microcatchments. With sparse data open to multiple interpretations, some observers question whether a ten-year cutting cycle is long enough in the face of the preexisting state of serious degradation and limited rainfall.

Nevertheless, the approach of involving the population directly in the management of Guesselbodi Forest, worked out by trial and error, has been copied widely in other NFM efforts in Niger.

Gorou-Bassounga

The Gorou-Bassounga forest occupies 8,800 ha in one canton of the Gaya Arrondissement of the Dosso Department. Its location at the southernmost point of the country near the Benin border results in relatively high annual rainfall of 800 mm, supporting a savanna forest of greater woody biomass diversity than most of Niger's forests. The Gorou-Bassounga forest is moderately degraded and suffers from heavy grazing and agricultural encroachment.

This forest's 300-km distance from the capital originally seemed to suggest that secondary products for local consumption would be more important than fuelwood in the NFM project. During the first few years of the firewood sales operation, however, huge transport trucks from Niamey have traveled the paved national road to buy wood from Gorou-Bassounga.

To a much greater degree than either Guesselbodi or Baban Rafi, the communities surrounding Gorou-Bassounga forest are urbanized. Of a total population of twenty thousand, some eighteen thousand people live in just three of the forestry cooperative's seven member communities. One impact of this population density has been persistent political pressure to allocate some land within the forest boundaries for agriculture.

Agricultural encroachment into the forest has been severe. When efforts were made in the 1970s to establish recognizable borders for the forest, more than 2,000 ha were lost to permanently established fields all around Gorou-Bassounga's perimeter. (Some eighty-seven of these border farmers, who illegally farm in the forest, became part of an earlier agroforestry project in which they plant and tend high-value trees in their fields in exchange for contracted farming rights.) Even with clear boundaries established, encroachment continues.

Other users also place demands on the forest. Gorou-Bassounga is of major importance to Fulani pastoralist groups, and the competition over resources is a major source of ethnic tension with sedentary Djerma farmers. The forest is the largest and most productive pasturage for herders in this part of the country. By informal census, more than seventy families of Fulani herders, all of whom are permanent residents in the region, use the forest to graze a still uncounted number of cattle and sheep. In fact, the forest has become a necessary part of their annual movements, providing forage while crops are growing in the surrounding fields. After harvest, the herders move their animals out of the forest to consume crop residues. Lacking permanent water points, herders have denuded patches of land by camping near seasonal ponds.

Initially, NFM activities in the Gorou-Bassounga forest were part of FLUP, which concentrated its first efforts in Guesselbodi. Intensive management activities actually date from 1988, when the U.S. NGO Lutheran World Relief assumed leadership in the provision of technical assistance. On-site supervision by a respected retired Nigerien forester is supported by a series of Peace Corps volunteer foresters and a CLUSA cooperatives assistant (as was the case in Guesselbodi's early days).

So new is the NFM effort in Gorou-Bassounga that woodcutters were still preoccupied with harvesting deadwood in early 1992. This has provided extra time in which to prepare the management plan and establish the cooperative structure. Partly because of the need to include the Fulani herders, both technical management and cooperative development got off to a slow start.

The level of urbanization and population density surrounding the forest also may help to explain the importance of political factions, increased occupational specialization, and intergroup tensions. Conflict between Djerma farmers and Fulani herders is on the increase. The forest management plan makes some accommodation of the Fulani population by providing for wells to be dug for animals at agreed sites of seasonal settlement in the forest. Some agricultural land also has been allocated to farmers by lottery, although not nearly as much as the Djerma have demanded.

The NFM effort at Gorou-Bassounga, even more than others in this study, suffers from an inability to constitute a local organization appropriate to the needs of forest management. By strict interpretation of the legal code for cooperatives (see page 251), all of the communities surrounding the forest and all of the Fulani groups that live in and near the forest are part of the newly formed forest cooperative. Hopefully, such externally imposed local institutions soon will be overturned by reforms, but they hamper the normalization of community involvement in NFM.

Baban Rafi

In sheer size, this forest, which covers approximately 70,000 ha and spreads over five cantons in two arrondissements of the Maradi Department, dwarfs the other two in this study. More than thirty villages are located in and around the forest. Baban Rafi is located just north of the border with Nigeria and some 40 km by secondary roads from Maradi, Niger's second-largest city, which receives at least 75 percent of its fuelwood from this forest.

One aspect of Baban Rafi that sets it apart from Guesselbodi and Gorou-Bassounga is that it is not a "classified" forest but, rather, a "protected" forest with somewhat fewer restrictions on use by the local population. (Classified national forests are meant to be under strict protection, while protected forests—which constitute the bulk of Niger's forest lands—have looser controls. Communities are situated not only around but within the periphery of these protected forests.)

Baban Rafi is one of the few remaining large forested areas in the country, and it is under intense pressure to provide fuelwood, farmland, and forage resources. Moreover, the forest suffered heavy tree mortality and resource destruction during the recurrent droughts of the last twenty-five years.

The forest has long been a major resource for Fulani transhumant herders. Research carried out in the summer of 1991 indicates that herding/farming populations in the forest are growing faster than village populations as increasing numbers of former transhumant herders have taken to clearing land and settling in the forest to farm.

The origins of NFM work in this forest date to preliminary inventories conducted by the FLUP unit in 1988, which in turn led to the involvement of CARE International in 1989. Under funding from the Danish governmental agency DANIDA, CARE provides technical and financial assistance from its major regional office in Maradi and is aided by a CLUSA cooperative assistant who lives in the forest village of Baban Rafi.

Like other NFM projects, the goals of the Baban Rafi effort combine environmental enhancement with economically productive resource utilization. Eventually, the Baban Rafi project's zone of intervention will include more than 40,000 ha, plus an extensive buffer zone of peripheral villages and farmland. In its current phase, the project is working in a pilot zone in and around the community of Baban Rafi. CARE and CLUSA have plans to help establish a second cooperative on the northern edge of the forest.

The major economic activity of the cooperative during its first two years was the harvest and marketing of deadwood from a 300-ha parcel delimited by the project. Local woodcutters were invited to harvest the wood—mostly *Prosopis africana*, a species that has suffered a high mortality rate in the region over the last decade—and sell it to the cooperative. Maradi's well-organized wood merchants were accustomed to securing wood without paying the full official tax, and they refused to purchase wood from the cooperative. Finally, in January 1991, the Maradi departmental head of the Ministry of Environment forced the merchants to buy out the cooperative's wood stock. The long-term viability of the relationship has not been resolved.

Problems of NFM Practice in Niger

Among sub-Saharan African countries, Niger must claim the dubious distinction of having one of the most rigidly controlled systems of "popular" organization. All areas of public life have been similarly circumscribed by limitations on freedom of association and exclusive sanctions to unitary institutions in social and economic spheres. This is not fertile ground for community-based approaches to conservation.

A prime example of the results of limiting free association is Niger's lack of NGOs. While national NGO movements have blossomed across Africa during the last two decades, the first truly indigenous Nigerien NGO struggled into existence less than five years ago. A number of others have followed suit, but Nigerien NGOs remain in legal limbo without clear statutes recognizing their right to exist. With few financial resources or trained cadres at its disposal, the national NGO movement in Niger will take years to become a force in civil society.

State-sponsored Institutional Structures for Local-level Organizing

The two elements of the state-sponsored system of popular organization that most directly influence and control current NFM efforts are the cooperatives and the Development Society. In Niger, the only legally recognized rural organizations are cooperatives. Until recently, these were an integral part of the Development Society. The Development Society was superimposed onto two preexisting national networks of government-sponsored institutions: cooperatives and the *Samariya*, or youth groups. At the village level, representatives of the Village Mutual Group (VMG)—the basic unit of the national cooperative network—and local representatives of the *Samariya* are to combine to form a Village Development Council (VDC). This structure does not permit Niger's citizens to organize as individuals or groups in self-defined relationships.

The national network of cooperatives is specifically intended to organize production in Niger. Since no other forms of economic entities are sanctioned for rural areas, cooperatives are the only organizing structure available for NFM projects and local resource user groups. On a policy level, the coupling of the cooperative movement in rural areas with the promotion of the idealized Development Society has led to an unusual membership definition: all adults in a given community are automatically members of the cooperative without any decision or desire on the part of individuals. Since a rural community is a complex, heterogeneous grouping, constituting a cooperative of the whole community ignores the essential nature of cooperatives as self-selected groups of individuals who choose to assemble out of common economic or other interests.

Not surprisingly, this approach to cooperative membership recruitment has been problematic for attempts to set up forestry cooperatives. Recent NFM efforts, however, have resulted in the development of new rural organizations that overlap and supersede the largely nonfunctional official cooperative structures. These forestry cooperatives have been constructed by associating the VMGs, producer groups, and/or village cooperatives.

Making the mandated cooperative structure serve the needs of natural forest management has been a major challenge of the community-based approach to resource management. Guesselbodi led the way and has set the tone for local participation. As this process is the model for all other NFM projects, its early development is instructive.

Transforming the Cooperatives in the Service of NFM

In 1985, FLUP, working with CLUSA, began serious discussions aimed at establishing a forestry cooperative in the nine communities surrounding the Guesselbodi Forest. During the painstaking negotiations, local political conditions were carefully respected, each canton chief's assistance was solicited, and geographic balances were struck in the election of cooperative officers.

FLUP and CLUSA had laid the groundwork for the forestry cooperative slowly. A CLUSA-trained extension agent had begun working in these communities the year before to study the social and cultural structures on which the cooperative would build. Also, in the year or more leading up to the cooperative's founding, villagers had participated in a long series of discussions on the forest management plan and policies governing forest use. Among the many concerns villagers expressed at these meetings were rights of animal passage and the hiring of workers for environmental work and guarding tasks.

As the notion of an overall plan for management of the forest began to gain acceptance among the communities, CLUSA and FLUP personnel introduced the concept of shared community responsibilities and benefits through partnership with the Forestry Service. If they were interested, this in turn would lead to the requirement for some sort of organization of all the participating communities, which would take the form of a forest cooperative.

The idea of an NFM project came from the outside and did not originate as a comprehensive idea from within the community. The difficulties that this population, long accustomed to top-down directives and with a well-honed distrust of the Forestry Service, faced in understanding this new interactive process are easily imaginable. These communities had little positive experience from previous government-mandated attempts to organize village cooperatives. This time, however, no one forced the people as FLUP and CLUSA questioned what level and kind of organization would be best.

Repeated discussions to develop a forest wood-cutting policy, including group analyses of local markets and a proposed system of individual cutters' permits, created an initial sense of the cooperative's possible functions. While FLUP (and the Forestry Service it served) was acknowledged as controlling technical matters, the people saw the co-op's potential to provide credit for donkey carts, manage the permit system, and assure fair fuelwood prices. Finally the people seemed ready to go ahead with the experiment.

Following the prescribed government policies for cooperatives, five VMG officers were selected in each of the nine communities surrounding the forest. These forty-five VMG leaders then came together as a "general assembly" of the new forestry cooperative and elected a nine-member administrative council, whose members would hold the posts of president, vice president, treasurer, secretary, two comptrollers, and three advisers.

Cooperative activities began slowly in the first year. Low-risk activities such as sales of improved planting seeds and fungicides generated income, allowed for a bank account and began developing skills and mutual confidence. Meanwhile, FLUP personnel developed a policy document in 1986 that spelled out the roles and relationships of each party in the management of Guesselbodi.

This policy document was crucial, since it would serve as the legal agreement among all the parties concerned. One element of the document is a contract between the government of Niger and the forestry cooperative that assigns the latter exclusive rights to exploit the Guesselbodi National Forest. More than six months of negotiations were required before the government, in 1987, finally signed this precedent-setting agreement. Like so much else done for the first time at Guesselbodi, this became the model for other NFM efforts in Niger.

At Guesselbodi and other NFM project sites in Niger, a signed agreement serves as the basis for forest management and institutional relationships. In addition to describing the general philosophy of the program, it details the action plan for resource use and environmental improvements, describes the financial arrangements for funds management, and legally binds the participating parties.

In general terms, NFM policy documents call for a forest manager resident in the forest to oversee conservation and restoration and work with the cooperative to ensure that exploitation policies are respected. This person is supervised by the Forestry Service. At Guesselbodi, in addition to exclusive rights to forest products, the co-op also has responsibility for financial management of the revenues generated by the exploitation of the forest.

The contractual aspects bind government and communities to the forest re-source-use plans in the document such as parcel-by-parcel wood cutting, control of animals, environmental activities, and so forth. Provisions cover the manner of fuelwood marketing and pricing, the arbitration of disagreements, the possibility of amendments and modifications, and the handling of revenues. Perhaps the most interesting aspect of this arrangement, from the standpoint of local partici-pation and control of natural resources, is the financial arrangement, since this is meant to be in the cooperative's hands.

In designing the management system for the Guesselbodi NFM project, finan-cial arrangements provided a litmus test for determining whether the local popu-lation genuinely benefited from the new scheme and whether the scheme would cover recurrent costs for the management of the forest. To exercise a meaningful level of control, local populations need not only benefit individually as woodcut-ters or straw gatherers, but must have some collective fiduciary responsibility and profit from the overall venture. At the same time, maintenance and improvement of the forest itself must be paid for if sustainable management is to be achieved. At Guesselbodi, the system is set up for just these possibilities.

In a somewhat simplified version, here is how it works: Co-op members can pur-chase permits for wood cutting (and eventually other activities) at the central stocking center. Salaried co-op staff members manage the center, and all buying and selling of forest products takes place there. When permit holders return to the stocking center with cut fuelwood, the co-op pays them for it and sells the wood to transport merchants at a profit. The money from permit sales goes directly into the forest management fund. The costs of exploitation and investment required for the year's cut are deducted from the annual gross profits of wood sales. The net profits are divided 25:75 between the cooperative and the forest management fund. Thus the forest fund gets all of the funds from permit sales and 75 percent of net sales profits from firewood; this money is used to cover general recurrent costs of forest management such as forest guards' salaries. The co-op receives 25 percent of net firewood profits. Together, the co-op and the Forestry Service de-termine the recurrent-cost budget, and the co-op retains any surplus after these costs have been covered. The co-op owns any capital investments. The co-op's profit from the use of other resources, such as hay, is not limited to 25 percent but is negotiable.

As a concept for increasing local control of sustained use of natural resources, the combination of a forest cooperative (or some other form of resource-users' grouping) and a forest fund for financial management appears quite attractive. FLUP personnel recount with obvious pleasure the general assembly at Guessel-bodi three years ago, after the first year's accounting. Stunned cooperative mem-bers were presented with hundreds of dollars—the cooperative's share of the project's net profits and an enormous sum by their reckoning—to do with as they pleased. Only time will tell if this level of revenue sharing will continue.

Incentives: Building Consensus among Local Resource Users

The assumption implicit in the desire to increase popular participation in natural-resources management is that the process will create or release incentives among the local population to exploit resources responsibly (i.e., sustainably). Incentives will consist of prospects for economic gain. At issue is the fact that prospects for economic gain may be perceived differently by individuals and households according to traditional user-group affiliation and habitual exploitation practices. Economic gain might be defined in terms of increased agricultural yields, revenues from the sale of fuelwood, or the conservation of forest for pasture. The significance of the incentives issue is that sustainable management will not be attained if large numbers of users see no benefit to participating according to the rules.

Local populations are far from homogeneous groupings. A major obstacle to local natural-forest management is the difficulty of establishing an organization across diverse groups that—although they have long and successfully interacted at the margins of their particular resource-management and exploitation systems—lack any kind of historical precedent or model for a comprehensive, jointly managed system over a large, defined territory. Indigenous tenure and management systems have not shown signs of evolving into a comprehensive system capable of both regulating resource conflicts among groups and operating according to the principles of sustainable exploitation.

A study of the early period of the Baban Rafi NFM experience illustrates that creation of broad-based incentives as a crucial element of sustainable management is likely to be more complicated than a simple transfer of management authority from the state to local populations.

User Groups

Women are major low-profile users of forest resources. They are often farmers, but, in the Baban Rafi forest, they are rarely field managers. Most women also own livestock, usually in small numbers and very often placed under the care of paid herders. On the other hand, women's exploitation of the forest to secure fuelwood for home use is significant and will have to be accounted for in any management system that is to prove sustainable in the long term. Yet, in this predominantly Islamic region, women are not encouraged to assume any type of active role outside the household. At least for the moment, the particular interests of women concerning the management of forest resources are not being articulated as new management structures come into being.

In addition to women, forest-resource user groups who assume low or nonexistent profiles in project or cooperative forums include traditional healers, sculptors, and hunters. These occupational groups continue to be active; however, to a significant degree, several of their major resource-exploiting practices have been driven underground, and practitioners are not likely to pursue their interests openly in cooperative or project forums.

High-profile user groups are those whose activities are recognized and addressed by the NFM project document and, generally, by external observers as having major environmental impact on the resources of the forest. We return here to the triumvirate of activities that make up the bulk of the threat: farming, herding, and the commercial exploitation of fuelwood.

The Baban Rafi cooperative was conceived by the project as a locally based mechanism for the rational exploitation and marketing of commercial forest resources. The single commercialized and marketable resource feasible on any significant scale is fuelwood. Wood cutting has long been important among many forest residents as a source of steady or intermittent income. That it is more common for Hausa farmers than Fulani herders to work as woodcutters is well known. From a random sample of resource users, thirty-five of forty farmers say they plan to participate as woodcutters in the next cooperative wood harvest; only three of twenty-eight herders have the same intention, although seven more say they may participate, depending on time availability. Clearly, this particular activity—wood cutting for market—holds greater appeal at this point in time for Hausa farmers than for Fulani herders.

Resident Fulani herders appear to have been slower to express support for the cooperative through the purchase of a membership card at a nominal fee. While thirty-four of a random sample of forty farmers state they have purchased a cooperative membership card, only twelve of twenty-eight herders say they have obtained the card. The only other statistical measure of participation—a rather tenuous and somewhat arbitrary indicator—is attendance at official co-op meetings. With five elected representatives from each of the eight VMGs that make up the co-op's general assembly, attendance per village has varied from a low of 1.2 to a high of 3.6 for different VMGs. Possible explanations for these differential rates illustrate both inter- and intragroup complexities of local NFM participation. However, high attendance rates among several VMGs that are exclusively Hausa confirm the pattern that Hausa farmers tend to participate at a higher rate than do Fulani or Bouzou herders.

Differential Participation and Inadequate Incentives

In the absence of an effective forum for the articulation of diverse interests, or in the event of a failure to represent these interests in processes of policy formulation, incentives adequate to induce the participation of diverse groups in a new management system may not be created and sustained. As a result, the question of incentives is of crucial importance. The presence in the forest of large numbers of resource users with little or no motivation to follow rules will undermine the sustainability of the system in the absence of an effective system of incentives.

The differential rates of participation suggest that the institutionalization of effective mechanisms to represent the varied interests and rights currently operating in natural forest management is a very complex matter. The differences between herders and farmers could mean that the substance of the incentive is more appealing to Hausa farmers than to Fulani herders or that the prospects for actual realization of the incentive are perceived differently by the two groups.

In the first case, a solution might be to broaden the appeal of participation to additional groups. For example, the development of straw harvesting and marketing at Baban Rafi along the lines of the Guesselbodi project might increase the appeal of participating in cooperative activities among herders, since the management of forage resources on a commercial basis should help to ensure supplies and provide for their distribution. Alternatively, the existing incentive of financial reward from the harvest and marketing of fuelwood may broaden its appeal to other groups as increasing numbers of herders expand their activities in the monetized economy and find it acceptable to sell their labor.

The concern raised by the second case is more problematic. While the financial incentives of commercialization may be as attractive to herders as to farmers, perceptions of attainability may, for perfectly practical reasons, differ from group to group at times. Several herder household heads state flatly that they do not have time to engage in wood harvesting activities sponsored by the cooperative. Such activities often are timed to take place during the dry season, a time of reduced activity for the farmer but a demanding time for herders attempting to secure the forage and water their livestock needs. Problems of communication between the village-centered VMGs and the scattered herder settlements are another complication that may prevent herders from realizing financial incentives (resulting from cooperative-sponsored commercial enterprises) on an equal footing with villagers.

Barriers to organizing and coordinating groups may be rooted in a diversity of worldviews and group histories that tend to encourage suspicion and isolationist sentiments among some groups more than others. Not only is this a common occurrence between such groups as herders and farmers, but it also may play a role in participation rates among factions within the same forest-resource user group. Thus the special needs of nonparticipating groups need to be recognized and addressed.

Sustainability

At the heart of all community-based conservation efforts is the issue of whether and how they can be sustained. The overlapping linkages that must be in place for sustained resource use are biological, economic, policy, and sociocultural. Given the paucity of hard data and the early stage of natural forest management experiments in Niger, perhaps the best response is to summarize what is known and to posit the conditions that must be in place if long-term sustainability is to be achieved.

Biology

The most straightforward criterion is biological. Preliminary analysis of the re-inventory data from earliest cuttings at Guesselbodi seemed to indicate that regeneration rates were significantly lower than predicted for the coppiced cutting, that forest composition was changing in favor of species less desirable for fuelwood, and that even the original estimates of standing fuelwood volume on which the management plan was based were incorrect. These findings, which are circumscribed by inadequate site maintenance and monitoring, appear to some analysts to call into question the ten-year rotational cycle and, hence, the biological sustainability of the forest's management plan. Subsequently, the methodology of the re-inventory researchers was questioned, and the validity of their findings is now clouded, although not completely discredited.

One element that further constrains the predictive value of data from the first years of natural forest management projects in Niger relates to the overmature state of most national forests, where trees have not been legally cut for many decades. Throughout the initial cutting rotation of an NFM project operating in such forests, the harvest of very large trees represents a one-time bonanza of fuelwood that completely skews statistical projections. The biomass in trees and other forest resources available for management in the future will result from a substantially different set of physical conditions.

Economics

The economic side of the sustainability equation presents more variables than constants. Demand for fuelwood at current prices is undeniable, as witnessed by the keen competition for Baban Rafi's wood resources and the long distances Niamey merchants will travel for wood. On the other hand, no one pretends that the high levels of investment required during the start-up phase of NFM efforts, such as expatriate technical assistance, aerial photography, and intensive conservation efforts, can be sustained in the long run from the proceeds of these Sahelian forests.

Some recurrent expenses, however, must be paid if economic sustainability is to be attained. At a minimum, forest guards' salaries, forest infrastructure maintenance, fire protection, oversight of forest product sales, management, and monitoring are all necessary NFM costs. During the initial, atypical period of NFM projects, marked by external investments, cutting in mature forests, and other noncyclical economic events, it is impossible to gauge long-term economic viability. Chronologically, no NFM effort has yet to enter the next period. As NFM participants gain more experience, pleasant surprises such as high levels of income from hay sales at Guesselbodi will be offset by less fortuitous developments such as the reportedly slow regrowth rates in that same forest.

In the NFM ledger book, both income and expenditures are susceptible to

manipulation, although not always in a favorable direction or with predictable results. The price of wood, set by the government, could be raised as some donors
have urged. Depending on how these increases are shared, higher proceeds
might benefit forest cooperatives, but increased prices might also encourage illegal cutting.

When budgets are tight, another temptation is to cut back on research, as was
the case at Guesselbodi when FLUP's level of investment dropped off. The risk in
such cases is the loss of invaluable monitoring data needed to inform both technical and management decisions affecting the viability of the entire effort. The economics of NFM is a complex matter, with many influences affecting long-term
fiscal sustainability.

Potential sources of NFM income yet to be realized could be a better-organized
grazing permit program for the forests and regulation of other nontimber forest
products in a manner that recovers some of the income. Honey production in the
forest and harvesting of plants for food and pharmaceutical purposes are examples of forest exploitation that could be subjected to income recovery. Negotiating
in-kind labor contributions from the major immediate beneficiaries of NFM
regimes such as wood and hay cutters and, eventually, holders of grazing permits
should be possible. Years will pass before these variables are sorted out and post-
project economic patterns emerge from NFM efforts. Sustainability on the economic level will depend on the proper functioning of management systems and
adherence to the principles of NFM, including multiple use and substantive local
involvement.

Policy

A third issue of sustainability concerns legislation and policy setting. Nigerien governmental policies are at the heart of misuse and mismanagement of forest resources over the last sixty years, and their reform is a prerequisite for NFM to function. Colonial administration and policies can not shoulder all the responsibility
for resource-management debacles. Nigeriens have controlled their government
for a third of this century—and they may, finally, be moving toward a more appropriate management approach.

The list of policies to be rationalized and harmonized is extensive. Land-tenure
rules need to be constructed and enforced to guarantee exclusive use while still
protecting all users' rights in multiple-user situations. Equally essential is establishment and exercise of the right of free association and organization of people
into self-defined, legally recognized entities, thereby ending the era of government-controlled cooperatives as the only legitimate form of organization.

A major grouping of required policy reforms fits under the rubric *decentralization*. At a minimum, decentralization requires deconcentration, or the handover of
some authority to lower levels within the government structure. This means increasing the scope for departmental-level technical ministries and lower-level ju-

dicial structures in order to bring government closer to resource users in exercising its sovereign responsibilities to legitimate management regimes, adjudicate disputes, and enforce decisions. A more involved form of decentralization required for NFM is *delegation*, or the transfer of specific functions to organizations outside the regular bureaucratic structure, such as the authority temporarily granted to NFM projects in their role as policy experiments. Delegation is happening more frequently, but only after lengthy negotiations and with a fair amount of international donor pressure.

A still more far-reaching decentralization effort is *privatization*, the divestment of certain heretofore governmental responsibilities to private entities. The term *privatization*, although maligned in some circles for hardships associated with structural adjustment programs, aptly describes the transfer of authority for forest management to locally constituted resource user groups. Perhaps a rough parallel exists between privatization of major government enterprises or parastatals and natural forest management privatization, in that the government divests itself of responsibility for functions it has proved incapable of adequately managing. Unlike the typical private-sector recipients of privatized functions, however, NFM privatization puts authority into the hands of local people. The normalization of this process (i.e., making it easier for rural communities to negotiate and making their right to do so permanent) is a precondition for sustainable NFM.

The evolving policy profile documents a growing consensus among Nigerien policy makers toward increasing popular participation in forest resource management by devolving a degree of authority over resources from the state to local populations. The significance of the policy trend is undeniable, yet it must be considered in conjunction with the recognition that, historically, state policies regularly have been distorted in the course of their implementation in rural settings. Such distortions have been the result of institutional shortcomings that have yet to be resolved.

Conclusion

Whether these policy reforms will take place and at what pace is unknown. It is tempting to posit a correlation between the increased demands of pluralism in national political life and the upswing in government acceptance of policy conditionality for NFM experiments that have opened the door for local resource control. It is even more tempting to imagine a freely elected democratic government assertively supporting NFM as part of the construction of a new civil society and the rescue of Niger's threatened forest lands.

Caution is in order. The national conference and extenuated negotiations toward multiparty elections that preoccupied a segment of the urban population left rural citizens on the sidelines with very little say in the process. Will an elected government controlled by urban elites treat rural producers differently than non-elected ones have? Is the shaky period of transition from military to civilian authority the best time to undertake decentralization, a process that works best when government legitimacy and policy direction are well established and accepted?

One thing that can be said about this period of major political upheaval and uncertainty is that it offers an opportunity to push ahead with bold and creative experiments in user-based resource management such as natural forest management—to prepare rural communities to exercise new responsibilities and increase the body of knowledge and practice in this field.

ACKNOWLEDGMENTS

Support for the preparation of this chapter was provided, in part, by the U.S. Agency for International Development through its Wildlands and Human Needs program.

CHAPTER 11

A Profile and Interim Assessment of the Annapurna Conservation Area Project, Nepal

Michael P. Wells

The 4,600-km^2 Annapurna Conservation Area in central Nepal, established in 1986, is perhaps the most geographically and culturally diverse multiple-use area in the world. The unique mix of ecosystems includes subtropical lowland oak, rhododendron, and bamboo forests; high alpine meadows; and desert plateaus—all mostly unaltered by human activity. The world's deepest river gorge, the Kali Gandaki, is located within the conservation area, along with some of the world's highest mountains, including Annapurna I (8,091 m). More than forty thousand people of different ethnic backgrounds inhabit the area.

The Annapurna Sanctuary, near the center of the conservation area, is a natural amphitheater surrounded by seven peaks higher than 6,700 m and several slightly smaller peaks (see Map 11.1). The southern slopes of these mountains receive more than 5,000 mm of rainfall annually and support a rich variety of birds and mammals, including Danfe pheasant, Himalayan tahr, barking deer, serow, goral, Himalayan black bear, musk deer, and the rare red panda. The dry northern slopes that extend to the Tibetan border contain snow leopard and blue sheep.

A variety of economic activities take place in the area. Settled agriculture and transhumant livestock keeping are more evident in the south, while trade (mainly with Tibet) becomes more important farther north. Income, education, and health in the Annapurna region are somewhat higher than the national average. Nevertheless, most of the people are poor farmers dependent upon the land for their livelihood. Infrastructure is extremely limited. The nearest large town, Pokhara (population 400,000), is a three-day walk from the conservation area boundary. There are airfields at Pokhara and at Jomsom. While road construction is gradually facilitating access to the southern edge of the conservation area, virtually all movement in and around the area takes place on footpaths. All goods purchased from outside are carried to their destination by porters or, at lower altitudes, by mules.

Map 11.1

Annapurna Conservation
Area

KEY

- ▬·▬·▬·▬· International Boundary
- - - - - - - - District Boundary
- ───────── Conservation Area II Boundary
- ▨ Stage I Area
- ▩ Pilot Program Area
- ∿ Stage I Area
- ▲ Major Peaks
- • Major Settlement
- ● Project Headquarters
- ○ Regional Office

Since Nepal was opened to foreign visitors in the 1950s, tourism has expanded rapidly to become the country's top foreign-exchange earner. Many tourists trek in the Himalayas, and two of the most popular routes are located in the conservation area: the Annapurna Circuit, a twenty-one-day route that circles the Annapurna Himal, and the Annapurna Sanctuary, a ten-day route into the center.

The large and growing numbers of tourists visiting Annapurna have had a severe negative impact on the natural environment. Large areas of forested land have been cleared to provide cooking, heating, and lodging services to visitors. At the same time, expanding agriculture, water pollution, poor sanitation, and littering of trails all have accelerated, compounded by a rapid growth in the resident population. These trends threaten the area's economic and cultural systems as well as its biological diversity.

In 1985, King Birendra made an unofficial visit to the Annapurna region and, based on his observations, issued a directive to improve and manage tourism development while safeguarding the environment. The royal directive stipulated the need to strike a balance between tourism, economic development, and nature conservation. The King Mahendra Trust for Nature Conservation (KMTNC), Nepal's largest and most influential conservation organization, took on the role of implementing the king's directive.

Initial surveys of the Annapurna region indicated that the traditional national park model, already well established in Nepal, would not be appropriate, and that a new protected-area concept would be required. After three years of intensive planning, the multiple-use Annapurna Conservation Area and the Annapurna Conservation Area Project (ACAP) were established. The project operates as a semiautonomous unit of the trust. The long-term objective is to benefit the inhabitants of the conservation area by providing a viable means to help them maintain control over their environment (KMTNC 1988). Participation of poor farmers, who constitute the majority of the population, was a primary goal. Using a grass-roots approach, small-scale conservation and alternative energy projects were to be the tools used to minimize the impact of visiting tourists and to improve the quality of life in the villages.

The discussion that follows is based on a visit to ACAP in November 1989 that included discussions with some of the intended beneficiaries of the project, periodic discussions from 1989 to 1993 with the key individuals involved in design and implementation, and a review of the literature cited in the bibliography. (The preceding section is based on Bunting, Sherpa, and Wright [1991]; Hough and Sherpa [1989]; KMTNC [1988]; and Sherpa, Coburn, and Gurung [1986].)

People of the Annapurna Region

The Annapurna Conservation Area is Nepal's most densely populated and ethnically diverse protected area, with a population of about forty thousand in three hundred villages (Stevens and Sherpa 1992a). Agriculture and trade have flourished in the Annapurna basin for hundreds of years. People from at least seven ethnic groups (including the Gurungs and Magars on the southern slopes, the Manganis to the east, and Tibetans and Thakalis farther north), each with distinct language, customs, and subsistence patterns, are found in the area. The Thakalis are involved principally in trade; the Gurungs comprise the majority in the conservation area.

Most people today follow some form of Hinduism or Buddhism, often blended with local variations on indigenous shamanistic beliefs. Until the rapid growth of modern tourism and penetration of media influences, principal links with the outside world came from trading with Tibet and service in foreign armed forces, especially via the Gurkhas of the British and Indian Armies (ACAP 1988). The most common occupation is farming, although a small number of people—many former Gurkha soldiers—more recently have become lodge owners.

As in most other parts of Nepal, people in the Annapurna region are heavily dependent on forest resources to meet their daily needs. A very high proportion of heating and cooking energy comes from wood. The forests also provide wood for construction and fencing, fodder for domestic animals, wild fruits and vegetables, medicines, fibers for ropes and cloth, and many other products and services for daily life. Bamboo is used to weave baskets and other goods. Rhododendron and pine are used to build houses and birch bark to make umbrellas and waterproof temporary dwellings; the leafy branches of oak, *sal*, and other subtropical species are fed to cows and water buffalo.

Tourism

Visitors have been drawn to Nepal by the country's cultural heritage and religious sites, the Himalayas, and the opportunities for wildlife viewing and trekking. Despite some uncertainties in the data, about 20 percent of Nepal's foreign visitors probably go to one or more of the country's protected areas. The economic value of tourism associated with Nepal's protected areas has been roughly but conservatively estimated to be about US$9 million (Wells 1993).

Annapurna accounted for about 36,000 of the 105,000 visits to Nepal's protected areas during 1990, almost four times as many as Sagarmatha (Mount Everest) National Park (ACAP 1988). The attractions of the Annapurna region are both spectacular and reasonably accessible. Two days' hiking from road's end brings trekkers to the foot of three 6,000-m peaks. Another few days' hiking up the rugged upper gorge of Modi Khola leads into the Annapurna Sanctuary, surrounded by nine massive peaks including Annapurna I, the world's tenth highest mountain (Stevens and Sherpa 1992b).

The number of foreign visitors to the Annapurna region grew rapidly during the 1980s but was relatively constant, in the 35,000 to 39,000 range, from 1989 through 1992. Each of these visitors is accompanied—on average—by one porter, and spends ten days in the area. Visitor numbers are highly concentrated in the spring and fall; in 1991, for example, more than half of the visitors arrived in the three most popular months (ACAP 1988).

Local villagers have been quick to respond to new economic opportunities from tourism. The growth in the number of visitors has led to a proliferation of tea shops and trekking lodges along the trails. In the Modi Khola Valley in early 1987, there were sixteen lodges and tea shops in the village of Ghandruk (site of the ACAP headquarters); another eleven in Chhomrong, the highest major settlement in the valley; twenty in the upper Modi Khola gorge; and six in the Annapurna Sanctuary. In all, there were more than 130 trekking lodges and tea shops by 1988, compared to a handful ten years earlier.

Virtually all of the lodges above Ghandruk have since been upgraded and enlarged. In the Modi Khola Valley, simple bamboo lodges have been replaced by substantial stone structures, some with metal roofs. Some of the relatively small lodges of five years ago have been converted into two- and three-story buildings with ten or more private rooms and a restaurant (Stevens and Sherpa 1992a).

Social and Environmental Impacts of Tourism

Although tourism has led to increased local incomes in the Annapurna region, it has brought new social problems. Tourism-linked social problems in the most-visited areas include "drug use and idle youth who seem unenthusiastic about taking up rural lifestyles . . . [and] . . . violations of religious customs and local standards of decency regarding dress and public behavior" (Stevens and Sherpa 1992b).

The environmental costs of the rapid growth in tourism have been considerable. Several recent studies of the environmental impact of mountain tourism in Nepal concluded that accelerated deforestation and negative environmental impacts appear clearly linked to the concentration of visitors in a few relatively small areas within a handful of parks. These areas are biologically fragile and already were under stress from the local population before the expansion of tourism (Banskota et al. 1990; ERL 1989; Gurung 1990; MFSC 1988; Touche Ross et al. 1989).

Although the extent of deforestation due to the energy demands of tourists has yet to be reliably established, there seems little doubt that it represents a serious threat to those mountain ecosystems where visitors concentrate. Environmental pollution is most evident along major trekking routes, at campsites, in small mountain villages, and at the base camps used by mountaineering expeditions. The most visible effects are increased amounts of nonbiodegradable garbage and littering, inappropriate disposal of human waste, contamination of water supplies, and pollution of creeks and streams. While the littering of trails with plastic is visually intrusive, waste-disposal problems appear to present a genuine health risk. Deforestation and waste-disposal problems have been particularly evident at

Annapurna, where these environmental costs have been compounded by wildlife hunting and the suppression of forest regeneration by grazing animals.

Project Origins and Objectives

The prospect of a protected area was far from popular in the Annapurna region. During the establishment of Nepal's existing national parks, the indigenous inhabitants either had been evicted or excluded from any role in management (Gurung 1992). This led to fears that the government would overturn traditional resource-use rights and management at Annapurna. Sensitive to these concerns, a small King Mahendra Trust survey team (two Nepalese and one expatriate) spent six months talking to villagers and collecting information in the area that eventually became the Annapurna Conservation Area. The team developed a provisional project design and management plan based on discussions with leaders and villagers throughout the region.

The results of this field survey indicated that environmental and human stresses in the Annapurna region were more pronounced than in any other region of Nepal. The trust survey team reported that local villagers were remarkably aware of problems of environmental degradation and generally claimed that in principle they would be supportive of corrective efforts. Assuming this moral support and some willingness to contribute time and energy, an effective framework was needed to allow villagers to control poaching and random forest cutting while providing viable, self-sustaining economic alternatives. The report suggested that it would be critical for planners, the King Mahendra Trust, regional conservation officers, and staff to consider the interests of the people in the region first, as true, long-term conservation can only arise from mutual trust (Sherpa, Coburn, and Gurung 1986).

The trust realized that designating the Annapurna region as a national park would have led to rapid international recognition, permitted the application of existing legislation, and enabled higher fees to be collected immediately. However, the staff feared that a national park designation and its associated restrictive management would generate the same negative local response experienced elsewhere in Nepal, e.g., at Chitwan, Langtang, and Sagarmatha national parks. The trust also was concerned that a national park might focus on wildlife and protection of the largely uninhabited areas at the expense of crucial education, development, and management activities in the populated areas.

The Conservation Area Concept

After consideration of various options, a new legal designation of the Annapurna region as a "conservation area" was recommended (HMGN 1973). The conservation area concept required new legislation and, in contrast to existing national parks, would allow specifically for hunting, collection of forest products, allocation of visitor fees for local development, and delegation of management authority to the village level. The draft plan was discussed in village meetings and revised on the basis of local input.

Following six years of intensive lobbying and negotiation, the Annapurna Conservation Area was officially gazetted in July 1992. The same legislation (HMGN 1973) also provided specific legal authorization for a nongovernmental organization (NGO) to manage conservation areas for a ten-year period. This landmark event considerably strengthened future prospects for conservation and development in the Annapurna region and provided a legal framework for the establishment of conservation areas based on similar principles in other parts of Nepal. Before the 1992 legislation, the project and its supporters had to fight a continual political battle against greater government control.

Resistance to the traditional national park concept (fences and fines) has a lingering effect. Some local people are still resistant to the project's initiatives because they remain convinced that the area eventually will be designated as a national park, leading to resettlement and/or a significant army presence. Legal designation of conservation areas may be more useful as a way to conserve new areas rather than as a technique to modify existing parks or reserves, where local people often have been alienated already and have become mistrustful of externally initiated conservation ventures.

In concept, the designated zones in the Annapurna Conservation Area are not particularly different from the idea of designating buffer zones outside and intensive visitor-use zones inside national parks. The approaches used to elicit local community involvement in its own economic development within the project should be transferable, in principle, to zones on the boundaries of existing national parks.

Project Objectives

The Nepalese conservation area concept is an innovative way to link conservation to development by emphasizing the role of villagers in using and managing natural resources. The objectives of ACAP are as follows:

- to involve local people in the conservation of their natural and cultural heritage,
- to utilize species and ecosystems sustainably to maximize current benefits while maintaining future options,
- to develop techniques for linking protection with community participation that may be applicable elsewhere in Nepal,
- to exploit the area's potential for tourism,
- to implement soil- and water-conservation programs,

- to develop service industries for tourism such as farms, orchards, poultry breeding and handicrafts,

- to educate villagers about conservation,

- to renew forest cover and prevent deforestation, and

- to introduce alternative sources of energy, principally hydroelectricity, as a substitute for fuelwood (Sherpa, Coburn, and Gurung 1986).

Land-use Zoning

The Annapurna Conservation Area was divided into a series of zones, each with specific regulations and management policies:

Special management zones   These are areas of conservation importance that have been degraded or are threatened by imminent degradation. These zones have the highest management priority. The popular trekking route from Chhomrong to the Annapurna Sanctuary and the Ghandruk-Chhomrong-Ghorepani Forest are included in special management zones.

Wilderness zones   These are areas above the upper-elevation limits for seasonal grazing (about 4,500 m). These areas are fully protected, with no development permitted.

Protected forest/seasonal grazing zones   These are generally areas that lie above the special management zones and below the wilderness zones. This category only includes areas that are more than one day's travel from villages on a forest-resource collection trip. Restricted collection of firewood and hunting is permitted, and local people may collect medicinal plants.

Intensive-use zones   These areas of human settlement on the southern slopes are characterized by intensive agricultural use and include areas that are less than one day's travel from villages. Management, administration, and conservation education activities are concentrated within these zones. Traditional forest- and pasture-management systems are encouraged and nurseries established. Hunting is strictly controlled.

Biotic/anthropological zones   These are characterized by natural areas where "the influence or technology of modern man has not significantly interfered with or been absorbed by the traditional ways of life of its inhabitants." Foreigners (except certain researchers) are not allowed to enter these areas.

In practice, project activities have been heavily concentrated in the intensive-use zones, and comparatively little attention has been given to the management of the other zones.

Project Implementation

Implementation of the project was planned in two stages. The first five-year stage would cover 800 km² of the southern slopes, mostly within a single political district. The second stage, contingent upon the success of the first, would comprise an 1,800-km² extension. A two-stage approach was considered necessary because sufficient trained project staff members were not available in 1986 (several experienced staff members were sent to the United Kingdom and New Zealand during 1987–89 for master's-level training in natural resources management). There was also a risk of prematurely committing and diluting resources over a large area before appropriate techniques had been worked out. Finally, future difficulties were expected in the designation of conservation-area status to the Stage II area, had it been excluded from the initial planning and legislation.

The project's first regional headquarters was established at Ghandruk village in the intensive-use zone in December 1986 (see Map 11.1). Since 1986 the project has had three Nepalese directors, the first two members of the initial survey team. Most of the other senior project staff members originate from other areas of Nepal, while junior staff members have been hired locally. No expatriate staff or technical consultants have been involved.

From 1986 until 1990, the project devoted most of its efforts to one small part of the vast region within the project area: the Modi Khola Valley and the Annapurna Sanctuary. This high alpine basin had experienced extensive adverse environmental impacts from trekking and mountaineering tourism.

The project is only now expanding into other areas on the southern slopes of the Annapurna range, including a second regional headquarters at Siklis. ACAP plans to establish regional headquarters at Jomsom and Manang to facilitate activities throughout the protected area (Stevens and Sherpa 1992a). Promotion of agroforestry among farmers of the region is a major new emphasis of the second stage.

The performance of the project's second stage will be critical. The first stage provided a valuable testing ground for community-based approaches but focused on too small an area to have a significant long-term effect on the entire ecosystem. The challenge now is to expand the project's promising beginning into a much larger area without suffering from the problems that plague many large-scale conservation and development projects.

Possible Future Expansion of the
Annapurna Conservation Area Project

Mustang—a vast region adjacent to the western boundary of the project area—recently has been opened to foreign visitors by the government of Nepal. The people of Mustang largely have been isolated from the outside world, and the area is full of virtually untouched biological and cultural treasures. Mustang will be extremely vulnerable to the dangers posed by excessive or poorly managed tourism. There is an urgent need for effective and appropriate precautionary action in this area. The government has asked the Annapurna project to expand into the Mustang area. This will be a formidable challenge, not least because the 7,000-km² Mustang is almost three times the size of the Annapurna Conservation Area. Mustang, however, represents an opportunity to protect an extraordinarily valuable area and test the utility of the Annapurna Conservation Area Project approach beyond the area for which it was initially designed.

Project Activities

The menu of Annapurna project activities is extensive. Some have progressed significantly, while others have not advanced beyond preliminary planning. The range of activities includes

- Community development: improved water supplies, health clinics, family planning, latrine and garbage-pit construction, trail and bridge repair, agricultural extension and training, lodge training and management committees, grazing-land rehabilitation, erosion control.

- Forest conservation: community nurseries, fodder and fuelwood plantations, fuel-efficient stoves, water and space heaters, solar technologies, microhydroenergy, kerosene depots, forest management committees.

- Conservation education: school programs, mobile audiovisual extension programs, house visits, posters, brochures, Minimum Impact Code for trekkers, public cleanup campaigns, displays at information centers.

- Research and training: wildlife biology and habitat studies, botanical surveys, forest-use and management studies, training for lodge owners and extension staff.

Project Activities Related to Tourism

One of the project's first priorities was to reduce the environmental impact of visiting trekkers and increase the local economic benefits from tourism. A lodge management committee was formed in Ghandruk to represent the lodge owners and oversee future lodge development. Many of the project-induced changes that affect the region's tourism began with extensive negotiations with lodge owners. Training courses to upgrade quality of service, standardize menus and prices, and improve levels of sanitation and waste disposal have been conducted for the owners of lodges and tea shops throughout the conservation area. The development of visitor centers and posts to check permits and provide information has created opportunities to educate visitors on issues of nature and culture, as well as on the potential environmental impact of their activities.

Several energy conservation measures have been introduced. Within the conservation area, lodges and expeditions are required to use kerosene, thus limiting collection of fuelwood to subsistence use. A kerosene depot has been established at Chhomrong to supply fuel to lodges and trekking groups in the conservation area. The project provided expertise, but not financing, for lodge owners who wanted to install backboilers to heat recycled water during cooking to further conserve energy. More than 120 lodges have installed the backboiler system so far (Gurung 1992). Lodge owners also have contributed to the cost of trail upgrading and maintenance. These accomplishments have greatly enhanced the status and influence of the project locally.

The value of the economic benefits lodge owners are accumulating has not been estimated. Even without exact estimates, the amount is considerable by local standards and has dramatically increased the average per capita income. How this new wealth has been used has not been systematically monitored. In the villages on the major trekking routes, the incomes of 100 to 150 families who own tea shops or lodges has increased significantly in the last decade. However, spin-off employment for nonfamily members appears to be very limited. With the notable exception of some seasonal vegetables, most lodges buy supplies in Pokhara, and many of these goods originate outside of Nepal. Some goods are purchased from traders who move up and down the trails, and employment for porters undoubtedly has increased because all goods must be carried on foot. The significant local economic benefits from tourism have not been distributed widely either among or within villages (Wells and Brandon 1992).

Project Activities Related to Forest and Pasture Management

Despite the extensive destruction of Nepal's forests during the twentieth century, a widespread tradition of community forest management existed until the enactment of the Private Forests Nationalization Act in 1957. This act made community forest management illegal. What followed was an extended period of confusion and rapid exploitation of formerly well-managed forests. A new phase began in the 1970s, as legislation gradually began to return control of forests to local people, a trend that culminated in the Decentralization Act of 1982. To date, reversion of control has progressed slowly, with many bureaucratic delays and unresolved local disputes.

Numerous reports note the existence of remote communities that were relatively unaffected by legislated changes and managed to retain effective control over nearby forests. Several examples were found in the Annapurna Conservation Area by the preliminary survey team (Sherpa, Coburn, and Gurung 1986). The project has sought to revive some of these traditional community organization structures by promoting the establishment of forest management committees.

The forest management committee decides major issues related to forestry and livestock use. When the committee is unable to reach a consensus, it tends to ask ACAP staff for input. Forest guards have been hired. The committee has responsibility for enforcing hunting regulations, fining poachers, etc. The committee also has the power to authorize the cutting of timber for specified purposes.

Livestock grazing in the forests threatens regeneration and is a significant environmental issue, although there is little or no data available on animal numbers. Some of the forest management committee members are also herd owners. The project staff has taken committee members to visit reforestation projects to help them understand the role of livestock in suppressing regeneration and to generate greater interest in stall-feeding, apparently with some success.

Community Participation in the Annapurna Conservation Area Project

The project's emphasis on community participation did not arise from an altruistic desire to apply an attractive theoretical concept but from the experiences of protected areas elsewhere in Nepal, particularly national parks. Many of the problems currently facing these parks and their surrounding lands can be directly attributed to management's insensitivity to local people's needs and constraints (Wells 1992). The clear message from these experiences, together with the findings of rural development programs worldwide, mandated a participatory approach.

Local support has been recognized as critical at a practical (not just rhetorical) level throughout the history of the project. Extensive consultations and local participation in decision-making have continued to be a feature of the project, and project managers have resisted, wherever possible, the unilateral imposition of regulations affecting local people. At the outset, the project recognized the need to establish trust in the minds of a skeptical local population, to convince them that they would benefit from—or at least not be harmed by—the project. A second step was to attempt to motivate people to make resource-management decisions, principally through the management committees described above. Expansion of the project beyond the initial target area had been planned for 1989 but was postponed for a year in the interest of developing stronger local support in the original project area.

The project has avoided investing in community projects as "gifts" and has consistently insisted on local participation, in cash or labor, in any community project. At least a 50 percent local contribution usually is planned, and wherever possible, project inputs are limited to contributions in kind (such as purchased goods). This is based on the belief that when local people are interested enough in a venture to invest in it—as opposed to receiving a perhaps unwanted gift—they will have a greater interest in ensuring that the venture succeeds.

A report on the first three years of the project describes five drinking-water projects, four school-assistance projects, two bridge-construction projects, three trail-repair projects, and two youth-development programs, all based on joint community-project inputs (Rana 1990). In other examples, local people in Ghandruk raised NR100,000 (US$5,000) as matching funds for a community health center, a process that took more than a year. For a 60 kW hydroelectric project in Ghandruk, a Canadian donor provided NR900,000 (US$45,000), the project provided NR350,000 (US$17,000), and the *panchayat* (the local political organization) obtained and took responsibility for a five-year bank loan to cover the remaining NR550,000 (US$27,000). The owners of small tourist-trekking lodges raised 50 percent of the cost of repairing and cleaning up the footpaths and trails in their area. This approach, although sometimes painstakingly slow, appears to be working extremely well and eliciting genuine local consideration and participation. Its success could be undermined by the eagerness of other donors to become involved in the conservation area and make large grants to the communities—something local leaders are well aware of and which previously has conditioned many villagers to expect development-agency or conservation-organization handouts. The Annapurna project staff so far has exhibited considerable skill in avoiding conflict over projects identified as locally desirable but inconsistent with conservation, such as road building. As Stevens and Sherpa point out,

> the initial relationship between the project and local people, and lines of communication, were given considerable attention, beyond the participatory nature of the initial survey and management plan development. For example, the Project's first director convinced a newly-formed lodge owners' committee to ban the use of fuelwood (and substitute kerosene) in lodges. This ban was later extended to some other stressed parts of the Conservation Area. This was not a grass-roots initiative— and neither was the establishment of the Conservation Area itself. The perception of a crisis and the need to address it originated from outside the region. But the early initiatives were worked out in face-to-face contact with people who would have to live with the results of any changes. Top-down regulations to be applied over large heterogeneous areas were avoided. Basing actions on local decisions has meant that the process of developing new conservation regulations and resource use practices has been very localized and slow. *(1992a:21)*

What has been gained has only come about through enormous time, effort, skill, and care, supported by quite large sums of money (in comparison with other rural programs in Nepal, if not with community-based conservation initiatives in other countries).

Financial Support

The project began with a grant from the World Wildlife Fund in 1985 through its USAID-funded Wildlands and Human Needs Program and has continued to receive grants from WWF. The King Mahendra Trust's United Kingdom trust underwrote the project's conservation-education program. In 1989, the project received funding from the Netherlands Development Corporation (SNV) for a five-year agroforestry and community-participation project. Several other donors have contributed to specific project activities. According to Rana (1990), total grants to the project amounted to NR4.7 million (then equivalent to US$185,000) in the 1988–89 fiscal year and almost NR8 million (US$280,000) in the 1989–90 fiscal year.

The project began collecting entry fees in the conservation area in 1989. The NR200 fee (equivalent to US$8 when established but worth less than $US5 by early 1992) is yielding annual revenues of NR4 million (equivalent to US$125,000 in the 1990–91 fiscal year). This amount is equal to half the revenues from all of the trekking permits issued in Nepal, or more than 40 percent of revenues from all of the country's national parks combined (Wells 1993). The revenues collected pass directly to the project and are deposited in an endowment fund. Financial self-sufficiency for the project from these invested entry-fee revenues is anticipated by 1995 (Gurung 1992).

The King Mahendra Trust for Nature Conservation

The King Mahendra Trust for Nature Conservation, established in 1984 as an autonomous, not-for-profit NGO following a special act of Parliament in 1982, is the largest and most influential conservation organization in Nepal. Royal patronage has contributed significantly to the trust's success. The trust also has close ties to influential politicians and has been given a remarkably autonomous and significant role in the management of the Annapurna Conservation Area. This is probably a unique arrangement for an NGO in Asia—or for any NGO on an issue of such global importance. The trust can raise money directly from overseas and has been able to lobby successfully for new legislation needed to guarantee its autonomy. Several of the trust's international committees raise both money and awareness in their respective countries. The trust has been able to bypass many of the inefficiencies and time-consuming procedures associated with government agencies and execute projects with a relatively slim and flexible bureaucracy. The Annapurna project is the trust's largest undertaking so far.

The trust's 1988 action plan describes two principal spheres of operation. The first is as an implementing agency, undertaking various projects; the second is to act as an influential coordinating and catalytic force. The action plan states that the trust's long-term objectives are to

- promote the concept of conservation for sustainable development in Nepal,
- promote the conservation of important biological resources through the maintenance of areas of high biological diversity,
- build self-supporting and self-sufficient conservation institutions, particularly in the nongovernmental private sector,

- integrate local development with conservation, and

- generate environmental awareness to bring about a balance between the needs for nature conservation and basic human needs (KMTNC 1988).

The trust has operated on a budget of less than US$1 million annually and recently completed the substantial task of preparing the environmental impact assessment of the proposed Arun III dam and hydroelectric project. The trust has been led by an outstanding Nepalese staff that has had a profound influence on conservation at a national level. However, the trust's overall management structure is stressed, and the organization is stretched to its capacity.

The relationship between the trust and the Department of National Parks and Wildlife Conservation (DNPWC) is informal but complex. The former secretary-general of the trust, as well as some of his senior staff members, were officially on secondment from DNPWC. Although some individuals made this move several years ago, their DNPWC positions have remained vacant.

There is an obvious contrast between the fund-raising abilities, financial resources, and autonomy (and, consequently, the effectiveness) of the two organizations. The trust has gone to considerable lengths to define its role as complementary to the department, mainly by concentrating on innovative pilot projects and special operations. The trust has neither the inclination nor the capacity to supplement the basic operational role of DNPWC, but many department staff members still resent KMTNC's involvement.

Recent political changes in Nepal have raised questions about the trust's future. Following the first democratic governmental elections in 1991, the trust's close ties to the monarchy—critical to its successes so far—now have become more of a liability than an asset. There is no indication at present, however, that these changes will have an adverse impact on the project, particularly now that the conservation area and the NGO's management role have been legislated. In addition, recent changes in the senior personnel of both the trust and DNPWC have considerably defused tensions between the two organizations.

Assessing the Project's Achievements

No systematic evaluation of the project has been attempted. Monitoring and evaluation of the project has been by limited internal review and occasional short visits from outsiders. Measures of progress and success are difficult to establish. The key indices to monitor may be qualitative rather than quantitative. Improvements in environmental awareness and basic needs are principal project goals, but no baseline measures were made. These variables are being monitored only through informal reporting from project staff. This deficiency of information—particularly about the activities of farmers outside the Ghandruk, Chhomrong, and Ghorepani areas, as well as the conservation area's biological diversity—will hinder future efforts to measure the impact of the project.

The project would benefit from regular independent evaluations, including socioeconomic and attitudinal surveys of the resident population and, possibly, of visiting trekkers. Such evaluations could be conducted effectively only by a Nepalese team prepared to spend considerable time in the field. Participant evaluations should be encouraged wherever possible. (For a general discussion on assessing the effectiveness of community-based conservation projects such as ACAP, see Brandon and Wells [1992] and Wells and Brandon [1992, 1993].)

Tourism and Conservation

The project's most immediate and visible results have been in reducing the environmental impact of foreign visitors and increasing the local economic benefits from tourism. Successful work with lodge owners through management committees has greatly enhanced the local status and influence of the project. The future of energy sources and their security is of major concern throughout Nepal and the Himalayas. Heavy consumption of fuelwood and insufficient replacement biomass is a special concern in parts of the conservation area. Establishment of the regulation requiring use of kerosene instead of fuelwood for all but subsistence purposes in the conservation area is one of the project's major achievements. This regulation was not imposed unilaterally but resulted from extensive discussions with the lodge management committee, whose members needed to be persuaded to make the relatively expensive investment in kerosene-burning stoves. A number of concerns remain, however.

The government of Nepal is understandably anxious to increase its foreign-exchange earnings from tourism. The number of foreign visitors therefore is likely to continue growing, and a significant proportion will continue to be attracted to Annapurna. However, the area has an upper limit in its tourist-carrying capacity beyond which ecological and cultural damage will make this type of exploitation unsustainable (Gurung 1990). So far, little consideration has been given to the possibility of redistributing, if not limiting, the number of visitors to particular areas.

The significant economic benefits of tourism have not been distributed widely, either among or within villages. Of the 100 to 150 families who own tea shops or lodges in the area, perhaps half have experienced very significant increases in income and wealth during the last decade. Economic impacts do not appear to spread far beyond these families into the local economy. Employment of non-family members in these businesses appears to be very limited, and many of the goods they use originate outside Nepal. Traders and porters may be benefiting. However, very little "trickle-down" economic growth appears to be taking place locally (Wells and Brandon 1992).

The value of the economic benefits accruing to lodge owners has not been estimated. The use to which this surplus is being put also has received little attention. There is some speculation that the additional savings are being invested in livestock, although some herd owners (only a small proportion of whom are lodge owners) seem anxious to reduce their herds. Some lodge owners have bought land in Pokhara. Others send their children to be educated at better schools in larger towns. There is no indication that lodge owners are interested in acquiring and managing additional lodges (although many are upgrading their facilities and expanding in size) or in using their accumulated savings to make loans to others. Local credit markets, either formal or informal, seem very limited. The possibility of new local industries to attract these surplus funds has not been explored.

Finally, significant waste and litter continues to accumulate in the conservation area, most originating directly or indirectly from tourism. The project has been successful in promoting collection and disposal of waste and litter in the southern part of the conservation area, particularly in comparison to other trekking areas such as Sagarmatha. An annual cleanup campaign for the Annapurna Base Camp, launched three years ago at Ghandruk School, has been so successful that in late 1989 the students found little obvious litter on the trails to collect. Lodge owners now collect and bury most litter, but, particularly in the case of nonbiodegradable materials, this solution is not viable over the long term and will require further attention.

Social and Economic Development

The Annapurna project's approach to community participation is probably the single most impressive aspect of the project. Successes in this area are due to the project leaders' and staff's familiarity with the region and its people and their consequent ability to judge the appropriate nature and timing of attempts to induce change.

Project achievements in development areas unrelated to tourism are difficult to identify and evaluate. Most inhabitants of the conservation area are poor farmers for whom the only direct impact of tourism is the higher prices they have begun to face for certain goods. Beyond the information collected during the initial project survey, little is known about farming systems employed in the more remote parts of the conservation area or their potential for improved productivity. At present, few indicators exist by which to measure the success of the project's efforts to significantly improve economic conditions for these farmers. The magnitude of this challenge is illustrated by the fact that throughout the Himalayas there are few convincing examples of successful agricultural or forestry development, either in Nepal or elsewhere. There is, however, ample evidence of continued population growth and environmental degradation.

Specific considerations for nontourism-related economic development include:

- Stage II of the project will emphasize community-level agroforestry initiatives as the principal tool for boosting farmers' incomes in an environmentally benign fashion. The technical approaches are to be worked out with assistance from outside experts and the agricultural research station at Lumle. Although appropriate technical packages will be important, any successes are likely to result from the project's high credibility in the region, the extent to which the project staff has been able to win over and influence local political leaders, and the extent of popular support for local institutions that enhance community participation.

- Physical and ecological constraints to the improvement of agricultural productivity in the Himalayas suggest that alternative income-generating activities should receive attention. Progress in this difficult and largely unexplored area has been modest. Hydroelectric power is an obvious area for investigation. Project personnel are currently conducting feasibility studies of a range of potential hydroelectric projects. The long-term need for diversification out of agriculture to protect the environment eventually may necessitate expensive investments in hydropower. Such investments are prone to collapse, as illustrated by several small-scale water projects in the region, all implemented before the project began, which now lie idle due to design deficiencies, inadequate local interest in maintenance, or lack of spare parts.

- The project is also training young people from the region and providing seed money for activities such as chicken farming, raising dairy cows, growing vegetables, etc. Others have been sent for training as electricians and mechanics. Some small industries also have been promoted, including a carpet factory in Ghandruk. The scale of these initiatives is very small, but the project hopes they will have a strong demonstration effect and catalyze local interest. Marketing is a major constraint, and tourists are likely to be seen as the most promising market for goods in the absence of transportation infrastructure.

- Several nurseries have been established and seedlings distributed either free or at low cost. Farmers have been encouraged to plant trees to stabilize slopes and to provide fuelwood and fodder. Although demand for seedlings has been relatively high, which in itself is a reasonable indicator of "success," little information is available on survival rates, making it difficult to tell to what extent the nurseries are an effective investment. As predictions of fuelwood deficits become more pessimistic, the successful promotion of high-altitude tree planting assumes critical importance. The project is also encouraging stall-feeding of livestock, a major shift in land use that will focus greater attention on the production of fodder trees.

Conservation of Biological Diversity

The absence of explicit linkages between the design of development programs and the achievement of biodiversity-conservation objectives has been identified as a recurrent weakness of community-based conservation programs (Wells and

Brandon 1992). Biodiversity conservation was not among the project's original objectives, perhaps because in the early to mid-1980s the term *biodiversity* had not achieved the ubiquitous (if poorly understood) position that it now holds. Individual project activities are related only indirectly to biodiversity conservation. But the project's overall focus has been to try to persuade local people that economic development need not be incompatible with conservation, and that there are long-term social and economic benefits to be gained from sound resource management. To the extent that this is being achieved, biodiversity is likely to benefit, even if indirectly and in an unquantified manner.

Prospects for Sustainability

The sustainablity of the project is difficult to assess at this stage. The formal gazetting of the conservation area provides a critical legal framework, and user-fee revenues should be a highly significant factor in assuring financial self-sufficiency. The recurrent-cost problem, upon which so many projects founder, thus may be avoided.

The extent to which viable local institutions can be promoted and eventually assume effective control over resource management will be critical. While a promising start has been made in terms of the forest and lodge committees, several years are likely to elapse before it becomes clear whether the project will be able to scale back project administration and allow true local leadership to take over. Several more years also will be required to assess whether the project will be likely to succeed in spreading economic benefits more widely to include farmers, who constitute the majority of the local population. This will be crucial in determining the "success" of the project.

The project undoubtedly has achieved some very impressive results during its first few years. Its highly professional and well-organized staff appears to have established a solid foundation for future expansion. However, to label the project an unambiguous "success" is premature. Such an evaluation is likely to result in unrealistic expectations and unjustified disappointment with future progress.

Replicability and Influence

The Woodlands Mountain Institute, a United States-based NGO, has cooperated with the Nepalese Department of National Parks and Wildlife Conservation to develop the Makalu-Barun Conservation Project, based on the Annapurna model. This community-based conservation and development project will be supported by the Global Environment Facility. This project will effectively extend the eastern boundary of Sagarmatha National Park and may become linked to a much larger and very ambitious multiple-use conservation project that has been proposed for southern Tibet.

The Annapurna project has attracted considerable international attention and receives a constant flow of short visits from VIPs and representatives of large and influential organizations. The project has been widely cited as a model that clearly demonstrates that development can be linked successfully to conservation and has won international awards on this basis. Possibly one of the most important and tangible achievements of the project has been its successful marketing of the concept of linking environmental conservation with participatory social and economic development, inspiring others to attempt to do the same.

ACKNOWLEDGMENTS

Thanks to Michael Wright for inviting me to write this chapter, which could not have been prepared without the cooperation of and extensive input from the first two directors of the Annapurna Conservation Area Project, Mingma Norbu Sherpa and Chandra P. Gurung (although they do not necessarily agree with what I have written). Others who have shaped my opinions about conservation in Nepal—particularly in Annapurna—include Teeka Bhattarai, Gabriel Campbell, Broughton Coburn, Harka Gurung, Hemanta Mishra, Ram Prakash Yadav, and Stan Stevens. My site visit to the Annapurna Conservation Area was financed by the World Bank and facilitated by the King Mahendra Trust for Nature Conservation. Responsibility for the opinions expressed here rests solely with me.

SOURCES

Annapurna Conservation Area Project (ACAP). 1988. *Annapurna Conservation Area Map and Guide*. Kathmandu: King Mahendra Trust for Nature Conservation (KMTNC).

Banskota, M., P. Sharma, S. Sharma, B. Bhatta, and T. Tenzing. 1990. *Economic Policies for Sustainable Development in Nepal*. Kathmandu: International Centre for Integrated Mountain Development.

Brandon, K., and M. Wells. 1992. "Planning for People and Parks: Design Dilemmas." *World Development* 20(4): 557–570.

Bunting, B. W., M. N. Sherpa, and R. M. Wright. 1991. "Annapurna Conservation Area: Nepal's New Approach to Protected Area Management." In *Resident Populations and National Parks: Social Dilemmas and Strategies in International Conservation*, ed. P. C. West and S. R. Brechin, 160–172. Tucson, Arizona: University of Arizona Press.

Environmental Resources Limited (ERL). 1989. *Natural Resource Management for Sustainable Development: A Study of Feasible Policies, Institutions and Investment Activities in Nepal with Special Emphasis on the Hills*. Report prepared for the Overseas Development Administration (ODA)/World Bank. London: ERL.

Gurung, C. 1992. "Peoples and their Participation: New Approaches to Resolving Conflicts and Promoting Cooperation." Paper presented at the World Parks Congress, Caracas, Venezuela, February 10–21.

Gurung, H. 1990. "Environmental management of mountain tourism in Nepal." Paper presented at the Economic and Social Commission for Asia and the Pacific (ESCAP) Symposium on Tourism Promotion in the Asia Region, November 12–15, Hangzhou, China.

His Majesty's Government of Nepal (HMGN). 1973. National Parks and Conservation Act, 1973 (Amended 1989). Department of National Parks and Wildlife Conservation, Kathmandu, Nepal.

Hough, J., and M. N. Sherpa. 1989. "Bottom-up versus Basic Needs: Integrating Conservation and Development in the Annapurna and Michiru Mountain Conservation Areas of Nepal and Malawi. " *Ambio* 18 (8): 434–41.

King Mahendra Trust for Nature Conservation (KMTNC). 1988. *Strategy for Environmental Conservation in Nepal: The Initial Five Year (1988/89–1992/93) Action Plan of the King Mahendra Trust for Nature Conservation (KMTNC).* Kathmandu: KMTNC.

Ministry of Forests and Soil Conservation (MFSC). 1988. *Plan for the Conservation of Ecosystems and Genetic Resources. Forestry Sector Master Plan.* Kathmandu: MFSC.

Rana, D. S., ed. 1990. *Annapurna Conservation Area Project: Three Year Retrospective Progress Report.* Kathmandu: King Mahendra Trust for Nature Conservation (KMTNC).

Sherpa, M. N., B. Coburn, and C. P. Gurung. 1986. *Annapurna Conservation Area, Nepal: Operational Plan.* Kathmandu: King Mahendra Trust for Nature Conservation (KMTNC).

Stevens, S. F., and M. N. Sherpa. 1992a. "Indigenous Peoples and Protected Area Management: New Approaches to Protected Area Management in Nepal." Paper presented at the World Parks Congress, Caracas, Venezuela, February 10–21.

———. 1992b. "Tourism Impacts and Protected Area Management in Highland Nepal: Lessons from Sagarmatha National Park and Annapurna Conservation Area." Paper presented at the World Parks Congress, Caracas, Venezuela, February 10–21.

Touche Ross, in association with Environmental Resources Limited (ERL), University of Surrey, New Era and METCON Consultants. 1989. *Nepal Tourism Development Programme.* Kathmandu: Asian Development Bank/Ministry of Tourism.

Wells, M. 1992. "Biodiversity Conservation, Affluence and Poverty: Mismatched Costs and Benefits and Efforts to Remedy Them." *Ambio* 21(3): 237–243.

———. 1993. "Neglect of Biological Riches: The Economics of Nature Tourism in Nepal." *Biodiversity and Conservation* 2:445–464.

———, and K. Brandon with L. Hannah. 1992. *People and Parks: Linking Protected Area Management with Local Communities.* Washington, D. C.: World Bank, World Wildlife Fund, and United States Agency for International Development.

———. 1993. "The Principles and Practice of Buffer Zones and Local Participation in Biodiversity Conservation." *Ambio* 22(2/3):157–162.

CHAPTER 12

The Farm Scheme of North York Moors National Park, United Kingdom

Derek C. Statham

The North York Moors National Park is a discrete block of upland country, 1,436 km² in extent, abutting the coast in the northeast of England (see Map 12.1). It attained its status as one of eleven designated national parks in England and Wales in 1952.

National Parks in the U.K. have two main purposes: conservation of their characteristic landscape and natural beauty and enjoyment of the landscape in appropriate ways by the general public.

These purposes are laid down in statute in the National Parks and Access to the Countryside Act, 1949. In 1976, following a government inquiry and the subsequent *Report of the National Park Policies Review Committee, 1974*, it was decided that in circumstances where the achievement of these two purposes would lead to conflict, the conservation objective has priority over recreational enjoyment. In carrying out their duties in the parks, the national parks authorities have to take into account the social and economic needs of each area. This statutory requirement is currently under review by the government, following the report of a committee asked to review the purposes, policies, and administration of the national parks (*Fit for the Future* 1991).

In the British situation, the needs of the resident populations inevitably have to be considered in the parks' management plans, since the country's parks are not wilderness, having been settled and farmed for several millenia. Their landscapes have been manipulated by man since prehistoric times and contain small towns and villages as well as large areas of seminatural vegetation. There are only small, isolated pockets of climax vegetation cover and a much diminished range of the original fauna.

Linkage with local communities is achieved via two policy processes: preparation of a development plan for each park under the Town and Country Development Plan system and a National Park Plan for management of the area. Both plans are prepared with considerable public involvement, including a public

Map 12.1

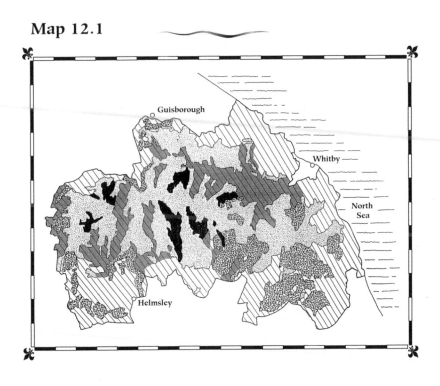

North York Moors
National Park

**Area Shown
in Detail**

KEY

Moorland

Forestry Areas

Farmland

Farm Scheme Target Areas

Established

Needed

inquiry. Support to local communities is further enhanced by the financing of the parks, each of which receives an annual central government grant to cover approximately 75 percent of its total budget. Remaining expenditures are financed by local council taxes and income generated by the park's activities. Currently, North York Moors' budget is around £3.3 million (US$4.95 million); £1.1 million (US$1.65 million) is to be spent on conservation works, £1.3 million (US$1.95 million) on recreation and interpretation, and £0.8 million (US$1.2 million) on planning control and other administrative costs.

North York Moors, a sparsely populated area with some 25,000 residents and large areas of seminatural moorland vegetation and forest habitats, admirably fulfills the specifications for a British national park. The area, which is of great beauty, is close to densely populated urban areas and easily accessible via the country's road and rail network. Local people and visitors from farther afield make some 13 million visits to the park annually. At the same time, North York Moors is a living place for farmers, foresters, hunters, fishermen, and other land users. Its landscapes are manmade and need constant management and expert skills.

In land-use terms, the area covered by seminatural heather moorland vegetation amounts to some 35 percent of the park's area. Farmland occupies about 40 percent, and the remainder is mostly woodland, of which recently planted coniferous plantations form the greater part. Only a few areas of ancient, broad-leaved woodland remain.

Geologically, the area consists of an up-faulted dome of Jurassic sediments of three distinct series. The oldest series is composed of shale, sandstone, and mudstone of the Lias and is mainly exposed along the coast and in valley bottoms. These are overlaid with freshwater sandstone—the "Ravenscar group" that forms the bedrock over much of the central moorland. The youngest series is the oolite group, which consists of clay, sandstone, calcareous grit, and oolitic limestone. This series forms the Tabular and Hambleton Hills, on the southern and western edges of the national park, which terminate in a spectacular northward-facing scarp.

The topography of the North York Moors owes much to the influence of the last ice age, which ended approximately seventeen thousand years ago. The moors were not covered by an ice cap but formed an area of tundra and glacial lakes surrounded by ice sheets. Glacial floodwater from this period, combined with river erosion and spring sapping, has dissected the underlying geology, creating deep, steep-sided valleys or dales.

At their highest point, the North York Moors rise to only 454 m. Their location on the east coast makes the climate more continental than most upland areas in Britain. Annual rainfall is 762–1015 mm, and mean winter and summer temperatures are 3°C and 15°C respectively—but with much variation according to altitude and exposure to wind. The climate and general exposure of the area have resulted in the moorland habitats supporting a range of species normally associated with far greater altitude.

Conservation Setting: The Main Habitats and Their Management

All of the principal habitat types in the North York Moors have been created or strongly influenced by man's activity. Conservation of the habitats continues to be a by-product of this traditional land use. Changes in the intensity and form of this activity will therefore have major environmental implications.

Moorland Habitats

The heather moorland lies between 250 and 400 m in altitude and is mainly un-enclosed (unfenced), although some sizable fenced areas occur, these being known as "intakes." Moorland habitat in this area is thought to be largely human-created, initially through burning to improve cover for game. Later a slash-and-burn type of agriculture was adopted, involving clearance of native oak, birch, and pine woodland and resulting in erosion and impoverishment of the upland soils. This process probably commenced in the Mesolithic (8,000–4,300 B.C.) and was largely complete by the end of the Bronze Age (800 B.C.). Certainly much of the moorland is thought to have been as it is now by the Roman period (A.D. 70–410).

Over most of the moorland the dominant vegetation is heather (*Calluna vulgaris*) and bilberry (*Vaccinium myrtillus*). The lower slopes often are dominated by bracken (*Pteridium aquilinum*). The moorland is generally poor in plant species, although many species-rich spring, stream, and flush areas occur. These wet areas are also of importance with regard to invertebrate fauna, which in turn support insectivorous birds such as curlew (*Numenius arquata*).

The moorland areas also provide an important habitat for reptiles such as the adder (*Vipera berus*) and common lizard (*Lacerta vivipara*). They are highly valued nationally and internationally for the communities of upland breeding birds they support (the area is proposed as a Special Protection Area for birds under the 1979 European Economic Community Birds Directive on the Conservation of Wild Birds).

The main forms of management are grazing of hardy upland sheep and rotational burning of heather to encourage high densities of red grouse (*Lagopus lagopus*) for sport. The red grouse, one of the fastest game birds in flight, is unique to Britain and highly prized internationally as a sporting target. By careful management, grouse numbers can be increased greatly beyond their natural population levels to form the basis of the shooting industry. Many moorland areas are managed primarily for grouse, and sportsmen and sportswomen pay high rentals for hunting rights.

Grouse shooting is controlled through the operation of the Game Laws and is permissable between August 12 ("the Glorious Twelfth") and December 10 for possessors of sporting rights and their authorized visitors. During organized drives across selected areas of moorland, sportsmen wait with their guns in hides or butts. Several thousand grouse are shot annually in the North York Moors, although bags depend largely on the breeding cycle, which fluctuates greatly over time. In the Moors, private owners and tenants pay some fifteen moorland gamekeepers to provide grouse shooting. The industry has become commercialized, and sporting costs are escalating. A typical driven-grouse day now costs £500 to £1,000 (US$750 to US$1,500) per gun.

Sheep grazing is the other main economic activity. The sheep remain in the open on the moors all year round, and hardy breeds have been established to survive the harsh winter conditions. The flocks are hefted to the moor, which means they have built up a homing instinct over several generations to graze certain areas. The hill sheep industry in the United Kingdom currently suffers from reduced income due to a variety of causes, and there is evidence that flocks have been withdrawn from the North York Moors.

Generally speaking, current management of the moors is in line with conservation of its wildlife. The large-scale reclamation of moorland to improved agricultural grass, which was seen as a major threat, has mostly ceased because of surpluses in the European Community and changes in subsidies. So too large-scale afforestation with alien conifers such as Sitka spruce and larch has come to an end; following public protest, the government prohibited further coniferous planting of the national parks in the mid-1980s. The United Kingdom currently imports 90 percent of its timber, but the latter threat could return if forestry became more profitable.

The high value placed on heather moors as a sporting resource and the fact that the majority of the moorland is part of private estates whose owners wish to maximize this value means that in the North York Moors, at present, the future of this habitat is not under any major threat.

Farmland Habitats

The earliest permanent agricultural settlements developed in the valleys, probably during the Bronze Age (2,100–800 B.C.). The present-day farming landscape is largely a product of the last five hundred years, although some field walls and boundaries have far older origins.

Farmland in the valleys contains a range of habitat types. On the upper dale sides adjacent to the moor, the large fields, often steep and rocky, contain heath vegetation, acid grassland, and flush communities. These fields form an important margin to the moor and are of particular value for breeding wading birds such as the lapwing (*Vanellus vanellus*).

Fields on the valley sides and floor traditionally have been managed for grazing and hay making. The dales still contain a range of seminatural grasslands of high quality that are of value at a regional level. These fields also contain marshy grassland and riparian habitats, including carr-woodland.

Native broad-leaved woodland, in deeply incised watercourses running up the valley sides, is a feature of the dales and often forms a link between moorland and river valley. Many of these native woods are classified as "ancient," i.e., they are likely to be remnants of primeval forest and thus are of considerable regional value. Woodlands traditionally have been the concern of the landowning estate, since most farms were tenanted. Traditional woodland management has aimed to produce fencing materials, fuel, and building timber; the result is varied and well-structured woodlands with considerable wildlife value.

Boundaries between fields and around woodlands mostly consist of drystone walls and hedges. Drystone walls, consisting of local undressed stone and built without mortar, are a characteristic feature of upland farming in Britain. Their construction and maintenance require considerable time and skill. Many walls are of historic interest, and they are a key feature in the landscape. Drystone walls are valued as shelter for stock and provide a habitat for amphibians, reptiles, invertebrates, and some nesting birds such as the pied wagtail (*Motacilla alba*).

Hedges consist of a managed belt of shrub vegetation, often of mixed species composition, but usually including a high proportion of blackthorn (*Prunus spinosa*) and hawthorn (*Crataegus monogyna*). Traditionally, hedges are managed by rotational cutting and laying every fifteen to twenty-five years. Hedge laying is a labor-intensive technique in which the main stems are partially cut through and laid over at an angle. Laying produces thick, vigorous regrowth that provides shelter and stockproofing and rejuvenates the hedge, ensuring its long-term survival. Hedges are excellent nesting habitat for small birds, and the predominance of berry-forming shrubs provides an abundance of winter food for birds and mammals.

Hedges are regarded as valuable wildlife corridors. Their thick, shrubby bases produce much cover for small mammals such as the bank vole (*Clethnonomys glareolus*), shrew (*Sorex* spp.), and weasel (*Mustela nivalis*) and protection for ground-nesting birds such as the gray partridge (*Perdix perdix*).

These varied and diverse farmland habitats combine to produce areas of considerable wildlife value and scenic beauty. Each habitat has relied on traditional upland farming practices for its creation and maintenance. In outline, management involves low-intensity mixed farming, mainly rearing of sheep and cattle, production of hay for winter fodder, and maintenance of soil fertility using farmyard manure from winter-housed stock.

The average hill farm consists of a strip of fields from the valley bottom to the moor's edge totaling 30 to 40 ha and employs at least two men. Such farms yield only low-to-moderate incomes, and most hill-sheep farms have been heavily subsidized in the postwar period, primarily to maintain family farms.

Threats to Farmland Habitats

Over the last forty years a combination of developing farming techniques, government policy, and funding for subsidized food has led to major changes in farming methods in the North York Moors. These changes can be summarized as intensification involving higher stocking rates, made possible by modern machinery and fertilizers and encouraged by production-based subsidies. The result has been far greater agricultural efficiency in terms of production, but this has been achieved at considerable environmental cost.

The main pastureland improvements have involved drainage; replacement of old, herb-rich pastures with more productive grass leas; increased use of nitrogen fertilizers; and use of broadleaf-specific herbicides. These improvements have led to loss of much of the seminatural and marshy grassland in the national park. Only 11.4 percent of grasslands in the park now can be classed as unimproved and seminatural; of these, 3.1 percent are neutral, calcareous, or marshy grasslands normally associated with valley-bottom fields. A switch from production of hay to production of silage on these pastures has further reduced their value to ground-nesting birds due to earlier cutting dates.

Many woodlands, having lost their economic value for timber production, have been used as wood-pasture to provide grazing and shelter for stock. An associated loss of woodland structure and, in some cases, complete loss of regenerating saplings has accompanied the change. In some cases, these ancient woodlands consist of little but mature and semimature trees and are in danger of dying out.

With increased agricultural production, the true value (i.e., the price received by the farmer) of produce gradually has declined. In hill-farming areas this trend has had a number of important effects. Farms have become larger, now averaging 85 ha, since smaller units are no longer economically viable, despite increased production. Much of the labor force on the land has been lost. Larger farms are managed by fewer people, as mechanization has replaced labor and the cost of additional employment can not be supported. In addition to its negative impact on the community, the loss of labor has had an important environmental effect. Many of the drystone walls and hedges have been neglected, replaced with modern alternatives such as wire fencing or, in the case of hedges, managed mechanically. The result has been environmental decline in both the long and the short term.

Finally, the reduction in value of produce has led to an intensification "treadmill": As incomes fall, production or efficiency has to be increased to compensate, leading in turn to larger farms, fewer farmers, and greater habitat loss. Increased production leads to lower prices, and the cycle continues. With the reform of the European Community Agricultural Policy (CAP), these trends are likely to intensify. For the traditional hill-sheep farms of the United Kingdom, the economic future is bleak, although recent policy decisions within the European Community attempt to address the problem of falling incomes, and expenditure in the hill environment is increasing. In addition, each European Community country is required to prepare a series of measures to conserve farm environments. The packages proposed for the United Kingdom by the Ministry of Agriculture, Fisheries and Food in 1993 contain a number of measures that will support hill farms.

Social and Economic Background
The population density of rural areas in the North York Moors is around 0.2 per ha. Density has been fairly stable over the last fifteen years, although the age structure and composition of the population have changed due to two principal influencing factors: The movement of people into the area, either to retire or to live in an attractive area remote from the workplace, has resulted in a substantial increase in the cost of housing and accommodation; this trend has been counterbalanced by young people moving out of the area, either to find employment or affordable housing. The result has been an "aging" population, an increasing proportion of which is retired (21 percent) or employed outside the national park.

The largest employment sectors in North York Moors National Park are agriculture (42 percent) and tourism (50 percent). Employment in agriculture has fallen considerably during the last twenty years, with a reduction in agricultural employment of 5.9 percent between 1985 and 1990. This figure hides a more important switch from full-time to part-time farming, with a greater portion of income derived from nonfarming activities. The proportion of part-time farmers is now 45 percent, compared with 42 percent in 1985 (1990 Ministry of Agriculture figures). The single largest employer in the park is the Cleveland Potash Mine at Boulby, where more than nine hundred people work. Another large employer is the Fylingdales Ballistic Missile Early Warning Station. Its six hundred employees live mainly in Whitby and Pickering, just outside the park.

To a certain extent the loss of employment in farming has been offset by an increased number of jobs in tourism. Many of these jobs, however, are part-time or seasonal and often poorly paid. Add to this the relatively high unemployment rate for the park, currently 7.1 percent, and the difficulties of the local economy become apparent. Across the park, economic profiles vary widely, from the depressed coastal zone to a more prosperous area along the Ryedale area in the south of the park.

The cultural makeup of the population is changing too. During the nineteenth century, mining of a variety of minerals, particularly iron ore (ironstone), supplemented the traditional farming economy. This led to an influx of laborers and their families from all parts of the United Kingdom and beyond. Although ironstone mining has now ceased, there is a legacy of fascinating industrial remains, including old railway tracks (admirably suited for recreational walking and riding) and "boomtown" buildings in some of the villages. Methodism and brass bands, both of which flourish in the area, also bear witness to this industrial past, as does the landscape itself. Today's immigrants, mainly the retired and the wealthy, cause social disturbance by buying up cottages for second homes or converting redundant agricultural buildings into holiday units. Some villages such as Robin Hood's Bay on the coast have a high proportion of second homes, leading to an imbalance in the community and an appearance of depression in the winter months, when most of the second homes are empty. On the positive side, the capital brought in by "offcomers," as the immigrants are known locally, has stimulated local trades and encouraged retention of traditional buildings.

The social and environmental changes affecting agriculture also can be seen as posing a long-term threat to the tourism industry. The North York Moors are viewed with great affection by the British public. The estimated 13 million visits per year bring in approximately £100 million (US$150 million) in revenues for local businesses. The principal draw for visitors is the scenic beauty of the area, which is largely a product of the traditional farming system. Conservation of biodiversity and landscapes is therefore very closely linked to the social structure and well-being of the agricultural community.

The use of the park for informal recreation has grown steadily since the nineteenth century, when people from newly urbanized areas began visiting the area using the new railway. Today, the park is heavily used by car-borne visitors. Of the 13 million visits, approximately 50 percent are for the day, mainly from residents of the surrounding urban areas of Cleveland and West Yorkshire. The remainder are made by tourists who stay in or near the park, and most of these come from the south of England. About 5 percent of all visits are by overseas travelers, mostly from Europe, North America, and the Commonwealth countries.

Most visitors tour the area and admire the scenery; about half undertake a walk of more than 3 km during their visit. The park is admirably suited for walking, especially on the open moors, but a wide variety of other pursuits, including angling, cycling, gliding, hang gliding, orienteering, horse riding, picnicking, canoeing, sailing, and nature study, also draw visitors.

Management of the park for recreation, especially the resultant traffic and car parking, is a major issue. Increasingly, measures are needed to control and restrict cars while encouraging more environmentally friendly modes of transport. The impact of these activities on the local agricultural community is considerable. Farmers experience problems of trespassing, litter, and disturbance of stock and wildlife, but they also gain opportunities for income from bed-and-breakfasts and farm-based recreation.

Background to National Park Involvement

Although designated a national park, the majority of the North York Moors is privately owned, a feature common to all the British national parks. The National Park Authority (NPA) therefore has to rely on the agreement and cooperation of the landowners to achieve its land-management aims.

A number of mechanisms help the NPA achieve its goals. Probably the most important is the ability to provide financial incentives and compensation in return for agreed works or management practices. This usually takes the form of a legally binding contract, known as a management agreement, between the land manager and the NPA. Such agreements can be used as a protective mechanism, if a site is under threat, or as an incentive, by providing a capital grant. In either case, the land manager's acceptance of an agreement is voluntary, since the NPA has limited power to enforce land-management prescriptions. The use of agreements is also constrained by financial considerations due to the limited budget of the NPA. Most land-use changes can be controlled by the NPA through the operation of the Town and Country Planning Acts, but farming and land-management activities usually are exempt from such controls. An ongoing debate centers around the proposed introduction of further controls over farming activities in the spheres of planning control and pollution prevention.

Objectives and Development of Approach

The objectives of the National Park Authority with regard to wildlife conservation on farmland are to halt the loss of habitats, encourage management to regenerate those in decline, and create new habitats where appropriate. In general, these objectives are achieved by promoting the continuation or reintroduction of traditional management by farmers. This benefits the community in additional ways by supporting labor-intensive works such as wall and hedge maintenance and local employment in these traditional skills.

Since 1975, the NPA has run a number of projects aimed at attaching a higher priority to conservation in farm management. These have included capital grants for planting trees and hedges, restoring walls, and managing woodland and management agreements that provide financial incentives for the retention and maintenance of important habitats. These schemes have been a great success in helping residents of the national park achieve conservation measures. A drawback is that the approach tends to be site specific, involving just the wood, field, or wall in question.

The early 1980s brought a move toward a more comprehensive approach, which would involve all of a farmer's land, by producing advisory documents, or Whole Farm Conservation Plans. These plans coordinated the various grants available and integrated them with the farmer's overall plans for the management of his land. The idea for farm conservation plans emerged from discussions with local farming representatives. The farmers felt that the park's schemes for tree planting, repairs to walls, etc., were of value, but the number of schemes, and the number of staff involved, was proliferating. Also, other government agencies such as the Ministry of Agriculture, the Forestry Commission, and the Countryside Commission offered grant aid for conservation. The situation had become very confusing to local farmers, who had only limited time and ability to find out about and evaluate the schemes.

Using experience gained from the operation of the grant schemes and conservation plans, a new approach, developed in 1987, was implemented on an experimental basis, with the approval of the North York Moors National Park's governing committee, in 1988. The approach aimed to promote farm conservation by providing financial incentives for both positive and protective conservation measures. This experimental scheme was based on a management agreement covering the whole of a farmer's land. Conservation earnings, in addition to those from food production, thereby became part of the farming business income.

The Experimental Farm Conservation Scheme was established on six farms in various locations, with agreements lasting three years. The farmers who took part in the experiment were people identified by park staff as particularly interested in conservation on their land. Again, the learning process proved to be very valuable and rapid. The experimental scheme was popular with the farmers involved and very effective in achieving results. The cost, averaging £1,700 (US$2,550) per farm per annum, was not excessive.

Within a year, park authorities felt that proposals should be drawn up for a more comprehensive scheme to be implemented on a wider scale. The experiment had attracted a great deal of interest from government agriculture and environment ministries and nongovernmental organizations (NGOs) such as the National Farmers Union and the Council for National Parks. The latter body, a national voluntary society, saw great potential in a "whole farm" conservation scheme, and its staff was helpful in drawing up the framework for the scheme.

Planning and Design of the North York Moors Farm Scheme

The involvement and input of other bodies, organizations, and individuals were essential in the development of the Farm Scheme. Park personnel held discussions with the National Farmers Union, Ministry of Agriculture, and Department of the Environment; the Countryside Commission and English Nature (both government advisory bodies); and local farmers and landowning organizations, as well as the Council for National Parks. This consultation was necessary in order to fully explore all aspects of the scheme and ensure that the design was right before implementation.

The involvement of local farmers was most valuable and enabled theoretical agreements to be drawn up to test the scheme's various implications. The government's Agricultural Development and Advisory Service (ADAS), which utilized its familiarity with farm businesses and the economics of hill farming, also was of considerable help.

The central concept of the Farm Scheme is reward for the production of conservation "goods." The conservation value of a farmer's land becomes an income asset in the same way as food production. The scheme's payments are based on results. The more a farmer is willing to put into environmental management and improvement, the more he or she can earn from the scheme.

Implementation of this approach achieves many aims:

- Important habitats and landscapes are conserved.

- The creation of an alternative income enables farmers to get away from the intensification treadmill.

- As conservation generates income, the farmer considers it when making day-to-day management decisions.

- The extra money available for traditional labor-intensive operations creates local employment opportunities.

The mechanism used to establish such an approach is a standard-format management agreement between the National Park Authority and the individual farmer. The agreement specifies annual maintenance and management payments and capital grants in an investment-and-return system. Once an agreement is completed, a farmer can "invest," for example, by fencing a wood or regenerating a hedge. When the work is completed, the investment earns an annual income for the farm.

The agreement includes a number of cross-compliance conditions, such as the protection of historic and archeological features. The result is a comprehensive, detailed scheme that is not overly complicated and is, above all, workable.

Implementation of the scheme was delayed for a short time while the National Park Authority sought funding. The money finally became available in 1990 through the National Park Support Grant, which is made up of approximately 75 percent central-government and 25 percent local-government funds. The incremental nature of the budget, with additional money being allocated each year, meant that implementation required a targeted approach in which an area of the park is identified as appropriate for establishment of the Farm Scheme. Within that area, all farmers are offered the opportunity to enter into an agreement. In this way, entire dales, or sections of dales, can be brought into conservation management with important cumulative environmental benefits.

The Farm Scheme was launched in April 1990, with Upper Farndale as the initial target area. This dale's recent management history provided the reason for its selection. The dale had been bought in the 1930s by the city of Hull, south of the park, with the intention of flooding it to create a supply reservoir. The threat of flooding was not lifted until the late 1970s, and the farms finally were sold to the sitting tenants in 1989. The result was run-down farms that had very little capital investment but a great deal of conservation potential. The new owners clearly would be looking to develop and improve their farms, and the Farm Scheme was an ideal tool to ensure that conservation played a central part in that development.

All farmers in Upper Farndale entered the scheme in the first eighteen months, resulting in eleven agreements covering 750 ha. Budget growth since then has enabled additional target areas to be brought into the scheme: Upper Rosedale, Middle and Lower Farndale, Snilesworth, Raisdale, Westerdale, and Glaisdale (see Map 12.1). The high level of uptake by farmers, at nearly 100 percent, has continued to date. By the end of 1993, there are likely to be around eighty Farm Scheme agreements covering approximately 5,400 ha.

All eleven Upper Farndale participants were Yorkshire family farmers who rely wholly or mainly on income from their small hill farms for their livelihoods. ADAS carried out a socioeconomic assessment of the first eleven farms to join the scheme. The assessment revealed that the £3,000+ (US$4,500+) payments to each farm from the scheme are becoming a valuable and important source of revenue and will help retain labor on these holdings and, in some instances, allow additional labor to be employed. Most of the farms had incurred a loss on the order of £1,780 (US$2,670) in 1990 and a profit of £3,000 (US$4,500) in 1991. The improved outlook in 1991 is in part a result of the payments made under the Farm Scheme. External factors, particularly the selling price of animals and payments from European Community farm subsidies, also had an influence. The farms' general position deteriorated in 1992, showing an average loss of £2,700 (US$4,050), but this loss was less than the average for hill farms in the area.

The considerable media publicity given the scheme gave the Upper Farndale farmers added interest and confidence in the project. Two became very adept at handling print, television, and radio media. This factor undoubtedly encouraged rapid expansion of the scheme into neighboring dales and continuation of the very high uptake.

Costs to the National Park Authority are around £3,400 (US$5,100) per agreement, inclusive of capital grant aid. The total budget available to the National Park Authority in 1993–94 for this work was £360,000 (US$540,000), including £23,000 (US$34,500) for staffing and administration costs.

The process of drawing up an agreement involves an initial survey of a farmer's land, followed by detailed negotiations over the content of the agreement. A mapped record is made of all features and habitats of value on the farm, with an assessment of their condition and management requirements. The land is classed in one of three categories: conservation grade, conservation woodland, or improved land. All walls, hedges, traditional farm buildings, and footpaths in good condition are measured. The farmer can then be given an estimate of the first year's payment available through the Farm Scheme and an indication of the conditions likely to be attached to the agreement.

As a general principle of the scheme, all existing habitats of value must be protected. However, the scheme does not aim merely to maintain the status quo; each agreement contains a program of environmental improvement works such as fencing to keep stock out of woodlands, drystone wall rebuilding, and hedge regeneration.

All aspects of the agreement are discussed with the farmer, and there is considerable scope for bargaining over the detailed content. When negotiations are complete, a final agreement document is prepared and signed by the farmer and a representative of the National Park Authority.

The eligibility rules require that a farmer spend at least 50 percent of his time working his farm and, more important, that he gain at least 50 percent of his income from the farm. These eligibility rules have been applied to agricultural grants by government departments in the United Kingdom for many years. In the North York Moors, the rules exclude only a very few farms owned by part-time farmers, usually professional people who farm as a hobby. These people normally are not short of capital and are still eligible for other national-park grant-aid programs for conservation works.

Since one of the main aims of the Farm Scheme is to retain the traditional hill farmers and their skills, applicants' compliance with these rules is seen as necessary. The rules also ensure that available funding is closely targeted where it is most needed.

Tenants also are required to notify their landlords of their participation in the scheme. Agreements are made with tenants when they are responsible for day-to-day management of their farms. The exception is the case of traditional farm buildings, whose repair usually is the legal responsibility of the landlord. In these cases, separate agreements are needed, and to date this has not presented any problems. The whole of the Rosedale estate, for instance, which includes fifteen tenanted farms, has been included in the scheme, with the full support of the landlord.

Payments to the farmer under the scheme are of two main types. First, annual payments are made in advance for area and linear features for management and maintenance. Second, grants for enhancement works are paid to each farm retrospectively and programmed over a five-year period. Once some of these enhancement works are completed, they can become eligible for annual maintenance payments, e.g., restoration and repair of a derelict stone wall. Payments can be made for the management of recreational resources as well as for conservation purposes. Thus the management and upkeep of public rights of way on foot and on horseback are eligible for annual payment.

Although the works program carries a good deal of flexibility, compliance with the management agreement is an essential part of the scheme. Failure to complete the improvement works is regarded as a breach of the agreement, as is the failure to maintain features or manage habitats in accordance with the conditions of the scheme. In the case of such breaches, the National Park Authority may choose to withhold part or all of the annual payment, terminate the agreement, or, in extreme cases, take court action to reclaim part or all of previous payments.

The park staff maintains contact with farmers, who receive assistance in the form of advice and help with grant claims, throughout the period of the agreement. At the end of each year, the farms are monitored for compliance with the terms of the scheme and to assess the following year's payment, taking improvements into account. Changes are recorded in the text and maps of the agreement documents.

A single park officer ran the scheme until 1992, when an assistant was appointed. Direct administration now involves approximately 1.5 staff members. In addition, park rangers are involved in settling agreements with farmers and, in particular, in assisting with management of the public footpaths and bridle ways. This approach has served to build up a strong working relationship between the farmers and the national park staff and established the National Park Authority as purchasers of the farmers' environmental "products."

Evaluation and Monitoring

In addition to annual monitoring of Farm Scheme agreements and frequent staff contact with farmers as part of the scheme's operations, a program of long-term monitoring has been established. The aim is to analyze the impact of the scheme in Upper Farndale over the five-year duration (1990–95) of the agreements. In outline, the monitoring program is set up to look at the botanical, landscape, and socioeconomic influences of the scheme.

The first two components have been assessed by independent consultants operating according to an agreed brief. So far, only baseline information has been gathered for the botanical and landscape elements. Final conclusions are not possible until comparative data become available in 1995. At this stage, it is possible to say that the scheme has halted habitat loss and resulted in improvement of some habitat types, e.g., woodlands and hedgerows. The condition and value of many landscape features also has improved. In the first two years of the scheme, improvements included 15.2 ha of woodland enclosed, 1.9 km of hedge regenerated, and 17.2 km of drystone wall brought into good repair.

ADAS is carrying out socioeconomic monitoring with two elements: a financial assessment of the scheme's impact on farm businesses compared with farms that do not have Farm Scheme agreements, and social monitoring involving a questionnaire that assesses the education, skills, and attitudes of the farmer and his family, and how these will affect their future plans and their attitudes toward conservation and the Farm Scheme. Again, only the first stage of socioeconomic monitoring has been completed, but it does suggest that

- The scheme has been well received by the participants.

- It will have a beneficial economic effect on the individual farm businesses.

- The scheme will have a major effect on the maintenance of landscape features by making capital available for the employment of outside labor.

- The scheme should have an immediate and long-term impact on local and nonlocal employment (a survey of the eleven Upper Farndale farms indicates that in this area alone approximately 2.5 full-time jobs have been created as a result of the Farm Scheme).

- A traditional approach to education and farming would work best.

From the results of the first two years, the North York Moors Farm Scheme appears to be achieving both its social and its environmental goals.

Botanical, landscape, and social monitoring are to be repeated in the final year of the scheme (1995). Economic assessment will be carried out annually.

Indicators and Achievements

Compared with other farm-support schemes, the North York Moors Farm Scheme is more labor intensive and more personal. The strong working relationship between the park's farm-conservation officers and the farmers appears to be one reason for the scheme's success. Despite the personal links, administrative costs are only 12 percent of total expenditures, a percentage that compares well with the administrative costs of other national schemes. In a short time, the scheme has produced substantial results on the ground and provides a good example of what can be achieved given a carefully designed local scheme and sufficient well-targeted resources.

Other advantages have accrued. After some years of suspicion of the national park within the farming community, particularly because of its control of development under the Planning Acts, there is now widespread recognition of the benefits the park offers local people and greater acceptance of the need to marry conservation on the farms with visitor activities. Much remains to be done in this important area of public relations, but the convergence of interests in promoting conservation is an encouraging sign.

The scheme has received support from a number of government departments and NGOs. Its widespread support and effectiveness have brought the North York Moors National Park recognition as a pacesetter for similar areas in Britain.

Prognosis for the Future

The long-term aim is for the Farm Scheme to extend implementation to all hill-farming areas within North York Moors National Park. Current implementation and future target areas, chosen from the "core conservation area" of the park as being most in need of assistance to maintain the traditional hill-farming landscapes, are shown on Map 12.1. Outside the core area, more change involving alternative uses of farmland, including planting and natural regeneration of woodland and conversion of farmland to heather moorland, will be encouraged. Extension of the scheme would involve approximately 520 farms covering 35,000 ha.

Such an expansion would rely on future funding of an estimated £2.2 million (US$3.3 million) per annum. All those involved in the scheme are confident that it provides a most cost-effective system for achieving conservation on farmland. Unfortunately, the National Park Authority is not likely to obtain funding at this level in the foreseeable future. The Farm Scheme therefore will have to be carefully targeted to the most important and vulnerable dales.

A series of nationally run schemes designed to encourage conservation management recently has been established. These, combined with changes in agricultural support systems under the European Community's Community Agricultural Policy (CAP), could remove some of the threats to valued and rare farmland habitats. Eventually, the North York Moors Farm Scheme could be absorbed into a broader national or European Community scheme, which in turn will benefit from the experience gained in implementing the local scheme.

The question of funding is obviously fundamental to the future of the scheme or its successor. Currently the government is proposing to extend the park budget to allow the scheme to expand. The British government also recently announced the establishment, as part of the United Kingdom's agri-environment package required under the European Community's CAP, of a further tranche of ESAs (Environmentally Sensitive Areas), in which payments and subsidies averaging £3 million to £4 million (US$4.5 million to US$6 million) per area will be available. The extension of this designation to the North York Moors (which is not among the areas currently proposed) in the future could enable the Farm Scheme to be subsumed within this national scheme. Against these larger budgets, the £2.2 million (US$3.3 million) needed to complete the scheme within the North York Moors does not seem excessive.

Other possibilities include more direct payment for conservation of the landscape by visitors or users of the park. At present, income from visitors—derived mainly from fees for various services, charges for publications, and car parking—amounts to £0.7 million (US$1.05 million), or approximately 16 percent of the park's budget. Public discussions and debates in recent years have explored ways of raising more income from visitors through charges such as a tax on accommodation in the park. Apart from the practical problems of implementing such a scheme, there is a consensus that this is not the best way to fund a British national park. Apart from the political and ethical considerations, imposition of visitor taxes in the North York Moors would be extremely difficult in practice. Numerous access points for vehicles and pedestrians connect with important principal roads serving places outside the park. Furthermore, much visitor accommodation is outside the park, in Scarborough and Whitby, for example; to implement a visitor tax scheme based on accommodation would involve drawing arbitrary boundaries around a park catchment area.

Collecting entry fees is not seen as a practical proposition, nor is it acceptable politically. The subsidy from state funds is seen as fairer and more efficient administratively. Tourists themselves, naturally, would be strongly opposed to such a scheme. It should be borne in mind that because the operation of the Farm Scheme results in a curb on production of food products, the extent of which will vary from farm to farm, there is a savings of public expenditure on farm subsidies through the operation of the European Community's CAP. The amount saved can be calculated only at the individual farm business level, and no figures are currently available. This is an area that needs research, as it is clearly important to the future of farm conservation schemes in countries where farm production is subsidized by the state. Bearing in mind the other economic benefits of such schemes (i.e., job preservation and creation, support for local tourism), the economic case for farm conservation appears to be a very strong one and would repay further study.

SOURCE

Fit for the Future: Report of the National Parks Review Panel. 1991. Cheltenham, England.

CHAPTER 13

Community-based Approaches to Wildlife Conservation in Neotropical Forests

John G. Robinson and Kent H. Redford

People living in and around protected areas frequently have been considered to have little interest in conserving biological diversity. Local communities traditionally exploited natural systems for food, fuel, medicine, material for housing construction, and so on. Until recently, conservationists largely have ignored traditional exploitation as a way to conserve biological diversity, preferring instead to protect natural systems by excluding people from parks and reserves—and, in so doing, denying them access to vital natural resources. Although useful as a way of protecting many natural areas, the protectionist approach is not totally satisfactory, even as a conservation strategy. The land area that can be so protected is limited, and human communities living in and around these areas all too often oppose the concept of protected areas.

More recently, many conservationists have suggested a different approach, arguing that empowering local people is the most effective means of conserving areas of high biological diversity. The argument goes as follows: Local people living in and around a protected area, if given access to its natural resources or some form of return, will assist conservation efforts. The benefit they receive need not be economic; resources can be exploited for cultural, social, and political reasons. Whatever form these benefits take, community-based conservation requires that these accrue to local people and that these people participate in the distribution and allocation of natural resources.

Community-based conservation is becoming increasingly popular as an approach to the conservation of protected areas (Wells and Brandon 1992; Brandon and Wells 1992). Despite this popularity, an internal contradiction persists at the heart of community-based management efforts: The exploitation of a species will lower its population density, usually decrease overall biodiversity, and tend to simplify ecosystem diversity (Robinson 1993). Such losses contradict the expressed aims of biological conservation. Community-based conservation thus requires a balance between meeting human needs on the one hand and ensuring that biological losses are not excessive on the other. But when is it possible to say that human needs have been met or that the ensuing losses of biodiversity and ecosystem functioning are acceptable?

The concept of *sustainability* presupposes that these conditions can be defined, agreed upon, and met. One approach to defining the extent to which human needs can be met is to recognize that overharvest will systematically deplete a resource. A resource can be depleted to the point where it no longer constitutes a signficant resource for local communities. Biological losses can be considered acceptable when they are consistent with the expressed conservation goals of an area such as maintaining a biological community, a given level of biodiversity, or a given species.

Tropical forests have attracted a great deal of conservation interest because of their immense biological richness. The importance of wildlife harvesting to human communities living in and around tropical forests is less appreciated. Studies of hunting are still in their infancy, and policy makers interested in conservation and development have largely ignored the issue. Forest animals seldom have been included in calculations of "forest value" (e.g., Peters, Gentry, and Mendelsohn 1989) or even featured in the list of benefits from forests (Myers 1988).

A much-needed exploration of the viability of community-based approaches to the conservation of tropical forest wildlife follows. Central to this inquiry is an understanding of the importance hunting holds for many rural communities. Application of various indices and models of sustainable harvest to hunting data derived from four neotropical case studies helps to clarify the impact of hunting on wildlife populations. Finally, the conclusions give some insight into the potential for tropical wildlife utilization to meet the dual objectives of conservation and human needs.

The Importance of Game

Meat from forest animals is important in the diets of virtually all people living in tropical forests. Unfortunately, the value of wild meat, either in traditional economic terms or as subsistence for forest-dwelling peoples, is inadequately quantified. Such figures as do exist are compelling:

- The annual sale value of consumed wild meat in Liberia in 1990 was estimated conservatively at UK£26.5 million (US$40 million) (Mayers 1991).

- Based on market prices of equivalent food, Caldecott (1986) estimates the monetary value of game meat in Sarawak to be Malaysian $166 million (US$66 million)/year, and that the 1.5 million inhabitants of the state consume some 18,400 metric tons annually.

- In a survey of global wild-meat consumption, Prescott-Allen and Prescott-Allen (1982) state that wildlife and fish contribute at least 20 percent of the animal protein in the diets of human inhabitants of at least sixty-two countries.

- Of those rural and urban people interviewed in a recent survey in southern Ghana, 95 percent claimed to eat wild meat on occasion (Falconer 1992).

- An older estimate from Zaire indicates that 75 percent of animal protein consumed in the country came from wild species (Heymans and Maurice 1973).

- Another survey indicates that 60 percent of the animal protein consumed each year in Botswana was of wild origin (von Richter 1969).

Information on the importance of wild game to people is more complete for the neotropics. In addition, there is more information on the impact of hunting on wild populations; also, considerable work has been done on the sustainability of subsistence hunting. Because of this, subsistence hunting in Latin America is the focus of this inquiry.

In some areas wild game provided all the animal protein available to people (e.g., Pierret and Dourojeanni 1966, 1967). Even when people have access to processed foods and meat from domestic animals, wild meat still constitutes a significant part of the diet (Ayres et al. 1991). As a general rule, wild game is more important to indigenous groups than to nonindigenous colonists (Redford and Robinson 1987), due perhaps to the stronger hunting traditions of indigenous peoples and their limited access to domestic animals and packaged meat.

Continent-wide estimates of the subsistence take of wild species are unavailable, but sample figures give a sense of the importance of game to local peoples. Redford and Robinson (1991) estimate that the half-million rural inhabitants of Amazonas state in Brazil annually hunt and consume at least 3 million mammals, 500,000 birds, and several hundred thousand reptiles. Expanded for the entire Brazilian Amazon, the estimate rises to a staggering 19 million individual animals.

Other estimates come from the Peruvian Amazon town of Iquitos, traditionally a major market town for Amazonian natural products. Gardner (1982) extrapolated from Castro, Revilla, and Neville's (1976) data from three commercial markets in the town to calculate the annual sale of wild game at about 200 metric tons. Castro and his colleagues estimated that approximately 11,000 individual primates were sold in the markets annually (about 5 percent of all wild game by weight), and that inhabitants of the Peruvian department of Loreto, which includes Iquitos, annually consume some 370,000 primates. Bodmer et al. (1990) provide a more recent estimate of some 30 metric tons of wild game sold in Iquitos markets each year. However, the sale of wild meat in Peru is now illegal, and they note that market sales represent "only a small proportion of the total amount of wild meat commercially sold in Iquitos" (Bodmer et al. 1990:54). Most wild meat is sold directly to households and restaurants.

The importance of wild game goes beyond its nutritional value (Redford 1993). In many indigenous languages, the word *hungry* literally means "hungry for meat," as distinct from hunger that can be satisfied by other foods (Wagley 1977). Wild game has a high social value; by securing game and sharing it with other members of the community, the hunter builds debts, acquires allegiances, and contributes to social cohesiveness (Stearman 1989). A number of studies (Paolisso and Sackett 1985) suggest a link between the increasing dearth of wild game and a breakdown of the traditional village social structure.

Impact of Hunting on Wildlife Populations

Hunting, whether subsistence or commercial, inevitably has a negative impact on prey-animal densities. Animal populations do not recover instantly from hunting, and any hunted site will have lower densities of hunted species. Yet the reduction in mammalian and avian densities in hunted areas frequently is far more dramatic than would be accounted for by the temporary reduction associated with offtake. In a broad comparison of densities across the neotropics, Redford (1992) finds that mammalian densities in areas subject to moderate hunting are 80.7 percent lower than in unhunted or lightly hunted areas; in heavily hunted areas, they are 93.7 percent lower than in unhunted sites. A similar comparison of avian densities indicates that game-bird densities under moderate hunting are 73.5 percent lower than in unexploited populations. The finding is supported by individual studies that have directly examined game densities in response to hunting intensity. Surveys of mammalian game indicate sharp declines with high hunting intensity (Freese et al. 1982; Johns 1986; Peres 1990; Glanz 1991). Similar patterns have been reported for birds. Silva and Strahl (1991) document very low densities of cracids (chachalacas, guans, and curassows) wherever they are hunted in Venezuela. Thiollay (1989) reports 94 percent lower densities of the macaw (*Ara chloroptera*) in hunted areas as compared to nonhunted sites in French Guiana.

Not all species are equally susceptible to hunting pressure. Large-bodied species tend to be preferred targets and frequently are exterminated in heavily hunted areas. The single-barrel 16-gauge shotgun is the hunting weapon of choice throughout the neotropics and generally has replaced more traditional weapons. Expensive shotgun shells encourage hunters to focus on the larger game species. In addition, colonists of European extraction tend to focus on large-bodied game species most closely resembling domestic animals in size, including ungulates, large rodents, and gallinaceous birds (Redford and Robinson 1987).

Neotropical forest hunters also prefer frugivorous, or fruit-eating, species, which are frequently described as "fat" or "tasty." Frugivorous primates such as spider and woolly monkeys are more sought after than folivorous (leaf-eating) and insectivorous species such as the howler or capuchin (Freese et al. 1982). Forest ungulates are generally frugivorous, and tapir and peccary species are preferred prey. Pacas generally are considered to be the tastiest rodent game species.

The impact of hunting on a species depends largely on its intrinsic rate of natural increase. Species with low rates are less able to withstand hunting and are much more susceptible to local extinction. As a general rule, in comparisons across species, the intrinsic rate of natural increase declines with increasing body mass (Robinson and Redford 1986). However, some species—for instance, primates—have much lower intrinsic rates than would be expected from their body mass alone. Others, such as peccaries, have higher rates than would be expected. As a result, members of the former group are more vulnerable to overhunting than the latter.

In general, large species, frugivorous species, and those with low intrinsic rates of population growth such as tapir, woolly monkeys, and cracids are most susceptible to overhunting. Large primates, for example, frequently disappear from heavily hunted areas (Freese et al. 1982). Some other species benefit from hunting through the removal of their predators and competitors. Such species tend to be small-bodied or are seldom considered tasty. Agouti populations were found to be higher in hunted areas in Brazil (Johns 1986). Smaller primates also can increase in less heavily hunted areas (Freese et al. 1982; Johns 1986; Mitchell and Raez 1991).

Case Studies

Four examples of indigenous or tribal peoples who exhibit a range of acculturation provide an opportunity to evaluate the sustainability of neotropical forest hunting. Bodmer (see AMAZON) details an additional example: the *ribereños*, traditional Amazonian peasants who live along watercourses. All five of these cases involve people hunting to meet their subsistence needs, although the *ribereños* in the Reserva Comunal Tamshiyacu-Tuhuayo also sell meat in local markets. The hunting patterns of each group are described here.

The Siona-Secoya

Vickers (1980, 1988) collected hunting information during the years 1973–1975 and 1979–1982 from Siona-Secoya living in and around the San Pablo settlement in the Ecuadorean Amazon. Information on the Cuyabeno Wildlife Production Reserve (Map 13.1) is based largely on the management plan for the area (Coello Hinojosa and Nations 1987).

Ecological and Socioeconomic Setting

The Siona-Secoya occupy a broad region in northeastern Ecuador, southern Colombia, and northern Peru. The forests where they live are of the lowland

Map 13.1

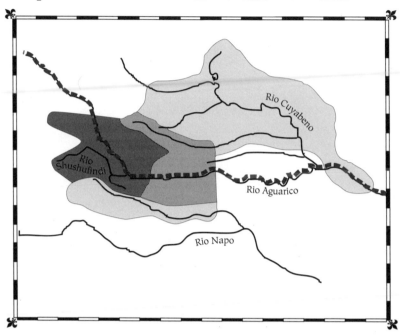

Cuyabeno Wildlife Production Reserve, Ecuador

KEY

Areas Hunted by Siona-Secoya Indians
from San Pablo, on the Shushufindi, 1973–82

Core Area (590 km^2) Hunted Daily

Area Hunted in All Months of the Year

Areas Hunted Intermittently or Seasonally

▬ ▬ ▬ Boundary of the Reserve along
the Rio Aguarico

type, with mean annual rainfall between 3,500 and 4,000 mm per year and little seasonality.

The Siona-Secoya today number about 1,000. In Ecuador, their largest settlement area is San Pablo, which has a population of about 375 people. Settlements are seminucleated, semidispersed villages that flourish for a period of years and then dissipate when people move up- or downriver. Settlers cultivate corn, plantains, manioc, and papaya and citrus trees. The Siona-Secoya are the most numerous indigenous group in the Cuyabeno Wildlife Production Reserve, an area of 2,547 km² managed, in theory, for the sustainable use of natural resources (Coello Hinojosa 1992).

San Pablo, a settlement on the Shushufindi River, a tributary of the Aguarico River, was Vickers' study site. The settlement site is just outside the Cuyabeno Wildlife Production Reserve boundaries, but part of the community's hunting area lies inside it. The community, established in 1973, initially was composed of about 100 people. By the late 1970s, the original settlement had grown to more than 250 people.

Hunting Patterns

Bamboo-tipped spears and shotguns are the traditional Siona-Secoya game-hunting weapons. Since the 1950s, single-shot 16-gauge shotguns have replaced these almost universally. Hunters take a wide variety of mammalian and avian prey, including woolly monkeys (*Lagothrix lagothricha*) (23 percent of kills over Vickers's ten-year study period), white-lipped peccary (*Tayassu pecari*) (16 percent of kills), collared peccary (*Tayassu tajacu*) (14 percent), Salvini's curassow (*Mitu salvini*) (7 percent), and piping guan (*Pipile pipile*) (6 percent). Vickers distinguishes between "preferred" species—those hunters always attempted to kill—and "less-preferred" species, those sometimes passed up. Tapir, peccaries, and large primates and birds were preferred, while deer, small primates, small birds, rodents, edentates, and reptiles were less preferred.

Throughout Vickers' study period, the community hunted primarily (81 percent of hunting man-days) in a 590-km² core area. Hunters spent an additional 12 percent of hunting time in an adjacent 560-km² area and the rest in a more distant 1,350-km² area. Other indigenous groups and colonists also hunted in the 2,500-km² catchment area but rarely ventured into the community's core hunting area.

Sustainability of Hunting

In Vickers' study, most hunting yields tended to decline during the first three years of the study but did not do so continuously throughout the ten years. The exceptions were woolly monkeys, curassows, and trumpeters (*Psophia crepitans*), for which continuously declining yields suggested that hunting was unsustainable. Some of the yields for less-preferred species increased over the period, possibly indicating increased use of the less-preferred species as the preferred species declined. Robinson and Redford's (1991) model indicates that the harvest of woolly monkeys is not sustainable anywhere within the catchment area. The harvest of collared and white-lipped peccaries, on the other hand, might be sustainable, even within the 590-km² core area. However, since Vickers' study, the human population in the San Pablo community has continued to grow (from 250 to 375 people), with an as yet unknown effect on harvests.

Management of Wildlife Resources

A management plan for the Cuyabeno Wildlife Production Reserve was submitted to the Dirección Forestal de Ecuador in 1987, funded in part by the World Wildlife Fund-U.S. The plan recognizes that management must take into account the needs of the indigenous groups but excludes their direct involvement in the management of the reserve and the surrounding area. The implementation of the management structure is still at a preliminary stage, so it is difficult to say who will manage the wildlife resources or whether they will do so effectively for the benefit of the local communities.

The Chimane

Hunting was surveyed for a three-week period in May 1987 at the end of the wet season (Redford and Stearman 1989; Stearman 1992). The results of this work largely agree with a more comprehensive but as yet unpublished study (Chicchón 1992). Information on the Beni Biosphere Reserve (Map 13.2) was mostly derived from Chicchón (1991) and Campos Dudley (1992).

Ecological and Socioeconomic Setting

The Chimane are an indigenous group of lowland Bolivia inhabiting a transitional zone between the lowland tropical forests extending outward from the base of the Andes Mountains and the westernmost edge of the Beni savannas. Annual rainfall averages around 2,000 mm, with a pronounced dry season between May and September.

The Chimane practice horticulture (planting upland rice, plantains, manioc, corn, squash, and a variety of fruits) combined with fishing and hunting. Although they have had contact with Europeans since the seventeenth century, they have retained their traditional culture and methods of resource extraction largely intact. The Chimane are seminomads who for generations have hunted and fished over a wide region centered in the modern Bolivian department of Beni. Many Chimane now work as day laborers on the large open-range cattle ranches in the grasslands of the Beni (for additional information, see Stearman 1992; Chicchón 1991, 1992).

Approximately five hundred Chimane who inhabit a zone at the northern edge of the Beni Biosphere Reserve (see Map 13.2) are the focus of this discussion of

Map 13.2

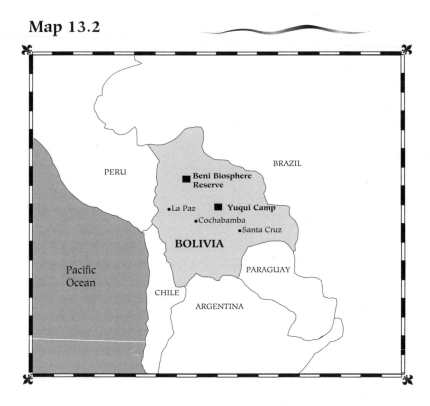

Beni Biosphere Reserve and Yuquí Camp, Bolivia

hunting. These Chimane have inhabited the area only for about five years and enter the reserve to hunt, primarily for subsistence needs. The reserve's isolated location provides little opportunity for commercial skin and meat hunting. The Chimane are responsible for most of the hunting within the reserve.

The Beni Biological Station, created in 1982, comprises some 1,350 km². The area was declared a biosphere reserve in 1986 and falls under UNESCO's Man and the Biosphere program. The reserve is part of a larger area known broadly as the Chimane Forest, which formerly comprised production forest, a cattle-ranching savanna area, and forested watershed protection areas. In 1990, the Bolivian government ceded significant portions of the Chimane Forest, including all of the biosphere reserve, to the Chimane and three other indigenous groups (for more information, see Chicchón 1991; Campos Dudley 1992).

Hunting Patterns

More than 85 percent of Chimane households hunt at least once a week. An additional 13 percent hunt once every one to two weeks. All households own and use bows and arrows, and 60 percent also own firearms. Hunters take a wide range of mammalian and avian prey including white-lipped peccary (44 percent of kills in Redford and Stearman's [1989] sample), collared peccary (7 percent), and a number of monkey species (32 percent). Peccaries, both collared and white-lipped, are preferred prey, although fish, monkeys, tapir, and deer are the choice of some people. Fish is the most frequently eaten food.

Sustainability of Hunting

Redford and Stearman's limited three-week survey focused on Chimane living away from towns. The data, nevertheless, are instructive. White-lipped peccary, the preferred prey, are taken by the Chimane at four times the harvest rate of the average Amazonian hunter (Redford and Robinson 1987). This rate yields more than 4.1 white-lipped peccaries/person/year within this Chimane community of about 500 people, or more than 2,000 individual animals/year. Using Robinson and Redford's (1991) population-growth model to calculate the catchment area required to produce this many animals gives a figure of about 2,500 km²—an area twice the size of the Beni Biosphere Reserve. This level of hunting, in other words, is not sustainable.

Management of Wildlife Resources

Clearly, Chimane hunting practices need to be integrated into the planning and management of the Beni Biosphere Reserve and its associated areas. At the time of the survey, only 7 percent of the respondents in Redford and Stearman's interviews had heard of the reserve in which they were hunting. This has since changed. The Chimane have no centralized form of political organization, which makes interaction with government and reserve planners difficult. Nevertheless, in 1990 the Chimane, supported by indigenous-rights activists, participated in a march that resulted in the establishment of the Chimane Territory, theoretically giving them considerable autonomy over the management of wildlife.

The Yuquí

The hunting patterns described here are largely based on a fifty-six-day study by Stearman undertaken in September-December 1983 and another completed during a comparable period in February-May 1988 (Stearman 1990, 1992).

Ecological and Socioeconomic Setting

The Yuquí dwell in lowland forest with annual rainfall that averages between 4,000 and 5,000 mm, broken by a two-month dry season. The land is flat and contains marshy areas flooded throughout the year and seasonally flooded areas dominated by *Socratea* palms. The region, about 60 km from the eastern edge of the Andes in central Bolivia (see Map 13.2), is marked by old river meanders and oxbow lakes.

The Yuquí are not as acculturated as the Chimane. Traditionally, they practiced no horticulture, and most of their caloric intake and animal protein came from game and fish. Up until very recently, fish provided the Yuquí with more than 50 percent of their animal protein intake. The Yuquí were first contacted by the New Tribes Mission in 1968. One group of forty-three people settled at a mission station on the banks of the Chimoró River. By 1982, the group had grown to seventy-three people. In 1986, a second band of twenty-three Yuquí joined the settlement. Recently, another group has been added.

Hunting Patterns

Traditionally, the Yuquí hunted with bows, but by 1983, hunters had acquired 16-gauge shotguns and .22 rifles. Newly contacted Yuquí still hunted with bows. Hunters take a wide variety of prey; in 1983, tortoises (*Geochelone* spp.) accounted for 11 percent of all kills, guans (*Penelope* spp.) for 9 percent, armadillos (*Dasypus novemcinctus*) for 9 percent, curassows (*Mitu* spp.) for 8 percent, capuchin monkeys (*Cebus apella*) for 8 percent, white-lipped peccaries for 6 percent, capybaras (*Hydrochaeris hydrochaeris*) for 6 percent, and collared peccaries for 5 percent.

The Yuquí primarily hunt within 5 km of the mission station using a core game catchment area of 78.5 km². In Stearman's 1988 study, 72 percent of all game, by weight, was harvested in this area. A larger, less intensively hunted area extends outward for some 10 km, defining a total catchment area of 314 km² (Stearman 1990, 1992).

Sustainability of Hunting

The Yuquí have been using a tiny catchment area, but the 1983 figures indicate that at the time game harvests also were low. Robinson and Redford's (1991) population-growth model was applied to the 1983 harvests to calculate the catchment area for selected important species, indicating the following: The capuchin monkey harvest requires a minimum catchment area of 433 km²; tapir, 216 km²; the white-lipped peccary, 71 km²; and the collared peccary, 22 km². These figures indicate that capuchin monkey and tapir were being overharvested in 1983, whereas the harvest of the two peccaries might have been sustainable. Yet by 1988, the three most important species by weight in 1983—capybara, white-lipped peccary, and tapir—were no longer being found by hunters. The species most frequently killed in 1988 were coati (*Nasua nasua*) (12 percent of kills), a species that, according to the Yuquí, "taste bad and make you sick"; tortoises (11 percent), guans (7 percent), and four species of monkeys (which jointly accounted for 23 percent of all kills). The Yuquí had not sighted or killed a white-lipped peccary since 1985. Collared peccaries still were being taken, if less frequently. Less-preferred species contributed significantly more to the Yuquí diet.

The drop in yields apparently resulted from colonists hunting and fishing in the area. Since 1986, colonists have encroached extensively into the territory of the Yuquí, primarily to grow coca. Colonists tend to remain on their farms only during the planting and harvesting seasons, returning to their highland settlements at other times. Colonists apparently have had a major impact on the fish and game available to the Yuquí, especially peccaries, tapir, pacas, and deer, which they often hunted with dogs. Colonists using dynamite and gill nets stretched across the river depleted fish populations, and forest-clearing impeded migration of the white-lipped peccary. By 1988, the Yuquí had lost some of their most important prey and were overhunting many species.

Management of Wildlife Resources

To ensure that game hunting is sustainable, the Yuquí require access to a much larger catchment area. Up until 1990, their legal holdings encompassed only 78 km² in a rough square around the main settlement. However, the area was included in a regional development project funded by the Interamerican Development Bank (IDB). As a result, the Yuquí now have legal access to a territory of 1,100 km². The express goal of this expansion was to assure the Yuquí of continued access to game resources.

The Xavante

Harvest information is based on a year-long study of Xavante hunting in the village of Pimentel Barbosa between February 1991 and January 1992 (Leeuwenberg 1991, 1992a, 1992b).

Ecological and Socioeconomic Setting

The Xavante occupy a transitional zone between the drier *cerrado* and the wetter Amazonia in the state of Mato Grosso in Brazil (see Map 13.3).

Traditionally, the Xavante were semimigratory and practiced extensive hunting, small-scale agriculture, and some fishing. In recent years, they have become more agricultural in response to incentives provided by FUNAI, the Brazilian Institute for Indian Affairs, and are raising some cattle.

The Xavante Indigenous Reserve of Pimentel Barbosa occupies some 2,200 km². Most of its 270 people live in the village of Pimental Barbosa, located in the center of the reserve. The hunting area for the community is restricted to a smaller area that extends outward from the village for some 25 km (comprising some 650 km²). A significant portion of the reserve is visited by the village hunters only rarely.

Hunting Patterns

During the course of a year, Leeuwenberg documented the harvest of 499 mammals of eighteen species. Ungulate species are the most important prey by both number and weight. Ranked by number, collared peccary accounted for 27 percent of kills, white-lipped peccary for 23 percent, giant anteater (*Myrmecophaga tridactyla*) for 18 percent, armadillos (*Euphractes sexcinctus*) for 9 percent, and pampas deer (*Ozotocerus bezoarticus*) for 7 percent. Most hunting occurred in the dry season between June and September.

The Xavante traditionally used fire to drive game and presumably manipulated its activity through vegetation management. Fires generally were lit at the end of the dry season on the advice of Xavante elders, who monitored the seasons, vegetation, and celestial conditions. Different habitats were burned at different frequencies: every one or two years for open grasslands, for example, and every four or five years for shrub woodland.

Sustainability of Hunting

Within the 650-km² catchment, Leeuwenberg was able to delineate the habitats available to different game species. His application of Robinson and Redford's (1991) model indicated that at least three of the ten most important species (pampas deer, grey brocket deer [*Mazama gouazibira*], and tapir) were being overhunted. In the case of the two deer species, this conclusion was supported by data showing a distorted age distribution of harvested animals, with few adults older than two years. In addition, density figures for giant anteaters indicated that this species also was being overharvested. The harvest of the two peccary species may have been sustainable, although the age distribution of white-lips raised doubts.

Management of Wildlife Resources

The community group Associação Xavante de Pimentel Barbosa is presently considering how to respond to overharvesting. It has proposed

- a temporary one-year moratorium on hunting pampas deer, grey brocket deer, tapir, and giant anteaters within the 650-km² main catchment area;

Map 13.3

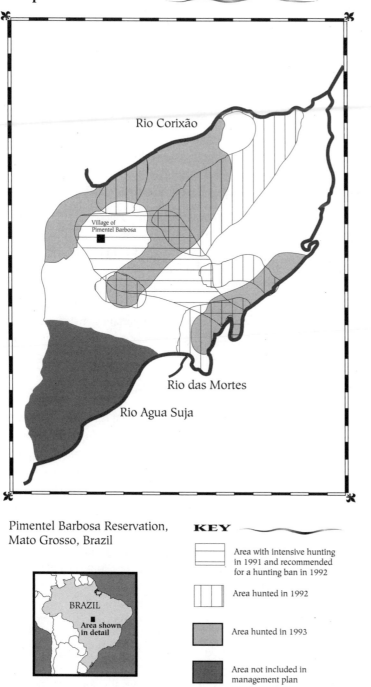

Rio Corixão

Village of
Pimentel Barbosa

Rio das Mortes

Rio Agua Suja

Pimentel Barbosa Reservation,
Mato Grosso, Brazil

BRAZIL

Area shown
in detail

KEY

Area with intensive hunting
in 1991 and recommended
for a hunting ban in 1992

Area hunted in 1992

Area hunted in 1993

Area not included in
management plan

- that hunting and fruit harvesting be extended to other areas of the reserve (this policy would also allow the Xavante of Pimentel Barbosa to patrol the boundaries of the reserve and exclude nonresident hunters, fishermen, and miners);

- reinstatement of traditional family hunting, a practice involving long hunting expeditions into distant areas (the practice also would instruct the younger generation in hunting traditions); and

- reinstatement of traditional fire management of habitats during nonfruiting seasons.

Potential for Community-based Conservation

All the cases examined here (as well as Bodmer's detailed coverage of the *ribereños* in AMAZON) are examples of community-based resource use. The question remains whether the exploitation patterns they present are good examples of community-based conservation. The community-based approach to wildlife use only meets conservation criteria if exploited species are used sustainably. This is more easily stated than achieved. In each example, the sociopolitical, economic, and ecological consequences of different harvest regimes are important considerations. In Robinson's (1993) definition, "sustainable use only occurs when the rights of different user groups are specified, when human needs are met, and when the losses in biodiversity and environmental degradation are acceptable." Let us briefly consider each of these requirements as they apply to community-based conservation:

- Local communities ideally have use rights over natural resources. However, in most countries, such rights are seldom recognized, although an argument for them can be made on moral, ethical, historic, legal, or pragmatic grounds. To the contrary, harvest rights frequently are assigned to outsider groups such as commercial operations, state or national wildlife agencies, trophy-hunting enterprises, and so forth, against the wishes or interests of local groups.

- The needs of the local communities must be considered. If these needs can be met without overexploiting the resource, then, in principle, wildlife can be used sustainably. Failing this, wildlife will be overharvested, and communities will be forced to turn to other economic activities.

- The loss of biodiversity associated with the harvest of wildlife must be acceptable to the interested parties, be they local communities, government agencies, or conservation organizations. The decline of harvested species, local extinctions, and impoverishment of the biological community must be within acceptable limits. But the question remains: Acceptable to whom? No community is homogenous (see PARTICIPATION), and interests vary according to age, gender, status, faction, and so on. Beyond the community, interested parties including government agencies, conservation organizations, and donors all have their own criteria.

In all the cases examined, there is evidence that some game species are over-harvested. In at least three of the cases (Siona-Secoya, Xavante, and the Tahuayo site described by Bodmer in AMAZON), however, some game species appear to be harvested sustainably. There are, moreover, management tools for regulating offtake. One generalization suggested by these cases is that catchment areas of about 2,500 km² seem to be necessary to provide for the subsistence hunting needs in human communities of a few hundred people in neotropical forests. Smaller catchment areas or larger human populations result in the over-harvest, and possibly the local extinction, of primates, tapir, and peccaries. Without an adequate resource base, community-based conservation based on wildlife use will be impossible, no matter how clearly the goals are defined or how effective the management structures.

The issue of who should manage wildlife harvests is a question on which there is little agreement. Community-based approaches presuppose a delicate balance between ecology, the needs of local communities, and the political interests of other user or interest groups. All decision-making power could, of course, be allocated to local communities—and this approach is certainly advocated by those who believe that, left to themselves, local communities will live harmoniously within their natural environment. In reality, most communities are involved in market economies; even if they were not, it is doubtful whether the "ecologically noble savage" (Redford 1990) envisioned by some conservationists ever existed. People everywhere act in their self-interest, especially in their economic interest. In addition, local communities rarely have the human resources to manage natural resources effectively and deal with regional and national markets (Browder 1992).

Another possibility is to assign the responsibility to regional and national government agencies. Yet throughout much of the world, governmental agencies traditionally have been insensitive to the socioeconomic needs of local communities and failed to conserve natural resources. Governments almost always favor policies that foster national economic development at the expense of resource conservation and the cultural and social integrity of local communities. Moreover, few governments have the resources to monitor resource utilization in remote areas.

Yet another possibility is to give the responsibility for managing wildlife areas to national nongovernmental organizations (NGOs). NGOs frequently are more idealistic and less economically motivated than governments. To an even greater degree than governments, however, they rarely have the expertise necessary for the task, and their goals tend to be even more narrowly focused.

It is likely, then, that for the foreseeable future, a loose alliance of local communities, NGOs, and government agencies will promote and contribute to community-based management efforts. The four cases reviewed here each show a different mix of players, and it is unlikely that a single management structure will emerge.

The challenge of community-based conservation will increase as populations grow and material expectations place greater pressures on the forest. Rural local communities will inevitably participate more in market economies (e.g., Stearman and Redford 1992) and thus step up their wildlife harvests. Other developments also will encroach on the wild lands needed to support sustainable harvests. The San Pablo Siona-Secoya settlement, for example, has grown from about 100 people in 1973 to 375 persons. Other interest groups also will compete more for the wildlife resources of the forest. In Tahuayo, to name just one instance, logging crews as well as commercial and subsistence hunters compete for wildlife with local communities.

Conclusions

Local communities can contribute to the conservation of natural systems, but only if their needs are met. To date, tropical forests have not proven able to support high human populations *and* retain a significant proportion of their biodiversity. As human populations climb, as local peoples' material expectations increase, and as other human groups benefit from the exploitation of the tropical forest, we can expect a progressive erosion in forest biodiversity. What is an acceptable loss of biodiversity? At what point do local communities cease to contribute to conservation and become net exploiters? Will local people, even if empowered, be able to manage their own resources? Who should define the overall goals of a community, and who should manage its affairs to meet these goals? The future of community-based conservation efforts depends upon the answers to these questions.

Acknowledgments

We thank David Western, Michael Wright, and the Liz Claiborne Art Ortenberg Foundation for encouraging us to address the issues explored in this chapter. Richard Bodmer, Avecita Chicchón, and Frans Leeuwenberg were generous in sharing unpublished information. Richard Bodmer, Frans Leeuwenberg, and John Payne provided useful comments on earlier drafts.

Sources

Ayres, J. M., D. de M. Lima, E. de S. Martins, and J. L. K. Barreiros. 1991. "On the Track of the Road: Changes in Subsistence Hunting in a Brazilian Amazonian Village." In *Neotropical Wildlife Use and Conservation*, ed. J. G. Robinson and K. H. Redford, 82–91. Chicago: University of Chicago Press.

Bodmer, R.E., N. Y. Bendayán A., L. Moya I., and T. G. Fang. 1990. "*Manejo de ungulados en la Amazonia Peruana: Analisis de su caza y commercializacion.*" *Boletin de Lima* 70:49–56.

Brandon, K. E., and M. Wells. 1992. "Planning for People and Parks: Design Dilemmas." *World Development* 20: 557–570.

Browder, J. O. 1992. "The Limits to Extractivism." *BioScience* 42:174–182.

Caldecott, J. 1986. "Hunting and Wildlife Management in Sarawak." WWF Malaysia Report. Kuching, Sarawak: World Wildlife Fund. Mimeograph.

Campos Dudley, L. C. 1992. "The Chimane Conservation Program in Beni, Bolivia: An Effort in Local Participation." In *Conservation of Neotropical Forests: Working from Traditional Resource Use*, ed. K. H. Redford and C. Padoch, 228–242. New York: Columbia University Press.

Castro, N., J. Revilla, and M. Neville. 1976. *"Carne de Monte Como una Fuente de Proteinas en Iquitos, con Referencia Especial a Monos."* *Revista Forestal del Peru* 6 (1–2):19–32.

Chicchón, A. 1991. "Can Indigenous People and Conservationists Be Allies?" *TCD Newsletter* (University of Florida) 23:1–5.

———. 1992. "Chimane Resource Use and Market Involvement in the Beni Biosphere Reserve, Bolivia." Ph.D. dissertation, University of Florida.

Coello Hinojosa, F. 1992. "The Cuyabeno Wildlife Reserve." In *Conservation of Neotropical Forests: Working from Traditional Resource Use*, ed. K. H. Redford and C. Padoch, 245–258. New York: Columbia University Press.

———. and J. D. Nations. 1987. *"Plan Maestro de La Reserva de Produccion Faunistica Cuyabeno, Provincia del Napo, Ecuador."* Report to Departamento de Areas Naturales y Recursos Silvestres de la Dirección Nacional Forestal del Ecuador. Photocopy.

Falconer, J. 1992. *Non-timber Forest Products in Southern Ghana*. Overseas Development Administration Forestry Series, No. 2. London: Natural Resources Institute.

Freese, C. H., P. G. Heltne, N. Castro, and G. Whitesides. 1982. "Patterns and Determinants of Monkey Densities in Peru and Bolivia, with Notes on Distributions." *International Journal of Primatology* 3:53–90.

Gardner, A. L. 1982. "Wildlife Management and Tropical Biology." Paper presented at the 33rd Annual American Institute of Biological Sciences meeting, Pennsylvania State University, University Park.

Glanz, W. E. 1991. "Mammalian Densities at Protected versus Hunted Sites in Central Panama." In *Neotropical Wildlife Use and Conservation*, ed. J. G. Robinson and K. H. Redford, 163–173. Chicago: University of Chicago Press.

Heymans, J. C., and J. S. Maurice. 1973. Introduction á l'Exploitation de la Faune come Ressource Alimentaire en République du Zaire. *Forum Universitaire* 2:6–12.

Johns, A. D. 1986. "Effects of Habitat Disturbance on Rainforest Wildlife in Brazilian Amazonia." Unpublished report to World Wildlife Fund-U.S.

Leeuwenberg, F. 1991. "Ethno-zoological Analysis and Wildlife Management in the Xavante Territory, Pimentel Barbosa, Mato Grosso State." Unpublished report to World Wildlife Fund-U.S.

———. 1992a. *"Manejo de Fauna Cinegética na Reserva Indígena Xavante de Pimentel Barbosa, Mato Grosso."* In *Manejo da Vida Silvestre para a Conservação* na *América Latina*, ed. R. E. Bodmer, 15–20. Proceedings of a Workshop. Photocopy.

———. 1992b. "Plano de Manejo da Fauna Cinegética." Report to the Associacão Xavante de Pimentel Barbosa. Photocopy.

Mayers, J. 1991. "Getting Back to Bushmeat." *BBC Wildlife* (January):16.

Mitchell, C. L., and E. Raez L. 1991. "The Impact of Human Hunting on Primate and Game Bird Populations in the Manu Biosphere Reserve in Southeastern Peru." Report to Wildlife Conservation International. Photocopy.

Myers, N. 1988. "Tropical Forests: Much More than Stocks of Wood." *Journal of Tropical Ecology* 4:209–221.

Paolisso, M., and R. Sackett. 1985. "Traditional Meat Procurement Strategies among the Irapa-Yukpa of the Venezuela-Colombia Border Area." *Research on Economic Anthropology* 7:177–199.

Peres, C. A. 1990. "Effects of Hunting on Western Amazonian Primate Communities." *Biological Conservation* 54:47–59.

Peters, C. M., A. H. Gentry, and R. O. Mendelsohn. 1989. "Valuation of an Amazonian Rainforest." *Nature* 339:656–657.

Pierret, P. V., and M. J. Dourojeanni. 1966. *"La Caza y la Alimentación Humana en las Riberas del Río Pachitea, Perù."* *Turrialba* 16:271–277.

———. 1967. *"Importancia de la Caza para Alimentación Humana en el Curso Inferior del Río Ucayali, Peru."* *Revista Forestal del Peru* 1:10–21.

Prescott-Allen, R., and C. Prescott-Allen. 1982. *What's Wildlife Worth?* Washington, D.C: International Institute for Environment and Development.

Redford, K. H. 1990. "The Ecologically Noble Savage." *Orion* 9:24–29.

———. 1992. "The Empty Forest." *BioScience* 42:412–422.

———. 1993. "Hunting in Neotropical Forests: A Subsidy from Nature." In *Tropical Forests, People and Food*, ed. C. H. Hladik, A. Hladik, O. F. Linares, H. Pagezy, A. Semple, and M. Hadley, 227–246. Paris: UNESCO.

Redford, K. H., and J. G. Robinson. 1987. "The Game of Choice: Patterns of Indian and Colonist Hunting in the Neotropics." *American Anthropologist* 89:650–667.

———. 1991. "Subsistence and Commercial Uses of Wildlife in Latin America." In *Neotropical Wildlife Use and Conservation*, ed. J. G. Robinson and K. H. Redford, 6–23. Chicago: University of Chicago Press.

Redford, K. H., and A. M. Stearman. 1989. "Local Peoples and the Beni Biosphere Reserve, Bolivia." *Vida Silvestre Neotropical* 2:49–56.

Richter, W. von. 1969. "Report to the Government of Botswana on a Survey of the Wild Animal Hide and Skin Industry." UNDP/FAO No. TA 2637. Mimeograph.

Robinson, J. G. 1993. "The Limits to Caring: Sustainable Living and the Loss of Biological Diversity." *Conservation Biology* 7:20–28.

———, and K. H. Redford. 1986. "Intrinsic Rate of Natural Increase in Neotropical Forest Mammals: Relationship to Phylogeny and Diet." *Oecologia* 65:516–520.

———. 1991. "Sustainable Harvest of Neotropical Forest Animals. In *Neotropical Wildlife Use and Conservation*, ed. J. G. Robinson and K. H. Redford, 415–429. Chicago: University of Chicago Press.

Silva, J. L., and S. D. Strahl. 1991. "Human Impact on Populations of Chachalacas, Guans, and Currasows (Galliformes: Cracidae) in Venezuela." In

Neotropical Wildlife Use and Conservation, ed. J. G. Robinson and K. H. Redford, 37–52. Chicago: University of Chicago Press.

Stearman, A. M. 1989. "Yuquí Foragers in the Bolivian Amazon: Subsistence Strategies, Prestige and Leadership in an Acculturating Society." *Journal of Anthropological Research* 45:219–244.

———. 1990. "The Effect of Settler Incursion on Fish and Game Resources of the Yuquí, a Native Amazonian Society of Eastern Bolivia." *Human Organization* 49:373–385.

———. 1992. "Neotropical Indigenous Hunters and their Neighbors." In *Conservation of Neotropical Forests: Working from Traditional Resource Use*, ed. K. H. Redford and C. Padoch, 108–128. New York: Columbia University Press.

———, and K. H. Redford. 1992. "Commercial Hunting by Subsistence Hunters: Sirionó Indians and Paraguayan Caiman in Lowland Bolivia." *Human Organization* 51:235–244.

Thiollay, J. M. 1989. "Area Requirements for the Conservation of Rain Forest Raptors and Game Birds in French Guiana." *Conservation Biology* 3:128–137.

Vickers, W. T. 1980. "An Analysis of Amazonian Hunting Yields as a Function of Settlement Age." In *Working papers on South American Indians*, ed. W. T. Vickers and K. M. Kensinger, 7–29. Bennington, Vermont: Bennington College.

———. 1988. "Game Depletion Hypothesis of Amazonian Adaptation: Data from a Native Community." *Science* 239:1521–1522.

Wagley, C. 1977. *Welcome of Tears: The Tapirapé of Central Brazil*. New York: Oxford University Press.

Wells, M., and K. E. Brandon. 1992. *People and Parks: Linking Protected Area Management with Local Communities*. Washington, D.C.: World Bank.

PART III

Themes

CHAPTER 14

Cultural Traditions and Community-based Conservation

Charles D. Kleymeyer

"Nosotros somos medio ambiente—We are environment."
—Evaristo Nugkuag, COICA (Coordinadora de las Organizaciones Indígenas de la Cuenca Amazónica) (Nugkuag 1991)

"Culture is like a tree. If the green branches—a people's language, legends, customs—are carelessly chopped off, then the roots that bind people to their place on the earth and to each other also begin to wither. The wind and rain and the elements carry the topsoil away; the land becomes desert."
—Mariano López, Tzotzil Indian, Chamula, Chiapas, Mexico (López 1990)

The Need for a Sea Change

Consider the following argument: Significant changes in the environmental degradation that we humans are causing will not result solely from new legislation and treaties, nor from increased enforcement of existing laws and treaties. More protection for selected areas and species and improved technologies for cleanup, prevention, and sustainable production also will prove insufficient. Nor will it be enough to attack the root causes of the problem by seeking reductions in poverty and decreases in population growth—as necessary as such actions may be. Even societies with stable, well-off populations, ample protections, and broad access to high technology continue to contribute to environmental degradation and suffer broad and lasting negative consequences. Their reform efforts help but basically amount to tinkering with a broken system. More tinkering and reform and science and technology alone will not be enough to save the earth. *Truly significant change will depend upon an antecedent sea change in the way people perceive the natural world, how it is used and abused, and what their relationship to that world must be.*

If this premise is correct, how can the needed sea change be accomplished? In everyday idiomatic language, we speak of having a change of heart. Can a sweeping change of heart regarding the environment be planned and carried out?

What would be the ingredients of such a change? And how, on a large scale, do we reach the human heart to effect this transformation—without which we too are an endangered species?

Do we invent new models and techniques for environmental caretaking from scratch, or do models for better designs and behaviors—perhaps disappeared or disappearing—already exist? Frequently, traditional peoples say they have time-tested ways. Chief Seattle's famous statement (valid in sentiment, whether or not poetic license was employed in recording it) is one of the more eloquent manifestations of this traditional conservation ethic (Seattle 1991; Gore 1992:259).

Perhaps we can incorporate and put into practice such strategies. At the very least, we may be able to enable traditional peoples to revive and maintain their time-tested strategies for their own benefit—and ours as well. On the other hand, this may be a hopeless indulgence—romantic and nostalgic—of modernized urban dwellers. Some would argue that these "ancient" strategies are no longer viable, except in zoolike conservation parks. Nevertheless, people at the grass roots may have some of the answers we seek. Because of the length and breadth of their experience and their proximity to current problems and challenges, such peoples frequently have a significant grasp of both the means and the ends of environmental conservation.

The Link Between Tradition and Change

To a degree not fully known or taken advantage of, some cultural values and practices at community level lend themselves to effective conservation. Some of these values and practices are disappearing and others may be presumed lost, but traditional peoples manifest many of them on a daily basis. In short, *culture itself should be considered a resource*, one to be preserved and sustained, transferred and used.

Cultural forms and traditions can be put to certain uses that can help meet the challenging task of producing the necessary massive change in human perceptions regarding the environment. In addition to being a resource to draw upon, *culture is a toolbox* full of means that can further mutually agreed ends.

A caveat: cultural forms and traditions, as a resource or as a toolbox, can be misused. In very different ways, historical fascist movements and vigilante hate groups as well as some forms of contemporary advertising provide many examples of such misuse. Moreover, culture can be distorted and weakened in the process of using it as a tool. Pieces of a culture can be made so undesirable that the original owners throw them away. On the other hand, case studies (including those gathered here) demonstrate that culture-based strategies for change can revive and strengthen cultural forms and traditions. The process of using them to produce a desirable end can refurbish and revitalize them (Kleymeyer 1993, 1994).

Much of what I have to say about culture as resource and toolbox I have seen in practice at the community level. This includes twenty-five years as a practicing development sociologist in Latin America (primarily in the Andean countries) and a similar period as a cultural activist (festival organizer, performing storyteller, and folklorist) devoted to the revitalization of folk culture in the United States and elsewhere in the Americas. In addition, I have drawn upon the sixteen case studies commissioned for the 1993 Airlie House workshop, twelve of which are reproduced in this volume. My recommendations are therefore practical rather than theoretical.

Were I to employ an anthropological definition of the term *culture*, even a book-length manuscript would not adequately cover the relationship between culture and conservation. Therefore, I will limit my discussion to the ways in which people manifest, draw upon, revitalize, and shape traditional cultural forms and strategies, and how these are sometimes lost or distorted in the process of carrying out grass-roots development and community-based conservation.

In no way do I propose the maintenance of traditional peoples in some static or pristine state, were this possible. Cultural traditions emerge and are maintained in a dynamic process of creative invention and reinvention, and they borrow and adapt traditions from other subgroups and cultures. This dynamic process readily lends itself to a strategy of using cultural forms and traditions to effect and preserve change. It also leads directly to a key issue: not whether a cultural tradition or form *should* change or be utilized for new ends, but *who should control* that process of change and utilization. This issue cries out for much reflection and debate in community-based conservation, a new approach that incorporates communities and traditional groups as coconservationists and cobeneficiaries (see Kleymeyer 1993, 1994).

Not all of the points I make are linked to field experiences that deal directly with conservation efforts. Nevertheless, many approaches developed at the grass-roots level are applicable to a variety of goals. For example, methods of teaching the prevention of cholera can be used to educate people about the use and abuse of pesticides. Furthermore, experiences in grass-roots development teach the value of putting aside the sectoral approach (health, agriculture, the environment, etc.) to problems in favor of examining their root causes (Kleymeyer 1991, 1992).

Finally, when speaking of traditional peoples, it is important to remember that this term does not refer to a few scattered cultural remnants tucked away in remote corners of forests and plains, with little potential impact on world society. Consider this statement by Pam Solo, former executive director of Cultural Survival:

> The politics of the 1990s will center on a single interlocking agenda: human rights, the environment, and development. At its heart are some 600 million indigenous people. Their fate is a pathway and a litmus test of our progress toward a peaceful and sustainable world order. From the periphery of political, economic, and social power, they are moving to the center of world attention. (*Solo 1992:1*)

Throughout this paper the term *traditional peoples* is used in place of a variety of terms such as *ethnic groups, indigenous peoples, cultural* or *ethnic minorities, tribal peoples,* and *natives.* Traditional peoples are groups of human beings who share and preserve direct, everyday connections to their distinguishable cultural roots (even though they may have willingly migrated or been forcibly moved from their homelands, including moves to cities). Traditional peoples consciously or unconsciously draw upon specific knowledge and strategies developed and tested by past generations to address current problems.

Culture as a Resource

Is tradition worth mining? Are village elders like volumes in a reference library? Are the forests and fields full of folk strategies to be harvested and transplanted in other ecological zones? Evidence in the environmental and social science literature, in the case studies in this book, and in empirical experience supports the argument that culture indeed is a resource (Alcorn 1994; Allman and Schrof 1990; Cabarle 1991; Chapin 1993; Chapin and Breslin 1984; Chumpí Kayap et al. 1993; Clay 1988; Cornista and Esqueta 1990; Davis 1993; Durning 1992; Goodland 1982; Irvine 1991; Morin-Labatut and Akhtar 1992; Palmer, Sanchez, and Mayorga 1991; Poffenberger 1990; Posey and Balée 1989; Reichel-Dolmatoff 1976; Richards 1975; Stahl 1992; Taboroff 1992; Verhelst 1990; Wali 1990; Warren 1992; Wolfe et al. 1992). There is also reason to exercise caution with this concept, so as not to romanticize it or portray it as an easy solution or panacea, thereby weakening its value over time (Cassidy and Dale 1988; Chapin 1988; Gill 1987).

Many people—from indigenous leaders, to environmental and development writers, to politicians—make the argument that traditional culture is a rich source of vital knowledge, concepts, and strategies for safeguarding the earth and addressing the challenges of survival and human advancement. Léopoldo Sédar Senghor, ex-President of Senegal, states the case for cultural preservation in the following ironic plea:

> White men, go into the distant villages of my land with your tape recorders, your cameras, and collect what the shamans, the street performers, and the old people tell you; the final keepers of a long human history, entrusted only to their voices. When they die, it will be as if for you, for your civilization, all the libraries were to be burned. (Gente 1978:21)

Alan Durning of the Worldwatch Institute argues strongly for the intrinsic value of traditional knowledge and techniques:

> First, indigenous peoples are the sole guardians of vast, little-disturbed habitats that modern societies depend on more than they may realize—to regulate water cycles, maintain the stability of the climate, and provide valuable plants, animals, and genes. Their homelands may harbor more endangered plant and animal species than all the world's nature reserves. Second, they possess, in their ecological knowledge, an asset

of incalculable value: a map to the biological diversity of the earth on which all life depends. Encoded in indigenous languages, customs, and practices may be as much understanding of nature as is stored in the libraries of modern science.

It was little appreciated in past centuries of exploitation, but is undeniable now, that the world's dominant cultures cannot sustain the earth's ecological health without the aid of the world's endangered cultures. Biological diversity—of paramount importance both to sustaining viable ecosystems and to improving human existence through scientific advances—is inextricably linked to cultural diversity. *(Durning 1992:6–7)*

Following are some of the ways in which cultural traditions represent a resource to be used in furthering conservation goals, as well as some of the issues surrounding such use:

Stewardship   The Aboriginals of Australia call it "looking after country" (see KAKADU); the Andean Quechuas speak of caring for Pacha Mama (Mother Earth). Undeniably, there is a tradition among these and many other indigenous groups of stewardship of the land and its natural resources (see INDIA). The reasons are myriad but largely have to do with survival and responsibility to younger generations: "The Aboriginal traditional owners see their deep and abiding commitment to 'looking after country' as a continuous legacy for their children and grandchildren" (KAKADU:152).

Chapin and Breslin recount a story, told by the Kuna of Panama, that uses cultural contrast to reveal lessons about stewardship:

In Panama, the zeal for development was personified in the figure of General Omar Torrijos, Panama's strongman ruler from 1969 to 1981. One day, four years ago, his helicopter skimmed over the San Blas rain forest towards a meeting of Kuna leaders on the island of Nuganá. The sight of so much virgin forest impressed Torrijos, and later that day, when he rose to speak . . . he chided the Kuna leaders: "Why do you Kuna need so much land? You don't do anything with it. You don't use it. And if anyone else so much as cuts down a single tree, you shout and scream."

A Kuna leader named Rafael Harris stood and responded: "If I go to Panama City and stand in front of a pharmacy and, because I need medicine, pick up a rock and break the window, you would take me away and put me in jail. For me, the forest is my pharmacy. If I have sores on my legs, I go to the forest and get the medicine I need to cure them. The forest is also a great refrigerator. It keeps the food I need fresh. If I need a peccary, I go to the forest with my rifle and—pow!—

take out food for myself and my family. So we Kuna need the forest, and
we use it and take much from it. But we can take what we need without
having to destroy everything as your people do."

. . . Torrijos was left speechless. He could only stride across the . . .
hall and wrap the Kuna leader in an emotional bear hug. *(1984:32)*

The packet of stewardship methodologies is not only there to be preserved for
its inventors or borrowed by others, it is available for hire. The Kuna have established their own self-managed park (facing a series of problems along the way), at
times employing Kuna youths as forest guards (Chapin 1993). In another among
numerous examples, Aboriginals are being employed as park rangers in Australia's Kakadu National Park (see KAKADU). The plan is to phase them into management positions as well. In Bolivar Province, Ecuador, a campesino federation,
FUNORSAL, established its own nature preserve, utilizing local traditional know-
how to take care of a piece of land that, although small, ranges from highland
peaks to subtropical forests.

Stewardship does not mean locking resources in a box and swallowing the key;
it can mean rational, sustainable use. Moreover, the connection between sustainable utilization of natural resources works both ways. Cultural values, for example, can help maintain wildlife, and the opposite is also true. NEOTROPICAL
FORESTS reports that "wild game has a high social value, and by securing game and
sharing it with other members of the community, the hunter pays debts, acquires
allegiances, and contributes to social cohesiveness. . . . A number of studies . . .
suggest a link between the increasing dearth of wild game and a breakdown of the
traditional village social structure" (303).

Reviving ancestral technologies   In numerous places throughout the world,
people are attempting to rediscover and put back into practice the traditional resource-management techniques of earlier generations (Allman 1990). Manuel
Huaya Panduro, project manager of HIFCO in Peru, makes an eloquent statement
about the purposes of these efforts:

> The monte [*rain forest*] is our mother. As long as the forest exists, we can
> meet all of our needs. We are trying to recapture our traditional knowl-
> edge. . . . Our forefathers knew how to reclaim land, and we are trying
> to capture that information. The land is our mother. If we don't take care
> of our mother, we will live as motherless children. *(Cabarle, Panduro,
> and Murayari 1993:1)*

These revival efforts sometimes entail ingenious archeological sleuthing, as in
the case of the raised-field agriculture techniques of the Tiwanaku on the Bolivian
altiplano (Obermiller 1990). Combining the Western scientific method with
modern-day campesino organization, this project has been able to rebuild the ancient raised fields with their surrounding water canals, which act as solar storage

batteries. A potato crop planted there recently took from the Dutch the world record for the highest yield per hectare. This project, although heavily funded and of uncertain replicability on a broader scale, certainly has received widespread and enthusiastic reactions from the scientific and development communities and from the media.

In other cases, revival efforts represent massive outlays of human capital (labor and training), much of it on a voluntary basis. An example is the construction of agricultural terracing in Chimborazo Province, Ecuador. In this case, not only does the effort draw upon ancestral know-how, it uses a pre-Columbian communal work form, the *minga*, to get the job done (see page 336 for further discussion of this mechanism).

In sum, the legacy of stewardship discussed above is not simply a philosophy but comes complete with methodology—specific sets of techniques for appropriate stewardship. These techniques can be rescued, adopted, and disseminated. Cornista and Esqueta describe a Philippine case:

> As conservation measures, the Kalahan Educational Foundation reintroduced old strategies the Ikalahans had stopped practicing, including *balka* or *barikes*, *gengen*, and *day-og*. *Balka* or *barikes* means "belt." The practice involves planting tiger grass, alnos, citrus, and pomelo along the contour to prevent soil erosion. In *gengen*, sweet potato vines derived from the harvested crop are laid laterally and covered with soil. *Gengen* is a technique of composting on the contour that rebuilds fertility while protecting from erosion. *Day-og* is similar to gengen but is generally practiced on level or flat lands. *(1990:144)*

The fact is, however, that the act of recuperating a disappearing or disappeared technique can change it. Of the traditional closed-access management technique found in the Maluku of Indonesia, Zerner points out, "in the process of reviving *sasi*, the institution was actually being reinvented" (MALUKU ISLANDS:101). Attempts to revive traditional techniques such as *sasi* should be rooted in local culture and social organization in order for them to take hold. In the case of the raised fields of Bolivia, for example, project management is in the hands of the indigenous campesinos, research being the responsibility of archeologists and agronomists.

Calling on a traditional conservation ethic   It is fashionable these days to refer to indigenous peoples as people who have a higher environmental ethic than the rest of us, and certainly higher than that of the modern industrialized world. Indeed, many indigenous groups such as the Australian Aboriginals and the original Amazonian rain-forest dwellers do have countless generations of experience in cohabiting with and managing the natural world. Whether out of a need to survive or from gratitude, these groups have developed a spiritual stance toward the environment that is often insightful, protective, visionary, and reverent. The language and images they use, often expressed in poetic and visual terms—"Mother Earth" and "looking after country," for example—make them easy to understand and remember. These strike a resonant chord with the rest of us in our growing ecological anxiety. It is tempting to hope that a traditional conservation ethic might be articulated in such a way as to remake our own stance regarding the environment (see Gore 1992, especially the chapter titled "Environmentalism of the Spirit," and LaDuke 1992).

We must approach these ethical imports, or implants, with caution because they are easily romanticized . . . and even fantasized (Redford 1990). We nonindigenous peoples to some extent may project our own idealized values regarding the environment upon traditional peoples, expecting of them behaviors we would not practice ourselves. Or we may reshape indigenous values into concepts that are more palatable to us (à la Chief Seattle). Certainly, we tend to talk about indigenous peoples as though they formed some monolithic group of loinclothed treehuggers. In the real world, however, some of them sell their timber rights (as the Chachis of coastal Ecuador have done, negotiating a thirty-year contract with a foreign–local consortium that will pay them a few dollars per tree and build roads restricted for use only by the companies), while others kill endangered species to sell their valuable pelts or clear the tropical forests to pasture cattle.

The "native ethic," to some extent, may be a function of poverty, traditional peoples being as destructive as the rest of us once they acquire tools such as power saws and motor vehicles. Once a group gains control over resources, traditional values are put to the test. The native corporations of southeastern Alaska, whose shareholders—just like those of any other company—pressure them to produce cash, provide a case in point.

As for the concept of Mother Earth, at least one author contends that this idea dates back only a hundred years or so, when whites began using it to refer to an amalgam of native female spiritual figures (Gill 1987). A similar entity, Pacha Mama, in the Andean region dates back much farther than a century. Nonindigenous peoples, through their own cultural prisms, also may view her as a single shared female earth deity. According to Ecuadorean educator and development worker Carlos Moreno (1993), however, Catholicism has reshaped the concept of Pacha Mama to encompass good and bad, sanctity and sinfulness; Pacha Mama, in some Andean people's minds, has become a mythic figure capable of reward and punishment. Originally, says Moreno, if humans treated the earth well, Pacha Mama responded positively. If not, no positive response (or punishment) was forthcoming. In either case, the symbolism is powerful and capable of affecting behavior in a positive manner.

Might there not also be as many ethical constructs as there are groups? And what happens when we encounter ethical systems that we dislike, clash with our own, or are incompatible with conservation of biodiversity? Some religious beliefs, for instance, have entailed killing endangered species, e.g., to obtain sacred eagle feathers. The Maasai claim that they traditionally used wildlife as "second cattle," killing them to eat during periods of drought (see AMBOSELI). Such clashes call for renewed emphasis on both tolerance and conflict-resolution strategies. Zerner raises the issue of ethics and the complexity of reshaping another group's ethical system to suit our own (and presumably their) purposes. He describes attempts to invent a "green *sasi*" (MALUKU ISLANDS:100) so as to limit access to endangered species. Nevertheless, saving traditions such as *sasi* may not be possible. Among the Kuna, elders, in league with a handful of young project leaders, hold local youths to a traditional conservation ethic that they very well may have ceased to care about.

In other cases, new ethics are being shaped from old ones. In Cotopaxi Province, Ecuador, impoverished campesino parents decided that perhaps the best inheritance they could leave their children was a forested mountainside (Herrán 1985). In nearby Bolivar Province, other campesinos came to the conclusion that traditional land defense based on legal claims and physical force could be expanded to include ecologically sound production practices and soil recuperation—thereby defending the health and fecundity of limited land.

Often, what is entailed is a balancing act, as the attempts to marry conservation ethics with the aspirations and traditions of the local people ("bearers of the longest continuous cultural traditions on earth") described in KAKADU (137) attest. The human family is notable for its variation and its capacity to change as conditions change. Western suggests that it is "more important to adopt and adapt existing value systems as a way of protecting biodiversity than to reach for any universal ideal" (1993:31).

Culture as a Toolbox

Can Anansi the Spider, known throughout Africa and the Americas for his guile in the face of adversity, be called upon to save the jungle? Can songs and murals raise consciousness enough to change behavior? Can a sociodrama or a folk dance festival get people to make the connection between reforestation and land defense? And what happens to cultural forms in the process of being so utilized? Numerous development projects have employed traditional cultural forms (music, dance, popular theater, puppetry, artisanal work, poster and mural art, oral tradition, and so on) in support of their goals. The Inter-American Foundation (IAF), for example, has supported culture-based development efforts in some thirty Latin America and Caribbean countries during the last two decades. Grass-roots groups and NGOs in these countries have carried out more than 250 projects in which cultural expression played an integral part (Kleymeyer 1993, 1994).

Using culture in this way—as a toolbox—encourages social and economic change by both drawing upon and reinforcing the cultural traditions of poor people, particularly ethnic minorities. This approach has evolved from efforts initiated in the developing world, as well as in poverty-stricken areas and ethnic enclaves of the industrialized world. This use of culture, rooted in respect for the wisdom and ways of traditional peoples, seeks to retain their special cultural strengths and contributions while enabling them to achieve change in their social and economic conditions; it does not try to maintain traditional peoples in an unchanged or "pure" cultural state.

In a nutshell, the argument is that a people's own cultural heritage comprises the foundation upon which equitable and sustainable development is built. The "cultural energy" thereby tapped and directed drives development efforts (Hirschman 1983; Kleymeyer 1992, 1993, 1994). And traditional forms of cultural expression can be employed as a means of realizing project goals.

The actual and potential uses of cultural traditions in grass-roots development and, especially, in community-based conservation are many:

Consciousness raising   Social movements throughout the world have used traditional cultural forms to raise people's consciousness about particular issues—sometimes so as to establish a given issue *as an issue* at the outset. Musicians and cultural activists such as folksinger Pete Seeger have effectively employed protest songs to make people aware of environmental degradation and encourage them to get involved in environmental action. In a now famous case, Seeger and the Sloop River Singers sailed up and down the Hudson River on the 100-ton sloop *Clearwater* in the 1970s, promoting river cleanup. According to Seeger, "Whereas only 10 or 12—a handful of—people knew about the fight to save the Hudson, now there are literally thousands from Sandy Hook to the Adirondacks. This is a result of years of work and Clearwater waterfront singing parties" (Lyman 1982).

Cultural expression is widely utilized in this way in the developing world as well. Donovan reports the importance of "consciousness-raising activities with community groups (e.g., films, puppet shows, theater, field days with games, fundraising contests) focusing on forests or sustainable development" in the BOSCOSA forest conservation and management project in Costa Rica (1993:18). In an intriguing statement that merits more study, he further reports, "By emphasizing reforestation with native species, constantly focusing on BOSCOSA's project goal of maintaining natural forest cover, and using this work to stimulate interest in natural forest management, the project has begun to have some success in creating a forestry culture among colonists with little or no cultural traditions as 'indigenous forest people'" (1993:22).

In highland Ecuador, the Feria Educativa (Educational Fair) has played a major role in raising consciousness about ethnic pride, self-managed development, and environmental protection (Kleymeyer and Moreno 1988). The Feria Educativa's young male and female Indian musicians have visited more than 750 indigenous villages in Chimborazo Province alone with their program of music, dance, and sociodrama. The program gets people to reflect—in their own language and with their own symbols and idioms—on local problems and publicly discuss issues, from racial discrimination to soil erosion, and identify innovative solutions, sometimes for the first time.

Cultural forms also are used to raise consciousness where people from developing countries live and work in industrialized ones. An Oregon-based theater company, Teatro Nuestro, travels to migrant farm workers to present live plays such as *El Pesticido*, which examines the issues surrounding pesticide poisoning. After one performance in California, an experienced farm worker remarked, "You might think this is a simple thing. Tonight everybody laughed. But there is a message. Slowly, the farm workers become more sophisticated, gain self-esteem and will fight for their rights" (Gilden 1988).

Teaching and training   Forms of cultural expression, such as stories, songs, and dances, effectively store and transmit information. They can be powerful teaching tools, since they preserve local history and lore, define and interpret dilemmas, and pass on lessons—especially to young people. They play a central role in the discovery of new possibilities and in encouragement of group reflection and awareness about poverty and development. They also can be used as a didactic technique in planning and evaluation efforts. By reminding people where they come from and who they are, cultural traditions help them shape a vision of where they should be going.

A Navajo teacher speaking at a public forum on intercultural education held on the Navajo Reservation in October 1985 had this to say about culture and teaching:

> Ethnic history is like a bow and arrow. The farther back you pull the bowstring, the farther the arrow flies. The same is true with historical vision: the farther back you look, the farther you can see into the future. If you pull the bowstring back only a little, the arrow only goes forward a short way. The same with history: if you only look back a short distance, your vision into the future is equally short.

Forms of cultural expression are effective ways of teaching because they capture people's attention and imagination in ways that other means of communication do not. In their very essence, whether used in formal and nonformal education and training programs or in the course of everyday life, they are culturally appropriate, using understandable language and symbols to transmit messages. Puppet shows and sociodramas can convey information and ideas in ways that are clear and easy to remember, and they frequently end with a group discussion that anchors the main points in the local context and helps build a consensus for action. This kind of audiovisual approach frequently has far more impact on people rooted in an oral tradition than printed materials.

On Costa Rica's Talamanca coast, high school students participated in an oral history project in which they went out into the villages to collect and publish local knowledge about the dangers of deforestation, snakebite cures, and uses of forest plants (Palmer 1982–83). Students not only learned and disseminated valuable knowledge about the region, they developed a better sense of their own identity and roots and a better appreciation for local indigenous practices. A broader effort to record local indigenous history and enhanced understanding of the environment soon followed (Palmer, Sanchez, and Mayorga 1991).

Other methods are effective as well. Fundación Natura, in Quito, Ecuador, has placed in a large number of Ecuadorean schools colorful posters that depict—far better than a book or article could do—issues such as the dangers pesticides pose to the environment and the ecological interconnectedness of the natural world (including how human beings fit into that world). As KAKADU suggests, even place names can be educational tools:

> The emphasis on Aboriginal interpretations of the park (e.g., the use of Aboriginal place names or Aboriginal interpretations of landscape, history, and culture) is an intangible element, but a benefit in which Aboriginal people place great emphasis and pride. This process also has a wider educational function, which leads to broader community understanding of Aboriginal culture and support for comanagement processes. *(152)*

Strengthening community-based organizations and the sense of community

Cultural traditions can be used to help strengthen local organizations and build a sense of community or shared identity at the village or regional level. Stronger local organizations with an enhanced sense of identity and community are more successful in carrying out all sorts of projects, including those that focus on environmental issues. Capable organizations and skillful leaders are concerned not only with the intellectual capacities of their members, but with their hearts and souls as well. Teamwork, sacrifice, communication, solidarity, and persistence are all elements of successful development efforts, and all of these elements can be enhanced through the application of a culture-based approach.

A strong sense of shared identity can energize people and inspire them to collective action to improve their lives. When people see themselves as proud members of a culture, they are more likely to organize and work for change. Organizations built on the bedrock of cultural identity are better able to single out common problems and collectively seek appropriate solutions.

Without a sense of community, individuals retreat into their families or themselves, to the detriment of collaborative efforts at survival and betterment. They may work individually to increase productivity and improve themselves, but collaborative social action withers or never even starts. Such expressions of culture as feast days; work parties; celebrations; and special songs, dances, and costumes establish and shore up a group's sense of identity and pride. Recognizing this, many groups actively promote such activities as an integral, vital part of everyday life.

Los Yumbos Chahuamangos, a music and dance group of lowland Quichua in the Amazonian region of Ecuador, exemplifies this use of cultural expression. Los Yumbos' members are drawn from a large agricultural cooperative made up of eleven communities and five hundred families. The group regularly plays music, sings, and dances at local festivals and important cooperative meetings, attracting broader attendance by injecting vitality into the proceedings and teaching and promoting organizational participation through lyrics and example. One of its songs explains in Quichua how a cooperative functions. Group members also are involved in mobilizing participation in a local federation that recently initiated a major forest-management project. Only a coalition of communities—not individual families or single communities—could have carried out a project of this scope and complexity.

Promotion of programs and generation of group energy   Many grass-roots groups and NGOs use traditional forms of cultural expression to promote development efforts and generate the energy and collective force necessary to begin and sustain group action (Kleymeyer 1993, 1994). The "cultural energy" produced in this way is an effective and inexpensive means of motivating and mobilizing people, and it is perpetually renewable. The more people use this energy, the more energy the process produces as a by-product.

Traditional forms of cultural expression can energize participants and instill in them strong feelings of group pride, reaffirmation, optimism, collective strength, and vitality. They are especially effective in calling forth and directing group energies toward shared goals—which might entail productive tasks, education and training, or conservation.

Examples of this use of culture can be found in development projects as well as in social movements. In highland Ecuador, I was present when a new campesino federation of twenty-six communities launched a major development project that included sustainable agriculture, reforestation, and terracing. As the central activity of this inauguration, the new federation invited each member community to send a dance or music group. In one of the dance presentations, a team of oxen, led by the festive music of a local village band, plowed a single furrow around the entire village plaza. Behind the plow, a line of women did a serpentine dance, reaching down at each beat of the music to plant a seed in the furrow, thereby celebrating the value of working with the soil. This was the largest such gathering by a local organization of indigenous people in living memory, and it stirred up a level of enthusiasm for organizational efforts that had a lasting effect on the surrounding population. The Feria Educativa, mentioned previously, also does effective promotional work with this and other federations, employing local music and dance to encourage collective action and tap into cultural energy, both of which are key ingredients necessary for carrying out development efforts such as the construction of an irrigation system or agricultural terracing.

This promotional approach, of course, can be abused (by political candidates, for example, or by advertising campaigns to sell pesticides that are banned in their countries of origin) as well as used for constructive purposes. The method only works as intended if its goals are clear and agreed upon and the participants in grass-roots development efforts have primary control over it.

Getting the work done   Among traditional peoples, cultural forms are closely related to work and production, although the relationship is often more contextual than direct. This is particularly true in settings in which music and dance have not been set off from the rest of the human enterprise as mere entertainment but are integral to social structure and to forms of work.

For example, an important traditional work form in the Andes is the *minga*, a pre-Columbian collective work system often used for harvests or for community projects (see Chumpí Kayap et al. 1993; and Herrán 1985). In Chimborazo, Ecuador, a federation of local communities built a major irrigation system with seven hundred *minga* days from each family. In the same region, federations have planted more than a million trees and are now building agricultural terracing using the *minga* system.

Collective work forms similar to the *minga* are known throughout the world (for instance, *tequio* in southern Mexico and barn raising in the United States). These traditional ways of organizing and managing work often are mobilized and ener-gized by songs and special foods, and a festive celebration commonly follows completion of the work. These sociocultural traditions promote group solidarity and pride, but they also get the work done—frequently far more effectively than more modern forms of mobilizing work such as wage labor and certainly better than coerced labor. Forestation projects give undeniable proof of the effectiveness of traditional forms. In the Cotopaxi case mentioned on page 331, the number of trees *minga* laborers planted in developing their own communal forests far sur-passed other local efforts by the government, USAID, and the private sector.

Significant reversals in certain environmental degradation trends such as ero-sion and desertification will not result simply from slowing or halting undesirable activities but will require massive amounts of labor. Cultural traditions can be called upon to get the work done, and do so in a less costly, more constructive, and effective manner.

Democratic discussion and social mediation   Forms of cultural expression can serve as a public forum for issues such as poverty, racial discrimination, or en-vironmental degradation and loss of species. It can, in addition, present the op-portunity for disparate groups to come together and seek increased under-standing, compromise, and tolerance.

From time immemorial, cultural expression has been used in democratic as well as totalitarian societies to protest and to pressure authorities. Caribbean calypsos and Colombian *vallenatos* are songs that frequently carry a critique; a well-known example is the music of the calypso singer Sparrow.

In Chile, the culture of protest has developed to a high form during the last two decades. Chilean protest songs and groups are some of the most popular in all of

Latin America, and Chile's poetry and theater is unsurpassed as social commentary. The successful Campaign of the No led by the opposition during the 1989 referendum on the Pinochet government was based on brilliantly executed songs, videos, posters, and other manifestations of cultural expression that touched and moved the Chilean people at the core. A scaled-down version of this campaign could be used to stop the importation of banned pesticides or clear-cutting of the Amazon for African palm oil plantations.

Cultural expression also can play a role in social mediation. In the right circumstances, it can contribute to reducing conflict by bridging sociocultural gaps between people and addressing issues over which they are divided. Sometimes such groups—such as blacks and Indians or Indians and colonists in the Amazon—otherwise would have little or no contact with one another.

The toolbox approach: a caveat   An overly utilitarian approach to culture can have unintended negative consequences. CRATER MOUNTAIN provides two illustrations of this phenomenon. Local Gimi leaders express "alarm about both the disappearance of rituals and the emptying of clan forests by young men who killed birds and marsupials for valuable plumage to sell or meat to use for food (199)," creatures that were the inspiration for much natural symbolism in Gimi dances and ceremonies. Later, after initiation of an ecotourism project in the area, Gimi dancers pander to the wallets of tourists by overemphasizing the sexual and the violent in their presentations of traditional ritual theater, causing distress among villagers who still view their rituals in strongly spiritual terms.

In sum, the reconstruction of traditions as tools of income production or environmental protection can backfire. The people targeted can reject or ignore such reconstructions, and sometimes the original tradition itself. We need to study such actions carefully. On the other hand, it is possible to revitalize old symbols, myths, and traditions without distorting, dismembering, or expropriating them and to make them vital agents once again. As the Feria Educativa in Ecuador demonstrates, this is often most likely when people are using their *own* traditions for their *own* purposes.

Joining Forces: The Potential for Alliance Between Traditional Peoples and Environmentalists

Are traditional peoples environment, as Evaristo Nugkuag claims? Or are these groups ultimately a threat to environment, as some others claim—the more so as they gain access to modern technology? Is an alliance between non-Western traditional peoples living in remote areas and urban-based, Western environmentalists viable? To some degree, the strategies and styles of these two disparate groups tend to clash. Historical differences abound: urban and modern versus rural and traditional, North versus South, restriction versus freedom, outsiders' interests versus ancestral territorial rights (e.g., parks versus homelands). On the other hand, shared goals are evident (although sometimes more so in assumption than in fact), particularly as both groups shed their.purist stances of the past and search for accommodation and sustainable use rather than confrontation and prohibition.

A good example is the case of the Indigenous-Environmentalist Alliance initiated by COICA (Coordinadora de las Organizaciones Indígenas de la Cuenca Amazónica, or the Coordinating Body for Indigenous Organizations of the Amazon Basin) at the First Summit Meeting between Amazonian Indigenous Peoples and Environmentalists held in Iquitos, Peru, in May 1990. COICA was formed in 1984, partly in response to the Amazonian Pact signed by South American nations with Amazonian territory. COICA also was a natural extension of a process of coalition formation among Amazonian indigenous groups during the preceding two decades, when scores of federations representing one or more tribal groups had been formed.

In several countries—particularly Ecuador, Peru, and Bolivia—confederations of these federations became effective voices for Indians throughout their Amazonian territories. Where Amazonian confederations do not yet exist, national-level confederations or other interest groups have helped coordinate the individual and combined efforts of tribal groups. COICA, in turn, is made up of these confederations and loosely knit coalitions and now entails all nine Amazonian countries: Brazil, Bolivia, Peru, Ecuador, Colombia, Venezuela, Guyana, Suriname, and French Guiana.

COICA works to coordinate its member organizations' human rights and development efforts. It also encourages and pressures national entities, international bodies (the United Nations, the Amazonian Pact, Amnesty International, etc.) and funding institutions (the World Bank, the Inter-American Development Bank, foundations) to more responsibly take into account the interests of indigenous peoples in the course of formulating and carrying out their development and political agendas. COICA has formed a number of alliances with other tropical indigenous peoples, with European cities whose inhabitants are interested in indigenous peoples and tropical environments, and with environmental organizations in Europe and throughout the Americas (although mainly from the East and West Coasts of the United States). (For a statement of COICA's agenda, see COICA [1991], Akwe:kon Press and Plenty Canada [1992:102–105], Davis [1993:85–91]. For discussions of alliances, see Alcorn [1993], Bedford [1992], Johnson [1993], Poole [1989], and Redford and Stearman [1993].)

In the case of the Indigenous-Environmentalist Alliance that emerged from the 1990 Iquitos meeting, early efforts centered primarily on coordinating lobbying activities and other contacts in Washington, D.C. This alliance so far has produced few concrete results and eventually languished due to heavy workloads among environmentalists and COICA personnel—and the usual difficulties of communicating and coordinating across institutions and over great distances. Despite this, the desire to mold the alliance into an effective force has continued on both sides. In May 1993, in a two-day meeting in Washington, D.C., original alliance members, plus representatives from human rights and development organizations, decided to form a broader coalition to cooperate with Amazonian indigenous groups, especially those represented by COICA.

Meanwhile, traditional peoples continue to argue that they are the appropriate caretakers of endangered areas, and thus should be entrusted with that task and duly supported:

> The physical and cultural survival of indigenous peoples of the Amazon, and the preservation of the Amazonian ecology and biodiversity, are not two separate topics. They are one and the same. That's why we are committed to this preservation.
>
> —*Valerio Grefa, president of COICA (Grefa 1993)*

> When the forest is leveled, the land destroyed, we cease being Shuar and Achuar people. For three decades we have been organizing to declare our presence in the forest, and we wish to strengthen our ties with outsiders to preserve this area. Our survival is linked to the planet's survival. . . . So for us, the land is not a commodity to be bought and sold for a price. It is what sustains us. The moment our land is lost, we are no longer Shuar and Achuar. When we cultivate the land, we honor its bounty, give it worth. We protect it because we have no place else to go. Outsiders often do not understand this. They see land as something a person can own and cash in. For us the land is part of our family, and because we are all one family here, we hold the land in common. This is why we have organized a federation.
>
> —*Miguel Puwainchir, President, Shuar-Achuar Federation, 1988–1992, Sucua, Ecuador (Puwainchir 1992:40)*

> We see it like this: it is as if we are all in a canoe traveling through time. If someone begins to make a fire in their part of the canoe . . . it will affect us all. And it is the responsibility of each person in the canoe to ensure that it is not destroyed.
>
> —*Ailton Krenak, Union of Indigenous Nations in Brazil (Solo 1992:1)*

In short, the traditional peoples of the Amazon are saying to us that they live in the Amazon and have been there for generations; if others want to save the Amazon, they need to join with traditional peoples and support their self-managed efforts. Many environmentalists agree, but some succumb to the temptation to romanticize the natural ability of traditional peoples to preserve their habitat. Others suffer from lack of experience with the complicated challenges of grass-roots development approaches. Nevertheless, there are enough tough-minded, imaginative environmentalists to make this innovative collaborative approach worth trying.

Over time, a combination of creative tension and shared goals could spawn an effective new conservation approach—an alliance strategy—entailing well-articulated divisions of labor in accord with the comparative advantage of each side of the traditional peoples/environmentalists equation. This alliance strategy could result in more effective lobbying in the industrialized world and more groundbreaking efforts in the developing world such as the HIFCO project in Peru (Cabarle, Panduro, and Murayari 1993) that combine traditional techniques with lessons and methods from Western science (Davis and Wali 1993). After all, such an alliance may be the most efficient way to provide access—on indigenous terms—to culture as a resource.

Youth, Culture, and Conservation

One large sector of the world population—young people—has a special present-day *and* long-term interest in conservation of the earth's resources. This group also happens to be particularly open to messages about the environment that appeal to the heart (Herman et al. 1991). From *Sesame Street* and the Children's Television Workshop in the United States to the songs and sociodramas of the Feria Educativa in highland Ecuador (Kleymeyer and Moreno 1988), children and youths can be reached quite effectively with an approach that draws upon culture as a toolbox.

We have on hand a powerful means of shaping the consciousness of young people regarding environmental issues, educating them in ecologically sound practices, and stirring them to action. Public schools and the mass media desperately need such effective educational techniques for teaching the necessary lessons about the environment, and about culture as well. If the connection between the two topics is made in the context of engaging media such as music and storytelling, so much the better.

Among traditional peoples, the young are most at risk of losing touch with their cultural roots and therefore with traditional knowledge and techniques. Observers such as Durning (1992) assert that the close relationship between cultural diversity and biological diversity makes the trend toward a transnational, urban-dominated monoculture worrisome. Even more disturbing is the fact that the twentieth century has seen the loss of more ethnic groups than any period in human history (Clay 1989). Sadly, this phenomenon is accelerating, and quite likely it is irreversible.

Nevertheless, we can and should attempt to maintain the earth's cultural and ethnic diversity. Much of the problem, of course, has to do with issues of human rights (including land rights), international peacemaking, and the halt of genocide, and thus lies outside the scope of this book. Some small but important steps can be taken to retard, if not prevent, the creation of a completely lost generation among the traditional young people who survive. Particularly when it comes to conservation themes, the means of using cultural forms to link the younger generations with the older ones—and thereby with ancestral, traditional knowledge and techniques regarding relations with the environment—are available. This is a conservation "growth market" in various senses, particularly since approximately one-third of the world's population is under fifteen years of age. The connections tying together children, culture, and conservation are naturally dynamic ones. They hold high promise, both for laying the groundwork for the broad changes that are needed and for getting the work done.

Conclusions

Just as trees are a resource and power saws are tools for harvesting them, so too are oral traditions a resource and songs the tools of harvest. Pesticides sprayed from airplanes are technology—and so are native remedies gathered from the forest below and *minga* work parties that replant where trees have been sawed down. Together, the songs, oral traditions, *mingas*, and other forms of traditional culture can be channeled into the efforts that will produce the sea change needed to defend and preserve the world's environment.

A conservation approach that views culture as a resource and a toolbox holds out the promise of adding to our collective repertoire of earth-saving methodologies. A number of activities should be carried out in order to enhance our capability to responsibly approach traditional culture for this purpose. First, we need to deepen our understanding and knowledge of both the actual and potential relationships between cultural traditions, philosophies, worldviews, and community-based conservation. Second, we need to learn to be more effective in enabling traditional peoples and others to draw upon and develop cultural traditions that are particularly useful in promoting a conservation ethic and plan of action. Third, we need to support the dissemination of information and experiences among traditional peoples, and between these people and scientists and conservation professionals. Fourth, we need to support and promote alliances and other forms of cooperation between representative organizations of traditional peoples and environmental action organizations. Fifth, we need to develop culture-based conservation strategies designed particularly with young people in mind. Finally, we need to support efforts to reflect upon and evaluate activities that link cultural traditions and community-based conservation, including exchange visits, workshops and conferences, and research.

In further developing a user-friendly earth ethic, we can turn to traditional peoples not only for what to include in this new way of relating to environment, but for useful tools for disseminating and promoting its adoption. In short, not only is cultural diversity a valuable world resource, but when harnessed and directed by local people, cultural energy potentially can drive more conservation efforts than nonsustainable energy sources such as fossil fuels and national budgets.

As we recognize the necessity of promoting knowledge and understanding of local traditions, culture, and language among nontraditional peoples, we must also keep in mind that the flip side of cultural arrogance—"They know it all," as opposed to "We know it all"—is equally misguided. Traditional knowledge and techniques have limits, as do "modern" or scientific ones. Neither system is immune from error or ineffectiveness. When the two systems collaborate, as in the case of HIFCO in Peru (Cabarle, Panduro, and Murayari 1993), some of those limits are pushed outward.

No single approach will be a panacea for the earth's ills. Each should be allowed to find its appropriate role and encouraged to thrive in it. Accountability, critical reflection, and mutual respect should be furthered.

Unquestionably, sensitivity toward all cultures is crucial, but this does not mean that a totally hands-off approach to cultural maintenance and change is always called for. Culture is not inviolate. It is possible to have profound respect and appreciation for other cultures and still challenge them to change. From wife burning in India and clitoridectomies in Africa, to the culture of weaponry in the United States and the slaughter of endangered species everywhere, no cultural group has the right to say, "It is none of your business; this is an internal matter." As members of a global village, it is the business of all of us to oppose destructiveness and lobby for caretaking. It is our business to ensure the participation of traditionally excluded groups such as women, young people, and lower castes and classes in decisions that affect them (see INDIA). We can believe in autonomy and self-determination and, at the same time, urge groups and societies to change themselves.

In searching for ways to achieve a sea change, speaking of the human heart may be risky. On the other hand, could the sea change that swept away totalitarian governments in Eastern Europe have happened without the power of the human heart? The heart alone, and the cultural traditions that it has created and nurtured throughout human history, is not enough, and it is not the end point. But the heart and its creations may be the point of departure in letting go of entrenched ways to use and control the environment—and actions that abuse it. It may enable us to embrace, like Evaristo Nugkuag, the view that we are environment.

ACKNOWLEDGMENTS

I would like to express appreciation to the following for their comments on earlier drafts of this chapter: Jim Adriance, David Bray, Lauren Spurrier, Shirley Strum, Ron Weber, and Michael Wright.

SOURCES

Akwe:kon Press and Plenty Canada. 1992. *Indigenous Economics: Toward a Natural World Order. Akwe:kon Journal* Special Issue 9 (2).
Alcorn, J. B. 1994. "Indigenous Peoples and Conservation." *Conservation Biology* 7 (2):424–426.
———. 1993. *Ethnobiology: Community, Culture, and Biodiversity.* New York: Columbia University Press.

Allman, W. F., with J. M. Schrof. 1990. "Lost Empires of the Americas: The Ancient Andean Empires Shed New Light on How Civilizations Arise." *U.S. News and World Report* 108(13):46–54.

Bedford, M. 1992. "Saving a Refuge: The Victory of Alaska's Gwich'in over the Energy Industry Suggests the Power of Alliances." *Cultural Survival Quarterly* 16 (2):38–42.

Cabarle, B. 1991. "Community Forestry and the Social Ecology of Development." *Grassroots Development* 15 (2):3–9.

———, M. H. Panduro, and O. M. Murayari. 1993. "Ecofarming in the Peruvian Amazon: The Integrated Family and Communal Gardening Project (HIFCO)." Case study prepared for the Liz Claiborne Art Ortenberg Foundation Community Based Conservation Workshop, October 18–22, Airlie, Virginia.

Cassidy, F., and N. Dale. 1988. *After Native Claims? The Implications of Comprehensive Claims Settlements for Natural Resources in British Columbia*. Oolichan Books and The Institute for Research on Public Policy/L'Institut de Recherches Politiques.

Chapin, M. 1993. "The Seduction of Models: Chinampa Agriculture in Mexico." *Grassroots Development* 12 (1):8–17.

———. 1988. "Recuperación de las Costumbres Ancestrales: El Saber Tradicional y la Ciencia Occidental entre los Kunas de Panamá." En *La Expresión Cultural y el Desarrollo de Base*, comp. C. D. Kleymeyer, 133–160. Quito: Abya-Yala; also in English 1994 as "Recapturing the Old Ways: Traditional Knowledge and Western Science Among the Kuna Indians of Panama." In *Cultural Expression and Grassroots Development*, ed. C. D. Kleymeyer, 83–102. Boulder, Colorado: Lynne Rienner.

———, and P. Breslin. 1984. "Conservation Kuna Style." *Grassroots Development* 8 (2):26–35.

Chumpí Kayap, M., M. Jempékat, C. Moreno, y C. D. Kleymeyer. 1993. "Trabajo y Tradición." En *La Expresión Cultural y el Desarrollo de Base*, comp. C. D. Kleymeyer, 225–251. Quito: Abya-Yala; also in English 1994 as "Work and Tradition." In *Cultural Expression and Grassroots Development*, ed. C. D. Kleymeyer, 149–166. Boulder, Colorado: Lynne Rienner.

Clay, J. 1989. *Indigenous Peoples and Tropical Forests: Models of Land Use and Management from Latin America*. Cultural Survival Report No. 27. Cambridge, Massachusetts: Cultural Survival.

———. 1988. "Radios in the Rain Forest." *Technology Review* 92 (7):52–57.

Coordinadora de las Organizaciones Indígenas de la Cuenca Amazónica (COICA). 1990. "Our Agenda for the Bilateral and Multilateral Funders of Amazon Development." In *IWGIA Yearbook 1990*. Copenhagen: International Work Group for Indigenous Affairs. Reprinted in *Indigenous Views of Land and the Environment*, 1992, ed. S. H. Davis, 85–91. World Development Report, Background Paper No. 10. Washington, D.C.: World Bank.

Cornista, L. B., and E. F. Escueta. 1990. "Communal Forest Leases as a Tenurial Option in the Philippine Uplands." In *Keepers of the Forest: Land Management Alternatives in Southeast Asia*, ed. M. Poffenberger, 134–144. West Hartford, Connecticut: Kumarian Press.

Davis, S. H. 1993. *Indigenous Views of Land and the Environment*. World Bank Discussion Paper No. 188. Washington, D.C.: World Bank.

————, and A. Wali. 1993. *Indigenous Territories and Tropical Forest Management in Latin America*. Policy Research Working Paper No. WPS 1100. Washington, D.C.: The World Bank.

Donovan, R. Z. 1993. "BOSCOSA: Forest Conservation and Management on the Osa Peninsula, Costa Rica." Case study prepared for the Liz Claiborne Art Ortenberg Foundation Community Based Conservation Workshop, October 18–22, Airlie, Virginia.

Durning, A. T. 1992. *Guardians of the Land: Indigenous Peoples and the Health of the Earth*. Worldwatch Paper 112. Washington, D.C.: Worldwatch Institute.

Gente. 1978. Display material quoting Léopold Sédar Senghor Gente 84:21.

Gilden, J. 1988. "The Perils of 'El Pesticido': Actors Tour Migrant Communities with a Play about Pesticides." *San Francisco Chronicle* 1988(39):A-7.

Gill, S. D. 1987. *Mother Earth: An American Story*. Chicago: The University of Chicago Press.

Goodland, R. 1982. *Tribal Peoples and Economic Development Human Ecologic Considerations*. Washington, D.C.: World Bank.

Gore, A. 1992. *Earth in the Balance: Ecology and the Human Spirit*. Boston: Houghton Mifflin.

Grefa, V. 1993. Talk presented to the World Resources Institute, February 23, Washington, D.C.

Herman, M. L., J. F. Passineau, A. L. Schimpf, and P. Treuer. 1991. *Teaching Kids to Love the Earth*. Duluth, Minnesota: Pfeifer-Hamilton.

Herrán, J. 1985. "Development, Environment and Culture: An Experience in Fieldwork." Paper prepared for the Global Meeting on Environment and Development for Non-Governmental Organizations, February, Nairobi, Kenya.

Hirschman, A. O. 1983. "The Principle of Conservation and Mutation of Social Energy." *Grassroots Development* 7 (2):6–8.

Irvine, D. 1991. "Amazonian Ecologists: Western and Indigenous Views of Conservation and Resource Management." Paper presented at the American Association for the Advancement of Science Annual Meeting, February 15, Washington, D.C.

Johnson, T. 1993. "Native Intelligence: Environmentalists and Native Americans Team up to Protect the Earth." *Amicus Journal* 14 (4):11–12.

Kleymeyer, C. D. 1991. "What is Grassroots Development?" *Grassroots Development* 15 (1):38–39.

————. 1992. "Cultural Energy and Grassroots Development." *Grassroots Development* 16 (1):22–31.

————, comp. 1993. *La Expresión Cultural y el Desarrollo de Base*. Quito: Abya-Yala.

————, ed. 1994. *Cultural Expression and Grassroots Development*. Boulder, Colorado: Lynne Rienner.

————, and C. Moreno. 1988. "La Feria Educativa: A Wellspring of Ideas and Cultural Pride." *Grassroots Development* 12 (2):32–40; reprinted 1993 as "La Feria Educativa: Una Fuente de Ideas y Orgullo Cultural." En *La Expresión Cultural y el Desarrollo de Base*, comp. C. D. Kleymeyer, 95–113. Quito: Abya-Yala; also in English 1994 in *Cultural Expression and Grassroots Development*, ed. C. D. Kleymeyer, 57–70. Boulder, Colorado: Lynne Rienner.

LaDuke, W. 1992. "Indigenous Environmental Perspectives: A North American Primer." *Akwe:kon Journal* 9 (2):52–71.

López, M. 1990. Conversation with the author, June, Chiapas, Mexico.

Lyman, F. 1982. "If I Can't Sing, I Don't Want to be Part of Your Revolution." *Environmental Action* (March):26–29.

Moreno, C. 1993. Interview with the author, February, Chimborazo, Ecuador.

Morin-Labatut, G., and S. Akhtar. 1992. "Traditional Environmental Knowledge: A Resource to Manage and Share." In *Cultural Identity and Global Change*, a special edition of *Development: Journal of the Society for International Development*, ed. L. Arizpe. 4:24–30.

Nugkuag, E. 1991. Conversation with the author, June, Washington, D.C.

Obermiller, T. 1990. "Harvest from the Past." *University of Chicago Magazine* 10 (Spring):26–33.

Palmer, P. 1982–1983. "Self-History and Self-Identity in Talamanca, Costa Rica." *Grassroots Development* 6 (2)–7 (1):2–9; reprinted 1993 as "Historia e Identidad de Talamanca, Costa Rica." En *La Expresión Cultural y el Desarrollo de Base*, comp. C. D. Kleymeyer, 133–160. Quito: Abya-Yala; also in English 1994 as "Self-History and Self-Identity in Talamanca." In *Cultural Expression and Grassroots Development*, ed. C. D. Kleymeyer, 113–120. Boulder, Colorado: Lynne Rienner.

———, J. Sanchez, and G. Mayorga. 1991. *Taking Care of Sibö's Gifts: An Environmental Treatise from Costa Rica's Kéköldi Indigenous Reserve*. San José, Costa Rica: Asociación de Desarrollo Integral de la Reserva Indigena Cocles/Kéköldi.

Poffenberger, M. 1990. *Keepers of the Forest: Land Management Alternatives in Southeast Asia*. West Hartford, Connecticut: Kumarian Press.

Poole, P. 1989. *Developing a Partnership of Indigenous Peoples, Conservationists, and Land Use Planners in Latin America*. Washington, D.C.: World Bank, Latin America and the Caribbean Technical Department; also in Spanish 1989 as *Desarrollo de Trabajo Conjunto entre Pueblos Indígenas, Conservacionistas y Planificadores del Uso de la Tierra en América Latina*.

Posey, D. A., and W. Balée, eds. 1989. *Resource Management in Amazonia: Indigenous and Folk Strategies*. Advances in Economic Botany, Volume 7. The Bronx, New York: The New York Botanical Garden.

Puwainchir, M. 1992. "The Voice of the Ecuadorian Amazon." *Grassroots Development* 16 (2):40.

Redford, K. H. 1990. "The Ecologically Noble Savage." *Cultural Survival Quarterly* 15 (1):46–48.

———, and A. M. Stearman. 1993. "Forest-dwelling Native Amazonians and the Conservation of Biodiversity: Interests in Common or in Collision?" *Conservation Biology* 7 (1):248–255.

Reichel-Dolmatoff, G. 1976. "Cosmology as Ecological Analysis: A View from the Rain Forest." *Man* 11 (3):307–18.

Richards, P. W. 1975. *Alternative Strategies for the African Environment: Folk Ecologies as a Basis for Community-Oriented Agricultural Development*. African Environmental Special Report No. 1: Problems and Perspectives. London: International African Institute.

Seattle, Chief. 1991. *Brother Eagle, Sister Sky: A Message from Chief Seattle*. New York: Dial Books.

Solo, P. 1992. "Who Do We Think We Are?" *Cultural Survival Quarterly* 16 (2):1.

Stahl, A. B. 1992. "Valuing the Past, Envisioning the Future: Local Perspectives on Environmental and Cultural Heritage in Ghana." In *Culture and Development in Africa: Proceedings of the International Conference Held at The World Bank, Washington, D.C., April 2 and 3, 1992*, Vol. 1, eds. I. Serageldin and J. Taboroff, 415–427. Washington, D.C.: World Bank.

Taboroff, J. 1992. "Bringing Cultural Heritage into the Development Agenda: Summary Findings of Report of Cultural Heritage in Environmental Assessments in Sub-Saharan Africa." In *Culture and Development in Africa: Proceedings of the International Conference Held at The World Bank, Washington, D.C., April 2 and 3, 1992*, Vol. 1, eds. I. Serageldin and J. Taboroff, 332–339. Washington, D.C.: World Bank.

Verhelst, T. G. 1990. *No Life without Roots: Culture and Development*. London: Zed Books.

Wali, A. 1990. "Living with the Land: Ethnicity and Development in Chile." *Grassroots Development* 14 (2):12–20; reprinted in Spanish 1993 as "En Comunión con la Tierra: Etnicidad y Desarrollo en Chile. En *La Expresión Cultural y el Desarrollo de Base*, comp. C. D. Kleymeyer, 253–269. Quito: Abya-Yala; also in English 1994 in *Cultural Expression and Grassroots Development*, ed. C. D. Kleymeyer, 167–178. Boulder, Colorado: Lynne Rienner.

Warren, D. M. 1992. *Indigenous Knowledge, Biodiversity Conservation and Development*. Ames, Iowa: CIKARD.

Western, D. 1993. "Conserving Savanna Ecosystems Through Community Participation: The Amboseli Case Study." Case study prepared for the Liz Claiborne Art Ortenberg Foundation Community Based Conservation Workshop, October 18–22, Airlie, Virginia.

Wolfe, J., C. Bechard, P. Cizek, and D. Cole. 1992. *Indigenous and Western Knowledge and Resource Management Systems*. Guelph, Ontario: University of Guelph.

CHAPTER 15

The Link Between Local Participation and Improved Conservation: A Review of Issues and Experiences

Peter D. Little

Since the 1970s, the role of local participation has been an important focus of rural development programs. In the same twenty years, the topic has generated a large literature. Local participation's utility for development has drawn both enthusiastic—almost evangelical—praise in certain quarters and wary criticism from others, with the latter usually decrying the concept's idealism and impracticality. Local participation has been used as a tool in the health, education, agriculture, forestry, water, and development sectors. Like so many other concepts in development, local participation usually is vaguely defined and unrigorously applied. Recently, conservationists, who see in local participation a possible means of achieving conservation goals, have utilized the concept in villages surrounding important national parks and protected areas.

While achieving meaningful local participation in rural development activities is difficult, the challenges are even greater in conservation programs. These confront contested trade-offs between rural development and environmental goals, often in situations of widespread poverty and pressing short-term needs. They also raise some key questions: Can conservation programs utilize participatory methods that empower communities to achieve conservation goals rather than development objectives? Can participatory development itself be utilized to achieve conservation goals?

The discussion that follows examines the linkages between local participation and conservation. It is meant to invoke debate rather than develop a definitive statement about the role of local participation in community-based conservation. Examples are drawn not only from the twelve case studies included in this book, but from many others in a massive and rapidly growing field of inquiry. For this reason, terminology and definitions need to be clear from the outset, to avoid confusion and the temptation to classify any effort that relies on local dialogue as a form of local participation.

For the purposes of this discussion, *community-based conservation,* or CBC, refers only to local, voluntary initiatives involving a minimum of several households in which at least one of the outcomes of local management practices is either the maintenance of habitats, the preservation of species, or the conservation of certain critical resources and another outcome is improvement of social and economic welfare. Conservation of biological diversity and the landscapes that support it receives emphasis in this definition, as does the development outcome that qualifies a project as community-based conservation and development. Utilization of concepts from the rural development field would be inappropriate if community-based conservation's only objective were conservation.

The origins and experiences of local participation and rural development constitute the first topic of discussion. The review presented below is not comprehensive but directs the reader to several works that explicitly address the theory and practice of participation in rural development (Cohen and Uphoff 1977; Oakley 1991; Cernea 1985; see Wells and Brandon 1992; West and Brechin 1991 for material specifically related to CBC). Local participation only recently has been invoked in conservation programs, and considerable ambiguity exists about what it actually entails. This brief historical exploration of a relatively new concept and the longer and richer history of its application in sectors such as agriculture and water management points to important opportunities and limitations in community-based conservation programs.

The discussion next turns to the important elements of local participation that could be used to guide considerations of participation and community-based conservation. Because of the variety of topics and processes that could be labeled as *participation* or *community,* a framework or list of important variables through which to filter the range of experiences and allow for comparison is very important. In this way, interested parties can be assured that they are discussing the same phenomena. Taking this tack also makes it easier to steer clear of simplistic notions that so long as local communities are consulted about a certain activity or are employed by a particular project, then the activity in question qualifies as local participation.

The development of this framework also reflects some recent general advances in ecological anthropology and political ecology with relevance to participation and community-based conservation (Schmink and Wood 1987; Blaikie and Brookfield 1987). Most social scientists now assume that conflict is inherent in most types of resource use or conservation, especially when the stakes are high or when "winners" and "losers" clearly are present. Different interest groups or "stakeholders" (Brown and Wyckoff-Baird 1992)—segments of the local "community" including rich and poor, male and female, private companies, the state, international conservation groups, local NGOs, and others—will have varied interests in a resource's use and conservation. While aims may be complementary at times, in most cases these varied interests are actively or potentially conflictive. This general pattern should influence how local participation is structured and point to the different interest groups that must participate in conservation activities.

Competition over forest resources among groups in the Amazon is a good example of this principle of conflict (Schmink and Wood 1987), but other cases can be found in virtually every region of the world (Homewood and Rogers 1991). Conflict may not always be so apparent as in the rubber tappers' movement in Brazil or in some of the grass-roots environmental movements in India, but a trained eye usually can ascertain underlying tensions. Noncompliance with a conservation program (e.g., trespassing on protected lands or failure to contribute labor to a conservation program) is the most common form of local protest in the presence of conflict. In short, it is better to assume that (potential) conflicts will be present, so that options such as written contracts or agreements specifying compensation can be considered. Community-based programs too often are initiated on the basis of an unrealistic understanding of local social dynamics; of competing interest groups, both within and outside the local community; and of the larger political and economic structures that spawn local competition and conflict.

Most social scientists have a favorite ethnographic example of sound community-based conservation. In this discussion, it is important to move beyond these site-specific examples in order to reach general conclusions about local participation's potential importance in community-based conservation. An improved understanding of the different social, political, and historical contexts under which local conservation takes place will help to debunk the false notion that all communities, if left alone, are able to defend and conserve their resources in a sustainable fashion.

The concluding discussion summarizes several unresolved issues surrounding local participation and conservation. Many areas require further observation and research before local participation can be said to improve local conservation definitively. In the meantime, the major lessons learned suggest new directions community-based conservation efforts can take to ensure that the links between participation and conservation are strengthened.

Participation, Rural Development, and Conservation: The Record to Date

Participation has been variously defined as

> an active process by which beneficiary or client groups influence the direction and execution of a development project with a view to enhancing their well-being in terms of income, personal growth, self-reliance or other values they cherish *(Paul 1987, cited in Oakley 1991:6).*

and as

> the organized efforts to increase control over resources and regulative institutions in given social situations on the part of groups and movements of those hitherto excluded from such control *(Pearse and Stiefel 1979, cited in Oakley 1991:6).*

These are not ideal statements, but in combination they include the two main elements of participation: *participation as a goal* in itself that allows communities to have greater control over their lives and resources; and *participation as a means* of achieving improved social and economic objectives. These two dimensions, of course, are not mutually exclusive; in many cases, the second element may prove elusive unless the first objective has been achieved. Several other interpretations of *participation* can be invoked, but conservation programs must confront the two cited above if they are to seriously consider participation as a means of achieving local conservation goals and if they are to borrow the methods and discourse of participatory development. Language is a powerful instrument; thus the extent to which terms such as *participation* are used to disguise what is actually taking place within the social science and development communities needs careful consideration.

The concept of *community-based conservation* as utilized in this discussion also calls for clarification. The literature and the case studies presented in this book rarely define the term (see BACKGROUND), but it seems to imply at least some of the following: local-level, voluntary, people-centered, participatory, decentralized, village-based management. Community-based conservation's terminology borrows heavily from the rural development literature, with implications for its utility in conservation programs. In this context, community-based conservation should involve resource conservation as at least one of its outcomes (although this may be secondary), and it should be linked to some material gain on the part of resource user(s). Cases in which local communities in low-income regions manage their resource bases with the prime objective of conservation—rather than improved social and economic welfare—are virtually nonexistent. On the other hand, many so-called community-based conservation programs (MALUKU ISLANDS; NEOTROPICAL FORESTS) are better described as local resource-management activities that are independent of a particular conservation program or objective.

Rural Development

Many of the lessons derived from local participation and rural development are directly relevant to the problems of community-based conservation. Elements of local participation can be traced to the community development and participatory education programs of the 1950s and 1960s. The concept took on increased importance in the 1970s, as disenchantment with large-scale, top-down development programs emerged. The expensive, centrally managed infrastructure projects that were so popular in the 1960s reflected a strong belief in trickle-down development. Local participation was associated with a new concern for the rural poor, many of whom never were reached by conventional development efforts. In the early 1970s, the so-called McNamara Doctrine of the World Bank and the New Directions of the United States Agency for International Development (USAID) emphasized the poor majority in developing nations and alternatives to large-scale, capital-intensive development interventions that benefited only elites and the urban, industrial sectors (Horowitz and Painter 1986). To reach the poor, these institutions posited, rural communities had to be actively involved in designing and implementing programs; top-down approaches that newly independent states had inherited from their colonial patrons had to be abandoned.

Development practitioners such as Robert Chambers and Norman Uphoff took the lead in advocating local participation in development planning and implementation. An enormous body of literature and experiences gradually began to emerge (Chambers 1983; Uphoff 1985). With considerable rhetoric devoted to local participation, the reality was often quite different; many rural development efforts still incorporated very little meaningful participation by local populations. In many cases, under the rubric *local participation*, an external body or agency decided what should be done, and the local community participated in its implementation and modification.

At approximately the same time, parallel concerns began to appear in three key rural sectors: agriculture, water (especially irrigation), and forestry. As these all involved the use and management of natural resources, they hold important lessons for community-based conservation programs.

In agriculture, researchers and practitioners began to question the wisdom of agricultural planning's reliance upon on-station testing (which opts for testing agricultural techniques and findings on "research stations" and precludes active participation by farmers in the development of suitable new technologies using their own fields), expensive technologies, and a research and extension model that permitted little dialogue with local farmers. Top-down planning had produced inappropriate agricultural practices that were irrelevant to the needs and resources of the small farmers who constituted the majority. By the mid-1970s, the critique of top-down agricultural planning centered around farming systems research and development (FSR&D). Definitions of the FSR&D approach usually include an emphasis on participatory research and extension approaches; a holistic view of the farm family in relation to its physical and social environment; and a focus on the farm family's goals and constraints. The development of new technologies is an important element of FSR&D, but its major emphasis is on building upon existing agricultural practices and knowledge. During the 1980s, several FSR&D programs were implemented, with some successes and some failures. The institutional rigidity that makes most agricultural ministries resistant to programs that call for strong farmer participation has been a problem. Another is donor and government impatience with the slow implementation rate for improved technologies.

Many institutions have withdrawn funding from FSR&D programs because results have not been achieved within a three-to-five-year project cycle.

Similar developments occurred in irrigation research and development of the 1970s and 1980s. Most conventional approaches to irrigation development were irrelevant to the bulk of small-scale farmers. Merrey's work on the Punjab irrigation schemes of Pakistan, for example, demonstrates that highly centralized irrigation management is incapable of dealing with waterlogging and other environmental problems manifested at the local level. These are the result of a management system that does not effectively control water flow to farmers' fields (Merrey 1987). By contrast, in the highly effective irrigation systems of Sri Lanka and parts of the Philippines, local farmers are organized into strong water-user associations, and management decisions are made locally (Coward 1985; Ostrom 1992; Esman and Uphoff 1984). Coward's work in Asia, for instance, shows that strongly participatory village-based irrigation schemes are more effective in responding to environmental and management problems than schemes with centralized management structures. Because many water-management problems manifest locally, they must be attacked at the same level by participants who are familiar with the systems. Perhaps more than any other sector, irrigation reveals the widest range of resource-management activities and the strongest participatory organizations. While this is especially true of South and Southeast Asia, it demonstrates the general importance of eliciting participation at several levels. Irrigation schemes often require participatory organizations at the farm (a group of irrigators), village, canal (usually a group of villages), and district (e.g., the headworks of the water management system) levels—as do many conservation programs.

Finally, the forestry sector began to undergo similar changes in the 1970s, when concepts such as *social forestry* and *community forestry* emerged. These countered the classical forest-management models developed in the North and disseminated to the South through colonial structures and, more recently, international organizations. Like the early rain-fed and irrigated agriculture programs, such forest-management systems were developed with very little input from local populations. Forest departments were perceived locally as sanctioning organizations that handed out fines and punishments to forest trespassers and offenders. Their programs were the antithesis of local participation, and in many developing countries, as Little and Brokensha (1987) point out, most forest management policies simply list what communities *must do* (for instance, build conservation terraces, plant trees, and set aside forest reserves) and *must not do* (cultivate on hillsides and near streams, burn grass, and cut down certain species of trees, or trees of less than a specified size). In many countries, including Kenya, forest departments seemed to invoke all that was restrictive and bad about colonialism, and only recently have local politicians dared to promote forest conservation programs.

In the mid-1980s a workshop on social forestry in eastern and southern Africa concluded that "some form of decentralization, and encouragement of local initiative, were desirable in the forest planning process" (Thomas et al. 1984:47). Most governments and forest departments in Africa simply did not have the capacity and the resources to carry out the level of reforestation and tree planting that is required for the next several decades. Therefore, the workshop participants reasoned, local producers and communities would have to be involved. Confronted with this reality and the acknowledgment that restrictive forest management programs were increasingly problematic, community-based forestry programs were encouraged throughout the 1980s and early 1990s. In response, an entire field of development practitioners—complete with its own journals and associations—emerged, and these groups remain very active. The case study (INDIA) on community resource management in eastern India reflects this new emphasis in forestry programs.

For community-based conservation, the lessons from social forestry and its experiences with local participation are important. Community- and social-forestry programs have had to address the well-publicized dilemma of conservation versus production or development. This issue is less important in farming systems and irrigation programs, because these are tied directly to production and income concerns. Weber and Hoskins point out, however, that this dichotomy may be false:

> Little is gained by trying to decide which of the two views [conservation versus production] is more important. Without adequate supplies of food and water, human lives are quickly placed in jeopardy. Yet, if the available land and water resources are over-used, the base is destroyed and production ceases regardless of availability of technological or capital inputs. (1984:6)

While this observation has validity, the conservation-production dilemma remains problematic and of critical importance in discussing any community-based conservation program.

The first and perhaps most important finding from community forestry programs is that local participation is a time-consuming process. It does not easily lend itself to the institutional environments of ministries, donor agencies, or even some larger nongovernmental organizations, especially those dependent on donor funding. A slow process of design and implementation is needed, as the hurry-up attitude of external funders can squelch local participation.

A second conclusion is that forest protection and reforestation is difficult if the local population does not perceive a crisis or threat. The local forestry case study (INDIA) demonstrates well the local initiatives that communities will take if they perceive a threat to their livelihoods—in this case the indiscriminate cutting of trees by outsiders. Farming systems and small-scale irrigation programs usually do not confront such problems, since farmers easily perceive a direct connection between participation and increased food production and improved welfare. Finally, as in participatory agricultural programs, an institutional environment that is not structured to deal with local participation has hindered social forestry.

The structural adjustment and liberalization programs that have marked donor activities in the 1980s, and thus far in the 1990s, have invoked a different perspective on local participation. Their effects still reverberate throughout the development community and impinge heavily on the conservation sector. Many countries with a strong interest in biodiversity issues such as Madagascar and Uganda currently are confronting massive structural adjustment programs, as well as strong pressure to introduce political reforms. At first, the national-level policy reform programs of the early 1980s seemed to have little direct relevance to local participation. More recently, an emphasis on political liberalization and democratization has been associated with the market liberalization programs of the structural adjustment era. Advocates of these reforms—seeing in local participation the potential for participatory democracy, increased involvement of the private sector, and a way of ensuring the delivery of local services and goods without state involvement—soon co-opted its vocabulary. Participatory local organizations became synonymous with democracy and the private sector, and a renewed vigor for their role in local social and political development emerged.

Thus despite the need to treat local participation and community-based conservation apolitically, the events of the last decade have made this virtually impossible. Structural adjustment and policy reform programs may have increased opportunities for local communities to manage and conserve their resources without government involvement, but, at the same time, it has also greatly politicized local conservation. From the perspective of local communities and organizations, the line between externally imposed economic and political reforms and indigenous environmental reforms grows increasingly blurred.

Participation and Conservation

In important ways, community-based conservation, like FSR&D and social forestry, is a reaction to the highly centralized and nonparticipatory programs of the past. The practice of carving large national parks out of native populations' lands without any local involvement, made possible by restrictive legislation and heavy-handed sanctions, is a classic example of the earlier approach. As pointed out previously, this top-down approach to conservation also was characteristic of many wildlife and forestry departments. Dissatisfaction with such restrictive conservation policies and programs opened the way for more participatory local programs that had conservation and development objectives. The realization that biodiversity conservation programs could not be limited to parks and protected areas also evoked concern for community-based conservation.

Unlike participatory rural development programs, community-based conservation programs are relatively recent, although elements of this approach appeared as early as the 1970s (see AMBOSELI). As with participatory initiatives in other sectors, it is easiest to describe community-based conservation by contrasting it with other approaches. Two decades of experience with local participation and biodiversity conservation has shown that local participation and conservation can not be pursued in isolation from development concerns if community-based conservation programs are to be sustainable. The CAMPFIRE program of Zimbabwe is a good example of a community-based conservation, or CBC, program that has a development outcome; the Amboseli National Park of Kenya is not (see CAMPFIRE and AMBOSELI). If a local population's role is to stay out of a certain (protected) land area or to stop certain management practices (e.g., herding or hunting) in order to preserve biodiversity, accepting compensation or development benefits in exchange, then according to our definition, such a program is not community-based conservation. If economic or other forms of compensation constitute the only means of effecting a biodiversity objective at the local level, then so be it. But language is important for clarity, and such activities should not be confused with community-based conservation, which implies household participation in management decisions and practices and builds upon existing patterns of community resource use. In certain case studies, including KAKADU, NORTH YORK MOORS, and BOSCOSA, monetary incentives are the predominant vehicle for enticing the local population into behavioral change with the goal of preserving biodiversity. By definition, these programs are not participatory CBC either, although members of the community have been involved.

A second lesson involves the importance of acknowledging that participatory CBC is not a panacea for environmental problems, including those related to biodiversity loss. Several case studies apparently assume that if a conservation activity is situated locally and involves local populations, then it is participatory. The presence of a national park or protected reserve administered by a central government entity almost inevitably means that participatory CBC will be highly constrained if not impossible and that strong monetary or other types of compensation will be required to offset losses in land or income. In this context, buffer-zone programs should not be confused with participatory CBC. Even though they are closely linked to a park or protected reserve, the existence of buffer zones has little to do with local decision-making or resource management systems. Neither INDIA, CAMPFIRE, nor MALUKU ISLANDS—the three case studies in this book that most resemble participatory CBC—is associated with a national park or protected area.

Third, using the earlier distinction between participation as a means of achieving certain objectives and participation as a method of empowering local communities, most of the case studies gathered here treat participation as a means rather than as a primary objective. Empowering local communities to manage their own resources without outside interference, sanction resource offenders, and decide upon conservation and development goals has not been a primary objective of most local conservation programs. Even in the case described in CAMPFIRE, a relatively successful local initiative, local communities do not have secure rights to their land and resources and can not make many decisions about land allocation without state involvement. Because contradictions between local development goals and conservation objectives often are glaring, empowerment of local communities may mean that they will decide not to pursue certain conservation goals. Most conservation groups avoid this potential problem by invoking the narrow definition of participation as a means of achieving certain objectives.

Does linking participation with local conservation initiatives really make a difference? Is environmental management or the preservation of biodiversity actually enhanced by promoting participatory efforts? These questions are difficult to answer, especially since the necessary ecological data over time are unavailable for most regions of the world. However, two related approaches may shed some light. The first approach accepts the reality that, since most biodiversity is found outside parks and reserves, conservation efforts must focus on these areas. Working in nonpark areas that are under some form of land ownership—whether communal or private—means that local communities must participate in conservation efforts in a meaningful fashion; any other approach would be politically unfeasible and unrealistic. In this situation, the type of participation that should be encouraged becomes the central question. Reality dictates that some type of local participation must be elicited, with or without empirical proof that local participation enhances conservation objectives.

The second approach proposes a with-or-without scenario for assessing the links between local participation and biodiversity conservation. (This approach is adapted from the work of a USAID-funded Cornell University team that has assessed the impacts of structural adjustment programs in Africa by looking at scenarios with and without reforms.) This tack suggests that, in the absence of strong empirical proof of a positive correlation between local participation and improved resource conservation, doing nothing about local participation produces worse results than trying to promote it. The no-participation scenario resulted in the deforestation problems described in INDIA, the poaching problems that have plagued East African parks (AMBOSELI), and other environmental problems elsewhere in the world. While eastern and southern Africa still face massive poaching problems, the approach described in CAMPFIRE demonstrates that participation can slow rates of resource depletion; INDIA makes a similar case for deforestation.

Critical Elements of Local Participation

The standard framework for discussing participation and development—usually in terms of the design, implementation, and evaluation phases of projects—is inadequate for treating community-based conservation programs, since other issues are important in determining the success or failure of participatory development. Change in the larger policy context of development and conservation calls for careful assessment of the ways in which this larger environment structures and channels local participation. Community-based conservation and development programs that support biodiversity raise additional special considerations. The concern for environmental conservation and loss of biodiversity is in large part a

"Northern" agenda. This means that the environmental agendas of local institutes and communities and the role that local institutes (governmental and nongovernmental) and researchers—rather than expatriate groups and individuals—can play in the design, implementation, and evaluation of conservation activities need careful attention.

Who Participates?

Local participation must start from a realistic appreciation of what a community is. *Community* is a commonly misused term that can invoke a false sense of "tradition," homogeneity, and consensus. Anthropological research during the last twenty years has confirmed that most rural communities are not free of conflict, nor are they homogenous. Participation becomes contingent on assumptions made about "community" members and their social relations. Can male members of the community speak for women? Are the interests of the poor represented by the actions of the rich? Is limiting input to certain members of the community— political leaders, for example—a sufficient condition of participation? In dealing with the question of participation, it is important to use a realistic notion of community, one that acknowledges different interests, competing groups, and negotiated consensus.

As a first step, community-based conservation programs should start with a simple model of who the major interest groups are; their current resource-use motives and whether these conflict with those of other groups; their behavior and its effects on resource use and conservation; and the potential winners and losers as a result of a conservation program. Brown and Wyckoff-Baird (1992) present many empirical examples of conservation problems that have resulted from failure to collaborate with important interest groups or segments of the local population. In the Oku Mountain Forest Project, Cameroon, goat producers (mainly women) were not consulted in the design phase and increasingly have encroached on forest lands with their herds. Local users of forest products other than pasturage, on the other hand, participated in the design of project activities and benefits, and they generally have followed the project's conservation strategies (Brown and Wyckoff-Baird 1992).

In some situations, only certain segments of the local community or region may seem to be appropriate participants. The Jahaly Pacharr irrigation scheme of the Gambia failed miserably because planners only involved male household heads and assumed that women laborers would follow the lead of their husbands. This did not take place, and the project has been plagued by severe labor shortages, land mismanagement, and a dismal economic performance (Carney In press).

Virtually none of the case studies in this volume document women's participation in resource-management decisions, although some point out that cultural norms inhibit their participation in decision-making. At a minimum, women are important resource managers—especially in the case of food production and forest management. Avoiding the issue of their participation in community-based conservation is likely to result in future difficulties, especially if programs assume that they will contribute labor and other resources to conservation efforts. If community-based conservation programs wish to address both environmental and developmental concerns, then they need to look more carefully at gender issues and learn from the experiences of rural development programs during the last two decades (Charlton 1984; Tinker 1990).

Conflict Resolution

The intense local conflicts and struggles that surround land and environmental issues in parts of Latin America and elsewhere raise further questions about the appropriateness of community-based conservation initiatives. In the Beni region of Bolivia (Jones 1990) and certain parts of the Amazon (Schmink and Wood 1987), age-old conflicts and struggles involving extremely powerful interest groups—as well as government policies that clearly favor certain user groups (ranchers and loggers) over others (indigenous peoples)—probably exclude these areas as good candidates for community-based conservation programs.

In the Beni, community-based conservation efforts actually were co-opted by powerful national interests, resulting in increased local conflict and environmental degradation (Jones 1990). Such cases require fundamental changes in land legislation and policy beyond the scope of any community-based effort. Similarly, the bitterness associated with a local history of broken promises regarding the Ngorongoro Conservation Area in northern Tanzania also calls into question the validity of implementing community-based conservation efforts without fundamental changes in conservation policies (Homewood and Rogers 1991).

Resolution of sensitive conflicts between different interest groups, however, is best handled within local and host-country institutions rather than by external institutions. This strategy of participation and conflict resolution is clearly most sustainable and politically palatable. In areas of intense conflict and differences (see BOSCOSA), some groups have been empowered without increasing local conflict and environmental problems. This requires commitment on the part of government. Many conservation problems related to wildlife poaching and deforestation are caused by outsider groups who take advantage of local resources and the community's inability to effectively defend their lands and resources. Communities increasingly find themselves without the authority to sanction outside violators— often because of government policies. The local forestry case study (INDIA) shows the importance of vesting authority to sanction offenders in local communities.

Sharing in the Definition of a Problem

Most community-based conservation programs are initiated on the basis of a perceived environmental problem, while most rural development programs are designed on the basis of assumed social or economic constraints. The critical questions are, whose definition of the problem is being invoked, and who shares in its meaning(s)? This issue often is not addressed. The extent to which the local population shares in problem definition and participates in its identification is a prime factor affecting program success. The matter is especially pertinent in biodiversity programs because so many of the debates on the subject have taken place in the North. Problem identification does not merely mean eliciting dialogue from local villagers but includes the extent to which local NGOs or research institutes participate in the definition of the problem and the degree to which the problem has been translated into terms or situations that have relevance to the local community.

A Maasai-based Tanzanian environmental NGO called Kipoc provides an example of how a local NGO can work with a community to define an environmental problem. Kipoc ("We shall recover" in the Maa language) was started about three years ago with the goal of helping pastoral communities in the northern part of the country to organize themselves and respond to environmental and development problems. Kipoc has worked closely with Maasai herders, helping them use legal and administrative means to recover lost lands and gain income from local wildlife conservation activities that previously had benefited mainly outsiders and tourists. While local herder communities recognize that land degradation is taking place, rarely are they asked to contribute to the definition of the problem or to the design of possible solutions. Discouraged by this exclusion, they "voice" concern or protest by poaching wildlife and grazing their animals within national parks.

Although the conservation and development problems of northern Tanzania are immense and conflict ridden, the presence of a *local* NGO—actually based in local communities, rather than in the capital city—has at least provided an institutional channel for problem identification and communication. As a result, Maasai views have reached the government and wildlife conservation groups. Donors and international NGOs now recognize the presence of this local NGO, and Kipoc has been approached to assist with local conservation and development efforts. While brokering groups potentially can create local dependencies and become part of the problem rather than part of its solution, Kipoc's presence in the region has made government and conservation groups more cognizant of the need to involve communities in the identification of problems and their solutions (see also BOSCOSA).

Rapid appraisal techniques often are used in development projects for initial investigations of local problems and needs. While these can provide a cost-effective and efficient means of eliciting some local input into problem identification, some problems need to be solved before the technique can be used in community-based conservation projects. In-depth investigation is needed to determine the right questions and how to phrase them for rapid survey. Otherwise, the result will be a list of canned problems and needs that may be more reflective of the appraisal team than of the local community. Furthermore, anecdotal survey data are unable to address important issues such as seasonality, intrahousehold resource use, or the history of resource conflicts in the area, nor can they serve as a baseline for measuring changes later in the project.

Many community-based conservation programs have overrelied on rapid or participatory rural appraisals; thus, unlike FSR&D, they have not made the required commitment to systematic data collection that is needed for effective design. A thorough understanding of resource use and management can not be acquired in a two-to-three-week period. Reliance on rapid appraisal techniques also is a major reason why so little baseline data currently are available for evaluating whether community-based conservation has improved either environmental or social welfare.

Very few of the case studies in this book illustrate strong local community participation in the definition of environmental problems and priorities. An exception is the local forestry initiative discussed in INDIA, in which a set of villages acknowledged the issue of a declining forest base and proposed regulations and techniques for dealing with the problem. In contrast to the Indian government and local politicians, the communities themselves pushed very hard for conservation measures: "Jyoti Naik and other village leaders since have met with local political representatives from the area and urged them to put pressure on the northside communities to begin protection activities" (INDIA:58). This is also a good example of a local initiative to improve local resource use and controls.

The CAMPFIRE effort is another community-based conservation program in which a local community participated in the identification of a conservation need—in this case, better management and regulation of wildlife resources (see CAMPFIRE). Although international and national organizations were instrumental in heightening local awareness of conservation problems, the communities themselves saw the linkages between economic benefits and sustainable management of wildlife. The CAMPFIRE program first was initiated in a very poor region of Zimbabwe and took on the appearance of a rural development rather than a conservation project. There, low-income producers saw the economic benefits that could accrue from tourism and hunting while recognizing the threat that poaching posed to these activities. The links between improved income and environmental conservation were especially apparent. There was no significant contradiction between the local goals of improved economic and social welfare and national and international concerns for maintaining the diversity of wildlife.

ANNAPURNA, in turn, presents an interesting Nepalese midpoint. Wells points out that "the perception of a crisis and the need to address it originated from outside the region. But the early initiatives were worked out in face-to-face contact with people who would have to live with the results of any changes" (ANNAPURNA:273). The Annapurna example may be the best that can be expected for many integrated conservation and development programs (ICDPs). In the long run, such an approach may be sustainable only to the extent that environmental problems are internalized locally. In other words, the notion of a conservation problem may be identified externally, but afterward, close work with the community is necessary to incorporate their concerns and communicate the problem in meaningful local terms. Such a process of participation may not involve the community in the initial appraisal of an environmental dilemma, but it ensures that they are strongly involved in how the problem is addressed locally. (For additional discussion of these issues, see Cabarle, Panduro, and Murayari 1993; Martins 1993.)

The Wider Political and Institutional Context

The manner in which a local community participates in development or conservation activities is strongly influenced by the wider policy context. Macro policies affecting access to land and natural resources obviously vary among different countries, reflecting varied political structures and governments. In addition, the extent to which particular states allow local communities meaningful political participation also varies by country. Where the macro policy and political environments are particularly strong determinants (or deterrents) of local participation in conservation programs (for example, as in NIGER), the political issue may prove more significant than any other variable in determining local participation.

In states in which local participation is heavily regulated by government policies, it is still possible—at least in the short to medium term—for meaningful community-based conservation to occur. Many successful local soil conservation programs in Kenya and Uganda have taken place without conducive policy environments and without large amounts of external funding. In a well-documented case in Machakos, Kenya, rates of soil erosion have been reduced since the 1930s, although human population in the area has increased more than 200 percent in the intervening decades. Local households and communities have responded to land shortages and severe soil erosion by shortening fallow periods, improving the quality and maintenance of hillside terraces, and shortening "the time lag between opening new land for cultivation and installing terraces to control erosion" (Thomas 1991:41). In Machakos, Meyers finds that 80 percent of households have bench terraces, and 62 percent have constructed cutoff drains (1981:93). While the macro policy environment has not been particularly conducive to local participation, population and land pressures motivated local communities to address acute environmental problems anyway.

The question of decentralization is a strong determinant of the extent to which local populations can be meaningfully involved in project-design activities. In each of the conservation cases from industrialized states, authority is strongly decentralized, and local communities and individuals enter into written contracts and agreements with the central government. Because the communities legally own land, either privately or collectively, and are represented by elected officials, the state is compelled to incorporate these communities into the design of any program activities. The programs presented in NORTH YORK MOORS and KAKADU could not have been initiated without the willing participation of the local communities. The involvement of local communities in institutionally complex societies often is formal and legalistic. For example, the Aboriginal community described in KAKADU has a lease arrangement with the Australian federal government that specifies the revenues and other benefits to be allotted them. The legal arrangements now provide for "termination of the lease if issues of detriment to the Aboriginal traditional owners can not be resolved" (KAKADU:147). Likewise, in NORTH YORK MOORS, each of the park's landowners has a written agreement with the United Kingdom government specifying legal conditions and economic compensation.

Certain programs in the Third World also have used formal contracts between local communities and government and other organizations to specify the responsibilities, obligations, and rewards of each. In areas where resource control is ambiguous and potential conflicts exist, contracts can be innovative tools for ensuring that participating groups are rewarded for their contributions. In rural Gambia, for example, a USAID-financed natural resources program is exploring possible land and forest-resource management contracts between communities and the state. These contracts will be entered into freely and will specify the government's and local communities' different responsibilities and incentives for improved conservation.

Design and Implementation

Local communities generally are more likely to be involved in project implementation than in design activities. Local populations' participation in design, when it takes place, often centers around issues of compensation and incentive infrastructure rather than resource conservation. Local involvement in the design phase does not necessarily ensure a successful project, since consensus on priorities and problems may never be reached. In the case of the Korup Project in Cameroon, for instance, local hunters participated in the design stage but were never convinced of the benefits of hunting alternatives. Therefore, contrary to project objectives, "hunting . . . has not declined significantly" (Brown and Wyckoff-Baird 1992:10).

AMBOSELI, KAKADU, and BOSCOSA describe conservation efforts in which communities were involved in the design of compensation activities to varying degrees. The most challenging of these, in terms of eliciting local participation in the design of activities, is the BOSCOSA project located in the conflict-ridden Osa Peninsula of Costa Rica. The project has dealt with an extremely diverse local population of small and large farmers, indigenous peoples, colonists/settlers, gold miners, ranchers, and others. Because of the tensions and heterogeneity of the population, the program designers proposed to work mainly through local grass-roots NGOs rather than deal directly with unorganized farmers. Within this institutional context, however, "local people would be the decision makers, selecting the forestry, agriculture, or other development alternatives that they wanted (i.e., ultimately they would design and implement their own projects)" (BOSCOSA:222). Local people decide which production activities and techniques should be supported and determine the "distribution of costs and benefits, and sharing of project financing" (BOSCOSA:222). The bitter conflicts surrounding conservation in the Osa Peninsula

PARTICIPATION 363

present an extreme example, and the BOSCOSA program has been prudent in trying to mediate and reconcile conflicts within networks of local institutions.

Many well-intentioned environmental initiatives have precluded much local participation because they were designed using technologies that are either too expensive or too labor intensive to maintain locally. Not a few small-scale irrigation programs in the Sahel and eastern Africa that were originally designed to be participatory have failed because the technologies could not be maintained without external assistance. The failure of motorized boreholes around Amboseli National Park in Kenya also illustrates how technology can preclude a local role in management and maintenance activities (although, in this case, the Maasai themselves requested this form of technology). This is true for water- and land-conservation programs that rely heavily on labor-intensive maintenance techniques. Many small-scale soil-conservation efforts in Ethiopia and northern Kenya exceed local capacities to contribute labor while still maintaining food-production activities.

Local Empowerment

Participation in policy decisions and program design usually is accompanied by some form of decentralization, which can result in real delegation of authority and empowerment of the local community. Too often, however, decentralization of resource-management activities means devolution of authority from the center to the periphery while power remains at the center. "Decentralization" then results in further concentration of power as technical ministries and central authorities carry out policies and programs from the top by placing their representatives in local areas. For the community, this type of decentralization means more responsibility in the management and implementation of activities but little real authority to affect resource use. Some important indicators of genuine decentralization include the extent to which financial decisions and revenue-raising activities are given over to local communities; community authority to negotiate with external bodies (including regional and central government entities) and agencies; and community power to sanction resource offenders as well as reward favorable practices.

Decentralization of decision-making has considerable implications for local resource use. While many rural communities have mechanisms—either formal or informal—for managing such critical resources as rangelands and forests (Brokensha et al. 1983; Sandford 1983), local regulations often prove ineffective in halting encroachment and environmental degradation by outside groups and organizations. The state itself plays a major role in undermining the power and autonomy of local organizations, leaving a vacuum in which outsiders can increase their control of local resources. In Sudan, for example, the government took control of range regulation from local authorities in the late 1960s (Haaland 1980), while in Botswana, indigenous institutions have been supplanted by district land boards that currently regulate access to land and water (Gulbrandsen 1980). In both cases, outsiders have benefited from the changes, and environmental degradation has been the result. In many cases, African states' usurpation of power has been incomplete, creating for farmers and herders what Runge (1981) calls a problem of "assurance." In such situations, producers lack confidence in state or local institutions' capacity to regulate access to resources, creating ambiguity about who has legal rights to forest, water, and other natural resources. In many cases, lack of assurance has resulted in the conversion of common-property systems (with well-defined rules and regulations) to open-access systems and widespread environmental problems (Little and Horowitz 1987; Little 1992).

Importance of Local Organizations

Local participation by community members usually is contingent upon the presence of one or more local organizations capable of channeling its opinions and inputs. These can be so-called indigenous organizations or newly formed local institutions that nevertheless represent different segments of the population. Emphasis on using indigenous or "traditional" organizations for eliciting local participation often is misplaced. What is traditional is not at issue but, rather, an organization's capacity as a vehicle for eliciting participation—a condition newly formed organizations often can meet.

Strong local organizations are the norm rather than the exception in industrialized countries. In general, the tradition of grass-roots organizations and NGOs is much stronger in Latin America and Asia than in Africa. In African countries, the state and, to a lesser extent, international agencies occupy so much of the political and organizational space that little room is left for the formation of strong grass-roots organizations. In Niger, for instance, the first local NGO was started only five years ago (see NIGER). In comparison to the organizational environments described in INDIA and BOSCOSA, sub-Saharan Africa is extremely undeveloped with regard to indigenous NGOs.

Whether working through traditional or customary organizations—rather than relatively new institutions—to promote participatory conservation programs offers any special advantages depends upon whether the organizations are truly representative of local interests and whether they are still viable under current circumstances. Resurrecting traditional institutions without addressing the factors that caused their decline is unlikely to be effective. In AMBOSELI, the project worked through newly created group ranch organizations, although it is difficult to know whether these organizations coincided with or competed against indigenous resource-management groups. The program described in CAMPFIRE also used relatively novel local organizations that have certain administrative responsibilities in Zimbabwe's hierarchy of government structures, but it is unclear to what extent they overlap with customary units of authority. The MALUKU ISLANDS case, which details marine resource management in Indonesia, makes the excellent point that it really does not matter whether or not *sasi*—an institution for regulating fish catches—is traditional. Its current functions and importance in local resource-management systems *are* significant, even though *sasi* originally may have been introduced by European traders.

In the end, so-called traditional organizations have to be evaluated according to the same criteria as any local institution. Experiences with local participation suggest that it is better to work through existing local organizations—customary or not—than to establish new institutions, which can be time-consuming and complex (see INSTITUTIONS). Where effective local organizations are absent, community-based conservation programs should attempt to introduce them (see BOSCOSA). Water management projects have enjoyed some success in crafting new institutions for resource management, and could serve as possible models for conservation activities (Ostrom 1991).

In many case studies, when local organizations are not community-based, a conscious effort has been made to use national NGOs and local research organizations in design and implementation and, in some cases, in monitoring and evaluation of activities. The CAMPFIRE program is a collaborative effort by a local NGO; the Centre for Applied Social Sciences, University of Zimbabwe; district councils; and the government's wildlife department. Virtually all of the research for the program has been carried out by or in collaboration with local organizations. The INDIA, MALUKU ISLANDS, and ANNAPURNA case studies describe strong research support by local NGOs and universities. This type of cooperation helps to ensure that local professionals and institutions have a vested interest in the program; that dialogue over policy and community participation is not dominated by expatriate researchers and institutes; and that local research capacity is strengthened while increasing the probability that research and monitoring efforts will be sustained after expatriate personnel withdraw. It also reduces the financial burden of the project, since large numbers of expatriate researchers are not brought in to carry out data collection.

Both CAMPFIRE and AMBOSELI point to the importance of involving district and other organizations in local conservation programs. Wildlife extends well beyond the boundaries of any single community or collection of communities, as do wetlands, lakes, and rivers. Decisions made at the district or regional level may prove critical for community-based conservation programs.

The Economics of Participation

The critical role that economic incentives play in motivating community-based conservation is now widely accepted. Yet certain activities or programs are more advantageous than others in their potential to generate economic benefits. Conservation interventions that are closely linked to production and income gains and build on existing production systems, for example, are most likely to elicit participation. Lucrative tourism (see KAKADU, AMBOSELI, CAMPFIRE, and ANNAPURNA) and

other programs that rely on a valuable natural resource such as a high-value marine or forest product (MALUKU ISLANDS; Martin 1993) also possess great potential for
generating both local income and community support. The presence of lucrative
crops, in turn, is an additional motivating factor for improved conservation. Referring again to the case of Machakos in Kenya, the data show a strong correlation between the cash value of a farmer's crops and his willingness to undertake soil-conservation work. Meyers notes that "the more important the crop sales are to the
farmer, the better managed is the shamba [farm]" (1981:97). Many conservation
programs, however, do not meet these criteria and rely on other types of incentives
that involve compensation or provision of social infrastructure. While the latter
approach may be the only way to acquire local support, such projects should not
be confused with community-based conservation that builds on local production
practices and is likely to be highly sustainable.

AMBOSELI, KAKADU, and BOSCOSA describe local communities involved in deciding
the types of compensation to be provided in lieu of access to certain resources or
in exchange for restrictions on certain economic activities. Community members
in KAKADU, BOSCOSA, and NORTH YORK MOORS are paid cash compensation (or rent) for
conservation investments. In the BOSCOSA project in Costa Rica, farmers received approximately US$700/ha over a five-year period following certain conser-
vation measures. Payments on a per-land-unit basis were considerably higher in
North York Moors in the United Kingdom. In Amboseli, Kenya, compensation to
local herders who lost access to dry-season waterpoints in the national park was in
the form of water infrastructure. The government, with support from international
organizations, provided a series of boreholes outside the park for herders to use.
Unfortunately, the government failed in its maintenance obligations, and considerable local resettlement and conflict resulted.

Economic benefits from community-based conservation are rarely documented
systematically. Exceptions are AMBOSELI, which presents useful data on the economic benefits of the program to local herders, and CAMPFIRE, which is more explicit
on the distribution of revenues to communities who have participated in the program. The KAKADU and NORTH YORK MOORS case studies detail the revenues paid to
local farmers and communities in two very different contexts. ANNAPURNA implies
that economic benefits have accrued but notes that very few economic data are
available. CRATER MOUNTAIN provides only sketchy information on the economic
benefits local communities and participants have received. Only AMBOSELI and
AMAZON attempt an opportunity-cost analysis that compares economic benefits
under the program with the likely accrual of benefits in the absence of a conservation initiative.

Monitoring and Evaluation

An important reason for the lack of understanding of economic benefits is the minimal monitoring or information gathering in many community-based programs.

Data rarely are provided on those segments of the community that have benefited the most, and revenue information is not categorized by gender or other social criteria. Thus while the authors of the case studies in this book seem to agree that economic benefits are an important ingredient for eliciting community participation in conservation programs, gauging just how important these have been is difficult in most cases. In this regard, however, NORTH YORK MOORS, KAKADU, and CAMP-FIRE leave little question that economic incentives have been the major factor in eliciting strong participation and support by local communities.

Monitoring and evaluation systems should be an integral element of any community-based initiative for other reasons as well. Most important is the need for timely information that can be used to adjust programs during their implementation. The full range of issues can not be covered in the design of a conservation program, and unexpected problems are likely to arise during implementation. Experience with community-based conservation is relatively recent, and it is important to learn from new initiatives. This means that data of good quality are needed and that information on baseline indicators should be collected prior to a program's implementation. At a minimum, it is important to have data on patterns of resource ownership and practices, local organizations, agricultural and other income-earning activities, labor availability, local knowledge systems, and community and household demographics. CAMPFIRE presents an important model for involvement of local researchers and institutions in these research and monitoring activities.

Research results also need to be accessible to local populations. Field seminars and workshops are excellent vehicles for discussing study results with local communities. Most communities have some literate members who can serve as local translators, but efforts to translate research findings into local languages should be encouraged. Under the Senegal River Basin Monitoring Program, the Institute for Development Anthropology (IDA) held several workshops and provided translations of their summary analyses to the community. These were used with considerable success in environmental negotiations with government and donor officials.

Conclusion

Several important points from the preceding discussion have implications for strengthening the links between local participation and community-based conservation. The first concerns the importance of a conducive institutional environment for promoting local participation. Considerable data support the finding that proper legal and institutional structures play a key role in supporting local participation in development and community-based conservation. Since many local conservation problems stem from encroachment by nonlocal interest groups, local communities' authority to sanction and reward resource users is important.

Whether community-based conservation programs constitute appropriate vehicles for implementing regional or national policy reforms remains doubtful. In many cases, empowerment of the local community through legislation and other means, so that its members can effectively manage and defend their resources from outsider infringement, is the major requirement. At a minimum, policies and laws should not preclude local communities' participation in conservation decisions or benefits. If land rights or other policies are skewed so that they make community-based initiatives ineffective, then community-based conservation activities probably should be avoided.

The earlier in the program cycle that local participation is encouraged—preferably at the problem-identification and design stages—the greater the probability that sustainable community involvement will occur in later phases. In many cases, communities have been only minimally involved in program design but are nonetheless expected to participate or, in some cases, provide labor and other resources during the implementation of program activities. Not surprisingly, under such circumstances local community members often show little enthusiasm for a program and react to it with considerable resentment and resistance. In the past, programs not uncommonly assumed community commitment ("participation"), including allocation of communally owned land, but did not allow communities a voice in the program's design.

There remains the question of whether participatory conservation programs should avoid areas of intense social and land-use conflict. Taking sides with certain groups and seeking participation only from them carries both risks and benefits. If conflicting interests are irreconcilable at the local or regional levels, externally funded community-based programs face a strong danger of subversion by local or outside interest groups, which could eventually accelerate both environmental problems and tensions. Resolution of sensitive conflicts between different interest groups is best handled within local and host-country institutions.

Local participation is almost always easier in the presence of one or more local organizations. Working through existing local organizations—customary or not—clearly is better than establishing new institutions, which can be an extremely difficult and time-consuming exercise. Particular attention needs to be paid to local organizations' and communities' participation in the definition of environmental agendas; the same goes for the role that local institutes and researchers can play in the design, implementation, and evaluation of conservation activities. Many well-intentioned community initiatives have precluded participation by local organizations because they introduce technologies that are either too expensive or too labor-intensive to maintain locally.

On the revenue side of local participation, the case studies hold valuable lessons. Although they describe programs in high-income countries, NORTH YORK MOORS and KAKADU demonstrate the central role that economic incentives assume in local conservation projects. If local priorities are incompatible with specific conservation objectives (e.g., conservation is not an important local priority), then economic compensation and negotiations must be an integral part of the activity. In such cases, local participation may be more narrowly defined in economic terms than in programs in which conservation and local development goals are not so far apart. Realistic ways of properly accounting for the real opportunity costs of conservation activities, including the costs of local land and labor and economic activities foregone by the local community, are urgently needed. Local participation can not be delinked from development concerns if community-based conservation is to be sustainable.

Participatory conservation efforts generally rely too heavily on rapid resource appraisals and do not make the necessary commitment to systematic data collection. CAMPFIRE and NORTH YORK MOORS demonstrate the importance of systematic monitoring of social and economic impacts and the need for local organizations' participation in this activity. Detailed socioeconomic data need to be gathered on a series of important baseline indicators (e.g., resource use and ownership, community and household demography, and income-earning strategies). Many countries place strong limitations on local research and institutional capacities; thus some support from expatriate researchers and institutions may be necessary, especially in a program's early years. In the latter case, some training of local staff may be required to ensure that the necessary skills are developed. Since the concept of ICDP is still at an experimental stage, it is absolutely necessary that periodic monitoring and data collection take place. In addition, programs should be designed with enough inherent flexibility that modifications to the design can be made on the basis of the monitoring exercise.

Community-based conservation should confront the pitfalls that integrated rural development (IRD) programs faced in the 1970s and 1980s. By trying to do everything—from agriculture and forestry to roads and water—IRD programs actually accomplished very little. They were spread over too many sectors and organizations and ministries and became implementational and institutional nightmares. While eradicating local poverty may be the most effective means of achieving environmental goals, this does not mean that community-based conservation must confront all dimensions of poverty. In many cases, conservation can be improved through the support of existing agricultural programs rather than through a new conservation initiative.

Local participation is a time-consuming process that does not easily lend itself to the institutional environments of ministries, donor agencies, and even some NGOs, especially those dependent on donor funding. There is a danger that the impatient attitude of external funders can stifle local participation and derail the slow process of design and implementation that is needed.

A potential problem also exists in that excessive expectations can be raised about the merits of participation and community-based conservation. The approach can become so overextended by diverse activities that it fails to achieve the goals of either local participation or improved conservation. Community-based conservation must acknowledge its limitations and downplay current perceptions of the concept as a panacea for all local conservation problems.

SOURCES

Blaikie, P., and H. Brookfield. 1987. *Land Degradation and Society.* London: Methuen.

Brown, M., and B. Wyckoff-Baird. 1992. *Designing Integrated Conservation and Development Projects.* Washington, D.C.: Biodiversity Support Program of the World Wildlife Fund, The Nature Conservancy, and the World Resources Institute.

Cabarle, B. J., with M. H. Panduro, and O. M. Murayari. 1993. "Ecofarming in the Peruvian Amazon: The Integrated Family and Communal Gardening Project (HIFCO)." Case Study 11 prepared for the Liz Claiborne Art Ortenberg Foundation Community Based Conservation Workshop, October 18–22, Airlie, Virginia.

Carney, J. In press. "Contracting a Food Staple in the Gambia." In *Living Under Contract: Contract Farming and Agrarian Transformation in Sub-Saharan Africa,* eds. P. Little and M. Watts. Madison: University of Wisconsin Press.

Cernea, M., ed. 1985. *Putting People First: Sociological Variables in Rural Development.* New York: Oxford University Press.

Chambers, R. 1983. *Rural Development: Putting the Last First.* London: Longman.

Charlton, S. E. 1984. *Women in Third World Development.* Boulder, Colorado: Westview Press.

Cohen, J., and N. Uphoff. 1977. *Rural Development Participation: Concepts and Measures for Project Design, Implementation and Evaluation.* Ithaca, New York: Rural Development Committee, Cornell University.

Coward, W. 1985. "Technical and Social Change in Currently Irrigated Regions: Rules, Roles, and Rehabilitation." In *Putting People First: Sociological Variables in Rural Development,* ed. M. Cernea, 27–90. New York: Oxford University Press.

Esman, M. J., and N. T. Uphoff. 1984. *Local Organization: Intermediaries in Rural Development.* Ithaca, New York: Cornell University Press.

Gulbrandsen, O. 1980. *Agro-Pastoral Production and Communal Land Use: A Socio-Economic Study of the Banqwaketse.* Gaborone: Ministry of Agriculture.

Haaland, G. 1980. "Social Organization and Ecological Pressure in Southern Darfur." In *Problems of Savannah Development: The Sudan Case,* ed. G. Haaland, 55–105. Occasional Paper No. 19. Bergen, Norway: Department of Social Anthropology, University of Bergen.

Homewood, K., and W. A. Rogers. 1991. *Maasailand Ecology: Pastoralist Development and Wildlife Conservation in Ngorongoro, Tanzania.* Cambridge, England: Cambridge University Press.

Horowitz, M. M., and T. Painter. 1986. *Anthropology and Rural Development in West Africa.* Boulder, Colorado: Westview Press.

Jones, J. 1990. "Native Movement and March in Eastern Bolivia: Rationale and Response." *Development Anthropology Network* 8:1–8.

Little, P. D. 1992. *Elusive Granary: Herder, Farmer, and State in Northern Kenya.* Cambridge, England: Cambridge University Press.

———, and D. Brokensha. 1987. "Local Institutions, Tenure, and Resource Management in East Africa." In *Conservation in Africa: People, Policies, and Practice,* ed. D. Anderson and R. Grove, 193–209. New York: Cambridge University Press.

———, and M. M. Horowitz, eds. 1987. *Lands at Risk in the Third World: Local-Level Perspectives.* Boulder, Colorado: Westview Press.

Martins, E. 1993. "Extractive Reserves: A Critical Analysis, Brazil." Case study prepared for the Liz Claiborne Art Ortenberg Foundation Community Based Conservation Workshop, October 18–22, Airlie, Virginia.

Merrey, D. J. 1987. "The Local Impact of Centralized Irrigation Control in Pakistan: A Sociocentric Perspective." In *Lands at Risk in the Third World: Local-Level Perspectives,* ed. P. D. Little and M. M. Horowitz. Boulder, Colorado: Westview Press.

Meyers, L. R. 1981. "Organization and Administration of Integrated Rural Development in Semi-Arid Areas: The Machakos Integrated Development Program." Unpublished report to USAID, Nairobi. Photocopy.

Oakley, P. 1991. *Projects with People: The Practice of Participation in Rural Development.* Geneva: International Labour Organization.

Ostrom, E. 1991. *Crafting Institutions for Self-Governing Irrigation Systems.* San Francisco: Institute for Contemporary Studies.

Paul, S. 1987. *Community Participation in Development Projects.* Discussion Paper No. 6. Washington, D.C.: World Bank.

Pearse, A., and M. Stiefel. 1979. *Inquiry into Participation.* Geneva: United Nations Research Institute for Social Development (UNRISD).

Runge, C. F. 1981. "Common Property Externalities: Isolation, Assurance, and Resource Depletion in a Traditional Grazing Context." *American Journal of Agricultural Economics* 63:595–606.

Sandford, S. 1983. *Management of Pastoral Development in the Third World.* Chichester, England: John Wiley and Sons.

Schmink, M., and C. H. Wood. 1987. "The 'Political Ecology' of Amazonia." In *Lands at Risk in the Third World: Local-Level Perspectives,* ed. P. D. Little and M. M. Horowitz, 38–57. Boulder, Colorado: Westview Press.

Thomas, D. B. 1991. "Soil Erosion." In *Environmental Change and Dryland Management in Machakos District, Kenya 1939–1990: Environmental Profile,* ed. M. Mortimore. Working Paper No. 53. London: Overseas Development Institute.

———, D. Brokensha, P. Little, and B. Riley. 1984. *Understanding Tree Use in Farming Systems.* Rome: Food and Agriculture Organization.

Tinker, I. 1990. *Persistent Inequality: Women and World Development.* New York: Oxford University Press.

Uphoff, N. 1985. "Fitting Projects to People." In *Putting People First: Sociological Variables in Rural Development,* ed. M. Cernea, 359–395. New York: Oxford University Press.

Weber, F., and M. Hoskins. 1984. "Farming Systems Research and Development and/or Agroforestry." *Farming Systems Support Project Newsletter* 2:3–6.

Wells, M., and K. Brandon. 1992. *People and Parks: Linking Protected Area Management with Local Communities*. Washington, D.C.: World Bank.

West, P. C., and S. R. Brechin, eds. 1991. *Resident Peoples and National Parks: Social Dilemmas and Strategies in International Conservation*. Tucson, Arizona: University of Arizona Press.

CHAPTER 16

Tenurial Rights and Community-based Conservation

Owen J. Lynch and Janis B. Alcorn

A growing number of conservationists have con-
cluded that secure property rights are essential elements for community-based
conservation (CBC) initiatives (Brown and Wyckoff-Baird 1992). According to at
least one analyst, it is more important for conservationists to promote recognition
or establishment of appropriate property rights in buffer zones and conservation
areas than to establish appropriate vegetation structures and land use in buffer
zones.

A major challenge for conservationists is to promote tenure incentives in situations where communities have no state-recognized tenurial rights. Conservationists need a solid understanding of the dimensions of tenure (particularly community-based tenure), the existing range of relationships between tenure and
conservation, and the procedural challenges that they may face if they choose to
pursue strengthening local tenure.

Several of the case studies in this book highlight the relationship between
tenurial security and conservation incentives. Only a few (KAKADU, AMBOSELI, and
CAMPFIRE) provide any detailed analysis of tenure considerations or explicitly lay
out any practical procedures used for addressing them.

Community-based conservation implies that local communities are making
management decisions. Communities must have or gain tenurial security in order
to make management decisions, either by themselves or as members of decision-
making boards that include other stakeholders.

Community-based Tenure:
Some Common Characteristics

Tenure is often misunderstood as defining relationships between people and property; in fact, tenure defines social relations between people. Those with tenurial
rights have a certain social status vis-à-vis natural resources in comparison to
those without tenurial rights to those resources. In other words, tenure determines

who can (and can't) do what with the property in question and under which circumstances they can (or can't) do it.

Tenurial rights may be held by the state, a corporation, an individual, a nuclear or extended family (clan), a neighborhood, or a community. Terms such as *ownership* and *leasehold* oversimplify the complex nature of rights and relationships. Rights often overlap and invariably encompass spatial, temporal, demographic, and legal dimensions. Tenure specialists acknowledge this complexity when they describe tenure as encompassing a "bundle" of rights and responsibilities. Natural resources rights, for example, may include rights of direct use, rights of indirect economic gain, rights of control, rights of transfer, residual rights, and symbolic rights (Crocombe 1971).

Community-based tenure systems usually include a complex mixture of group and individual property rights. As with state-created property rights, none is absolute or permanently fixed. The distinguishing characteristic of community-based tenure systems is that they draw their primary legitimacy from the community in which they operate and not from the nation-state in which they are located. In other words, local participants, not the national government, are the primary allocators and enforcers of local rights to resources. This is true whether the community-based tenurial system covers areas the state deems to be private or public.

Although community-based tenure systems are extremely variable, complex mixtures of individual and common-property rights, they often share several characteristics. Community-based tenure systems, for example, tend to be flexible and ever evolving. They are more than just a set of rights; they are institutional systems that include processes for establishing and allocating property rights to groups or individuals, including tenurial rights to specific agricultural lands, trees, or other resources within the community's territory. Traditional tenure systems also include conflict-resolution mechanisms and strategies of varying effectiveness for defending the local resource base against incursions by outsiders and resolving intracommunity disputes.

Rights to use or manage a given patch of forest, particularly its trees, wildlife, or water resources, may overlap in a community-based tenure system. As seen in NIGER, seasonal migrants may have forest-access or wildlife-use rights at certain times of the year. Seasonal flooding of agricultural land under individual tenure may create ponds to which the entire community has fishing rights. The rights of pastoralists, foragers, fishers, and peripatetics to move across a given space further demonstrates the complex political nature of group rights over resources (Casimir and Rao 1992).

Community-based tenurial rights and responsibilities can be inherited in complex ways, and bundles of rights often get reorganized in each new generation. For example, an individual's lifelong right to farm a particular piece of land may be returned to his or her community upon death, and the elders may allocate that land to an unrelated person. Rights to protected fruit trees in the forest or to certain fishing grounds may be allocated to someone else. At the same time, however, people may not think of themselves or of anyone else as having "ownership" in the sense that land can be sold; instead, land is an inalienable part of the community. As a Pacific Melanesian man told John Cordell, "I couldn't sell you my land. That would be like cutting off my arm and selling it to you. It would be of no use to you." Likewise, indigenous peoples commonly say that the land owns the people. These complexities make it difficult for outsiders to fully understand or accurately codify the structure of a given community's tenure system and hence presents a particular challenge for community-based conservation.

Perhaps most important from a conservation perspective, community-based property systems generally evolve with the changing availability of the resource. As a resource becomes scarce, communities often restrict use rights and institute enforcement mechanisms. Local ecological feedback can have an impact on the system. Likewise, community-based systems evolve with changing historical relationships between different communities, including relationships with outsiders (such as conservationists, the military, or commercial buyers). Community-based systems are not operated by "ecologically noble savages" living in harmony with nature (see NEOTROPICAL FORESTS:315), nor by individuals whose best interest is always to seek short-term gain, but by individuals responding to tenurial and other incentives to act in their own best interest and maintain the collective resource base (Berkes 1989; McCay and Acheson 1987; Gadgil and Berkes 1991; Ostrom, Walker, and Gardner 1992).

Community-based Tenure: Private or Public?

In supporting community-based conservation, it is important to clarify the distinctions between public and private ownership on the one hand and individual and group rights on the other. *Public* is the legal label applied to natural resources owned by the government. *Private* refers to resource rights owned by nonstate entities, whether individually or as groups. Thus as with individual ownership, community-based tenure systems can involve private rights. The second point to be made is that community tenure systems almost always include *both* individual and group (or common-property) rights.

Most tenure theorists, meanwhile, use a different topology that recognizes four basic types of property rights: private, common, state, and open-access (situations in which no property rights or no rules limiting access have been defined). There are two fundamental flaws in this topology. First, private ownership usually is deemed synonymous with individual ownership, when, in fact, group ownership also can be private. Second, the topology virtually requires that community-based tenurial systems that include both individual and group rights must be disentangled and separated before any of these rights can be recognized by the nation-state concerned. The very process of separating individual group rights may render the community-based system ineffective. Furthermore, group rights often overlap, and within a given community, there may be several distinct groups.

An alternative classification scheme that has advantages for conceptualizing and implementing improved laws and policies for supporting community-based conservation entails four tenure combinations: private individual, private group, public individual, and public group. Each combination refers to a bundle of rights. Private-group and public-group tenure often include overlapping individual and common-property rights located within the perimeter of a particular area.

While private individual tenurial rights can be legitimized through titles or leases the state grants to legal entities (individuals, corporations, etc.), private-property rights (whether individual or group) need not always be contingent on state grants or documentation. Some private-property rights predate and are independent from the nation-states where they are located; many traditional community-based tenure systems fall within this category.

Property rights are not, and should not, always be contingent on state grants or documentation. More often than not, however, long-established community-based tenurial rights are not recognized by nation-states (Lynch 1990; Siriat et al. 1992). Instead, most national governments promote expansive claims of state ownership and insist that community-based property rights are not legally recognizable unless they are established and documented pursuant to grants from the state. There are exceptions, and some states have recognized preexisting community-based tenurial rights through innovative mechanisms such as the Panamanian semiautonomous *comarca* and the Aboriginal Trust described in KAKADU. Such recognition enables communities to maintain customary law within their "private" territories.

The advantage of private community-based property rights is that there is usually more local control and less governmental regulation than if property rights were deemed "public" and owned by the state. As will be discussed, ineffective government regulation has resulted in a substantial loss of biodiveristy. NORTH YORK MOORS reveals that holders of private-property rights can legally oblige the government "to rely on the agreement and cooperation of the landowners to achieve its land-management aims (290)." They also oblige the government to give better notice and pay compensation before expropriating rights for public purposes. Private rights generally provide the holder with greater bargaining leverage and therefore tend to establish a more durable comanagement structure for sharing both rights and responsibilities between communities and government.

But no property rights, including private ones, are absolute; all property rights located within the boundaries of nation-states are subject to some degree of regulation. The recognition or grant of private rights therefore does not preclude governments from taking steps to ensure that conservation objectives are being met by the holders of these rights and from intervening when they are not. Zoning laws are a prime example of this governmental prerogative. In some instances, forest zoning laws, wildlife laws, and other restrictive policies can assist communities in achieving conservation objectives.

How tenure is officially classified depends in large measure on the state's interest in the resources in question. In most developing countries, large areas (including areas gazetted as forest land), water, and mineral resources are deemed by the nation-state to be "public." Communities living within these areas, by contrast, often consider the natural resources within their locales to be "private." More often than not, however, nation-states do not recognize such community-based tenurial rights. Instead, most national governments promote expansive claims of state ownership and insist that local property rights—whether group or individual—are not legally cognizable unless they are established pursuant to documented grants from the state. The conservation issue is whether these state claims of ownership promote or weaken the conservation of resources.

Finally, the difference between what is legally or formally the case and what actually occurs on the ground should be recognized. While forest or other natural resources may be owned by the state or by indigenous peoples on paper, the people who live in or use a given area often determine what happens to its resources. The tenurial security necessary for effective community-based conservation does not only mean rights on paper, but also state acceptance and exercise of its responsibility to assist communities in exercising their right to defend their territories and their biodiversity.

Relationships Between Tenure and Conservation

With these tenurial complexities in mind, what are the general relationships between tenure and conservation? What are the known problems associated with strong, "public" tenure, or "state ownership"? When does strong private, community-based tenurial security contribute to conservation success? What kinds of balances between state and community tenurial rights can have positive impacts? When might private individual titling be viable as a conservation option? Comparison of the conservation effectiveness of public or state tenure versus community tenure is important because these represent the two primary conservation options in areas of relatively high biological diversity.

By briefly assessing states' performance in managing forest, wildlife, and fishery resources under "public" tenure; considering under which range of conditions community-based tenurial security may contribute to reaching conservation objectives (including situations of comanagement as well as situations in which communities have semi-independent status); and briefly considering situations in which conservation ends can be served by granting private individual tenure, we can attempt to answer these questions.

Conservation Performance under "Public" Tenure

No global assessments of the success of state-owned parks and protected areas exist. The Nature Conservancy's assessment of parks in Latin America found that the ecological integrity of many of the parks surveyed was at risk. An informal survey of knowledgeable field biologists from Latin America, Africa, and Asia yielded the uniform opinion that states everywhere are failing to carry out their full responsibilities to manage biodiversity and in fact may be contributing to its destruction. The status of the world's "public" forest reserves is better studied; rapid deforestation of these forests has been recognized as a global crisis.

Conservation failures under strong public tenure are, in part, the result of factors noted in NEOTROPICAL FORESTS and POLICY: government's tendency to support economic development, its lack of sensitivity to socioeconomic needs and conservation interests, and its lack of resources to monitor resource conditions. In addition, many case studies (see NIGER, AMBOSELI, INDIA) cite widespread evidence to conclude that strong public tenure has failed to support conservation because states have followed colonial patterns of mining natural resources for quick capital to maintain state coffers and the political status of its elites.

Negative impacts on biodiversity have paralleled the erosion of traditional community-based tenurial rights that occur as states impose "public" rights. The most well-documented causal links between loss of tenurial security and biodiversity loss come out of studies seeking the causes behind the loss of the world's tropical forests.

States historically have assumed rights over forests, particularly for revenue generation; these include rights to decide harvest schedules, royalties, who can harvest (timber permits), export tax, and rights to nontimber forest products, etc. (see INDIA, ANNAPURNA). In this process, states generally have ignored customary property rights. In India, for example, the state incrementally overcame local resistance and community-level assertions of rights to manage forests by slowly shifting from granting communities forest "rights" to restricting communities to more limited "usufruct (use) rights" and "privileges," and finally to denying all rights to forest products and other privileges altogether. Local communities fought to retain forest management rights, but over several decades, the state eliminated all community-level tenurial security.

Historical records show that India's forests were biologically rich, despite being used by high populations of people and livestock for thousands of years prior to central control under British colonization. Tribal authorities, local elites, and princes enforced strict local forest management rules through methods including taxes, fines, land-use zoning, required labor commitments, and community forest guards. The British ignored these local institutions and transformed community-managed forests into state forests that became de facto open-access areas. Now, after the forests and their biodiversity have become severely degraded, various Indian states are granting certain tenurial rights to local communities in recognition of strong empirical evidence that communities can effectively manage and, in this case, regenerate their own forests (see INDIA).

The degradation of biodiversity under public control is not limited to forests. That inappropriate management and ignorance of traditional regimes have contributed to the degradation of grasslands and wildlife in Africa is widely accepted (see AMBOSELI, CAMPFIRE). Establishment of parks and wildlife reserves sometimes has led to degradation or destruction of biodiversity by people who view the park as territory taken from them by outsiders for outsiders' benefit. Likewise, numerous cases in which traditional communities have attempted to defend their fishing territories against outside fishing interests are well documented in Oceania and other coastal zones throughout the world. The resulting degradation of fisheries has been especially well documented in India but applies globally.

By insisting that biologically rich lands are owned by the state (under public tenure), national governments often create conditions of "open access." Garrett Hardin's (1968) "The Tragedy of the Commons" was actually about the tragedy of open access, a situation that is promoted when community-based resource management systems are delegitimized and states fail to manage the resource (McCay and Acheson 1987; Berkes 1989). When community-based tenure is weakened, biodiversity is often pillaged in a wide-open race for short-term gain. In effect, public land, or other public resources, belong to no one in particular but to everyone in general. This ambiguous official status acts as a magnet that pulls charcoal makers, loggers, landless farmers, and other short-term users onto "public" forest land.

In practice, however, access generally is not equally open to all when profits can be made from exploiting public resources. Many nation-states grant legal privileges either to favored elites (e.g., logging concession holders, plantation developers) or to troublesome "excess" populations of the landless rural poor through planned or incentive-assisted resettlement schemes. As an example of such political use of public resources, in many countries, land tenure laws reward new settlers with titles if they "improve" land by clearing it of trees (see BOSCOSA). In a twist on the usual story, an indigenous Sarawak community made the hard choice to cut down their forest when the state designated it as a public forest reserve. If they had tried to fight the reserve, arguing that the forest was theirs, the community would have lost its village lands as well as the right to harvest the forest. On the other hand, migrants following logging roads would have been permitted to cut down the trees with the legal protection of the government and granted title to the same land. By cutting down all the trees, the existing community was able to secure tenure to the land, since village lands are deemed "agricultural land" once they are cleared. The village paid a small fine and then planted rubber trees.

When communities traditionally have managed resources sustainably, government claims may destroy any incentive to continue to do so. Without official recognition, communities do not have access to the formal legal structure to exclude those who encroach on their rights and overexploit their resources, be they local elites, multinational corporations, or landless migrants. Lacking legal recognition, indigenous peoples and migrants living on "public" lands can not legally benefit from exploitation of the local natural resources base. Deprived of the legal means and incentives to exclude newcomers and manage the forest for long-term sustainable benefit to themselves, many communities become increasingly responsive to market pressures to overexploit and join in the free-for-all.

In the case of wildlife, public management is often nonexistent, although most states claim the right to regulate hunting. As noted in AMAZON and CAMPFIRE, local communities tend to carry out wildlife management in rural areas more effectively than government authorities.

In summation, rational human beings face disincentives to make long-term improvements and take short-term losses to sustainably manage their local resource base when they lack assurance that they and their successors will continue to profit from their investments. The growing clamor for tenurial security by rural people around the world demonstrates the importance of this assurance. Simply stated, tenurial security is an important precondition for sustainable resource management, principally because it encourages long-term planning and greater investments of labor and resources. In the words of Harvard economist Theodore Panayotou,

> Property rights need to be *secure*. If there is a challenge to ownership, risk of appropriation (without adequate compensation), or extreme political or economic uncertainty, well-defined and exclusive property rights provide little security for long-term investment such as land improvements, tree planting, and resource conservation. *(1989)*

Communities' Conservation Performance under Private Tenure

How do communities manage and conserve biodiversity under a range of community-based tenure situations (except in the case of individual titles)? Communities may have community title, a lease, or some other type of specific legal instrument—such as a *comarca* (Panama), a *comunidad* (Mexico), or an indigenous reserve (as in several South American countries)—that recognizes their special authority to regulate tenure within their borders. More frequently, however, communities have no legal instrument from the state that recognizes their tenurial rights. Tenurial security, as discussed here, is not defined merely by the existence of a legal instrument but by strong legal and institutional mechanisms (e.g., customary law and institutions, or support from national judicial or police systems) that enable a community to defend tenurial claims against outsiders, make decisions about how to allocate resources among its members, and retain the authority to resolve conflicts among its members.

Community-based tenure often is associated with strong community-based resource management regimes. Conservationists' concern for tenurial security should translate not only into concern for state-sanctioned de jure tenurial security, but also into concern about the strength and authority of the underlying community-based resource management institutions.

Most of the world's biodiversity is found outside protected areas. Often areas with high biodiversity and areas where traditional community-based control over resource access and management are also in place overlap—creating situations in which local people possess community-based de jure tenurial security and effectively exclude others. Yet no national-level assessments to ascertain the extent to which traditional management systems are responsible for the presence of high diversity have been carried out.

Throughout the world, biologists have identified biologically rich areas and selected them for protected-area status. These areas include territories that are occupied by indigenous communities and/or migratory pastoralists that rely on utilization and management of wild resources as part of their livelihood strategies. For example, in Central America, more than 85 percent of all protected areas are occupied by indigenous peoples, and a similar percentage applies to many countries. Communities living in what are currently high-biodiversity areas generally enjoy, or have enjoyed until recently, de facto tenurial security and consequently have regulated resource access among themselves and excluded outsiders. These are often communities of ethnic minorities or indigenous peoples.

Many local people believe they have played an active role in maintaining biodiversity. A Karen headman in northern Thailand recently spoke of a village threatened with loss of tenurial security and resettlement:

> [The conservationists] think they created this World Heritage Site by filling out a bunch of papers and encircling this area on a map. They didn't create it. This forest and these animals wouldn't be here if we hadn't kept others out. We took care of this forest that our ancestors left us. We Karen are responsible for creating this World Heritage Site, not the conservationists.

While community agricultural lands often are held under rights that Westerners might consider to be very close to private individual property rights, the forests, reefs, grasslands, and other ecosystems used by community members are generally under complex, often overlapping tenure rights that share benefits across a broad range of the community, restrict community use, and work to exclude non-community members. Overlapping rights protect the system from outsider acquisition or exclusive use by any one entity that might destroy it; such traditional systems, in effect, are a partnership between individuals and the broader community to maintain the community's resource base. As MALUKU ISLANDS relates, rules for using and protecting biodiversity generally are enforced by the threat of religious sanctions and social ostracism. On a more pragmatic level, enforcement is carried out by resource "bosses," appointed committees, and rotating forest/reef guards who regularly monitor resources and extractive activities. Penalties can be severe, including expulsion from the community.

Peoples who have traditionally lived in a given area for long periods of time generally have deep ecological knowledge about their area and the impact of their activities. For example, they often utilize sophisticated agricultural systems that rely on ecological processes. Extensive research has demonstrated that many traditional shifting cultivators possess local knowledge bases and operate swidden systems that are well suited for sustainably managing local resources (Warner 1991; Lynch 1990; Alcorn 1989). Communities operating these swidden agricultural systems generally manage a wide range of nonagricultural resources as well. For example, they may carry out agroforestry, maintain freshwater fisheries, manage harvest of nontimber forest products and game, and protect sacred forest areas.

Customary rights to wildlife are understudied, but they appear to be most frequently allocated in one of two ways. If there is a chief, headman, or other powerful leader, wildlife may be owned by the leader, who has the authority to give out rights to hunt particular species within the group's lands, usually on a day-by-day basis. The hunter often is required to share the hunt with the entire community. It is the chief's responsibility to regulate hunting in order to maintain game stocks. Outsiders must seek permission to hunt from him and may be required to pay a fee or give some portion of the meat to the community. Also common is the allocation of rights to hunt or trap in specific places. In these systems, regulation of hunting pressures may be the purview of a boss (or council) who makes sure that game populations are not severely depleted.

Alternatively, hunting and trapping in a family's territory customarily may be done only at particular times of the year, resulting in reduced impact on game species. Rights to hunt certain species may be held by particular groups—by certain castes in India, for example. In other cases, however, there is no apparent ownership of game beyond the communal right to hunt in a particular territory—which may overlap with the hunting rights of other communities. In such cases, however, there is still the expectation that meat will be shared. CAMPFIRE illustrates an adaptation of these kinds of rights to a cash economy where the animal has high value to outsiders. These outsiders, in effect, purchase the right to hunt from an authoritative body representing the community and the state, which, under the CAMPFIRE program, share comanagement decisions.

Indigenous management systems do not always maintain maximum levels of biodiversity; rather, community-based systems (just as in biological evolution) appear to evolve to be "good enough" to maintain ecosystems that provide a wide variety of resources and situations to buffer livelihoods in the face of changing weather, population growth, public tenurial claims, market demands, and other factors. The institution is good enough to maintain levels of biodiversity that are also good enough. The level of how well the institution functions (what makes the institution good enough) and the level of how much biodiversity is good enough depends on costs of maintenance, return on investment (e.g., is it worth dying in confrontation with the military or local elites to protect the forest?), other resource options, degree of political cohesion, and cultural values. Good enough, in such institutions, may be the same as what is good enough in evolution: adequate to ensure survival of the biotic populations, communities, and ecosystems in question. Any system's current configuration depends on history, chance, selective pressures, and the "material" (social and ecological) that is available as grist for evolution in the face of changes.

Communities' standards of what constitutes good enough levels of biodiversity may not be the same as biologists' standards for parks and strict reserves. In areas where high or medium levels of biodiversity exist, community standards are used to maintain viable populations of most species in the habitats that are managed for diversity. At the other end of the scale are the standards of good enough applied by suburbanite Americans who apply weed killer to eliminate diversity in their immediate environment. Forestry departments apply similar good-enough standards as they cut down natural forest (for profit) and put in plantations. As BOSCOSA reminds us, the indigenous Guaymi community was the only community interested in natural forest management at the start of their project. The Guaymi standard for good enough valued high diversity; the settler community had lower standards. The standard managers use inside parks is also under question. Often, management seems to be guided by whatever is good enough to maintain populations of large mammals. Recently, there has been some debate over whether this strategy is indeed always maintaining overall diversity.

Levels of biodiversity under community-based tenure may or may not be different from those of reserves under state management. In some areas of high biodiversity (particularly in Amazonia), human population density is extremely low, participation in the market economy is minimal, and few outsiders have threatened to destroy forests. In these situations, large game animals are the species most likely to be affected by community hunting pressure (see AMAZON, NEOTROPICAL FORESTS), but the effect on overall biodiversity levels may be small. In other areas, communities are struggling to adapt to a wide variety of internal stresses to their systems, as well as struggling to stave off escalating threats from outsiders who are either extracting resources without regard for local regulations or who are actively settling on communities' lands. All of these stresses affect traditional tenurial security, but there is widespread evidence that many communities continue to fight to maintain their own authority over their resources (Lohmann 1991). As their territories shrink before colonists' penetration (or incursions by outside fishing boats), communities often set aside forest areas (or selected reef systems) in their now reduced territory as reserves where hunting, tree-cutting, or other extractive activities are forbidden, or they may enact stricter laws, perhaps outlawing hunting and fishing for sale. Embara communities in the Darien region of Panama and some Indonesian communities (see MALUKU ISLANDS) currently are taking such action.

When the stresses of social change or encroachment by commercial resource

exploiters occur, communities may have difficulty in adapting (see MALUKU IS-
LANDS). In some cases, after a community perceives an initial drop in the populations of exploited species, effective restrictions are established, but in other cases,
accommodation never occurs. If the resource is overharvested, the population of
the exploited species may be radically reduced or destroyed. This may lead to loss
of the market, and then the population may be able to recover. In CRATER MOUN-
TAIN, AMAZON, and NEOTROPICAL FORESTS, new monetary values of biota led to new
pressures on those populations not found in the subsistence system that were difficult to address through existing social norms.

In the face of stress, then, many communities adapt their strategies for maintaining biodiversity. In some cases, especially when outside pressures on forests
have intensified and communities recognize that specific species are being lost,
communities have opted for extraordinary efforts to maintain those species. Some
Brazilian indigenous groups, for example, have sought World Wildlife Fund assistance to combine new scientific methods with their traditional knowledge in
order to develop monitoring systems to track the impact of increased hunting on
their lands and develop improved management techniques (see AMAZON, NEOTROP-
ICAL FORESTS). Some maintain high levels of biodiversity by tightening up community regulations and introducing new conflict-regulation mechanisms.

Some communities, however, are unable to adapt to stress due to a variety of
factors often related to the strength and interests of community leadership, loss of
traditional culture, etc. As a result, biodiversity levels, or the population levels of
particular species, drop radically (see AMAZON, NEOTROPICAL FORESTS). The reasons
for variations in adaptive capacity, and the relative number of systems that adapt
versus those that fail to adapt, have not been well studied. The biology of the
species or ecosystem in question certainly plays a role. The degree of de facto
tenurial security also seems to be important, yet there are instances of two neighboring communities, one of which was able to conserve biodiversity while the
other was not. (Such micro-level variation between communities is not uncommon in other realms, such as communities' adaptation/adoption of modernization options.)

Where stress is "internal" due to increasing population or decreased access to
traditional resource areas, some communities elect to intensify one aspect of their
livelihood system in order to maintain biodiverse zones. For example, Southeast
Asian groups often have opted for labor-intensive terraced agricultural systems,
thus maintaining biodiversity in forested areas elsewhere in their territories instead of clearing their entire area for agricultural purposes. Mexican Huastec
Mayan families with secure communal tenure (at densities of more than 100
people per km^2) have opted to intensify cash crops on 25 percent of their communal land and dedicate 50 percent to short-fallow swidden fields that produce
corn and fuelwood, so that the remaining 25 percent of their holding can retain
biodiverse forests. The reasons they give for their decision to maintain biologically
diverse managed forests include direct access to products (firewood, fruits, medi-

cine, construction materials, and unknown products they may find useful in the future); the superior quality of life offered by fresh breezes, shade, clean water, and clean air; protection of the earth; and ecological services such as soil-quality protection, prevention of erosion, and site improvement for swidden agriculture.

Where the stress of resource scarcity is caused by outsiders, it is not uncommon for communities to respond by seeking government assistance. Given the generally poor support they receive from the state, however, recently they have also sought assistance from NGOs (see AMAZON) and formed alliances with other communities that have the same problems (although some states view such activities as antigovernment).

The tenacity of community-based management of biodiverse areas under stress offers evidence of many communities' commitment and ability to maintain biodiversity under changing conditions. Numerous theorists have tried to explain why and how rural communities have resisted incorporation into the global economic system, despite colonial and market pressures. While explanations vary, it is clear that rural communities and traditional groups have struggled to retain their territories, their self-reliance, their cultural identity, and their biodiversity, even when engaging in wage labor outside their community lands. Maintaining biodiversity reserves is one strategy that enables communities to maintain their identity and self-reliance; biological resources, as the ultimate safety net for the poor, also serve to secure survival.

In addition to state expropriation, a number of stresses can cause changes in biodiversity-maintaining traditional systems: demographic changes, cultural changes, failure to educate young people in traditional-systems management or traditional ecological knowledge necessary for decision-making, new market demands, community institutions that are unable to interface effectively with outsiders, technological changes, and crop changes. Many of these factors also directly contribute to changes in community tenurial regimes, and it is change in tenurial regimes that is often the ultimate cause of biodiversity degradation.

An observer of the buffer zone of Ranthambhore National Park in India, for example, would be tempted to blame communities for the extremely degraded forest that exists there. A more careful analysis would reveal that the state is largely to blame. State-sponsored logging was followed by overuse condoned by corrupt officials. Rather than try to engage buffer-zone communities in comanagement, park officials increased the number of armed guards. Even in the face of such degradation and lack of government assistance, Ranthambhore communities continue to struggle to establish and enforce social regulations to control access to biodiversity in their section of the buffer zone (Sarabhai et al. 1990).

Communities under stress often do what they can to adapt their land use in ways that retain biodiversity, but tenurial erosion (and the concomitant erosion of biodiversity) often continues. In cases under stress, it is not uncommon for communities to practice a form of triage to secure the survival of certain species while allowing other types to disappear. For example, despite the depletion of terrestrial biodiversity under increasingly intensified farming, some Bangladeshi communities have continued to use common-property regimes to regulate access to highly biodiverse fisheries in floodplain and wetland waterways. These food-rich waterways also provide habitat for a wide array of migratory birds. This last bastion of biodiversity is now threatened by loss of tenurial security as waterways under community-based tenure and management are now being appropriated by wealthy private individuals who engage in capital-intensive fish farming. The development schemes include lucrative loans that provide payoffs to corrupt officials and often never require repayment. These fish-farming systems probably will fail, but loans, not profitable production, are the main "profit" sought by the elite. The resulting depauperate fish communities are likely to be further depleted under open access since traditional tenure and regulatory institutions will lose their legitimacy during the farming takeover.

In sum, strong evidence suggests that erosion of community-based tenure is linked to erosion of biodiversity, and that, even under stress, communities will strive to retain biodiversity. There is insufficient information to identify which succession of factors predicts whether communities will be able to adapt their community-based management systems to stresses that threaten their conservation success, particularly when these stresses are externally generated.

Biodiversity levels are being maintained or improved where efforts are made to recognize existing private community-based resource-management regimes; create new community-based systems that are quasi-public, quasi-private, or a combination of public and private rights; and develop comanagement systems that usually operate under strong "public" tenurial rights (see INDIA, NIGER, AMBOSELI). These efforts have grown in the last decade. Unfortunately, few of these efforts are being closely monitored from a biodiversity perspective, so it is difficult to point to "successes" or learn lessons from "failures."

Despite enthusiasm for these new approaches, few researchers actually have generated and reported measurable results to assess whether, or under which circumstances, tenurial security leads to conservation success. An exception may be the case of the semi-independent Kuna *comarca* established in Panama more than fifty years ago and since awarded Biosphere Reserve designation. Aerial photography and historical knowledge of the forests and reefs indicate that the Kuna are effectively using their strong tenurial security to manage biodiversity successfully and keep outsiders from encroaching on their forests and reefs. Some Philippine groups who hold community forest leases can tell a similar story.

Some of the most ambitious (and most important, from the biodiversity point of view) efforts to support community-based conservation through improved tenurial security involve creation of indigenous reserves in Latin America—efforts widely supported by international conservationists as a means of protecting biodiversity in tropical forests. The tenurial security these reserves offer varies widely. The highly publicized Colombian reserves in fact give only limited tenurial security and decision-making authority to local institutions or communities. The state re-

tains rights to make management decisions about forest, water, and mineral resources. This same pattern marked the start of tenurial erosion and concomitant
forest destruction in India.

Many field-workers on the front lines of conservation activism are now convinced that tenurial security is an essential—but not necessarily a sufficient—condition for conservation. It is very important to remember, however, as Western ob-
serves in AMBOSELI, that however just empowerment may be, it does not
necessarily lead to conservation. There is no guarantee that better defined and
more secure tenurial rights automatically will result in a slowing of deforestation
or reef destruction or lead to more sustainable systems of production.

The challenge of predicting the outcome of efforts to involve people in conservation is immense. Community-based systems do not guarantee the success of
conservation efforts. Suspicious of relying on communities, some scientists promote comanagement through partnerships of NGOs, the state, and communities
under strong state guidance. KAKADU demonstrates success under strong community comanagement. Globally, however, there is insufficient evidence upon which
to evaluate the track record for conserving high biodiversity through comanagement or to ascertain whether it succeeds best when communities initiate comanagement through requests to the government. Comanagement, as in INDIA, works
in some situations where biodiversity is severely degraded, of little commercial
value, and therefore of minor interest to the state. On the other hand, even when
communities have expressed a strong willingness to protect their healthy forests,
comanagement generally has not been acceptable to the Indian government for
forests that have monetary value. This is changing, however, in Indian states such
as Orissa, where tribal communities are gaining control over and protecting still-
forested areas.

Evidence from the field supports the premise that tenurial security, especially
where communities are relatively intact, is generally a strong conservation tool.
Local situations, tenurial systems, and community cohesion vary widely, however, and traditional systems and communities often disintegrate in the face of
more powerful interests. The difficulties and mixed results, at best, of efforts to
revive defunct community-based systems (particularly after resettlements or other
social upheavals) and efforts to create new systems should be acknowledged. An
exception may be parts of Southeastern Asia, where, through the centuries, communities have developed institutional and cultural methods with which to maintain community cohesion under resettlement. Success is much more likely if conservationists work to support tenurial security for intact communities with strong
traditional institutions that can effectively regulate common-property management and adapt existing institutions to new stresses.

The conservation incentives most appreciated by communities with strong
tenurial security include security necessary for long-term management planning,
expectations that ecosystem management decisions will be made by the local
community, expectations that the community will be able to exercise power to

evict or manage the behavior of users in accordance with long-term management objectives, and the freedom to evolve appropriate management institutions and conflict-resolution mechanisms as conditions change.

State Recognition of Local Rights

In areas where local people have a demonstrable concern for the environment, a stated desire to manage it sustainably, and a desire for state recognition, the best governmental response to community-based tenure would be to officially recognize community-based rights and delineate the spatial perimeters of existing systems. When existing systems are rooted in the local ecology and already possess legitimacy in the minds of local people, recognition facilitates more environmentally and culturally appropriate evolution and development.

However, there is a tension between broad state recognition of traditional rights and codification of its intimate details. The latter may be impossible due to their complexity, will certainly be time-consuming, and may, in fact, destroy the flexibility and adaptability of the system—one of the greatest virtues of traditional systems.

Despite the complexities of community-based tenure systems, recognition of them in governmental laws and policies should not be contingent on project planners' and implementers' first becoming familiar with the intricacies and nuances of these regimes. Only general familiarity with the existence and viability of community-based tenure systems is necessary. Requiring that intracommunity tenurial variations be specifically addressed in policies, programs, and projects will complicate and even block widespread systemic efforts to support and gain legal recognition for community-based tenure systems. Such requirements will make recognition efforts more complicated, prolonged, and expensive than they need be.

In most instances, customary laws are based on oral traditions that allow the flexibility necessary to respond to changing conditions. Codification of existing tenurial rights and processes at a particular moment in time is a common—and often well-intentioned—attempt to validate traditional rights for incorporation into modern systems. Codification efforts, especially by outsiders, reify customary laws at a particular moment in time and therefore provide outsiders with an inappropriate tool that disrupts internal community functioning. Furthermore, codification fails to preserve the traditional flexible system of conflict resolution. Thus the traditional system dies, since it must evolve on its own terms to remain valid, and authority shifts from the community to the state.

The solution may be simply to delineate the perimeters of community-based tenurial systems. Perimeter delineation would obviate the need for national governments to conduct more expensive and culturally disruptive surveys of individual property rights. More important, it would enable governments to determine the exact location and range of community-based tenure systems. If this information were in hand, governments could better formulate more appropriate natural resources policies.

Powerful political and economic interests' opposition to recognition strategies—and their insistence that legal rights to natural resources are contingent on detailed state grants and documents—ensures that efforts to promote the recognition of community-based tenurial rights in most countries will require long-term effort. With the exceptions of Great Britain and Papua New Guinea, official strategies for securing community-based tenurial rights in the case study countries only appear possible by way of grants made under the auspices of government-sponsored conservation and social forestry programs.

Private Individual Titling and Private Title Holders in CBC

By definition, community-based conservation appears to require an intact community capable of reflecting collective interests and exercising appropriate authority. What occurs in the absence of such a cohesive community? The information available about the effectiveness of individual private titling programs for community-based conservation efforts is insufficient to allow for generalization.

Inequities in the distribution of rights to arable lands may spur migration into ecologically fragile areas rich in biodiversity, especially when landless farmers have no alternative but to migrate into fragile forest areas. In such situations, land-titling programs that stabilized the frontier would seem to be an effective way to conserve still-intact forest areas. Land-reform programs that offer individual titles in an effort to stem migration onto public lands, however, are not necessarily the conservationist's best answer to resource distribution problems, since land reform can have negative impacts on biodiversity. For example, some land-reform programs in Africa that focus on individual documentary titling at the expense of community-based tenure have contributed to increased landlessness and destruction of biodiversity (Porter, Allen, and Thompson 1991). In countries with frontier forests, such as Costa Rica, the availability of individual titles and homesteading laws encourages the clearing of forests on public land, thereby "improving" it and establishing state-sanctioned rights that lead to titles. Often these titles are later sold (frequently to ranchers who encouraged the initial settlement), and the settlers move to a new forested area. During times of land speculation, these incentives for individuals to benefit from titling programs are especially strong.

Experience shows, furthermore, that the benefits of individual titling may not actually reach the desired resource users. When procedures for individual titling do exist, they tend to be overly complex, culturally inappropriate, time-consuming, and expensive, especially for people living on traditionally owned forest lands. Influential outsiders, meanwhile, often possess the wherewithal and knowledge needed to meet the procedural obstacles and thus acquire state-sanctioned legal rights to land that is already occupied and, in many instances, customarily owned.

In theory, however, individual titling should help traditional resource owners defend at least some of their rights against powerful outsiders. Unfortunately, as noted above, too often in practice one of the dangers of titles is that once acquired, the land is then sold to someone outside the community. Individuals not protected by community-based tenure often lose their land rights this way. Nevertheless, it may be appropriate to provide individual titles or leaseholds as one element of a conservation strategy when the territory of a group seeking community-based tenure has been invaded by noncommunity members who can not be made to respect the legitimacy of the community system. For example, one proposal to protect Cuyabeno Reserve in Ecuador suggested giving titles to colonists in return for their agreement to defend their parkside borders against incursions by other settlers. Indigenous residents (the Siona-Secoya) allowed to live inside the Cuyabeno Reserve have community-based tenure, but they are unable to keep the colonists out by themselves. By using two different types of tenure recognition, conservationists planned to stem invasion and destruction of the park by working with all local residents.

Community-based efforts also can be built around situations in which individuals hold individual titles. NORTH YORK MOORS, for example, describes a comanagement arrangement between individual English title holders and the state. In a few other such situations in Latin America, particularly in Costa Rica and Mexico, communities of people with individual holdings have sought special reserve status to prevent unwanted development that would destroy forests.

Conclusions

Support for state recognition and defense of community-based tenurial rights is an essential element of any community-based conservation initiative. What, then, are the obstacles to strengthening such tenure? The key limiting factor in most developing countries is that the nation-state claims ownership of most environmentally important areas, or ownership of specific resources of conservation interest such as forests or wildlife. For example, 80 percent of all forest areas in Peru, Bolivia, Brazil, Venezuela, the Dominican Republic, Panama, Belize, Jamaica, and Trinidad and Tobago is considered to be state owned. Similarly high percentages of state ownership have been reported in Africa and tropical Asia. The only reported exceptions are Zambia, Zimbabwe, Botswana, and Papua New Guinea and other Pacific Island nations. In many countries, states are effectively executive committees of elites who make policies and laws enabling politically, socially, or economically powerful interests to use state and public resources for their own benefit. While states often allow community-based tenurial regimes to continue in areas where they do not presently conflict with these interests, they generally refuse to acknowledge their presence when they present obstacles to elite profiteering from natural resources exploitation, as in the case of timber sales to political allies.

As a result, most forest dwellers are considered, regardless of their length of occupancy, to be squatters on "public" (i.e., state-owned) land. In many countries, including Indonesia and many Latin American countries, de jure squatter status is less obvious to outsiders because constitutional provisions theoretically protect undocumented customary rights. But these undocumented rights are often ignored within national legal systems that promote expansive claims of public ownership (Davis and Wali 1993).

Despite dramatic improvements in the rhetoric of community-based conservation of natural resources—and a growing number of programs, projects, and, in some instances, even national laws and policies—most national governments still do not recognize in any effective, broad-based manner the tenurial rights of forest- and fishery-dependent people or their contributions to conservation and sustainable management. Neither do most countries, as Feldmann notes in POLICY, provide rural people with effective access to decision-making processes involving conservation and resource management.

The democratic foundation for popular sovereignty has been reiterated in the constitutions of many countries. Yet the transition from colonies to republics resulted in little change in state laws, policies, and practices for allocating power and wealth among the nations' citizens. Instead, the new republics largely mirror the policies and designs of the former colonial government.

The underlying problem is that many modern nation-states usually fail to reflect, in a supportive and substantive way, native values and aspirations, especially those that endure on local levels among impoverished and disenfranchised poor rural majorities. This phenomenon appears to be widespread. Despite positive rhetorical developments, most national policies and legal systems, including most conservation policies and programs, still tend to benefit international and domestic elites and disenfranchise hundreds of millions of people who inhabit or are directly dependent upon, environmentally fragile and important areas for their subsistence and livelihood. These outcomes reinforce an inequitable legal distribution of the benefits of natural resources conservation and utilization. They directly contribute to accelerating rates of tropical deforestation, biodiversity loss, and coastal degradation.

ACKNOWLEDGMENTS

We gratefully acknowledge the assistance and insights gained from discussion and debate with Michael Wright, Tom Fox, Forrest Swick, David Anderson, Frances Seymour, Jorge Tejerina, Kent Redford, and Marvic M. V. F. Leonen. In addition, this chapter draws upon unpublished work and discussions with the following researchers: Henry Chang, Eric Worby, Mac Chapin, Gerald Murray, Peter Herlihy, John Butler, Shelton Davis, Elizabeth Reichel, Nickie Irvine, Miguel Piñedo-Vasquez, John Cordell, Bob Johannes, Jeff Campbell, G. Raju, James Thompson, Mark Freudenberger, George Dei, Nancy Peluso, Tania Li, Theo Panayotou, Arturo Gómez-Pompa, Harold Conklin, Witoon Permpongsacharoen, and Felipe Montoya.

SOURCES

Alcorn, J. 1989. "Process as Resource: The Agricultural Ideology of Bora and Huastec Resource Management and Its Implications for Research." In *Natural Resource Management by Indigenous and Folk Societies in Amazonia*, ed. D. Posey and W. Balée, 63–77. New York: New York Botanical Garden.

Berkes, F., ed. 1989. *Common Property Resources*. London: Belhaven Press.

Brown, F., and B. Wyckoff-Baird. 1992. *Designing Integrated Conservation and Development Projects*. Washington, D.C.: Biodiveristy Support Program.

Casimir, M. J., and A. Rao., eds. 1992. *Mobility and Territoriality: Social and Spatial Boundaries Among Foragers, Fishers, Pastoralists, and Peripatetics*. New York: Berg/St. Martin's.

Crocombe, R. 1971. "An Approach to the Analysis of Land Tenure Systems." In *Land Tenure in the Pacific*, ed. R. Crocombe, 1–17. Melbourne: Oxford University Press.

Davis, S. H., and A. Wali. 1993. *Indigenous Territories and Tropical Forest Management in Latin America*. World Bank Working Paper. Washington, D.C.: World Bank.

Gadgil, M., and F. Berkes. 1991. "Traditional Resource Management Systems." *Resource Management and Optimization* 8:127–141.

Hardin, G. 1968. "The Tragedy of the Commons." *Science* (December 13): 1243–1248.

Lohmann, L. 1991. "Who Defends Biodiversity?" *Ecologist* 21:5–13.

Lynch, O. 1990. *Whither the People? Demographic and Tenurial Aspects of the Tropical Forestry Action Plan*. Washington, D.C.: World Resources Institute.

McCay, B. J., and J. M. Acheson, eds. 1987. *The Question of the Commons: The Culture and Ecology of Communal Resources*. Tucson, Arizona: University of Arizona Press.

Ostrom, E., J. Walker, and R. Gardner. 1992. "Covenants With and Without a Sword: Self-governance Is Possible." *American Political Science Review* 86: 404–417.

Panayotou, T. 1989. *The Economics of Environmental Degradation: Problems, Causes and Response*. Cambridge, Massachusetts: Howard Institute for International Development.

Porter, D., B. Allen, and G. Thompson. 1991. *Development in Practice*. New York: Routledge.

Sarabhai, K. V., G. Raju, K. Desai, P. Kathuria, and R. Khandelwal. 1990. *Buffer Zone Restoration in India: Issues and Approaches*. New Delhi: VIKSAT.

Siriat, M., S. Pradodjo, N. Podger, A. Flavelle, and J. Fox. 1992. "Mapping Customary Land in East Kalimantan, Indonesia: A Tool for Forest Management." Paper presented at the International Association for the Study of Common Property (IASCP) meeting, Manila, Philippines.

Warner, K. 1991. *Shifting Cultivators: Local Technical Knowledge and Natural Resource Management in the Humid Tropics*. Rome: Food and Agriculture Organization.

CHAPTER 17

Community Environmental Action: The National Policy Context

Fabio Feldmann

Since the Earth Summit in Rio in June 1992, environmental questions have become increasingly entangled with international relations and international economic issues. Action at the community or village level may seem far removed from the Rio conference and demands related to the core relationships between highly industrialized and poor countries. Transnational factors, however, have created a new international context within which environmental protection must be considered. A parallel exists between North-South power relationships at the global level and the need to alter the debate between national and international conservationists and poor local communities at the village level.

The current political transition under way in many developing countries poses a constant threat of disruption for community-based projects. Among the reasons for political instability are the fragile history of citizens' rights, difficulties in obtaining access to justice, hindrances to the application of law (even when legislation exists and is adequate), low levels of education, lack of even minimal survival conditions, and political and economic conflict resulting from inequality within and between nations.

As the first environmentalist congressman in Brazil, elected with the task of negotiating the inclusion of an environmental chapter in the constitution, I have experienced this reality in the front lines of public life for the last eight years. I have learned firsthand that national environmental policy lies at the intersection of two larger problems that have molded the permanent social and economic crisis of the poor: the ambiguous role of the state and the extreme disparity in distribution of social benefits and national wealth. These difficulties are further exacerbated by underlying weaknesses in the political structures of many countries.

The State and Conservation Policy

Far from being the solution to environmental mismanagement, the state often is unable to generate, manage, or implement the necessary integrated public policies. The particular difficulty of shaping environmental policy is the need to link a wide range of interrelated policies that guide and influence the utilization of natural resources. Rich countries experience this dilemma, but in developing countries the use of power as an instrument of short-term sectoral interests can more directly—or at least more obviously—frustrate more farsighted policy initiatives.

Historically, developing countries have followed a strategy of intense exploitation of natural resources and the export of raw materials. This development model has created the belief, still prevalent today, that an exploitive attitude toward natural resources is always preferable, provided that it maintains at least a minimal level of economic activity and generates employment and foreign currency. Thus conservation policies such as the creation of a system of protected areas are ineffective, since the state's inability to enforce them creates an open-access situation. This cultural context pervades the acts of the state, which does not see maintenance of protected areas as a priority. The fundamental discrepancy between legal establishment of protected areas and effective implementation is captured in the term *paper parks*. Promulgating appropriate policies is insufficient if, at the same time, the state winks at the survival strategies of its people, which may include trespassing in parks and overexploitation of resources by elites, activities that ultimately lead to resource destruction.

Many states adopt the newest environmental trends and fads and speak of "sustainable development" but prove unable or unwilling to build and enforce coherent public policies. This ambivalent attitude means that, in many cases, the state is a completely ineffectual agent for negotiating the relationship between society and the environment. This underlying weakness of national political systems is a particular problem for community-based approaches to conservation. As a result, the first priority among those concerned with community-based conservation should be political empowerment at village level. The goal should not be the creation of specific national environmental policies but, rather, establishment of channels for increased local social participation in the national political system and guarantees of a transparent process of decision-making. Political pluralism and a strengthened democratic process are the most fundamental preconditions for conservation.

In Latin America, for instance, the minimal restoration of democratic rule during the last decade has yet to lead to effective democratic operation of society and the exercise of citizens' individual and collective rights. With the departure of most authoritarian regimes during the 1980s, the situation has improved but, as a result of deteriorating social conditions and political and economic deadlocks, remains potentially unstable. Much of the developing world is consumed with trying to overcome social paralysis and instability. Concentration on these problems is at the expense of creating stable and adequate rules for future democracy, not to mention the complex task of establishing coordinated national policies for natural resources management.

Poverty and the Question of Enforcement

In addition to the basic lack of democratic civil processes, the severe impoverishment of most of the population in the developing world is a barrier to the creation of environmental policies. Poverty-induced environmental problems include growth and deterioration of urban areas; insufficient or nonexistent basic sanitation; alarming public health conditions; environmental disasters promoted by misallocation of land in urban areas; and, in rural areas, loss of arable land, deforestation, and poisoning and silting of rivers. Rather than face localized wars and violence over land, protected areas become easier targets of opportunity for the poor. Elites also use such areas to divert pressure that otherwise would be directed against their holdings.

At national level, the need for farsighted environmental planning to avoid future ecological and human disruption conflicts with the perceived short-term need to sacrifice nature in the name of alleviating poverty and maintaining political stability. Combining local action and coupling conservation to the economic and social interests of involved communities, as articulated at the Rio Earth Summit, thus becomes a powerful source of political legitimacy for environmentalism.

Integrating Local and National Policy

The case studies in this book demonstrate the considerable progress that has been made in involving communities with conservation, but the dangerous gap between individual locally based conservation actions and the state's ability to plan and carry out public policies at national level remains. Individual community activities may succeed but may never be translated into a wider pattern of behavior. In fact, as the Brazilian constitutional experience attests, it is not uncommon for the promising start of a project to be reversed due to sudden changes in national policy, ultimately resulting in an even more destructive situation. Such reversals do not invalidate the importance of demonstration cases in community-based conservation, but they do suggest caution in developing countries, where local action must be supplemented by other equally important activities: institution building, internalization of social participation, and creation of a more stable and reliable role for the state.

For national environmental policy to be maintained over time in the face of multiple claims, local institutions must be able to petition and act on behalf of their constituencies. Community-based conservation must strengthen the cultural, political, and organizational sophistication of local implementing institutions. Outside NGOs' arguments for change are not enough; local institutions, at both national and community level, must be able to affect the operation of national legislative and executive bodies. These institutions must operate with sufficient fairness to gain legitimacy in the face of overwhelming pressure from other political interests outside the community. Successful examples or models of community-based conservation become important sources of strength in resisting such external special interests. Thus at its foundation, the movement toward community-based conservation requires action to build local institutions and empower communities. In this light, concepts such as environmental education are not simply a matter of explaining the operations of a physical ecosystem but must involve assisting communities in the exercise of their full rights as citizens.

Integrating environmental concerns into political decision-making structures presents a dual challenge. First, local-level prejudices against the existence of protected areas must be overcome. Protected areas must be linked to community interests in the short and, ultimately, in the long run. Such areas must be seen as important prerequisites for local survival through maintenance of ecological balance, the basis for adequate and improved continuation of nature's productivity. The second challenge, at national level, is to generate pressure to integrate planning and public policy based on sustainable development. For this to be accomplished, the environmental movement must reach beyond its particular areas of self-interest into the broader field of politics, focusing on strengthening rules that encourage the desire for participation, diversity, and openness that accompanies demands for maintenance of ecological balance.

From either the local or the national perspective, there is no one "right" policy. Policies, tailored for each country's particular stage of national development, must be capable of evolving and changing as economic transition occurs. Flexibility and feedback are essential components in the implementation and evolution of policy. The ability to monitor and carry out ongoing evaluation are equally important elements. Successful community-based policy is, in many ways, indistinguishable from the process of debate and negotiation that underlies the basic political process.

The Role of International Funding

International funding has both a positive and a negative influence on the process of environmental destruction in developing countries. Environmental protection should not be used to create conditionalities and constraints on the autonomy of recipient countries. On the positive side, however, funds can provide incentives for integrating the environmental factor into social and economic planning. Within the programs of development-assistance institutions, environmentalists need to particularly emphasize incorporation of protected areas that involve promotion of community participation coupled with conservation.

The national political settings delineated in the case studies range along a continuum from institutions that are a historical inheritance of the colonial era to more contemporary institutional barriers, particularly in countries where the state is struggling to accommodate the complex demands of an emerging democratic society. Knowledge of the historical underpinnings of current difficulties is fundamental to understanding the functioning of community-based conservation. For example, despite having obtained formal independence, a history of colonialism appears to strongly limit the ability of governments to organize the use of natural resources as part of their process of development (see NIGER and INDIA). Historical analysis can be critical to understanding resistance to decentralization or delegation of authority and the power of institutional paralysis which, in most cases, stems from central authorities' deep and complex interference in the natural development of communities and societies.

Cultural and Historical Constraints to Integration

At the other end of the spectrum, a people's cultural, spiritual, and religious traditions affect communities' ability and willingness to play an effective role in managing natural resources within the larger national framework. The role of culture is seen most clearly in CRATER MOUNTAIN, AMBOSELI, and KAKADU. Even as national authorities establish national rights and strategies to protect resources, such strategies may be ineffective if they are incompatible with customary or traditional rights recognized at community level.

The traditional approach to environmental action, undertaken independently of community concerns and with strict protection as its objective, also has its problems. Government agencies face difficulties in negotiating their priority issues with other government institutions. The trend toward associating conservation action with community participation, human survival, and improved living standards creates even greater complexity. Other public institutions not traditionally associated with environmental concern, such as a ministry of local government, become necessary partners in the process of imparting social awareness. Each additional agency involved in the process brings its own institutional perspective and priorities. In addition, the natural bureaucratic resistance to relinquishing authority to local communities increases as more institutions become involved in the debate. Despite their individual uniqueness, every case consistently presents a picture of difficulty in coordinating the activities and priorities of competing government institutions.

For community-based projects to be more than isolated individual actions, they must form part of a national strategy that is both flexible and adaptable to experience. Reconciliation of intra-institutional jurisdictional mandates and responsibilities is also essential. In Zimbabwe, for example, the use of nonarable land, totaling about 80 percent of the country's territory, is planned by a wide range of government agencies. The National Conservation Strategy (NCS), with the CAMPFIRE project as its vital center, seeks to provide the necessary coordinating strategy; however, rather than providing interagency coordination, the NCS is really a list of priorities. Federal agencies are "vertically integrated," operating jointly with those local district bodies with which they share a common mandate, rather than coordinating horizontally with key government ministries at the same level. The NCS seeks the slow process of building consensus about the links between conservation and development, but in the meantime, the need to make decisions on resource issues is immediate and pressing. In Zimbabwe, efficient horizontal cooperation among sectoral agencies is required, as is the establishment of an independent professional body within the bureaucracy to strengthen relations between government and society. As in most countries, no national policy mechanism exists that can deal with these coordination and reconciliation issues (see CAMPFIRE).

Without some unifying national strategy supported by a clearly articulated national policy, resource agencies traditionally have been marginalized, unable to compete with more politically powerful agencies. In England, as exemplified by the North York Moors National Park, environment clearly is a peripheral sector in the formulation of government policy. "Environment" is understood as a mechanism for conservation of green areas and parks, tied to a low-budget government body with little power or influence. CAMPFIRE and NORTH YORK MOORS paint a picture of unarticulated public policies on the environment or of institutions so compartmentalized that they are unable to insert the concept of environmental sustainability into the strategy of other ministries.

In addition to the basic horizontal problem of policy coordination between conservation-oriented and other sectoral agencies, there is the vertical issue of effective delegation or devolution of authority from the center to the periphery of society. Relationships between the central government and regional and local decision makers are a key factor in community-based conservation policy. The degree and direction of support or interference from central governments may foster or frustrate local initiatives.

Simple decentralization of authority to more local levels of government is not the same as actual devolution of rights to communities. Difficult as it is to convince central government to relinquish real power, the underlying structure by which authority is delegated is equally complex. Even well-intentioned devolution or allocation of natural resources policy rights may fail if they are incompatible with customary or traditional rights. In addition, delegation of authority, if it is to result in the conservation of natural resources, requires that local authorities accept long-term accountability for the state of those resources.

For example, AMBOSELI reflects the complexity inherent in trying to integrate so-called modern natural resources policy with a traditional system. Until two decades ago, the Maasai system was marked by communal use and ownership of land, with authority flowing from the elders. In the postcolonial government, elected members of Parliament created a power structure parallel to and in conflict with this traditional system. The process of power sharing between central government and the local people has been marked by the force of Maasai conservatism and the aggressive paternalism of government policy. In addition, the Amboseli project has been negatively influenced by the political practices of local parliamentary candidates, who exploit the Maasai's fear that their land might be annexed by central authorities. This fear is reinforced and apparently confirmed by inconsistent government actions. While strategically placed individuals in key government and NGO positions have now established a dialogue, the events described in AMBOSELI stress that the primary impediment to conservation action has been governmental and institutional. In Kenya, insistence upon preservationist policies coupled with paternalism, lack of institutional continuity, failure to comply with economic commitments, corruption, and nepotism—all associated with political and economic crisis—creates a picture often seen in many countries throughout the world.

While significant devolution of authority to the local level is critical for community-based conservation, devolution must be supported by an appropriate legislative framework and implemented through a process of public consultation involving all the relevant stakeholders. Few of the community approaches to conservation described in the case studies have any clear legislative foundation. In some cases (see particularly NIGER), lack of environmental legislation goes hand in hand with poor political development in the country as a whole. Disagreement between existing legislation and the real need for community dialogue with guidelines on how to integrate conservation and economic development are not the only problem. Even the existence of advanced environmental legislation, as in the case of the Brazilian constitution, does not assure implementation. Much effort has been expended nationally and internationally to produce thoughtful, occasionally ideal legislation on resource management and community authority that has no prospect of ever being applied. The best legislative mandate is of no avail if a country fails to provide the minimum conditions necessary for its enforcement. Such conditions must flow from the full exercise of citizenship, which is not possible in the majority of countries where political and institutional instability or economic disorder prevail.

More than the issue of policy coordination between sectoral agencies and the underlying legislative framework's adequacy to support decentralization of authority is involved. For community-based approaches to conservation to succeed, we must look to the fundamental relationship between the state and its citizens: the issue of political pluralism and the condition of civil society. While it need not take any particular prescribed form, a democratic or multiparty framework is necessary for the interests and rights of communities to be fully expressed and enforced.

NGOs and the Role of Government

Particularly relevant to community-based conservation is the relationship between the government and nongovernmental organizations (NGOs). The case studies clearly reveal how strongly NGOs can influence public actions. An active, vibrant NGO movement suggests great vitality in the civil society and in citizens' ability to promote institutional advancement. At the same time, we need to evaluate the extent to which NGOs may be usurping the proper role of government. While they may be able to catalyze action, the vigor of NGOs may indicate paralysis on the part of the government. The government is the center of the decision-making process within any society and must not abandon its functions to NGOs because of lack of capacity. Although in some situations NGOs performing quasi-governmental tasks may generate very positive social results, this role also can obscure responsibility. Often, particularly if the NGO is international and responding to the needs of its supporters, it is unclear to whom NGOs are accountable.

With this very important caveat, the leadership of NGOs and their greater capacity for initiative and innovation in community-based conservation, compared with that of governments, is undeniable. NGOs supply human, technical, and financial resources when the state lacks them, as occurs in CRATER MOUNTAIN. They introduce innovative managerial concepts such as sustainable management, as in NIGER. They play a quasi-governmental role in testing the feasibility of new protected-area categories, as occurs in ANNAPURNA, and as CAMPFIRE demonstrates, they undertake implementation of national programs for environmental protection.

NGOs encourage the exercise of citizenship within involved communities and induce new behaviors on the part of government agencies. To a certain extent, government agencies depend on NGO initiatives to explore innovative approaches and build the necessary base of political support for their implementation. Flexibility and feedback are essential components in implementation and evolution of community policies. Timely and continuous monitoring to allow for adaptation is important. These are particularly challenging characteristics for government agencies and areas where NGOs may be uniquely qualified. Ultimately, though, political relations between communities and national institutions must be adopted through government structures, legislation, and policy if continuity and sustainability are to be ensured.

Linking Benefits to Participation

National policies that devolve authority to communities are fine in principle, but the case studies demonstrate that, in order to succeed, community-based conservation must provide real economic alternatives. Incentives are essential to generate local commitment to environmental management which does not or can not exist otherwise. Benefits need not be solely financial but may include access to markets, increased accessibility or control of resources, or elimination of cost and risk. In addition, community-based projects must provide some national-level as well as community benefit in return for the national contribution to any comanagement scheme. KAKADU presents a successful example of such a policy of comanagement and benefit sharing. Aboriginal people's participation in Kakadu National Park's management plan is guaranteed, and the communities' ability to manage the park is encouraged by their involvement as members of the park's advisory board. At the economic level, the institutional arrangement involves a leasing agreement with payments and mining royalties that benefit the Aboriginal people. The government's benefit is the establishment of a protected area with less social cost and less conflict.

NORTH YORK MOORS presents the most systematic policy of linking economic benefits to conservation. The benefits program evolved over time as the National Park Authority entered into voluntary cooperative agreements with landowners, the key element being financial incentives. Eventually, this piecemeal approach was replaced by a plan for the whole agricultural area of the park, establishing coordination among different incentive programs and integrating several existing agricultural programs into a coherent management arrangement. In 1987, this experience was further refined as a Farm Scheme aimed at conservation and protection measures in agricultural areas. It involved participation of farmers' representatives, ministers of agriculture and environment, owners' organizations, and the Council for National Parks. Farmers' participation was critical in assessing the effectiveness of the agreements.

The fundamental policy underlying the Farm Scheme is conversion of conservation action into a source of income supplemental to the production of food as an agricultural business. The benefits are conditioned on compliance with legally enforceable obligations. ANNAPURNA, AMBOSELI, and BOSCOSA provide additional examples of policies of benefit sharing between national and local entities. The complexity and sophistication of the NORTH YORK MOORS experience, however, provides a challenge for these programs.

Conclusions

The case studies are located in a rural setting that, from the viewpoint of national power, is seen as a nonmodern sector, resistant to change or, at the very least, risk aversive. The fragile ecosystems involved feature high biodiversity, unique natural resources and conservation problems that require for their solution local community involvement associated with appropriate resources. Although such communities might be expected to react positively, since they are reputed to be the main beneficiaries of the conservation process, institutional factors in fact create powerful incentives to the contrary.

First, for community-based conservation to succeed, there is need for greater clarity of the concept of community benefit itself. Among the cases, what the promoting institution and the community understand as a benefit are often significantly different. More problematic still is identification of the appropriate relationship of authority and accountability to community participation and local and national governmental power structures. Whether any of the complex relationships described in the cases have created a decision-making model capable of sustainable development is highly questionable.

Second, the extent to which any individual project, aimed at long-term objectives, can truly provide effective conservation alternatives directly linked to a process of development in regions featuring fragile ecosystems and plagued by predatory economic activities is open to question. The goal of a project may be to link conservation to a community through its committed involvement instead of simply isolating the area from that community; however, long-term sustainability of agreements between central governments and historically weak rural communities that are still marginal to most decision-making structures may be doubtful. The ability to simply reassign a sympathetic bureaucrat or reverse policies when governments change can undercut the most carefully and elegantly designed community-based project. Without fundamental change in societal relationships as a whole, it is possible that no community-based approach will be effective.

Even when central bureaucratic institutions are committed to effectively sharing power and resources with the periphery, the nature of their relationship remains complex. On the one hand, devolution is fundamental to allowing greater community participation in decisions, but on the other, some degree of centralization is also desirable to guarantee integration between local conservation alternatives and national public policies. Some centralization of responsibility can help to avoid periodic destruction of promising experiments that can be overwhelmed as a result of national policy. Continued involvement of national institutions also can help to ensure that short-term local self-interest will not be at the expense of society's interest in longer-term resource preservation.

Local politicians' awareness of the new conservation intention—to overcome past indifference or hostility toward local needs—will be an important first step in assuring long-term success. A clear perception of effective and concrete benefits also must exist, because any poor community and the individuals within it can not be concerned only with protection of ecosystems but must think also of their quality of life. Where tangible benefits can be established, conservation can move from an externally imposed, socially insensitive set of goals to a community conservation partnership.

ACKNOWEDGMENTS

Sincere thanks go to Maristella Bernardo, Maria Celeste Guimarães, and Fernanda Gabriela Borger for their assistance in the preparation of this chapter.

CHAPTER 18

The Role of Institutions in Community-based Conservation

Marshall W. Murphree

The term *community-based conservation* contains an objective—conservation—and an organizational approach through which to achieve this objective—the community. Communities are not, however, monolithic, undifferentiated entities. They contain categories of people distinguished by age, sex, interest, and power. Nor do they exist in a political or economic vacuum; they are linked in various ways with the larger society that surrounds them. For communities to act as effective agents of conservation, they must be structured so as to accommodate internal differences for collective goals. Equally, their links with the larger society must be structured in a productive and sustainable relationship that is both stable and dynamic. The organization of these structures is the topic of this chapter.

In this review, the term *institution* is used to refer primarily to an institutional actor, rather than in the more abstract sociological sense, which employs the term to indicate a recognized normative pattern that applies to a particular category of relationships. As used herein, *institutional actors* roughly equates to *organizations*, although institutional actors can be highly individualized, particularly in the case of private-sector entrepreneurship or tenure.

For the purpose of presenting a broad overview, categories and typologies have been highly compressed. This poses analytic problems, since it implies a generalization that may omit important detail. Institutional structures are multiplex and dynamic, but the case studies presented in chapters 2 through 13 are often silent on their own details—a circumstance that is difficult to avoid at this level of abstraction. Any treatment of institutional issues in the case studies necessarily intrudes on topics taken up in the other theme reviews. Although other sections of this book deal with important issues such as tenure, national policy and legislation, community structures, and process dynamics, I have not hesitated to bring them into this analysis where necessary.

Contextualizing Issues

Three general contextual issues need consideration before examining the specifics of institutional structures found in the case studies. In contemporary conservation-strategy debates, the community-based approach overlaps with the advocacy of local "participation" and "involvement" and is frequently linked to protected-area concerns. There are common strands of approach in all of these, but it is important to identify points at which community-based conservation differs from other strategies. This section thus analyzes important differences in motive and perspective, the issue of proprietorship, and the links between community-based conservation and protected areas.

Institutional-Actor Motives and Objectives

At the outset, the subject matter presents a paradox: Of the twelve case studies presented in this book, only one describes conservation developments that could be described as having been conceived and initiated by communities (INDIA). True, other case studies demonstrate attempts to revive or build upon indigenous conservation traditions and interests, but these programs are, in various degrees, externally initiated and imposed (see INITIATION).

I suspect that this paradox says something important about the institutionalization of conservation concerns. In the contemporary postcolonial developing world—and, indeed, in the developed capitalist world (NORTH YORK MOORS)—"communities" rarely articulate conservation concerns as an isolated set of activities. The institutionalization of conservation as a discrete set of concerns and actions is a product of governments, interest groups, and scholarship. Community perspectives on conservation are usually more holistic and integrative and more likely to view conservation as a means rather than an end.

The implications of this paradox increasingly have caught the attention of the conservation establishment during the last decade, leading to the "new paradigm for conservation" that Western discusses (1993:35). This new paradigm, which seeks to co-opt community support for exogenously derived conservation objectives, is an advance upon older confrontational and strictly protectionist stances. Conservationists now often prefer treating local people and their behaviors as a most effective vehicle for furthering their aims rather than as unfortunate stumbling blocks. This change of attitude does not, however, resolve the paradox. By definition, community-based conservation must be of, by, and for the community. Such a configuration is likely to involve different motives and objectives than those of externally derived conservation interventions. In some circumstances, this may produce fundamental incompatibilities; in these cases, governments and the conservation establishment must seek means other than community-based strategies to further their objectives. After all, imposed community-based conservation is a contradiction in terms and implies an exercise in futility.

In other circumstances, however, the motives and objectives of internal and external actors will be compatible and can create a productive synergy between different institutions. Then the promotion of community-based conservation can be viable, if the community itself sets the priorities. In this way, the community uses external institutional actors for its own integrated conservation and economic ends, rather than as the means for an external institution's ends. Differences in the objectives of various external institutional actors also must be recognized. When differences between external institutions are incompatible, failure is likely (Martins 1993). Yet objectives can be diverse and compatible. The collaborative support for the CAMPFIRE Programme in Zimbabwe includes organizations with different objectives: conservation, rural economic development, and the furtherance of local governance. In fact, the community focus can bring together frequently diverse "sectoral" interests (see MALUKU ISLANDS), often most apparent among donor agencies working on rural development. Rural development agencies' new interest in "off-farm" use of natural resources by the rural poor make them increasingly important institutional actors on the conservation scene, perhaps outstripping mainline conservation agencies in their importance.

The Institutional Centrality of Proprietorship

Advocacy of community-based conservation is largely driven by several perceptions: the importance of areas outside direct state control for biodiversity (AMBOSELI); the impotence of state agencies to manage conservation areas; the potential for cost-effective local management, using informal social pressure and drawing on detailed local knowledge of ecological dynamics; and local communities' enhanced motivation to conserve natural resources when conservation is of direct economic benefit to them. The literature is full of plans to decentralize conservation management, to involve local people in planning, to encourage their participation in projects, and to increase the economic benefits of natural resources to them. However well intentioned, such plans generally fail to achieve their aims of sustainable natural resources management and utilization. "Participation" and "involvement" turn out to mean the co-option of local elites and leadership for derived programs; "decentralization" turns out to mean simply the addition of another layer to the already obstructive bureaucratic hierarchy that governs natural resources management (Murphree 1993:5).

The reason for this is that participation usually is undertaken in ways that segregate responsibility from authority. The concept of community-based conservation implies that "the community" has an adequate institutional base for management, and this in turn implies that it has a sanctioned authority that implements its responsibilities. In practice, participation rarely incorporates such authority. What is required to make the concept of participation viable is proprietorship, which means sanctioned use rights, including the right to determine the mode and extent of management and use, rights of access and inclusion, and the right to benefit fully from use and management. Proprietorship provides the necessary tenurial component for an adequate institutional framework. It can be put in place through private-property arrangements (NORTH YORK MOORS) in which individual land and resource owners collectively manage a common property resource; or it can be instituted through a communal property-rights regime, which is likely to be the more viable option for most contexts in the developing world.

Delegation of proprietorship over natural resources to communities requires the state to relinquish considerable authority and responsibility. Such relinquishment, of course, is never total, any more than the privatization of land holdings implies total withdrawal of state authority over land. But relinquishment of authority does run contrary to the bureaucratic impulse to retain central authority. The establishment of communal natural resources management regimes will require strong policy directives to overcome this tendency, since the political will to relinquish control is weak in most governments. Furthermore, the ethos and interests of nongovernmental conservation agencies are generally inimical to this "radical" approach. Thus genuine policies of devolution of authority in conservation matters (as opposed to decentralization) are as rare today as they were sixty years ago, when Leopold (1933:404–412) made a strong case for them.

If the objective is community-*based* conservation, proprietorship in some significant form must be in place or projected to the community itself. In its absence, other forms of community "involvement" or "participation" must be understood for what they are: co-optive, cooperative, or collaborative arrangements. These arrangements, in certain circumstances, well may be appropriate and productive, but they do not on their own constitute community-based conservation.

There remains the question, Whose proprietorship? *Community-based conservation* implies that we are talking about communities, but *community* is an ambiguous term that eludes unequivocal definition. Nevertheless, the concept persists, indicating that it subsumes certain enduring and relatively ubiquitous organizational and institutional principles. It is sufficient to say that we are talking about social units with members who interact directly and have a collective identity both self- and other-defined. Relationships in such units are principally primary rather than secondary, and conformity to group norms is achieved mainly by peer pressure.

These criteria impose certain limits of scale upon "communities," both in terms of membership and spatial extent. Beyond a certain group size, relationships, decision-making, and management become bureaucratized. Beyond certain spatial limits, the same effect follows. Thus communities usually have a spatial dimension, and the terms *community-level* and *local-level* frequently are used interchangeably, even if, strictly speaking, they are not synonymous. One other loose usage of the term *community* has less to do with spatial considerations and applies to groupings of social units with common interests—in other words, "communities of interest." Perhaps, more accurately, these should be understood as interest-group associations that are small enough to foster primary relationships, collective interest, and peer control among proprietary units.

These definitional considerations, presented in hierarchical form in Table 18.1, have a bearing on our analysis of cases of community-based conservation. What is meant by a "community focus"? Is it level 7 or 6 or 8 in the table? While disputes can arise on this subject, any initiative with management focused at higher levels (e.g., levels 3, 4, or 5) has weak credentials as a *community*-based program or project, however appropriate or effective it may be in other terms.

On this issue, the cases reflect ambiguity in intent and/or shifts over time; for example, in AMBOSELI, the Kajiado County Council was the proprietary focus at an early stage, and the group ranches became the focus later. Finally, we must note differences in intent and actualization. CAMPFIRE's principles clearly are community-based, but as Metcalfe points out, the realization of this principle has been different in various community settings (see CAMPFIRE).

The conditions for community-based conservation are that it must be both community-*based* (the proprietary issue) and *community*-based (the scale issue). Other institutionally structured conservation management approaches, however laudable or appropriate, are something else and must sail under different colors. This is not to suggest that other management forms are incompatible with community-based conservation or that they can not mutate into community-based conservation.

Protected Areas and Proprietorship

I do not advocate devolution of rights as a panacea for all conservation concerns. Governments (or substate regional entities—levels 3 to 5 in Table 18.1) remain responsible for national conservation concerns, which may be managed best by state (or substate) agencies. These concerns may relate to a common property resource (e.g., water), a national economic asset (e.g., a tourist attraction), or maintenance of biodiversity. In such cases, the state assumes the role of proprietor and legislates, controls, and assumes the responsibilities of direct management. This well may be the only viable approach, given the nature of the resource. There is, however, an important condition: Viability also depends upon the state's capacity to perform the managerial role it has assumed as proprietor.

Particularly in respect to biodiversity concerns, governments have tended to create protected areas under state or regional proprietorship. Brandon and Wells note that the "global network of protected areas has improved dramatically during recent decades" (Brandon and Wells 1992:558). This trend may not be an unmitigated good. First, even if the trend continues, protected areas are unlikely to assuage biodiversity concerns, since most biodiversity lies beyond parks (AMBOSELI). Second, the caveat about limits on state capacities applies. States that extend "paper parks" or protected areas beyond their management capacities are assuming a proprietorship that will be spurious in practice. Third, expansion of protected areas usually takes place at considerable cost to local people in terms of access to land and resources and, sometimes, the predations of certain wildlife

Table 18.1

```
╔═══════════════════════════════════════════╗
║                                           ║
║     Levels of decision-making and activity  ║

                    **1**
              International level

                    **2**
               National Level

                    **3**
        Regional (State or Provincial) Level

                    **4**
                District Level

                    **5**
              Subdistrict Level
     (e.g., *taluk* in India or *thana* in Bangladesh)

                    **6**
               Locality Level
    (a set of communities that have cooperative/commercial
    relations; this level may be the same as the district level
         where the subdistrict center is a market town)

                    **7**
              Community Level
    (a relatively self-contained socioeconomic and residential unit)

                    **8**
                Group Level
       (a self-identified set of people who have some common
        interest; may be a small residential group such as a
          neighborhood, an occupational group, or some
            ethnic, caste, age, sex, or other grouping)

                    **9**
              Household Level

                    **10**
               Individual Level

     *Source:* Uphoff 1986:11
```

408

species. The conflict this creates between protected areas and their neighbors can block the achievement of conservation objectives.

This third issue most frequently has evoked what Western calls the "new paradigm for conservation": seeking to obtain the cooperation of protected-area neighbors by making such areas a source of economic and developmental benefit to surrounding communities. The variety of schemes implemented in this mode include revenue sharing, resource sharing, buffer zones, compensation, and promotion of local development projects as usage substitutes. Brandon and Wells subsume these initiatives under the title Integrated Conservation-Development Projects (ICDPs), with the following description:

> While the core objective of these projects is protected area conservation, the projects aim to achieve this by promoting socioeconomic development and providing local people with alternative income sources which do not threaten to deplete the plants and animals within the PA. (1992:557)

Many of the schemes that operate under the rubric *ICDP* turn out to be relational: Their core objective is to *improve relationships* between state protected areas and their neighbors through trade-offs on terms determined by the state. Few are proprietary in essence, seeking to *devolve proprietorship* of the protected area to local communities or to create proprietary units on the periphery of protected areas. A notable exception is found in KAKADU.

Projects that focus on improving relationships are not necessarily inappropriate. But they frequently run into problems with the trade-offs. The state often deals with indeterminate partners ("villages," "groups") or with regional administrative units that can not satisfy the criteria of community-based proprietorship. With undefined partners, the potential to establish local responsibilities and enforce the required regulations is small. Proprietary schemes have far greater chances of long-term success, since they provide the basis for conflict resolution between authorities of equal status in an open and transparent manner. For most protected areas, devolution of proprietorship involves negotiations between the state and several proprietors, or between the state and a coalition of proprietors.

Finally, communal (or coalitional proprietary) natural resources management regimes that fulfill the criteria of community-based conservation may create their own protected areas (although they rarely are called by this name) independently of the state. Zimbabwe offers two examples. First, there are the rhino conservancies, in which groups of private ranchers have entered into mutually binding agreements to provide appropriate range and management arrangements for a discrete rhino population, an instance of coalitional proprietorship (DNPWM 1990). Second, in the CAMPFIRE Programme, some communities—Kanyurira Ward, for example—have, through land-use planning, designated portions of the areas under their jurisdiction for exclusive wildlife use. In an area of 400 km², 380 km² have been set aside for wildlife use, with the 20 km² reserved for human settlement and agriculture protected by electric fencing (see also INDIA).

Thus community-based conservation schemes may or may not be linked to state protected areas. Often they are, and this is commonly the case when state or conservation agencies have initiated them. But community-based schemes can stand alone in their essential characteristics. Thus ICDPs and community-based conservation initiatives are not necessarily synonymous. ICDPs can be purely relational in character, or they can be proprietary. Proprietary schemes can involve a variety of relationships: negotiated cooperation between the state and individual or communal proprietary units, proprietorship resident in a coalition of actors, or creation of protected areas solely within the jurisdiction of a single proprietary unit.

Institutional Actors in Community-based Conservation

The roles, resources, and relations of institutional actors commonly found in community-based conservation are important in determining program success or failure. This section categorizes these actors and analyzes the roles, resources, and relationships involved.

The Actor-oriented Approach

Most organizational analysis treats organizations in a political vacuum. The same is true of much program and project planning. These may give some attention to government policy and legal structures but generally assume that planning is largely a matter of "packaging" organizational structures and performance. In contrast, Abel and Blaikie put forward the following suggestion:

> The utilization of natural resources at a particular place and time is the outcome of conflicting interests between groups of people with different aims. Usually there is no absolute dominance by one group, so there are commonly a number of different ways of using resources at the same place and time. (1986:735)

The actor-oriented approach is a way to explore the political dimensions of environmental management, both at micro and macro levels. It argues against treating "the community" as a homogenous, undifferentiated entity.

Both the community context and the community/external intervention nexus can be examined, giving a clearer understanding of organizational roles and dynamics:

> Rather than viewing intervention as the implementation of an action plan, it should be visualized as an on-going transformational process in which different actors' interests and struggles are located. (Long 1992:9)

The concept of *actor*, however, is a social construction rather than simply a synonym for *individual*. Nor is *institutional actor* a synonym for *group*. An institutional actor, the focus of this chapter, is an entity organized for the interests of some group or set of goals. Groups and individuals are considered within the context of organized institutional arrangements.

Institutional Actors

Table 18.2 displays the spectrum of institutional actors in community-based conservation programs or projects. The table is not exhaustive, nor are all the actors listed likely to be found in a specific case. They are briefly analyzed here:

Traditional Authority Structures

These are structures of authority and power whose legitimacy is based on a shared value system and collective cohesiveness. This often includes a shared history and leadership derived from kinship and descent. Where such structures are present (AMBOSELI, MALUKU, KAKADU, CRATER MOUNTAIN), they can be a powerful institutional factor, even though they are often ignored in formal planning and implementation (Murphree 1993).

Local Governance Structures

These are elected or appointed bodies. They are accountable to a local constituency and have authority to deal with development and regulation.

Local Party Political Structures

These usually are most significant at local levels in states that have adopted a one-party state model. There they assume a quasi-administrative role (NIGER). With the decline in the popularity of this model, they are of decreasing significance.

Self-interest Organizations

These are local associations organized to promote specific interests, usually economic in nature. They may address multiple objectives of common interest (e.g., women's clubs) or specific objectives (e.g., a water-users' association). They may be cooperatives, with pooled economic resources involved. In certain instances, they may be termed local NGOs (BOSCOSA). Where such organizations have proprietorship over a resource, they may structure a coalition (INDIA).

Service Organizations

These may have a religious, charitable, or community-service function.

Private Entrepreneurial Actors

These may be individuals or corporate individuals operating as a business entity within the community. Only ANNAPURNA discusses these, but they can represent a powerful local dynamic and focus of leadership.

Regional or Subregional Administration

These institutional actors represent administrative extensions of the state under a ministry of local government, state administration, or similar designation. They

Table 18.2

Categories of institutional actors

1

Internal or Community Institutional Actors

Traditional Authority Structures
Local Governance Structures
Party Political Structures
Self-interest Organizations
  Multiple Task
  Specific Task
  Cooperatives
  Local NGOs
Service Organizations
Private Entrepreneurial Actors

2

External Institutional Actors

Government or State Political Actors
  Regional or Subregional Administration
  Government Line Ministries/
  Agencies/Project Administration
Nongovernmental Institutional Actors
  Donor/Aid Agencies
  Consultancy Agencies
  International NGOs
  National NGOs
  Universities and Research Organizations
  National Interest Associations
  National Service Organizations
  Private Sector Entrepreneurial Actors
  Neighbors

have various degrees of autonomy, depending on state decentralization policies, and their constituencies may be either national or regional. They are staffed by bureaucratic hierarchies that foster one-way, top-down decision-making. Thus their core constituency is often the state/bureaucratic center.

Government Line Ministries/Agencies/Project Administration

These institutional actors normally have the functional responsibilities of extension and regulation, although they may assume elements of administration in specific sectors. Their constituency is the same as for government administrations.

National Political Party Organizations

These institutional actors are usually transitory, appearing at community levels only at seasons of national electoral activity. They can not be dismissed, since the messages they give or receive and pass on at national level can influence policy.

Donor and Aid Agencies/Consultancy Agencies/International NGOs

Donor agencies usually do not attempt to implement programs or projects directly but prefer to work through government agencies or NGOs. They may assume a de facto implementing role through conditions placed on grants. They also may control implementation by contracting out project management to consultancy agencies directly accountable to them. Consultancy agencies increasingly are involved in implementation as well as planning. These may be private for-profit actors, but they also may be NGOs or university/research organizations or consortia involving two or more of these categories. International NGOs may be donors, implementors, or both.

National NGOs

National NGOs generally are differentiated from international NGOs on the basis of their national, regional, or local constituencies; their indigenous expertise and perspectives; and their scale. National NGOs allegedly are less bureaucratized and more capable of working at local levels. For these reasons, donors' and international NGOs' increasing use of national NGOs has led to their proliferation. Sometimes this creates problems of capacity and bureaucratic overdevelopment in national NGOs; it also may distance national NGOs from their originally intended beneficiaries.

Universities and Research Organizations

Primarily organized for research and training purposes, these can play an influential role in policy formulation and in program and project planning and monitoring. Sometimes they are involved in implementation through participatory research or through consultancies.

National Interest Associations

These are formally distinguished from national NGOs by representing proprietary or producer interests with clear lines of accountability; NGOs tend to be issue-focused actors with a more diffuse and self-defined constituency. The CAMPFIRE Association in Zimbabwe is an example.

National Service Organizations

These are the national equivalents of local service organizations, often religious.

Private-Sector Entrepreneurial Actors

These are national rather than communal actors but can have a powerful impact on community-level plans to manage the environment. Their capital and managerial expertise are particularly important when natural resources use involves marketing outside the community (AMBOSELI, CAMPFIRE, MALUKU ISLANDS, BOSCOSA).

Neighbors

This category refers to spatially proximate communities or proprietors. These may include areas where the state is the proprietor, as well as private landowners or other neighboring communities (INDIA).

Roles, Resources, and Relationships

Table 18.2 demonstrates that there are a large number of possible institutional actors involved in community-based conservation. For this synopsis, there are three main groupings: community institutional actors, government institutional actors, and nongovernmental institutional actors. The analysis briefly examines the roles of these actors, their resources, and their interrelationships.

Roles and Resources

The resources held by community, government, and nongovernmental institutional actors and the roles they play vary considerably. These are briefly analyzed below, along with the relationships between these actors.

Communities   Communities are by no means homogenous or undifferentiated entities. The community itself has conflicting interests and different aims. Community-based conservation makes the implicit assumption that these ongoing dynamic conflicts can be contained by collective agreement and compliance. Communities have been able to do this historically. Whether they can do this in contemporary contexts is more problematic. Economic transformation, colonization, and bureaucratization have ripped apart traditional sources of community organization. If the community is to serve as a viable principle of social organization in the contemporary world, it must be institutionalized in a way that allows effective interaction with external institutional actors.

This institutionalization requires a clear definition of the community and its vested constituent units of social organization. As Cernea comments in regard to participatory afforestation strategies, "Operationally, it is not only a challenge but an absolute necessity to desegregate the broad term 'people' and to identify precisely *who* and *how*" (1989:25). After this identification is made, the institutionalization must be responsive to local relational dynamics, accountable to collective community interest, and able to articulate views and positions effectively with external institutional actors.

This requires external actors who can exercise caution in carrying out interventions. One such intervention would be state legal policy that legitimates the proprietary status of communities. The intracommunal institutionalization of social actors is more problematic. Particularly in the developing world, long colonial histories have denied communities the authority to act autonomously, making them dependent on political and economic outsiders. The ability to plan and function is thus new to the generations that now people these communities. Extension agencies are needed to assist communities in structuring their institutional organization, particularly at national or international levels. However, external actors tend to impose their own formulations, often inconsistent with community circumstances and perspectives. In spite of the dependency into which some have been cast, communities usually have far greater organizational resources than are acknowledged. These may be inhibited rather than enhanced by external interventions insensitive to local context.

Few case studies specifically address intracommunal organizations explicitly— a fact that is revealing in its own right. Some (MALUKU ISLANDS) describe approaches that appear to have little concern for these factors. BOSCOSA pays considerable attention to the identification and institutionalization of interest groups and their relationship to external actors, but it is questionable whether this program is community based. This general lack of clarity in the definition of community institutional actors is a matter that needs to be addressed.

Government institutional actors   The role of governments and their agencies in community-based conservation should be enabling and supportive, providing extension, coordination, and regulation. In practice, this is frequently not the case. The inbuilt tendency of government structures is to assert power and claim authority, even when they lack the resources to fulfill the implied responsibilities. Furthermore, governments are bureaucratic in nature, and bureaucracies generally resist the devolution of authority, within their own hierarchies or beyond. The tendency of bureaucratic hierarchies to foster top-down, one-way communications and decision-making strengthens this characteristic. Bureaucracies are often extractive rather than supportive and either regard communities and their resources as sources of raw materials, revenue, and labor for the state or for important elite constituencies of the state (AMBOSELI, CAMPFIRE).

State institutional actors derive much of their strength from their status as "gatekeepers": coercively backed authorities that determine what communities can and can not do. They also derive strength from their ability to control the flow of fiscal and other resources from the center to the periphery. Rarely do flows to communities offset what has been extracted from them. Finally, state agencies act as gatekeepers for donor grants and aid projects.

Why would state-agency actors support community-based projects at all? In part, the answer may be political: States need to be seen as responsive to the needs of their rural constituents. Another factor may be the state's need to co-opt local organizational resources without genuine devolution of proprietorship and benefit. Genuine devolution is rare, and KAKADU presents an outstanding exception. In CAMPFIRE, the program witnesses the acceptance in principle and initiation of devolution by one government agency, but the process is hampered by the reluctance of other government agencies.

Government agencies are by no means unified in perspective and action, nor are the legislation and policy that drive them. Wildlife agencies and agricultural extension agencies, for example, are frequently in conflict and deliver different messages at the community level.

Nongovernmental institutional actors   Nongovernmental institutional actors differ from the other two major categories in focus and permanence. With the exception of universities and research organizations, national interest associations, and national service organizations, the nongovernmental actors listed in Table 18.2 (page 412) are issue- or problem-specific in focus. Communities and governments are organizational responses to multiplex and enduring structural and societal requirements. As such, they have the character of permanence, although their profiles may change radically over time. Nongovernmental actors arise in response to perceived need, and their raison d'être falls away when the need (or the perception of it) changes. Thus, in a constant contradiction, their character includes potential obsolescence, even though their internal dynamics may strive for permanence. Often the response is to change objectives within the organization. This may be a healthy stratagem, denoting a flexible and capable agency, but such moves need to be scrutinized carefully to ensure that they are not supply driven or an accommodation of agency leadership's entrepreneurial interests.

Impermanence may be a problem for nongovernmental agencies, but it also provides the basis for their strengths. Being issue- and problem-specific, they can mobilize financial and personal resources comparatively quickly and efficiently. They have become the financial conduits and managers of global environmentalism, with resources that dwarf those of national governments. This places them in an uneasy relationship with national government agencies. They have the money, personnel, and rapid-response capacity for programs and projects, while national governments claim sovereignty and gatekeeping authority.

Relationships
Institutional actors in each major category tend to see themselves as internally unified in opposition to actors of other categories and as internally differentiated in

terms of their role within their own category. Thus community institutional actors see themselves as having common interests when faced with external actors, but as having different interests in juxtaposition to each other. Just as "local people relate all outsider-generated activities" (CRATER MOUNTAIN:205), external actors see themselves as a common category dealing with the community, but sharply differentiate between governmental and nongovernmental categories. Both subcategories tend to perceive a unity in opposition to each other but assume competitive stances with respect to members of the same subcategory. The frequent differences in the perspectives and objectives of government wildlife and agricultural extension agencies is a good example.

The important exception to this generalization lies in the exploitation of internal divisions to forge alliances across the major category boundaries. Thus, for instance, an external actor such as a national NGO may ally itself with a community cooperative to further mutual objectives.

The personal factor   While institutional actors are not synonymous with individuals, the personal factor should not be ignored. It is individuals who critically shape and reshape the roles and performance of institutional actors. An organization, regardless of how appropriate its structure is, is only as good as the people who operate it. This recognition usually emerges only explicitly in organizational strategies for training and hiring but not in program planning. Differences in the performances of two organizations may be due more to the performance of individuals than to differences in structure.

While the personal factor is difficult to pin down, it is useful to examine the role of individuals in two contexts: within institutional structures and between them. For the first category, INDIA provides a good example of the importance of individuals in the initiation and leadership of community-based conservation. Program intervention should provide the flexible context for leadership. Beyond this, organizations should allow for leadership that seizes on individual potential as it arises and develops.

The second category includes individuals who work between institutional actors. This critically important function requires special skills (AMBOSELI). A cultural go-between or ombudsman is often crucial to integration of internal and external actors' perspectives and concerns. This role is best filled by an individual with long-established local and national credentials who can operate independently of any specific institution. Greater effort should be made to identify and facilitate the work of individuals who can play this role.

Key Implementational Issues

Of the broad spectrum of issues in the implementation of community-based conservation programs and projects, the two most important are linkage and process.

Linkage

The assertion that small-scale proprietary activities provide the basis for genuine community-based conservation implies that discrete communities implement these by and for themselves. If so, the linkages of primary concern are those between the intracommunity actors that may produce conflicts and compromises.

This analysis is not, however, an argument for community autarky or isolated community autonomy. There are several reasons why, in the contemporary world, communities can not act in an autonomous, isolated mode. Communities are bound by modern market systems into larger economic structures that may fragment collective community economic interests. National political interests and bureaucratic regulations erode communal authority. "Integration into larger systems means that the social and economic center of gravity shifts away from the community, and rural institutions become politically marginalized" (Lawry 1990:415). Thus communities need allies, including the state, if they are to realize proprietary claims. They also need assistance with collective arrangements to overcome internal division and reach external actors. Communities themselves seek integration with and need the assistance of actors in the outside world.

These circumstances have prompted schemes of "comanagement" between communities and government (Lawry 1990). Comanagement is a broad concept that covers an assortment of managerial arrangements. In one sense, almost all land and resources are comanaged by the state and other actors, from the urban plotholder subject to municipal regulations to the farmer subject to veterinary and cropping quotas. But proposals for state-community comanagement usually suggest far greater direct state involvement in hands-on management. Given the different authority and resources that the state and communities possess, it is not surprising that comanagement usually turns out to be state management.

The arguments in favor of comanagement usually are based on perceptions of different levels of management skills and resources. A parallel rationale for external intervention in community management is based on mutual interest. This approach, called stakeholder analysis, examines the groups and social actors with a real or putative stake in communal environments and their use. As with comanagement, *stakeholding* is a concept with wide application. It usefully delineates the broad circle of actors with an interest in a community's resources: private entrepreneurs, the state, academics, planners, NGOs, and the international conservation establishment. All of these, in some form and in various degrees, "use" the community's resources and therefore have a stake in them. The danger is that this perspective easily can transform interest into a conceptual collective proprietorship by a vast and amorphous circle of stakeholders. Those stakeholders who have invested the most in professional expertise and monetary capital form the board of directors. But this accounting procedure is false. Communities' investment in their environments—their land, their resources, their labor, their local environmental knowledge, their managerial presence, and their stake in the future—is in the aggregate and, by social accounting, is far higher than that of all external actors put together.

Stakeholder perspectives and comanagement stratagems each have value, but both reveal the dangers inherent in links between community and external actors. External interventions easily can shift from facilitation to co-option.

Community-based conservation programs thus pose a dilemma: They require the very community-external linkages that have such high potential to subvert the community itself. To counter this potential for subversion, clear priorities should be specified for all linkages and their components. Communal interests, responsibility, and authority should be paramount. Specific regulatory authority retained by the state should be clearly defined, both in scope and mode, and exercised in a sensitive and supportive manner. This approach to comanagement is well illustrated in KAKADU. The reciprocal rights and responsibilities specified in these linkages also need to be reviewed and revised periodically. Finally, external actors should recognize the potential danger of linkages subverting rather than facilitating community-based conservation (communities usually are fully aware of this). Regular dialogue between communities and external agencies should help to monitor the situation.

Intracommunity Linkages

Community-based conservation implies a community with proprietary rights, institutionally structured so that collective interest subsumes and reconciles internal and sectional division. Generally, the institutional instrument for this is the local government authority or the traditional authority structure, or both. They integrate the interests and activities of other institutional actors at the internal or community level. Unfortunately, in much of the developing world, local government structures are poorly evolved and traditional authority structures eroded. This Achilles' heel of community-based conservation is often the root cause of failure in initiatives of this type. This weakness in itself is not a reason to abandon such approaches; community-based conservation schemes can play an important role in strengthening the development of effective institutions of local governance.

The strengthening of local institutions is determined in large part by the character of extracommunity alliances. For the community, these linkages can be divisive or unifying. The divisive tendency can be unleashed when, for instance, a government or aid agency promotes an intracommunity fishing cooperative and supplies it with resources that make it more powerful than overall community authority. This tendency can be exacerbated if multiple alliances of this type are present in the community. The community then fragments into a number of institutional actors, each with a powerful external ally, which receives its allegiance in place of the community.

The direction of primary accountability is a key issue in intracommunal linkages. My own view is that the tendency toward fragmentation is best contained when proprietorship of the common property resources of a community clearly is vested in the community's coalescent authority structure. Then resource use by other intracommunal actors (or external actors, for that matter) is governed by lease or other agreements with the authorities. The case studies devote little analysis to this important issue.

Community–External Actor Linkages

This type of linkage, of course, is the critical nexus for initiatives in community-based conservation, with inherent necessities and dangers. In an ideal situation, the community "will" is cohesive, the state reinforces local authority effectively, and external actors respond in coordinated fashion to the initiatives of local authorities.

Unfortunately, this ideal is rarely in place (INDIA). Where such conditions do exist, they should be allowed to continue evolving in tune with internal community dynamics. Such ideal conditions are not, however, commonly found, and external initiatives often are required. The nature of such interventions, how they are structured, and the mode of their delivery then become important factors.

Centripetal direction   Intervention should lead to a collective institutional base for communal management that overcomes intracommunal divisions. It should be channeled through the communal "gatekeepers." The extent to which this practice has been operative in the case studies gathered here is not always clear. In KAKADU it is clearly present and in CAMPFIRE, incipiently so. In MALUKU ISLANDS, it seems to be absent.

This general prescription is not appropriate in all circumstances. Subcommunity institutional actors may show better organizational characteristics, and it *may* be appropriate for external actors to use them as an initial entry point (AMBOSELI, CAMPFIRE, ANNAPURNA). BOSCOSA presents a detailed example of this strategy. While effective care must be taken to avoid intracommunal fission, the sensitive approach of BOSCOSA's principal participatory tool, the gradual development and consolidation of local NGOs as advocates for sustainable development, is appropriate—although the consolidation of local NGOs is only one component in the institutional consolidation of communities. If community-based conservation is the larger goal, alliances or linkages between subcommunity and external actors must be carefully monitored and, if necessary, changed, recognizing that initial justifications may not remain valid.

Role definition   "Local people relate all outsider-generated activities, however unconnected they may seem from an external perspective," CRATER MOUNTAIN (205) asserts. Indeed, these activities *are* interrelated, either positively or negatively. Coordination improves the impact but requires clear definitions of the roles of each external actor to produce complementarity rather than competition. Generally—using the idiom of the theater—the script for community-based conservation calls for the community to be the lead actor, with government and

NGO agencies cast in supporting roles. Government agencies have a primary responsibility to provide the support of higher authority and coordinate external inputs. They also may have an extension role to play. NGO agencies generally have the role of resource conduit, either in terms of funding, research, or extension personnel, to the community. External actors' clear understanding and acceptance of these respective roles is necessary but not in itself sufficient. The understanding must be held by the community, too, requiring external actors to communicate within the community itself. A further step would be to suggest that the community participate in the specific role designations of external actors. This shifts the locus of accountability for external actors toward the community. It also points to the need for continuous and direct interaction between communities and external actors. Finally, it implies that the role of external actors can change.

Coordination and scale   Coordination between all significant external actors is desirable. There are, however, certain practical constraints. Effective collaboration becomes more difficult as the number of collaborators increases, and the community may not be able to handle a plethora of external actors. Comprehensiveness and efficiency represent a trade-off in the external package delivered to the community. On balance, efficiency in coordination should have priority, implying limitation of the number of external actors directly involved in implementation at community level.

External funding and community institutional development   External actors, particularly NGOs, often come bearing the promise of gifts. The dangers of external funding for community development are now widely recognized, even if they frequently go unheeded. They include the perpetuation of dependency relationships in which communities and external agencies play extractive games with each other; the initiation of unsustainable capital development projects and localized bureaucratic structures; communities' tactical acceptance of objectives that are inconsistent with their own perspectives; and the introduction of power differentials within the community.

Despite these dangers, judicious donor funding of community programs is still warranted, particularly at the beginning. Technological innovation in the management and use of natural resources may be appropriate but beyond the means of cash-starved communities. The communications needs of a developing institution may require recurrent budgets that communities are not able to meet. Where programs involve new marketing arrangements, communities may need start-up capital to enable them to enter the market competitively. These are good reasons for donor funding, and eight of the case studies make reference to such inputs. What is important is that donor funding should further community interests rather than buy the donor a stake in the community's resources.

It is also important that donor funding is carefully structured to avoid the associated dangers:

- Care should be taken to avoid grants for capital development over which the community has little control or interest in maintaining. The CRATER MOUNTAIN discussion is instructive on this point.

- Avoid funding that drives a rapid buildup of unsustainable bureaucratic and managerial overheads and diverts benefits away from the community. CAMP-FIRE provides a warning example, indicating how some district councils have a tendency to use donor funds and wildlife revenues to follow this path.

- Indirect use of donor funds should be considered. Some donors with a conservation mandate refuse to fund nonconservation projects. Certain circumstances, however, may call for indirect solutions (such as the provision of a cattle-watering point or fencing of a vegetable garden) linked to the community's ability to manage wildlife (AMBOSELI).

- The use of donor funds to provide soft loan facilities for communities is an important but usually neglected consideration. As a mechanism for linking community performance with assistance, it provides the community with capital not usually available through commercial loan agencies. Donor funds also can enhance a community's bargaining position with private entrepreneurs, who also can be a source of capital inputs.

- Properly directed, donor funding can be used as an instrument for fiscal management, particularly if accountability for funds is located in the community. Donor agencies and governments are often reluctant to do this, citing financial inexperience and the extension training involved. Initially, local actors need help, to "write proposals, manage project funds, write financial and technical reports, and do quality control," as BOSCOSA points out. The BOSCOSA effort is an excellent example of one agency's grasp of institution building, made possible with donor assistance.

- Donor agencies frequently propagate unrealistically short timeframes for project successes. The donors have their own criteria, often of the move-a-lot-of-money-quickly variety. Such criteria are often incompatible with the pace of community institutional development. Generally, long-term grant facilities with small-scale increments are better than short-term, large-scale inputs.

Linkages Between External Actors

A major fault line exists between governments and NGOs, particularly between international donors and NGOs, in terms of their constituencies, objectives, and resources. Governments must be responsive to broad constituencies whose concerns are primarily political and economic. Their objectives therefore are to institute and implement policies that reflect these concerns, thus retaining their legitimacy. Retention of authority is a major political objective of governments, one that is also necessary for their role as coordinator. What governments in the developing world generally lack are the economic and skilled-manpower resources needed to promote the rapid rural development expected by their constituencies. Coupled with the general bureaucratic tendency to resist devolution and retain authority at the center, this creates conditions inimical to the development of community-based conservation.

Comparatively speaking, international environmental actors (donors and NGOs) are well endowed with the financial and skilled-manpower resources developing nations lack. They have different constituencies, comprised of the long-term conservation interests of the societies that sponsor them. They therefore seek to introduce long-term conservation directions into societies governed by short-term needs and development imperatives. This contrast between long-term conservation perspectives and short-term political and economic imperatives is not, of course, simply a First World–Third World contrast; it is an internal political conflict within the societies of the First World themselves. When First World states, or their conservation establishments, seek to impose long-term sustainability policies on Third World societies, an ecological neocolonialism emerges, one that is particularly pernicious, since the neocolonials operate internally in response to their own short-term imperatives.

The legitimacy of international agencies' efforts to influence developing-country conservation policy is thus open to question. If this drive is understood as a trade-off in First World–Third World relationships, the answer may be positive. The developing nations hold the bulk of the world's wealth of biodiversity, and the developed world holds most of the world's economic and technological wealth. This suggests the desirability of an equitable trade arrangement between the two. But then, donor inputs into Third World conservation must be understood for what they are: components of trade, not paternalistic charity.

This rather different understanding of relationships is a good start, but as the basis of TRADE, NOT AID, it requires contracts that recognize the status and role of national agencies. Since this particular trade relationship is rarely recognized, let alone institutionally well developed, donor agencies and international NGOs tend to operate in a contractual vacuum. Having received authorization from bureaucratic gatekeepers, donors have to rely on functional relationships with national institutions that evolve and change over time. Some of them do this very well and rightly perceive their role as including national institution building (BOSCOSA).

Linkages between international and national agencies thus drive and determine the impact of external actors on community-based conservation programs. The national proprietorship implied in TRADE, NOT AID programs is usually best implemented at community levels by national governments and national NGOs. International donor and international NGO inputs should be directed through these channels. National agencies then need to develop close and continuous collaboration, and donor and international agencies must adapt their own administrative and bureaucratic cultures to the capacities and styles of the national actors they use.

Scale and continuity are two important variables in creating linkages and coordination. Practical constraints suggest that the number of lead agencies in a program or project should be limited if they are to collaborate effectively. The Collaborative Group strategy—channeling policy on external inputs to communities through a five-member consortium (CAMPFIRE)—has been a major factor in the cohesiveness of the CAMPFIRE program over time. This group has no formalized regulatory status but derives legitimacy from its track record, accepted by the two group members with formal authority, the Department of National Parks and Wild Life Management and the CAMPFIRE Association of district councils. It is an arena for the rendition of accountability by its three NGO members—CASS, WWF, and ZimTrust—and it is small enough to allow this accountability to be continuous rather than sporadic.

Continuity in the membership of collaborating external actors is equally important, even if their roles change over time. This argues in favor of using national agencies that, as long-term actors, are therefore best suited to implement the long-term objectives of conservation concerns. International donors and NGO agencies come and go, according to the dictates of their mandates and the interests of their constituencies. For example, Amboseli was a spatial and historical terrain into which certain donors entered and from which they subsequently retreated. Transient donors and international NGOs generally do not have to live with the consequences of their actions. In its more extreme manifestations, this can lead to gunpowder interventionism: placing the fuses for institutional combustion and leaving before the explosion occurs. Communities evolve more comfortably with established national agencies with continuity and accountability closely linked to the community's own political voice.

Fry (1991), following a visit to Kanyurira Ward, has described the importance of linkages that bind relevant institutional actors into a relationship of mutual responsibility and benefit:

> However much Campfire involves the active participation of the local community, it could not succeed without the simultaneous involvement and commitment of a number of non-local people and institutions. I think that a complete analysis and understanding of the project would reveal that whatever successes it achieves will be the result of a symbiosis of government, NGOs, local community and the big game hunters. This is an important point for me. Far too often in the analysis of development projects the role of the intermediaries is underplayed. Usually because the donors prefer to imagine that local communities can be masters of their own destiny—surely an illusion given the external constraints on all members of society, not least on the poorest! The people of Kanyurira are citizens of Zimbabwe as well as inhabitants of Dande. Like it or not, they are situated within the confines of a particular social and cultural nexus and a specific state and economy. Surely the villagers have their own perspective on life. But so do CASS, WWF,

the Zimbabwe Trust, the safari operator, the Council and others. And they are also citizens of Zimbabwe, with their own specific hopes and ambitions. It is the interplay between these various actors that is the strength of the Campfire idea. Without any one link in this chain the project would not be viable.

Process

I strongly support Western's assertion that "locally-based approaches must be flexible and responsive to change above all else. The prevailing pattern of change from traditional to consumer societies underway in much of the developing world, as well as demographic and political changes, present a moving target for conservationists. What works now will not necessarily work in a few years" (Western 1993:37). Furthermore, programs and projects themselves generate internal changes. Institutional development is evolutionary, proceeds in phases and may take unanticipated directions (CRATER MOUNTAIN). Programs proceed stochastically, and initial success may generate conflict later as institutional actors' roles change and their power bases shift (BOSCOSA).

This combination of contextual change and internal program evolution dictates a strategy of "adaptive management" in community-based conservation programs. Adaptive management assumes that no planning or initial design can encompass all the relevant variables or anticipate all the consequences of the complexities of environmental management. Bell argues that, for wildlife conservation,

> the profession of wildlife management as a whole must be consciously structured to cater for these uncertainties, as well as for changes in value system, policy and technical capabilities. This means that the profession as a whole must be organized as a self-testing and self-evaluating system operating by negative feedback in relation to clearly defined objectives. (1984: 3)

In addition, I suggest that the system should be self-adjusting. To apply an adaptive management strategy to programs of community-based conservation, a process of rigorous self-evaluation and role adapatability must be put in place.

Programs of community-based conservation frequently rely on formal reviews for self-evaluation. This is understandable; these can be discretely budgeted and conveniently conducted by others rather than by hard-pressed program staff. While they can be a useful component in evaluation, they are not sufficient for the self-evaluation required by adaptive management, for a number of reasons.

First, they may be superficial or self-serving, since external agencies have an interest in justifying their performance to government or donors. Rather than success, absence of conflicts or problems may well denote the absence of any significant institutional change. Tension and confrontation, on the other hand, may indicate that dynamic institutional change has been initiated. Second, the results of formal reviews usually are presented in a form that is not readily accessible to communities. The monitoring process is then less than transparent, and the community has a marginal role in it. Third, such exercises are intermittent and can not provide the continuous feedback evaluation required for self-adjustment in adaptive management. What is required is something far more onerous: a sustained and continuous dialogue between the community and external actors that is both evaluative and adjustive. This requires time, tolerance, candor, and communications skills—resources that are sometimes scarce. But any agency serious about promoting community-based conservation must make provision for them, at the expense of restricting other activities if necessary.

The adaptive management strategy also needs adaptability in roles. This is particularly the case with national agencies, which, because of their continuity, are usually appropriate channels for external intervention. Actor continuity does not, however, imply immutability. Indeed, it may imply the opposite: a dynamic process of role redefinition responsive to institutional growth and evolution. CAMP-FIRE illustrates some actual or projected agency role shifts: the Department of National Parks and Wild Life Management moving from a predominantly regulatory to an extension mode; CASS making the transition from first-phase initiatory mode to a role more analytic and advisory; the CAMPFIRE Association resolving to change from an association of district councils to an association of producer communities. Such shifts require difficult internal adjustments but are necessary to make programs of community-based conservation responsive to their inherent shifting dynamics.

Conclusions

Schemes for community-based conservation have as their objective the sustainable use of the environment at community levels. But they are predicated on the existence of sustainable institutions of community management. The emergence of such institutions, against the background of a long era in which the importance of the communal context has been ignored, is a protracted and dynamic process. There are few shortcuts that can accommodate the impatience of external actors who wish to accelerate the process, and attempts to do so are counterproductive. On the other hand, external actors easily can retard or obstruct the process by inappropriate interventions. Attention to the participation and community issues embedded in the institutional framework of community-based conservation may prevent misdirected planning and implementation, thereby facilitating rather than frustrating the process. Community-based conservation in essence is about sustainable institutions. Recognition of this fact provides the basis for sound policy and effective implementation.

ACKNOWLEDGMENTS

The author wishes to gratefully acknowledge the support of the International Development Research Centre of Canada (IDRC) and the Ford Foundation, whose assistance to the Centre for Applied Social Sciences at the University of Zimbabwe made possible the research on which this chapter is based.

SOURCES

Abel, N., and P. Blaikie. 1986. "Elephants, People, Parks and Development: The Case of the Luangwa Valley, Zambia." *Environmental Management* 10 (6):735–751.

Bell, R. 1984. "Adaptive Management." In *Conservation and Wildlife Management in Africa*, ed. R. Bell and E. McShane-Caluzi, 3–7. Washington, D.C.: U.S. Peace Corps.

Brandon, K., and M. Wells. 1992. "Planning for People and Parks: Design Dilemmas." *World Development* 20(4):557–570.

Cernea, M. 1989. *User Groups as Producers in Participatory Afforestation Strategies*. Washington, D.C.: World Bank.

Department of National Parks and Wildlife Management (DNPWM). 1990. *National Conservation Strategy for Black Rhinoceros*. Harare: Department of National Parks and Wild Life Management.

Fry, P. 1991. Letter to the author reporting on a visit to Kanyurira Ward, Zimbabwe, as the Ford Foundation representative in Harare.

Lawry, S. 1990. "Tenure Policy Toward Common Property Natural Resources in Sub-Saharan Africa." *Natural Resources Journal* 30:403–422.

Leopold, A. [1933] 1986. *Game Management*. Madison: University of Wisconsin Press.

Long, N. 1992. "Introduction." In *Battlefields of Knowledge*, ed. N. Long and A. Long, 3–15. London: Routledge.

Martins, E. 1993. "Extractive Reserves: A Critical Analysis, Brazil." Case study prepared for the Liz Claiborne Art Ortenberg Foundation Community Based Conservation Workshop, October 18–22, Airlie, Virginia.

Murphree, M. 1993. *Communities as Resource Management Institutions*. Gatekeeper Series No. 36. London: International Institute for Environment and Development (IIED).

Uphoff, N. 1986. *Local Institutional Development: An Analytical Sourcebook With Cases*. West Hartford, Connecticut: Kumarian Press.

Western, D. 1993. "Ecosystem Conservation and Rural Development: The Amboseli Case Study." Case study prepared for the Liz Claiborne Art Ortenberg Foundation Community Based Conservation Workshop, October 18–22, Airlie, Virginia.

CHAPTER 19

Economic Dimensions of Community-based Conservation

Daniel W. Bromley

Community-based conservation (CBC) of biological resources recently has come to be regarded as a feasible concept with which to augment or supplant traditional approaches. These older models, based on the idea that only national governments could bring sufficient knowledge and authority to the task, are now largely discredited. The traditional approaches did not work for two fundamental reasons.

First, biological resources can not be managed by proclamation alone, and many national governments—having declared certain areas part of a system of national reserves or parks—were powerless to implement what they had declared. Governments do not "own" what they can not control. Lacking effective means of matching proclamations with actions, many national reserves became inviting targets for people on the very margin of survival.

The second reason for failure, which is related to the first, is that creation of such islands of biological abundance in areas often suffering from severe resource degradation offers enticements that no amount of enforcement and wardens could overcome. In a word, the incentives were clearly awry. The problem is now of far greater importance than previously. With the declaration of the 1992 Convention on Biological Diversity, the international community appears prepared to expand the nature and extent of biological reserves on a scale deemed impossible only a decade ago. The failures of the traditional model would simply be compounded many times over if it were the only institutional form on which governments could draw in implementing this expansion. Fortunately, there are alternatives, and CBC appears to be the method of choice at the moment.

Community-based conservation seems compelling because it starts from the most fundamental principle: Individuals will take care of those things in which they have a long-run, sustained interest. National preserves—the traditional model—violate this principle by driving a legal and bureaucratic wedge between local people and the resource base in need of protection. Community-based conservation seeks to locate arenas of mutuality between those who want biological resources to be managed on a sustained basis and those who must rely on these same biological resources for the bulk of their livelihood.

The major problem to be addressed in community-based conservation is how to structure the working rules of such resource-management regimes so that local people have a robust and durable interest in the conservation of biological resources of interest to the larger international community. The answer, in brief, is to be found in the structure of entitlements (often called property rights) and in the constellation of incentives and sanctions that emanate from them. If we think of these new entitlement structures as resource-management regimes, then the incentives and sanctions constitute the working rules of those regimes. These working rules define domains of choice for local people as participants in the sustainable management of biological resources. The economic problem is to craft working rules that are incentive compatible for CBC.

Incentive Compatibility

The economic dimension of CBC centers around the search for new institutional arrangements that will align the interests of local people with the interests of non-local—and often distant—individuals and groups seeking sustainable management of particular ecosystems. In essence, we seek new resource-management regimes in which the interests of those living in such regimes coincide, to the greatest extent possible, with the interests of those living at some remove.

Economics usually is thought to concern markets, prices, or the buying and selling of particular objects. While these are indeed part of the economist's domain, at the most fundamental level, economics is about particular behaviors in response to specific choice domains. Economists are interested in the choices that people make, given the context in which individuals find themselves at a particular moment. The economic dimension of CBC is precisely concerned with the context of choice throughout a hierarchy of biodiversity conservation interests. The connection between behavior and reward is found in incentives—grounded in entitlements—that define choice domains for individuals.

If the relatively rich in the industrialized North are able to enjoy the benefits of biodiversity conservation at scant individual cost—while restricting the choice domain of poor individuals in the tropics, where a particular ecosystem such as Rondônia in Brazil has attracted international attention—then incentive problems abound. This situation is unworkable because the interests of local people—on whom the fate of ecosystems depends—are discounted relative to the interests of those who care for the ecosystem but not for its human inhabitants.

Incentive compatibility is established when local inhabitants acquire an economic interest in the long-run viability of an ecosystem that is important to people situated elsewhere. The interests of locals need not be identical to those of the international conservation community; sustained conservation of local resources requires only that the local stake in conservation becomes somewhat greater than in the previous resource-use patterns deemed inimical to conservation. Such ecosystems represent benefit streams for both parties: those in the industrialized North who seek to preserve biodiversity and those who must make a living amid this genetic resource.

The world's genetic resources are under constant threat from a range of land-use changes and economic pressures. This threat is the more serious because of the failure of existing institutional arrangements to guide and control individual and group behaviors with respect to these genetic resources. Recent international efforts, including the 1992 Earth Summit held in Rio de Janeiro, suggest that many of the world's leaders are prepared to make a commitment to the preservation of biodiversity. New policy initiatives with respect to biodiversity conservation are being pursued on several fronts. These initiatives must be understood as only part of a larger institutional transformation necessary to affect the way in which local people use and manage genetic resources.

Public policy with respect to community-based conservation of biodiversity consists of three components: the goals or intentions of CBC; a structure of new institutional arrangements predicated on these intentions; and a constellation of enforcement mechanisms that will induce compliance with the intentions. That is, policy is more than just the expression of abstract goals by national leaders. Policy must be seen as a coherent process whereby goals are transformed into meaningful operational strategies and programs that will render them attainable. The starting point of any (new) policy is the intention(s) that it aims to achieve.

Figure 19.1 depicts what can be called the policy hierarchy. At the policy level, goals and intentions are discussed and articulated. From these flow a set of institutional arrangements with the purpose of creating organizational structures—or modifying existing organizations—so that various aspects of biodiversity conservation can be improved. The Convention on Biological Diversity can be regarded as the policy declaration, which is then followed by specific rules to be followed by the contracting parties. These rules—the new institutional arrangements—will call for the designation of protected areas, guidelines for management of those areas, the restoration of degraded ecosystems, and systems to regulate the use and management of such areas in the future.

These institutional arrangements hold organizational implications, as the figure suggests. Some governmental agencies will be created, while existing agencies will be given new writs with the intent of carrying out the policy intentions of the convention. In Figure 19.1, this is the organizational level. Here, a lower level of institutional arrangements will be formulated. Examples include particular criteria for designating certain areas worthy of protection, management guidelines for allowable uses and activities in those areas, etc. These second-level institutional arrangements then bear on behaviors at the operational level. At this level, individuals interact with each other—and with environmental resources—in a way

Figure 19.1

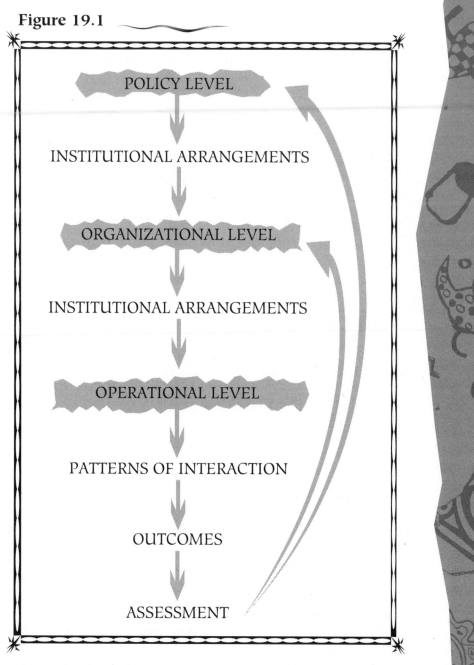

POLICY LEVEL

INSTITUTIONAL ARRANGEMENTS

ORGANIZATIONAL LEVEL

INSTITUTIONAL ARRANGEMENTS

OPERATIONAL LEVEL

PATTERNS OF INTERACTION

OUTCOMES

ASSESSMENT

The policy hierarchy

that is either conducive to sustainable management of such resources or leads to their destruction.

Finally, Figure 19.1 illustrates the feedback that is part of any policy process. The patterns of interaction among local people—their economic activities, land-use practices, and individual and collective use of the local ecosystem—result in particular outcomes that may or may not be conducive to sustainability of the ecosystem. Mechanisms and procedures for assessing outcomes against the declared purposes of conservation policy, and allowing correction and modification when discrepancies arise, must be in place. That feedback can pertain to either the policy or the organizational level. At the policy level, perhaps the goals and intentions were unrealistically optimistic or too vague. At the organizational level, perhaps bureaucratic turf battles have precluded the development of a coherent policy-implementation framework.

Regardless of where in the hierarchy fault lies, the fundamental problem is that the institutional arrangements defining choice domains at the operational level are inappropriate. That is, the resulting patterns of interaction fail to bring about individual and group behaviors that will result in conservation of biological resources.

These points suggest that local individuals can become part of a system of community-based conservation if they are given an interest in the benefit stream flowing from the newly managed biological domain. However, it is important to pay particular attention to the relationship between systems of property rights and economic incentives (see TENURE).

Entitlements

A fundamental issue is how institutional arrangements in general, and systems of property rights in particular, constitute an essential structure of economic incentives that operate on individual economic agents. Customarily, the outcomes of market processes—prices, quantities, and costs—are regarded as "economic incentives" while the legal arrangements—property rights—are regarded as "constraints" on economic behavior. This view has the twin disadvantage of both being incomplete and comprising a fallacy of composition. Prices and costs are simply artifacts of the prevailing institutional structure that indicates which factors of production must be paid for and which can be obtained free of charge. Hence, "cost" is a function of underlying legal arrangements.

The economic incentives at the operational level in Figure 19.1 are embedded in a particular legal structure. If property rights are unclear or perverse, then human action that degrades the environment will proceed without any mechanism for making the responsible party bear the costs of such behavior. The destruction of local habitat in the trekking regions of Nepal illustrates this problem (see ANNAPURNA). Similarly, poaching of wildlife in southern Africa reflects incentives at the operational level, which programs such as CAMPFIRE seek to rectify (see CAMPFIRE). The prevailing property structure therefore forms the very core of economics—and therefore of the incentives that individuals face (Bromley 1989, 1991).

In the language of property relations, we say that current resource users stand in a position of privilege with respect to the interests of those who care about biological resources. This means that resource users are free to disregard the costs their actions impose on others. Under the prevailing legal setup, those who care about biological resources have no rights.

In Madagascar, the logging of timber threatened the habitat of the golden bamboo lemur and the greater bamboo lemur (Wright 1993). Under the prevailing legal setup, loggers were free to disregard the costs imposed on those who hoped to protect the lemur's habitat. In other words, both the government and the loggers dismissed as unimportant the interests of those who care about the lemur. The loggers and those who care about habitat preservation were defined by the legal correlates of privilege and no rights respectively. Loggers were free to harvest timber at the lowest possible cost of those things for which they must pay: labor, fuel, machinery, permits, operating capital, and the like. For the loggers, the associated habitat was not a resource, but merely an impediment to the expeditious removal of timber.

The legal structure, in this way, defines what constitutes a resource. The legal system (and the embedded property regime) creates incentives for behavior through its recognition—or nonrecognition—of what is a "cost." The destruction of genetic resources in the vicinity of logging was not a "cost" to loggers because the prevailing legal relations failed to force the government to regard them as such. Therefore, changes in property regimes can offer fundamental changes in the economic incentives for loggers and others whose behaviors hold important implications for the world's biological resources.

The essence of the Ranomafana National Park Project was redefinition of the legal relations between those who saw only the forest's trees, and those who saw the forest as habitat for a complex of biological resources. Under the new legal regime—Ranomafana National Park—loggers face vastly different incentives. These different incentives flow inexorably from a different legal structure. The loggers now have a duty to protect genetic resources on pain of financial sacrifice, and those who care about biodiversity conservation have a right to expect careful treatment of the area's biodiversity. Ranomafana National Park is simply a new legal regime for resource management.

Community-based conservation is an effort to assign rights and duties to local communities so that they behave in certain ways with respect to particular biological resources. The rights come in terms of the secure expectation that local management in the interest of biological conservation will be rewarded in some way. The duties come in terms of the obligations that local groups agree to undertake in order to reap the benefits of biological conservation.

These rights and duties concern who is excluded from use of the biological resource; how that exclusion will be defined, monitored, and enforced; how the group will create new rules when circumstances dictate; and how the group will interact with external bodies—both national and international—in redefining rule structures. These rules, and the rights and duties of which they are a part, constitute the necessary conditions for the existence of the new resource-management regime. The management of that regime is then defined by a secondary set of rules that indicate acceptable behavior on the part of all who use the biological resources; procedures for assuring compliance with the management rules; criteria for deciding when the existing rule structure no longer serves its purpose; and procedures for changing the constellation of management rules.

In the international sphere, when we say that a particular nation has rights over its biological resources, it means that others—whether individuals or nation-states—have duties with respect to those biological resources. The Ranomafana National Park is a perfect example of international collaboration in the redefinition of legal regimes over biological resources.

The international Convention on Biological Diversity aims to bind nation-states together in a structure of quasi-right–quasi-duty relations that will carry the force of moral—if not legal—authority. The governments of various nations will have a moral commitment to protect biological diversity within their sovereign territories. The critical missing element, of course, is an ultimate authority that will prevent nation-states, having accepted the conditions of the convention, from defecting. Long-run compliance, however, might be secured through a number of means including changes in foreign economic assistance, trade sanctions, or withholding of other "benefits" of the international community (Young 1989).

These and other issues will require careful analysis if the international community is to succeed in crafting durable and incentive-compatible means for managing the world's biodiversity on a sustainable basis.

Economic Incentives

In biological conservation, a fundamental problem is understanding the critical interrelation between the interests of individuals, groups, and national governments as manifested in behaviors with implications for the world's genetic resources. Behaviors, informed and driven by interests, are mediated through various property regimes that entail prospects of perceived gains and losses for various agents in the system. In brief, individuals and governments face incentives for certain behaviors. Some of these are often thought to be economic in nature, but rarely are incentives regarded as legally based. As the foregoing makes clear, however, economic incentives can not exist without predication upon some legal relation.

If the destruction of biological resources—by virtue of the legal arrangements—is of no consequence to the responsible party, then there is no incentive with which to encourage greater care in preventing such damage. On the other hand, if the legal regime shifts, so that parties responsible for resource destruction are also responsible for compensating those harmed, the economic incentives shift dramatically as the potentially responsible party now contemplates the financial implications of the required compensation payments.

Economic instruments for biological conservation can not be regarded in isolation from the legal regime that makes those economic instruments both relevant and binding to economic agents. A situation in which those who cause destruction of genetic resources stand absolved of compensation requirements is the very essence of a perverse economic incentive. The perversity can be corrected not by finding some more clever economic instrument, but by changing the legal regime within which the particular economic instruments are embedded. A shift from a legal situation of privilege to one of duty for polluters is precisely the necessary first step in rectifying perverse economic incentives.

The challenge of community-based conservation is to create mechanisms for articulating values in biodiversity conservation and then permit those values to be manifested in incentive-compatible policy instruments. Finally, compliance procedures must be implemented to assure that conservation actually results. CBC programs with any hope of success will contain all three elements.

Facilitative policies build on the existing conservation tendencies of individuals living among valuable biological resources. Such policies are pertinent when the interests of the local community coincide with the interests of those who seek to conserve biological resources. Here, CBC could succeed if the policy process simply reinforced certain preexisting tendencies among the local population. CAMPFIRE discusses an effort to align the interests of local individuals in Zimbabwe with enhanced prospects for biological conservation. Programs such as CAMPFIRE seek to give local inhabitants a stake in the sustainable management of a range of ecological resources. Kakadu National Park in Australia, created from a combination of commonwealth and Aboriginal land, also seems to have borne this element in mind (see KAKADU).

When the interests of local communities are not consistent with enhanced conservation of biological resources, then it will be necessary to move beyond facilitative policies to actions that appear more regulatory in nature. Where it is possible to rely on inducement of certain conserving activities, then the domain of volition is largely preserved. Where compulsion is necessary to realize conserving activities, then the domain of choice for individuals is constrained.

Inducing policies attempt to realign incentives so that individuals and groups will be more inclined to engage in CBC activities. ANNAPURNA presents one example of this phenomenon. In this case, the drastic increase in trekkers to the Annapurna region of Nepal threatens a range of biological resources. The local inhabitants had become unwitting participants in the degradation of the ecosystem as commercialization of the area proceeded unchecked. While local residents certainly benefited from the increased commercial activity, the new development path was not sustainable. The Annapurna Conservation Area Project seeks to reintegrate local individuals into decision-making so that they can retain some control over their immediate surroundings. The communities undertake both small-scale conservation measures and efforts to provide alternative energy sources to preserve the area's dwindling forest resources. The intent is to reintegrate local individuals into decisions about local biological resources so that they manage those resources in a sustainable fashion. This is an example of policies that induce change in local behaviors.

Policies that compel certain behaviors attempt to force individuals to avoid actions that threaten biological conservation. The traditional approach to biological conservation—national parks, preserves, and other protected areas—is an example of compulsion in practice. The essence of community-based conservation is to replace compulsion with a mixture of facilitative and inducing approaches.

Property Regimes in Resource Management

Two general types of property regimes are pertinent to community-based conservation programs. The first (and traditional) way in which biological resources are protected is by creating national parks or national reserves. This is known as a state-property regime. In these regimes, ownership and control of environmental resources rests with the state, while management is carried out through its agents (government). Individuals and groups may be able to make use of the environmental resources, but only with the forbearance of the administrative agency charged with carrying out the wishes of the larger political community. The state may either manage and control the use of state-owned environmental resources directly, through government agencies, or it may lease the resources to groups or individuals, who are then given usufruct (use) rights for a specified period of time. In the extreme, state-property regimes result in the complete eviction of those with customary-use rights (see INDIA).

State-property regimes remove most managerial discretion from the user and generally convey no long-run expectations in terms of tenure security. To be successful, such regimes require governmental structures and functions that can match policy pronouncements with meaningful administrative reach.

The conservation community seems divided about the record of such regimes. A state-property regime is an example of compulsion. Those who live in or near such areas are generally prevented from using most parts of the local ecosystem. One graphic illustration of this is found in AMBOSELI, where such exclusion certainly does not appear to be conducive to aligning the interests of the Maasai with long-run conservation in Kenya.

Recently, buffer zones have been established around some biological reserves. These buffer zones still operate as examples of state-property regimes, with the provision that certain uses are allowed. These are still basically compulsory regimes, with strict rules originating outside the group of locals prescribing acceptable resource-use patterns and rates.

While buffer zones were thought to solve the enforcement problems associated with the artificiality of preserves, the solution is only partial. The next logical step is to recognize that conservation may be best enhanced if local people can be incorporated directly into the ecosystem as part of the management regime (see NEOTROPICAL FORESTS, BOSCOSA, AMAZON). Indeed, at the extreme, conservation is often enhanced to the extent that local people can be vested with a long-run interest in resource management.

Two approaches can be pursued. The first, as illustrated by KAKADU, is to create a state-property regime on lands that are acknowledged to belong to local people. Kakadu National Park in the extreme north of Australia encompasses both Aboriginal land (under lease) and commonwealth land. Along with this joint ownership of land, a system of joint decision-making governs many aspects of park use and management. Under this comanagement arrangement, local people become an integral part of the structure of resource use.

Where this option is not available, it is possible to develop an alternative ownership regime that gives locals a stake in the future-benefit streams arising from the ecosystem. This ownership structure would resemble what we call a common-property regime. Of course many common-property regimes around the world have been destroyed as a result of the relentless march of "modernization" and individualization. However, as suggested earlier, the essence of a common-property regime is that it strives to get the incentives right in a most fundamental way. Granting ownership rights to a group of local inhabitants and allowing them to craft a set of management rules for controlling use of their biological resources potentially resolves much of the conflict of interest that attends the preservation of local biological resources.

The literature concerning the feasibility of common-property regimes is broad (Bromley 1991, 1992; McCay and Acheson 1987; Ostrom 1990; Stevenson 1991). Much of this literature addresses the robustness of common-property regimes against competing claims from those outside the group of co-owners. As with private property, a common-property regime requires the willing legitimacy of the political hierarchy in which it is located. Private property would be nothing if the owner(s) did not have the capacity to call upon some authority system to enforce the sanctity of the regime. The same condition of authority also must exist for common-property regimes if they are to survive.

Is the legitimacy of that ownership drawn from the community or the nation-state? The answer hinges on the question of who the local community turns to when the legitimacy of its claim is challenged by outsiders. Arguing that legitimacy rests with the locals when the very security of the local natural resource is under threat from others who covet its bounty is not enough. Community claims address only the origins of the ownership interest of local people, not how that property right is to be upheld against potential incursions by others.

Whether we like it or not, the only authority available for that task is the nation-state and its government. Indeed, as suggested elsewhere, the breakdown of many common-property regimes is traceable to the fact that the nation-state regarded local communities as politically marginal and therefore not worthy of the effective protection that only the state can provide. There are no rights in a state of nature; rights only exist in the presence of an authority system that agrees to protect, with violence if necessary, the interests it finds legitimate. Individuals effectively have only those rights that the nation-state agrees to protect with its monopoly on coercion. The protection brought to those interests by the state consists of duties for non-owners. Only with effective duties assigned to others can rights exist (Bromley, 1992, 1993).

The community reserves of the Peruvian Amazon appear to meet this condition of external legitimacy for the common-property regime and the internal legitimacy for the rule-making authority of the group (see AMAZON). The government acts as an authorizing agent for these management regimes but seems to rely on the local inhabitants to operate the regime. When resource degradation becomes too severe, nonresidents are precluded from extracting resources. This decision apparently is the foundation of a renewed commitment on the part of locals to manage the resource base in a sustainable fashion.

The impetus for the community management scheme came from locals reacting to the extraction of resources they regarded as their own (see AMAZON). With external legitimacy recognized by the nation-state, the way was clear for the locals to undertake the hard work of crafting improved management rules conducive to enhanced resource management over the long run.

As with a number of similar situations, in formulating policies for CBC, careful analysis of the feasibility of rehabilitating these common-property regimes is essential. However, it is necessary to recall that policy requires more than good intentions. Coherent policy also requires rules of implementation and rules of enforcement. The history of destruction of common-property regimes is dominated by failures of rules and by failures of enforcement mechanisms (see INSTITUTIONS).

A true common-property (*res communes*) regime requires, at a minimum, the same thing as private property: exclusion of non-owners. While property-owning groups vary in nature, size, and internal structure across a broad spectrum, they are all social units with definite membership and boundaries, certain common interests, some interaction among members, some common cultural norms, and their own endogenous authority systems. Tribal groups and subgroups, subvillages, neighborhoods, small transhumant groups, kinship systems, or extended families are all possible examples of meaningful authority systems within common-property regimes. These groupings hold customary ownership of certain natural resources such as farmland, grazing land, and water sources. In the absence of authority, there can be no property. When the authority system breaks down, the coherent management of environmental-resource use can no longer exist. Under these circumstances, any property regime—private, common, state—degenerates into open access (*res nullius*).

The various property regimes elaborated upon here reflect economic conditions of land and related environmental resources, as well as the social overlay that reflects how those resources are to be used for the benefit of individual users—and those individuals from outside the immediate area who seek to influence how local biological resources are used and managed.

An essential element of biological conservation is to determine which areas should remain in the freehold domain, which areas should remain state property, and which areas should be restored to common-property regimes. In some places, national governments will need to declare their commitment to owning and managing certain critical areas. Existing national parks and preserves fit this notion. But state-property regimes may be created, as well, where several competing user groups are unable to reach sustainable agreements among themselves.

In other areas, governments only need to assure the external legitimacy of boundaries, thus allowing the evolution of common-property regimes over large expanses of important biological resources. Note that national governments may be required to protect new common-property regimes from intrusion by others, but they can then delegate management to the users themselves. Under this assured boundary protection, co-owners are presumed to be able to innovate institutional arrangements for managing natural resources on a sustainable basis. This management, in addition to concern for the nature and extent of natural resources use, also would be concerned with mobilizing and implementing investments in these resources. Such investments, in all probability, would constitute joint property among the co-owners of the regime.

Governance Issues in Community-based Conservation

Community-based conservation strategies will be successful only with recognition that the local management entities ("communities") are themselves embedded in a political regime that may be indifferent to conservation and the role of local communities in that process. At this stage, national governments must be presumed to have agreed to a program of enhanced biological conservation and that the problem is how to devolve that new (or enhanced) interest down to the local community, whose actions will be central to successful conservation outcomes. In other words, national governments will face the problem of determining the best locus for engaging in a particular policy discussion about biological conservation, formulating particular policies that will bring about enhanced biological conservation, and implementing the working rules and enforcement mechanisms associated with a particular policy.

First, there is a need to develop criteria whereby the policy dialogue on biological conservation can be properly located in a vertical dimension. The failure in most environmental policy discussions is that they do not start with a logic for identifying which level in the political hierarchy is the necessary and sufficient one for choice about particular environmental matters. "Political hierarchy" here means the national level, the regional level, and the local level. Most environmental policy fails to articulate a coherent reason why practically all policy dialogue is presumed to be at national level, while the regional and local levels are ignored or assumed to be so subservient to the national level that no conversations need be held there. This failure led to the traditional approach, in which national governments presumed that they were the only entities competent to protect and manage biological resources.

The task of developing criteria that will help national governments understand that some environmental issues are best addressed at the local level, some at the regional level, and still others at the national level is still before us. Given the extreme sensitivity to local and regional concerns in many nations, these issues will continue to plague the development of conservation policy.

The second imperative is to understand the proper role for executive, legislative, and judicial decisions. Of course, nations differ in how these three functions work and interact, and it is not possible to develop, in great specificity, a template that works in all places. In spite of this, some general conceptual work to help explain the logic of certain actions being determined in an arena of bargaining (the legislature), certain actions being determined in the arena of administrative rules (the executive), and other actions being determined in the arena of conflict resolution (the judiciary) clearly is needed.

The interplay between the legislative domain and the executive domain is often the most troubling. Legislatures are given to grand proclamations that are passed to executive-branch departments for implementation. Before these sweeping goals can be implemented, however, they must first be rendered coherent and meaningful. What, for instance, does a legislature mean by "protecting" biodiversity? What does a legislature mean when it declares that it wants the nation's waters to be "clean"? And how does it perceive "sustainable development"? Executive branch agencies are left with the difficult task of giving content to such broad declarations.

Similar problems will arise under various programs to promote community-based conservation. Which aspects of local ecosystems will become the focus of conservation? Which levels of use will be regarded as consistent with conservation? Who will arbitrate disputes over decisions that have been taken? Policy development for community-based conservation must include careful attention to these matters.

As a third point, most environmental discussions and environmental program proposals are silent on the critical link between individual economic agents and the new policy environment intended to change individual behaviors. Predictions about the good things about to happen as a result of a particular program leave out the role of the individuals whose large and small behaviors—which must be modified as a necessary condition for change—led to the current undesirable situation.

The relationship between the individual economic agent and the state usually is treated as a box into which new programs are dumped. By assumption, behaviors will be instantly modified, so that a better environment automatically results. Unfortunately, there are at least two forms of slippage in this policy. First, its makers often fail to understand the primary causes of environmentally destructive behaviors, and so the presumptive corrective policy instruments are ineffectual or miss the mark. Second, policy makers too commonly assume that compliance with the new policy will be immediate and total.

Policy makers need some guidelines that help them see the critical role of incentives in inducing compliance at minimal cost. Merely passing laws or developing administrative rules can be trivial and often counterproductive if compliance does not follow. Indeed, most environmental problems arise not from the absence of laws, rules, guidelines, and mandates but, rather, from the fact that individual economic agents can ignore those strictures with impunity. Often, a nation does not need more laws or rules, only smarter laws and rules that are cunning in their effect. Cunning rules induce different behavior in ways that minimize the individual's interest in cheating. In economic terms, cunning rules are incentive-compatible rules.

Finally, we come to the problem of deciding a logical sequence of steps. A meaningful program of biological conservation requires criteria for identifying problems that require immediate attention, those that can be addressed next, and, finally, those that do not currently represent a serious threat to the society under consideration. The great need here is development of environmental assessment criteria that are not dependent upon the disciplinary composition of a particular team of experts charged with conducting an assessment of the biological resources in particular places. This requires a wide range of environmental knowledge as an underpinning, but the payoff from more comprehensive assessment seems obvious. This work must also develop criteria for deciding which problems require immediate attention, and in what form.

By way of general guidelines, care should be taken to investigate current patterns of environmental resource use in particular locales, with special attention given to management of these resources in the commercial and subsistence sectors. Development of indices of local resource degradation and an understanding of the current situation in terms of long-run sustainability will be important. Throughout, it will be essential to pay particular attention to local power structures; existing laws, rules, and customs influencing natural resources use; and household responses to these institutional conditions in terms of their survival strategies.

Helpful steps can be taken to engage local communities in a participatory process to determine desired future development scenarios (see PARTICIPATION). These scenarios must recognize environmental sustainability, the economic and social empowerment of local people, and the reorientation of natural-resources-use regimes toward community needs and aspirations. The work should call attention to impediments to reallocating various natural resources, and it should suggest local, regional, and national mechanisms and instrumentalities with which to effect reallocation.

Individual and group access to particular natural resources must be documented and the major factors—or lack thereof—that influence that access determined. Special attention should be paid to current use patterns, the causes of resource degradation, sources of current conflicts over environmental resource use, and the institutional arrangements—rules, laws, customs—that have given rise to this situation.

For each local area, it will be essential to develop several feasible scenarios of natural resources use. These development scenarios should emphasize environmental sustainability, the economic and social empowerment of local people, and the gradual reorientation of resource use toward community needs and aspirations. Probable impediments to reallocations of various natural resources should be made and local, regional, and national mechanisms and instruments to effect that reallocation suggested.

Resource Values and Resource Valuation

The economic approach to biological conservation is often thought to require that markets be established so that "economic values" might be revealed. This confusion of price with value not only gives rise to disparaging jokes about the density (or arrogance) of economists, it confuses sources of value. Values, as artifacts of prevailing social norms, reside in the minds of individuals (Vatn and Bromley 1994). Not until diamonds became associated—through clever and relentless advertising—with durable love did they acquire such "value," thereby allowing a "market" in which high prices seemed eminently "reasonable" to work.

Markets do not exist to reveal true values; markets simply allow willing buyers and sellers to come together for mutual gain. The prices emanating from the market carry no normative significance in the absence of a long list of assumptions that allow us to infer, if the assumptions hold, that exchange prices reveal true social values. But if genetic resources are not to be bought and sold like loaves of bread, we need not despair that we can not discover their true value. The social problem is not to discover "true values" for genetic resources (for such a quest is bound to fail) but to ensure that genetic resources are managed under legal regimes that prevent their destruction at zero cost to the responsible parties. After all, if legal regimes are nonperverse, and if the potentially responsible parties are thereby precluded from making decisions about genetic resources with little financial sacrifice, then we would find rather more "conservation" of genetic resources taking place. Is it "enough" conservation? Who knows? But it is an improvement over the status quo in which certain economic interests are at liberty to squander valuable biological resources at no personal cost.

Values, after all, can be articulated through several mechanisms. Yosemite National Park did not need to spend its early years embroiled in some market process that enabled individuals and groups to ascertain its very considerable "value." Its social value was determined by intuition and reason, not by empirical observation. Economists tend to be wary of such "political" (or extramarket) revelations of value, warning that free riders will thereby be able to "overstate" the value of such places in order to preserve them without actually having to pay for them. Of course, we often forget that such objections not only beg the ultimate question of what represents "true value" but also seem to imply that markets will reveal such truth. Markets *may* reveal truth—but they may not. When irreversibilities are present, it may be prudent to take steps to avoid the small probability that our actions may set in train events leading to the disappearance of certain presumptively valuable biological resources. We call this the safe-minimum-standard of conservation (Bishop 1978, 1980; Pearce and Warford 1993).

Many questions on how to value resources, define policy, design property regimes, institute legal structures, decide equity, and arbitrate differences and disputes must be present at the heart of any coherent policy dialogue over biological conservation. It seems reasonable to consider a dual approach to the problem of biodiversity conservation. The first step is to move quickly to ensure that existing biodiversity is preserved; this is the short-run imperative. Next, it will be necessary to set in place legal and economic regimes that enhance long-run sustainable management of diverse biological systems. That is, the future must first be secured from destruction. Only then can we implement coherent management regimes of long-run benefit to all participants in this complex human and biological system.

To date, the Convention on Biological Diversity provides only the first component—a set of intentions or goals—of public policy. The hard part, now, is to create new institutional arrangements that will transform good intentions into modified behaviors on the part of both individuals and national governments. Articulating good intentions is the easy part and, although necessary, is very far from sufficient to assure biodiversity conservation over the long run. Biological conservation is enhanced to the extent that we are clear about the sources of "value" in biological resources and create institutional arrangements to recognize and distribute part of that value to those who undertake the hard work of resource management in the interest of conservation.

Two essential aspects of the value of biological conservation are implicit in the foregoing discussion. The first, called the intrinsic approach, sees value in biological resources independently of any direct use by humans. This view regards the conservation of biological resources as important in its own right without any further justification (see LINKAGE). The intrinsic approach starts from the ethical position that humans lack the moral sanction to destroy natural habitat. The second, the utilitarian approach, regards biological conservation as important because of the need to preserve the option that we may someday discover valuable products from such resources. This position is one of consequentialism and proceeds from the notion that nature is our storehouse. Biotechnology based on the extraction of genetic materials is part of the utilitarian view of biological conservation.

These two world views are not necessarily at odds in a practical sense. Indeed, both views together support the widest possible preservation or conservation of biological resources. Under the right terms, the moral position of the intrinsic-value approach might well accede to the extraction of certain genetic material for utilitarian pursuits. But the essential trait of both these views is that biological resources must be conserved at almost any cost.

The problem, of course, is that the "cost" of this preservation is likely to fall on those least able to pay. Suppose the maintenance of large reserves of genetic materials—undertaken to please a number of signatories to the Convention on Biological Diversity—requires a sacrifice in the living standards (or cultural practices) of local people. How can this new structure of imposed rights and duties be made to seem fair to the locals who must bear much of the cost of biodiversity conservation? A more subtle "cost" arises when local people, who may have nurtured a particular genetic complex, fail to enjoy the enormous economic wealth that arises from commercial application of genetic resources. How can the extraction of genetic material be conducted so that those who "created" this particular genetic complex will share in the future income stream from its widespread use?

We have here an economic problem with two distinct components. The first concerns the potential benefits from ecosystems that are maintained in their "natural" state against the onslaught of "development." In other words, indigenous peoples must be compensated for the reduced level of economic and social well-being that maintaining particular ecosystems in their "natural state" may necessitate. The second concerns how local people might share in the benefits. This involves developing contracts with the protectors and managers of indigenous ecosystems with the prospect of future payoffs from commercial development of local materials. Clearly, the two aspects of the problem are not unrelated. Part of the potential compensation from the simple act of sustained management may well be the probability of a significant windfall from the commercialization of genetic materials it has preserved. I call these the economics of forbearance and the economics of serendipity.

The Economics of Forbearance

The economics of forbearance refers to resource-management regimes crafted to manage local ecosystems on a sustainable basis. The word *forbearance* is appropriate for the simple reason that the choices indigenous communities make in favor of conservation may relegate them to a lower level of economic "development" than otherwise might be possible. Sustainable management of important ecosystems does not automatically sentence communities to relative penury, but the presumption is necessary in order to anticipate possible threats against the resource base.

In such instances, we must imagine two possible developmental trajectories for local communities and reckon the difference in economic well-being arising from the one that is imposed from the outside in the interest of biological conservation. As previously mentioned, when relatively wealthy inhabitants of the industrialized world impose developmental trajectories on poor peoples in the agrarian tropics, incentive compatibility suffers severe distortion. The incidence of benefits and costs from this situation are not only inimical to durable conservation behavior in the local area but manifestly inequitable. Cost-sharing schemes to remunerate local "managers" of externally valued ecosystems are essential on pragmatic grounds, as well as on grounds of simple equity.

The Economics of Serendipity

Particular ecosystems, managed on a sustained basis by indigenous peoples, occasionally produce natural resources or genetic materials that give rise to prodigious wealth for the party able to control the associated income streams. The economics of serendipity refers to the need for careful institutional crafting to ensure that local groups enjoy the fruits of commercial developments arising from locally produced genetic materials.

As a model, we might consider fashioning such income-sharing schemes along the lines presently used in the extraction of hydrocarbons, plus a bonus for the embedded effort that has gone into the development of that genetic resource. Note that fossil fuels are entirely passive with respect to the local community, while genetic materials must be understood as the willful product of human action and choice. The Lockean idea of acquiring some presumptive claim to an income stream from the expenditure of labor is pertinent here. Royalty schemes prevalent in the fossil-fuel business therefore represent a minimal approach to compensation of local resource managers.

Conclusions

The economic dimension of community-based conservation seeks to emphasize the critical role of incentives operating on those who will have the responsibility of resource management and on those who insist—from their distant material comfort—upon conservation of biological resources. The incentives must be right at the community level before indigenous peoples will knowingly enter into such agreements. Getting the incentives right at the international level, so that those who declaim the wonders of biological conservation are not absolved of the financial responsibility conservation implies, is equally important. After all, celebrating the wonders of biodiversity preservation is cheap and facile if no costs are thereby incurred. It is doubly disingenuous if the declaimers stand to reap untold wealth through the careful marketing of derivative products made possible by the sweat and forbearance of the unseen poor.

Within the nation-state, community-based conservation must be seen as an essential reform in nations' environmental policies. At the most fundamental level, programs to enhance CBC necessarily locate different rule-making powers at different levels (at the center, at the regional level, at the local level) in a national system. Emphasis must be given to the implied organizational structure and institutional dimensions of environmental policy in general and land-use policy in particular.

The international community can facilitate community-based conservation to the extent that the citizens of the industrialized North are prepared to underwrite a good share of the perceived opportunity costs of widespread conservation of areas that might otherwise fall under the curse of modernism. This will require collaborative programs with the sovereign governments in places where biological conservation is desired. Incentive problems are therefore pertinent down through the nested structure of interests. CBC will be successful only if the rules—and the incentives—are right all the way through that hierarchical system.

ACKNOWLEDGMENTS

The author wishes to thank the editors, Shirley Strum, David Western, and Michael Wright, and the copyeditor, Lisa Lawley, for their help in making this chapter more readable.

SOURCES

Bishop, R. C. 1978. "Endangered Species and Uncertainty: The Economics of a Safe Minimum Standard." *American Journal of Agricultural Economics* 60:10–13.

————. 1980. "Option Value: An Extension and Exposition." *Land Economics* 58(1):1–15.

Bromley, D. W. 1989. *Economic Interests and Institutions: The Conceptual Foundations of Public Policy.* Oxford, England: Basil Blackwell.

————. 1991. *Environment and Economy: Property Rights and Public Policy.* Oxford, England: Basil Blackwell.

————, ed. 1992. *Making the Commons Work.* San Francisco: ICS Press.

————. 1993. "Regulatory Takings: Coherent Concept or Logical Contradiction?" *Vermont Law Review* 17(3):647–82.

McCay, B. J., and J. M. Acheson, eds. 1987. *The Question of the Commons.* Tucson, Arizona: University of Arizona Press.

Ostrom, E. 1990. *Governing the Commons.* Cambridge, England: Cambridge University Press.

Pearce, D. W., and J. Warford. 1993. *World Without End.* Oxford, England: Oxford University Press.

Stevenson, G. G. 1991. *Common Property Economics.* Cambridge, England: Cambridge University Press.

Vatn, A., and D. W. Bromley. 1994. "Choices Without Prices Without Apologies." *Journal of Environmental Economics and Management* 26(2):129–148.

Wright, P. 1993. "Ranomafana National Park, Madagascar: Rainforest Conservation and Economic Development." Case study prepared for the Liz Claiborne Art Ortenberg Foundation Community Based Conservation Workshop, October 18–22, Airlie, Virginia.

Young, O. R. 1989. *International Cooperation: Building Regimes for Natural Resources and the Environment.* Ithaca, New York: Cornell University Press.

CHAPTER 20

Ecological Limits and Opportunities for Community-based Conservation

Nick Salafsky

There is a fundamental tension between the proces-
ses of biodiversity conservation and human development (Robinson 1993). The
strict preservation of natural ecosystems essentially requires that humans be excluded from the system. In contrast, the process of development basically demands that natural resources be used to improve human welfare. Having worked
as both a tropical forest ecologist and a rural village economist, I can attest that
there is thus a certain personal and professional schizophrenia involved in simultaneously trying to do both conservation and development work.

Despite the inherent contradictions, the spatial, ethical, and organizational
overlap of conservation and development concerns inevitably meant that these
two fields would be linked together. Unfortunately, the missionary zeal with which
this linkage was promoted often did not have grounding in proven results.

Perhaps the greatest casualties of this new paradigm were the ecological concepts that were trampled on or co-opted in the stampede to produce rhetorically
correct project proposals. One example is the term *biodiversity*, which had long
been used by ecologists to refer strictly to "the variety and variability among living
organisms and the ecological complexes in which they occur" (Office of Technology Assessment 1987). All of a sudden, this term expanded into a buzzword
used to describe biological resources in general (van Schaik et al. 1992). As a
result, any type of "green" development effort such as planting monocultures of
fast-growing, exotic tree species for fuelwood was billed as a biodiversity-
conserving project. Not to be outdone, however, conservationists also jumped on
the bandwagon and began applying the phrase "sustainable development"—
which had been used primarily to describe the maintenance of ecological
processes and life-support systems (IUCN/UNEP/WWF 1980)—to describe their
preservation efforts (Robinson 1993). Thus any type of strict conservation project
such as the gazetting of a remote nature reserve was promoted as having sustainable development benefits such as watershed protection. Meanwhile, both sides

seemed to ignore the deep underlying threat of ecological collapse latent in the ticking timebombs of human population growth and expanding consumerism (Meffe, Ehrlich, and Ehrenfeld 1993).

My purpose in raising these contradictions is not to criticize the underlying intentions and objectives of community-based conservation. Indeed, I strongly believe that the concept of CBC is the only possible means of finding common ground between humans and the natural world and thus healing this schizophrenia. My point is that CBC projects can be successfully developed only with knowledge of ecological limits and opportunities.

The case studies included in this book (and the others written for the Airlie House workshop) provide an opportunity to consider the CBC concept within the context of ecological theory and practice. Three critical questions must be addressed: Can CBC projects stop our slide toward ecological collapse? Can CBC projects accomplish meaningful biodiversity conservation? And can CBC projects develop ecologically sustainable land-use systems? The process of examining potential answers to these questions also should help to demonstrate the relevance of ecology to community-based conservation.

A Graphic Model for Examining Ecology within CBC

As a device for discussing the role of ecology in CBC, I would like to propose a simple graphic model. Like any model, it is an abstraction of complex problems and is not intended to be a perfect analogue of the real world, but, rather, a framework for discussion and debate. The model begins by plotting the welfare of the natural world as a function of human-induced ecosystem alteration (see Figure 20.1). The x-axis is scaled so that movement to the right indicates increasing human impact on the environment, be it at local, regional, or global level. The y-axis, by contrast, is a unitless measurement of welfare that, like the analogous concept of utility in microeconomics, is ordinal rather than cardinal. In other words, we can not measure how much welfare is represented by any single point along the y-axis, only state that a point higher up on the axis represents relatively greater welfare than one lower down.

Almost all ecologists probably would agree that the welfare curve for the natural world would look something like the solid line in Figure 20.1. Depending on the scale under consideration, at the left-hand side of the curve there might be an initial dip (dotted line A) as a result of extirpation of species that are extremely sensitive to disturbance and a subsequent rise (dotted line B) as a result of increased diversity of habitats and ecotones (habitat borders that, in general, seem to be preferred by many species). In addition, at the right-hand side of the curve there might be an extended tail (dotted line C), resulting from the survival of human-adapted species such as cockroaches, rats, and kudzu. Nonetheless, particularly

Figure 20.1

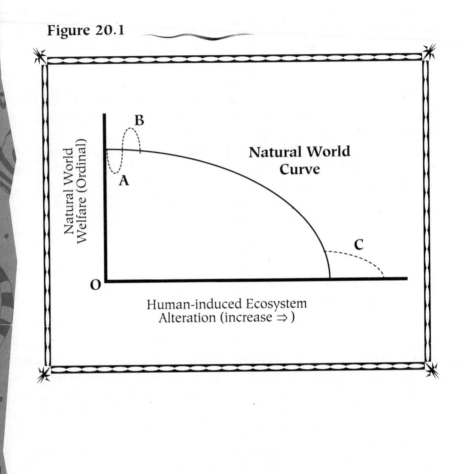

on a global scale, the solid line is probably a reasonable approximation of the welfare of the natural world.

As shown in Figure 20.2, the human-welfare curve starts at the origin by definition of the x-axis. After this, however, there is a great deal of debate as to the shape of the curve. On one side of the spectrum is Simon's curve, named after economist Julian Simon, in which human welfare increases without limit due to the use of ever-improving technology to shift from one natural resource to another. On the other side of the spectrum is the Club of Rome curve (after the authors of the 1971 *Limits to Growth* study), in which human welfare gradually increases and then dramatically crashes as nonrenewable resources ultimately are used up. A middle-ground position between these two extremes is the general human-welfare curve, in which there is an initial increase in welfare, a steady-state period, and then a subsequent decline as habitat conversion and resultant pollution accumulation erode the quality of life. In reality, this curve is probably nonlinear and may have several local maxima. Furthermore, as evidenced by the considerable debate between ecologists and economists, there is some question as to whether decline is inevitable. Nonetheless, for the purposes of my argument, the simple linear function shown in the figure is a sufficient representation.

In Figure 20.3, the general human-welfare curve is superimposed on the natural world's welfare curve. Although in the figure the natural world curve is drawn as "greater" than that of the human curve, the fact that two ordinal y-axes are being used means that differences in vertical position between the two curves are meaningless. What is important, however, is the relative shape of the two curves at different points along the common x-axis. In particular, three regions need to be considered: Region I, in which the human welfare curve is ascending; Region II, in which the human-welfare curve is relatively flat; and Region III, in which the human-welfare curve is descending.

The next three sections of this chapter explore the ecological implications of this model, focusing in particular on the role that CBC projects can play in finding solutions to the three questions posed earlier. For each question, I provide a brief theoretical background to the ecological concepts involved in relation to the model presented in Figure 20.3 and then examine how these concepts are treated in the case studies.

Question 1: Can We Avoid Ecological Collapse?

In looking at the model presented in Figure 20.3, one of the first questions that comes to mind is where along the x-axis are we located today? Many, if not most, ecologists would argue that the world as a whole is at least in Region II and, more likely, in the initial stages of Region III—on the precipice of the drop toward the depths of ecological collapse (Meffe, Ehrlich, and Ehrenfeld 1993). Although living standards have improved dramatically for much of the world during the last few centuries, this economic expansion has been possible only through the

Figure 20.2

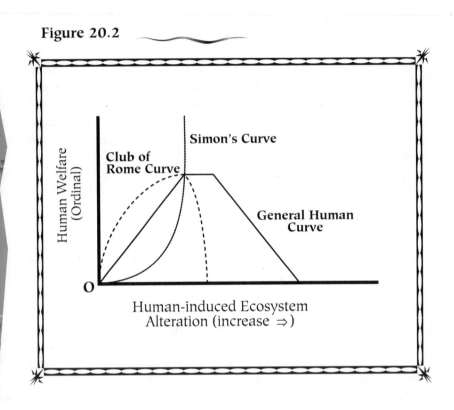

Figure 20.3

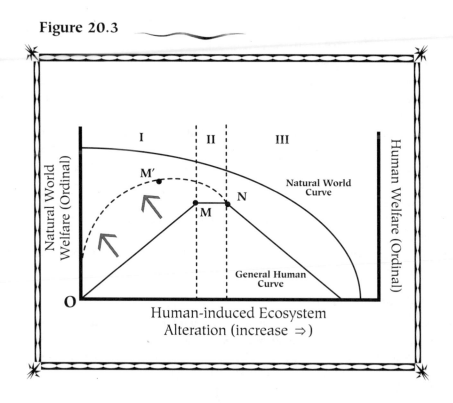

unsustainable exploitation of rapidly diminishing stocks of fossil fuels, forests, fish, and farmland. The harbinger of the future seems all too apparent in the poorest parts of the world such as Haiti, Bangladesh, the Sahel, and even rural Mississippi, where natural ecosystems are being completely expended in the desperate quest for survival.

The Open-access Resources Problem

If we are indeed in Region III, the next question is: Why are we here when it is clearly a nonoptimal position for society as a whole? The answer to this question seems to be rooted in different incentives for individuals as opposed to society or, as an economist would put it, in an externality problem owing to an incomplete allocation of the costs and benefits of resource extraction. In other words, there is an open-access resources problem in which individuals and nations face perverse incentives to convert habitat and exploit natural resources at a faster-than-optimal rate since they receive all the benefits while the costs are spread over society as a whole.

The case studies in this volume present a number of potential CBC solutions to this open-access resources problem such as the community forest management system in INDIA or the *sasi* system in MALUKU ISLANDS. These solutions, however, generally seem to be more socioeconomic than ecological, and hence beyond the scope of this paper.

The Population Problem

I would be highly remiss in my role as an ecologist if I did not emphasize the ultimate open-access resources problem: explosive growth in human populations (Meffe, Ehrlich, and Ehrenfeld 1993). The idea that population growth is an open-access resources problem is not new. Garrett Hardin (1968) developed his famous model of common pastureland as a means of illustrating the overpopulation that might be expected if society subsidizes the education and upbringing of children, so that there is an incentive for each family to have more offspring than it can afford. A similar perverse incentive also exists on an aggregate level, as ethnic groups and nations seek to outgrow one another, so as to wrest political and military control from their opponents by sheer numbers.

Exponential growth in human population is hardly surprising to ecologists. A fundamental tenet of ecology is the concept of carrying capacity, which is defined as the maximum population that a given environment can sustain (Daily and Ehrlich 1992). As countless experiments with paramecia in jars, rats in boxes, and deer on islands have shown, a population in a closed system with no predators will expand exponentially until it reaches the carrying capacity—and then crash.

Humans are different from other species in that continual advances in technology have enabled us to keep the system open and thus maintain higher and higher populations. But as Hardin (1968) points out, these technological fixes merely ratchet population levels one notch higher without addressing the underlying social problems. Ultimately, simple mathematics dictates that we will never achieve true sustainability unless society actively provides a system of incentives and constraints to ensure that the average number of children per woman is two or less. This need for population control is as much or more important in the developed world as in the developing world, especially given the vastly greater amounts of resources consumed by residents of the former.

Most of the case studies explicitly mention human population pressure as one of the critical factors motivating and affecting their CBC programs. Several of the case studies also report specific population growth rates, including 4 percent per year in AMBOSELI and 4.7 percent in CRATER MOUNTAIN. A few of the case studies address human carrying-capacity issues. For example, CAMPFIRE states that Zimbabwe's "population will exceed its total production capacity by the year 2030" (171) and tries to differentiate between ecological and economic carrying capacity. Martins (1993) examines human population density in the various reserves and suggests that high densities mean that subsistence hunting may not be sustainable. Finally, NEOTROPICAL FORESTS discusses the carrying capacity of the local environment in the context of both animal and human populations. The authors conclude, based on their findings, that "catchment areas of about 2,500 km^2 seem to be necessary to provide for the subsistence hunting needs in human communities of a few hundred people in neotropical forests" (315).

Unfortunately, however, none of the other case studies even mentions the concept of carrying capacity, let alone attempts to estimate what the capacity of the local environment might be. Furthermore, none discusses the inclusion of family planning efforts in their project, save for CRATER MOUNTAIN, which states that "until recently, local people have rejected any notion of population control, citing the need for sons as warriors, as protection against sorcerers, or as gardeners" (210).

Finally, none of the case studies mentions developing strategies to deal with the influx of poor migrants that might be expected if the project does indeed succeed in raising the standard of living relative to surrounding areas. This situation has already occurred in the Indian village of Chandana, whose forests are under constant attack from neighboring villages (see INDIA).

Question 2: Can We Enhance Biodiversity Conservation in Modified Landscapes?

For a society in Region III of the model in Figure 20.3, where the human welfare curve is declining, optimal actions would be those that reduce habitat alteration so as to move the society back to point N on the graph. A society in Region II, on the other hand, should, from an anthropocentric perspective, be largely indifferent to being anywhere between point N and point M, where human welfare is stable. If, however, even the smallest amount of biocentric perspective enters into the equation, then the optimal amount of habitat conversion becomes point M, since it maximizes the welfare of the natural world without cost to humans. The question then becomes: How can society preserve natural habitat in the face of incentives for individuals to overexploit resources? In the following sections I discuss two approaches to solving this problem.

Biodiversity Conservation in Buffer Zones Around Parks and Reserves

The traditional answer to this question has been to set aside land in parks and reserves dedicated to conservation. Without a doubt, parks and reserves are important; probably almost all ecologists would agree that from a conservation perspective, the more parks and reserves, the better. Nonetheless, parks and reserves have a number of limitations.

Foremost among these limitations is the size of parks. Conservation biology theory holds that small, isolated parks generally will not provide sufficient habitat to maintain viable populations—the minimum number of individual members of a species necessary to avoid deleterious inbreeding effects and allow for random fluctuations in population size (Shaffer 1981; Thomas 1990). This need for extensive areas is particularly true in the case of large predators at the top of the food chain, which need hundreds and even thousands of square kilometers of habitat to survive (Noss 1993). Large parks are also less susceptible to edge effects (Lovejoy et al. 1986) and to invasions of exotic and parasitic species (Wilcove 1985). Finally, and perhaps most important, very large parks also can allow for the maintenance of ecological and evolutionary processes and the movement of ecosystems in response to normal long-term and/or human-induced climatic change (Noss 1993).

Few, if any, existing parks and reserves are sufficiently large, given the above criteria. Accordingly, in the mid-1970s, conservationists developed the biosphere-reserve concept, in which the core conservation area of a park is surrounded by a ring of buffer zones (UNESCO 1974). These buffer zones were seen as fulfilling two basic functions: extension buffering, which extends the core habitat of plants and especially animals, and sociobuffering, which provides goods and services for people (MacKinnon et al. 1986). Over time, the biosphere concept expanded from the initial simple ring design to encompass complex mosaics of multiple-use areas connected to one another via corridors or linkages along rivers and uplands (Harris 1984; Schelhas 1994). At its extreme, proponents of the concept have developed maps in which entire continental regions are organized into interlinked networks of core preserves and buffer zones (Noss 1993).

A number of the case studies include elements of the augmentation of conservation in traditional parks and reserves through the development of buffer zones and multiple-use areas. For example, the Baban Rafi case in NIGER describes efforts to develop a 40,000-ha zone of intervention and an additional extensive buffer zone of peripheral villages and farmlands around the 70,000-ha core protected forest. Likewise, BOSCOSA discusses project efforts centered on Costa Rican communities located on the fringe, or buffer area, of an existing national park or reserve.

A number of other projects, although not linked to explicit, hard-edged conservation areas, also promote the development of a holistic mosaic or spectrum of land uses. For example, Metcalfe describes the CAMPFIRE project's zoning of land in Zimbabwe into "a regional landscape plan which integrates the primary conservation ethic of protected areas with the ascendent development ethos of the communal lands" (21). Similarly, NORTH YORK MOORS describes a U.K. national park as containing a mosaic of habitats including heather moorland, farmland valleys, and broad-leaved woodlands.

Although a number of the case studies mention as project goals the creation of buffer zones, only a few explicitly describe efforts to determine which types of land-use patterns would be suitable in these areas. For example, BOSCOSA discusses the testing of tree species for inclusion in Costa Rican buffer-zone agroforestry systems that could potentially provide products for both household consumption and market sale.

Furthermore, the few studies that report testing potential land-use systems have done so exclusively from the standpoint of socio-buffering functions. None of the studies reports efforts to examine the suitability of these buffer-zone land-use systems for extending animal habitat. The need for this type of study is of greatest importance in the humid tropics, where only a few studies of animal use of agroforestry systems, plantations, and other typical buffer-zone habitats have been made (Terborgh and Weske 1969; Duff, Hall, and March 1984; Steubing and Gasis 1989; Salafsky 1993).

Overall, community-based conservation projects have an important role to play in developing buffer-zone land-use systems that can both provide goods and services to people and habitat for wildlife. The best strategy for developing such buffer zones is not to import or try to invent completely new land-use systems. Instead, wherever possible, the range of existing local land-use systems should be evaluated in terms of their economic return and suitability to provide key resources to animals and plants. The most promising should then be tested and evaluated in trial plots, in conjunction with local residents, to learn how to improve them further. Finally, the system needs to implemented. Since it is unlikely that it will be completely in local people's interests to plant systems in an optimal conservation pattern (see below), developing an incentive system to induce residents to adopt the system also may be necessary.

Biodiversity Conservation in Managed Habitats

In addition to size, the other major limitation of parks and reserves is that, historically, they tend to be established only when there is little or no opportunity cost to humans (see Figure 20.3). The low-opportunity-cost criterion means that most parks are located in marginal lands that have little or no alternative value. A look at an ecological map of the United States reveals that while numerous parks are located in deserts and mountain ranges, none is on fertile prairie. Similarly, in Zimbabwe "more than 90 percent of communal lands are located within the less productive regions III, IV, and V" (CAMPFIRE: 169). Likewise, in Australia, the entire Kakadu National Park is located on soils that are described as being "acidic, shallow, and infertile" (KAKADU:136). Furthermore, the low-opportunity-cost criterion means that if parks do include valuable lands, they are subject to intense conversion pressure from both local people (gold miners and farmers in the Osa Peninsula in BOSCOSA) and established interests (loggers and ranchers in the United States).

Given these limitations of parks and reserves, it is clear that they are not the sole answer for biodiversity conservation. At the core of the CBC concept is thus the idea of promoting conservation in nonpark lands that make up the vast majority of the world's land surface. The downward slope of the natural world's welfare curve in Figure 20.3 means that it will never be possible to conserve a complete natural ecosystem in a modified landscape. Instead, CBC projects need to focus on certain achievable goals that explicitly address the trade-offs between the welfare of humans and that of the natural world. The challenge for CBC project staff is thus to determine how to define these conservation goals, how to design and implement conservation practices necessary to reach these goals, and how to monitor progress and measure success toward achieving these goals.

Definition of conservation goals   The first step in establishing a biodiversity-conservation program in modified lands is to define the goals of the program. As discussed above, the term *biodiversity* refers to the "variety and variability among living organisms and the ecological complexes in which they occur" (Office of Technology Assessment 1987). With regard to conservation, this definition traditionally had focused on preserving individual species (groups of interbreeding individuals). The definition can be extended, however, both downward, to cover genetic variability within a population (differences between individual organisms), and upward, to include habitat and ecosystem diversity (different types of communities).

One potential goal for CBC projects would be to preserve viable populations of all native species found in the area of the project. If this goal were to be adopted, it would not be necessary to work with every last species. Instead, conservation efforts should focus on those species that are rare and/or adversely impacted by human activities. A good model for the process of selecting critical species can be found in the ranking system developed by The Nature Conservancy in conjunction with State Heritage Programs (agencies that are responsible for cataloging and tracking species and habitats within each of the United States). This ranking assigns all species to a five-point scale based on their relative global and statewide rarity (Noss 1993).

Although desirable in principle, the goal of preserving all species may be extremely difficult or impossible to attain in a modified landscape. A more pragmatic goal would be to select certain target species for conservation efforts. Criteria for this selection process might include degree of endemism (is the species found elsewhere in world, or only in this one site?), function as a keystone resource (how many other species depend on this species for food or other resources?), role in the ecosystem (is the species an important and/or unique pollinator?), cost of protection (would conservation require extensive modification of existing land-use practices or only minimal changes?), and probability of success (will the species respond to conservation efforts, or is it likely to go extinct anyway?). A number of moral and ethical criticisms can be applied to this process of targeting only certain species for conservation action. Nonetheless, if a project's conservation resources are limited, it seems sensible to make decisions based on rational and informed deliberation rather than by default.

Finally, an alternative (but not necessarily exclusive) goal for CBC projects would be to focus less on individual species and more on ecosystems and ecosystem functioning. Under this goal, a project would try to preserve ecosystem functioning such as hydrological and nutrient cycles, topsoil accumulation, and food chains or webs by using a combination of native species and management efforts.

In addition to the question of the conservation goal, a major issue in any CBC project, of course, is who sets that goal, particularly when both communities and external institutions are involved.

A few of the case studies do explicitly define how they might measure success from a species perspective or list a species-based indicator in their list of successes. For instance, AMBOSELI concludes that "ecologically, the success of the program can be judged by the data . . . [that] show that the ecosystem has remained open, migrations . . . viable, and populations . . . healthy" (46). Similarly, CRATER MOUNTAIN cites one success as "the restoration of rare bird populations whose numbers had declined steeply during the previous decade" (211). Other case studies implicitly set goals that are oriented toward maintaining viable species populations. For example, AMAZON speaks of the goal of obtaining an ecologically sustainable resource harvest.

Most of the case studies do not define what they are trying to attain with regard to biodiversity conservation. In some instances, it is difficult to tell whether this lack of explicit conservation goals reflects the status of the actual project or merely the focus of the author of the report. In other case studies, however, an implicit or explicit decision was made not to focus directly on biodiversity. For instance, Martins states that while some reserves do seem to cover areas of significant biodiversity, others do not, and it is "left to chance to explain the favorable situations regarding biodiversity that can be found" (1993:11). Similarly, and perhaps most tellingly, BOSCOSA explicitly states that the project "was not designed or envisioned as a biological conservation project" (221); instead, it was "to complement a separate, unrelated protection program by fomenting grass-roots-level sustainable economic alternatives for people in Corcovado's buffer zone" (221). The author of BOSCOSA goes on to conclude, however, that this approach did not work and that "unless a program explicitly incorporates biological conservation (i.e., forest or species conservation) as a criterion for evaluating project activities, it is likely that the rate of deforestation will continue" (Donovan 1993:41).

Implementation of conservation practices   The second step in establishing a biodiversity conservation program in modified lands involves determining which conservation practices will be tested and implemented. The actions that any CBC project can take are, of course, completely dependent on the site-specific ecological, socioeconomic, and cultural environments and on the goals and resources of the project. Thus steps that would be required to promote conservation of marine animals in the Maluku Islands are very different from those that would be required to promote conservation of rare plants in the North York Moors. Nonetheless, the case studies elucidate a few general principles.

The first and perhaps most important of these principles is to focus primary attention on conservation actions that minimize the trade-off between human and natural-world welfare. Although from the global perspective of Figure 20.3 these welfare curves have a smooth appearance, at local level, it is much more likely that these curves have all sorts of vertical variations, as shown in Figure 20.4. Local variability may offer effective but relatively cost-free opportunities for biodiversity conservation. The most desirable conservation practices to implement are those that improve the welfare of the natural world while simultaneously either benefiting (step A) or at least coming at little or no cost (step B) to humans. Conversely, the practices that should be avoided are those that neutrally (step D) or negatively (step E) impact the natural world while benefiting humans. In between are steps that benefit the natural world but come at a cost to humans, thus setting up a trade-off situation (step C). An efficient conservation plan would thus call for first taking all type-A and type-B steps and then ranking the type-C steps on the basis of anticipated effectiveness and cost and choosing those that are feasible within existing project constraints.

The real-world decisions that CBC projects make, of course, will not be as simple as the theoretical steps discussed above, especially given that costs and benefits can be difficult to quantify. The problem is further compounded, since the heterogeneous nature of communities means that there can be winners and losers within or between groups as a result of a particular conservation action. Nonetheless, as the following examples illustrate, most project actions can be categorized, at least roughly.

Modifying traditional *sasi* techniques to allow populations of marine organisms to remain unmolested during critical breeding times is an example of a type-A win-win situation, since it both allows for growth in the population levels and enhances future harvests (see MALUKU ISLANDS). Implementing a control program for tsetse flies, on the other hand, is an example of a type-E lose-win situation because it is beneficial to livestock and their human owners but reduces the habitat

Figure 20.4

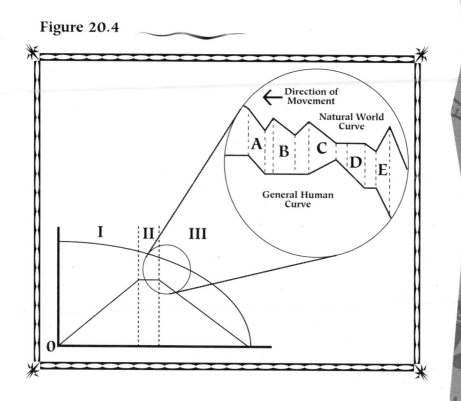

available for wildlife (see CAMPFIRE). Finally, while instituting a marginal fee increase for nature tourists to gain local-community cooperation in protecting a park is an example of a type-C trade-off situation in which the benefits are great in relation to the costs. Spending vast sums of money on ex situ efforts to conserve highly endangered species (such as the California condor) is a trade-off in which the cost (from a global perspective) is high in proportion to the benefit.

The second principle is to promote, wherever possible, land-use practices that maintain the structure and function of the natural ecosystem(s) in the region and employ native species. Use of ecologically appropriate land-use systems and native species has a number of potential benefits for humans (see the discussion of ecosystem agriculture in the next section). As a rule, however, these systems also would be expected to provide the most suitable habitat for indigenous wildlife.

For example, in humid tropical regions multispecies agroforestry systems or the circular garden techniques employed by the HIFCO project in Peru (Cabarle, Panduro, and Murayari 1993) are more likely to provide habitat for forest wildlife than monocrops of exotic grains. In arid savannah regions in Kenya or Zimbabwe, by contrast, open-range cattle herding is more compatible with the conservation of migrant ungulate herds than the division of the range into small agricultural plots. A better system still would be the direct use of these wild herds as "second cattle" (AMBOSELI:20), or even as primary cattle, assuming controlled harvests proved to be economically and culturally feasible.

The third principle is to pay attention to the biological needs of target species and the conservation-biology theory discussed above in the context of buffer zones. Adherence to this principle means asking questions for each proposed action: Does the action provide foraging or breeding habitat or other critical resources for target species? Does it take into account time periods when populations are more sensitive, such as breeding seasons? Does it minimize the impact on a population's reproductive capability? Does it protect key migration routes or provide corridors linking natural areas? Does it allow for the movement of populations over time? Does it promote the formation of large, holistic land-use complexes?

Examples of conservation actions that provide key resources include the efforts to protect dry-season water sources described in AMBOSELI and the establishment, discussed in NORTH YORK MOORS, of hedges that "are excellent nesting habitat for small birds" (287), "provide an abundance of winter food for birds and mammals" (287), and "are regarded as valuable wildlife corridors" (287). An example of an action that makes use of biological knowledge about population dynamics is the institution of regulations that promote male-directed hunting of deer, peccaries, and large rodents in the Tamshiyacu-Tahuayo Communal Reserve of Peru discussed in AMAZON. Finally, NORTH YORK MOORS also provides examples of holistic landscape design in which park policy promotes the maintenance of "native broad-leaved woodland in deeply incised watercourses running up the valley sides . . . [that] forms a link between moorland and river valley" (287).

The fourth principle involves the need to anticipate and minimize conflicts between humans and the natural world. These conflicts can include competition for scarce resources such as grass or water, dispersal of weed plants from nonagricultural areas, crop or livestock damage by marauding animals from nearby wildlands, and even (in very rare instances) attacks on human populations by large predators such as tigers in India. CBC projects thus need to anticipate which types of conflicts will occur and how their cost can be minimized for both sides.

AMBOSELI provides one example of the complexities inherent in trying to resolve this type of conflict. In Kenya, where crops planted by local agriculturalists suffer from wildlife depredations, the Kenya Wildlife Service proposes the fencing of all park lands to protect people from animals, and vice versa, as a solution. This fencing, which perhaps might have solved the immediate problem, would have stopped animal migrations and led to gradual biological impoverishment of the national parks "due to insularization effects" (AMBOSELI:xxx). CAMPFIRE discusses another approach to the crop-raiding problem, tried in Zimbabwe as part of the CAMPFIRE program. There, a compensation program was established to repay farmers for damage caused by wildlife. Problems develop with this system, however, in that "compensation claims against the trust lacked any built-in mechanism for balancing individual costs against group benefits" (CAMPFIRE:176).

The fifth and final principle is to understand that there are limitations to what community-based conservation can achieve. Inevitably, some species will not survive in a modified landscape. For instance, populations of disturbance-sensitive animal species will be difficult to maintain in any system regularly frequented by humans. Furthermore, most wild tree species and other large plants are likely to be excluded from agriculturally based land-use systems. Finally, certain ecosystems generally do not seem to be compatible with human activities and the human psyche.

For example, even ecologically sensitive agroforestry projects such as those being implemented in the Osa Peninsula of Costa Rica involve replacing native forest with domesticated species (see BOSCOSA); thus in this modified landscape, not all plant species will be preserved. Likewise, my own experience living and working for more than a year in a pristine tropical rain forest in Kalimantan, Indonesian Borneo, provides an example of the incompatibility of ecosystems and the human psyche. Although on many levels the forest was the most beautiful place I have ever been, it was also very clearly not a human environment. Inevitably, I felt a sense of relief whenever I stepped from under the canopy into the small clearing of the research station. While a few indigenous forest tribes such as the Guaymi of the Osa may prefer to live in the deep forest (see BOSCOSA), most peoples probably prefer to live in cleared areas. Thus large tracts of unbroken forest will likely be maintained only in parks and reserves or in dedicated timber and nontimber forest-product-extraction areas in which people work but do not live (Wilson 1984).

Monitoring results   The final step in establishing a biodiversity conservation program in modified lands is to establish a mechanism for monitoring the results of the program so that corrective actions can be taken if target goals are not achieved. If a species-based criterion for conservation has been adopted, then biodiversity can be measured in one of several ways. As usual, the choice of a given technique depends on a trade-off between accuracy of the results and the cost. Project staff members thus need to decide which type of monitoring best fits their needs.

The most rigorous technique involves systematic censuses of target populations. In a forest ecosystem, for example, trained observers can walk established census routes and record all animal encounters, either as a linear distance from the trail (Burnham, Anderson, and Laake 1980) or as a radius around fixed observation points (Reynolds, Scott, and Nussbaum 1980). These observations then can be analyzed using simple statistical techniques or a geographical information systems (GIS) program to estimate the density (number of individuals per unit area) or biomass (total weight per unit area) of target species in the habitat. For territorial species, it is also possible to map territories to get similar estimates of density or biomass (Brockelman and Ali 1987).

Since the census-based methods must be rigorously conducted to have meaning and thus require the presence of trained observers, they tend to be relatively expensive (although in the greater scheme of things, professional ecologists generally come pretty cheap). A less labor-intensive approach is to target select indicator species (species known to be sensitive to certain types of habitat disturbance) for censusing (Noss 1990). Finally, a quick-and-dirty approach is to rely on ad-lib observations of species or reports from knowledgable local people (Salafsky 1993). Monitoring of ecosystem-based approaches to biodiversity conservation requires different techniques to ensure that important parameters (e.g., water quality or soil-nutrient levels) are being maintained. These types of monitoring efforts also can suffer from logistical problems such as those experienced in the Guesselbodi site discussed in NIGER, where vandals stole fencing and other items that demarcated test plots.

A number of the case studies explicitly describe efforts to monitor population levels of critical species, primarily large vertebrates. For example, the Amboseli Project in Kenya tracks the populations of all large-mammal species (see AMBOSELI). Similarly, CRATER MOUNTAIN describes surveys of plant and animal species in Papua New Guinea. BOSCOSA refers to the results of botanical- and faunal-inventory efforts in Costa Rica and the establishment of a Conservation Data Center for the Osa region. Finally, NORTH YORK MOORS discusses the project's selection of a subset of areas on which to perform detailed monitoring of plant communities.

Other case studies, however, include little or no mention of monitoring efforts.

At best, they express the hope that since "natural areas" exist, conservation must be occurring. For example, the natural forest management project of NIGER describes what seems to be highly disturbed secondary forest with little or no reference to species composition. INDIA mentions that in the village of Chandana, where community forest management is under way, more than 214 species of flora and fauna are present in the forests; the discussion of Mahapada Village, by contrast, makes no mention of the species present, save for one anecdotal tale of a bear emerging from the forest. MALUKU ISLANDS does not mention monitoring of the species in the marine areas by marine-resource-management institutions in Indonesia. Finally, KAKADU claims that "the mere existence of Kakadu [National Park in Australia] is a major contribution to nature conservation, not only nationally but internationally" (151), but does not say more.

Question 3: Can We Sustainably Increase Production?

To this point in the paper, and indeed throughout most of human history, the human welfare curve in Figure 20.3 has been assumed to be fixed in place. In other words, human welfare can be increased only by moving along the curve toward an optimal position in Region II. A more intriguing approach to this problem, however, is to see if it is possible to increase production while maintaining a given level of habitat disturbance (shift the curve upward) or, even better, increase production while reducing habitat disturbance (shift the curve upward and to the left, as illustrated by the dashed line in Figure 20.3). Ideally, this shift could result in the establishment of a new optimum point (point M') that is better for both humans and the natural world. Such a shift could occur in two ways.

Shifting the Curve I: Developing Sustainable Land-Use Systems

The first way in which the curve potentially can be shifted upward is by developing land-use systems that provide returns to humans with minimal ecosystem disturbance. This research is covered in the fields of agroecology and ecosystem agriculture and the concepts of extractive reserves and ecosystem management.

The basic tenet of agroecology is that human-derived agricultural systems also are ecosystems. Accordingly, they must be understood and studied from an ecological perspective (Marten and Saltman 1986; Hecht 1987; Gliessman 1990). The concept of ecosystem agriculture goes a step further and holds that the ideal agricultural systems, from an ecological point of view, are those that mimic the naturally occurring ecosystem(s) of the region (Jackson 1980). For example, in the humid tropics, a diverse agricultural system based on multistrata tree crops would be the most appropriate farming method. At the broadest levels, both agroecology and ecosystem agriculture are not merely a set of scientific or farming methods but a complete philosophical outlook on life based upon farmers working in partnership with nature, rather than in opposition to it (Hecht 1987).

Extractive reserves and ecosystem management involve maintaining a steady return of products for household consumption and/or market sale from a relatively intact natural ecosystem. These management systems most often are thought of in the context of harvesting timber and nontimber products from forests, but similar principles apply to the harvest of marine resources from coral reefs or game from savannahs. Although the extractive-reserve concept generated considerable excitement when first developed (Peters, Gentry, and Mendelsohn 1989; Allegretti 1990), a growing body of research indicates that it is best seen not as a universal panacea for sustainable development, but rather as one component of an overall land-use strategy (Browder 1992; Salafsky, Dugelby, and Terborgh 1993).

The CBC case studies present a number of examples of potentially sustainable land-use systems. Examples of ecosystem agriculture include the cattle-herding and game-ranching efforts described in AMBOSELI and CAMPFIRE, the agroforestry systems being developed in the Osa Peninsula in Costa Rica (see BOSCOSA) and, especially, the raised beds and circular-garden farming systems being developed in the rain forests of Peru (Cabarle, Panduro, and Murayari 1993). Examples of extractive systems and ecosystem management include the forest management projects of NIGER and INDIA, the marine harvesting system of MALUKU ISLANDS, extractive reserves in Brazil (Martins 1993), and subsistence hunting efforts discussed in AMAZON and NEOTROPICAL FORESTS. In looking at these various systems, several important ecological issues arise that need to be considered in project design.

The first of these issues involves how to define *sustainable use* in theoretical and practical terms. The basic definition of this term involves employing resources "at rates within their capacity for renewal" (IUCN/UNEP/WWF 1991) or, in economic parlance, spending the interest and not the principle (Robinson 1993). Although translating this simple theoretical definition into practical terms can be difficult, a few of the case studies do deal with this issue. For example, the natural forest management project described in NIGER monitors forest regeneration rates to try to determine whether rotational cycles are sufficiently long to allow for maintenance of forest stocks. The case study authors conclude that initial harvest projections were overly optimistic, perhaps due in part to the fact that the initial harvesting efforts did not take into account the "one-time bonanza of fuelwood" (257) that comes from the initial harvest of mature forests. A similar one-time bonanza occurred in the Maluku Islands in Indonesia, where initial harvests of trochus shells after a lull during World War II turned out to be much greater than harvests in subsequent years (see MALUKU ISLANDS). Perhaps the best treatment of sustainability, however, is in NEOTROPICAL FORESTS, which explicitly discusses a number of ways in which population growth rates and observed hunting yields can be used to estimate the sustainable yield from populations of neotropical mammals.

The second issue involves understanding the ecological constraints on the system. In the case of agricultural systems, important considerations include choice of species (which plants and animals will be used in the system?), interactions between species (are plants stratified, or do they compete for space and light?), and nutrient cycling (are nutrient budgets balanced, or will inputs be required?). A few of the studies, including BOSCOSA, discuss testing various species for inclusion in agroforestry systems. Furthermore, Cabarle, Panduro, and Mura-yari (1993:25-26) discuss how the integration of trees into the raised-bed system optimizes use of vertical and horizontal space and how the use of leaf litter main-tains the nutrient balance in the circular gardens. Overall, however, there is room for much more on-farm research into ways of further improving these systems.

In the case of extractive systems, important considerations include the density of the exploited species (how long does it take to locate, harvest, and transport the product to the point of sale?), the phenology or temporal availability of the product (is the product available year-round or only at certain times?), and the sustain-ability of the extraction system (does harvesting the product interfere with repro-duction or kill the species?) (Salafsky, Dugelby, and Terborgh 1993). Here again, some of the case studies suggest ways of improving extractive systems along these lines. For example, as mentioned above, the wildlife management project in Peru discusses how promoting the harvest of males can enhance sustainable yields of deer and large rodents (see AMAZON). Again, however, there seems to be a need for considerably more research on these topics.

The third issue involves the fact that most potentially sustainable land-use sys-tems currently only seem to support low human population densities. In general, low population density seems to be characteristic of most of the land-use systems described in the case studies, especially those oriented toward resource extrac-tion. For example, the extractive reserves in Brazil support only 0.8 to 21.5 in-habitants/km² (Martins 1993), and the huge Kakadu region in Australia only sup-ported an Aboriginal population of around 2,000 individuals (KAKADU:137). By contrast, the HIFCO circular farms in Peru support a density of around 100 in-habitants/km² (calculated by dividing an assumed 6 individuals per household by the reported 0.06 km² plot size (see Cabarle, Panduro, and Murayari 1993:26). Unfortunately, however, population densities in many parts of the world already are much higher. Although in theory it may be correct to argue that many large populations supported by modern high-input agricultural systems are inherently unsustainable, in practice, this argument is moot unless radical population-reduction measures are enacted. Sustainable systems thus will have to become even more productive.

The final issue is that a sustainable system is not necessarily a biodiversity-conserving system. As Robinson (1993) writes, hunting-control efforts can pro-duce a short-term sustainable yield while still holding a species at a relatively small population level at which it can not perform its traditional ecological services such as seed dispersal. Similarly, a tree plantation can be managed to provide a sustainable yield of fuelwood, but it may not provide habitat for many animals, compared to a natural forest. This argument is apparent in NIGER, which describes forests "from the perspective of productivity" (243) as being "overmature due to protective policies [so that] conservative cutting would help to remove older growth and promote regeneration through coppicing and natural seeding" (243).

Although from an economic viewpoint, cutting old growth may indeed make sense, from an ecological viewpoint this is likely to be damaging to biodiversity conservation. CAMPFIRE also makes a similar distinction between ecological and economic sustainability with regard to the carrying capacity of the rangeland in Zimbabwe.

Shifting the Curve II: Making Natural Systems a Part of Human Welfare

The second way in which the human-welfare curve can be shifted as shown in Figure 20.3 is to incorporate the natural world's curve into the human curve. In other words, if the largely artificial dichotomy between these two curves were dissolved, then the value that humans place on the survival of the natural world should influence the extent of habitat conversion that we choose. Wilson has termed this value of the natural world *biophilia*, and it is closely related to the economic concept of existence value, which states that people value knowing that wildlife and wild habitats exist in the world, even though they may never see or experience these themselves. Empirical evidence for the presence of positive existence values can be found in the substantial sums of money donated to conservation groups around the world and through use of various economic techniques used to estimate people's valuation of biodiversity (Loomis and Walsh 1986).

An important consideration in trying to develop biophilia in a CBC project is that biodiversity tends to be a luxury good (an item for which demand increases as income rises). A poor farmer may enjoy the variety of animals around the forest in her village, but if given the choice between clearing the land to feed her family and preserving the habitat for the animals, her decision is very clear-cut, so to speak. Her wealthy neighbor, on the other hand, might choose to maintain the forest (van Schaik et al. 1992).

Although a number of indigenous societies such as the Gimi-speaking peoples of New Guinea, who pattern their initiation rituals on hornbill behavior (see CRATER MOUNTAIN), may have a deep reverence for wildlife, the majority of people in the world seem more like the Maasai in Kenya, whose "attitudes toward wildlife . . . have ranged from indifference to antagonism" (AMBOSELI:20). Effective CBC projects thus will need to help create systems in which people have a vested interest in wildlife such as those described in AMBOSELI and CAMPFIRE, in which local peoples share in the return from wildlife earnings in the form of infrastructure and cash dividends. Furthermore, these projects will need to include conservation education such as the "'farmer-to-farmer' horizontal exchanges of local knowledge" (Cabarle, Panduro, and Murayari 1993:10) promoted by the HIFCO project in Peru, which helps to "encompass and articulate the particular group's understanding and cosmological vision of the surrounding natural environment and its management of various goods and services" (Cabarle, Panduro, and Murayari 1993:10).

Ultimately, the interlinked nature of the global economy, in which the ecosystems in the most remote regions of the earth are affected by consumption patterns in cities on the other side of the world, means that this education process can not be restricted merely to the rural communities in developing countries that are the primary focus of the case studies in this volume. Instead, as much or more of this work needs to be conducted in the urban regions of the developed world. Ironically, perhaps the best tool for creating such a vested interest in the natural world among the residents of these urban areas lies in fostering a sense of community among these increasingly fragmented societies. In this light, the education process becomes not a one-way imposition of unshared values, but a two-way flow of mutually beneficial information among and between communities throughout the world.

Conclusions

The basic premise of the graphic model presented in Figure 20.3 is that human-induced ecosystem alteration is an independent variable that directly affects both human and natural-world welfare. We humans can control this variable. It is within our power to control the forces of expanding consumerism and population growth and reverse our slide toward ecological collapse. It is within our power to create holistic land-use complexes that expand parks and reserves to encompass entire ecosystems and actively promote biodiversity conservation in modified landscapes. And it is within our power to develop sustainable land-use systems that enable us to improve both human welfare and that of the natural world.

Taken as a whole, the case studies prepared for the Airlie House workshop demonstrate that community-based conservation projects are an important means with which to address these issues. To be sure, as outlined above, a great number of questions and challenges need to be resolved. In particular, biological conservation is often in conflict with human development. Ultimately, however, there is truth in the platitude that conservation will never be successful without human development, and vice versa. CBC projects should be able to accomplish both if they are grounded in the knowledge of ecological limits and opportunities.

ACKNOWLEDGMENTS

I thank Randy Kramer, Deborah Lawrence, Priya Shyamsundar, Carel van Schaik and, especially, Annie Kennedy, Shirley Strum, John Terborgh, David Western, and Michael Wright for their input into various drafts of this chapter.

SOURCES

Allegretti, M. H. 1990. "Extractive Reserves: An Alternative for Reconciling Development and Environmental Conservation in Amazonia." In *Alternatives to Deforestation: Steps Toward Sustainable Use of the Amazonian Rain Forest*, ed. A. B. Anderson, 252–264. New York: Columbia University Press.

Brockelman, W. Y., and R. Ali. 1987. "Methods of Surveying and Sampling Forest Primate Populations." In *Primate Conservation in the Tropical Rain Forest*, ed. C. W. Marsh and R. A. Mittermier, 23–62. New York: Alan R. Liss.

Browder, J. O. 1992. "The Limits of Extractivisim." *BioScience* 42(3):174–182.

Burnham, K. P., D. R. Anderson, and J. L. Laake. 1980. "Estimation of Density from Line Transect Sampling of Biological Populations." *Wildlife Monographs* 72:1–202.

Cabarle, B., with M. H. Panduro and O. M. Murayari. 1993. "Ecofarming in the Peruvian Amazon: The Integrated Family and Communal Gardening Project (HIFCO)." Case study prepared for the Liz Claiborne Art Ortenberg Foundation Community Based Conservation Workshop, October 18–22, Airlie, Virginia.

Daily, G. C., and P. R. Ehrlich. 1992. "Population, Sustainability, and the Earth's Carrying Capacity." *BioScience* 42(10):761–771.

Donovan, R. Z. 1993. "BOSCOSA: Forest Conservation and Management on the Osa Peninsula, Costa Rica." Case study prepared for the Liz Claiborne Art Ortenberg Foundation Community Based Conservation Workshop, October 18–22, Airlie, Virginia.

Duff, A. B., R. A. Hall, and C. W. Marsh. 1984. "A Survey of Wildlife in and around a Commercial Tree Plantation in Sabah." *Malaysian Forester* 47(2):173–213.

Gliessman, S. R. 1990. "Applied Ecology and Agroecology: Their Role in the Design of Agricultural Projects for the Humid Tropics." In *Race to Save the Tropics: Ecology and Economics for a Sustainable Future*, ed. R. Goodland, 33–47. Washington, D.C.: Island Press.

Hardin, G. 1968. "The Tragedy of the Commons." *Science* 162:1243–1248.

Harris, L. D. 1984. *The Fragmented Forest: Island Biogeography Theory and the Preservation of Biotic Diversity*. Chicago: University of Chicago Press.

Hecht, S. B. 1987. "The Evolution of Agroecological Thought." In *Agroecology: The Scientific Basis for Alternative Agriculture*, ed. M. A. Altieri, 1–20. Boulder, Colorado: Westview Press.

IUCN/UNEP/WWF. 1980. *World Conservation Strategy: Living Resource Conservation for Sustainable Development*. Gland, Switzerland: International Union for the Conservation of Nature (IUCN).

———. 1991. *Caring for the Earth: A Strategy for Sustainable Living*. Gland, Switzerland: International Union for the Conservation of Nature (IUCN).

Jackson, W. 1980. *New Roots for Agriculture*. San Francisco: Friends of the Earth.

Loomis, J. B., and R. G. Walsh. 1986. "Assessing Wildlife and Environmental Values in Cost-Benefit Analysis: State of the Art." *Journal of Environmental Management* 22(2):125–131.

Lovejoy, T. E., R. O. Bierregaard, Jr., A. B. Rylands, J. R. Malcolm, C. E. Quintela, L. H. Harper, K. S. Brown, Jr., A. H. Powell, G. V. N. Powell, H. O. R. Schubart, and M. B. Hays. 1986. "Edge and Other Effects of Isolation on Amazon Forest Fragments." In *Conservation Biology*, ed. M. E. Soulé, 257–285. Sunderland, Massachusetts: Sinauer.

MacKinnon, J., C. MacKinnon, G. Child, and J. Thorsell. 1986. *Managing Protected Areas in the Tropics*. Gland, Switzerland: International Union for the Conservation of Nature.

Marten, G. G., and D. M. Saltman. 1986. "The Human Ecology Perspective." In *Traditional Agriculture in Southeast Asia: A Human Ecology Perspective*, ed. G. G. Marten, 6–19. Boulder, Colorado: Westview Press.

Martins, E. 1993. "Extractive Reserves in Brazil: A Critical Analysis." Case study prepared for the Liz Claiborne Art Ortenberg Foundation Community Based Conservation Workshop, October 18–22, Airlie, Virginia.

Meffe, G. K., A. H. Ehrlich, and D. Ehrenfeld. 1993. "Human Population Control: The Missing Agenda." *Conservation Biology* 7(1):1–3.

Metcalfe, S. 1993. "The Zimbabwe Communal Areas Management Programme for Indigenous Resources." Case study prepared for the Liz Claiborne Art Ortenberg Community Based Conservation Workshop, October 18–22, Airlie, Virginia.

Noss, R. F. 1990. "Indicators for Monitoring Biodiversity: A Hierarchical Approach." *Conservation Biology* 4(4):355–364.

———. 1993. "The Wildlands Project Land Conservation Strategy." *Wild Earth* (Special Issue):10–25.

Office of Technology Assessment, United States Congress. 1987. *Technologies to Maintain Biodiversity.* Washington, D. C.: U.S. Government Printing Office.

Peters, C. M., A. H. Gentry, and R. O. Mendelsohn. 1989. "Valuation of an Amazonian Rain Forest." *Nature* 339:655–656.

Reynolds, R. T., J. Scott, and J. A. Nussbaum. 1980. "A Variable Circular Plot Method for Censusing Bird Numbers. *Condor* 82:309–313.

Robinson, J. G. 1993. "The Limits to Caring: Sustainable Living and the Loss of Biodiversity." *Conservation Biology* 7(1):20–28.

Salafsky, N. 1993. "Mammalian Use of a Buffer Zone Agroforestry System Bordering Gunung Palung National Park, West Kalimantan, Indonesia." *Conservation Biology 7(4):928–933.*

———, B. L. Dugelby, and J. W. Terborgh. 1993. "Can Extractive Reserves Save the Rain Forest? An Ecological and Socioeconomic Comparison of Non-Timber Forest Product Extraction Systems in Petén, Guatemala, and West Kalimantan, Indonesia." *Conservation Biology* 7(1):39–52.

Schelhas, J. 1994. "Policy Review: Building Sustainable Land Uses on Existing Practices—Smallholder Land Use Mosaics in Tropical Lowland Costa Rica." *Society and Natural Resources* 7(1):67–84.

Shaffer, M. L. 1981. "Minimum Population Sizes for Species Conservation." *BioScience* 31(2):131–134.

Steubing, R. B., and J. Gasis. 1989. "A Survey of Small Mammals within a Sabah Tree Plantation in Malaysia." *Journal of Tropical Ecology* 5:203–214.

Terborgh, J., and J. Weske. 1969. "Colonization of Secondary Habitats by Peruvian Birds." *Ecology* 50:765–782.

Thomas, C. D. 1990. "What Do Real Population Dynamics Tell Us about Minimum Viable Population Sizes?" *Conservation Biology* 4(3):324–327.

UNESCO. 1974. *Task Force On: Criteria and Guidelines for the Choice and Establishment of Biosphere Reserves.* Final Report. Paris: UNESCO.

van Schaik, C., R. Kramer, P. Shyamsundar, and N. Salafsky. 1992. *Biodiversity of Tropical Rain Forests: Ecology and Economics of an Elusive Resource.* Durham, North Carolina: Duke University Center for Tropical Conservation.

Wilcove, D. S. 1985. "Nest Predation in Forest Tracts and the Decline of Migratory Songbirds." *Ecology* 66(4):1211–1214.

Wilson, E. O. 1984. *Biophilia.* Cambridge, Massachusetts: Harvard University Press.

CHAPTER 21

Are Successful Community-based Conservation Projects Designed or Discovered?

Frances J. Seymour

Are successful community-based conservation projects designed or discovered? Are they the result of planning and implementation orchestrated from the outside, or is their success based primarily on community resource management systems already in place at the time of project initiation? The design-versus-discovery question focuses attention on the role of the outsider in project initiation. Representatives of donor agencies and the intermediary organizations that they support to implement projects are often both literally and figuratively distant from project sites. They seek roles—as designers or discoverers—in promoting community-based conservation. Motivated by commitments to both human and biological communities, such outside agents seek ways to broaden the array of economic choices open to resource-dependent people while encouraging them to conserve and enhance biodiversity. In other words, they seek to promote both development and conservation.

What roles are available to outsiders that are legitimate, effective, and minimize adverse risk? Conscious of the limited financial and human resources that can be brought to bear in either the design or the discovery mode in comparison to the challenges at hand, they question whether resources are being squandered in vain attempts to design projects while the existing potential of community initiatives is allowed to wither from neglect. Given current rates of resource degradation, time may be the scarcest commodity of all. The cases studies in this book shed light on the comparative effectiveness of the two modes of project initiation and on the long-term sustainability of the resulting projects.

Beyond the imperative to be responsible stewards of scarce project resources, the risk of unintended consequences is another reason to consider the question of design versus discovery. The business of design always includes the possibility of doing harm to the very people and ecosystems being "assisted." Similarly, "discovery" of a successful, small-scale community-managed conservation regime can easily bring increased money, attention, and expectations to the community, ultimately undermining the foundations of its success. Whether the design and discovery modes of project initiation carry any inherent risks and whether these can be anticipated or minimized are additional topics on which the case studies can provide guidance. Issues of site selection, leadership, timing and incentives, scale and replicability, and sustainability for the two modes of project inititiation are also part of the discussion that follows.

The twelve case studies in this volume provide a convenient portfolio of projects with which to inform a discussion of design versus discovery in community-based conservation projects. While the small number and heterogeneity of these cases (plus a few others and some of my professional experiences cited in the text) precludes rigorous testing of hypotheses, they nevertheless offer sufficient material for the development of working propositions. The intention is to stimulate dialogue among practitioners through consideration of recent project experience, so the discussion does not attempt a treatment of the bulk of relevant scholarly literature.

While the nature of outside intervention is different in designed and discovered projects at the time of project initiation, the strategies of successful community-based conservation projects converge on a synthesis of the two approaches, linking site-specific interventions to macro-level policy and institutional reform. The sustainability of both kinds of projects ultimately may be linked to political relationships and processes. By identifying nurturing roles for outsiders—particularly donor agencies and the intermediaries that they support—it may be possible to facilitate an integrated design-and-discovery process for community-based conservation initiatives.

The Design-Discovery Continuum

The design and discovery modes of community-based conservation development can be defined in caricature. *Design mode,* in this discussion, refers to externally catalyzed initiatives focused on particular project sites. In the design mode, individuals or institutions outside the community take the initiative in organizing a response to a problem also identified and defined by outsiders. Usually, the project is in response to biodiversity under threat and in need of protection. Project design assumes that something is wrong with the existing resource-management regime and that external intervention is needed. Designed projects have external human- and financial-resource inputs as key strategic elements.

Discovery mode refers to efforts to identify and support conservation activities initiated by communities themselves. Usually, discovered projects target community resource-management systems under external threat. Project discoverers assume that appropriate local resource-management regimes already exist, and that the role of external actors is to assist in legitimizing them. Discovered community-based conservation regimes, of course, are not projects at all at the time of their discovery; the very word *project* connotes external intervention. In the discovery mode, donors and other outsiders often adopt a programmatic approach. Their efforts may focus on policy changes with the potential to affect communities across an entire region rather than on interventions targeted to one particular site.

These definitions of *design* and *discover*, of course, present a false dichotomy. Rather than two distinct modes of project initiation, these definitions describe the two ends of a spectrum of approaches that combine elements of both design and discovery. The specific nature and timing of outside intervention places any given project nearer one end or the other. The case studies in this book, being a fairly heterogenous lot, differ in the amount and nature of detail provided on the key events and actors involved at the point of project initiation. Nevertheless, for the purposes of discussion, the projects and programs described in the cases can be arrayed along a continuum ranging from design to discovery *at the time of their initiation.*

The portfolio of projects is weighted toward the design end, with fewer examples of those initiated in the discovery mode. At the discovery end of the spectrum is INDIA, a case in which, prior to the initiation of programmatic support from the Orissa Forest Department, some thirty forest protection committees already were functioning in one area alone. Still near the discovery end of the spectrum is the support for existing local resource management regimes in Brazilian extractive reserves described by Martins (1993). In MALUKU ISLANDS, local community leaders and outsiders jointly "discover" *sasi*, an indigenous marine resource-management system, and adapt it to contemporary circumstances.

In these three cases, the outsider's primary role is to assist communities in gaining external recognition and support for indigenous resource management regimes. NEOTROPICAL FORESTS briefly mentions initiatives *ribereño* communities in Peru have taken to regulate overexploitation of fish and game, but the authors give no indication that these efforts have been the targets of project support since their discovery.

At the design end of the spectrum is CRATER MOUNTAIN, as well as the cases described by P. Wright (1993) in Madagascar; Glick, Neary, and Rasker (1993) in Yellowstone National Park in the United States; and Cabarle, Panduro, and Murayari (1993) in the Peruvian Amazon. These projects were initiated, financed, and primarily managed by outsiders in the interest of modifying the conservation behavior of local landowners and/or resource users at particular sites.

The bulk of the remaining case studies gathered here also describe projects initiated by outsiders, but somewhere nearer the middle of the spectrum, since the communities got involved in project design and management, and the projects linked site-specific innovation to national-level policy change, at an early stage. This set includes AMBOSELI, ANNAPURNA, BOSCOSA, CAMPFIRE, KAKADU, NIGER, and NORTH YORK MOORS.

The arrangement of cases along the continuum depends on which aspect of project initiation is emphasized. Beyond the moment of project initiation, the distinct features of design and discovery begin to blur further. Indeed, one element of a project may be used to illustrate a feature of the design mode, while another element of the same project can be used to describe an aspect of the discovery mode. A project's placement along the continuum also can change over time. Those at each end tend to move toward the center as they mature, and this convergence foreshadows a tentative answer to the question posed in the title of this chapter.

Site Selection in the Discovery Mode

How a site is selected is an obvious starting point for this discussion. Knowing who chose a particular site for a community-based conservation initiative and why helps to place the project along the design-discovery continuum. Through their selection of sites with particular features, outside intervenors implicitly state their priorities. Site selection also has implications for project management and political support, which in turn affect a project's prospects for long-term sustainability.

Community-based conservation regimes subject to "discovery" are initiated by the communities themselves. The sites of such indigenous community management systems are thus not "selected" according to externally imposed criteria. Nevertheless, some educated guesses are possible about the characteristics of community management regimes most likely to be discovered and the circumstances under which they are most likely to become targets of external project initiatives.

While occurrence is not selected, the "discovery" of community-initiated conservation regimes is no doubt biased. The literature on common-property resource management (including papers presented at the National Academy of Sciences Conference on Common Property Resource Management [NAS 1986] and the first four conferences of the International Association for the Study of Common Property) provides a wealth of examples of community resource-management systems. Yet these represent only a subset of the total number, and those that come to the attention of more casual observers are particularly unlikely to constitute a random sample of the whole (Chambers 1980, 1983). Outsiders are perhaps less likely to notice marine conservation systems, the boundaries of which are invisible to the casual observer, than terrestrial ones. Outsiders are less likely to "see" the management of forests that appear to be "natural" than the management of those that have been visibly altered.

Outsiders—prospective donors in particular—are more likely to learn of systems championed by an articulate community leader or local government official. In MALUKU ISLANDS, the village of Ihamahu in Indonesia is nominated by the provincial university's environmental studies center for the national Kalpataru environmental achievement award. Other examples become known if they are the site of a well-publicized conflict over resource use between a community and an outside government or private interest. The world most likely would not know the name of Chico Mendes had there been no political confrontation between the Brazilian extractivists and their competitors for the Amazon's resources. Community-based conservation regimes without such characteristics may be like dogs that don't bark in the night: As long as their resources are well managed and not a source of overt conflict, they do not attract outsiders' attention.

The community-initiated conservation regimes described in the case studies, including the West Bengal and Orissa forest protection movement in INDIA, the *sasi* systems in MALUKU ISLANDS, and extractive reserve management in Brazil (Martins 1993) appear to have evolved in conditions of relative resource scarcity. For example, the West Bengal villagers described in INDIA respond to the negative impacts of forest degradation resulting from clear-cutting in the 1940s and increasing pressures from adjacent villages. *Sasi* is depicted in MALUKU ISLANDS as a system that evolved to organize, regulate, and distribute the benefits of commodity trade with outsiders and optimize the harvest of marine resources. In Brazil, the extractivists' traditional management practices were threatened by encroaching colonists and ranchers (Martins 1993). Although threatened, these systems retained a relatively high degree of functional integrity at the time of their discovery.

In contrast, several case studies nearer the design end of the spectrum allude to traditional resource management systems that have broken down over time and proved unable to respond to new scarcity-inducing pressures. The nature and timing of increasing pressures on resources are likely to influence the concerned community resource management system's ability to respond. Where resource scarcity develops slowly and is a function of the behavior of community members, there may be an appropriate timeframe and institutional setting in which a community management regime can evolve to meet the new challenge. Communities may be less able to respond to resource scarcity that develops suddenly or is precipitated by the actions of people and institutions outside the community's control.

The case studies, however, present a more complex picture. MALUKU ISLANDS describes the breakdown of traditional *sasi* restraints on trochus shell exploitation as a function primarily of increasing community desires and suggests that the system is constantly being "reinvented," according to the interests of each, by community leaders, government authorities, and even environmental NGOs. NIGER describes resource degradation as a function of both internal and external dynamics, the cumulative impact of drought, demographic pressures, and centralized resource-management practices and policies.

In CAMPFIRE, traditional ownership worked well until conditions changed and resources became less plentiful. Eventually, the resource base declined because the community had not developed resource-allocation systems appropriate to periods of stress. Why some traditional systems are able to adapt to changing conditions and others are not remains an intriguing question. For our purposes, the important point is that intact community resource management systems are candidates for discovery, while those that have broken down are eligible targets for project designers. The potential influence of the macro policy environment on the evolution of traditional systems is discussed below.

Finally, the case studies suggest that the "discovery" of community resource management and granting of support by outsiders does not necessarily proceed according to biodiversity conservation priorities. Martins (1993) says that in the case of Brazil's extractive reserves, social issues were as pressing as the need to maintain biodiversity, and that the former often strongly affected decisions taken in support of the latter.

As Western has suggested, projects located on the discovery end of the spectrum may be more concerned with sustainable resource utilization than those at the design end, which may focus on resource protection (M. Wright 1993).

Site Selection in the Design Mode

Site selection for projects that originate in the design mode depends on the designers' primary objective. Reference is seldom made to site-selection criteria as such. Instead, particular circumstances often lead to a project's development. Within this eclectic site-selection process, however, are two countervailing tendencies: Sites tend to be selected primarily for their intrinsic conservation value or for their potential as models for dispute resolution or community resource management.

Projects Focused on Biodiversity Conservation

Several of the projects described in the case studies were initiated by external actors concerned with conservation of biological resources at a particular site. In a few cases, during the course of field research, a scientist became concerned about threats to the ecosystem and/or a particular species under study. By attracting the attention of a donor, a government agency, and/or an NGO, the scientist set into motion a chain of events that led to design and external funding of a project. The project in Papua New Guinea described in CRATER MOUNTAIN began when an anthropologist studying birds of paradise as an inspiration for traditional dances launched an effort to conserve them and intensified after the New York Zoological Society's curator of birds visited the site.

Despite their initial concerns with biological conservation, project initiators sooner or later recognize that conservation objectives are inextricably tied to local socioeconomic development and design their interventions accordingly. While some projects start out with a community-based approach, others such as BOSCOSA may move in that direction only after other approaches prove inadequate.

While these projects were initiated primarily with biological conservation objectives, a systematic site-selection process based on biological criteria was not necessarily employed. In only a few instances were sites selected according to some national or international framework of conservation priorities. The MALUKU ISLANDS case aside, in Indonesia international donor and domestic NGO attention has been focused disproportionately on community-based conservation at terrestrial rather than marine sites, despite the value and precarious status of the country's coral reefs. The interest and advocacy of a particular individual with

personal or professional ties to the area appears to have been the key factor dif-
ferentiating project sites from other similar sites with equal or greater biodiversity
value.

Sites chosen under these circumstances tend to be relatively remote—both
physically and in the political sense—and relatively pristine from an ecological
perspective. Indeed, their pristine state, in addition to the attraction of a particular
ecological community or species, probably was the reason some were chosen as
sites for biological research in the first place. Such sites may be located just
beyond the frontier of significant human disturbance. Projects are then designed
to "hold the line"—to protect the interiors of national parks through buffer-zone
development, for example, or to control habitat loss or the direct exploitation of a
particular threatened species—in order to ensure that ecosystems remain un-
spoiled. Sites that are still relatively pristine appear to offer better chances for success; protecting an intact ecosystem is easier than rehabilitating a degraded one.
AMAZON, however, with its description of the significant hunting pressure on mammals in the Peruvian Amazon, provides a reminder that the association between
remoteness and abundance does not always hold.

Remote project sites, however, may be least likely to have the institutions necessary to support a project. While indigenous resource-management institutions
are likely to be highly sophisticated, their function may be opaque or even invisible to outsiders. And although well adapted to extant conditions, they may not be
positioned to deal with rapid demographic change or other sources of environmental stress. The few "discovered" community-based conservation regimes
among the case studies appear to have evolved in conditions of relative scarcity
in the presence of external threats. If biological resources are abundant and
threats are remote, the local community may have no rationale for expending the
energy to organize and to make and enforce rules on resource use.

Relatively remote communities also may be less likely to have formal institutions such as cooperatives to serve as vehicles for project implementation. BOSCOSA
suggests that buffer-zone development projects typically must deal with "communities that are critically located from a conservation viewpoint . . . [but have no]
appropriate organization, thus necessitating the formation of organizations" (223).

A second difficulty of project design for remote sites is their low priority with
government agencies charged with conservation. The more distant the site from
the national or provincial capital, the less likely the concerned agency knows the
site well or has the resources to post staff members there, even to serve as "counterparts" for project-supported staff. In Costa Rica, BOSCOSA reports, the Osa was
regarded "as a Costa Rican Siberia— a place for new, inexperienced, or problematical staff" (220). A sympathetic Ministry of Forestry official in Indonesia once
confided that "nobody cares about Irian Jaya [the country's easternmost
province]; it takes a day to get there!" Agency staff members also may share ma-
jority-culture prejudices against traditional peoples: Some Kenyans considered
the Maasai's resistance to modernization a sign of backwardness (AMBOSELI).

Government agencies also may find allocation of scarce resources to relatively pristine sites hard to justify under political pressure to respond to more imminent threats to better-known protected areas closer to capital cities. Officials of the Indonesian Ministry of Forestry suggested that start-up problems encountered by a USAID-funded project, including the ministry's failure to post counterpart staff to the site, were the legacy of a disagreement concerning the choice of project site. Ministry officials claimed that they had argued strongly for a threatened protected area close to the provincial capital, but that USAID project designers had insisted on a remote location that occupied a low position on the ministry's list of priorities (MOF 1992).

At remote or frontier sites, the institutional vacuum may extend to all sectors, tempting projects to take on matters of both governance and basic service delivery more appropriate to the state. In Niger, national policies sometimes appear irrelevant in rural areas due to "the presence at the village level of non-state authority systems and institutions and the general absence at the village level of resident administrative or advisory installations of the state" (NIGER:239). The Nigerien communities' lack of access to basic formal institutions of governance such as courts and representative assemblies means that the project must rely on alternative mechanisms for dispute resolution and decision-making. While traditional institutions may work well for this purpose when conflict is confined to one ethnically homogenous community, their scope and externally recognized legitimacy may be insufficient to deal with issues involving larger geographic scale and third-party actors such as commercial fishing, logging, or mining interests.

This institutional vacuum is the central problem of indigenous communities facing the impact of commercial logging in Irian Jaya: They simply do not have access to conflict resolution fora that the communities, the concessionaires, and local government and military officials all deem legitimate. Communities located closer to government centers or that have a native son trained in law are more likely to seek—and sometimes obtain—redress of their grievances through formal administrative or judicial procedures (Tjitradjaja 1991).

The lack of basic government services in remote sites may lead *conservation-oriented* projects to take on other community needs such as health, education, and infrastructure improvements. Providing such services may create a linkage between the conservation project and the community, but the decision to do so entails some risks. As P. Wright (1993) says of the project in Madagascar, involvement in such enterprises increases the complexity of project coordination and threatens to exceed the mandate, expertise, and capacity of implementing organizations. Such activities tend to absorb an increasingly larger proportion of project resources at the expense of conservation objectives. While providing general infrastructure and services may successfully promote conservation in the short term, these activities are not likely to be effective in the long run if pressures on resources are increasing (Brown and Wykcoff-Baird 1992).

Projects Focused on Demonstrating Community Management

If projects targeting biodiversity conservation tend to be located at relatively remote and pristine sites, projects more explicitly focused on conflict resolution and the development of models for community-based conservation evidence a countervailing tendency. These projects tend to be located where resource degradation and conflict are relatively well-advanced and where communities, government agencies, and interested third parties have reached some degree of consensus that a crisis exists. Such sites—often characterized by higher population densities, heterogenous communities influenced by in-migration, and open conflict over resource rights and access—tend to be more accessible and to have a higher profile among responsible government agencies at the national level.

BOSCOSA presents one example of a project intentionally targeted in this way, where the perception was that a project—the primary purpose of which was not conservation of biological resources—could not have made things worse. Another example is a project being developed in Indonesia on a site encompassing four provincial government jurisdictions and a host of problems. According to a World Bank official, the project, to be funded under the Global Environmental Facility (GEF), is intended to serve as a model for conservation planning and will enable project proponents to say, "If we can do it here, we can do it anywhere" (World Bank 1993).

Projects sited to address national-level political conflict include Amboseli—"the most controversial wildlife area in Kenya at the start of the program" (AM-BOSELI:44)—where national and provincial governments were at odds over the control of revenues, and Kakadu in Australia, where recognition of Aboriginal land title was an issue of extreme political sensitivity at national and provincial levels (KAKADU). The natural forest management cases cited in NIGER are targeting degraded areas to develop models for joint resource management, and the Guesselbodi project staff's proximity to capital-city decision makers is mentioned as an advantage of the site.

Ironically, such high-profile sites may be least likely to achieve policy breakthroughs in certain political climates due to the bureaucratic behavior that they induce (Craven 1991). The Indonesian Ministry of Forestry selected for its social forestry program sites where conflict between local communities and the ministry over forest management was known to exist. One site in Irian Jaya was literally across the street from the ministry's provincial office. In part because of the attention from high-level officials, the ministry staff was unwilling to approve the deviations from existing forest land-use regulations necessary for the project to demonstrate the effectiveness of more participatory resource management approaches and recognition of traditional landowners' rights. In contrast, a similar project initiated by the World Wide Fund for Nature in a more remote area of the province had greater freedom from the limitations of official policy and was able to recognize communities' traditional land rights in the conservation area.

The natural forest management projects in Niger appear to face an analogous dilemma with respect to organizational forms for forestry cooperatives. While government policy, reflecting its "antidemocratic instincts," does not recognize the legitimacy of organizations outside its own narrow cooperative framework, more appropriate de facto organizational forms are evolving at project sites (NIGER). In both cases, the question becomes whether, when, and how to seek de jure legitimacy for such a de facto innovation. (The ethical dilemma that arises when outsiders engage local institutions not recognized by the state is discussed in Seymour and Rutherford 1990).

A final point regarding site selection in crisis areas is that some threshold of resource degradation may exist beyond which continued utilization is not possible without at least a temporary decline in community incomes. AMAZON calculates the specific decrease in hunting revenues that would result from imposition of a management regime with long-term sustainability. In INDIA, the participating West Bengal and Orissa communities face a near-term shortfall of fuelwood while the village forest is allowed to regenerate, but in areas where degradation is so advanced that root stock no longer exists, even this sacrifice may not be sufficient to achieve sustainable production.

According to a framework for Integrated Conservation and Development Project (ICDP) site selection proposed by Dinerstein (1993), such sites would not be a priority for conservation intervention. Dinerstein's framework synthesizes a site's biological interest, social feasibility, and conservation feasibility, giving priority to those that score high in all three factors rather than one or two.

The striking conclusion of this brief survey of project site selection is that few sites are selected according to formal criteria. Instead, site selection appears to be driven by eclectic factors related to personal and political interests on the part of individuals and institutions. Ironically, the leadership a project-specific constellation of individuals and institutions provides may function as a proxy for social feasibility.

Leadership

Very few of the project sites, designed or discovered, were selected for their intrinsic conservation value or feasibility. This is less surprising considering the critical role individual and institutional leadership plays in project development.

Individual Leadership

The portfolio of cases provides fewer insights into the dynamics of leadership in discovered than in designed projects—perhaps a natural result of the lack of outsiders on the scene to document the process by which indigenous systems evolve. However, we do get a glimpse of the importance of individual charismatic and traditional leaders. In INDIA, an illiterate West Bengal small farmer takes the lead in raising local awareness and organizing his neighbors for forest protection. MALUKU ISLANDS' description of the *sasi* system introduces a chief *kewang*, whose role combines the knowledge, prestige and functions of a ritual practitioner with the "responsibilities of a resource monitor with the power to enforce community resource management rules" (80). Chico Mendes is an example of a charismatic leader acting on behalf of community management on a larger political stage (Martins 1993).

What happens to the leadership dynamic after a community-based conservation initiative is "discovered"? In MALUKU ISLANDS, the *kewang* of Ihamahu, upon receipt of the national Kalpataru environmental award, is inspired to further expand and elaborate the conservation activities included in the village's reinvented *sasi* system. Outside attention and support can, in some cases, enhance the effectiveness of a local leader. But detrimental shifts in accountability can occur after the advent of outside intervention as well. The local leader may begin spending more and more time interacting with outsiders (even attending international conferences) or may become the subject of envy and suspicion regarding funds management and other donor-supplied benefits. Discoverers and designers should consider the risk that contact with outsiders may adversely affect the effectiveness and/or legitimacy of local leaders.

Individuals also play key roles in the development of designed projects, but, in contrast to discovered projects, these individuals tend to be outsiders. Several cases convey, either implicitly or explicitly, the author's role as a critical actor in the events described (see KAKADU and AMBOSELI).

The leadership of outside individuals has both advantages and disadvantages. Outsiders often must contend with nationals' sensitivities about expatriates, or those of regional or ethnic groups toward each other. Due to the history of their involvement in conservation in East Africa, expatriates involved in the Amboseli project met with initial suspicion (AMBOSELI). Similarly, The Nature Conservancy, working in the Greater Yellowstone area of the United States, has noted the "perceived difference between locals and outsiders, especially regarding the level of trust and participation extended them" (Glick, Neary, and Rasker 1993). Ironically, the neutral position that allows outside individuals to serve as "honest brokers" between communities, government agencies, donors, and others also raises questions of whose interests they represent and to whom they are accountable.

By definition, the initiative in a project conceived in the design mode comes from outsiders, but various patterns of leadership development emerge thereafter. Often, people skilled in advocacy play the initial leadership roles. As projects develop, however, leadership needs shift from advocacy to diplomacy and management, skills with which initial project leaders may be less favorably endowed. In the CRATER MOUNTAIN case, a resident anthropologist spends years building consensus for conservation in local communities; this same individual, in his capacity as a board member, later causes friction with national staff by unilaterally deciding on how grant funds will be used.

Projects initiated by outsiders may induce emergence of project leaders from within the community. In CRATER MOUNTAIN, an individual took the initiative to build an airstrip, which led to additional donor funding commitments, assignment of Peace Corps volunteers, and increased marketing opportunities for the village. In AMBOSELI, a shift in the level and nature of Maasai participation occurs in the second phase of the project. Externally catalyzed projects also may facilitate leadership within government agencies and political bodies. Again in AMBOSELI, a game warden and a member of parliament play key roles in developing the program and pushing for its political acceptance.

In designed projects, the dynamic of contact with outsiders also may serve to delegitimize community leadership. In consensus-oriented Melanesian societies, anyone who steps forward and presents himself to outsiders as a representative of the community for a transaction involving community resources is immediately suspect (Henry 1993). Like evangelical and commercial interests before them, designers of conservation projects are in danger of engaging such communities in leadership norms inappropriate for the cultural context. Identifying community representatives, and understanding the institutions and processes that confer legitimacy upon them at the local level, may be one of the most difficult tasks facing project designers.

Institutional Leadership

The institutional dimension of leadership has a different character in designed projects than in discovered projects, particularly at initiation. Perhaps the most attractive feature of a "discovered" community-based conservation initiative is that its leadership is already embedded in a local institution. Such leadership presumably is more legitimate and sustainable than that initially provided by outsiders in designed projects. However, MALUKU ISLANDS cautions against romanticizing the origin and contemporary function of community management systems, reminding us that they are not necessarily egalitarian in purpose or effect. AMBOSELI describes authority in Maasai society as resting with the ruling elders, giving women no formal decision-making role.

Institutional leadership in designed projects originates outside the concerned community. Often three or more external institutions eventually are involved in project management, including a government agency, an intermediary such as a national nongovernmental organization or project management unit, and an international donor. Sorting out leadership roles among these various institutions and the community is always complicated, particularly at the time of project initiation.

Discussions of preconditions for successful community-based conservation projects often neglect the need to identify sources of support and leadership within the government bureaucracy. Supportive officials may be necessary to legitimate and replicate community-based conservation initiatives, if only in renouncing their own claims as primary managers of the resource in question.

Project leadership within government agencies may be constrained by bureaucratic cultures that inhibit risk taking. In CAMPFIRE, government agencies are extremely reluctant to devolve authority to local communities. A history of antagonism between the concerned government agency and local communities may be present due to previous law-enforcement-oriented interactions. In NIGER, "farmers and pastoralists live in fear and disdain of Forest Service agents who appear to do little more than impose fines" (241). In BOSCOSA, local communities are suspicious, resentful, and cynical toward government agencies, while government-agency staff members hold prejudices toward local communities that preclude effective leadership at the time of the project's initiation.

Project leadership within an independent, national-level intermediary institution appears to be an effective alternative to government-agency leadership. Sometimes the national counterpart of an international conservation organization plays this role; in other cases, community-development or advocacy-oriented NGOs mediate between concerned communities and other outsiders. Such organizations apparently are well placed to facilitate alliance building among other concerned parties. Examples include the role of the Zimbabwe Trust described in CAMPFIRE, the King Mahendra Trust in ANNAPURNA, and, in BOSCOSA, the project entity initiated by the World Wildlife Fund and the Neotropica Foundation. MALUKU ISLANDS also alludes to the important role of national-level NGOs as intermediaries in *sasi*.

Interestingly, few of the case studies describe donor agencies taking up leadership or activist roles. This may reflect an ambivalent attitude toward the donors' role more than lack of involvement in project initiation and management. In Ranomafana National Park in Madagascar, the donor presence at meetings hinders frank discussion (P. Wright 1993), while in AMBOSELI, the attraction of outside funders lends prestige and legitimacy to the project at a critical point in its development. In CRATER MOUNTAIN, a succession of visits from prospective donors threatens to produce cynicism within the local community.

Although donor agencies without in-country staff will have difficulty exercising responsible leadership from afar, those with field staff can perform important roles as honest brokers among the various institutions involved in project management and related policy reform. The Ford Foundation staff in Asia has pursued active, programmatic strategies in several countries to build national-level alliances in support of community resource-management project implementation and policy reform among concerned government agencies and communities, academic researchers, and NGOs (Seymour 1987; F. Korten 1988; Poffenberger 1990). Donors as facilitators of community-based conservation characteristic of this approach are described later.

Timing and Incentives

If site selection sets the stage, then individual and institutional leadership define the players in the initiation of community-based conservation projects. Timing and incentives characteristic of the design and discovery modes of project initiation animate the dramas that follow.

The emergence and continuation of community-initiated conservation in the context of both design and discovery are related to favorable national-level policies and political support. The evolution of community-initiated conservation regimes appears to be strongly influenced by policy environments (see NIGER, INDIA). The flip side is that initiatives assisted by supportive polices also can be set back by policy reverses. According to Martins (1993), Brazilian policies supporting the price of rubber underpin the economic viability of extractive reserves, but render them vulnerable to removal of such supports.

The discovery of community initiatives and the takeoff of designed projects appears to be related to national-level political support. The construction and recognition of a "green *sasi*" system in Indonesia is linked to national-level political currents articulated by the minister of environment and population (MALUKU ISLANDS). Support from political elites is important in AMBOSELI. Often projects can position themselves strategically to take advantage of changing policy environments. In ANNAPURNA, royal patronage for the project and implementing institution is a key factor in the project's success. On the other hand, sustainability of a politically favored project may then become vulnerable to the fortunes of its political champions.

While the external policy environment may have a significant impact on the timing of a community-based conservation project, many of the incentives project participants face are inherent in the nature of the project itself. The community-initiated resource management regimes described in the case studies appear to have occurred in conditions of relative resource scarcity and function to conserve resources for communities' long-term use. Common property theory suggests that people will invest in developing institutions to control resource management when the benefits exceed the costs of doing so.

Such incentives can not necessarily be relied upon in designed projects, which may target conservation of resources such as the birds of paradise in CRATER MOUNTAIN, with value external to the local community. To the extent that those outside the community enjoy the benefits of conservation, some sort of subsidy is necessary to compensate the community for the real and opportunity costs incurred locally. In AMBOSELI, a wildlife utilization fee distributed to the Maasai explicitly addresses this need. Payments made to landowners for investments in conservation in NORTH YORK MOORS are based on the same principle. The sustainability of community resource management practices supportive of conservation appear to be dependent on long-term continuation of such subsidies. Local leaders involved in the Crater Mountain project were indignant when tourism revenues—the quid pro quo for bird-of-paradise protection—dropped off in the late 1980s (CRATER MOUNTAIN).

Community-based conservation projects initiated by outsiders also are vulnerable to all of the familiar perverse incentives inherent in development projects

(Wells and Brandon 1992). Donor-agency staff members move money according to the funding cycle and financial scale characteristic of that organization—and will look for opportunities to do so. P. Wright (1993) complains that USAID's three-year funding horizon is hardly sufficient to get a project started. While donors' financial contributions to particular projects may seem to be too little, too late, the opposite problem—too much, too soon—is also widespread. Leaders of the Annapurna project are reportedly concerned that the project's requirement for a cash or labor contribution from target communities will be undermined by donors eager to make grants to become involved in the conservation area (ANNAPURNA).

Donors and the recipients of their grants are under pressure to demonstrate success as early as possible and minimize deviation from the implementation plan initially agreed upon. The Campfire Collaborative Group is concerned that the project not become "a mosaic of donor funded five year 'blueprint' projects, driven by log frame approaches, insensitive to the needs of adaptive management" (Metcalfe 1993). The Madagascan Ranomafana project has received funding from nineteen donor organizations, "each [with] its priorities and restrictions; no single one will fund all parts of such a project" (P. Wright 1993:6). There is also "donor fatigue." Donor-agency staff members face pressure to move on to "new" initiatives after a certain period of time; the result often is the packaging and repackaging of the same project to address the eccentricities of a series of donors. If donor relations are so burdensome for designed projects, such multiple and changing demands can quickly overwhelm discovered projects.

Scale and Replicability

If community-based conservation projects are to have any significant impact on the welfare of rural communities or on the maintenance of biodiversity in natural habitats, they must be implemented on a large scale and/or embody characteristics that lend themselves to rapid replication. Projects initiated in either the design or the discovery mode implicitly or explicitly attempt to address this requirement through different strategies.

Designed projects focus on specific problems at specific sites, or at least start at that scale. Scale, in most community projects, is defined by the size of the concerned protected area, although activities often start with individual households within the communities (ANNAPURNA) or particular communities within a larger set (NIGER) as targets. Several of the designed projects were developed with the stated intention that they should serve as models that could later be replicated in other sites, and some had as their explicit objective the task of influencing the national policies and practices of government agencies.

There are clear advantages to the site-specific "project" approach. Project proponents—including leaders of concerned communities, external donors and intermediaries, and even sympathetic government officials—can use a project as a vehicle with which to circumvent cumbersome or inappropriate regulations, supplement insufficient budgets and staffs, and secure special concessions on an experimental basis. The special status of a project also can work against its ability to serve as a model for broader replication. Even so, the resources and time necessary to achieve project objectives often are underestimated by project designers. Communities, donors, or government agencies often are frustrated when, after so many years of project implementation, the problem is not yet "solved." Indeed, even after several years, there may be no institutional framework in place through which to continue addressing project objectives after the withdrawal of external support, much less extend the project to new sites and communities.

Project horizons beyond a specific site depend in part on the goal: Is the point to work within the existing legal, policy, and administrative framework, or to use the project to change that framework? In attempts to engage the larger bureaucratic infrastructure responsible for conservation and work through existing channels to facilitate community-based conservation, project proponents can find their efforts at the mercy of a wide range of systemic problems. These may include civil-service restrictions on staff recruitment, salaries, and career paths and other problems that are far beyond their capacity to reform. Setbacks described in AMBOSELI were due to the the decay of the Wildlife Conservation and Management Department (WCMD) in the early 1980s.

On the other hand, only through direct engagement can community members, external donors and intermediaries, and government officials learn about structural constraints on community-based conservation and experiment with generally applicable ways to get around them. Then the specific project site functions as a laboratory in which to identify community-level constraints and gradually adjust the project focus upward to provincial-level planning and national-level policy.

Projects designed for specific sites sooner or later may add national-level policy change and reorientation of government agencies to their agendas (see the fifth element of the designers' strategy in BOSCOSA).

Early surveys conducted in the development of the Annapurna project indicated that a new legal designation, conservation area, was needed as an alternative to the restrictive national park classification. After six years of lobbying and negotiation, project advocates achieved recognition of the conservation area concept, as well as a legislative mandate for NGO involvement in conservation area management (ANNAPURNA). In NIGER, donors pressure the government to change national legislation to recognize customary resource rights. In Zimbabwe, CAMPFIRE has established itself as a catalyst in the natural resources policy reform process. Similarly, in AMBOSELI, implementation of the project plan depended on the establishment of new policies under the national plan. For these projects, indicators of success can be measured at two levels:

- success in achieving specific conservation and community-management objectives at a particular site, and

- success in catalyzing change in the more general policy and institutional environment necessary for the sustainability and replicability of the site-specific experience.

In this way, specific projects that "fail"—in the sense that they do not lead to functional and legitimized community resource management regimes in specific sites—can still be useful if participating institutions come away from the experience with knowledge and attitudes that will serve to support community-based conservation in the longer term. In my experience, a Ford Foundation-supported social forestry program in the outer islands of Indonesia exemplifies this paradox. During five years of project implementation, the program failed to achieve its goal; forest-edge communities and the Ministry of Forestry made no comanagement agreements. The program was, however, very successful in educating ministry officials about the nature of forest-management conflicts and the inadequate response of ministry policy and field staff members. Through participation in the project, these officials developed an appreciation for the value of social science research, the potential role of NGOs as intermediaries, and the need to develop alternative policies for communities in forest management. Whether this benefit is ultimately worth the disappointment the project's target communities suffered remains debatable, especially given the rapid turnover in government and donor-agency staff and the failure of most institutions to actively and effectively internalize and disseminate the lessons learned.

Unlike designed projects, community initiatives are not input intensive, so the potential scale of their replicability is not initially limited by externally supplied project staff or finances. They thus have the potential to make dramatic impacts on the landscape in relatively short amounts of time, as the West Bengal forest protection movement has demonstrated (WBFD 1989).

Expansion leads to variation in both the geographic scale of individual sites and the intensity of management. The question of scale and replicability often leads outsiders directly to consideration of the policy environment following "discovery" of a community initiative: If the local management system is part of the solution, then the problem must lie elsewhere.

Indigenous management units operate on the village level, where individual participants are able to deal with each other face to face. The West Bengal and Orissa villagers in INDIA are able to patrol their protected forests effectively because they can recognize individuals who have the right to enter and those who do not. The young boy who fears discovery in the coconut grove in MALUKU ISLANDS knows he will be recognized and shamed if he is caught violating *sasi*.

The need to articulate community systems within larger government structures arises when threats to the local resource management regime exceed the reach of an individual community's authority. Government agencies' as well as neighboring villagers' recognition of the local system is critical to the community's ability to enforce rules of exclusive access. National-level fisheries law is used to legitimize community-level resource management authority not recognized by commercial fishermen in MALUKU ISLANDS. Forest protection committees in West Bengal and Orissa (INDIA) need official government recognition so that the forest department will back up their enforcement efforts vis-à-vis outsiders, and so that the court system can be used to adjudicate boundary disputes between villages.

Achieving national or state-level recognition of indigenous community management regimes is only the first step, however, and does not in itself guarantee rapid replication. Once policy makers confer legitimacy on local initiatives, challenges arise in the articulation of informal community resource management systems within formal laws and institutions. Not the least of these challenges is communication of the new policies to potential beneficiaries. Poffenberger and his colleagues have detailed the myriad legal and institutional issues that have arisen as the forest protection movement has been recognized by government agencies in the context of comanagement (INDIA). These include the official recognition and demarcation of protected areas, coordination of enforcement activities between communities and forest department officials, and the development of procedures for timber harvesting and revenue sharing.

Thus while outsider interventions to support "discovered" community initiatives often start by advocating policy change, they often end up in site-specific project interventions more characteristic of designed projects.

Sustainability

Many features characteristic of designed and discovered community-based conservation projects influence the long-term viability of initiatives. Government agencies may have difficulty sustaining support for projects at remote sites when problems closer to home demand attention. Conversely, innovative projects in out-of-the-way places may have more freedom to press the limits of government tolerance than high-profile initiatives near the capital. Designed projects face the challenge of making the transition from external to indigenous leadership. Initiatives that require compensation of communities for conservation costs require indefinite subsidy. The sustainability of discovered community resource management regimes depends on external recognition and effective policy reform.

These examples illustrate that the long-term sustainability of community-based conservation initiatives ultimately is political in nature. Operationalizing innovative community management structures that result from designed projects and legitimizing systems that are targets in discovered projects requires national-level policy change. The implications of these policies, which deal with issues such as indigenous resource rights and administrative decentralization, are among the most sensitive any society has to face. Even when relevant policies are in place at macro level, the political will to enforce them at community level must be present. Such conditions are likely only when concerned communities have the power to access and hold administrative, political, and judicial institutions accountable.

Designing for Community Initiative
The dichotomy between designed and discovered projects implies a choice for outsiders. One choice allows for selection of sites according to conservation priority
but embraces the many pitfalls of designed projects, including structural constraints on sustainability and replicability inherent in the project approach to development. The other implies enhancing community initiatives where they already
exist as the limit of outside intervention, precluding the possibility of intervening
at sites where such systems are not in place or have broken down. However, the
case studies point toward a strategy that combines the best of the design and discovery modes, supporting community initiatives where they exist and designing
and inducing them where they do not. While starting points differ for the two approaches, as the two kinds of projects mature, outsiders' roles rapidly converge.

Where community management regimes exist, there are roles for outsiders including donors and other intermediaries. In the discovery mode, initial programmatic support may take the form of documentation of existing systems, networking
with similar groups to facilitate information exchange and alliance-building, and
advocacy for national-level recognition. The next step, however, is to assist in articulating informal local systems with formal national structures. This articulation
process often leads to site-specific, project-type interventions to assist communities in obtaining legal recognition of their rights and accessing the technical assistance needed to optimize resource management. Thus programs initiated in the
discovery mode must move toward site-specific interventions characteristic of designed projects if they are to be effective in operationalizing policy change.

Where community management regimes do not exist, have broken down, or are
embroiled in conflict, external catalysts also have a legitimate role to play in facilitating community initiatives (i.e., in the design mode). In AMBOSELI, it "was unrealistic [to think that] the Maasai would come up with their own plan" (26) when
the government threatened to take over their land. In ANNAPURNA, recognition of
the crisis and the impetus for addressing it through establishment of the conservation area designation and other actions comes from outsiders.

During the last ten years, development practitioners increasingly have recognized the pitfalls of the "blueprint" approach to project design, and the case
studies in this book indicate that the conservation community has been quick to
take advantage of lessons learned. Several projects explicitly provide for participation in which the character, timing, and scale of implementation are driven by
community initiative.

In several cases, a sophisticated combination of site-specific intervention and
engagement of the national policy framework utilizes progress at one level to stimulate change at the other in an iterative fashion (see AMBOSELI, BOSCOSA). The CAMP-
FIRE case study recognizes the difficulty (and, indeed, the inappropriateness) of
separating the two. Thus projects that start out in the design mode must move
toward more programmatic interventions at policy level to ensure the sustainability of site-specific initiatives.

In the long run, then, successful community-based conservation projects seldom are exclusively designed or exclusively discovered; rather, they are the result of an iterative process between the two. Starting points may be different, but once the project is under way, the external agent's role is the same: to empower, legitimize, or otherwise assist the potential for community management in specific localities. This involves both creation of an enabling environment at the policy level as well as direct assistance at the community level to make new policies operational. The bureaucratic reorientation process necessary to achieve this goal is what D. Korten has termed "micro-policy reform" (1986).

To summarize, designed projects start out as site-specific initiatives providing technical support to particular communities, but move toward the discovery end of the design-discovery continuum as they facilitate community initiative and begin to articulate the project with national-level policy and bureaucratic structures. Programs initiated in the discovery mode start out by advocating the legitimation of existing community management systems but must move toward the design end of the continuum as they assist particular communities in taking advantage of new policies.

Roles for Donors and Other Outsiders

Providing financial support appears to be secondary in importance to other roles that outsiders such as donors and intermediaries play. The case studies suggest several specific roles outsiders can play to induce and support community initiatives in the context of designed or discovered projects. These include alliance building among various stakeholders, provision of support for intermediary institutions such as NGOs, and facilitation of diagnostic research, study tours, and conferences and workshops. These roles are described briefly below.

Alliance Building

Donor agencies and/or intermediary institutions (see below) can serve as facilitators among various parties with interests in community-based conservation. Regular communication between government officials and environmental advocacy groups, or between foresters and anthropologists, is unlikely to occur unless actively promoted. Neutral outsiders such as donor-agency staff members can create opportunities for such communication in a way that is constructive and oriented toward problem solving. Several case studies, including AMBOSELI and CAMPFIRE, describe the effectiveness of coalition-building across government, NGO, and academic organizations in achieving and operationalizing policy changes necessary to support community-based conservation.

Support for Intermediary Institutions

Another donor role is to support the development of intermediary institutions, which appear to be uniquely positioned to facilitate site-specific innovation and linkage to government policies and institutions. Based on its ability to inspire confidence in this role, the Zimbabwe Trust successfully facilitates devolution of authority to district councils, a key feature of the CAMPFIRE concept (CAMPFIRE).

In ANNAPURNA, the King Mahendra Trust "has been able to bypass many of the inefficiencies and time-consuming procedures associated with government agencies and execute projects with a relatively slim and flexible bureaucracy" (274). The King Mahendra Trust's relationship with Nepal's Department of National Parks and Wildlife Conservation is reported to be "informal but complex (ANNA-PURNA:274)," including the secondment of several senior staff members from national parks to the trust.

BOSCOSA's initiators, the Neotropica Foundation and the World Wildlife Fund, saw the project as largely an NGO effort (BOSCOSA) because a strong NGO identity was central to obtaining the cooperation of parties who were unwilling to work with a government agency. Because of their apparently neutral position, these independent entities can build alliances among local communities, government agencies, and other institutions to achieve the necesary policy and institutional change.

Support for Diagnostic Research

In both the design and discovery process, diagnostic research sponsored by outsiders appears to play a strategic role in defining and analyzing resource-management issues at particular sites and in building a consensus for change among concerned individuals and institutions. Western describes the development of his own understanding of the issues over the course of his research and suggests that research on the Amboseli ecosystem's diversity, wildlife migrations, and interactions between the Maasai and wildlife was essential in drawing up an effective plan for conflict resolution (AMBOSELI).

The description of forest protection committees in West Bengal and Orissa in INDIA is an example of the policy-relevant information that can be obtained through rapid appraisal exercises. Diagnostic research played a key role in identifying problems and marshaling support for solutions in social forestry programs throughout Southeast Asia (Poffenberger 1990). Diagnostic research also can document the existence of community-based conservation systems to provide leverage for policy makers.

Facilitation of Study Tours

Study tours are a potential means of accelerating support for community-based conservation among both community members and government agencies. For community members, a visit to an area that is suffering from inappropriate resource management can provide motivation to avoid a similar outcome at home. Villagers in CRATER MOUNTAIN observe the adverse impacts of an international mining company's operations in a nearby village and determine to exercise control over extractive activities on their own land. In ANNAPURNA, forest management committee members' visits to reforestation projects are effective in promoting understanding of livestock's role in suppressing forest regeneration, as well as the advantages of stall feeding (Wells 1993). World Neighbors, a private, United States–

based voluntary agency, has utilized farmer-to-farmer exchange visits as a key element of rural development activities in its programs in Latin America and Asia.

Study tours also can be used strategically to socialize government officials to more participatory approaches to resource management. Ford Foundation–supported study tours of the Philippines introduced Indonesian forestry officials and NGOs to the idea of granting stewardship rights to indigenous communities in classified forest areas and provided examples of NGO intermediary roles between such communities and government agencies. A subsequent study tour to West Bengal stimulated discussion of the possibility of sharing the proceeds of timber sales with Javanese villagers.

Thus study tours and exchange visits allow communities to consider the experience of others with similar problems and objectives and selectively adopt features of other projects and programs appropriate for their own situations.

Support for Workshops and Conferences

A final role for outside facilitators of community-based conservation is the sponsorship of workshops and conferences at local, national, and international levels. Such events provide legitimacy for project initiation and may serve as turning points in achieving consensus on policy change (see NIGER, CAMPFIRE, AMBOSELI).

Conclusions

In recent years, tropical foresters have begun to question the effectiveness and efficiency of plantation-based strategies for forest rehabilitation and management. Recognition of the resource intensity of plantation establishment, the ecological risks associated with introductions of exotic species, and high failure rates have led them to consider natural regeneration and natural forest management alternatives. Such alternatives build on ecosystems' existing structures and resilience, and respect diversity and natural ecological processes. But a decision to pursue a natural forest management strategy does not preclude roles for foresters; the natural regeneration process requires protection from disturbances such as fire and can be accelerated with judicious enrichment planting and thinning. Naturally occurring climax forests serve as laboratories for deepening foresters' understanding of how these complex systems function.

Community-based conservation practitioners' increasing sophistication in donor and intermediary institutions is analogous. They have recognized the expense, risks, and constraints on sustainability and replicability associated with traditional project design. They are learning to look for, value, and build upon indigenous knowledge and existing community institutions. Yet, even when functioning community-based conservation regimes are already in place, outsiders can play a role in facilitating establishment of a policy and institutional environment favorable to long-term project survival, deepening understanding of how they arise and function, and nurturing the development of such regimes where they do not yet exist or have broken down.

The cases reviewed here present the following principles about site selection, leadership, timing and incentives, scale and replicability, and sustainability associated with project design and discovery:

- "Discovered" community initiatives appear to have evolved in response to resource scarcity or external threat; they tend to focus on sustainable resource utilization rather than on conservation. Discovery of such initiatives by outsiders, and their selection as targets of external assistance, is limited and biased in favor of those most visible, championed by articulate spokesmen, or engaged in overt conflict.

- Site selection in designed projects is driven by the primary objective of the designer; those with a conservation orientation tend to focus on remote and pristine sites, while those with a demonstration/conflict-resolution orientation usually focus on more degraded sites.

- Neither design nor discovery approaches tend to utilize formal biodiversity conservation priority frameworks or other formal criteria in site selection. Site selection appears to be an eclectic, ad hoc process driven by the interests of individuals and institutions with ties to particular sites.

- Individual leadership is key to the success of both designed and discovered projects. There is a risk that community leaders will be misunderstood by outsiders or compromised by contact with them. Outside leadership has advantages and disadvantages, and needed leadership skills and roles change over time.

- Institutional leadership of government agencies is constrained by risk aversion and previous negative interactions with and attitudes toward communities. Leadership by independent intermediary organizations such as NGOs appears to be quite effective. Donor-agency leadership is constrained by distance and internally driven funding cycles, but donors with resident staff can serve as facilitators in alliance building and in other useful roles.

- Community initiatives are strongly influenced by the constraints and opportunities created by the macro policy environment. The discovery of community initiatives and the likelihood of designed projects' takeoff are to some degree functions of national-level political support.

- Donor-agency funding modes and project-approach dynamics introduce perverse incentives and distortions to both designed and discovered projects.

- Designed projects focus on specific sites, but their resource intensity and special project status unencumbered by bureaucratic constraints preclude replication. Community initiatives are based on a local management unit; replication is constrained not by resources but by articulation difficulties within larger legal frameworks and institutions.

- Designed projects start out focused on specific sites but sooner or later have to deal with structural and policy issues. Interventions to assist discovered projects start out focused on structural and policy issues but eventually have to assist particular communities with articulation of external policies and institutions.

- The long-term sustainability of projects, whether designed or discovered, depends on national-level political support and local-level political empowerment.

- Donors and the intermediaries that they support can play a facilitative role through support for alliance building, strengthening of intermediary institutions, diagnostic research, study tours, and meetings and conferences.

ACKNOWLEDGMENTS

The author gratefully acknowledges the insights provided by colleagues during professional assignments at the Ford Foundation in Jakarta, Indonesia, and the Biodiversity Support Program in Washington, D.C., that contributed to the analysis contained in this chapter. Special thanks are due to Janis Alcorn for comments on an earlier draft. Particular appreciation is extended to Michael Wright, for the many ideas and questions raised in our discussions, and for his generosity with deadlines, without which this chapter would not have been possible.

SOURCES

Brown, M., and B. Wyckoff-Baird. 1992. *Designing Integrated Conservation and Development Projects.* Washington, D.C.: The Biodiversity Support Program.

Cabarle, B., with M. H. Panduro and O. M. Murayari. 1993. "Ecofarming in the Peruvian Amazon: The Integrated Family and Communal Gardening Project (HIFCO)." Case study prepared for the Liz Claiborne Art Ortenberg Foundation Community Based Conservation Workshop, October 18–22, Airlie, Virginia.

Chambers, R. 1980. *Rural Poverty Unperceived: Problems and Remedies.* Staff Working Paper No. 400. Washington, D.C.: World Bank.

———. 1983. *Rural Development: Putting the Last First.* London: Longman.

Craven, I. 1991. Conversation with the author.

Dinerstein, E. 1993. "Integrating Principles of Conservation Biology in the Strategic Planning Process at WWF-US." Internal World Wildlife Fund document. Photocopy.

Glick, D., D. Neary, and R. Rasker. 1993. "Conservation in Greater Yellowstone." Case study prepared for the Liz Claiborne Art Ortenberg Foundation Community Based Conservation Workshop, October 18–22, Airlie, Virginia.

Henry, D. 1993. Conversation with the author.

Korten, D. C. 1980. "Community Participation and Rural Development: A Learning Process Approach." *Public Administration Review* 40(5):480–511.

————. 1986. "Micro-Policy Reform: The Role of Private Voluntary Agencies." In *Community Management: Asian Experience and Perspectives*, ed. D. Korten. West Hartford: Kumarian Press.

Korten, F. F. 1988. "The Working Group as a Mechanism for Bureaucratic Transformation" In *Transforming a Bureaucracy*, eds. D. Korten and R. Siy. West Hartford: Kumarian Press.

Martins, E. 1993. "Extractive Reserves in Brazil: A Critical Analysis." Case study prepared for the Liz Claiborne Art Ortenberg Foundation Community Based Conservation Workshop, October 18–22, Airlie, Virginia.

Metcalfe, S. 1993. "The Zimbabwe Communal Areas Management Programme for Indigenous Resources (CAMPFIRE)." Case study prepared for the Liz Claiborne Art Ortenberg Community Based Conservation Workshop, October 18–22, Airlie, Virginia.

Ministry of Forestry (MOF), Indonesia. 1992. Conversations between the author and ministry officials.

National Academy of Sciences (NAS). 1986. *Proceedings of the Conference on Common Property Resource Management*. Washington, D.C.: National Academy Press.

Poffenberger, M., ed. 1990. *Keepers of the Forest: Land Management Alternatives in Southeast Asia*. West Hartford: Kumarian Press.

Seymour, F. 1987. "The Ford Foundation's Rural Poverty and Resources Programming in Indonesia: A Strategy for Making a Difference." Internal Ford Foundation report. Photocopy.

————, and D. Rutherford. 1990. "Contractual Agreements in Asian Social Forestry Programs." Paper presented at the First Annual Meeting of the International Association for the Study of Common Property, September 27–30, Duke University, Durham, North Carolina.

Tjitradjaja, I. 1991. "Differential Access to Resources and Conflict Resolution in a Forest Concession in Irian Jaya." Unpublished manuscript. Jakarta: University of Indonesia.

Wells, M. P. 1993. "A Profile and Interim Assessment of the Annapurna Conservation Area Project, Nepal." Case study prepared for the Liz Claiborne Art Ortenberg Foundation Community Based Conservation Workshop, October 18–22, Airlie, Virginia.

Wells, M., and K. Brandon with L. Hannah. 1992. *People and Parks: Linking Protected Area Management with Local Communities*. Washington, D.C.: The World Bank.

West Bengal Forest Department (WBFD). 1989. *Forest Regeneration through Community Protection*, eds. K. C. Malhotra and M. Poffenberger. New Delhi: The Ford Foundation.

World Bank. 1993. Conversations between the author and staff members.

Wright, M. 1993. Conversation with the author.

Wright, P. C. 1993. "Ranomafana National Park, Madagascar: Rainforest Conservation and Economic Development." Case study prepared for the Liz Claiborne Art Ortenberg Community Based Conservation Workshop, October 18–22, Airlie, Virginia.

PART IV

The Workshop

CHAPTER 22

Linking Conservation and Community Aspirations

David Western

Conservation must be embedded in local communities if it is to flourish as a voluntary rather than a coercive effort. Some communities practice conservation quite successfully themselves and need no outside help. Ideally, this is what community-based conservation is all about. Unfortunately, such initiatives are exceptional in today's world due to population growth, poverty, economic exploitation, weak policies, and lack of localized skills and resources. The success of community-based conservation therefore will depend on outside forces and how conducive they are to the growth and spread of conservation within and between communities. For the most part, local and outside views on conservation are in opposition. Bringing these opposing views into alignment will be essential to successful promotion of grass-roots conservation. This was the subject of the first session of the workshop.

The growth of grass-roots conservation also depends on a clear understanding of conservation and community interests. What is conservation all about, who promotes it and why, and how different are the goals of its many advocates? What does the term *local community* mean? How do local communities differ from national and global society? What are the inherent strengths and weaknesses of community action as opposed to national and international action? Can these respective strengths be built upon to promote local conservation and redefine the role of outside support? Finally, how can conservation and community interests be linked, and which criteria should be used to judge the success of community-based conservation? In short, effective community-based conservation depends on a firm grasp of two concepts—*conservation* and *local communities*—and an understanding of how the two can be linked to advantage. It is still too early for clear answers; the questions at least need to be explored.

Conservation

Conservation, as BACKGROUND makes clear, incorporates a wide variety of interests loosely bound by a common concern for saving nature, natural products, and planetary processes. Each conservation group has a distinctive agenda, whether the sustainable use of natural resources, recreation, biodiversity, or the right of nature to exist. Interests vary geographically and taxonomically: One group may champion national and global conservation; another, a specific area or single taxa, whether whales or wolves. Transcending each special interest are the claims of those who are opposed to conservation. The most legitimate claim to natural resources and biodiversity comes not from rival conservation bodies, however loud their thunder, but from rural communities with historical claims to both land and resources. Special-interest groups and local communities clash in conservation programs the world over.

Wherever conservation involves local communities, local interests have to be considered in relation to the interests of outsiders. Half the battle is in finding the right fit between local and external conservation interests—a task rather like playing one of those fit-the-block games children use to learn shapes: Blocks slide straight into the right slot but stubbornly resist a mismatch. Most conservation failures are the result of mismatched interests.

Conservation, in other words, may or may not be in a community's interest, and local community activities may or may not be compatible with those of outside conservationists. The role of community-based conservation is to build up local initiatives in cases where local and outside interests match. Where a match is not immediately apparent, the challenge is to find solutions acceptable to all the parties concerned. In AMBOSELI and CAMPFIRE (and in Yellowstone National Park; see Glick, Neary, and Rasker 1993), local people and outsiders explore tourism, hunting, and compensation for stock killed by wildlife as possible solutions.

Justifying Conservation

An essential first step in the process of finding a workable match is for conservationists to explicate as many reasons as possible to conserve a particular resource, in order to gain support. Wide support for conservation initiatives plays an essential role in increasing the rural landscape's perceived value among local communities. The more a community values the resources in its landscape, the more reasons its members will find to justify its conservation.

Among local communities, two types of value most often come up: namely, utilitarian and nonutilitarian value. A third value based on strategic importance is just beginning to emerge.

Utilitarian Value

The need to conserve natural resources needs no elaboration for communities intimately rooted in the land. The Maluku Islander is as aware of the need to sustain fish stocks as the Maasai herder is of the need to sustain cattle herds. Every human being—indeed, all life—depends on renewable supplies of air, water, and soil to replenish the nutrient cycle. Nonetheless, a number of obstacles interfere with the sustainability of these essential ecological cycles. The task of conservation is to remove these obstacles, as INDIA and NIGER discuss in some detail.

The case for conservation is less obvious when resource use is not intimately linked to immediate needs or obviously related to environmental destruction. Upstream forest destruction, for example, may decrease water supplies to downstream irrigation plots over such a protracted period that farmers do not relate cause with effect. All the same, making the connection clear can highlight a resource's utilitarian value and provide a justification for conservation.

Nonutilitarian Value

Justifying conservation through the nonutilitarian value of resources is more difficult. The distinction between utilitarian and nonutilitarian conservation can be traced back to the Hetch Hetchy Dam controversy in the United States' Yosemite National Park (see BACKGROUND). The divide between Gifford Pinchot's wise-use strategy and John Muir's preservationism has grown deeper in recent years as nature's instrumental (utilitarian) and intrinsic (nonutilitarian) values have become more clearly defined.

The division would not be so problematic were it not for its political, economic, and racial overtones. Most preservationists, including animal rights advocates, biocentrists, deep ecologists, and so-called Greens, are largely rich, urban, and Western; most biodiversity exists on tropical lands owned by poor communities who possess a strong utilitarian view of nature. Few such communities see any connection between biodiversity and human welfare. They tend to dismiss nature preservation as Western mawkishness at best and land grabbing at worst. Understandably, justifying conservation based on nature's nonutilitarian or nonconsumptive value among such groups can be difficult.

If biodiversity does have intrinsic value for a small percentage of the world's wealthy, the equitable solution, of course, is for the rich to compensate the poor who do the conserving (Myers 1979). In reality, the conscience money that finds its way to the rural poor who bear the cost of conservation is a pittance.

Strategic Value

Ecologists and natural resource economists are exploring another more promising avenue: justifying conservation through the strategic global value of biodiversity. Biodiversity, if shown to maintain essential biological cycles, biospheric processes, and genetic diversity indispensable to agriculture and the pharmaceuticals industry (Wilson 1988), assumes worldwide strategic importance on a par with food and energy sufficiency (Myers 1986). Valued in this way, biodiversity becomes too vital to whittle down without risking the health and welfare of New York stockbrokers and Ituri Forest hunters alike.

A decade ago, arguments about the strategic significance of biodiversity fell on deaf ears. The connection, too rarefied for public taste, was dismissed as the railings of ecofreaks and the Green fringe. Today, a thinning ozone shield, greenhouse warming, acid rain, and urban pollution have brought home the link between natural-resources conservation and development after decades of environmental degradation. As a result, politicians and planners now take biodiversity's national and global security implications seriously (Myers 1987).

This more penetrating view does help narrow the divide between utilitarian and intrinsic values of nature. The need to preserve biodiversity, seen in terms of global welfare and intergenerational equity, overshadows local costs and narrows the gap between outside and local interests. One consequence is that lack of a short-term payoff for society at large no longer brings conservation plans grinding to a halt.

Put another way, biodiversity's strategic value is useless unless conservation assures local communities' security. As has been widely pointed out, even the Brazilian rubber tappers' demand for extractive reserves was inspired by the need to save jobs; the need to save monkeys only occurred to the community when the time came to elicit international support (Hecht and Cockburn 1990). Ecotourism, wildlife utilization, fisheries, forestry, extractive reserves, agroecological farming, and the preservation of culturally valuable landscapes are just a few of the avenues through which community-based conservation projects have tried to make tangible biological diversity's value to local communities (see ANNAPURNA, CAMPFIRE, MALUKU ISLANDS, NIGER, NORTH YORK MOORS, KAKADU, and the other case studies in this book).

The Risks of Exploitation

Using nature's diversity, particularly for commercial purposes, always carries the risk of overexploitation (see NEOTROPICAL FORESTS). This is as true in the rich North as it is in the poor South. The North Atlantic fisheries and the Northwest lumber industry in the United States are two cases in which short-term profitability, jobs, and reelection promises have resulted in overexploitation.

This is not to say that commercially sustainable offtake of various resources is a pipe dream. According to Rosenberg et al. (1993), a number of European and American fisheries have proved sustainable. However, successes are few and limited to situations in which property rights are well defined, offtake is monitored and adjusted scientifically, and enforcement is in place. Under open-access conditions, North American fishermen are as likely to destroy fish stocks to buy new Toyotas as Maluku Islanders are to overexploit trochus to feed their families. While conservationists are not necessarily averse to exploitation that turns out to be sustainable, they are justifiably wary of the sort of short-term profit incentives and ownership uncertainties that accelerate environmental degradation.

Limits of Acceptable Change

Anxiety about exploitation comes down to ecology as much as economics. What are the limits of acceptable change globally, nationally, locally? What are the critical thresholds beyond which natural processes can no longer recover?

Ehrlich and Ehrlich (1981) use the analogy of rivet poppers to demonstrate the folly of considering environmental destruction only in economic terms. How many rivets can we pop from a fuselage before an aircraft falls out of the sky? they ask. Which rivet is one too many, given the long delay in ecosystem and planetary response? Acidification of lakes in Europe, for example, lagged seventy years behind the onset of sulfur emissions (Stigliani and Salomons 1993). Even total elimination of chlorofluorocarbons before the end of the century would do little to prevent the ozone layer from thinning dangerously for another decade or more.

Worse still are ecological uncertainties. The carcinogenic effects of DDT only became apparent decades after its introduction. By then, many raptors—including the national bird of the United States, the bald eagle—were brushing against extinction.

Who will decide the limits of acceptable change anyway: biologists, economists, politicians, the general populace? In whose interest are decisions to be made: that of our own communities? Neighboring communities? Humanity? Our children and grandchildren? These questions can not be ignored. They will surface with increasing urgency and regularity as resources diminish. When it comes to justifying conservation, ecological truths are just as important as economic truths.

Local Communities

Just as conservation is not homogenous, so too interests within and between communities are varied. The reasons are plain enough: National interests embrace many divergent economic and political factions, often heavily biased toward urban aspirations and international relations; local communities, by contrast, are characterized by greater parochialism.

The national perspective, however essential to societal interests, tends to homogenize local aspirations. National goals generally are concerned with human development and contingent on economics, natural-resources exploitation, and technological advancement. Resource economists are beginning to note, however, that traditional economic development as measured by gross domestic product (GDP) distorts real growth by ignoring the depletion of natural capital (Repetto 1988). National plans also tend to ignore local aspirations, value systems, cultures, politics, and land-use practices. The objections of minority groups such as the Kayapo in the Amazon, the !Kung in the Kalahari, and the Aboriginals of Australia usually are brushed aside in the interest of mainstream society.

Centralized decision making and the denial of traditional rights widens the rift between national and local aspirations. According to most of the case studies, governments have assumed control over resources, even when they lack the means to manage them effectively. A bad situation has been made worse by the widespread collapse of traditional exploitation and conservation practices.

Finally, by undervaluing resources, governments impose heavy costs on local communities. These costs, whether due to deforestation, overfishing, protected-area designation, or mineral exploitation, fall hardest on communal landowners and disenfranchised minorities. The outcome everywhere is a tussle between the center and the periphery over who has the political right to make decisions and use the land and its resources (see INSTITUTIONS).

This tussle is most contentious when it comes to resources that traditional communities regard as God-given. Biodiversity is another element in the tussle—one that local communities contest hotly because of its abstract nature. Ironically, the conflict over wildlife ownership in the developing world has taken on an element of economic and class warfare, echoing a similar battle in North America a century ago (Tober 1981).

An Evaluation of Strengths and Weaknesses

The strengths and weaknesses of community participation outlined here are no more than illustrative of the many points raised in the workshop. Variation from one community to another is so great that workshop participants suggested case-by-case evaluations as an integral part of building up local conservation capacity.

Strengths

Perhaps the greatest strength of localized conservation is that it limits the number of stakeholders. Closed membership and clear rights and responsibilities prevent the scourge of open-access abuses. Once localized and personalized, the costs and benefits of conservation can directly influence individuals. One example is the NIMBY (Not in My Backyard) syndrome that arose as a backlash to pollution and toxic waste dumping in the West. The reverse syndrome, just beginning to surface, is the PIMBY (Please, in My Backyard) response to clear-cut conservation benefits. The grass-roots reforestation efforts in INDIA and the farmers in NORTH YORK MOORS are good examples of the PIMBY syndrome.

Vested interest, ownership, and a sense of belonging carry with them several other positive connotations. These include commitment to exploration of issues and agreed goals, a sense of pride, and custodianship. Small closed-membership groups and close proximity also add immediacy and flexibility in the recognition and response to problems. Commitment opens up prospects of communitywide monitoring and enforcement based on social ostracism.

Finally, localized conservation can draw on the deep knowledge, traditions, ethics, and adaptive practices of rural communities intimately linked to the land and nature.

Weaknesses

The major drawback of community-based conservation is parochialism. Local communities are often ignorant of the larger political, economic, and environmental forces that touch every society. A good example, presented in AMBOSELI, is traditional Maasai elders' strenuous resistance to change in faltering subsistence practices, despite cautions from their more worldly political leaders.

Parochialism crops up in many aspects of locally based conservation. Ignorance or denial of forces likely to weaken the community (see AMBOSELI) is but one example. Other obstacles to local conservation include ignorance of population growth and its impact, cultural conservatism, Machiavellian politics, corruption, greed, market forces, or simply the failure to grasp opportunities open to other societies.

The intense conservatism of rural communities also reinforces an us-versus-them mentality that obstructs the integration of cultures so essential in an increasingly secular world. The same conservatism blinds communities to the ecological impact they have on other people and, generally, to any sense of responsibility to outsiders.

Other shortcomings arise from lack of knowledge, values, skills, and institutional capacity. These shortcomings can be circumvented if they are recognized, as in the innovative case of comanagement between Aboriginal communities and the Australian National Parks and Wildlife Service described in KAKADU.

Poverty and the desire for progress also encourage overexploitation and environmental destruction in rural areas. Poor people put survival above all else, while those in search of progress often ignore environmental costs. In both cases, the outcome is the same: Sustainability goes to the wall.

Finally, the mixed voices emanating from local communities, particularly those drifting away from traditional practices and not yet moored to new values, stand in the way of communal goals and action. Nepotism, cheating, and corruption often are no less problematic in local settings than in the national arena. On the other hand, the tyranny of countless small, self-interested decisions in fractious communities can be just as environmentally prejudicial as the greed of a few robber barons or big businesses.

Linking Conservation and Community Interests

The litmus test of community-based conservation is whether it improves conservation—as distinct from the dispensation of social justice or redress of economic inequity—in rural areas. Whether community participation is synonymous with conservation is an open question. Clearly, the answer hinges on the degree to which conservation fulfills local aspirations, and on whether links between the two can be made and strengthened.

Ecological Diversity and the Rural Landscape

There are many reasons to think that rural areas can support significant habitat and wildlife (Western 1989). Many rural lands, remote as well as inhospitable, are seldom exploited heavily. The polar circles, high mountains, arid rangelands, moist forests, and flooded forests and wetlands are some of the earth's most sparsely populated regions, yet include some of the world's richest habitats. In part, this serendipitous state of affairs arises because areas of high agricultural potential are low in biodiversity (Huston 1993).

Various land-use practices, including pastoralism, ranching, shifting cultivation, fishing, forestry, sport hunting, tourism, and recreation, also conserve biodiversity. In addition, some habitats and many wild animals are resilient in the face of human exploitation. Then, too, large numbers of people are abandoning extensive rural areas, including farmland in Europe and North America and rangeland and deserts in Africa and Asia, due to economic changes and urban drift. Finally, habitat restoration, natural recolonization, and conservation easements are likely to restore degraded and abandoned lands during the coming century (Jordan, Gilpin, and Aber 1987).

These facts support the belief that rural lands will retain biodiversity—perhaps far more than all protected areas put together. The problem is that depending on these trends alone amounts to conservation by default—clearly an inadequate response to a biodiversity crisis. If communities can become active and central players in biodiversity conservation in the coming decades, their participation could go a long way toward alleviating the crisis.

In general, the case studies in this book put forward the view that community-based conservation is workable. Unfortunately, as Wells and Brandon (1992) conclude, the evidence in support of this view is neither as compelling nor as widespread as conservationists would like to think. Development specialists who attended the workshop echoed a similar view: Conservation and development, they stressed, will go nowhere until local communities achieve both resource and social security.

Intangible Conservation Incentives

Local communities seem to be primarily concerned with tangible benefits, according to most of the case studies. Tangibility, however, is neither sufficient nor always necessary. Other factors enter into the conservation deliberations of local communities.

One example is empowerment. In a supportive atmosphere (see ANNAPURNA), giving a community a say in its own affairs can bring out dormant conservation attitudes. The same can be said of participation. Broad participation often brings out the commitment and insights of otherwise ignored members of a community, including women and minority groups (see INSTITUTIONS, CULTURE). Bringing these unheard and underrepresented voices into the participatory process strengthens widely shared, if weakly expressed, values. Industrial pollution in the West, for example, went unchecked until media coverage and special-interest lobbyists whipped NIMBY sentiments into an effective campaign for policy reforms, legislation, and enforcement. The participatory process gave a strong, unifying voice to diffuse feelings of indignation, which later proved itself in the ballot box.

A sentimental connection to the land and a strong land ethic (Leopold 1949) also can stretch conservation beyond utilitarian concerns. Several authors cogently argue that the rise of modern environmental ethics really is an ancient land ethic still widespread in Africa and Asia (Engel and Engel 1990). If the land ethic indeed is a return to ancient holism, then traditional values and cosmologies have a lot to contribute to community-based conservation.

Others argue that traditional values are not enough. One workshop participant, John Marrinka, a Maasai from Kenya, insisted that conservation education is a primary step in sensitizing communities to the larger issues at stake. How else could a traditional community ever learn of new opportunities and threats to its well-being, he asked?

Weak Conservation Linkages

These caveats are useful reminders that conservation is not just a matter of dollars and cents. But latching on to intangible values as an excuse for ignoring economic realities is socially callous. Empowerment, participation, awareness, education—these may be essential ingredients of community-based conservation, but they seldom provide the yeast that can raise community members' lives above the material and physical hardships that stand in the way of conservation.

Conservation, paradoxically, can be linked to development in a roundabout way, according to the workshop participants. That is, development itself can lead to conservation. This assumption is present in many of the case studies, although it is never explicitly spelled out (see INSTITUTIONS). The development-for-conservation approach can be thought of as *weak*, or *indirect*, *conservation*. Its rationale goes something like this: Improved security and economic circumstances bring changes in outlook and life-style. The resulting smaller family size, attainment of higher education, and greater economic security hasten the process of demographic and economic transition, lowering the ultimate population size (Robey, Rustein, and Morris 1993). The upshot is greater freedom of choice and expanded sensibilities. Nash (1967) has argued that conservation in North America followed in the wake of urbanization and prosperity.

Taking the cynical view, weak conservation may be the only hope for the poor world, where no strong conservation incentives exist. According to most workshop participants from the Third World, this is no reason to dismiss weak conservation as irrelevant, since conservation through development well may present the only (and perhaps best) route to global sustainability in the long run.

Strong Conservation Linkages

Given current and projected rates of environmental degradation, weak conservation probably will be altogether too little too late to sustain much of the earth's productivity and biological wealth. The only hope, according to the conservationists at the workshop, is *strong conservation*. Strong conservation entails bringing about welfare improvements through personal action. Soil-erosion control and energy conservation are two strong conservation measures familiar to communities and development agencies.

How can such strong conservation linkages be firmly established in local communities and actively reinforced in their members' behavior? The answer depends on the perceived costs and benefits of conservation and, in social terms, comes down to who bears the costs and who reaps the benefits. Apportioning costs and benefits equitably is no easy task. It often involves complex ecological and socioeconomic research and calculation (Pearce and Turner 1990; Swanson and Barbier 1992)—skills far beyond the comprehension and capacity of local communities.

This is not to say that traditional and illiterate societies are incapable of figuring out the costs and benefits—and the inequities—of conservation. The Maasai have a sound grasp of the trade-off between wildlife and livestock when it comes to pasture consumption (see AMBOSELI). Outsiders and local communities, or even different interest groups within a single community, on the other hand, do not always perceive the terms of such trade-offs in the same way.

If making the link between action and reward is difficult for natural resources conservation—particularly where improvements are measured in decades—how much harder is it for biodiversity? How can projected national or global benefits during the course of the next century help improve the lot of a peasant community today? How can the values ecologists, animal rights advocates, and armchair nature lovers perceive in the natural world and the costs borne by local people such as the Yanomami ever be calculated, much less reconciled? Such calculations may be feasible for a few charismatic species such as elephants, but what of the millions of tropical invertebrates still unknown to science?

Even if there is no satisfactory answer to these questions, the complexity of the task should not stand in the way of solutions. The World Bank, for example, has calculated the cost of conserving biodiversity within the present protected-area system—increased by half—at around US$2.4 billion (World Development Report 1992). Sustainable development practices would involve an annual investment of 3 to 4 percent of developing countries' GDP (World Development Report 1992). Participants in the Rio Earth Summit recognized that environment is fast becoming the third pillar, along with security and economic issues, in the emerging international system (Holmberg, Thomson, and Timberlake 1993). The resulting Agenda 21, a program for implementing the charter of the Earth Summit, and the promise of US$2 billion in expanded financial support through the World Bank's Global Environment Facility is a modest beginning. It is a signal, however small, of a long overdue political willingness to confront the assault on the global environment. The new funding highway no doubt will speed the flow of conservation money from North to South, from rich to poor nations; the more vexing question, however, is how such funds can be channeled to local communities and linked to conservation performance.

Making the connection on the ground will not be easy. National governments still insist on retaining financial control of donor funds destined for rural communities. International donors are still administering large grants over short funding cycles in the interest of financial and administrative expediency. The misguided view that paying landowners to conserve biodiversity is a bribe, rather than a payment for services to society and global security, also persists.

The manner in which costs and benefits are calculated and reconciled will determine how soundly the link between conservation and individual reward is made. Should revenue earnings from tourism or sport hunting, for example, be channeled to communal programs or to individual shareholders (see CAMPFIRE)? The weakness of communal facilities is that community members regard them in the same light as open-access resources: There is no strong link between individual conservation effort and reward. The weakness of individual dividends, on the other hand, is that individual shares are diluted to insignificance when divided among thousands of members.

Making and reinforcing the link between communities and conservation involves several other factors. These include biological and socioeconomic monitoring, enforcement, and arbitration procedures (see INSTITUTIONS). Openness and accountability are also vital elements in overcoming the corruption, cheating, and nepotism that so often weaken community-based conservation.

Finally, if community-based conservation is to be judged a success or a failure—and lessons learned—conservationists, donors, and communities need clear-cut criteria for making such evaluations.

Success Criteria

Determining success criteria is a process fraught with difficulties and largely ignored in the majority of the case studies. One big hurdle has been conservation bodies' reluctance to admit failure for fear of turning away donors (Bonner 1993). A definition of goals, whether involving natural resources, biodiversity, or wildlands, nevertheless is a necessary starting point. How goals can be met also needs clarification. Is conservation to be achieved indirectly, through development, or more directly, through changes in attitude and behavior and the benefits that accrue from strong conservation?

Whatever the goals and methods, the end result ultimately must be measured in terms of real conservation improvements, not empowerment, participation, tenurial rights, or any other surrogate measure. Community-based conservation still could be judged a relative success, despite continuing environmental degradation, if it slowed degradation more effectively than alternative conservation methods under similar circumstances. Buying time in which to explore better options is, after all, a success of sorts.

Does conservation improve as a result of community action? Is a community better off for having participated in conservation? These related questions lie at the heart of community-based conservation. Yet another factor concerns the extent to which communities (rather than outsiders) adopt and sustain conservation. Still, as INITIATION points out, whether action originates within or outside the community may be unimportant, as long as it is effective and sustained.

Finally, natural-resources and biodiversity conservation may call for different success criteria (see INITIATION). In the first case, the link between human welfare and resource exploitation is strong; in the second, the link between welfare and biodiversity conservation is weak. Resource use therefore may be more easily achieved and sustained than biodiversity. Moreover, sustainable resource use does not imply biodiversity conservation. On the contrary, most exploitation systems, even if sustainable, narrow food chains and reduce biodiversity. Biodiversity conservation therefore may have to originate outside and require a greater degree of subsidization than natural-resources conservation.

This difference apart, success in community-based conservation ultimately must be measured by how deeply the effort is embedded in each community's aspirations and how effectively its members' efforts sustain it.

SOURCES
Bonner, R. 1993. *At the Hand of Man: Peril and Hope for Africa's Wildlife.* New York: Knopf.
Ehrlich, P., and A. Ehrlich. 1981. *Extinction: The Causes and Consequences of the Disappearance of Species.* New York: Ballantine.
Engel, J. R., and J. G. Engel, eds. 1990. *Ethics of Environment and Development: Global Challenge, International Response.* Tucson, Arizona: University of Arizona Press.
Glick, D., D. Neary, and R. Rasker. 1993. "Conservation in Greater Yellowstone." Case study prepared for the Liz Claiborne Art Ortenberg Community Based Conservation Workshop, October 18–22, Airlie, Virginia.
Hecht, S., and A. Cockburn. 1990. *The Face of the Forest: Developers, Destroyers and Defenders of the Amazon.* New York: Harper Perennial.
Holmberg, J., K. Thomson, and L. Timberlake. 1993. *Facing the Future: Beyond the Earth Summit.* London: Earthscan.
Huston, M. 1993. "Biological Diversity, Soils, and Economics." *Science* 262: 1676–1680.
Jordan, W. R., M. E. Gilpin, and J. Aber. 1987. *Restoration Ecology: A Synthetic Approach to Ecological Research.* Cambridge, England: Cambridge University Press.
Leopold, A. 1949. *A Sand County Almanac.* New York: Oxford University Press.
Myers, N. 1979. *The Sinking Ark.* Oxford, England: Pergamon Press.
———. 1986. "Economics and Ecology in the International Arena: The Phenomenon of 'Linked Linkages'." *Ambio* 15(5):296–300.
———. 1987. *Not Far Afield: U.S. Interests and the Global Environment.* Washington, D.C.: World Resources Institute.
Nash, R. 1967. *Wilderness and the American Mind.* New Haven, Connecticut: Yale University Press.

Pearce, D. W., and R. K. Turner. 1990. *Economics of Natural Resources and the Environment.* Baltimore: Johns Hopkins University Press.

Repetto, R. 1988. *The Forest for the Trees? Government Policies and the Misuse of Forest Resources.* Washington, D.C.: World Resources Institute.

Robey, B., S. O. Rustein, and L. Morris. 1993. "The Fertility Decline in Developing Countries." *Scientific American* 269(6):30–37.

Rosenberg, A. A., M. J. Fogarty, M. P. Sissenwine, J. R. Beddington, and J. G. Shepherd. 1993. "Achieving Sustainable Use of Renewable Resources." *Science* 262:828–829.

Stigliani, W., and W. Salomons. 1993. "Our Fathers' Toxic Sins." *New Scientist* 140(1903):38–42.

Swanson, T. M., and E. B. Barbier. 1992. *Economics for the Wilds: Wildlife, Diversity and Development.* Washington, D.C.: Island Press.

Tober, J. A. 1981. *Who Own the Wildlife? A Political Economy of Conservation in Nineteenth Century America.* Westport, Connecticut: Greenwood Press.

Wells, M., and K. Brandon. 1992. *People and Parks: Linking Protected Areas with Local Communities.* Washington D.C.: World Bank.

Western, D. 1989. "Conservation Without Parks. Wildlife in the Rural Landscape." In *Conservation for the Twenty-first Century,* eds. D. Western and M. Pearl. New York: Oxford University Press.

Wilson, E. O. 1988. *Biodiversity.* Washington, D.C.: National Academy Press.

World Development Report. 1992. *Development and the Environment.* New York: Oxford University Press.

CHAPTER 23

Lessons Learned

Shirley C. Strum

Two things are certain about community-based conservation: It is possible, and it is difficult. In recent years, the technique may have been oversold as a viable solution, as the pendulum of opinion swung from one extreme (Outsiders know best) to the other (Locals know best). What makes community-based conservation difficult? What contributes to success?

Although CBC is still a new approach, as the case studies in this book attest, many lessons already have accrued about what works and what doesn't. These lessons cut across case studies and across themes because they are essentially about how human beings act, react, and interact. When two or more people get together in the context of a volatile mix of values, rights, and responsibilities; of power and enforcement; and of disproportionate costs and benefits, problems always arise—and sometimes, also, solutions.

Community action is never easy, and those attempting community-based conservation have learned a great deal from the recent but relatively longer history of development projects (see INSTITUTIONS). Other efforts to build communities in the political, social, and economic context of emerging nations and regional networks have provided additional insights (see POLICY, INSTITUTIONS).

Building or mobilizing a community is an arduous task. The obstacles range from simple tension to outright conflict of interest among the participants, from the lack of any sense of community to the necessity of including too many communities, from social and cultural mechanisms that no longer work to sociocultural forms that are tenaciously opposed to the kind of community and the kind of conservation that CBC requires.

Even when community issues seem resolved, a wealth of problems remain. Social conditions are constantly changing. New conditions present unique challenges and opportunities. Should the response to new conditions be to use or resurrect old solutions, or is innovation required? What is the appropriate scale of social action for successful community-based conservation? And how can local solutions circumvent the impact of externalities: factors originating from the outside over which the community has no control?

This is the *community* half of community-based conservation. But CBC breaks new ground by trying to link community needs and aspirations with the needs of the environment. The goal is conservation of the ecological processes that maintain biodiversity. The issues and conundrums are obvious (see LINKAGE), but the conservation half provides fewer lessons to draw upon.

The discussion in this chapter derives from small-group sessions at the Airlie House workshop. These focused on the important factors of culture, institutions, participation, tenure, and policy already explored in Part III's themes. These discussions also brought economic, regional (Asia/Pacific, Africa, Latin America, Developed Countries), donor, and technical perspectives to bear. Despite the different perspectives, the participants agreed to a remarkable degree about the lessons already learned.

Who Decides

CBC's most diagnostic characteristic is its shift of the locus of decision from the top (government, institutions, donors) to the bottom (local communities). This builds on the lessons to be found in development projects. Success in community development has been much greater when decisions, plans, and implementation of projects involve community members (see INSTITUTIONS). Not all bottom-up projects based on community participation succeed, but almost all top-down projects that exclude community involvement fail. The question of who makes the decisions embodies crucial dimensions of both empowerment and participation.

Yet the shift in who makes decisions is not a self-contained solution. New as well as old difficulties stalk community efforts. Sometimes communities are so disintegrated that decision and action can not be engendered. Many communities must first learn about how to participate, how to create dialogue. Even when they have managed to do so, often they must be empowered, both legally and in practice, so that decision-making does not become a futile exercise. Because of the government's reluctance to give communities land tenure and legal rights, the CAMPFIRE program in Zimbabwe was designed and accepted ten years before it finally was implemented (see CAMPFIRE).

Shifting down does not necessarily mean going all the way to the bottom. When the individual is the unit, a war of all against all often results, as each person seeks to act in his or her self-interest. The community focus helps to create a higher—but still local—level of commitment that can help balance individual rights and responsibilities. Who participates and who makes the decisions is also context specific, and the *conservation* context is particularly complex. Successful conservation often involves diverse participants, even at the local level, and can include more than one community or cut across ethnic and cultural boundaries. The deceptively simple move from the top to the bottom level of social action makes clear that communities should be the decision makers but generates a host of other problems in the process.

Conflicts of Interest

Conflicts of interest are inherent and inevitable, even within relatively homogenous communities. Conflict at the local level is heightened by the breakdown of traditional systems. When interests diverge (often most dramatically between generations), the means of arbitration may no longer function. Even when communities are still viable and have ways of dealing with their internal conflicts, they seldom have methods (except violence) with which to resolve disagreements between communities.

Conflict increases as the number of participants and the number and levels of social groupings expand. The Osa Peninsula of Costa Rica is a good illustration. Any biodiversity conservation on the Osa must reconcile the interests of indigenous people and immigrants, nationals and foreigners, farmers, miners (both legal and illegal), and loggers, along with those of a multitude of government agencies and NGOs (see BOSCOSA).

Conflict at any level impedes the success of community-based efforts. This is true when nation-states are reluctant to devolve the tenurial rights essential to local communities; when existing institutions resist delegating power; when different agencies have conflicting agendas, often reified in contradictory policies; or when one individual co-opts the rights of others in the community.

Ignoring conflict is unrealistic. In many cases, outside arbitration may be the only solution. The main thrust of community-based conservation has been to wrest control and power away from governments, reinvesting it at the local level. Government still plays a crucial role when it comes to the adjudication of disputes within and between communities and between levels of society. Yet the involvement of government in community-based conservation often generates new conflicts, since the interests of governments seldom coincide with community interests.

Arbitration is one method of resolving conflicts of interest. Building consensus by focusing on common needs or problems is another tactic. A variety of different peoples inhabit the Sierra Nevada de Santa Marta mountains and the surrounding area in Colombia. These people have little in common except the need for water, which the mountains provide. Water became a focus for joint action that is leading to community-based conservation in the region (Mayr 1993). Another alternative may be partnerships and comanagement between communities and other actors. This approach minimizes antagonism and creates new strategies for dealing with conflicts. The comanagement between a government agency and Aboriginal people described in KAKADU helps keep open the lines of communication. Potential problems find acceptable solutions, successfully inhibiting the development of a destructive us-versus-them mentality.

Tension Between Insiders and Outsiders

Who has the right to initiate action and participate in implementation of CBC projects? If the participatory process is a crucial way of achieving linkage of community and conservation needs, what constitutes participation? What role should outsiders play?

Ideally, CBC projects should be initiated by the communities themselves, but often this proves impossible (see INITIATION), particularly in biodiversity conservation. Few societies around the world value diversity for its own sake. How can any traditional community learn the value of biodiversity and benefit in some tangible way without an external trigger? Outsiders can play an important role in this and other aspects of CBC projects. For example, outsiders can stimulate and facilitate local participation and skills. They also may have to do what locals can not do for themselves in the interim: help create dialogue within and between communities and link communities to the "outside." These roles should change over time, as projects develop and local people acquire their own skills.

Tension between outsiders and insiders emanates, in part, from CBC's shift of focus. After a history of experience with government projects, communities often view their own government as an outsider. Both governments and communities frequently feel international agencies are outsiders who interfere as much as help when they try to insert their own inappropriate agendas. But this is only part of the problem. Tension also arises when outsiders—be they governmental agencies, international donors, or committed individuals—are reluctant to let go, to give up power and control when they should, once the project develops its own momentum. External funding often is used heavy-handedly to reinforce outsiders' efforts to remain involved.

Governmental or international outsiders are well-known villains. But the tension between outsider and insider permeates CBC at all levels. There will always be a shifting line between insider and outsider in the complex and diverse conservation context, with its context-specific participatory process. In the effort to save remnant forests (see INDIA), West Bengal and Orissa communities involved in forest management view neighboring communities who do not subscribe as outsiders, despite great similarities in their cultural traditions and even the existence of social ties between them. Once a group joins the cause, its members quickly change status, leaving the outsider appellation for other communities who still exploit the forest. Government enforcers are seen as insiders when they work in partnership with the forest management committees and as outsiders when they oppose the community.

Problems of trust and communication underlie most insider/outsider tensions.

An outsider is often anyone whom community members view with suspicion. Restoring trust and dialogue can change perceptions and alter alliances. The Nepalese conservation-area project spent its first year trying to create a dialogue, which then formed the basis of future joint action between diverse participants (see ANNAPURNA).

Values, Rights, and Responsibilities

The current environmental crisis is as much about changes in values as it is about economics and politics (see BACKGROUND). Solutions to the crisis also will have to involve values. Fortunately, in the rural landscape that is the focus of CBC, traditional societies whose values do or can make the link between behavior and conservation still exist. Often, tapping into these values makes for successful conservation, even when the people themselves don't think of their actions and beliefs in conservation terms.

Values

Sometimes values simply need to be reinforced. In other cases, existing values must be redirected toward appropriate issues (see CULTURE). Where values are dormant because the society is in transition, they may have to be revived. But in many circumstances, new values are required. How to create and disseminate these new values is perhaps the most provocative challenge for community-based conservation (see CHALLENGES).

Rights

Rights are formally encoded values. A variety of legal, cultural, and political rights are central to CBC. At the core of legal rights is secure tenure vested at the local level (see TENURE, INSTITUTIONS).

Tenure

Tenurial rights can take many forms. The best options for community-based conservation may not be individual ownership or the introduction of exotic tenure systems. In many contexts, the greatest success comes when community-based tenure systems or other traditional systems are used. A good illustration comes from Papua New Guinea, where 97 percent of the land is communally owned by some seven hundred clans, rather than by individuals or the government. The community-based conservation plan discussed in CRATER MOUNTAIN successfully employs this preexisting communal tenure system.

Culture

Cultural rights also are involved. These range from the simple right of cultural survival to the right of traditional people to their own knowledge, particularly knowledge about the natural world and how to manage it. Many areas of high biodiversity are also areas where traditional peoples reside. Resident people, who see themselves as having safeguarded these areas, also regard themselves as stakeholders. As a result, they claim proprietary rights over their knowledge, particularly when biotechnology is being extracted from biodiversity within their territory. The Rio Earth Summit served to showcase this struggle over ownership of genetic resources in the world's tropical forests.

Politics

Political rights go beyond ownership of land, resources, or knowledge. Even when tenurial rights are in place or cultural rights are guaranteed, if "political power" resides elsewhere, rights often go unimplemented or remain ineffectual (see TENURE, POLICY). Devolution of rights must go hand in hand with increasing democratization of power, and with education that builds both awareness and political skills. This is well illustrated in the successful people-centered agricultural improvement programs in Latin America, which operate on the principle of "evolving response." Starting slowly and on a small scale, these programs build momentum through education and demonstrations under the leadership of villager extensionists (Bunch 1982).

Responsibilities

Values entrain rights, but they also prescribe responsibilities. Although responsibility is a central issue in community-based conservation, understanding of how it functions is still rudimentary (see CHALLENGES). There are two vacuums in the realm of responsibility. The first occurs when modern legal systems replace traditional systems. As individual rights become sacrosanct, the state, which devolves these rights, can not and does not replace the inbuilt checks and balances of tradition. Without the incessant watchful attention of others, individuals' sense of responsibility disappears. The other vacuum results from the new context of interests. In a framework that runs the gamut from individual to community to national to regional to global interests, the distribution of rights and responsibilities is still unclear. Definition and linkage of rights has progressed further than the exploration and attachment of responsibilities.

Fortunately, the sense of responsibility can be re-created in several ways. One approach is to forge new common values about community and conservation that connect rights and obligations. Another approach is to legislate responsibilities with each set of rights (see INSTITUTIONS). In either case, CBC participants need to have the means and the capabilities required to fulfill their responsibilities. These often come from education. In NORTH YORK MOORS, farmers are educated about the aims of the program and their responsibilities in it, as well as about their rights. Conserving some parts of the landscape requires traditional skills that are fast disappearing. The program revives the art of building stone walls, enabling farmers to meet that part of their responsibilities.

Even when values, rights, and responsibilities are in place, any participant, whether an individual or a government, sometimes may fail to conform. Enforcement is necessary in such cases. The need for coercive enforcement increases when values, rights, and responsibilities do not correlate.

Problems of Scale

Shifting the focus of decisions and the locus of action from the top to the bottom by empowering local communities does not guarantee success. The shift usually introduces problems of scale. Scaling down gets rid of corruption and ineptitude at the top and gives the bottom the chance to make its own decisions. But scaling down often reveals that communities have their own corruption, nepotism, and ineptitude, which can subvert common goals. These characteristics must be controlled.

Equally critical is the realization that communities do not exist in isolation and can not act alone. For local action to be effective, it must be linked to the larger network of power and policy. This is particularly true in conservation. The resources that need safeguarding often encompass large areas and several communities. Scaling up from one community to several, from community level to higher levels, is imperative. The challenge is to maintain the integrity of community goals and aspirations in the process. The CAMPFIRE program in Zimbabwe began in just a few locations but expanded throughout the country, keeping a sensitivity and adaptive response to local concerns (see CAMPFIRE). By contrast, the natural forest management projects discussed in NIGER have yet to find an answer to the same problem.

Change

Folk wisdom claims that the world is a stable place and that its parts (behaviors, cultures, traditions, institutions, even ecosystems) are also stable. The most recent scientific thought, on the other hand, appreciates the dynamic nature of just about everything. Change is both inevitable and incessant. Change abounds, even in simple situations: Social relations change, traditions and values change, relationships between people and their environment change, and the environment itself changes. There are degrees of change, of course, and communities demonstrate well its range and implications. Within communities, constant minute changes occur in the daily re-creation of culture, although these changes often go unnoticed by community members when they occur. Ignorance gives the illusion of permanence and stability in cultural traditions. Other changes, whether they originate inside or outside a community, are perceived and seen as acceptable. Yet these may have unexpected and challenging consequences. At the other end of the spectrum are catastrophic, demoralizing changes that result in trauma because they jeopardize cultural meanings and understanding.

Change takes on new dimensions when participants and actions scale up. Different communities, ethnic groups, and cultures change in their own way and at their own pace. When they are linked to each other, and to policies and institutions that also change in an individualistic manner, often they are out of sync. Institutions and cultural traditions probably are the slowest to change; individual behavior can evolve very fast. Conservatism and rigidity, whether in institutions or in individuals, present real obstacles to both development and conservation. These tasks require flexible, quick, and adaptive responses to the realities of constantly changing situations, since obstacles can emerge in many guises. Traditional hunters in the Peruvian Amazon, for example, continued using their preexisting philosophy of hunting after they acquired modern technology (see NEOTROPICAL FORESTS). The results were devastating for the forest and its wildlife.

Costs and Benefits

The biodiversity crisis stems, in part, from economics. How natural capital has been valued and should be valued is one critical dimension. Undervaluation has led to overexploitation. If the current market price of tropical hardwood were its true value, few nations' workmen could afford to use it as temporary supports in the construction of concrete buildings. Equally pernicious has been the disjunction between those who benefit from and those who pay the cost of irresponsible use of natural resources. Most often, wealthy nations or transnational corporations profit enormously, while poor countries, and the even more impoverished people who live at the source, pay the cost of the resulting environmental degradation.

The CBC approach aims to rectify one type of inequity. This involves transferring an increased share of benefits to local communities. Benefits can take many forms, among them cash payments, social services, or control of marketing. CBC projects have provided two striking lessons about benefits. The first is that to be effective, benefits need not be very large, at least by Northern standards. The second is that no matter how great the necessity for long-term planning, communities need to see acceptable short-term benefits in the interim if CBC is to succeed. Papua New Guineans view revenue from ecotourism as their reward for implementing conservation practices and as an important bridge to future options both for the community and for conservation in CRATER MOUNTAIN. When ecotourism founders, the entire project is in jeopardy. The success of forest management groups in INDIA is closely linked to use of other forest products or to the presence of alternative sources of income. Groups lacking these can not afford to delay extracting timber, although they know the environmental cost.

Innovation

If past approaches haven't worked, and change is constant and inevitable, what are the solutions? Contradictory lessons apply to the question of whether it is best to enhance, strengthen, and otherwise improve existing traditions, institutions, policies, and governments, or whether innovation is needed in the form of new traditions, new institutions, and new policies. A possible argument is that if old institutions didn't work, why should new ones function any better? If old policy was never implemented, is there any guarantee that new policy will be? In many cases, sound approaches exist but have never been put into action. For example, some countries already have legislation that grants indigenous rights and legitimizes community resource-management systems, but these laws and policies have never been implemented. Perhaps the first step should be to fix what is wrong with what already exists.

On the other hand, CBC is revolutionary in its shift of focus. Existing policy, legislation, and institutions may be inadequate in the face of this reorientation. New ways of doing business, including creation of partnerships and dialogue, changes in economic relations, and changes in donor roles, may be required. Realistically, a mix of old and new is likely to be the answer.

Linkages Between Community and Conservation

Not all conservation can or should be community based, and mobilizing communities certainly is not, in itself, a guarantee of conservation. For reasons already discussed, many CBC projects will not achieve the desired link between improved conditions for people and conservation of biodiversity. Despite this difficulty, there are reasons to believe in the efficacy of this approach.

One is the possible link between cultural diversity and biodiversity. An array of areas that contain high biodiversity happen to coincide with the residence of traditional peoples. If this relationship turns out to be causal, then helping to ensure cultural survival and cultural diversity through community-based efforts could itself be a technique for conserving biodiversity. Traditional resource users tend to be strongly motivated to maintain their important and often diverse resources. The argument also works in the other direction: Attempts to conserve cultural diversity and ensure cultural survival may require the presence of biodiversity. Much cultural distinctiveness, after all, is the result of selection of resources and development of different ways of using them.

Even when traditional links become increasingly tenuous under the impact of modern circumstances, the situation sometimes can be turned to advantage if new incentives are created. CBC, armed with such incentives, can make fresh connections between community and conservation. The practice of *sasi* in Indonesia (see MALUKU ISLANDS) originally aimed to maximize harvests. When fishing becomes commercialized, the old system results in rapid depletion through overfishing. Using a set of new incentives, *sasi* is reinvented, and communities are rewarded for successful conservation rather than for maximum exploitation of marine resources.

While the principle of linkage should be paramount in community-based conservation, current projects provide the lesson that no simple rules can be applied in diverse contexts to guarantee successful linkage. Each effort needs to be tailor made. The irony is that success brings changes that require additional adjustments.

Externalities

Even the most promising CBC efforts are affected and often jeopardized by factors outside the immediate context and beyond community control. These externalities can range from bad governmental policies to vagaries of climate. The externalities of most concern to those involved in CBC are remarkably similar and ominously interconnected: poverty, runaway population growth, disproportionate consumption of resources, inappropriate economics, unfavorable international terms of trade, constraining history, political instability, and political pressure for democratization.

Poverty and population growth, while distinct phenomena, are tied together as important externalities. Poor people are desperate people. Poverty prevents long-term planning and makes issues of sustainability irrelevant. The rate of population growth relative to the level of development constrains the potential for development. Major increases in population, coupled with poverty, create disastrous conditions for both people and biodiversity.

The disproportionate consumption of resources complicates the population question. Some analysts say as little 5 percent of the world's population consumes as much as 40 percent of its resources (Myers 1979), setting in motion many other externalities and causing major losses of biodiversity. The culture of consumerism is itself a major threat, as it becomes diffused throughout the world.

Current economic principles and the international terms of trade that they create are another external source of environmental sabotage, as well as a stumbling block for community-based conservation. Biodiversity, in its parts and in its whole, is inappropriately valued. As long as this is true, natural capital will be used wastefully, and many stakeholders and stewards will not get their proper recompense. With the present set of economic relationships, CBC projects can only make small inroads into both community development and the conservation of biodiversity. Current international terms of trade create ever more desperate situations for those who live at the edge—the edge of survival and the edge of biodiversity.

Less momentous but still constraining is the legacy of history. Recent history, particularly colonial occupation, is often an obstacle both to change and to better ways of doing things. Because policies, institutions, and leadership traditions are slow to change, colonial attitudes are still enshrined in postcolonial contexts. Many of these run counter to the basic premises of community-based conservation.

If fossilized, antithetical institutions and policies aren't enough of an impediment, many developing countries also have to cope with political instability. This makes effective planning and implementation of projects impossible or unrealistic. Even more serious for conservation is that political instability often generates wars. Armed conflicts and ethnic disputes usually mean the rapid disappearance of biodiversity, no matter what safeguards are in place or which innovative new plan is in the works.

Finally, the recent trend toward political democratization, particularly in developing countries, may be an obstacle as well as an opportunity for community-based conservation. A political climate that favors democracy facilitates the community-based approach, since democracy and effective community participation rely on the same principles of empowerment. But there are dangers in democracy. Some forms of democracy enshrine extreme individualism, giving individuals the right to use and abuse each other and the environment. Both kinds of behavior are antithetical to CBC. By contrast, many traditional systems that are not democratic or egalitarian can be springboards for successful community-based conservation. Forcing these systems to be truly democratic, causing social disintegration and hampering conservation action, could prove counterproductive.

These and other externalities limit and, at times, undermine CBC and should be cause for concern. On the positive side, experience indicates that CBC programs can begin to ameliorate some of the impact externalities have on communities. They attempt to redress inequities, albeit modestly, and contribute mechanisms that allow the community voice to be heard beyond the conservation context, on many issues.

Conclusions

The lessons in the history of development work and formative CBC efforts seem almost self-evident in retrospect. Modest as these lessons are, they do point out the complexity of the issues, the myriad interaction of factors, and the inevitability of problems when humans try to work together. They also provide insights about obstacles to be overcome if community-based conservation is to succeed.

The lessons learned can be summarized as pressure points in the community-based conservation approach. These are

- the opposition between *center and periphery* in the struggle for power, in the exercise of rights and responsibilities, and in costs and benefits;

- the disjunction between *short-term and long-term costs and benefits* in both natural-resources use and biodiversity conservation;

- the difference in *valuation* of natural resources and biodiversity;

- the difficulties of mobilizing community action, particularly when *societies are in transition;*

- the clash of *insiders' and outsiders'* values, interests, and agendas;

- the *context specificity of problems and solutions,* requiring each program to be tailor made, adaptable, and flexible; and

- the diversity of linkages that are both necessary and possible, generating a *complex landscape* for community-based conservation.

SOURCES

Bunch, R. 1982. *Two Ears of Corn: A Guide to People-centered Agricultural Improvement.* Oklahoma City, Oklahoma: World Neighbors.
Mayr, J. 1993. Conversation with the author, October, Airlie, Virginia.
Myers, N. 1979. *The Sinking Ark.* New York: Pergamon Press.

CHAPTER 24

Recommendations

R. Michael Wright

        The Airlie House Community Based Conservation Workshop produced no unanimous agreement, made no pronouncements to a breathless world, issued no press releases. The third week of October 1993 was one of intense debate, with wisdom shared, opinions passionately expressed, cultural perspectives pondered, friendships made, and differences respected. We found the issue of partnerships between communities and conservationists too new, the views too varied, the time too short, and the need for learning still too great for a tidy set of simple answers.

These recommendations are drawn from the presentations, discussions, and written contributions offered at the workshop. They have been constructed from the bottom up, beginning with reports from the thematic discussion groups, followed by those of the regional groups, with additional input drawn from the case studies and the lively general debate. While the workshop is the genesis of these recommendations, the participants certainly would not endorse them in their entirety or in their particular wording. Nevertheless, they represent areas of broad and significant agreement. If they are not the final answer, perhaps they are the beginning of wisdom—or at least the end of ignorance—concerning conservation undertaken by and for communities.

The recommendations address with a global perspective a topic that in its very essence is local. Community-based conservation focuses on villages and hamlets, on wattled huts in Zimbabwe's *miombo* woodlands or thatched cottages in the North York Moors of England. In these places, the day-to-day challenges of balancing conservation and survival are often small scale, undefined, complex, and unique to their social and ecological settings. As we seek recommendations for building a general framework for CBC, we must remain cognizant of the reality that if community-based conservation is to succeed, it must always address local problems that communities feel directly and remain rooted in their local reality and values.

Culture

Whether we are speaking of an indigenous community in Peru, a complex mosaic of peoples around Annapurna, or the more recent cattle culture of Costa Rica, the complexity and diversity of local cultures have been missing elements in most recent conservation initiatives. Not only is culture ignored, multiple cultural adaptations to unique environmental challenges represent a resource as valuable, and as threatened, as biodiversity itself. The failure to tap this resource must be corrected in the following ways:

Empowerment

The power and integrity of groups and communities and their traditional cultures and values must be protected. Particularly where local cultures have long-standing traditional claims to resources and a history of maintaining them, opportunities exist for collaboration between environmental and human-rights organizations.

Concept of Culture

Externally initiated conservation projects that impact upon traditionally owned resources should recognize and make themselves compatible with local people's integral concepts of culture. This will require a level of local knowledge rarely found at present.

Cultural and Land Rights

Intellectual and cultural property rights, as well as the land and other resource rights of indigenous peoples, must be recognized and accommodated in conservation decisions. Allocation of such rights will be a major point of conflict within societies and in international forums.

Economics and Values

When devising market-oriented conservation solutions, economics may be an inappropriate measure of value in culturally diverse areas. In addition, the commercialization of resources that previously played a subsistence role can lead to increased income disparity and impoverishment, particularly of female resource users.

Human Impact

Linking conservation and culture must be based on the reality that not all customary or traditional activities are environmentally beneficial. In balancing conservation with cultural practices, the need is for an independent assessment of the positive and negative impacts of human behaviors on biodiversity.

Flexibility

Cultures are diverse and constantly in transition. They also defy complete external understanding. In response, conservation approaches must be flexible and transparent, allowing indigenous peoples to manage the process, degree, and pace of cultural change.

Innovative Partnerships

Conservationists should undertake an active search for innovative partnerships that build on the enormous diversity of traditional knowledge and unique conservation solutions. Control of the fruits of that knowledge, however, should reside with its creators.

Participation

Broad-based (although not necessarily universal) local participation is inherent in the concept of community-based conservation, but such participation is not synonymous with conservation. Participation ensures that conservation investments or costs are balanced by equivalent rewards; where relevant local stakeholders are not participating, real needs are not being addressed. Democratic processes and local power to make decisions are prerequisites to effective participation. The recommendations to broaden participation in conservation decisions include:

Local Leadership

Creative, motivated, and diversified local leadership needs to be identified and supported while local institutional capacity is emerging.

Involvement and Empowerment

Only through active involvement in all stages of planning and management can local groups gain power and articulate a shared vision. If their power is to be real, these groups must be involved at the earliest stages of problem definition, data gathering, and data analysis so that they can adapt and control the process of their own development.

Building Capacity

A sense of immutability based on past experience can frustrate community solutions. Participatory capacity and confidence often must be built, particularly for poorly represented groups or sectors such as women and minorities. Capacity building requires projects with sufficient time for consensus to emerge, access to timely information, an appropriate scale of activities, and funding to strengthen local capabilities. Confidence comes from success built on existing activities that are locally tested and culturally calibrated.

Conservation Context

Communities are not homogenous. The crucial groups to participate in CBC activities therefore are defined by the nature of the resource and the extent of human impact. Thus effective participation in management of a communal forest area may require several communities, while the fate of an endangered species might depend on only a few village hunters. Often, elites whose survival is not dependent upon the resource nevertheless dominate the participatory process.

Government

CBC requires more than romanticizing the local. Participation of governments is indispensable. Extension, training, arbitration, and consultation between and within communities all commonly fall within the purview of governments. Government's most fundamental role in CBC is to establish a civil context that allows free and open participation in the political process by all levels of society.

Resource Ownership

Perhaps the single greatest obstacle to conservation is lack of secure tenure to land, wildlife, and other resources. Community-based conservation requires creation of clear and unequivocal property rights that create a vested interest in managing resources sustainably. Secure tenure includes the right to use a resource, determine mode of use, benefit from use, determine the distribution of benefits, and establish rules of access to the resources. The workshop participants had the following recommendations regarding this issue:

Traditional Tenure

Conservation organizations that have relied on governmental or "modern" legal systems in the past should recognize the legitimacy and potential of traditional or customary tenure systems as a basis for conservation.

Demarcation

Demarcation of physical boundaries and ownership patterns in relation to land, resources, and wildlife are prerequisites to sustained environmental management of resources. Unless demarcation is undertaken with great sensitivity, however, codification of such details can reify customary laws and destroy their essential flexibility. Prerequisites include informed consent of the community, effective prior notice, community retention of the primary responsibility of self-definition, and open negotiations over benefits and project plans.

Denationalization

Where governmental incapacity has created situations of open access and where local commitment to conservation and capacity exists, nationalized resources should be returned to local ownership and a management regime that the community knows and accepts. Reversing decades of centralization will require substantial political will.

Guarantees of Security

In addition to legislative grant or acknowledgment of preexisting tenurial rights, governments need to guarantee and enforce local rights to land, resources, and wildlife against infringement by external parties. Tenurial rights also need to be reinforced by increasing local capacity to manage resources.

Individual Rights

Where cohesive communities do not exist, a well-documented, financially and procedurally accessible national system of individual property rights may be the only available means through which to address tenure insecurity. However, application of individual rights to resources previously held communally frequently has been culturally and ecologically devastating.

Comanagement

Governments may retain some rights or demand responsibilities when devolving tenurial rights. Comanagement limitations balance the immediate needs of resource owners with the longer-term societal interest in maintenance of resources. Comanagement should be introduced with procedural safeguards and remain subject to periodic review.

Production of Benefits

Resolution of tenure insecurity alone will not achieve sustainability. Individual or group benefits, as well as near- and long-term community benefits, must be assured to justify deferred exploitation. For example, access to capital or credit may be necessary to convert ownership into long-term benefits.

Policy

The centralization of power in the nation-state as enshrined in national policies must be reversed if localized conservation efforts are to flourish. Community-supporting policies need to encapsulate the foregoing specific recommendations within a national strategy that empowers and implements them through the political process. This can be achieved through the following means:

Community Participation

National policies should require that communities participate in the decisions that affect them and the resources that they in turn affect. Community-based conservation requires opening the political process at all levels to a broader range of people, including the traditionally excluded underclasses. Policies supporting participation require transparent government decision-making, with mechanisms for adequate and timely public disclosure, and a political process that holds government institutions and officials accountable to citizens.

Policy of Local Management

The goal of government policy should be removal of barriers to the implementation of community projects. Rights and responsibilities for and means to manage natural resources must be granted to successively more localized entities. The most local institution is not always ideal, and each resource needs to be analyzed to determine the level at which conservation can be achieved best. Management of a fishery, for example, may require a regional strategy to incorporate the impact of forestry and farming practices.

Population and Resources

For conservation to succeed, policies must address the issue of population and the ultimate carrying capacity of land. Such policies should be undertaken within the context of concern for women's health, education, and economic roles.

Impact of Policy

The impact of policies or policy changes should be subjected to environmental assessment. Particular attention should be given to the inadvertent or perverse environmental impacts of macro policies such as national economic plans, export or transportation strategies, and subsidization of excessive resource exploitation (which may include underpricing water and irrigation systems). All of these may render community projects unsustainable.

National Environmental Strategy

Creation of a national strategy for the sustainable use of resources provides a framework that supports community-based activities. Such strategies need to reconcile conflicting interagency mandates and encourage coordination of planning and management. They also need mechanisms with which to resolve competing values, interests, rights, and claims over resources within society.

International Environmental Strategy

International agencies and donors should not ignore governments in their zeal to support communities. The long-term viability of CBC projects requires strong government involvement. External agencies, particularly, should support national policies devolving authority and underwrite basic institutional changes such as national land-titling programs.

North-South Issues

Donors and international NGOs need to develop a broad understanding of North-South policy issues (debt, equitable terms of trade, biotechnology, intellectual property rights, international trade agreements) and exercise policy influence on their *own* governments and multilateral institutions to create a supportive context for community-based conservation activities.

Institutions

Government policies are no better than the strength and responsiveness of the institutions charged with their implementation. Community-based conservation requires unprecedented collaboration—horizontally, often between competing institutions, and vertically, through institutions at different levels of society. Recommendations to improve institutional performance on CBC include:

Institutional Environment

A supportive institutional environment is a necessary condition for village-level conservation to prosper. Such an environment will include establishment of local resource proprietorship and community capacity for self-definition. A conducive institutional environment entails a variety of institutions at multiple levels—national, regional, local, and community—and supportive linkages between them.

Information

The flow and availability of timely, relevant information is essential to enable institutions to be effective, responsible, and accountable to communities.

Training

For community conservation partnerships to succeed, investments in training and development of local institutions' capacity, particularly managerial capacity, are needed. Training may include university courses, in-service training, or leadership development. Because community initiatives are often stimulated by crisis, mediation and conflict-resolution skills are particularly relevant.

Appropriate Institutions

Despite the almost unwavering tendency to the contrary, strengthening of institutions should favor preexisting institutions rather than creation of new ones. Local institutions should be simple, self-adjusting, adaptive, and resistant to externally generated priorities. Governmental natural resources agencies need expanded mandates that allow them to support community activities outside the narrow geographic confines of their institutional focus.

Catalytic Role of NGOs

The difficulties of marginal communities acting in isolation create a role for external organizations to act as brokers with national institutions, bringing in expertise and new perspectives, assisting with realization of proprietary claims, and building local capacity to deal with more powerful entities. These outside agencies must take care to avoid usurping local initiatives, institutions, and leadership.

Skills and Knowledge Transfer

The concept of an external expert on internal resource management contains a readily apparent contradiction. Although substantial local capacity and personnel experienced in community approaches exist, donors and governments rarely draw upon them. In fact, conservation through community empowerment is predominantly a developing-world phenomenon transferred North in vehicles such as the partnership movement in the United States. Here are some recommended means of rectifying existing imbalances:

In-country Expertise

Governments and external agencies need to identify and use in-country expertise. Where local capacity is lacking, building individual skills and strengthening institutions is essential if activities are to be truly community based.

Local Knowledge

Local knowledge and experience need to be recognized, reinforced, and disseminated by external agencies. This can be accomplished through partnerships and exchanges between communities and intermediary institutions. South-South exchanges between communities, practitioners, and other participating institutions are particularly effective means of replication.

Documentation

Community experience should be documented and in-country information gained from research made accessible to other communities, NGOs, and governments through case studies, regional exchanges, and networks.

Research and Evaluation

As part of a collaborative agenda-setting process, the links between traditional values, local techniques, and biodiversity conservation should be investigated. Community-based research should focus on developing options and technologies that are environmentally sound and affordable but do not require great community sacrifice or increased individual risk. In general, the best tool or technique for CBC is the simplest one that will do the job.

Methodology

Methods that more fully realize the economic, subsistence, and spiritual value of biodiversity and incorporate this value into political decision-making processes will greatly strengthen community management of resources.

Donors

Paternalistic conservation is antithetical to community-based resource management. Top-down approaches to resource transfers must cease, and this will require a major reorientation of the way in which donors and recipients operate. The existing giver-taker relationship needs to evolve into one of partnership. CBC then can become a hunt for agreements or bargains openly arrived at and based on balanced self-interest. Recommendations for bringing about this evolution—perhaps revolution—include:

Change Policies and Practices

Donors need to relinquish control over projects once initial agreement over objectives has been negotiated, a task perhaps as difficult as the one governments face in devolving rights to local communities. Donor policies and practices should foster partnerships based on mutual interest directed toward local initiatives. The characteristics of such partnerships include responsiveness to local initiatives and context, including appropriate scale and pace; risk taking and maintenance of long-term involvement; flexibility and adaptiveness; acceptance of complexity and uncertainty; the practice of open, transparent, participatory agenda setting; and engagement in activities based on mutual trust, respect, and joint learning.

Change Methods of Operation

If activities are truly community led, donors should not have a vested interest in pushing any activity in a predetermined direction. They should support people, institutions, and processes rather than projects, infrastructure, and specific outcomes. Local communities should set criteria, including social and cultural as well as economic objectives, against which the activity will be evaluated. In consultation with their external partners, communities need to determine the appropriate scale for budgets and accept reciprocal obligations for financial accountability and performance.

Resource Brokers

Multilateral and bilateral agencies and other donors should reconfigure themselves to become resource brokers. They can assist communities in living sustainably by brokering a variety of activities. These might range from reinforcing existing community resource management to helping communities acquire transfer payments for environmental services valued by the global society.

Regional

Although workshop participants included a staff member from the World Bank and a Maasai tribesman, a political leader from Brazil and an ambassador from Papua New Guinea, a British park manager and a native American from Canada, a philosophy professor from the American Midwest and a community-development expert from the Philippines, their global advice and concerns were strikingly similar. There is a sense of universality in the CBC approach, but this universality is subject to regional nuance. Because of their different circumstances, each region emphasized particular and unique issues that will affect implementation of community approaches around the world.

Africa

The image of vast African savannas belies the continent's overriding problem of population growth in relation to resource availability and land capacity. Unresolved, the population problem undermines per capita economic growth rates, and the fragile resource base unravels further. Alleviation of poverty is the first step in developing options for long-term sustainability, productivity, and conservation. Human survival is nowhere more intimately tied to maintenance of biological resources, particularly for women farmers, than on this, the earth's poorest continent.

Colonial history followed by centralized, often authoritarian, governments that did not concede to traditional tenurial systems has led to widespread open-access use and abuse of resources in Africa. One of the major needs in this region is definition of community membership in relation to property, land, and resources and broadening of membership to include women. Once membership has been recognized, security of tenure will be a critical next step, preferably through recognizing traditional tenure systems or, where this option no longer exists, by granting legal title to land and resources.

Africa has few formal nongovernmental environmental institutions, and those that exist are generally weak. The Africans at Airlie House gave special emphasis to developing and strengthening institutions, particularly at local level, and to linking them at local and national levels. Traditional village-based structures continue to provide a potential base for local resource management in many parts of Africa; however, the continent has been following a halting path in pursuit of the global trend toward political pluralism and decentralization that is the foundation of CBC approaches.

Asia

Natural resources in the Asia and Pacific region present an extremely varied picture. In many countries, resources are under intense threat due to a high rate of economic development combined with enormous population pressure. As a result, many East Asian CBC projects are focused on restoration of biologically degraded lands. As in Africa, local property rights and tenure are critical issues in some parts of Asia; in contrast, however, local ownership rights over resources are better defined in the Pacific, particularly in Papua New Guinea, than almost anywhere else in the world. There is a need to strengthen local organizations, but, although the NGO movement started later here, the number of Asian NGOs now may have surpassed Latin America's. These organizations are seeking direct access to information and funding for biodiversity conservation and community-based conservation. Since the major impact on the region's resources, particularly forests for energy use, is the result of economic growth and sheer human numbers, the Asian/Pacific participants placed emphasis on finding alternative economic opportunities that are less environmentally damaging.

Latin America

Latin America has more in common with Asia than with Africa. Here, too, economic growth and disparities in wealth have a more significant impact on resources than population growth, although parts of Central America and the Andes are exceptions. Within Latin America, some regional areas—particularly the tropical forests of the Amazon and Central America—bear striking similarity to Africa, with problems of open access, lack of tenure, and poverty. The issues of indigenous land rights and the relationship between traditional peoples and the dominant culture are here closely linked to CBC.

Latin America has a young but highly developed nongovernmental institutional framework that needs to be strengthened. Its activities also need to be coordinated through information exchanges. The nongovernmental sector is increasingly sophisticated and advocacy oriented; it provides considerable political and technical support to communities seeking to renegotiate their relationship with government authorities. The Latin Americans stress, more than Africans or Asians, the need to immediately use their own institutions for CBC activities. They expect international donors to route funding through national institutions rather than through international intermediaries.

Developed Countries

The developed world generally does not perceive population growth as a significant factor in environmental degradation. Instead, its consumption of resources is the driving force behind much global biodiversity loss. On the one hand, this loss results from direct importation of developing countries' resources and, on the other, from low commodity prices and protection of markets that frustrates development in the South and leads to poverty-driven environmental destruction. The developed countries have highly evolved and often subsidized resource systems (including fisheries, forestry, and, particularly, agriculture) that have an enormous negative impact on biodiversity. Because of overproduction, there is now an opportunity to convert these subsidies into incentives for conservation. One of the major areas for conservation action in the developed world is landscape restoration and ecosystem rehabilitation.

Unlike developing countries, industrialized countries have an opportunity and the financial resources to create CBC programs through land-use planning managed by well-established local government units and supported by a formalized set of legal procedures. Like other regions, however, developed countries do not present a unified picture, as seen in the contrast between the effectiveness of land-use planning in British protected landscapes compared to the sancrosanct nature of individual land rights in the United States and its adversarial approach to problem solving.

At Airlie House, the former communist states of Eastern Europe and the former Soviet Union drew special attention. Centralization of authority and land in these countries is inimical to CBC activities and has led to the greatest environmental degradation in the North. High priority should be given to the issues of property rights and localized decision-making in order to reverse this trend. North-North exchanges are one approach. The nongovernmental sector, as a catalyst in the toppling of communist regimes, retains a unique degree of legitimacy for undertaking community conservation.

Acknowledgments

I wish to thank my wife, Pam, and my children, Melina and Brendan, who tolerated prolonged absences with unfailing good humor throughout the production of this chapter and the entire book.

CHAPTER 25

A Few Big Challenges

*David Western, Shirley C. Strum, D. Tuzin,
K. Sayre, and R. Michael Wright**

The workshop participants struggled hard with the question of how to link conservation with local community interests, the lessons learned from experience around the world, and recommendations for further improvements. What emerged was no more than a stab in the dark. As in any workshop, particularly on a topic so new and diverse, enormous uncertainties and challenges remained unresolved at the end. The future of community-based conservation depends to a great extent on identifying and tackling those challenges, however formidable they may seem. We have pulled together a few of the big challenges that run throughout the workshop proceedings. If these do not offer immediate solutions, they at least perform the essential task of reminding CBC advocates how much more they must yet ponder and tackle.

Ecology

The challenge of community-based conservation is as formidable for ecologists as for economists. By stepping into rural areas, ecologists abandon their familiar and reassuring natural world and enter a realm long shunned as too unnatural to merit serious academic attention. Natural populations and natural ecosystems rest on the high altar of ecological research, while ecologists usually regard human-modified landscapes disdainfully as aberrations. The intellectual switch required for professionals to accept such landscapes as the norm and also as a fitting new scientific frontier will not happen overnight. Biodiversity conservation came to be seen as a legitimate and, eventually, noble intellectual challenge in biology only after a slow process of change that took years. We can only hope that the next step, into the humanized world, will be quicker.

*Sections on "Ecology" and "Economics" by David Western; "Values of the South, Ethics of the North" section by Shirley C. Strum, D. Tuzin, and K. Sayre; "Policy" section by R. Michael Wright.

However formidable, the biological challenges of conserving biodiversity in the rural landscape are not insurmountable. The challenges revolve around identifying the sources of biodiversity, safeguarding species in situ, or, failing that, rescuing and restoring species and habitats threatened with extinction. Advances in identification, safeguarding, and rescue, in turn, depend upon improvements in biological theory, criteria for intervention, and conservation management techniques.

Identification

The distribution of biodiversity with respect to the protected areas presents a big challenge. Until we have a better sense of how species are distributed relative to human land uses, exactly how important rural lands outside protected areas really are in terms of biodiversity will remain unknown. The few data available reveal surprising and encouraging results. In Kenya, for example, more than 70 percent of large mammals occur outside parks. National parks and protected areas worldwide include less than 10 percent of extant moist tropical forests and, presumably, a minor portion of species, given their localized distributions. The proportions of biodiversity in rural areas in the industrialized world, where protected areas are few and far between, is likely to prove higher yet.

Inventorying biodiversity will take decades using conventional taxonomic surveys. Biologists are now devoting some attention to rapid-appraisal methods based on indicator species. Whether the incoming data will lead to improved theoretical predictions of biodiversity distribution or whether the patterns will have to be pieced together area by area from surveys is still unclear. Even with data in hand, new methods for aggregating and weighting information and prioritizing sites will be needed to speed up and improve the process of biodiversity inventories. How fast this happens will determine how effectively humans can conserve species, habitats, and ecological processes.

Safeguarding

Safeguarding biodiversity in rural areas comes down to a question of how ecosystems are structured and how they function. Ecology and its application to wildlife, fisheries, and forestry management, for example, has been heavily influenced by the view that equilibrium is the norm in ecosystems and populations. Recent studies suggest that nonequilibrium models may describe natural systems more accurately. Whatever the relative importance of these two theories, most rural lands undergo far more rapid and extensive change than natural systems.

Understanding how these changes affect biodiversity is the necessary basis of any rural-based conservation: What is the relationship between the type and degree of human disturbance and biodiversity? Which species are affected? How are the structure and property of ecosystems modified? What does this imply for conservation in terms of the minimum area needed to conserve habitats and species and the frequency and magnitude of disturbance needed to maintain biodiversity? Which species are critical to the maintenance of essential ecological processes? Can any other species act as surrogates?

The biggest challenge for ecologists is to look decades and centuries ahead to anticipate how they can take advantage of the shifting landscape mosaic to maintain biodiversity. Can we anticipate the direction and type of change? Where are opportunities likely to open up and close down? Can we identify habitat bridges and species translocations for spanning the gap? Will carbon emissions cause a global change in climate and habitat? We can't be sure.

What we can be sure of is that changes in human activity will affect habitats on a global scale, one way or another. The inevitability of change calls for a fluid view of ecology if the pitfalls of the parks approach are to be avoided. The uncertainties may recede but are unlikely to vanish in the foreseeable future. We can at least minimize the risks by coming to grips with the dominant landscape and confronting the reality of habitat modification and change. This includes elevated rates of species interchange between ecosystems where habitats merge and lowered rates where they fragment and isolate.

Rescue

Intervention is still something of an anathema to conservationists dedicated to the preservation of the natural world. Yet, inevitably, human activity will continue to modify the natural world, and conservationists will overcome their reluctance to step in to rescue species from extinction and habitats from degradation. Knowing when to intervene, and how, will call on insights and skills that conservationists have barely acknowledged so far, let alone developed. The challenges include choosing which species to rescue and what to do with them when their habitat disappears, as well as which habitats to rehabilitate and how, in rural as opposed to protected areas.

Rural lands offer enormous potential for conservation, even if they are shaped by human activity. The overriding question is, How far should we go in trying to save nature the way it is, rather than let a new set of ecological relationships linking the human and natural world emerge? Ultimately, this issue concerns the direction of future selective pressures. What are the implications of a ruralized world for global ecology and evolution? Can species unadapted to human impact continue to thrive, or will the more coevolved and better-adapted species continue to increase, spread, and evolve into new and perhaps no less diverse forms?

If outcomes are uncertain, we can at least be reasonably sure that innovative ideas, local initiatives, new incentives, and ecological tinkering that blends utility and conservation will help to arrest the drift to monoculture and ecological impoverishment.

Economics

The different values and views of nature held by people around the world consti- tute the primary justification for community-based conservation. Out of this di- versity of viewpoints, however, springs a differential perception of who wins and who loses in conservation—the biggest obstacle to community efforts. The vari- ance in views over winners and losers is a good deal less in the case of sustainable utilization than it is in the case of biodiversity conservation.

Humankind's sense of the finiteness of nature is still altogether too rare. Where finiteness is well understood, the need for sustainability is tacitly acknowledged, if not practiced. Even so, sustainability is more the exception than the rule. What is lacking, in either case, is a strong incentive to forego immediate gratification in the interest of long-term sustainability. In failing to live within their means, local communities face the universal problem addressed by the Brundtland Commis- sion and the Earth Summit: sustainability—beyond question the biggest challenge of the postindustrial age.

What distinguishes most local groups from others is motive. In the industrial- ized world, incentives to deplete usually come down to open-access uncertainties and market incentives. In poor communities, the motive more often is poverty. The poor must eat today in order to have any future options, sustainable or otherwise. Exhortation, coercion, and practical demonstration are equally sterile paths to sustainability without assured survival and realization of short-term improve- ments in welfare.

The problem of overcoming poverty and directing communities down the path to sustainability still taxes developmentalists and conservationists alike. The dif- ficulty is not so much ignorance of what this task requires; thousands of commu- nities around the world have moved beyond hand-to-mouth existence, and the catalytic forces are understood and have been widely documented. More accu- rately, the willingness to introduce stimulatory policies and channel essential re- sources all too often is lacking. Even where the will is present, the global scale of poverty is daunting. Each year 75 million new mouths, more than half of them poor, are added to the growing breadline. How can growth be slowed, poverty eliminated, and sustainability given a chance? How can these things be accom- plished fast enough to bring the ultimate population ceiling to levels compatible with reasonable quality and diversify of life? No other challenge has such mo- mentous implications for community-based conservation or, indeed, the future well-being of our species.

Escape from poverty, unfortunately, is no assurance of sustainability. Rich na- tions consume most of the world's resources and will continue to do so into the foreseeable future. How can incentives for sustainability be brought to bear di- rectly on individual behavior? How can Green economics create tight feedback linkages between remotely connected consumption and production processes, so that incentives to sustain supersede incentives to deplete?

These questions are hardly new, and the answers, although promised by environmental economics, still elude us. We are a long way from melding ecological truths with economic truths, whatever the rhetoric. The question of sustainability is elusive enough in the case of natural resources on which we depend. How much more elusive sustainability will be in the case of biodiversity, where the link between action and consequence is far weaker and more remote.

The fate of our biosystem is a distinctly recent concern of industrialized nations. Few societies value biodiversity for its own sake or have any sense that nature brings benefits when sustained or imposes costs when degraded. Fewer still have any notion that global processes that influence the entire planet are under threat.

Sustainability concerns are so recent that we hardly know which questions to ask, let alone what the answers are. What is the value of biodiversity anyway? Is it strategically important to human survival and productivity? If so, to what extent? How much biodiversity do we need, and which essential ecological processes must we maintain? Is biological diversity important to our well-being in a more spiritual sense? If so, are societies that have been deprived of biological diversity spiritually poorer than those living in a more diverse world?

These are areas of great uncertainty, however much conservationists may insist otherwise. Assuming that we can begin to put figures on the strategic value of biodiversity globally or nationally, how do we calculate, let alone apportion, the costs and benefits between different communities and respective generations?

This question brings us to the nub of community-based conservation. How do we link biospheric and ecosystem processes and compute the value of conservation undertaken by a local community for society at large? The computations are hard enough in cases where economic analysis is widely accepted. How much harder will the calculus be when it involves cultures with different perceptions and values? And how much harder still where cultures are in a state of rapid change and embody many different value systems? How can transfers be made in ways that local communities understand and want, rather than as outsiders calculate?

These uncertainties only get us down to the community level, not within it. What of the complex question of how costs and benefits are perceived and apportioned within a community? How do we calculate the costs that any particular individual bears, and what it will take to bring about positive conservation action? Who makes these decisions, and who allocates benefits? How can benefits be apportioned in such a way that they are perceived to be positively linked to individual conservation efforts?

These are some of the many uncertainties and challenges the workshop raised. The answers, even when resolved by economists and ecologists in principle, still will need to be implemented in simple, innovative ways that local communities can understand and accept.

Values of the South, Ethics of the North

The consequences of human population size and ecological limits are not the only big challenges. Culture, cultures, communities, values, and ethics each could constrain or facilitate community-based conservation as much as ecology or economics. Two crucial issues in community-based conservation are *who* and *how*. The simple answers of a decade ago are no longer sufficient.

For a start, failing to understand the important distinctions between culture, cultures, and communities could create serious obstacles and result in missed opportunities for community-based conservation. *Culture* refers to the socially transmitted understandings that pervade all human activity: the values, cognitions, and emotions through which humans relate to each other and to their environment. Without the formation, internalization, and propagation of values, whether they are about community or about conservation, the community-based conservation approach will lack legitimacy and cultural authenticity. It could be written off as a program based on coercion or on the alien wisdom of external authority.

These internalized constructs are dynamic, not fixed or static. Cultural values have always arisen from circumstances. This makes the changing conditions of our modern world a double-edged sword for culture. On the one hand, change is disruptive. Yet change presents new opportunities as well—a chance to enlarge cultural systems of meaning and values. Because culture is not immutable, new ideas or new approaches can be inserted.

Culture changes by its own momentum. The pace accelerates when *cultures*—the embodiment of culture within spatial and temporal boundaries—come into contact. The recent widespread and remarkable rate of contact makes change the status quo; culture and cultures in transition are the norm. Despite this, many community-based conservation efforts tend to reify culture and romanticize what went before. This naive sentimentality is anachronistic and possibly perilous.

On-the-move populations are vast and growing. If predictions of global warming prove correct, and if population doubles as anticipated, the next generation will witness human dislocations of a new magnitude. Community-based conservation will have to deal with "environmental refugees" who, through no fault of their own, have lost their birthright. These nonindigenous people will have lifestyles that are not adapted to their new ecological settings. Moreover, they will see themselves as having rights equal to those of peoples who have lived in the area longer. But migrants often come from different places, bringing with them a diversity of cultures. To resolve this situation, institutions that maximize cultural flexibility and transcultural values are needed. Community-based conservation has the potential to become one of these institutions, but only if it can recognize the realities of cultural diversity, disruption, and conflict. Championing indigenous rights may be a useful first step for some CBC efforts, but not if it becomes a retreat into notions of ethnic purity and priority. The exclusion of "outsiders" based on a cultural ideal will not halt mass movements of humans, nor will it help to save biodiversity in the places where they end up.

Culture is dynamic, cultures disintegrate or assimilate, and people move. This is an infinitely more complex situation than most CBC practitioners realize. To complicate the labyrinth, communities as we have known them are disappearing with increasing frequency. In the past, communities were forged in relative isolation, through close and prolonged social integration, emotional bonding, and shared values. They were remarkably homogenous by today's standards. Modern secular and mobile society has destroyed most traditional communities. If we have no social "community" as the locus of action for community-based conservation, what are the prospects?

The geographical or ecological focus that is necessary for conservation may help to define a new community. Creating or recreating a sense of community, even among diverse people, can happen through the very same processes that operated in the past: proximity, interaction, and common interests—this time, in the ecological context. Although this new community may be different from traditional social communities, it meets the prerequisites for community-based conservation. We might even be building the kind of community (more open; more diverse, with a vision and cohesion that is locational; situated in an environmental context linking community to nature in a sustainable fashion) that is more appropriate within the realities of this small planet.

New communities also will need new environmental values. Are the events in the North a preview of what is to come? Until now, the environmental behavior of the North has been marked by domination, exploitation, eradication, paternalism, and protectionism. Yet the emerging international economic networks, the political aftermath of the Cold War, and scientific advances such as thermonuclear fusion energy and the Human Genome Project are the sort of revolutionary developments that could create a transcultural, transnational "community" and new contexts for values. The time may be at hand for a shift to codependence, sustainable utilization, preservation, fraternalism, and custodianship. What makes this shift possible, and can the North be a model for all the world? Some have argued that it is all a question of "rights." The issue of rights is central to community-based conservation, yet it is rarely evaluated or placed in cultural or historical perspective.

Moral systems can be viewed as responses to the threats that particular societies face. Values and the moral norms that implement them tend to motivate people to act in a fashion that enhances their chances for survival. Moral theory gains currency as the codification of moral components of value systems that are already in place in a particular society. For example, warfare was a serious threat to resource security among ancient Greek pastoralists and farmers. Within their heroic society, virtue and honor could be seen as values critical to survival, giving force to Aristotle's virtue theory. Similarly, John Stuart Mill's utilitarianism made sense during the time of the British commercial empire, but utilitarianism would have been implausible in the Golden Age of Greece.

This way of conceptualizing moral norms has several important implications for the issue of rights. First, both values and moral theories are culturally and historically specific, and this is true of the attendant rights as well. Second, as with any form of adaptation, moral structures, along with the rights they embody, reflect adjustments to past circumstances. When change occurs—particularly rapid or dramatic change—the past system may no longer be adaptive.

Morality, ethics, and rights have special relevance for community-based conservation efforts because of the diversity of culturally based moral systems and because conservation action tends to import alien moral structures that may or may not be appropriate. Practitioners of community-based conservation daily face the realities of a culturally diverse world, the challenges of how to translate culture and mesh divergent cultural systems in the service of conservation.

One solution that CBC champions may hold hidden dangers. A basic tenet of community-based conservation is that secure tenurial and resource rights should be vested at the local level. Action, however, is often couched in a Western—not a local or traditional—framework. This has unexpected and far-reaching consequences. First, the nature of rights and the character of the moral community differ in modern and traditional societies. Traditionally, conventions are maintained by moral suasion, peer pressure, shame, and fear of ostracism; law is synonymous with custom. The rights of individuals are closely wedded to communal responsibilities enforced by other community members. By contrast, modern Western law is formalized as a separate institution that often shifts the focus away from communal rights to individual ones. Formal police and the judicial powers of the state enforce the law. The result is that even when individual rights and responsibilities are part of the same legal package, responsibilities more often than not disappear through the cracks in the system. The exercise of rights without the imposition of responsibilities inevitably leads to abuses of human and natural resources. Thus when community-based conservation advocates individual legalistic rights to replace traditional systems, it sets in motion new and powerful forces that may need to be contained.

Even more pernicious is the possibility that the current Western notion of rights, itself an adaptation to events of the past, might be inappropriate in the modern situation. These ideas about rights can be traced to new conditions created by the Industrial Revolution, the rise of consumerism, and the increasing division of the social world into haves and have-nots. One tradition of rights derives from the utilitarian theory of obligation and communal benefit, while the other is rooted in social-contract theory and the theory of justice.

We know that current social and ecological conditions are no longer those of the Industrial Revolution. At a minimum, we need to examine whether these kinds of rights and the values they enshrine are still relevant. If not, extending them to others (and continuing to perpetuate them in the North) may hasten rather than prevent social and environmental collapse—certainly the wrong foundation upon which to build community-based conservation.

If the old values and ethics are no longer appropriate, what is? Given the rapid rate of social and ecological change and the small window of opportunity that remains, is there enough time for cultural systems, particularly value systems, to adapt to the new circumstances by natural processes? Perhaps it is necessary to search actively for answers and carefully create a new set of values, morals, and rights. If so, the biggest challenge will be to gain cultural legitimacy and authenticity for the new moral system so generated.

Perhaps the first tentative steps—not in terms of actual rights or moral systems, but in regard to what constitutes the moral community—have been made. Conflict between humans and between humans and their environment is not new. Human history has never known any shortage of exploiters, oppressors, and victims. What is new today is the framework of extended equity used in the resolution of conflict. We are beginning to claim that fairness and justice should stretch beyond self-interest to encompass others in the human and natural worlds, in our generation as well as in future generations, in the South as well as in the North. Although it is not yet a universal opinion, value, or ethic, extended equity may be a real change in the rules of the game and an important meeting point for the values of the South and the ethics of the North.

Policy

The chasm that separates the world of the village from that of a policy maker in the capital is both physical and psychological. While distance and deteriorating infrastructure often make the journey arduous, the true barriers more often are power, culture, and tradition. Yet virtually every case study stresses that community-based conservation projects must be supported by appropriate centrally initiated policies. They call for a reversal of most natural resources policies, built on centralized power, based on detailed practices and behavior defined and micromanaged by government agencies.

Given this historical predilection, how can central authorities be influenced on behalf of the people in the countryside? Which policies actually will encourage wise local management of resources, not simply locally inspired extinctions? How shall we encourage central power brokers to devolve authority to otherwise poor and generally disenfranchised people? How do we design incentives that can create self-enforcing rules—rules that are sufficiently in tune with local needs and values that they will be enforced through local social mechanisms and norms? How do we identify policies that are goal based, that do not demand the impossibility of specific local solutions mandated in detail by policies from the top? Is it possible to establish policies that provide some necessary certainty but remain flexible and capable of evolution?

Much of the promotion of CBC relies on equity arguments in favor of a policy of devolving authority to local bodies. Generally, such arguments do not acknowledge, much less resolve, the issue of balancing the winners and losers that result from such a shift. Certainly, the urban elites who often profit from ready access to resources will be reluctant to abandon such advantage. Likewise, government agencies whose status and power derive from their ability to influence resource decisions have little incentive for self-diminution. But the situation is not without hope. Through subsidies (grants and foreign aid), external agencies can encourage devolution. Governments' very inability to manage resources may leave them little choice but to share responsibility locally. The democratic forces of political pluralism, most importantly, increase pressure on governments to relinquish exclusive and authoritarian approaches to resource utilization.

Even when reluctance to share power has been overcome, switching to incentives-based policies remains a challenge. The goal of such policies is to induce changes in national (or local) behavior to lessen the negative impact of human activity on natural resources and to encourage positive (e.g., sustainable) use of resources. When moving from general principles to specifics, however, complexity compounds. Can national resource-management policies be designed with sufficient particularity to mesh with daily survival decisions? National-level policies may have very different impacts in and within communities, and addressing these differences can lead to centrally designed micromanagement, often with perverse consequences. In addition, policies alone will be ineffective, in the absence of sufficient education, local leadership, scientific knowledge, and institutional capacity, which often are lacking.

Incentives are particularly difficult when applied to biodiversity, which, as noted in ECONOMICS, can not readily be converted to financial terms. Few are the circumstances in which a clear, mutually reinforcing linkage exists between sustainable use of resources and communitywide well-being. As a result, in most communities, CBC will require policies of comanagement that are inherently more complex to implement than either completely local or unequivocal government management.

A narrow focus on environmental policy is insufficient, as CBC projects may be undercut by policies apparently unrelated to resource conservation such as changes in economic-development policy, banking laws, and tax policy. The question is not simply whether policies are right or wrong, but whether policies that are valid in their own sectors result in outcomes that conflict with maintaining resource sustainability. Pricing of agricultural products to favor urban voters, export-oriented development plans, or national road building may cancel out a protected area or undercut locally marketed commodities that are keystones for CBC projects. In addition to designing affirmative policies, hard as that may be, virtually every country needs to clarify such jurisdictional confusions and conflicts.

On the other hand, nonenvironmental policies provide opportunities to support CBC activities. The policies likely to produce the highest net benefit are those that establish appropriate valuation for environmental benefits and costs (and the internalization of that value) and clear resource tenure that allows individuals to improve their welfare by deferring use or enhancing resources. A particular challenge in many countries is to make national systems of property rights compatible with customary and traditional rights.

Despite these multiple challenges, around the globe a clear move toward policies of decentralization or localization of resource decision-making is discernible. In developing countries (which, as the case studies demonstrate, are in the lead in community-based approaches to conservation), the move toward policies of local management may be inspired primarily by governments' inability to implement national policies (even theoretically ideal policies) in the rural countryside. Recognition of the need to better manage resources, coupled with their own inability to do so, provides governments with a motivation for seeking communities as allies in conservation.

Many developing countries are used to extensive government intervention in economic decision-making (for example, national five-year plans or industrial policies). Industrialized countries, on the other hand, tend to rely primarily on monetary, tax, and trade policies to implement social goals. As a result, developing-country governments are more likely to intervene with policies that support CBC—although not necessarily successfully, due to a history of "government failure." In country after country, supportive policies have been created through considerable effort, only to languish unimplemented. Many governments are simply unable to influence change within their own borders due to political weakness, poverty, and bureaucratic inefficiency. Taxes go uncollected, so changes in tax policy designed to influence conservation decisions are meaningless. In rural areas, policies often go unenforced, as the case of wildlife laws in Peru demonstrates (see AMAZON). Despite the creative energies documented in the case studies, it is clear that for policy to be effective, the fundamental need is for increased governmental capacity.

In contrast, industrialized countries may be forced to seek local involvement as a result of enforceable legal entitlements, as in the United Kingdom (see NORTH YORK MOORS), or in response to the limits of regulation. In the United States, for example, the cumulative effect of overlapping regulations and legalistic enforcement mechanisms actually may prevent efficient resource-management decisions (witness the stalemate over old-growth forests in the Northwest or the virtual extinction of salmon fisheries on both coasts of the United States) and are beginning to generate a backlash. The result has been the recent emergence of the "partners movement." In this movement, local industry, conservation groups, government agencies, scientists, residents, and other diverse interest groups seek to create a radical center of reasonable people who can work together to move away from the gridlock and polarization of advocacy toward consensus on a local agenda. The goal of the partners movement, paralleling the experience of CBC projects around the world, is to define in very specific local settings a set of ecosystem-economic-community objectives and for communities to reclaim from federal authorities the right to determine their fate. Many challenges remain in this fledgling movement, which is still primarily (with some notable exceptions) conflict and crisis driven;

very time-consuming; and subject, over time, to being captured by the same industry or elite forces that overexploited resources initially. The movement also does not eliminate the need for some mechanism with which to enforce negotiated agreements. In these circumstances, the United States has much to learn from the developing world's experience with CBC.

This simple fact remains: At the national level, we do not yet understand how to balance policies between centrally mandated enforcement to address long-term societal goals for the preservation of species and the need to involve local people in management decisions that affect their livelihoods in order to ensure that such decisions are respected in the field. If national policy presents a challenge, that challenge is dwarfed by macropolicies driven by international social, economic, and political forces. The growth in numbers of the earth's human inhabitants, waves of migration, abject poverty, excessive consumption, international economic inequalities, and predatory terms of trade can overwhelm the most elegantly designed national CBC policies and projects. Changing such macropolitical realities defies the limited capacities of existing global institutions. Global uncertainty, however, must not become an excuse for failing to act locally wherever possible.

CHAPTER 26

Vision of the Future: The New Focus of Conservation

David Western

The global changes of the last half century have been disastrous for the environment. Human numbers have tripled; energy consumption has quadrupled; pollution has fouled our atmosphere, oceans, and soils. Natural habitat is being reduced to vestigial fragments, and thousands of plant and animal species are being driven over the precipice of extinction.

Push the trends another fifty years into the future, and the outlook is calamitous. The exponential curves of consumption and degradation show a world running out of agricultural land and essential resources. Global climate will be several degrees hotter and the ozone layer dangerously thin. City skies will be acrid with pollution, rivers and lakes heavily acidified, and groundwater contaminated with toxic waste. Perhaps half of all species will have disappeared in a mass extinction spasm.

These apocalyptic scenarios are based on computer predictions made during the course of the last twenty years. Any conservationist brave enough to look ahead is sure to be demoralized. There is no glimmer of hope in a future viewed through the prism of past human excesses. Conservationists might as well pack up and enjoy nature as long as it lasts—or should they?

Fortunately, there is scope for change and room for hope—if we take our cues from the positive trends. Several recent projections take a more sanguine view of the future. I share this optimism, not so much because of any giant strides yet taken, but because of the changes now fermenting in the human mind and examples, here and there, where the distillation process has manifested itself in the first small steps in a new direction. My optimism is based on a quarter-century of improvements in and around Kenya's Amboseli National Park, an area that was regarded as a conservation basket case in the 1960s. The improved outlook for the ecosystem (see AMBOSELI for details) convinces me that conservation, when alert and responsive to local needs, can find an enduring place in our future.

From Despair to Hope

In addition to changes in the human mind that portend changes in our behavior toward the environment, a number of more visible trends run counter to the apocalyptic scenario. These trends suggest that awareness and action can slow and ultimately reverse the precipitous slide toward environmental catastrophe.

In 1798, when Thomas Malthus made his abysmal forecast of a Europe plunging into overpopulated misery, Britain had fewer than 10 million people, most living in poverty. Today, Britain's population is six times larger, and its people are wealthier and healthier. In other words, the link between population size and poverty is weak at best. This is not to dismiss the Malthusian theory of limits to growth; the ceiling is simply higher than Malthus and many ecologists allow. This in itself is important, since we have more time than anticipated before the crunch—time in which to do something about the warning signs showing up in the environment.

The significance of time becomes all the more apparent when we consider the momentous changes of the last century. World population growth only began to climb steeply from the mid-1800s. By the 1950s, the growth rate peaked and has been in steady decline ever since. As a result, present projections predict world population will level off between 10 and 14 billion people, one-third of the number the 1960s growth projections predicted. Today, demographers are concerned less about running out of food and space than they are with a powder-keg world divided into rich and poor.

Even more significant for environmental pressure points is urban drift. At present rates, withdrawal to urban areas will cause populations in rural areas to peak in 2050, at numbers about a third greater than at present. The figures will fall rapidly thereafter, repeating the drift that saw the Western switch from an agrarian to an urban society in less than a century. Rural depopulation, among other factors, saw the recovery of wildlife populations in much of the eastern and southern United States.

If changes in sensibilities toward nature that accompanied urbanization in the West are anything to go by, the future urban population of the developing world will become more sympathetic toward nature, as well as a financial force in keeping it intact. Environmental awareness is already on the rise, alongside education and urbanization, in Africa. In Kenya, the Wildlife Clubs movement has enrolled well over a million schoolchildren eager to see the lion and cheetah they have heard about only in fables. Similar youth movements have sprung up throughout Africa and the rest of the Third World.

Countertrends are present in other indices of environmental quality, too. Many airborne pollutants are declining in major industrial nations. An increasing number of lakes and rivers, including Britain's once foul Thames, are being cleaned up at public insistence. Habitat-restoration and species-recovery plans constitute something of a growth industry in the conservation world.

More hopeful yet are the welter of new policies, laws, and enforcement measures aimed at cleaning up the environment. Environmental impact assessments have become mandatory in many countries. Endangered-species legislation and national conservation strategies are commonplace. The Wetlands Convention (RAMSAR), the Convention on International Trade in Endangered Species (CITES), the Mediterranean Treaty, the Convention on Climate Change, and the Biodiversity Treaty are just a few of the dozens of international conservation agreements that have come into force during the last two decades. The growth in numbers of conservation organizations has been nothing short of phenomenal. Peru alone has more than five hundred nongovernmental conservation organizations—up from a handful in the 1970s. By 1990, virtually every major bilateral and multilateral donor agency had adopted environmental policies.

The rise of the environmental movement and its influence on national and global politics culminated in the Rio Declaration of 1992. Although the declaration fell short of expectations in several respects, the fact that the Earth Summit took place reflects the new global environmental agenda adopted by many heads of state.

These countertrends show that environmental degradation can be slowed and reversed. Societies freed from poverty are choosing cleaner and more diverse environments in which to live, and they are willing to pay for that privilege. The encouraging trends anticipate future directions in conservation. If promoted energetically, the future need not be some nightmarish rendition of the past. In the most paradoxical twist of all, development is no longer seen as the archenemy of conservation. Conservation and development are complementary, according to the new paradigm. Development eliminates poverty and paves the way for conservation. In a reciprocal link, conservation preserves the resources essential for sustaining development (see LINKAGE).

Changing Our Minds

Although the trends are encouraging, the positive signs don't yet signify a sea change in our relationship to the environment. To catch the winds heralding such a change, we have to look for subtle cues—the first small eddies and ripples. Step back and the signs are there, in changing behavior patterns, in the attitudes that mold behavior, and, most of all, in the awareness that precedes changes of attitude and behavior.

The rise of environmental awareness in the last two decades is captured in the new words entering popular speech: *ecology, ecosystem, biosphere, green labeling, greenhouse warming, ozone hole, ecotourism, biodiversity,* and dozens of others. Several events helped to raise public consciousness, among them the 1970s oil crisis; the Torrey Canyon and *Exxon Valdez* oil spills; the destruction of the Amazon; the slaughter of whales, elephants, and tigers; and the fragile appearance of our blue planet seen from outer space. The regular press coverage of population growth and environmental destruction is almost impossible to ignore. The message of earthly bounds and limits finally has been driven home to the general populace.

The recognition of bounds and limits is hardly new to ecologists. They justifiably claim that governments are finally coming around to their position. Margaret Mead's admonition—"Never forget that a small group of thoughtful committed citizens can change the world; indeed this is the only thing that ever has"—is germane to their cause.

Evidence suggests that coercive governments can bring about improvements. Fertility control in China and the establishment of protected areas around the world are two examples that come to mind. Coercion has limits, though, and is as futile as rowing up a waterfall when it runs against the perceptions and wishes of a population. The litter of paper parks around the world is a reminder of how fruitless token conservation can be. Conservation can not spread as long as its roots are confined to the high ground of the wealthy or academic few. Coercive programs are everywhere wilting before the strong winds of liberty and ensuing proprietary claims eddying around the world since the collapse of the Cold War (see BACKGROUND).

The new environmental awareness is no longer constrained by class and race. Environmentalism has entered the collective public consciousness on a monumental scale. Forty-eight top commercial companies led by Swiss industrialist Stephan Schmidheiny, for example, came together as the Business Council for Sustainable Development to prepare their own contribution to the Earth Summit. Their message? Markets must reflect environmental as well as economic truths.

Environmental awareness is not confined to urban areas, either; encouraging signs are cropping up in rural areas, too. Local communities are taking a fresh interest in the conservation of renewable resources, natural habitats, and wildlife, as the case studies in this volume illustrate. These, admittedly, are small steps, but steps—we must remember—taken in the face of enormous obstacles, and often without outside help.

From Awareness to Action

Only by looking back at the distance already covered is it possible to get a glimpse of the way ahead. The schism between nature and humanity caused by industrialization, commercialism, urbanization, and population growth over the last half-century reflects a profound loss of contact with the land. The centralization of authority, particularly in totalitarian and authoritarian states, made matters worse by dishonoring traditional property rights and encouraging open-access resource abuse. Knowledge, respect, and caring for the land died for lack of contact.

The small, localized efforts taken here and there around the world amount to a renewal of sorts. They reflect grass-roots changes and a profound shift in the center of gravity among developmentalists and conservationists. Conceding that local people can become the chief beneficiaries and custodians of natural resources and biodiversity is a truly momentous stride; this one leap opens the door to a rural conservation long thwarted by misguided policies.

Perhaps the most encouraging aspect of community-based conservation is that it is happening spontaneously. Many communities close to the land that have suffered the costs of mismanagement are taking the initiative. Conservationists and developmentalists who take the time to look, learn, and think about natural justice—and what works and fails in conservation—are buoyed by these grass-roots initiatives. As a result, conservation policies are nudging the locus of action from the center to the periphery.

One last link in the chain running from awareness to attitudes to behavior is necessary in order for community-based conservation to work. That link is responsibility. Behavior well may mirror concern, but whether that behavior helps or hinders conservation is another question altogether. Tens of thousands of campers feeding grizzly bears in Yellowstone National Park in the United States have turned the animals dangerous, causing their destruction. Nature lovers en masse have destroyed high Himalayan pastures. When it comes to nature, destruction is destruction, whether the cause is poverty, greed, or the crush of admirers.

Few governments are willing to empower communities without some assurance of their capacity and sense of responsibility. A community's future security, no less than society's, is jeopardized by environmental abuse. Environmental responsibility, then, is the flip side of freedom. Without responsibility, individual freedom tramples over the rights of other individuals, communities, nations, humanity, and future generations. The NIMBY mentality described in LINKAGE advocates, for example, that pollutants should not be dumped in our own backyard but fails to engender the responsibility to see that they are disposed of in an environmentally harmless way.

On the positive side, localizing conservation action is likely to foster the responsibility that goes with rights. Thinking globally and acting locally closes the circle of action and consequences in three essential ways: environmentally, economically, and socially. Localization rebuilds the connections lost in today's amorphous and transient society. If the responsibility that comes of living within a community and on the land can not be established locally, can it ever be established in the less personal and less intimate global setting? If caring and responsibility do start locally, will it not be easier to expand the sensibilities they engender from individuals to communities, nations, humankind, and even future generations?

Changing Roles

If the gulf between conservation and development has closed, however slightly, what does this augur for the future? What will it take to fulfill the promise of conservation in the rural landscape? And what are the challenges for conservationists?

In practical terms, community-based conservation calls for sweeping policy re-forms on a grand scale. If the locus of action is to be the community, conservation policies and practices must be turned on their heads. The approach must be bottom-up rather than top-down, and local rather than national. Diverse (rather than uniform) environmental values and conservation practices also must be encouraged.

Here is where community-based conservation becomes more revolutionary than evolutionary: Such changes call for nothing less than a turnaround in en-trenched political norms.

Every aspect of conservation, from user rights to donor roles, must be rethought (see RECOMMENDATIONS). Local initiatives and skills must become the driving force of conservation. The role of government must move from center stage to the pe-riphery and change from coercive to supportive. Governments must think in terms of integrating the activities of many conservation-oriented groups and individuals and arbitrating their disputes.

The future, for conservationists, lies not in trench warfare fought by ecowar-riors, but in building local awareness and local capacity. The role of national non-governmental organizations lies in linking up interest groups and encouraging rec-iprocal exchanges between them. Local communities will become the real conservation practitioners who experiment with new techniques and disseminate them by example. National and regional conservation organizations will become the partners of local communities. International conservation bodies will become the antennae, technical innovators, and watchdogs of conservation. They will look ahead for the pressure points and devise new and better tools and skills for conservation. They will become global monitors who advocate compliance and change. Conservation organizations, together with bilateral and multilateral donors, will become resource brokers looking for innovative conservation enter-prises to support and foster.

Community-based conservation should draw strength from connections be-tween the many groups and individuals with a stake in conservation. Yet, however many connections may be built, the problems standing in the way of environ-mental sustainability still must be solved. Populations can not continue to grow and poverty can not deepen without threatening the future (see ECOLOGY). Rapid cultural change, with its attendant problems of community breakdown and loss of traditional values, is an equally big if overlooked threat. At the opposite extreme lies the tyranny of factionalism: equating freedom with political separation. Solving every cultural difference by division traps human beings in an infinite re-gression and removes an important incentive for accommodation. Learning to live with our own differences is the first step on the road to learning to live with other species.

The problems of free trade are no less a threat to self-determination and community conservation. The General Agreement on Tariffs and Trade (GATT) and the North American Free Trade Agreement (NAFTA), among many other global and regional free-trade agreements, risk scuttling local conservation efforts and progress made at the Earth Summit—unless, that is, trade agreements are sensitive to environmental and local concerns. The ecological truths acknowledged by the Business Council for Sustainable Development, in other words, must quickly assume the stature of economic truths.

The list of problems goes on. In some cases, breaking with the past is as difficult as embracing the future. Institutions in the developed world have become so atomized and bureaucratized that reintegrating their activities will be no less formidable than building up skills and institutions from scratch.

A New Vision

Locally based conservation calls for a brave new vision rooted in interconnections. If conservation is to become embedded in our daily activities, nature and society must be intimately linked in our minds. This is a radical departure from the Western view of the separateness of Man and Nature—one that rekindles a holistic, ancestral way of thinking about our species in relation to the rest of the natural world (see BACKGROUND). Research, knowledge, and education all will have a central role to play in the conceptual shift if we work on the premise that rural communities have as much to teach others as they have to learn about how to live in a more integrated world.

Holism has an important contribution to make in balancing the widespread reductionist and purist view of science. Ecologists will need to come to grips with biodiversity and biological processes within human-modified landscapes. They also will need to develop new theories to accommodate the complex and shifting mosaic of habitats occurring over millions of square kilometers and many centuries. Discrete ecosystems in steady-state and coevolved species almost certainly will be the exception rather than the rule in the future, whether or not this was true in the past. Economists also will need to deal with the externalities in conservation, with the enormous social inequities, with the long-term sustainability of renewable resources, and with the maintenance of genetic adaptability.

The possibility exists that sustainability in a single location is an illusion, a romantic ideal made wholly unattainable by the tremendous flux in cultures, populations, economies, and land-use practices. If this turns out to be true, there will be all the more reason to view sustainability in global and generational terms. Humans will need to think big to exploit the niches opened up by the continually changing modes and shifting centers of production. In this event, conservationists will have to learn how to deal with a moving target of opportunity and threat.

Conservation will cease to be a singular activity based on biology and resource use. Instead, it will be the sum of many interrelated and integrated activities that contribute to the sustainability and maintenance of biological diversity. How well we succeed in embedding conservation in daily practices depends on the extent to which its precepts become basic rights and freedoms we value and insist upon.

Sensibilities and rights have expanded continually in modern times. There is reason to believe our environment and the natural world will be drawn deeper into that expanding circle.

Conservation arose as a singular, distinctive human activity based on scarcity, threat, and aesthetics. It follows that if humans embed conservation in their psyches and behavior, and if they tackle scarcity and poverty with the same zeal given to space exploration, conservation will cease to be a discrete human activity.

If this vision is ever realized, conservationists will become redundant. It will be time to hang up our consciences and our indignation and retire on the pension fund of nature we have so regularly paid into for decades. Until then, there is much to be done. The best hope for sustaining life's diversity lies in embedding conservation values in the lives of rural people.

If conservationists can take up the challenge of this new and unfamiliar terrain, they will help move the impetus from North to South and from center to periphery. They will, in the process, help conservation become multiethnic and multiethical, thus healing its deep schisms with an array of approaches no less diverse than biodiversity itself.

RECOMMENDED READING

Clark, W. C., and R. E. Munn, eds.1986. *Sustainable Development of the Biosphere.* Cambridge, England: Cambridge University Press.

Constanza, R., B. G. Norton, and B. D. Haskell, eds. 1992. *Ecosystem Health: New Goals for Environmental Management.* Washington, D.C.: Island Press.

Ehrlich, P. R., and J. P. Holdren, eds. 1988. *The Cassandra Conference: Resources and the Human Predicament.* College Station, Texas: Texas A&M University Press.

Engel, J. R., and J. G. Engel, eds. 1990. *Ethics of Environment and Development: Global Challenge, International Response.* Tucson, Arizona: University of Arizona Press.

Herman, E. D., and K. N. Townsend, eds. 1993. *Valuing the Earth: Economics, Ecology, Ethics.* Cambridge, Massachusetts: MIT Press.

Hudson, W. E., ed. 1991. *Landscape Linkages and Biodiversity.* Washington, D.C.: Island Press.

Kemf, E., ed. 1993. *The Law of the Mother.* San Francisco: Sierra Club Books.

Malthus, T. R. [1798] 1970. *An Essay on the Principle of Population.* Hamondsworth, England: Penguin Books.

McCormick, J. 1989. *The Global Environmental Movement: Reclaiming Paradise.* London: Belhaven.

Meadows, D., D. L. Meadows, and J. Randers, eds. 1992. *Beyond the Limits: Confronting Global Collapse, Envisioning a Sustainable Future.* Post Mill, Vermont: Chelsea Green.

Nash, R. F. 1989. *The Rights of Nature: A History of Environmental Ethics.* Madison, Wisconsin: University of Wisconsin Press.

Piel, G. 1992. *Only One World: Our Own to Make and Keep.* New York: Freeman.

Repetto, R., ed. 1985. *The Global Possible: Resources, Development and the New*

Century. New Haven, Connecticut: Yale University Press.

Shabecoff, P. 1993. *A Fierce Green Fire: The American Environmental Movement*. New York: Hill and Wang.

Southwick, C. H., ed. 1985. *Global Ecology*. Sunderland, Massachusetts: Sinauer.

Thomas, K. 1983. *Man and the Natural World: A History of the Modern Sensibility*. New York: Pantheon.

Weiner, J. 1990. *The Next One Hundred Years: Shaping the Fate of Our Living Earth*. New York: Bantam.

Western, D., and M. Pearl, eds. 1989. *Conservation for the Twenty-first Century*. New York: Oxford University Press.

World Commission on Environment and Development. 1987. *Our Common Future*. New York: Oxford University Press.

World Development Report. 1992. *Development and the Environment*. New York: Oxford Univeristy Press.

Participants

Liz Claiborne Art Ortenberg
Community Based Conservation Workshop
Airlie, Virginia
October 18–22, 1993

Janis Alcorn
Biodiversity Support Program
U.S.A.

Hilary Barbour
World Wildlife Fund
U.S.A.

Martha Belcher
SEJATI
Indonesia

Gail Bingham
RESOLVE
World Wildlife Fund
U.S.A.

Fernanda Gabriella Borger
University of São Paulo
Brazil

Antonio Brack-Egg
UNDP/Amazon Cooperation Treaty
Ecuador

Daniel W. Bromley*
University of Wisconsin–Madison
U.S.A.

Roland Bunch
COSECHA
Honduras

Bruce Byers
Office of Environment and Natural
    Resources
USAID
U.S.A.

Liz Claiborne
Liz Claiborne Art Ortenberg Foundation
U.S.A.

Laura Cornwell
Chesapeake Biological Laboratory
University of Maryland
U.S.A.

Sandy Davis
Social Policy and Resettlement Division
World Bank
U.S.A.

Gustave Doungoube
Reserve Dzanga-Sangha/Parc National
    de Dzanga Kdoki
Central African Republic

Fabio Feldmann
House of Representatives
Brazil

Tom Fox
Center for International Development
    and Environment
World Resource Institute
U.S.A.

Cindy Gilday
Department of Renewable Resources
Government of the Northwest
    Territories
Canada

Bruce Goldstein
University of California, Santa Cruz
U.S.A.

*Mr. Bromley's theme paper on economics was commissioned after the workshop (which he did not attend), pursuant to the participants' discussions and recommendations.

Chandra Prasad Gurung
King Mahendra Trust for Nature Conservation
Nepal

Michael Hill
Australian Nature Conservation Agency
Australia

Michael Jenkins
John D. and Catherine T. MacArthur Foundation
U.S.A.

Twig Johnson
Office of Environment and Natural Resources
USAID
U.S.A.

Dennis King
Chesapeake Biological Laboratory
University of Maryland
U.S.A.

Chuck Kleymeyer
InterAmerican Foundation
U.S.A.

Ronald Léger
Community Based Exchange
Costa Rica

Andreas Lehnhoff
Defensores de la Naturaleza
Guatemala

Peter Little
Institute for Development Anthropology
U.S.A.

Owen Lynch
World Resources Institute
U.S.A.

Cynthia Mackie
Conservation International
U.S.A.

Maria Angela Marcovaldi
Fundação Pro Tamar (TAMAR)
Brazil

John Marrinka
Olgulului Group Ranch
Kenya

Thirtha Maskey
Department of Parks and Wildlife Conservation
Nepal

Juan Mayr
Fundación Pro-Sierra Nevada de Santa Marta
Colombia

Jeffrey A. McNeely
IUCN
Switzerland

Simon Metcalfe
Centre for Applied Social Sciences
University of Zimbabwe
Zimbabwe

Marshall W. Murphree
Centre for Applied Social Sciences
University of Zimbabwe
Zimbabwe

James Murtaugh
Liz Claiborne Art Ortenberg Foundation
U.S.A.

Julius Ningu
East Usambaras Conservation and Development Project
Tanzania

Tri Nugroho
Lembafa Alam Tropika Indonesia (LATIN)
Indonesia

Perez Olindo
African Wildlife Foundation
Kenya

Art Ortenberg
Liz Claiborne Art Ortenberg Foundation
U.S.A.

Enrique Ortiz
Conservation International
U.S.A.

Esther Prieto
Centro de Estudios Humanaetarios
Paraguay

David Quammen
Liz Claiborne Art Ortenberg Founda-
tion
U.S.A.

Alison Richard
Peabody Museum of Natural
History
Yale University
U.S.A.

John Robinson
Wildlife Conservation Society
U.S.A.

Nightingale Rukuba-Ngaiza
Northeastern University
Uganda

Nick Salafsky
Biodiversity Support Program
U.S.A.

Kenneth Sayre
Department of Philosophy
University of Notre Dame
U.S.A.

David R. Schmidt
Linn County, Oregon
Board of Commissioners
U.S.A.

Frances J. Seymour
World Wildlife Fund
U.S.A.

Phil Shabecoff
Greenwire
U.S.A.

Rebecca Sholes
AMID East
American Mideast Education
Training Service, Inc.
U.S.A.

Derek Statham
North York Moors National Park
Great Britain

Shirley Strum
Department of Anthropology
University of California, San Diego
U.S.A.

Liying Su
International Crane Foundation, China

Krisnawati Suryanata
University of California, Berkeley
Indonesia

Margaret Taylor
Ambassador to the United States
Papua New Guinea

Aurora F. Tolentino
Institute for Global Environmental
Strategies
U.S.A.

Amy Townsend
Institute for Global Environmental
Strategies
U.S.A.

Ellen Trama
Liz Claiborne Art Ortenberg Foundation
U.S.A.

Don Tuzin
Department of Anthropology
University of California, San Diego
U.S.A.

John Waugh
IUCN
U.S.A.

W. William Weeks
The Nature Conservancy
U.S.A.

David Western
Wildlife Conservation Society
Kenya

Michael Wright
World Wildlife Fund
U.S.A.

Patricia Wright
Ranomafana National Park Project
Madagascar

Index